Interrogative
Investigations

CSLI Lecture Notes
Number 123

Interrogative Investigations

The Form, Meaning, and Use of English Interrogatives

JONATHAN GINZBURG ◆ IVAN A. SAG
King's College, London   Stanford University
Hebrew University of Jerusalem

CSLI
PUBLICATIONS
Center for the Study of
Language and Information
Stanford, California

Library of Congress Cataloging-in-Publication Data

Ginzburg, Jonathan, 1964–
    Interrogative investigations : the form, meaning, and use of English interrogatives / Jonathan Ginzburg,
Ivan A. Sag.
        p. cm. -- (CSLI lecture notes ; no. 123)
    Includes bibliographical references (p.) and index.
    ISBN 1-57586-277-8 (cloth : alk. paper) -- ISBN 1-57586-278-6 (pbk. : alk. paper)
    1. English language--Interrogative. I. Sag, Ivan A., 1949– II. Title. III. Series.

PE1395 .G56 2001
425--dc21

                                                                                    2001017172

Please visit our web site at
http://cslipublications.stanford.edu/
for comments on this and other titles, as well as for changes
and corrections by the author and publisher.

Contents

Preface

This book began as conversations that took place as the alphabetically prior author was writing his doctoral dissertation at Stanford University. Geography and complex personal and professional circumstances are responsible for the considerable time it has taken to bring the work to completion. Along the way, there were fleeting but crucial conversations in Columbus, Edinburgh, Prague, Ithaca, Brussels, Stanford and London, without which our collaboration could never have succeeded.

We would like to acknowledge our debt to a number of colleagues who have provided much feedback on the ideas presented here. Carl Pollard and Eric Potsdam (serving as CSLI reviewer) provided such useful, detailed, yet highly critical comments on an earlier version of this book, that the final year of preparation and revision amounted to a vast overhaul of our theory. We owe both of them an extraordinary debt. Our debt to Pollard goes beyond this, however, as countless interactions with him over the years about the grammar of interrogatives have left their mark throughout Chapters 5 and 6.

We want to thank Farrell Ackerman, Emily Bender, Elisabet Engdahl, Georgia Green, Shalom Lappin, Bob Levine, Rob Malouf, Adam Przepiórkowski, and Peter Sells for detailed comments on various drafts. In addition, we thank the following people for helpful discussions, useful suggestions, and/or corrections: Anne Abeillé, Ralph Albrecht, Ash Asudeh, David Beaver, John Beavers, Emily Bender, Francis Bond, Bob Borsley, Chris Callison-Burch, Luis Casillas, Brady Clark, Robin Cooper, Ann Copestake, Elisabet Engdahl, Anke Feldhaus, Tim Fernando, Charles Fillmore, Edward Flemming, Dan Flickinger, Itamar Francez, Danièle Godard, Georgia Green, Howard Gregory, Jim Higginbotham, Erhard Hinrichs, David Johnson, Andreas Kathol, Paul Kay, Ruth Kempson, Jongbok Kim, Tibor Kiss, Dimitra Kolliakou, Manfred Krifka, Shalom Lappin, Alex Lascarides, Bob Levine, Jean-Philippe Marcotte, Rob Malouf, Detmar Meurers, Larry Moss, Doris Penker, David Pesetsky, Stanley Peters, Ellen Prince, Frank Richter, Mark Steedman, Shiao-Wei Tham, Rich Thomason, Enric Vallduví, Carl Vogel, Tom Wasow, Gert Webelhuth, Yael Ziv, and Arnold Zwicky. Thanks also to Carl Vogel for his bibtex macros, to Kim Lewis Brown, Brady Clark, Max Etchemendy, and Chris Sosa for their hard work during the copyediting process, and to Jerry Torres for fleshing out a woefully incomplete bibliography. Special thanks in addition to both Dikran Karagueuzian and Lauri Kanerva for their sage advice and special assistance with just about everything having to do with the production of this book.

Finally, the research reported here was conducted in part under the auspices of CSLI's LINguistic Grammars Online (LINGO) project. In that connection, we gratefully acknowledge support from Germany's Bundesministerium für Bildung, Wissenschaft, Forschung, und Technologie (BMBF), who supported LINGO's participation in the Verbmobil project under Grant FKZ:01IV7024. This material is also based in part on work supported by the National Science Foundation under grant number IRI-9612682. We further acknowledge the support of the UK Economic and Social Research Council (grant number R000222969 *Phrasal Utterance Resolution in Dialogue*). Ginzburg was supported by an Alon Young Researcher Fellowship from the Israeli Inter-University Planning and Budget Committee and a series of visits at the Department of Linguistics at Göteborg University was supported by INDI (Information Exchange in Dialogue), Riksbankens Jubileumsfond 1997-0134.

1

Introduction

1.1 Prolegomena

Interrogative constructions have played a central role in the development of modern syntactic theory. Characterizing the constraints on the 'dislocation' of *wh*-phrases in interrogatives, for example, has been at the heart of work in generative grammar since the mid 1960s. Indeed, within the paradigms known as *government and binding* (GB) or *principles and parameters*, phenomena pertaining to interrogatives have long been considered among the most compelling for postulating a syntactic level of 'logical form' (LF), a level that has survived and continues to play an influential role in the paradigm of the *minimalist program*.

Most work within these paradigms has been driven by concerns largely internal to the respective frameworks, drawing little motivation from formally oriented semantic and pragmatic work on interrogatives. Although there has been a significant amount of work on interrogatives across a variety of languages, there are few comprehensive syntactic and semantic treatments of a wide range of interrogative constructions and uses in a single language. In this book, our aim is to provide an account that rigorously integrates syntax and semantics and at the same time covers a wide range of English constructions.

The development of large-scale descriptions is a crucial step to take. Only when comprehensive grammar fragments are commonplace will it become possible to meaningfully compare available frameworks for grammatical description. More than forty years of applying mathematical tools to the study of syntax, for example, has failed to produce a consistent, large-scale generative-transformational description of any single human language. In linguistics today, one is not required to demonstrate that all assumptions being made in a given treatment are consistent with one another, let alone capable of providing a more systematic account than other known treatments. Theoretical linguists are free to pick and choose whatever subset of the phenomena in one or many languages they want to discuss and to selectively draw from a combination of ideas from fragmentary proposals in the literature. The analytic proposals one encounters, often formulated in terms that appear formally rigorous to an outsider, are often simply untestable. Most current theoretical discussions about the formal or architectural properties of vaguely articulated models are not grounded in any systematic, comprehensive empirical descriptions. Hence the debates about metatheory in these discussions are, at best, premature.

By constructing a consistent large-scale description of an interesting and complex domain, we hope to provide a basis for more meaningful theoretical discussion and cross-framework comparison. The tools we have selected for this task are the grammatical framework of Head-Driven

Phrase Structure Grammar (HPSG) and the semantic framework of Situation Semantics. Building on the grammatical constructions developed in Sag 1997 and the comprehensive semantics for interrogatives developed in Ginzburg 1992, 1995a,b, we develop a treatment of the syntactic and semantic properties of English interrogative constructions. Although we confine our attention here to English, we believe our general approach can be extended both to *wh*-stacking languages, such as Polish, and to *wh*-in-situ languages, such as Hindi and Japanese.

1.2 Syntactic Preview

In this section, we place our work in a broader syntactic context and outline some of the leading ideas of our syntactic analysis.

1.2.1 Generative Grammar

Our work falls squarely within the domain of the enterprise of generative grammar, which we define, following Chomsky (1966: 12) as follows:

> A *generative grammar* (that is, an explicit grammar that makes no appeal to the reader's 'faculté de langage' but rather attempts to incorporate the mechanisms of this faculty) is a system of rules that relate signals to semantic interpretations of these signals.

Note also the following quotation from the preface to Chomsky 1975:

> A grammar constructed in accord with the principles postulated in such a theory [of generative grammar] gives an explicit characterization of a language and its structure—and within the broader semiotic theory envisioned but not developed here, an explicit characterization as well of the meaning and reference of expressions and conditions of appropriate use.

We hope that it will soon become clear that our work, like related work in the tradition of HPSG, has as its goal the development of "explicit characterization[s]" that deal with "language and its structure" and their relation to 'semantic interpretations', and even to a 'broader semiotic theory'.[1]

Although few well-informed readers will doubt that the analyses presented qualify as generative grammar, there are significant differences between our approach and that of investigators working within the framework of Government and Binding or the Minimalist Program. These latter two frameworks, implicitly or explicitly, reject the following two theses:

1. **Constraint-Based Architecture**: Grammar is a system of constraints that govern the relation between form and meaning. There are no operations within grammar other than constraints. This precludes, for instance, transformational operations.
2. **Constructionism**: Grammatical constructions play a fundamental role in the theory of grammar.

1.2.2 Constraint-Based Grammar

Our work also falls within a particular tradition of work in generative grammar, often referred to as Constraint-Based Grammar (CBG).[2] The fundamental idea of CBG is that grammars consist

---

[1]We emphasize this point only because, as noted by Smith (1999), there is now a second meaning of 'generative grammar' that renders it interchangeable with 'generative-transformational' grammar. This misleading usage should be rejected, in our view.

[2]The tradition of CBG starts with the pioneering work of Johnson and Postal (1980). Grammars of this sort are also sometimes referred to as 'Unification-Based' grammars. This term is misleading, however, as unification is but one of many procedures that can be used to solve systems of identity constraints.

of correlated constraints that are satisfied by modeling structures. A grammar is thus straightforwardly a theory of a language: a set of statements in an appropriate feature logic (constraints) that are satisfied by certain models, each of which is a specified correlation of sound, syntactic information, and meaning. We assume that the modeling structures in HPSG are directed graphs that specify values for features such as PHONOLOGY, (syntactic) CATEGORY, (semantic) CONTENT and CONTEXT (of use).

Following a long analytic tradition, phenomena that have been treated by transformational movement are treated exclusively in terms of constraints.[3] A particular construction type, for example, allows a 'fronted' element as its first daughter and an appropriate sentential phrase as its second (head) daughter. This head daughter is further constrained to bear an appropriate specification for the feature, named SLASH in HPSG, encoding information about elements missing within that constituent:

(1)

$$\begin{bmatrix} \text{S} \\ \textit{fin} \\ \text{SLASH} \ \{ \ \} \end{bmatrix} \rightarrow \boxed{1} \begin{bmatrix} \text{S} \\ \text{SLASH} \ \{\boxed{1}\} \end{bmatrix}$$

General principles of the theory, also formulated as constraints, ensure that this head daughter's value for the feature SLASH match the SLASH value of its own head daughter. Various constraints that we discuss in detail in Chapter 5 interact to ensure that an appropriate lexical head (the verb *likes* in (2)) appears without its object, just in case the indicated SLASH information is 'percolated' up through the structure and identified with the appropriate filler:

(2)

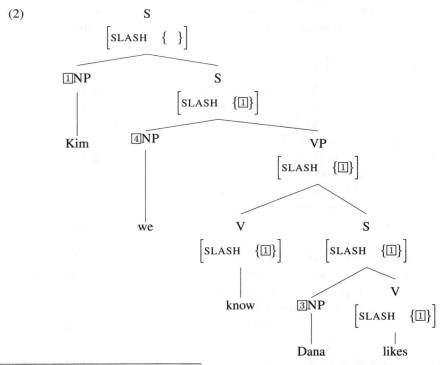

---

[3] See Brame 1978, Johnson and Postal 1980, Gazdar 1981, Ades and Steedman 1982, Kaplan and Bresnan 1982, Bresnan 1982b, Gazdar et al. 1985, Kaplan and Zaenen 1989, Pollard and Sag 1994, and Steedman 1996, among others.

Thus what looks like movement is not analyzed as movement at all. An 'extracted' element (like the NP *Kim* in (2)) is permitted only when a corresponding element is missing within the body of the sentence. This follows from the CBG account because it is only in this way that a structure with the extracted element can satisfy all the constraints of the grammar, as explained in detail in Chapter 5.

In this book, we treat some of the most theoretically central and recalcitrant phenomena in English syntax, including *wh-*'movement' (Chapter 6), 'pied piping' effects (Chapter 5), inversion ('I-to-C movement'), and the restricted distribution of auxiliary *do* (Chapter 2). Our analytic method is always that of CBG: simple constraint satisfaction. We should add that for the last thirty years, transformational theories have always assumed, but never precisely specified, a theory of features and values—and hence, *ipso facto*, a theory of feature structures. CBG, in making no use of transformational operations, thus streamlines the architecture of grammatical theory, analyzing more data with less theoretical apparatus.[4]

There is a further argument in favor of the CBG approach to grammar, if it can be shown to be empirically adequate. As argued forcefully in a number of works,[5] CBGs are psycholinguistically plausible. An unordered set of constraints fits well into a psycholinguistic model where linguistic and nonlinguistic information are smoothly and incrementally integrated in on-line language processing (Tanenhaus and Trueswell 1995). CBG approaches lexically encode significant grammatical information, which squares rather well with recent research in psycholinguistics (see MacDonald et al. 1994 for an overview). In addition, it has been known (at least since Fodor et al. 1974) that independent psycholinguistic evidence for the existence of transformations is lacking.

For these reasons, a precise, comprehensive description of a significant empirical domain in CBG terms is significant. If transformational operations *can* be eliminated from grammatical theory they *should* be.

1.2.3 The Primacy of Constructions

Although syntactic work within the transformationalist tradition frequently uses the term descriptively, '(grammatical) construction' has been a *theoretical* taboo at least since the 1980s. Briefly, Chomsky argued that transformations like 'passive' and 'raising', common in earlier versions of transformational grammar, could be eliminated in favor of general conditions on structures that would allow a single operation—Move NP—to do the work of a family of such transformations. This has guided the subsequent evolution of transformational analysis where one now finds discussion of even more general operations, such as 'Move α' or 'Move'. This evolution has tended to move away from construction-specific proposals toward a discussion focused almost exclusively on general principles from which the idiosyncrasy of individual constructions are supposed to be derived.

However, as already noted by McCawley (1988) in his review of Chomsky 1986, Chomsky's discussion of the passive construction did not touch on crucial issues like the relevant verb morphology, the choice of the preposition *by*, and the role of the verb *be*. As McCawley pointed out, these properties of the construction followed from nothing under Chomsky's proposals. Rather, they would have to be stated in a fashion that would render Chomsky's proposal comparably stipulative to the alternative it sought to replace.

---

[4]Students of CBG sometimes think otherwise, as the feature structures of transformational theories often appear simpler by comparison. In point of fact, this is an illusion arising from the incomplete and inexplicit nature of the transformational alternatives.

[5]See Kaplan and Bresnan 1982, Sag and Wasow 1999: Chapter 9, and Johnson and Lappin 1999.

Closely related to these issues is the distinction Chomsky makes between 'core' phenomena and the 'periphery' of language. The core phenomena consist of 'pure instantiations of Universal Grammar', while the periphery consists of 'marked exceptions (irregular verbs, etc.)' (Chomsky and Lasnik 1993).[6] The move away from constructions thus leads to the study of 'Core Grammar'.

There is a problem here as well: that of knowing which phenomena are core and which are peripheral. The literature offers virtually no criteria for distinguishing the two, though this is critical if the distinction is to have empirical content at all.[7] Be that as it may, there is a more serious difficulty facing any attempt to justify the move away from constructions ('anticonstructionism', if you will) on the basis of a concern for core grammar: the fact that there is no inconsistency between the concern for general principles of grammar (even Universal Grammar in Chomsky's sense) and a construction-based approach to grammar.

The construction-based approach developed here illustrates the significant convergence of recent theoretical work on grammatical constructions and their properties within the CBG generative tradition. Early work in HPSG[8] adapted multiple inheritance hierarchies, already used in computational work in knowledge representation and object-oriented programming, to express cross-classifying generalizations about words. This same general approach has subsequently been applied in various ways to the grammar of phrases by other linguists. Two notable examples of such work are Hudson's Word Grammar[9] and the framework of Construction Grammar developed by Fillmore, Kay and their collaborators.[10] See also Zwicky 1994, Kathol's (1995) analysis of German clause types, and Sag's (1997) treatment of English relative clause constructions. All of these researchers have treated generalizations about constructions in terms of cross-classifying type hierarchies.

The type-based approach to constructional analysis also has the advantage that it allows generalizations of varying grain to be expressed naturally. For example, Fillmore (1999) points out that English has various kinds of 'inverted' clauses, including the exclamatives in (3), the 'blesses, wishes and curses' in (4), the conditionals in (5), and polar interrogatives like (6):

(3) a. Boy, *was I stupid*!

    b. Wow, *can she sing*!

(4) a. May they live forever!

    b. May I live long enough to see the end of this job!

    c. May your teeth fall out on your wedding night!

(5) a. *Were they here now*, we wouldn't have this problem.

    b. *Should there be a need*, we can always call for help.

(6) a. Were they involved?

    b. Can she sing?

---

[6]Recent work in the Minimalist Program, though seldom discussing the core/periphery distinction explicitly, adheres to it in practice. In fact, most work in this tradition focuses on an even narrower subset of putatively core data.

[7]For independent, highly convergent arguments that the core-periphery distinction is both unmotivated and largely inconsistent with independently motivated, more data-driven approaches to learning, see Jackendoff 1997 and especially Culicover 1999.

[8]See, for example, Flickinger et al. 1985, Flickinger 1987, and Pollard and Sag 1987.

[9]See Hudson 1990, 2000.

[10]See Fillmore 1999, Fillmore and Kay 1999, Fillmore et al. to appear, Koenig and Jurafsky 1994, Goldberg 1995, and Koenig 1999.

These are clearly distinct constructions, each involving a language-particular correlation of inverted form with a particular semantic type, as well as other kinds of idiosyncrasy. Yet these constructions are a family: they are all finite, they all realize the subject post-verbally, and they are all incompatible with uninvertible finite auxiliaries like *better*. In Chapters 2 and 6, we develop an analysis of these constructions in terms of the supertype *subject-auxiliary-inversion-phrase* (*sai-ph*). This is itself a subtype of *headed-phrase* (*hd-ph*), a general property of which is the presence of a head daughter. As the researchers cited earlier have argued, natural language generalizations typically manifest themselves at diverse classificatory grains. This fact is accurately modeled by a hierarchical system of construction types of the kind we assume here, where constraints can be placed on the most specific type of construction, on the most general type *phrase*, or on any of the intermediate types recognized by our grammar. In addition, as argued convincingly by Johnson and Lappin (1999), there are certain kinds of cross-linguistic generalizations that are quite difficult to state without a notion of construction type.

Moreover, as Ackerman and Webelhuth (1998) have suggested, a type-based system of grammar can reasonably posit that certain types are part of a universal inventory, assuming Chomsky's extremely strong version of UG. Alternatively, Ackerman and Webelhuth propose a notion of *archetype*—a recurrent type in human languages that emerges in response to more general functional and cognitive factors, yet is not 'hard-wired' as such.[11] These are divergent views of UG, but they are both compatible with the view that a grammar is based on the notion of construction, analyzed in terms of types, type hierarchies, and type constraints.

Let us illustrate the construction-based approach in more detail. 'Topicalized' clauses, *wh*-interrogatives, *wh*-relatives, and *wh*-exclamatives in English are another family of constructions. Each consists of an initial extracted element followed by a sentential head that contains an appropriate gap. However, only matrix *wh*-interrogatives involve auxiliary inversion. Moreover, topicalized sentences disallow a *wh*-word in the extracted position, and each *wh*-clause requires the presence of a different kind of *wh*-word within the extracted constituent:

(7) a. [That desk], my friend from Denmark built __ .

    b. *What* did they build __ ?

    c. [*What* an ugly desk] they built __ !

    d. the desk *which* they built __ ....

As we note in Chapter 5, the three classes of *wh*-word are not interchangable, though, for historical reasons, they have common members. And of course each construction has its own kind of meaning.[12]

One could stipulate the properties of these constructions piecemeal, by positing five unrelated constructions like those in (8):

---

[11] For an insightful discussion of a similar notion that seems to us entirely compatible with our framework, see Langacker 1991.

[12] There are further differences (e.g. having to do with the category of the extracted element) that we will ignore for present purposes.

(8) a. *topicalized-clause*:

$$
\begin{bmatrix} \textit{fin} \\ \text{ROOT} & + \\ \text{SLASH} & \{\,\} \\ \text{CONTENT} & \text{decl} \end{bmatrix} \rightarrow \boxed{1}\begin{bmatrix} \text{WH} & \text{none} \end{bmatrix} \quad \mathbf{H:} \begin{bmatrix} \textit{fin} \\ \text{INV} & - \\ \text{SLASH} & \{\boxed{1}\} \end{bmatrix}
$$

(S → S, H: S)

b. *inverted-wh-interrogative-clause*:

$$
\begin{bmatrix} \textit{fin} \\ \text{ROOT} & + \\ \text{SLASH} & \{\,\} \\ \text{CONTENT} & \text{int} \end{bmatrix} \rightarrow \boxed{1}\begin{bmatrix} \text{WH} & \text{wh-int} \end{bmatrix} \quad \mathbf{H:} \begin{bmatrix} \textit{fin} \\ \text{INV} & + \\ \text{SLASH} & \{\boxed{1}\} \end{bmatrix}
$$

c. *uninverted-wh-interrogative-clause*:

$$
\begin{bmatrix} \textit{fin} \\ \text{ROOT} & - \\ \text{SLASH} & \{\,\} \\ \text{CONTENT} & \text{int} \end{bmatrix} \rightarrow \boxed{1}\begin{bmatrix} \text{WH} & \text{wh-int} \end{bmatrix} \quad \mathbf{H:} \begin{bmatrix} \textit{fin} \\ \text{INV} & - \\ \text{SLASH} & \{\boxed{1}\} \end{bmatrix}
$$

d. *wh-exclamative-clause*:

$$
\begin{bmatrix} \textit{fin} \\ \text{SLASH} & \{\,\} \\ \text{CONTENT} & \text{excl} \end{bmatrix} \rightarrow \boxed{1}\begin{bmatrix} \text{WH} & \text{wh-excl} \end{bmatrix} \quad \mathbf{H:} \begin{bmatrix} \textit{fin} \\ \text{INV} & - \\ \text{SLASH} & \{\boxed{1}\} \end{bmatrix}
$$

e. *wh-relative-clause*:

$$
\begin{bmatrix} \textit{fin} \\ \text{ROOT} & - \\ \text{SLASH} & \{\,\} \\ \text{CONTENT} & \text{rel} \end{bmatrix} \rightarrow \boxed{1}\begin{bmatrix} \text{WH} & \text{wh-rel} \end{bmatrix} \quad \mathbf{H:} \begin{bmatrix} \textit{fin} \\ \text{INV} & - \\ \text{SLASH} & \{\boxed{1}\} \end{bmatrix}
$$

But this somewhat redundant formulation is quite distinct from current views of construction grammar and certainly distinct from the theory we present here.

A construction-based grammar, in fact, derives constraints like the ones shown in (8) as theorems of a more abstract system of phrasal types. As already noted, by organizing phrases into a multiple inheritance hierarchy, one can posit higher-level types and formalize the relevant cross-cutting generalizations. Thus all of these clauses are subtypes of what we call *head-filler-phrase*—a kind of phrase whose immediate constituents are a filler daughter (the extracted element) and a 'slashed' clausal head daughter. This type is a subtype of *headed-phrase* and is subject to the Generalized Head Feature Principle, which requires that the syntactic and semantic properties of the mother and the head daughter be shared *by default*. These constraints govern the relevant superordinate types and their subtypes. Thus, all phrases of type *topicalized-clause* must obey the properties of *head-filler-phrase* and *headed-phrase* in addition to whatever constraints are imposed directly on the type *topicalized-clause*. This constraint inheritance is violated only when a constraint on some subordinate type contradicts a *default* constraint on some superordinate type, e.g. the GHFP.

In parallel, the types in (8) inherit constraints from other supertypes. For example, the type *wh-interrogative-clause* is a subtype of *interrogative-clause*, from which it inherits the requirement that its content is a question. The treatment of the other types of clause in (8) is similar, involving the supertypes *exclamative-clause*, *relative-clause* and *clause*. Once the proper type hierarchy is constructed and the relevant constraints are defined for all these supertypes, the stipulations specific to the types in (8) become minimal. They reduce in fact to something like those shown in (9):

(9) a. *topicalized-clause*:
$$\begin{bmatrix} \text{S} \\ \text{ROOT} \quad + \end{bmatrix} \rightarrow \begin{bmatrix} \text{WH} \quad \text{none} \end{bmatrix} \; \mathbf{H}\text{:}[\textit{fin}]$$

b. *wh-interrogative-clause*:
$$\text{S} \rightarrow \begin{bmatrix} \text{WH} \quad \text{wh-int} \end{bmatrix} \; \mathbf{H}$$

c. *wh-exclamative-clause*:
$$\text{S} \rightarrow \begin{bmatrix} \text{WH} \quad \text{wh-excl} \end{bmatrix} \; \mathbf{H}\text{:}[\textit{fin}]$$

d. *wh-relative-clause*:
$$\begin{bmatrix} \text{S} \\ \text{ROOT} \quad - \end{bmatrix} \rightarrow \begin{bmatrix} \text{WH} \quad \text{wh-rel} \end{bmatrix} \; \mathbf{H}$$

1.2.4 Some Syntactic Consequences

The simplified analysis just sketched only approximates the one we develop in this book. Our analysis will account for numerous more subtle facts about these constructions, for example the following:

- *Wh*-interrogatives and *wh*-relatives (but not topicalizations or exclamatives) can be a subjectless infinitival:
  - (10) a. I wonder [who (*for Sandy) to visit].
    - b. The person [in which (*for you) to place your trust] . . . .
    - c. *Bagels, (for) Sandy to like.
    - d. *How big a bagel (for) Sandy to like!
- In English, subjunctives never appear in interrogatives:
  - (11) a. *What be he careful of?
    - b. *I wonder what he be careful of?
    - c. *I wonder whether he be careful.
- The filler phrase in all *wh*-constructions need not be the *wh*-word, but may be a phrase properly containing the appropriate *wh*-word, subject to constraints that we specify:
  - (12) a. I wonder [[whose pictures]/*[pictures of whom] they liked]?
    - b. The person [[to whose mother] they were talking] . . . .
    - c. [What a/*What some nice person] he is!

- Uninverted *Wh*-interrogatives appear only in embedded environments:
  - (13) a. *Who(m) Kim will visit?
  - b. I wonder [who(m) Kim will visit].
- Certain auxiliaries must head inverted clauses; other auxiliaries may not:
  - (14) a. Aren't I allowed to go?/*I aren't allowed to go.
  - b. What aren't I allowed to see?/*They revealed [what I aren't allowed to see.]
  - c. Aren't I the cutest thing you ever saw!
  - d. *What be/being/been he careful of?
- Subject *Wh*-interrogatives appear in both embedded and unembedded environments:
  - (15) a. I wonder [who left].
  - b. Who left?
- Only interrogatives allow multiple *wh*-expressions:
  - (16) a. Who read what?
  - b. I wonder [who read what].
  - c. *How many presents they gave to how many people!
  - d. *The person [[whose pictures of whom] they liked best]...
- In a multiple *wh*-interrogative, only the first *wh*-expression can be modified by *the hell*, *in tarnation*, and the like:
  - (17) a. I wonder [who the hell saw Kim/*who the hell].
  - b. *Lee visited who the hell?
- Only interrogative *wh*-words can be modified by *the hell*, *in tarnation*, etc:
  - (18) a. *Anyone [who the hell saw them].
  - b. *What the hell a nice person she is!
- There are also topicalized interrogative, exclamative, and imperative clauses:
  - (19) a. That kind of antisocial behavior, can we really tolerate in a civilized society? (Radford 1988)
  - b. People that stupid, am I ever fed up with!
  - c. The Roman Forum, be sure to visit when you're in Rome!
- 'Root' is the wrong notion for restricting the constructions in (9); 'main clause phenomena' may also appear in certain embedded environments:
  - (20) They argued convincingly *(that) [problems of this sort, they would never be able to deal with].
- In simple finite VPs, which also determine the grammar of subject *wh*-interrogatives in our analysis, only 'polarized' forms of the auxiliary *do* may appear:
  - (21) a. Kim didn't go to the store.
  - b. Kim did not/TOO/SO go to the store.
  - c. *Kim dĭd go to the store.
  - (22) a. *Who dĭd leave?
  - b. Who dĭdn't leave?
  - c. Who dĭd not leave?
  - d. Who DID leave?

- Counterexamples to standard accounts of 'superiority' violations exist in multiple *wh*-interrogatives, in reprises and more generally, when accentual prominence is properly considered:

    (23)　　Who wondered what WHO was doing?

    　　　　(= Who are the x, y pairs such that x wondered what y was doing?)

    (24) A:　What did Agamemnon break?

    　　 B:　What did WHO break?

    (25) a.　Who took WHAT WHERE?

    　　 b.　What did WHO take WHERE?

    　　 c.　Where did WHO take WHAT?

We hope that the subsequent chapters, where all these matters are analyzed in detail, will serve to illustrate the explanatory power of construction-based approaches to grammar.

Clauses are pervasive in this book. The *clause*, in our view, is a special kind of construction that correlates a particular syntactic combination (a subject with a VP head; a *wh*-less filler with a sentential head, etc.) with a kind of *message*. Messages, as detailed in Chapter 3, are the semantic kinds most fundamental to communication: propositions, questions, facts, and outcomes. 'Smaller' entities in our ontology (e.g. atomic individuals, SOAs, and situations) serve as the building blocks from which atomic messages are constructed. A clause is thus a kind of construction that packages constituents into a communicatively significant unit. Not all message-denoting phrases are clauses, however. For example, two clauses can be coordinated into a phrase whose content is a complex message, but the coordination construction is not clausal because it must also allow non-clauses to be coordinated. Thus clauses in a certain sense serve to ground the recursion of complex messages in our theory.

1.3　Semantic Preview

In this section, we place our work in a broader semantic context and provide an overview of the semantic proposal we argue for in subsequent chapters.

1.3.1　Beyond Montague Semantics

In a series of ground-breaking works published in the late 1960s and early 1970s (see Thomason 1974a), Richard Montague showed how to analyze certain aspects of the meaning of natural language expressions using tools from mathematical logic. He also demonstrated that such an analysis could provide a precise alternative to Russell's (1905) view that the outward form of language is misleading and hence not amenable to *direct* semantic analysis. Montague's framework provides a formalization of an essentially Fregean view of semantics.[13] However, Montague's framework has been criticized with respect to at least three fundamental issues:

1. **Cognitive construal**: Montague's theory of propositions, in contrast to Frege's (unformalized) version, is subject to the problem of *logical omniscience*.[14] This impairs significantly its ability to serve as the semantic component of a broader cognitive theory of mind.

---

[13] Albeit one that Frege might not have endorsed. Frege analyzed propositions in terms of senses that have internal structure. However, the fine-grain achieved in Frege's analysis gets lost in Montague's formalization. Of course, the formalization was motivated by the need to clarify the nature of the units that make up Fregean senses.

[14] *Logical omniscience* is the property of assigning identical content to logically equivalent sentences. There is by now a large literature on this problem. For a succinct illustration of the problem in a doxastic context, see Kamp 1990.

2. **Ontology**: Montague's possible worlds-based ontology is an intensionalized version of the sparse entity/truth value ontology advocated in Wittgenstein's Tractatus (see Thomason 1974b). Montague's ontology is hence both cognitively unwieldy and impoverished. (See Bealer 1982 and Barwise and Perry 1983 for detailed discussion.)

3. **Context**: Montague's framework offers an account of context dependence by relativizing interpretation to a pragmatic index. However, as already pointed out by Cresswell (1973), this latter notion is quite arbitrary. The components of an index are determined in an essentially ad hoc way and, moreover, such a view of context lacks the external coherence needed to underwrite complex notions like deixis and bridging reference (see, for example, Clark 1977).[15]

All three issues are crucially important when constructing an account of the meaning and use of interrogatives. It is obvious that if a semantic theory is to serve as a component in a theory of how agents interact in conversation, then it must have the potential for cognitive construal. For example, it must be possible to explain how queries and assertions function in affecting the information states of agents in dialogue.[16]

The importance of integrating contextual factors into the grammatical analysis of interrogatives becomes evident in connection with the notion of answerhood, which lies at the heart of explaining what interrogatives mean. As discussed briefly below and at length in Chapter 3, existing accounts of interrogative meaning have seriously underestimated the extent to which context influences answerhood.

Ontological analysis is also vital to a proper explanation of the meaning of interrogatives. The predicates *believe* and *know* are commonly thought of as selecting for a propositional argument. However, as Vendler (1972) pointed out, this view is highly problematic. To take one example from the many we discuss in Chapter 3, the word *know* licenses inference patterns such as (26), whereas the word *believe* is incompatible with both *fact*-NPs and interrogative clauses:

(26) a.   Bo knows/believes that Mo left.
    b. A: Who left?
       B: Bo knows a fact that resolves that question.
           Hence, Bo knows who left.
    c. A: Who left?
       B: #Bo believes a fact that resolves that question.
       B′:   #Bo believes who left.

That such facts cannot be reduced to idiosyncratic syntactic subcategorization is demonstrated by (27) and, more intriguingly, by the fact that such patterns are cross-linguistically universal:

(27) a. A: Jo left yesterday.
       B: Bo knows/believes that.
    b. A: Who left yesterday?
       B: #Bo believes that.
    c. A: Who left yesterday?
       B: Bo knows that.

---

[15]Groenendijk and Stokhof (1991a) and Chierchia (1995) provide a new version of Montague's theory that allows interesting aspects of context dependence and contextual change to be modeled.

[16]We use 'interrogatives' as a cover term for a class of constructions, 'questions' for the class of entities denoted by interrogatives, and 'queries' for speech acts that involve posing questions.

As we discuss in Chapter 3, such universals remain unaccounted for in existing Montagovian approaches to interrogatives (e.g. those of Karttunen 1977 and Groenendijk and Stokhof 1984). The importance of working out the ontology of natural language is recognized in lexical semantics (see for instance the program initiated by Pustejovsky 1995). However, with some interesting but isolated exceptions (e.g. Bach 1981, Chierchia 1985, Moens and Steedman 1988, and Asher 1993), the issue of an adequate ontology for natural language semantics has been neglected in contemporary formal semantics. Many insights that have arisen in the philosophical literature, most influentially those of Vendler, have not led to significant attempts to develop a theory that supplants the existing overly sparse Montagovian ontology. As Kamp (1996) has observed with respect to research on the distinctions between events, facts, and propositions, "that so many of those questions remain unanswered and so few have been answered deserves to be considered one of the great scandals of semantics." (p. 106)

Deferring detailed argumentation to later chapters, we suggest here that various intrinsically problematic aspects of Montague Semantics affect its ability to elucidate the meaning and use of interrogatives. What, then, is a viable alternative?

1.3.2 Situation Theory and Situation Semantics

In their book *Situations and Attitudes*, Barwise and Perry (1983) present a new approach to semantics, which they argue should supplant Montague's framework. Two aspects of their program should be mentioned:

(28) a. **An information-conditional approach to semantic modeling:** Barwise and Perry suggest that the logical underpinning for semantics be a theory of the information that agents can acquire as they interact in the world. Given this, the framework they develop provides tools for describing external reality in terms that can capture the resource-bounded nature of perception.

b. **An utterance-based formulation of semantics:** Barwise and Perry argue that context dependence should not be tackled by viewing context as an incidental modality that somehow affects sentences. Rather, semantics should take utterances, spatio-temporally located speech events, as the entities whose contents it analyzes. In their view, meanings pertain to types of utterances. Indexicality is then accommodated directly as the dependence on features that characterize a speech event.

In essence, semantic work inspired by *Situations and Attitudes* branched in two distinct directions, which correlate with (28a) and (28b). One direction, involving formally oriented work, came to be known as Situation Theory (ST). The second direction, concerning itself with more grammatically oriented work using tools developed by situation theorists, acquired the name Situation Semantics (SitSem).

By far the most influential contribution of ST has been the recognition that the semantic ontology needs 'sub-world' entities such as situations or events to explain, among other things, the semantics of naked infinitive constructions and domain restriction in quantification. At the same time, despite the initial interest created by ST, its impact on working semanticists has been limited. One limiting factor has been the lack, until recently, of stable modeling techniques in ST. Possibly more important is the perception that an ST approach requires buying into a very rich ontology whose empirical justification has been insufficient. One can relate this concern to the dearth of work that tries to simultaneously combine on a large scale: (a) a linguistically well-motivated ontology, (b) a well worked-out model theory, and (c) formal grammatical analysis. As we mentioned above with respect to syntax, as long as attention is focused on highly restricted sets of phenomena, theories are intrinsically underdetermined by data. Without integrative work of the sort just described, the illusion emerges that all semantic theories are essentially equipotent.

One of the central aims of this book is to demonstrate the viability and vitality of a situation semantics approach. To this end, we provide extensive linguistic argumentation for an ontology needed to analyze the contents of all the major types of finite clauses in English, with particular focus on interrogatives. We use the framework developed by Seligman and Moss (1997) to ground this ontology model-theoretically. We then show how to represent this model theory within a version of the well-developed formalism of Typed Feature Structures. On one hand, as is shown in Chapter 3, the ontological approach of Montague Grammar can be related to that of ST, rather than viewing the former as being disconnected from the latter.[17] On the other hand, we believe that a situation semantics approach provides particular benefits as semantics begins to confront the radical context dependence of actual dialogue. The analyses of reprise and ellipsis phenomena that we present in Chapters 7 and 8, including accounts of short answers (29a), direct sluicing (29b), reprise sluices (29c), and literal reprises (29d), will provide a particularly clear illustration of how situation semantics can be applied to radically context-dependent semantic problems:

(29) a. A: Who managed to annoy no one?
          B: No one.
      b. A: Did anyone call?
          B: Yes.
          A: Who?
      c. A: Did you meet Makriyannis.
          B: WHO?
      d. A: Did Mo dupe the judges?
          B: Mo?

1.3.3   Some Semantic Theses

We now wish to point out a number of concrete areas in which we believe our account constitutes a significant advance over previous work, and indeed points to flaws in fundamental assumptions that have dominated past work on the meaning and use of interrogatives.

Questions and Answerhood Conditions

The semantic universe we create allows us to formally ground a common intuition about questions, namely that they are akin to open propositions. Specifically, we identify questions with propositional abstracts. In fact, the open-proposition view has a long history which goes back at least to Jespersen (1924) and Cohen (1929). However, although this view resurfaces periodically, it has to date not managed to survive in the face of competition from alternatives which we call Exhaustive Answerhood Conditions (EAC) approaches, whose most influential representatives are Karttunen (1977) and Groenendijk and Stokhof (1984, 1989, 1997). As we discuss in Chapter 3, existing proposals to treat questions as open propositions run into significant formal

---

[17]This point has been emphasized in work by Cooper (for instance, Cooper 1993).

and empirical problems, for instance in the domain of coordination. Moreover, they leave several crucial issues entirely unanswered.

Perhaps the most serious of these inadequacies is a failure to offer an account of so-called *exhaustive* answerhood as needed to explicate the meaning of interrogatives embedded by factive predicates (e.g. *know, discover*, and *reveal*), which license inferences like the following:

(30) a. Mo discovered who participated in the heist.

  b. Hence, Mo discovered a fact that resolved the question who participated in the heist.

Indeed, providing an account of such clauses served as the defining problem of EAC approaches like Karttunen's and Groenendijk and Stokhof's. Nonetheless, as we detail in Chapter 3, EAC approaches do not ultimately deliver an adequate account of answerhood. This is for two main reasons. First, such approaches ignore the intricate contextual factors that play an important role in the notion of exhaustiveness. Second, other equally important semantic notions of answerhood exist, such as the notion of *aboutness* (Ginzburg 1995a). It is *aboutness* that underlies the intuitions speakers have about the coherence of replies to queries, regardless of their truth or specificity. As we will see, EAC accounts of *aboutness* that derive this notion from exhaustiveness are inadequate.

We will show that, within the semantic universe we define, the various formal and empirical problems facing an open-proposition approach to the semantics of interrogatives can be solved. Furthermore, we will demonstrate that a variety of answerhood notions needed for semantic and pragmatic explanation can readily be defined. Thus, the notion of question we provide is not identified with any particular notion of answerhood; rather it constitutes a means of *underspecifying* answerhood.

Wh-Expressions Are Not Generalized Quantifiers

Our view of what questions are leads to an extremely simple view of *wh*-phrase meaning. Essentially, a *wh-phrase* does two things: (1) it enables an abstraction to occur, over the parameter that the *wh*-phrase associates with the semantic argument role it fills and (2) it introduces certain restrictions over that argument-role—personhood for *who*, inanimateness for *what*, the common-noun property for *which*-phrases, etc. We say 'essentially' because we argue in fact that interrogative *wh*-phrases have three distinct types of use:[18] (1) an *independent* use, which is our primary focus in this book; (2) a *functional(ly dependent)* use; (3) a *reprise* use. We demonstrate in Chapters 6 and 7 that, in spite of these differences, a single constraint captures the commonality of these three uses in building up a question. The differences among the three types of use arise from independent mechanisms—lexical, in the case of functional readings, and constructional, in the case of reprise readings.

This view of *wh*-phrase meaning, which we claim accounts for all interrogative uses in English, contrasts with a view of *wh*-phrases as generalized quantifiers. The syntactic motivation for this highly entrenched view, particularly among syntacticians, is examined below.[19] The quantificational view also has some semantic motivation, such as the need to account for the ambi-

---

[18] We also provide analyses of *wh*-phrases as they occur in exclamative and (to a lesser extent) relative clauses. These, we suggest, behave somewhat differently from interrogative *wh*-phrases.

[19] The view of *wh*-expressions as quantifiers has antecedents in remarks made by Carnap (1937) and Reichenbach (1947).

guity manifested in sentences such as (31a) given that they can elicit responses such as (31b) or as (31c):

(31) a. A: Which movie did each senator condemn?
      b. B: *Naked Lunch*.
      c. B: Helms condemned *Huckleberry Finn*, Lieberman condemned *Crash*, ...

As argued in Chapter 4, such ambiguities are anything but straightforward 'scope ambiguities'. We consider past treatments of this phenomenon and show that accounts treating *wh*-phrases as quantifiers are forced to adopt otherwise unmotivated mechanisms to account for the ambiguity. In contrast, we will defend the strategy of Engdahl (1980, 1986), who proposes tackling the ambiguity in terms of an additional *functional* use of *wh*-phrases. We also provide additional arguments for a non-quantificational view of *wh*-phrases, the most detailed of which concerns the presuppositions associated with *which*-phrases.

Wh-Phrase Meaning and Dislocation

The utterance-based formulation of semantic theory pioneered by situation semantics (see above) has for the most part been perceived as obscure, and thus has rarely been pursued. This apparent obscurity is the result of a pervasive simplifying assumption and a frequently asserted dogma. The simplifying assumption, almost universally shared by generative grammarians and formal semanticists, is that a grammar should describe a homogeneous speech community. The dogma, promoted in various writings (see, for example, Chomsky 1986), holds that the proper domain of study for linguistics is something Chomsky calls 'I(nternalized)-language', as opposed to 'E(xternalized)-language'. E-language is described as "a collection of actions, utterances, linguistic forms (words, sentences) paired with meanings, or a system of linguistic forms or events" (Chomsky 1986: 19), whereas I-language is described as a biologically endowed "notion of structure in the mind of the speaker" (Chomsky 1986: 21).

We believe that this is a false dichotomy. One may agree that grammatical theory is a subfield of cognitive science and, as such, needs to contribute to mental, and even biological, modeling. However, this in no way entails adopting a solipsistic perspective on the agents whose grammatical systems are being modeled. Quite to the contrary, a variety of evidence requires us to adopt a realist position, where grammars describe types of speech events in which embodied agents *interact* with one another. Reprise utterances, a detailed analysis of which we provide in Chapter 7, constitute some of the evidence for this claim.

The issue of whether or not grammars can be assumed to pertain to homogeneous speech communities and the issue of E-language vs. I-language might seem remote from the more concrete task of developing a grammar for interrogatives. In fact, there is an interesting connection between these issues, mediated by the assumption that *wh*-phrases are syntactic operators. This view, taken together with the possibility of movement at distinct derivational levels, often has been offered as an explanation for a putative linguistic universal, namely that *wh*-phrases are obligatorily fronted. With this approach, languages can be partitioned into those where *wh*-phrases obligatorily move 'in the syntax', such as English, and those where such movement takes place at an abstract level of Logical Form, such as Mandarin. Indeed, the role played by LF in such explanations played an important role in its achieving canonical status in linguistic theory. Sentences such as (32)—in particular (32a,b), where the wide scoping *wh*-phrase occurs within an island—have rarely been thought to pose a threat to the assumption that *wh*-fronting is obligatory:

(32) a. Merle knows who ate WHAT?

   b. Mo dislikes Merle and WHO ELSE?

   c. You're leaving WHEN?

The reason for this is the commonly held belief that (1) such sentences can only be used as *reprise* questions—Bolinger's term for a class of uses which includes, but is not limited to 'echo' questions—and furthermore (2) the syntax and semantics of such forms are outside the purview of grammar proper. In Chapter 7, we argue that both these assumptions are false. We show, based in part on insights of previous research, that reprise uses obey various well-known grammatical constraints. Moreover, given a theory of utterance processing, which we sketch briefly, a variety of reprise utterances can be described simply, without postulating additional theoretical apparatus. Of course, in order to develop a grammar for reprising one must drop the assumption that grammars pertain to homogeneous speech communities, since the very point of a reprise is to highlight differences in the information states of speech participants. Indeed, one must allow utterances as entities in the grammatical ontology since utterances are indeed the antecedents of reprise queries.

Given an analysis of the semantics of reprise utterances, we will be able to demonstrate that English also allows for non-reprise *wh*-interrogative constructions in which no *wh*-phrase is dislocated. For instance:

(33) Lester: I've been working here for 14 years. You've been here for how long? A month?
      [from the movie *American Beauty*]

The analysis we develop for such constructions extends surprisingly to yield an analysis of so called intonation questions—declarative constructions used to pose polar questions:

(34) Bo will also attend the convention?

1.4 Conclusion

The chapters of this book are interconnected to an unusual degree. The consequences of a proposal in one chapter are often intimately involved with the details of another. For this reason, we have included three appendices that lay out the overall theory of the book in a manner more uniform and complete than the presentations in any one chapter.

Finally, we note that many of the analyses presented here have made their way into the large-scale computational grammar of English developed by the LINGO project at Stanford University's Center for the Study of Language and Information. For the beginnings of a computational implementation based directly on the grammar of this book, see Callison-Burch 2000 and Ginzburg et al. 2000.

2

HPSG: Background

2.1 Introduction

In this chapter, we outline the basics of a particular version of HPSG. We begin with the lexicon and its organization, turning next to the important consequences of our decision to model phrases as feature structures. A multidimensional hierarchy of phrases is introduced, along with a sketch of how this allows cross-classifying generalizations about constructions to be expressed. We build up an account of simple finite clauses—both indicative and subjunctive, and then extend this account to subjectless infinitival clauses. Finally, we provide a few examples of lexical entries whose complement selection properties can be simplified, given the semantic types associated with the clausal constructions presented here. We leave until Chapter 5 a presentation of our treatment of filler-gap constuctions, the inheritance of *wh*-specifications, and an account of quantifier scoping, all of which play a role in the analyses of interrogatives developed in subsequent chapters.

2.2 Feature Structures

Utterances in HPSG are modeled as feature structures of type *sign*. Since the features associated with structures of this type include PHONOLOGY and SYNSEM, the latter specifying both syntactic and semantic information, the constraints we impose on signs correspond to the general conventions governing the sound-syntax-meaning relation in a given language. A system of signs thus provides a finite specification of an infinite set of utterance kinds.

But linguistic information can be complex. Within the feature structures specified as values of SYNSEM, numerous grammatical distinctions must be made: *noun* vs. *verb* vs. other parts of speech; *nom* vs. *acc* case; *vowel* vs. *consonant*, and so forth. In order to make such distinctions, a grammar must posit many kinds of linguistic entities 'smaller' than the signs, and must provide an account of the specific properties of each such kind. The grammar of a language thus must include:

- an enumeration of the set of types (sometimes called 'sorts') that play a role in the grammar—a linguistic ontology,
- a statement of which features are appropriate for each type,
- a statement what type of value is appropriate for each such feature, and
- a specification of all constraints that instances of particular types must satisfy (usually referred to simply as 'type constraints').

The modeling assumptions of HPSG have provided a novel way of working with certain traditional notions of grammar (e.g. 'lexical entry' and 'phrase structure rule') that allows increased precision and analytic uniformity. Lexical entries are descriptions of (or constraints on) feature structures that belong to the type *word*; construction rules (or phrase structure rules, or 'immediate dominance schemata') are partial descriptions of feature structures of type *phrase*. These are the immediate subtypes of the type *sign*. Hence, the lexical entries and construction rules work together: the lexical entries define a set of words; the construction rules define a set of phrases built from words or phrases. A language can then be viewed in various ways, for example as the set of feature structures of type *sign* that satisfy the constraints of the grammar, the set of feature structures of type *phrase* that satisfy all relevant constraints, as the set of PHONOLOGY values of those signs, etc. Each such characterization may have its own utility.

2.3   Words

In the case of words, then, an HPSG grammar specifies an inventory of lexical types and the various constraints that instances of those types must obey. We follow the common practice of formulating lexical descriptions (constraints on objects of type *lexeme* or *word*) in the language of attribute-value matrices (AVMs):[1]

(1)

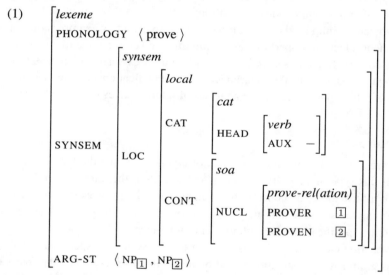

Lexical descriptions like (1) specify complexes of phonological, syntactic and semantic information that are satisfied by a family of feature structures. These feature structures are structured according to a particular nonarbitrary feature geometry. For example, *synsem* objects (the syntactico-semantic complexes that serve as values of the feature SYNSEM) encapsulate precisely the information that heads can select for, and thus play a key role in the HPSG account of the locality of subcategorization. Similar considerations motivate the supposition of *local* objects (these encapsulate the information transmitted in raising and extraction dependencies), and the other embedded feature stuctures illustrated in (1).

---

[1]We abbreviate feature names as needed, e.g. CAT (CATEGORY), CONT (CONTENT), ARG-ST (ARGUMENT-STRUCTURE), NUCL (NUCLEUS), LOC (LOCAL) and SS (SYNSEM). For a complete list of abbreviations used in this book, see the List of Abbreviations.

The feature geometry illustrated in (1) is a consequence of the linguistic ontology specified by the grammar. In particular, a grammar provides a complete specification of what types of feature structure exist and how those types are organized into a hierarchy, i.e. for each type, what its immediate supertypes (IST) are. The grammar also specifies which features are appropriate for each grammatical type, as well as what type of value is appropriate for each feature, as in (2):[2]

(2)

TYPE	FEATURES/TYPE OF VALUE	IST
sign	$\begin{bmatrix} \text{PHONOLOGY} & list(form) \\ \text{SYNSEM} & synsem \\ \text{CONTEXT} & conx\text{-}obj \end{bmatrix}$	*feat-struc*
phrase	$\cdots$	*sign*
lex-sign	$\begin{bmatrix} \text{ARG-ST} & list(synsem) \end{bmatrix}$	*sign*
lexeme		*lex-sign*
word		*lex-sign*
synsem	$\begin{bmatrix} \text{LOCAL} & local \\ \text{SLASH} & set(local) \\ \text{WH} & set(scope\text{-}obj) \\ \text{BCKGRND} & set(fact) \end{bmatrix}$	*feat-struc*
local	$\begin{bmatrix} \text{CATEGORY} & category \\ \text{CONTENT} & sem\text{-}object \\ \text{STORE} & set(scope\text{-}obj) \end{bmatrix}$	*feat-struc*
category	$\begin{bmatrix} \text{HEAD} & part\text{-}of\text{-}speech \\ \text{SUBJ} & list(synsem) \\ \text{COMPS} & list(synsem) \\ \text{SPR} & list(synsem) \end{bmatrix}$	*feat-struc*
$\cdots$	$\cdots$	$\cdots$

We will add further details about types, features, and type constraints as we present particular analyses. The type system for the English grammar fragment developed in this book is summarized in Appendix A.

---

[2]The feature WH correponds to the feature QUE of Pollard and Sag (1994). This feature has two related functions: (1) to distinguish interrogative and exclamative *wh*-words from all other words, and (2) to distinguish phrases containing such words from those that do not. WH and the feature SLASH—used to encode information about extracted elements in filler-gap constructions—are discussed in Chapter 5. The feature BACKGROUND (BCKGRD), which plays a significant role in the analyses of Chapters 7 and 8, is discussed in Chapters 3, 4 and 5. Finally, it should be noted that in the feature geometry we assume, the feature CONTEXT (CTXT) is declared at the level of SIGN, not LOCAL, as in previous proposals. Nothing essential hinges on this aspect of our analysis. *Conx-obj* abbreviates *contextual-object*.

This particular organization of linguistic information seeks to provide an account of the empirical fact that subcategorization (category selection in the familiar sense), case and role assignment, semantic selection, and head-valent agreement all operate in highly constrained local domains. Agreement with or selection for the complement of a complement, for example, is systematically precluded, as is case or role 'assignment' to a complement's complement. By constraining head-valent constructions so that the head daughter's value for valence features like SUBJ(ECT), COMPLEMENTS (COMPS), and SPECIFIER (SPR) is identified with the SYNSEM value of the relevant valent daughter(s), it follows that lexical heads have restricted access to information about the elements they combine with: they may select for only information that is encoded within a valent's *synsem* object. The relevant locality effects are thus a consequence of the interaction of the geometry of *synsem* objects and the theory of head-valent constructions.[3]

Let us return to lexical entries. Note first that very little of the information in a lexical entry like (1) must be listed in the lexicon. This is true because lexical types, type inheritance, and the theory of linking[4] allow complex lexical information like that shown in (1) to be derived, rather than stipulated. That is, much of this information is inferred via the 'logic of the lexicon'. For example, inflectional rules build words from lexemes whose basic subcategorizational properties are diverse. These lexemes are in turn organized into families whose members share grammatically significant properties, stated as constraints on particular lexemic types (corresponding to particular lexical natural classes). The resulting lexical architecture is represented as a multiple inheritance hierarchy where, for example, 'part of speech' and 'argument selection' provide independent dimensions of classification and constraint, as shown in (3).

(3)

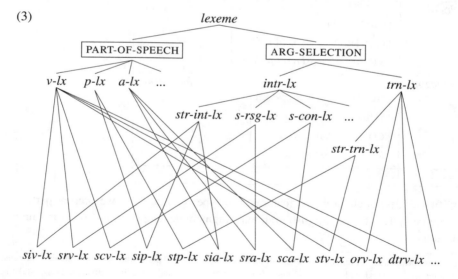

---

[3]The *synsem* architecture presented here is not yet entirely satisfactory in this respect, as it makes arbitrarily deep semantic structures available for local selection. For recent work that provides the basis of a solution to this problem, see Copestake et al. 2000.

[4]See Wechsler 1995, Davis 1996, 2001, Davis and Koenig 1999. It should be noted that these researchers utilize semantic roles of a coarser grain (e.g. ACTOR, UNDERGOER) than those assumed here. Nothing in this book turns on the issue of role granularity.

Here we use the following abbreviations for non-maximal types:

(4)   a.   *v-lx*: *verb-lexeme*
      b.   *p-lx*: *preposition-lexeme*
      c.   *a-lx*: *adjective-lexeme*
      d.   *intr-lx*: *intransitive-lexeme*
      e.   *trn-lx*: *transitive-lexeme*
      f.   *str-int-lx*: *strict-intransitive-lexeme*
      g.   *s-rsg-lx*: *subject-raising-lexeme*
      h.   *s-con-lx*: *subject-control-lexeme*
      i.   *str-trn-lx*: *strict-transitive-lexeme*

And the maximal lexemic types (the lexemic 'species' in the sense of King (1989) at the bottom of this hierarchy can then be assumed to be those shown in (5).[5]

(5)   a.   *siv-lx*: *strict-intransitive-verb-lexeme* (e.g. *die*)
      b.   *srv-lx*: *subject-raising-verb-lexeme* (e.g. *seem*)
      c.   *scv-lx*: *subject-control-verb-lexeme* (e.g. *try*)
      d.   *sip-lx*: *strict-intransitive-preposition-lexeme* (e.g. *of*)
      e.   *stp-lx*: *strict-transitive-preposition-lexeme* (e.g. *in*)
      f.   *sia-lx*: *strict-intransitive-adjective-lexeme* (e.g. *big*)
      g.   *sra-lx*: *subject-raising-adjective-lexeme* (e.g. *likely*)
      h.   *sca-lx*: *subject-control-adjective-lexeme* (e.g. *eager*)
      i.   *stv-lx*: *strict-transitive-verb-lexeme* (e.g. *prove*)
      j.   *orv-lx*: *object-raising-verb-lexeme* (e.g. *believe*)
      k.   *dtrv-lx*: *ditransitive-verb-lexeme* (e.g. *believe*)

Note that *of* is here classified as an *sip* because it takes only one argument—its object.[6] The preposition *in*, by contrast, is transitive because it has two arguments. In modificational uses (e.g. *the nail in the bowl*), the first argument of *in* is the modified nominal (*nail*). In predicative uses (e.g. *The nail is in the bowl.*), the first argument is the unexpressed subject of *in*, which the copula identifies with its own subject (*the nail*).[7]

This mode of lexical analysis, pioneered by early work in HPSG, reflects the fundamental fact that lexical regularities are cross-cutting in a way that is elegantly modeled by lexical type hierarchies and constraint inheritance. Some of the particular constraints we assume for particular lexical types are illustrated in (6):[8]

---

[5]For convenience, we are here ignoring a number of lexical types that this system of classification is easily extended to accommodate.

[6]At least this is the most common classification. *Of* also leads a life as a transitive preposition, for example, in *This is of the utmost importance.*

[7]For further discussion of this distinction, see Sag and Wasow 1999, chap. 7.

[8]'⟨ XP ⟩' designates a list containing exactly one phrasal element; '⟨ ⟩' designates the empty list. Note that the analysis of raising assumed here (unlike the one presented in Pollard and Sag 1994, for example) involves identifying just the LOCAL value of the raised argument and the unexpressed subject of a following argument. By sharing only LOCAL information in raising constructions, we allow certain discrepancies between the raised argument and the relevant unexpressed subject. As shown by Miller and Sag (1997) and Abeillé et al. (1998), non-local information distinguishing 'clitic' arguments (realized as pronominal affixes on the verb) must not be transmitted through raising dependencies. Similarly, in the analysis of extraction dependencies we present in Chapter 5, the extraction information encoded in the value of the nonlocal feature SLASH must not be transmitted in raising.

(6) a.
$$v\text{-}lx \Rightarrow \left[\text{SS}|\text{LOC}|\text{CAT} \begin{bmatrix} \text{HEAD} & v \\ \text{SPR} & \langle\,\rangle \\ \text{SUBJ} & \langle\,\text{XP}\,\rangle \end{bmatrix} \right]$$

b. $p\text{-}lx \Rightarrow \left[\text{SS}|\text{LOC}|\text{CAT}|\text{HEAD} \quad p \right]$

c. $a\text{-}lx \Rightarrow \left[\text{SS}|\text{LOC}|\text{CAT}|\text{HEAD} \quad a \right]$

d. $trn\text{-}lx \Rightarrow \left[\text{ARG-ST} \quad \langle\,\text{NP}\,,\,\text{NP}\,,\,...\,\rangle \right]$

e. $str\text{-}intr\text{-}lx \Rightarrow \left[\text{ARG-ST} \quad \langle\,\text{NP}\,\rangle \right]$

f. $s\text{-}rsg\text{-}lx \Rightarrow \left[\text{ARG-ST} \quad \langle\,[\text{LOC}\;\boxed{1}]\,,\,[\text{SUBJ}\,\langle[\text{LOC}\;\boxed{1}]\rangle]\,\rangle \right]$

g. $s\text{-}ctrl\text{-}lx \Rightarrow \left[\text{ARG-ST} \quad \langle\,\text{NP}_i\,,\,[\text{SUBJ}\,\langle\text{NP}_i\rangle]\,\rangle \right]$

h. $str\text{-}trn\text{-}lx \Rightarrow \left[\text{ARG-ST} \quad \langle\,\text{NP}\,,\,\text{NP}\,\rangle \right]$

i. $orv\text{-}lx \Rightarrow \left[\text{ARG-ST} \quad \langle\,\text{NP}\,,\,[\text{LOC}\;\boxed{1}]\,,\,[\text{SUBJ}\,\langle[\text{LOC}\;\boxed{1}]\rangle]\,\rangle \right]$

j. $dtrv\text{-}lx \Rightarrow \left[\text{ARG-ST} \quad \langle\,\text{NP}\,,\,\text{NP}\,,\,\text{NP}\,\rangle \right]$

. . .

The type constraints in (6) should be understood as stating general properties (as particular feature-value specifications) of particular lexemic types. Individual lexemes assigned to an appropriate maximal lexemic type (a leaf type in a type hierarchy like (6)) inherit the constraints associated with that type and all its supertypes. Some of these constraints involve default specifications that may be overridden by conflicting constraints on subtypes or by idiosyncratic individual lexemes. All the defaults we employ here (based on the theory outlined in Lascarides and Copestake 1999) are non-persistent. That is, though the 'initial description' of the lexeme hierarchy may involve the use of default constraints, these defaults are either overridden or rigidified through the process of constraint inheritance. Thus, in each description of some instance of a maximal type (e.g. a full description of the lexeme *give*) there are only hard constraints.[9]

---

[9]Thus the lexical descriptions we posit could be formulated within a logic like SRL (King 1989) or RSRL (Richter 1999, 2000). However, the latter foundations provide no means for expressing default regularities of the sort that we claim constitute linguistically significant generalizations about lexemes, words, and constructions. By contrast, the foundations adopted here allow default generalizations to be expressed and are highly restrictive in addition. For example, relations, negation, and full quantification are all lacking, a fact that prevents certain kinds of HPSG analyses that are in the literature from being expressed *directly*. The trade-off for this, however, is computational tractability—the immediate possibility of developing precise, wide-coverage grammars that can be used in practical applications involving both parsing and generation. On this last point, see Flickinger et al. 2001.

Finally, consider the following principle (essential to our treatment of words) that relates ARG-ST lists to the valence features SUBJ, COMPS, and SPR:[10]

(7)   Argument Realization Principle (ARP; preliminary version):

$$
word \Rightarrow \begin{bmatrix} \text{SS|LOC|CAT} & \begin{bmatrix} \text{SUBJ} & \boxed{A} \\ \text{SPR} & \boxed{B} \\ \text{COMPS} & \boxed{C} \end{bmatrix} \\ \text{ARG-ST} & \boxed{A} \oplus \boxed{B} \oplus \boxed{C} \end{bmatrix}
$$

This formulation of the ARP simply ensures that all arguments are realized on the appropriate valence list—and hence are selected by a given word in a headed construction (see below). Note that if a word is specified as [SUBJ ⟨ ⟩] and [SPR ⟨ ⟩], it then follows from the ARP that all of that word's arguments appear on its COMPS list. A word like *proves*, on the other hand, is an inflected form of the lexeme *prove* and hence, through the interaction of the constraint in (6a) and the ARP, it must include the following information:

(8)
$$
\begin{bmatrix} \text{SS|LOC|CAT} & \begin{bmatrix} \text{SUBJ} & \langle \boxed{3} \rangle \\ \text{SPR} & \langle \ \rangle \\ \text{COMPS} & \langle \boxed{4} \rangle \end{bmatrix} \\ \text{ARG-ST} & \langle \boxed{3}\text{NP} , \boxed{4}\text{NP} \rangle \end{bmatrix}
$$

The valence properties of the inflected form *proves*—that it must combine with an object complement and a subject, but no specifier—are thus appropriately related to the argument structure specified for the (*stv*) lexeme *prove* in (1).[11]

Of course there is considerable cross-linguistic variation in argument realization. In the approach adopted here, the various well known patterns, e.g. the realization of unexpressed arguments as pronominal affixes in Romance languages (Miller and Sag 1997, Monachesi 1999) and so-called 'pro drop' phenomena, are treated as language-particular variations of the ARP. All these realizations are intuitively 'subtractions'—that is, they involve *synsem* elements that belong to a word's ARG-ST list, but which fail to be realized in any of its valence lists (SUBJ, COMPS, or SPR). In Chapter 5, we present a modification of (7) that treats extracted complements in terms of a discrepancy between a word's ARG-ST list and its COMPS list.

2.4   Features of Verbals

We follow Sag (1997) in assuming that the part of speech types (the values of the feature HEAD) associated with verbs (*v*) and complementizers (*c*) are subtypes of a common supertype called *verbal*. Taking into account the theory of gerunds developed by Malouf (1998, 2000), where

---

[10]Here and throughout we use capital letters to distinguish tags designating lists.

[11]The relation between lexemes and words can be captured either via lexical rules or else by a type system where words are simultaneously classified in two dimensions: lexeme and inflection. For proposals along the latter lines, see Koenig 1999, Miller and Sag 1997, Abeillé et al. 1998, and Bouma et al. 2001. For convenience, we will adopt the lexical rule approach here. For more on lexical rules in HPSG, see Copestake 1992, Meurers and Minnen 1997, Copestake and Briscoe 1992, Meurers 2000, and (for a more elementary presentation) Sag and Wasow 1999. Bouma et al. (2000) provide an overview and comparison of various approaches to expressing lexical regularities in HPSG. See also Briscoe et al. 1994.

gerunds and verbs also share a common supertype—*verb*, we have the following part of speech hierarchy:[12]

(9)

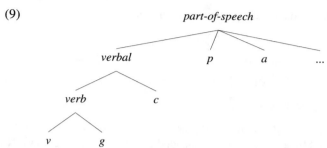

The features VERBFORM (VFORM) and IC (INDEPENDENT-CLAUSE) are declared to be appropriate for the type *verbal*, i.e. for both verbs and complementizers. Other features, e.g. AUX(ILIARY), and INV(ERTED), are appropriate only for instances of type *verb*. Verbs and gerunds are distinguished in terms of their valence properties, as explained briefly in Chapter 5.

2.4.1 Distinguishing Verbal Forms

The values of the feature VFORM—*finite (fin)*, *infinitive (inf)*, *base*, *present-participle (prp)*, *perfect-participle (pfp)*, and *passive-participle (pas)*—are organized into a (multiple-inheritance) hierarchy as shown in (10):

(10)

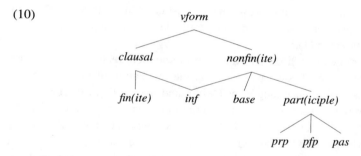

These correspond to familiar distinctions among verb forms; the types in this hierarchy are motivated in part by subcategorization. For example, *pfp* is the VFORM value of perfect participles, e.g. those heading VPs selected by the auxiliary *have*. By contrast, modals select for a VP whose head daughter is [VFORM *base*]. In both cases, the VP complement's VFORM specification is the same as that of the VP's head daughter, in virtue of the (Generalized) Head Feature Principle discussed in the next section. The nonfinite auxiliary verb *to* is the only verb specified as [VFORM *inf*]. The complementizer *for* is also so specified, however, making *to*-phrases and *for-to* phrases a syntactic natural class.

Since the analysis sketched here differs in a variety of ways from previous work in the tradition of GPSG/HPSG, we will briefly consider the evidence for the grammatical distinctions we have made. The groupings in (10) are motivated by various criteria. First, the supertype *clausal* is used to distinguish the verb forms (those specified as [VFORM *fin*] and [VFORM *inf*]) that head

---

[12]Malouf also classifies the HEAD values of gerunds and nouns as having a common supertype *noun*, thus providing a treatment of gerunds as a 'mixed' category.

clausal constructions. All of the clauses we study here (declaratives, interrogatives, exclamatives, relatives and imperatives) are headed by verbs specified as [VFORM *clausal*].

Our second, partially overlapping, classification of verb forms has an independent motivation. The grammar of negation, for example, makes reference to the *fin/nonfin* distinction. Constituent negation of verbal phrases is possible in English only when the phrase modified is headed by a [VFORM *nonfin*] form, as illustrated by the contrasts in (11).

(11) a. *Kim [not [walks]].   ([VFORM *fin*])
      b. I prefer to [not [be nominated]].   ([VFORM *base*])
      c. I prefer [not [to be nominated]].   ([VFORM *inf*])
      d. [Not speaking French] is a disadvantage.   ([VFORM *prp*])
      e. I would have [not finished in time].   ([VFORM *pfp*])
      f. [Not given any awards at the banquet], Sandy went home disgruntled. ([VFORM *pas*])

Moreover, auxiliary verb forms that are [VFORM *fin*] (and indicative or conditional, in addition) are the only ones that can select *not* as a complement, so as to express sentential negation:[13]

(12) a. Kim is not going.
      b. If Kim were not going to the party, then....
      c. *I prefer that Kim be not put in charge.
      d. *Be not overly concerned!
      e. *Being not a Republican is a disdvantage.
      f. *Pat has been not to Paris.
      g. *Sandy was visited not.

Note that imperative forms (e.g. *Go!*, *Eat!*) are [VFORM *fin*] in our analysis, predicting that they cannot be modified by constituent negation:

(13)   *[Not [go to the store]]!

The type *part* is motivated by the grammar of modification. The participles (but not [VFORM *base*] VPs, for example) all share the ability to modify nominals. The lexical rules that characterize such modifiers make reference to the specification [VFORM *part*]. The hierarchy of VFORM values thus serves the grammar of selection and modification in a variety of ways.

Finally, we should point out that cutting across the distinctions discussed in this section is the dichotomy between predicative and nonpredicative forms, which is crucial to a number of English constructions. We treat these in terms of the binary feature PRED, which distinguishes predicative from nonpredicative forms of verbs, nouns, prepositions, and adjectives. Among inflected verbal forms, only the passive and present participles are [PRED +] (See Sag and Wasow 1999, chap. 11).

---

[13]We thus assume that finite auxiliaries allow argument structures like the one shown in (i).

(i) $\left[\text{ARG-ST} \ \langle \text{NP} , \text{ADV}_{neg} , \text{VP} \rangle \right]$

On this analysis of sentential negation, see Warner 1993, 2000, Kim and Sag 1995, In press, and Sag and Wasow 1999. We will not have much to say about counterfactual conditionals in this book, but it should be noted that we break with tradition in classifying verb forms like the one in (12b) as 'conditional', rather than 'subjunctive'. Conditional forms in fact have little in common with subjunctive forms of the sort that appear embedded in examples like (ii).

(ii) I suggest that they *be* considered.

2.4.2 Distinguishing Verbal Meanings

The content of a verb specifies a state-of-affairs, or *soa*. *Soa*s are the building blocks of the various kinds of message—*proposition*, *outcome*, *fact*, and *question*—that are described in detail in Chapter 3. But there is reason to draw a distinction between two kinds of *soa*. For example, the content of the sentence *Kim Sanderson left* is a proposition whose truth or falsity directly involves the real world. And the content of *whether Kim Sanderson left* is a question that is similarly realis—it is resolved according to whether the proposition that Kim Sanderson left is true or false (at a given real world spatio-temporal location). By contrast, the meaning of an imperative sentence like *Get out of here!* makes no direct reference to the real world; nor do subjunctive or infinitival clauses like *that Kim Sanderson leave* or *for Kim Sanderson to leave*. Intuitively, these clauses make reference to future outcomes involving Kim Sanderson's leaving. Thus, the distinction between these two types of content, which we refer to as realis and irrealis, seems fundamental to the semantic interpretation of clauses.

In our analysis, this bifurcation of clausal meanings is reflected in terms of a bifurcation of the type *soa* into two subtypes, which we will call *realis-soa* (*r-soa*) and *irrealis-soa* (*i-soa*). The strategy is to impose a lexical restriction on finite indicative verb forms (*loves*, *went*, *is*, etc.) requiring that they have an *r-soa* as their content. Conversely, imperative and subjunctive verb forms, though finite, will have a CONTENT value of type *i-soa*. These lexical restrictions, taken together with type constraints guaranteeing that propositions must be constructed from *r-soa*s, while outcomes must be constructed from *i-soa*s, will modulate the kinds of meaning that can be associated with the phrasal constructions allowed by our grammar.[14]

Inflected forms of verbs are derived from verbal lexemes that specify only the nucleus of the *soa* in the verb's content. Verbal lexemes specify their content type simply as *soa*, the immediate supertype of *r-soa* and *i-soa*. The lexical rules forming finite indicative verb forms will impose the further restriction that the CONTENT value be of type *r-soa*, as illustrated in (14)—the lexical description of the 3rd-singular present indicative form *proves*:[15]

---

[14]Fixing the CONTENT type of verbs as one or another kind of *soa* (rather than as, say, a proposition) also aids the treatment of preverbal adverbial modification, which is possible in all kinds of clauses:

  (i) Kim always wins.
  (ii) Does Kim always win?
  (iii) Always wear white!
  (iv) What a mess Kim always makes of things!

Because verbs and the VPs they project are uniformly treated as *soa*s, there can be a uniform semantics for the combination of a VP and its modifier. This happens at a lower level of structure and gives rise to a more complex *soa* that is incorporated into the meaning (proposition, question, etc.) of the clause.

  Similarly, quantifiers may be assigned scope within any kind of message:

  (v) Kim wrote three letters.
  (vi) Did Kim write three letters?
  (vii) Write three letters!
  (viii) How seldom Kim writes three letters!

This uniformity too is accounted for by the fact that all messages are constructed from *soa*s (and the fact that quantifiers are scoped within *soa*s).

[15]The features POL(ARIZED) and AUX(ILIARY) are discussed in the next section.

(14)

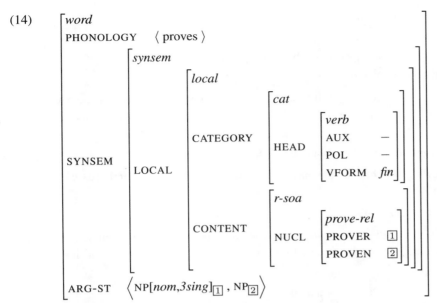

All inflectional rules forming nonfinite forms, e.g. participles or *base* verbal forms, say nothing about the content type, and hence preserve the lexeme's semantic indeterminacy. This allows the content of a participle, for example, to be the *r-soa* required by a proposition (as in (15a)) or the *i-soa* required by an outcome (as in (15b)):

(15) a. Kim Sanderson is *proving* an important theorem at this very moment.

b. Be *proving* a theorem when your math teacher walks in!

We may now assume one more inflectional rule creating (uninflected) finite forms with content of type *i-soa*. These finite forms, like the one illustrated in (16), will appear in imperative clauses like (17) or in subjunctive clauses like (18).

(16)

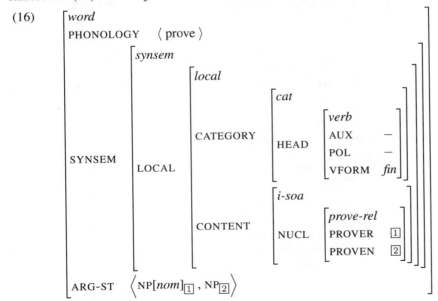

(17) a. *Prove* that theorem!

　　　b. *Be* waiting for me!

(18) a. I suggest that she *prove* that theorem right now.

　　　b. I suggest that you *be* waiting for me.

Note that here the subject argument's case must be nominative. We take this case assignment to be valid for all finite verb forms in English, a conclusion that is easy to justify for subjunctive uses:

(19) 　　I suggested (that) they/*them *be* made available.

In fact, the following kind of example may provide independent support for this case assignment, even for imperative uses:[16]

(20) 　　You and he *be* quiet!

In previous GPSG/HPSG proposals, it has sometimes been assumed that subjunctives are the same ([VFORM *base*]) forms that occur elsewhere, e.g. in the complements of raising verbs:

(21) a. Kim expects to be nominated.

　　　b. I expect Merle to be nominated.

But there is reason to doubt this. The subject of a non-subjunctive infinitival form may be either nominative or accusative in case, depending on the nature of the 'raised' constituent with which it is identified:

(22) a. *They* expect to be nominated.

　　　b. I expect *them* to be nominated.

Hence lexically, the subject (i.e. the first ARG-ST member) of this form bears no case restriction (or else is restricted to bear the non-maximal type *structural-case*).[17] Since the subjunctive/imperative forms, as we just saw, assign nominative case to their subject, we conclude that subjunctive/imperative forms, though homophonous with base verb forms, should not be identified with them.

2.4.3   Some Auxiliary Issues

There is a further curiosity about imperatives and subjunctives that remains to be discussed. This has to do with sentential negation, which appears to be expressed in subjunctive clauses via preverbal *not*:

(23) a. I urged that they not attend the reception.

　　　b. *I urged that they attend not the reception.

---

[16]The difficulty with this argument is the variation of case marking in NP conjuncts, possibly tied to shifts of register. Thus (i) is also acceptable, but apparently only in an informal register where (ii) is also possible.

　(i) You and him *be* quiet!

　(ii) You and him should *be* quiet.

Note, however, that many languages have full imperative paradigms and that it is a general property of Indo-European languages that imperative verb forms are finite, assigning nominative case to their subject argument.

[17]HPSG Analyses of case based on this distinction between *structural-case* and *lexical-case* can be found in Pollard 1994, Heinz and Matiasek 1994, and Przepiórkowski 1999.

However, as Potsdam (1996) notes, the *not* that appears in subjunctive clauses allows VP Ellipsis:

(24)   I don't really want you to use my name; in fact I must insist that you not _ , because I have concerns about my family.

Since VP Ellipsis is licensed only by auxiliary verbs (Bresnan 1976, Sag 1976), the possibility of (24) suggests that there is a homophonous *not* that functions as a subjunctive auxiliary verb.[18] We will assume this analysis, which is similar to Potsdam's (and quite like the analysis of Italian negation suggested on independent grounds by Kim (1995)). The result is a simple account of sentential negation in subjunctive clauses: the auxiliary *not* has a negative *i-soa* as its CONTENT value. We block analogous examples involving matrix imperatives, e.g. (25), by restricting this auxiliary to embedded clauses, i.e. by an [IC −] lexical specification.

(25)   *Not go to the store!

(The feature IC is discussed in more detail in section 2.7 below.)

Our analysis of the English auxiliary system builds on previous GPSG/HPSG work that has posited the feature INV(ERTED) (Gazdar et al. 1982), which is used to distinguish auxiliary verbs heading inverted phrases from all other verbs. The lexical encoding of this information allows us to accommodate lexical exceptions to inversion—both positive and negative.[19] However, the present analysis diverges in one crucial way from previous work in the PSG tradition. Following Sag (2000), we utilize the specification [AUX +] not to distinguish auxiliary verbs from other verbs, but rather to identify auxiliary constructions. Thus inversion constructions, instances of sentential VP Ellipsis, and finite verbs that are positively or negatively 'polarized' will be specified as [AUX +] and auxiliary verbs—lexically unspecified for AUX—will be the only verbs that are compatible with these constructions.[20]

This shift in the interpretation of the feature AUX provides a simple lexical account of the restricted distribution of unfocussed *do*: *do* is lexically specified as [AUX +] and hence is compatible ONLY with the auxiliary constructions. This excludes examples like (26), as explained in section 2.6 below.

(26)   *Kim díd leave.

2.5   Phrases as Feature Structures

Phrases too can be modeled as typed feature structures, as they have been within HPSG. Features such as HEAD-DAUGHTER (HD-DTR; whose value is a sign, i.e. a word or phrase) and DAUGHTERS (DTRS; whose value is a list of signs) encode roughly the same information that branches do in conventional phrase structure trees.[21] The figure in (27) presents a simplified analysis in

---

[18]It is interesting to note that in Modern Greek there is a negative particle *mi* that is confined to subjunctive and imperative clauses. Thus something quite like the distinction we posit here is lexicalized in at least one other language.

[19]For discussion, see Gazdar et al. 1982, Gazdar et al. 1985, Green and Morgan 1996, Warner 2000, Kim and Sag 1995, In press, and Sag 2000.

[20]In Sag's analysis, there are three kinds of polarized auxiliary forms:

- *Not*-contracted forms: *haven't, won't*, etc.
- Forms selecting a polarized adverbial (*not*, SO, or TOO) as a complement, e.g. *Kim will not/*SO/*TOO do that*.
- Positively polarized forms, i.e. focussed finite auxiliaries, e.g. *Kim WILL/DID go to the store.*

All [POL +] verbs belong to one of these three classes.

[21]This application of feature structures remains less familiar within linguistics, largely for historical reasons having to do with the ubiquity of rewrite rules, tree structure derivations, and other foundational tools adapted to natural language in the 1950s.

feature structure terms of the sentence *Leslie drinks milk*:

(27)
$$
\begin{bmatrix}
hd\text{-}subj\text{-}ph \\
\text{PHON} \quad \langle\, \boxed{1}, \boxed{3}, \boxed{4}\, \rangle \\
\text{SYNSEM} \quad \text{S} \\
\text{DTRS} \quad \left\langle \begin{bmatrix} \text{PHON} & \langle\, \boxed{1}\text{Leslie}\,\rangle \\ \text{SYNSEM} & \text{NP} \end{bmatrix}, \boxed{2} \right\rangle \\
\text{HD-DTR} \quad \boxed{2} \begin{bmatrix} hd\text{-}comp\text{-}ph \\ \text{PHON} \quad \langle\, \boxed{3}, \boxed{4}\,\rangle \\ \text{SYNSEM} \quad \text{VP} \\ \text{HD-DTR} \quad \boxed{5} \begin{bmatrix} word \\ \text{PHON} \quad \langle\, \boxed{3}\text{drinks}\,\rangle \end{bmatrix} \\ \text{DTRS} \quad \left\langle \boxed{5}, \begin{bmatrix} \text{PHON} & \langle\, \boxed{4}\text{milk}\,\rangle \\ \text{SYNSEM} & \text{NP} \end{bmatrix} \right\rangle \end{bmatrix}
\end{bmatrix}
$$

It may not be obvious that there is any significant difference between the sign-based (feature structure) representation of this phrase and the corresponding, more familiar tree structure. However, there are several advantages of this new analytic perspective, as pointed out in Sag (1997). The most important consequences of the sign-based theory of phrases is that it allows us to address such questions as the following, that were touched on in Chapter 1:

- How are specific constructions related to one another?
- How can cross-constructional generalizations be expressed?
- How can constructional idiosyncrasy be accounted for?

Once phrases are modeled as typed features structures, the types of phrase can be organized into a hierarchy, in much the same way as the lexical types discussed earlier in this chapter. By introducing appropriate supertypes into the hierarchy, one can model the fact that phrase types come in families—i.e. that there are family resemblances cutting across the various types of phrase. Moreover, a type-based analysis can express high-level generalizations (e.g. as a constraint on the type *phrase*), idiosyncratic constructional properties (as a constraint on some maximal (leaf) phrasal type) or generalizations involving 'family resemblances' (via constraints on some intermediate-level phrasal type, e.g. *headed-phrase*, *declarative-clause*, or *head-complement-phrase*). As noted in the previous chapter, there is considerable evidence that this is precisely the way natural languages are organized. Natural language grammars are systems of constraints of varying grain.

The sign-based approach plays a particularly useful role in the theory of clause types we develop below. For example, it provides a unified framework for describing the 'correspondence rules' that constructions encode. This is because such correspondences, as we will show in detail, involve syntactic, semantic, phonological and even contextual information. Our approach also allows us to extend the application of general grammatical constraints to more and more 'peripheral' constructions, without having to posit a bifurcation (otherwise unmotivated, as far as we are aware) between the 'core' and 'periphery' of language.[22]

Although we believe the shift in analytic perspective embodied in our analysis is highly significant, the fact remains that most linguists are accustomed to thinking of grammatical structure in terms of trees. For this reason, we will often describe phrases in terms of more familiar tree diagrams. A feature structure like (27), for example, can be represented in tree-based terms, as shown in (28).

(28)

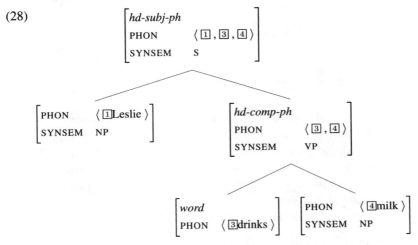

In fact, whenever possible, we will abbreviate tree diagrams like (28) in an even more familiar format, e.g. (29).

(29)

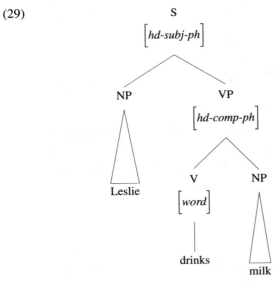

---

[22]See Chapter 1. Also relevant is the discussion of Fillmore and Kay 1999, Fillmore et al. to appear, and Bender and Flickinger 1999.

In addition, since all our constraints on phrasal signs are local (making reference only to a mother and its daughters), we will write them in the familiar notation of context-free rewrite rules.

We claim that all phrases found in natural languages are classified according to the following hierarchy of phrasal types:[23]

(30)

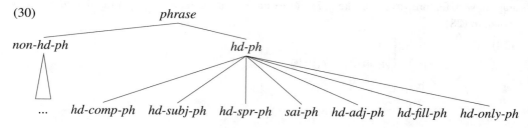

That is, phrases are classified as either *headed-phrase* (*hd-ph*) or *non-headed-phrase* (*non-hd-ph*), with each type exhibiting various subtypes. Among the headed-phrases, seven subtypes are recognized, including: *head-adjunct-phrase* (*hd-adj-ph*), *head-filler-phrase* (*hd-fill-ph*), *head-only-phrase* (*hd-only-ph*), *head-subject-phrase* (*hd-subj-ph*), *head-complement-phrase* (*hd-comp-ph*), *head-specifier-phrase* (*hd-spr-ph*), and *subject-auxiliary-inversion-phrase* (*sai-ph*), as indicated.[24] We will illustrate each of these types in due course.

Phrases are governed by the feature declarations shown in (31):[25]

(31)

TYPE	FEATURES/TYPE OF VALUE	IST
sign	PHONOLOGY *list(speech-sound)* SYNSEM *canon-ss* CONTEXT *conx-obj*	*feat-struc*
phrase	DTRS *nelist(sign)*	*sign*
hd-ph	HD-DTR *sign*	*phrase*

Each headed phrase must have some value (possibly the empty list) for DTRS because it is also of type *phrase*, for which that feature is appropriate and necessary. Similarly, all phrases must have some value for PHONOLOGY and SYNSEM, because they are also of type *sign*, for which those features are both appropriate and necessary.

---

[23]At this more abstract level of contemplation, *subject-auxiliary-inversion-phrase* is no doubt too specific a rubric and should be renamed as *head-initial-phrase* or *head-subject-complement-phrase*. For our present, English-specific purposes, however, we will keep the present name. Our analysis of *sai-ph* is based on the SAI construction of Fillmore 1999.

[24]Note that we make no use here of the type *hd-marker-ph*, although this may in fact need to be recognized for the treatment of English conjunctions.

[25]*Nelist* stands for *non-empty-list*.

Phrases are subject to the following general constraint:[26]

(32)   Empty COMPS Constraint (ECC)

phrase:

$$\left[\text{CAT}\left[\text{COMPS}\ \langle\ \rangle\right]\right] \rightarrow \ldots$$

By requiring that all phrases be [COMPS $\langle\ \rangle$], (32) guarantees that within any phrase, the complements have already been 'consumed' by the phrase's lexical head. Complements are introduced as sisters of the lexical head (as guaranteed by the constraint introduced below on head-complement phrases) and hence they must be more deeply embedded than specifiers, subjects, or fillers, all of which combine with head daughters specified as [COMPS $\langle\ \rangle$]. (This follows without further stipulation, because the head daughter of a head-complement phrase can never be phrasal.)

Just as in the case of the lexicon, certain kinds of phrase obey type-specific constraints. For example, our generalization of the Head Feature Principle (analogous to the 'X' identity condition of '$\bar{\text{X}}$ Theory') can be formulated as a constraint on phrases of type *hd-ph* (The symbol 'H' here is used to indicate the head daughter of a given phrase.):

(33)   Generalized Head Feature Principle (GHFP)

hd-ph:

$$\left[\text{SYNSEM}\ /\ \boxed{1}\right] \rightarrow \ldots \mathbf{H}\left[\text{SYNSEM}\ /\ \boxed{1}\right]\ldots$$

The '/' notation (Lascarides and Copestake 1999) here indicates a default constraint—specifically one requiring that the SYNSEM value of the mother of a headed phrase and that of its head daughter be identical by default. Specific subtypes of *hd-ph* may override the GHFP, but by formulating (33) in defeasible terms, it will require that the features of a head daughter and those of its mother have identical values, except in cases where this is explicitly contradicted by constraints on those subtypes.[27]

The GHFP allows considerable simplification in our grammar. Earlier work in HPSG posited principles such as the (nondefault) Head Feature Principle and the Valence Principle (P&S–94, chap. 9)), which required the head daughter's SUBJ, COMPS, and SPR specifications either to be 'cancelled off' (analogous to function application in categorial grammar) or else to be inherited by the mother in a headed phrase. Since these valence features are part of the SYNSEM value, the GHFP ensures that the head daughter's values for all these features will be inherited by the mother, unless the phrase in question is subject to a particular constraint requiring that there be a discrepancy between head daughter and mother (a cancellation) for the value of some particular

---

[26]Henceforth, abbreviations of an obvious sort will be used, where no confusion should arise. For example, [COMPS $\langle\ \rangle$] in (32) abbreviates [SS|LOC|CAT|COMPS $\langle\ \rangle$].

[27]Note that one could replace the GHFP with a set of nondefault constraints, each of which specifies the relevant identities on particular subtypes of *hd-ph*. Our use of defaults could thus be regarded as abbreviatory. However, our system of constraints is conceptually quite different from one cast in a pure monotonic system. By using defeasible constraints, we express generalizations about construction types that appear to be beyond the reach of monotonic logics like (R)SRL. We thus achieve a significant gain in descriptive simplicity which, as noted by Lascarides and Copestake (1999), is typical of systems using default constraints.

valence feature.[28]

One such cancellation affects instances of the type *hd-comp-ph*, which permits a lexical head to combine with exactly as many complements as it selects via the COMPS feature:[29]

(34)   *hd-comp-ph*:

$$[\ ] \ \rightarrow \mathbf{H} \begin{bmatrix} word \\ \text{COMPS} \ \ nelist(\boxed{A} \oplus list) \end{bmatrix}, \ \boxed{A}$$

The constraint in (34) factors out only the information that is specific to phrases of this type. The synsems of the complement daughters are identified with an initial sublist of the head daughter's COMPS list. Moreover, by default, there are no further elements on that COMPS list. Thus, if no subordinate type says otherwise,[30] the synsems of the non-head daughters of a head-complement phrase will correspond exactly to the list of complements selected by the head daughter. Finally, observe that because the list of non-head daughters must be nonempty, a strictly intransitive lexical head—one whose COMPS list is empty—cannot head a *hd-comp-ph*. Our phrase structure is thus 'bare', in the sense of Chomsky 1995a.

The following two constraints factor out what is specific to phrases of the type *hd-subj-ph* and *hd-spr-ph*.

(35)   *hd-subj-ph*:

$$\begin{bmatrix} \text{SUBJ} & \langle \ \rangle \end{bmatrix} \rightarrow \begin{bmatrix} \text{SS} & \boxed{1} \end{bmatrix}, \ \mathbf{H} \begin{bmatrix} \text{SPR} & \langle \ \rangle \\ \text{SUBJ} & \langle \boxed{1} \rangle \end{bmatrix}$$

(36)   *hd-spr-ph*:

$$\begin{bmatrix} \text{SPR} & \langle \ \rangle \end{bmatrix} \rightarrow \begin{bmatrix} \text{SS} & \boxed{1} \end{bmatrix}, \ \mathbf{H} \begin{bmatrix} \text{SPR} & \langle \boxed{1} \rangle \end{bmatrix}$$

In both cases, only one non-head daughter is allowed and this daughter's SYNSEM value is identified with the value of the appropriate valence feature (SUBJ or SPR) of the head daughter that selects it. The phrase itself has an empty value for the corresponding feature.

The GHFP interacts with these last three type constraints to specify appropriate values for all valence features. All valence features not mentioned in the individual constraints will have identical values on the mother and head daughter, as shown in (37a–c). These represent the unification of the GHFP and the ECC with the particular constraints in (34)–(36).[31]

---

[28]Our account thus builds on the insights of Borsley (1993), who argues that the HFP should be viewed in default terms. See also Gazdar et al. 1985.

[29]The notation in (34) is intended to be equivalent to the following:

(i)

$$hd\text{-}comp\text{-}ph \ \Rightarrow \begin{bmatrix} \text{HD-DTR} \ \boxed{1} \begin{bmatrix} word \\ \text{COMPS} \ \ \texttt{signs-to-synsems}(nelist(\boxed{A} \oplus list)) \end{bmatrix} \\ \text{DTRS} \ \langle \boxed{1} \rangle \oplus \boxed{A} \end{bmatrix}$$

Here the `signs-to-synsems` function relates a list of signs to the corresponding list of the synsems of those signs. In the revised construction theory of Sag 2001 (which draws a fundamental distinction between constructions and phrases), the function `signs-to-synsems` is eliminated.

[30]For example, the *elliptical-vp* phrase Sag (2000) posits for the treatment of VP Ellipsis. See below and also Bender 2000.

[31]For the moment, we ignore the features SLASH, WH, STORE, and BACKGROUND whose values the mother and head daughter will agree on in all these constructions. See Appendix A.

(37) a. **GHFP** & ECC & *hd-comp-ph*:

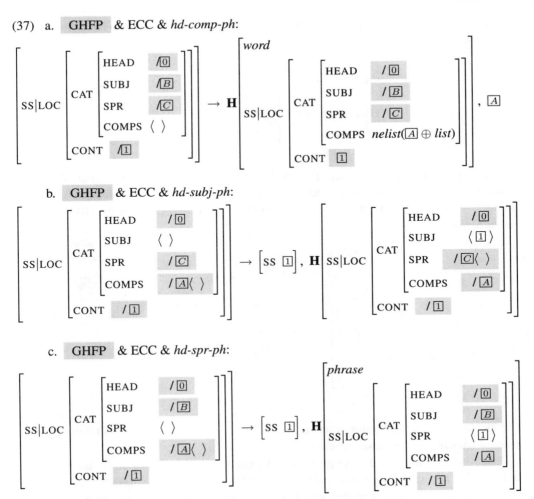

  b. **GHFP** & ECC & *hd-subj-ph*:

  c. **GHFP** & ECC & *hd-spr-ph*:

Here the head daughter and mother have identical values for every feature within SYNSEM that can be identified in a way that is consistent with the nondefeasible constraints associated with the particular construction. The complex pattern of identities (indicated here by shading) is a direct consequence of the GHFP (given the default logic of Lascarides and Copestake 1999), without which all the identities of (37a–c) would have to be stipulated piecemeal in unrelated constraints, i.e. in a completely ad hoc manner. Because none of the types illustrated here are maximal, all the shading in (37) involves default identities, that will possibly be overriden by hard constraints on subordinate types. Finally, note that ARG-ST is a feature that lives 'outside' of SYNSEM. Hence, although the mother of a head-complement phrase has no ARG-ST specification (it is a phrase) while the head daughter must have some non-empty ARG-ST list, this is in no way inconsistent with the GHFP.

Let us now turn to the type *sai-ph*, all instances of which are subject to the following constraint:[32]

(38)   *sai-ph*:

$$
\left[\text{SUBJ} \; \langle \, \rangle \right] \rightarrow \mathbf{H} \begin{bmatrix} word \\ \text{INV} & + \\ \text{AUX} & + \\ \text{SUBJ} & \langle \boxed{0} \rangle \\ \text{COMPS} & \boxed{A} \end{bmatrix}, \boxed{0}, \boxed{A}
$$

Thus in this kind of phrase, which must be headed by an inverted ([INV +]) auxiliary verb, elements are 'cancelled' from both head daughter's SUBJ list and its COMPS list. Again, the further constraints on such phrases illustrated in (39) are a consequence of the GHFP and ECC and need not be stipulated.

(39)   **GHFP** & ECC & *sai-ph*:

$$
\left[\text{SS|LOC} \begin{bmatrix} \text{CAT} \begin{bmatrix} \text{HEAD} & /\boxed{0} \\ \text{SUBJ} & \langle \, \rangle \\ \text{SPR} & /\boxed{C} \\ \text{COMPS} \; \langle \, \rangle \end{bmatrix} \\ \text{CONT} & /\boxed{1} \end{bmatrix} \right] \rightarrow \mathbf{H} \left[\begin{matrix} word \\ \text{SS|LOC} \begin{bmatrix} \text{CAT} \begin{bmatrix} \text{HEAD} & \boxed{0} \begin{bmatrix} \text{INV} & + \\ \text{AUX} & + \end{bmatrix} \\ \text{SUBJ} & \langle \boxed{2} \rangle \\ \text{SPR} & \boxed{C} \\ \text{COMPS} & \boxed{A} \end{bmatrix} \\ \text{CONT} & /\boxed{1} \end{bmatrix} \end{matrix} \right], \boxed{2}, \boxed{A}
$$

The identity of CONTENT values illustrated in (39) will in fact be overridden by the particular inverted constructions we discuss below.

The types just illustrated serve to classify the maximal phrasal types of our analysis. Finite verb phrases, for example, are analyzed by a kind of head-complement phrase we call *finite verb-phrase (fin-vp)*. This type of phrase, which allows us to incorporate the treatment of auxiliaries developed by Sag (2000), is subject to the following constraint.

(40)   *fin-vp*:

$$
[\;] \rightarrow \mathbf{H} \begin{bmatrix} \text{HEAD} & \begin{bmatrix} \text{AUX} & \boxed{1} \\ \text{POL} & \boxed{1} \end{bmatrix} \\ \text{COMPS} & \boxed{A} \end{bmatrix}, \boxed{A}
$$

This construction inherits the constraints shown in (41). Shaded values again mark the effects of the GHFP, i.e. those identities that are not defeated by hard constraints on subordinate types.

---

[32]If we allow ellipsis in this construction (in order to handle examples like *Is Kim?*), then the constraint in (38) must be subtly modified to avoid unwanted interaction with the GHFP. Such a revision of (38) could take the following form:

(i)   *sai-ph*:

$$
\left[\text{SUBJ} \; \langle \, \rangle \right] \rightarrow \mathbf{H} \begin{bmatrix} word \\ \text{INV} & + \\ \text{AUX} & + \\ \text{SUBJ} & \langle \boxed{0} \rangle \\ \text{COMPS} & nelist(\boxed{A} \oplus \boxed{B}) \end{bmatrix}, \boxed{0}, \boxed{A}
$$

(41) 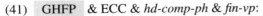 **GHFP** & ECC & *hd-comp-ph* & *fin-vp*:

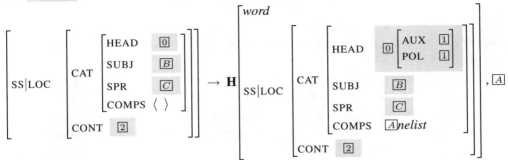

Note that since *fin-vp* is a maximal type in our analysis, there is no more specific type that will override the identities enforced by the GHFP. Hence these are all hard constraints, as indicated in (41).

The type *fin-vp* allows a treatment of phrases like the following.

(42)

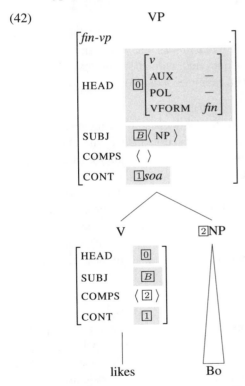

The identification of AUX and POL values here may seem puzzling at first. Intuitively, this is just a way of collapsing what would otherwise be two constructions (polarized and non-polarized finite VPs) into one. Recall that *not*-contracted auxiliaries are all [POL +], as are focussed finite auxiliaries and those that select for polar adverbs (see note 20). All other verb forms are lexically specified as [POL −]. Given this, and the fact that only auxiliary verbs are unspecified for the feature AUX, it follows that an instance of the *fin-vp* construction will be [AUX +] just in case it is polarized and is headed by an auxiliary verb, as in (43).

(43) a.   Kim won't go to the store.
      b.   Kim has not/TOO/SO gone to the store.
      c.   Kim HAS gone to the store.

Any *fin-vp* not headed by a polarized verb form will be [AUX −], even if it is headed by an auxiliary verb, as in (44b):

(44) a.   Kim went to the store.
      b.   Kim has gone to the store.

This reinterpretation of positive AUX specifications as distinguishing auxiliary constructions (instead of distinguishing the auxiliary verbs, as in previous analyses) provides the key to analyzing the much discussed distribution of unfocussed *do*. As noted earlier, the auxiliary verb lexeme *do* is exceptionally specified as [AUX +]. Given what we have said about VPs so far, this predicts that *do* can head a *fin-vp* construction only when it is polarized, accounting for familiar contrasts like the following:

(45) a.   Kim didn't go to the store.
      b.   Kim did not/TOO/SO go to the store.
      c.   *Kim dĭd go to the store.

This is not the whole story of *do*, of course. Following Sag (2000), we treat VP Ellipsis via a separate construction (*elliptical-vp*—also a subtype of *hd-comp-ph*) that allows an [AUX +] verb to appear with a proper subset of its complements. Unnegated, unfocussed *do* may head such a construction and is thus predicted to occur in elliptical examples like (46):

(46)   Kim *dĭd* __ .

This construction requires that some complements selected by the head remain unexpressed.

Nonfinite VPs are to be handled in terms of a distinct construction that we will refer to simply as *nonfinite-head-complement-phrase (nf-hc-ph)*.[33] As discussed by Sag (2000), when nonfinite auxiliaries head such phrases, they are always [AUX +].

Finally, it should be noted that we assume a finer grained analysis for the type *hd-subj-ph*. Declarative instances of this type can be distinguished from those head-subject phrases that involve accusative subjects (so-called 'Mad Magazine' sentences, e.g. *What, [me worry?]* (Akmajian 1984, Zhang 1990, Lambrecht 1990), or absolute constructions, like [*My kids in college now*], *I'm going to have lots of free time*). We will not present an analysis of these constructions here.[34]

2.6   Clause Types

To express generalizations about the shared properties of diverse construction types, we propose (following Sag 1997) to classify phrases not only in terms of their 'X̄' type (e.g. whether they are headed or not; if they are headed, what kind of daughters are involved, etc.), but also relative to an independent dimension of 'clausality'. On our theory, each type of phrase is cross-classified: each maximal phrasal type inherits both from a CLAUSALITY type and from a HEADEDNESS type.

---

[33] If certain refinements are made, it is possible to modify this construction so that it encompasses most other unsaturated ([SUBJ ⟨YP⟩]) XPs, as well as VPs.

[34] We have not said anything about the principles of linear ordering that guarantee the proper sequencing of PHON values in these signs. This is an issue too far afield fom the present study. Though we will identify the head daughter with a particular member of the DTRS list and will continue to represent constructions in terms of ordered trees, the reader should bear in mind that the linear order of constituents in our theory should in fact be determined by linearization constraints of greater generality. For relevant further discussion, see Pollard and Sag 1987, Chap. 7, Reape 1994, and Kathol 1995, 2000.

(47)

```
                              phrase
                    ┌────────────┴────────────┐
               CLAUSALITY                 HEADEDNESS
              ┌─────┴─────┐              ┌─────┴─────┐
          clause      non-clause      hd-ph       non-hd-ph
         ┌───┴───┐
     core-cl   rel-cl
  ┌──────┼──────┐
imp-cl decl-cl inter-cl excl-cl
```

hd-comp-ph hd-subj-ph hd-spr-ph sai-ph hd-adj-ph hd-fill-ph hd-only-ph

This classification recognizes a distinction between clauses and nonclauses, and also identifies at least the following subtypes of *clause*: *decl(arative)-cl(ause)*, *inter(rogative)-cl(ause)*, *imp(erative)-cl(ause)*, *excl(amative)-cl(ause)*, *core-cl(ause)* and *rel(ative)-cl(ause)*. [35] Our analysis lets us express generalizations about phrases with the same simplicity and precision that is standard in work on hierarchical lexicons. With the phrasal multiple inheritance hierarchy, we also have no need to posit phantom formatives—the inaudible functional heads that are routinely assumed in many competing analyses of clausal structure. The work done by these elements is replaced by constraints associated with the various types of clause.

The subtypes of *clause* are the locus of constraints that will be highly relevant to our treatment of interrogatives. Before proceeding, however, we must clarify our assumptions about the subtypes of *synsem*. Both the analysis of unexpressed controlled subjects and our account of filler-gap dependencies lead us to distinguish various subtypes of *synsem*. We follow familiar terminology and refer to the type of unexpressed controlled subjects (of nonfinite phrases) as *pro-synsem (pro-ss)*[36] and to the type of the 'gap' argument in an extraction construction as *gap-synsem (gap-ss)*.[37] We assume that instances of all such types exhibit exceptional properties (for example, they cannot be locally realized through simple combination of a head with its subject, complement, or specifier) and are hence 'noncanonical'. To reflect this, we posit the hierarchy of *synsem* subtypes shown in (48). (Here *canon-ss* abbreviates *canonical-synsem* and *noncan-ss* abbreviates *noncanonical-synsem*.)

(48)

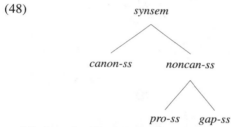

All signs (both words and phrases) are governed by the following principle, already built into the type declaration for *sign* in (31) above:

(49)   Principle of Canonicality:

$$sign \Rightarrow \left[\text{SYNSEM} \quad canon\text{-}ss \right]$$

The Principle of Canonicality ensures that every overt linguistic expression has a SYNSEM value of type *canon-ss*. Since overt complements, subjects, and specifiers must have a *canon-ss* SYNSEM value, the constraints already illustrated for head-complement, head-subject, and head-specifier phrases guarantees that whenever some head selects for a *noncan-ss* argument, that argument cannot be a daughter of any such phrase.

In our grammar, clauses are the constructions that are used exclusively to build phrases whose content is communicatively complete, i.e. whose CONTENT value is some subtype of *message*: *proposition*, *question*, *outcome*, or *fact*. The following constraint ensures this:

---

[35] The hierarchy assumed here may well require revision as the analysis is extended, e.g. to purpose, rationale, absolute, gerund, and conditional clauses.

[36] The type *pro-ss* is analogous to the type PRO proposed by Pollard (1989) and shares its properties, in the main.

[37] For languages that allow missing arguments with distinctive properties, further subtypes of *synsem* may be necessary.

(50) *clause*:

$$\left[\text{CONT}\quad message\right] \rightarrow \cdots$$

(50) guarantees, for example, that no clause can have a *soa* as its content.

The intuition our analysis encodes is that verbs and the verb phrases they project have *soa* content, i.e. their content is not yet a proposition (or any other kind of message). Hence neither verbs nor the VPs they project can function as independent utterances; nor can they serve as complements of verbs like *believe* or *think*, which select propositional arguments. In order to build a phrase whose content *is* a *message*, it is necessary to embed a VP within a clausal construction. As noted in Chapter 1, the clausal constructions thus serve to ground a recursive process that generates message-denoting signs.

Let us now turn to the constraints governing the various subtypes of *clause*. Core clauses (declaratives, interrogatives, exclamatives, and imperatives) cannot be modifiers, as is guaranteed by the following constraint:[38]

(51) *core-cl*:

$$\left[\text{HEAD}\quad\begin{bmatrix}verbal\\ \text{VFORM}\quad clausal\\ \text{MOD}\quad none\end{bmatrix}\right] \rightarrow \cdots$$

(51) also guarantees that core-clauses are headed by verbs whose VFORM value is (a subtype of) *clausal*, i.e. by finite verbal forms or the auxiliary *to*.[39]

Of the clause types considered here, only relative clauses may be used as modifiers. The constraint in (52) allows for this possibility.

(52) *rel-cl*:

$$\left[\begin{array}{l}\text{HEAD}\quad\begin{bmatrix}\text{IC}\quad -\\ \text{INV}\quad -\\ \text{MOD}\quad \left[noun\right]\end{bmatrix}\\ \text{CONT}\quad fact\end{array}\right] \rightarrow \cdots$$

Relative clauses have *fact* as the type of their CONTENT value, yet the content of a relative clause always contains an index that is identified with the index of the nominal that the clause modifies.

The feature IC (INDEPENDENT-CLAUSE—see section 2.7 below) is a variant of Uszkoreit's (1987) MAIN-CLAUSE feature; the [IC −] constraint in (52) ensures that relative clauses cannot serve as independent clauses, and hence that they have no status as (non-elliptical) independent utterances. The specification [INV −] in (52) guarantees not only that post-auxiliary subjects are in general impossible in relative clauses, but also that forms like first-person singular *aren't*, lexically specified as [INV +], can never head a relative clause:

(53) a. *The person [(that/who) are they visiting] is Sandy.

    b. *The person [(that/who) I aren't visiting] is Sandy.

---

[38] For discussion of modifier analyses based on the feature MOD, see Pollard and Sag 1994.

[39] Note that core clauses may also be headed by complementizers, as their part-of-speech is also a subtype of *verbal*. Thus, as sketched below, we will treat diverse kinds of CP as instances of type *core-cl*.

We now introduce further constraints on the immediate subtypes of *core-cl*:

(54)   *decl-cl*: $\begin{bmatrix} \text{CONT} & \begin{bmatrix} austinian \\ \text{SOA} & / \boxed{1} \end{bmatrix} \end{bmatrix} \rightarrow \dots \mathbf{H}\begin{bmatrix} \text{CONT} & / \boxed{1} \end{bmatrix} \dots$

(55)   *inter-cl*: $\begin{bmatrix} \text{CONT} & question \end{bmatrix} \rightarrow \dots$

(56)   *imp-cl*: $\begin{bmatrix} \text{CONT} & outcome \end{bmatrix} \rightarrow \dots$

(57)   *excl-cl*: $\begin{bmatrix} \text{CONT} & fact \end{bmatrix} \rightarrow \dots$

The effect of these constraints is to establish a correlation between clausal construction types and types of meaning. As explained earlier, the semantic type *austinian* mentioned in (54) has two subtypes: *proposition* and *outcome*. Indicative declarative clauses (see Chapter 3) denote propositions,[40] while subjunctive clauses (analyzed here as a kind of *decl-cl*) denote outcomes. Note that the content of the head daughter of a declarative clause (a *soa*) is embedded as the mother's SOA value by default.[41] The treatment of exclamative clauses in terms of facts is explained in Chapters 3 and 6.

We are now ready to analyze more fully our previous example *Leslie likes Bo*. The more embedded phrase *likes Bo* is an instance of the *fin-vp* construction illustrated in the previous section. However, in order to combine a finite VP with the subject NP *Leslie* we need a new type of phrase, which we will call *declarative-head-subject-clause* (*decl-hd-su-cl*). This is a subtype of both *decl-cl* and *hd-subj-ph*:

(58)

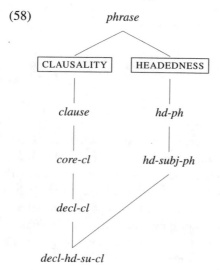

The only constraint particular to *decl-hd-su-cl* is shown in (59):

---

[40] In fact, as motivated in Chapter 3, we allow indicative declarative clauses to denote either a proposition or a FACT. We introduce a construction 'promoting' proposition-denoting signs to fact-denoting clauses in section 2.10 below.

[41] The reason this is a default is that the analysis of elliptical declarative clauses developed in Chapter 8 will construct a SOA value from contextual information, rather than the head daughter's CONTENT.

(59)   *decl-hd-su-cl*:

$$[\ ] \rightarrow [\ ], \left[\text{HEAD} \begin{bmatrix} \text{VFORM} & fin \\ \text{INV} & - \end{bmatrix} \right]$$

Simply declaring the existence of the type *decl-hd-su-cl* and indicating its place in the hierarchy of phrasal types is sufficient to predict (through constraint inheritance) that all instances of this type have the properties shown in (60):[42]

(60) ECC &   GHFP   & *hd-subj-ph* & *core-cl* & *decl-cl* & *decl-hd-su-cl*:

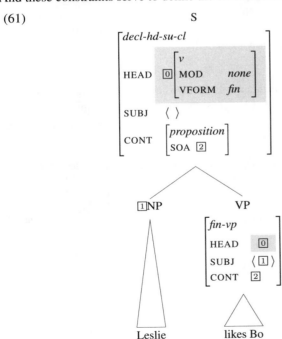

And these constraints serve to define the existence of phrases like the following:

(61)

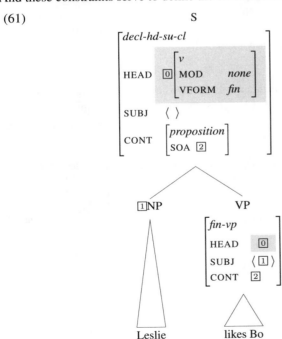

---

[42]Perhaps the [INV −] constraint assumed here should apply to *hd-subj-ph*, rather than directly to *decl-hd-su-cl*. But the constraint would then have to be a default, assuming some instances of *hd-subj-ph* are nonverbal (and hence incompatible with the feature INV).

Here the VFORM value *clausal* has been resolved to *fin* and the CONTENT value *austinian* has been resolved to *proposition*. These resolutions are a consequence of the lexical properties of the indicative verb *likes* and their interaction with various of the type constraints we have discussed. In particular, a finite verb has either an *r-soa* (indicatives) or an *i-soa* (subjunctives) as its content. The type *austinian* has the subtypes *proposition* and *outcome*. The former type is constructed from (has as its SOA value) an *r-soa*; the latter only can be constructed only from an *i-soa*. Hence, it follows that instances of the *decl-hd-su-cl* construction like (61), i.e. those that are headed by an indicative verb form, can only denote a *proposition*.

Conversely, when a *decl-hd-su-cl* is headed by a subjunctive/imperative verb, the content can only be of type *outcome*. This construction therefore gives rise to (embedded) subjunctive clauses like (62) and (independent) imperative utterances with subjects, like those in (63):

(62) a. they be careful

      b. he go home

(63) a. Everyone get out of here!

      b. Nobody move!

      c. Somebody help me!

      d. Kim take the high road! (The rest of you are with me.)

Although imperative sentences like (63) have many mysterious properties that we cannot try to unravel here, it is a pleasing consequence of our approach that it generalizes to these, as well as to indicative clauses.

Finally, it should be noted that, in consequence of the constraints in (59), all instances of *decl-hd-su-cl* are headed by a noninverted, finite verb or VP.[43] This means, among other things, that infinitival clauses like (64) are systematically excluded:

(64)   *[Sandy [to go to the store]]

This discussion has provided only a preliminary glimpse of how our constructional analysis will assign meanings to phrases. The phrasal types introduced so far are summarized in (65). Among the further details yet to be presented is an account of quantification, a matter we take up in Chapter 3 and in section 5.3.[44]

---

[43]When the finite verb is strictly intransitive, it cannot serve as the head daughter of any head-complement phrase (the head daughter of such a phrase must have a nonempty COMPS list). In this case, the verb itself is the head of the *decl-hd-su-cl* (e.g. *Kim left.*). When a finite, noninverted verb selects complements, it first combines with those complements by the *fin-vp* construction.

[44]We will not discuss imperative clauses in this book. However, a first cut at formulating the constraint governing the subjectless imperative construction (*no-subject-imperative-clause*—a subtype of *imp-cl* and *hd-only-ph*) might be (i):

(i) *ns-imp-cl*:

$$\left[\text{CONT}|\text{SOA } \boxed{1}\right] \rightarrow \begin{bmatrix} \text{VFORM} & \textit{fin} \\ \text{SUBJ} & \langle \text{NP}[\textit{2nd}] \rangle \\ \text{CONT} & \boxed{1} \end{bmatrix}$$

(65)

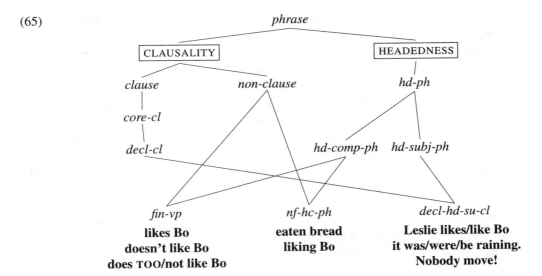

2.7 Main and Embedded Clauses

A grammar must specify what kinds of phrase can be used as an independent utterance. In standard presentations of context-free grammar, for example, this is done by designating 'S' as the 'start symbol'. In a system of feature structures like the one developed here, this is often done by positing a distinguished type—*root*—whose constraints must be satisfied by any 'stand-alone' utterance. Fragments present a special case, of course, one that we return to in Chapter 8. Here we present a preliminary statement (one that we will revise in Chapter 7) of the constraints to be associated with the type *root* so as to predict which phrases can function as independent utterances.

In earlier discussions, we introduced the feature IC to distinguish between independent clauses and others. If a clausal construction is specified as [IC −], then it cannot function independently (modulo elliptical fragments); rather it must be an embedded clause. However, in light of the fact that independent clause phenomena sometimes appear in subordinate clauses (Hooper and Thompson 1973, Green 1976), we must keep the notions 'independent clause' and 'main clause' distinct. Simplifying what is a complex issue well beyond the scope of this monograph (for discussion, see Green 1996), a clause can appear independently only if it is [IC +]. However, certain embedded environments, as we will see in the next section, also allow [IC +] phrases.

To guarantee this effect, we build an [IC +] condition into the *root* type constraint, which we formulate as follows:

$$(66) \quad root \quad \Rightarrow \quad \begin{bmatrix} \text{HEAD} & \begin{bmatrix} verbal \\ \text{IC} & + \\ \text{VFORM} & fin \end{bmatrix} \\ \text{CONT} & message \\ \text{STORE} & \{\,\} \\ \text{SLASH} & \{\,\} \\ \text{WH} & \{\,\} \end{bmatrix}$$

(66) says that a root phrase must be an [IC +], finite verbal projection (i.e. one whose HEAD value is either of type *v*, *g* or *c*). This of course allows an instance of *decl-hd-su-cl* like (61) above to serve as an independent utterance. Gerund phrases (e.g. *Les liking Bo*) will be excluded

as independent utterances because gerunds are lexically specified as [IC −], and hence are incompatible with *root*.

Our decision to in addition allow CPs (discussed below) as independent utterances is somewhat speculative. The treatment of *that*-clauses and *for-to*-clauses that we will outline requires them to be [IC −], and hence incompatible with *root*. However, we leave open the possibility that other expressions, e.g. *how come*, are [IC +] complementizers, and hence that the clauses they project are [IC +] CPs, as proposed in Chapter 6.[45]

The constraint in (66) also requires that the CONTENT value be some subtype of *message*. This constraint allows for *root* phrases whose content is of type *proposition*, *fact*, *question*, or *outcome*, but it rules out phrases whose content is of type *soa*.[46] Finally, (66) requires in addition that the values for STORE, SLASH and WH must be empty. These features are all discussed in Chapter 5.

How then do embedded clauses acquire the specification [IC −]? The answer to this is partly lexical. We assume that there are lexemic types specifying ARG-ST lists that include sentential complements, i.e. verbal complements whose CONTENT value is some subtype of *message*. The relevant lexemic types are constrained so that each such argument must be [IC −] as well.[47] Sentential complements of all kinds[48] will be specified as [IC −].

2.8 Complementizers and *To*

As noted above, the part of speech types associated with verbs and complementizers share a common supertype *verbal*, for which the features VFORM and IC are both appropriate. Given these assumptions, we may formulate the lexical entry for the complementizer *that* as shown in (67):

(67)

$$
\begin{bmatrix}
\text{PHON} & \langle \text{ that } \rangle \\[2ex]
\text{SS|LOC} & \begin{bmatrix}
\text{CAT} & \begin{bmatrix}
\text{HEAD} & \begin{bmatrix} c \\ \text{IC} & - \\ \text{VFORM} & \textit{fin} \end{bmatrix} \\[3ex]
\text{SUBJ} & \langle \, \rangle
\end{bmatrix} \\[4ex]
\text{CONT} & \boxed{1}\,\textit{austinian}
\end{bmatrix} \\[6ex]
\text{ARG-ST} & \Big\langle \overset{S}{\begin{bmatrix}
\text{INV} & - \\
\text{VFORM} & \textit{fin} \\
\text{SUBJ} & \langle \, \rangle \\
\text{CONT} & \boxed{1}
\end{bmatrix}} \Big\rangle
\end{bmatrix}
$$

---

[45]The decision to let CPs be compatible with *root* is of course independently motivated in many languages, including French (the exclamative complementizer *comme*), Gascon (the affirmative complementizer *que*), Hindi (the interrogative complementizer *kyaa*), and Arabic (the intensifying complementizer *inna*). This analysis might also be independently motivated for English by examples like (i), pointed out to us by Carl Pollard:

    (i) That it should come to this!

This motivation would turn on showing that such clauses are not better analyzed in terms of ellipsis.

[46]This semantic condition may be an independent factor ruling out gerund phrases as independent utterances.

[47]An alternative would be to introduce a further classification of phrases, placing an [IC −] condition on any sentential daughter. This would have the virtue of providing a unified treatment of the 'embeddedness' of complements and other subordinate clauses, if indeed a uniform treatment is warranted.

[48]Except perhaps complements of direct quotation, depending on how these are analyzed.

As just noted, *that* is [IC −]; and hence *that*-clauses cannot function as independent utterances. There is a further effect of the constraints in (67): because (1) the VFORM and CONTENT values of *that* are shared with those of its sentential complement and (2) that shared content is of type *austinian*, *that* allows both indicative and subjunctive complements. These can be simple declarative clauses (e.g. instances of the type *decl-hd-su-cl*), topicalized clauses (in certain restricted circumstances discussed below), or coordinations of such.[49]

The lexical entry for the complementizer *for* is similar to (67).[50] We assume that *for* differs from *that* in taking two syntactic arguments, instead of one. In addition, the LOCAL value of the first argument is identified with that of the unexpressed subject of the second argument:

(68)

$$
\begin{bmatrix}
\text{PHON} & \langle\, \text{for}\, \rangle \\[4pt]
\text{SS}|\text{LOC} &
\begin{bmatrix}
\text{CAT} &
\begin{bmatrix}
\text{HEAD} &
\begin{bmatrix}
c \\
\text{IC} & - \\
\text{VFORM} & inf
\end{bmatrix} \\[6pt]
\text{SUBJ} & \langle\,\rangle
\end{bmatrix} \\[10pt]
\text{CONT} &
\begin{bmatrix}
outcome \\
\text{SOA} & \boxed{1}
\end{bmatrix}
\end{bmatrix} \\[20pt]
\text{ARG-ST} &
\left\langle
\begin{bmatrix}
canon\text{-}ss \\
\text{LOC} & \boxed{2}
\end{bmatrix},
\overset{\text{VP}}{
\begin{bmatrix}
\text{VFORM} & inf \\
\text{SUBJ} & [\text{LOC}\ \boxed{2}] \\
\text{CONT} & \boxed{1}
\end{bmatrix}}
\right\rangle
\end{bmatrix}
$$

As noted by Sag (1997), if we assume that *for-to* clauses, but not *that*-clauses, project a flat (ternary) structure, we obtain an immediate account for contrasts in (69), first noted by Emonds (1976: 196).

(69) a. Mary asked me if, in St. Louis, John could rent a house cheap.

　　b. He doesn't intend that, in these circumstances, we be rehired.

　　c. *Mary arranged for, in St. Louis, John to rent a house cheap.

　　d. *He doesn't intend for, in these circumstances, us to be rehired.

This argument assumes that these sentential modifiers must have a sentential constituent to modify. On our analysis, there is a clause for the adverbial to modify only in the case of *that*-clauses like (69a,b), not in the case of *for/to*-clauses like (69c,d). And no other analysis of (69c,d) is possible because any such analysis would require that two complements be allowed to right-shift over an adverb. However, as (70) shows, this possibility must be disallowed on independent grounds:

(70) a. *Kim persuaded in St. Louis Sandy to rent a house cheap.

　　b. *Lee believed in these circumstances Sandy to be in the right.

---

[49] *Coordinate-phrase* is not a subtype of clause, though (as noted above) the semantics we assume allows such non-clauses to have propositional content.

[50] It no doubt makes sense to organize the complementizers via a lexical type, factoring out all common properties as constraints on that type. However, we will not concern ourselves with such matters here, simply presenting the individual lexical items that would result from such an analysis.

Observe that the object of *for* is required to be of type *canon-ss*. This is inconsistent with that object being a *gap-ss* and hence correctly predicts that the object of *for* cannot be extracted:

(71) *Who did you prefer for __ to get the job?

Finally, the semantics of *for* is an outcome formed from the *soa* of the infinitival VP complement. Like subjunctive clauses, the meaning of a *for-to* phrase is irrealis in nature.

Since these complementizers have a lexically assigned content of type *austinian* (*that*) or *outcome* (*for*),[51] in order to provide *that*-clauses and *for-to*-clauses with the right semantics, we identify the complementizer's content with that of the CP it projects. To this end, we posit the clause type *CP-clause* (*cp-cl*), which is subject to the following constraint:

(72)   *cp-cl*:
         [ ] → **H**[HEAD *c*] , ...

Nothing more needs to be said about this clause type except that it is a subtype of both *core-cl* and *hd-comp-ph*:

(73)

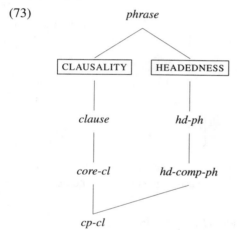

The inheritance of content and all other feature specifications from the head daughter to the CP is guaranteed by the GHFP:

---

[51]Or *question*, as is the case for the complementizers *whether* and *if*, discussed in Chapter 6. Similarly, French exclamative clauses like (i) are likely best analyzed as an instance of this type, with the lexical entry for *comme* specifying a CONTENT value of type *fact*.

  (i) Comme il fait   beau!
     How   it makes beautiful
     How beautiful it is!

For discussion, see Desmets in preparation.

(74) GHFP & ECC & *hd-comp-ph* & *clause* & *core-cl* & *cp-cl*:

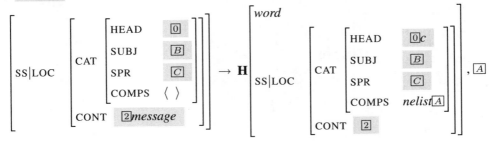

This clause type accounts for clauses like (75) and (76).

(75)

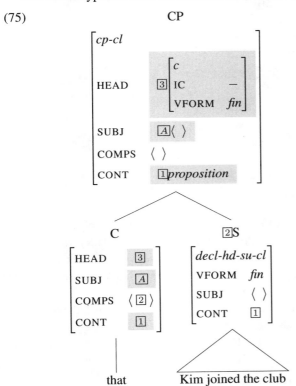

(76)

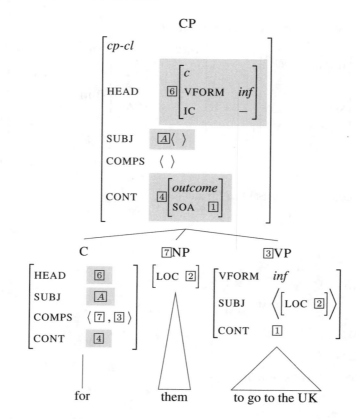

In (75), the CONTENT value must resolve to *proposition*—the only subtype of *austinian* constructible from the *r-soa* provided by the indicative verb *joined*. The CONTENT value of *to* is lexically underspecified (as type *soa*), but in contexts like (76) (where *for* introduces a content of type *outcome*), it is resolved to type *i-soa*. Elsewhere, as detailed below, a *to*-phrase can denote a *proposition*, requiring that *to*'s CONTENT value be resolved as an *r-soa*.

A final observation: although the complementizer *that* is specified as [IC −], the IC value of its complement is left unspecified. This has the effect of allowing 'main clause phenomena' [52] in certain embedded ([IC −]) environments, but only if the complementizer *that* is present. This appears to be a correct prediction:

(77)   a. She subtly suggested (that) we had to visit France.

   b. She subtly suggested *(that) [problems of this sort, our analysis would never account for].

(78)   a. They believed (that) they were oppressed.

   b. They believed *(that) [never again would they have to do housework].

(79)   a. The kids were under the impression (that) they had to leave.

   b. The kids were under the impression *(that) [out from under the bush would appear a small animal].

---

[52]We mean to include here most of the phenomena discussed by Emonds (1976) under the rubric of 'root transformations'.

We make no attempt here to explain the pragmatic circumstances governing when independent clauses can appear in embedded environments.[53] However, the fact that a complementizer, an unambiguous marker of syntactic embedding, is required in order for independent clauses to be embedded is both surprising and descriptively challenging. Our (admittedly partial) account of the matter is strikingly simple.

To-phrases are more complex. As shown by Pullum (1982), the word *to* is profitably analyzed as a defective (i.e. paradigmless), nonfinite auxiliary verb—that is, a verb that is lexically unspecified for the feature AUX. This treatment, for example, provides an account of why *to* 'licenses' VP Ellipsis, as in (80).

(80) a. They ordered us to leave, and we *will, should, are* __ .

　　 b. They ordered us to leave, and we want *to* __ .

Crucially, this is a property not shared by complementizers or by nonauxiliary verbs, as the impossibility of ellipses like the following show:[54]

(81) a. *Pat preferred for Sandy to get the job, and we preferred for __ , also.

　　 b. *Kim ordered us to leave, and Sandy ordered us __ .

　　 c. *They ordered us to leave, and we want __ .

We therefore formulate the lexical entry for *to* as shown in (82).

$$
(82) \quad
\begin{bmatrix}
\text{PHON} & \langle\, \text{to}\,\rangle \\[2mm]
\text{SS}|\text{LOC} &
\begin{bmatrix}
\text{CAT} &
\begin{bmatrix}
\text{HEAD} &
\begin{bmatrix}
v \\
\text{AUX} & + \\
\text{VFORM} & \textit{inf}
\end{bmatrix} \\[4mm]
\text{SUBJ} & \left\langle\; \boxed{7}\begin{bmatrix} \text{LOC} & \boxed{2} \\ \text{SLASH} & \{\,\} \end{bmatrix} \;\right\rangle
\end{bmatrix} \\[6mm]
\text{CONT} & \boxed{1}
\end{bmatrix} \\[10mm]
\text{ARG-ST} & \left\langle\; \boxed{7},
\begin{bmatrix}
VP \\
\text{VFORM} & \textit{base} \\
\text{SUBJ} & \left\langle \begin{bmatrix} \text{LOC} & \boxed{2} \end{bmatrix} \right\rangle \\
\text{CONT} & \boxed{1}
\end{bmatrix}
\;\right\rangle
\end{bmatrix}
$$

This is quite similar to the entries required for other auxiliary verb lexemes. It is distinctive, however, in that it is the only element specified as [VFORM *inf*]. Hence (since is a subtype of *clausal*; see (10) above), *to* is distinctive in being the only nonfinite verb form that can project

---

[53]For some discussion, see Hooper and Thompson 1973, and Green 1976, 1996.

[54]For arguments that apparent counterexamples, e.g. (i), are a phenomenon distinct from VP Ellipsis, see Hankamer and Sag 1976, Hankamer 1978 and Pullum 2000.

　(i) Kim ordered us to leave, and we agreed.

a clause. In addition, note that the element on its SUBJ list is specified as [SLASH { }]. The consequences of the latter constraint will be explained in a moment.

The auxiliary *to* projects a head-complement phrase as an instance of the type *nf-hc-ph* introduced in section 2.6 above. A non-clausal *to*-phrase is illustrated in (83):

(83)

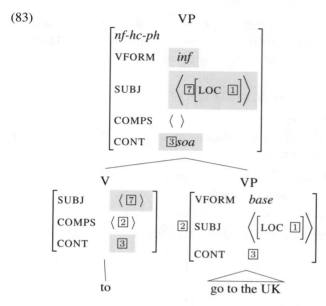

Note that the content of this phrase, like that of *to* and *to*'s VP[*base*] complement, is constrained only to be a *soa*. Hence, a phrase like (83) may be resolved as either an *r-soa* or an *i-soa* in the appropriate context. A *soa*-denoting phrases like (83) can be selected as a complement by a raising verb (in which case its content is generally resolved to type *r-soa*) or by the complementizer *for* (in which case its content is resolved to type *i-soa*).

However, in other contexts, *to*-phrases convey more than just a *soa*. For example, as a controlled complement,[55] a *to*-phrase denotes an *outcome* and many uses of *to* phrases appear to denote propositions with a so-called 'arbitrary' interpretation of the unexpressed subject. Thus we claim that both kinds of meaning are possible for *to*-clauses:

(84) a.   Lee wants [to be happy]. (*outcome*)

  b.   They claimed [to know the answer to that question]. (*proposition*)

And when *to*-phrases stand alone as elliptical utterances or as short answers, they also acquire the force of a message.

(85) a. A: What do you want?

    B: *To go home.* (*outcome*)

  b. A: What are they claiming now?

    B: *To be able to read Hangul.* (*proposition*)

---

[55]For an overview of the properties that distinguish control and raising, see Soames and Perlmutter 1979 or Sag and Wasow 1999.

The auxiliary *to* can give rise to such clauses in virtue of a further clause type: *declarative-nonsubject-clause* (*decl-ns-cl*), a subtype of *hd-only-ph* and *decl-cl*:

(86)

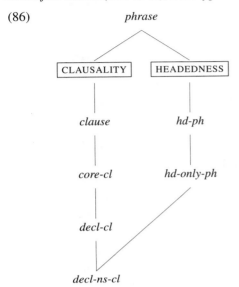

Instances of this type are constrained as follows:

(87) *decl-ns-cl*:

$$\begin{bmatrix} \text{HEAD} & \begin{bmatrix} v \\ \text{INV} & - \end{bmatrix} \\ \text{SUBJ} & \langle\, \text{XP}\,\rangle \end{bmatrix} \rightarrow \ \dots$$

Constraint inheritance of a now familiar kind gives us the information in (88).[56]

(88) GHFP & ECC & *decl-cl* & *hd-ns-cl*:

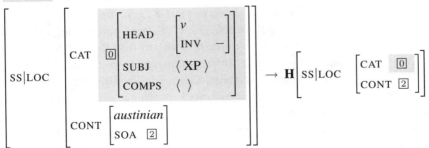

---

[56]Our rule notation does not provide a perspicuous presentation of the information contributed by the type *hd-only-ph*, namely that the REST of the DTRS list is the empty list. See Appendix A.

This allows for *to*-clauses like (89) to be built from *soa*-denoting *to*-phrases like (83), once the effects of the GHFP and the constraint on the type *decl-cl* are taken into account:[57]

(89)   'S'

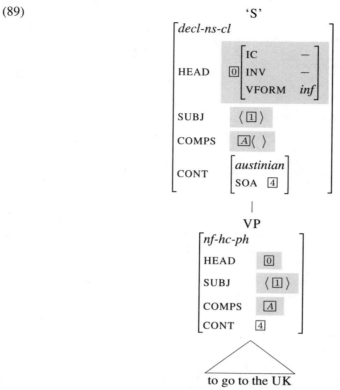

to go to the UK

Recall that there is a constraint on type *decl-cl* (see (54) above) requiring that declarative clauses have *austinian* content. Thus, because (87) says nothing about CONTENT, instances of this clausal type may have either subtype of *austinian*—*proposition* or *outcome*—as their content. As we will see in Chapter 6, it is this potential for *to*-phrases to denote propositions, as well as outcomes, that allows them to appear in *wh*-interrogative constructions (e.g. *who to visit*).

Crucially, other *soa*-denoting VPs, e.g. *going to the UK, gone to the UK* cannot serve as the head daughter of the *decl-ns-cl* construction. Such VPs are specified as [VFORM *prp*] or [VFORM *pfp*], both of which are incompatible (see (10) above) with the [VFORM *clausal*] constraint on this kind of phrase that is inherited from its supertype *core-cl* (see (51) above). That this constraint must be true of both mother and head daughter follows from the GHFP. Our claim, then, is that *to*-phrases are unique in being ambiguous between a nonclause whose content is a *soa* and a clause whose content is either a proposition or an outcome.

When a *to*-phrase has *soa* content, e.g. in raising contexts, no restrictions are placed on the unexpressed subject of that phrase (the element on its SUBJ list). That subject, whose LOCAL value is identified with the raised NP, can be any kind of nonreferential element, for example, as long as the verb heading the complement of *to* selects for a nonreferential NP of that particular kind:

---

[57]We abbreviate such clauses as 'S', rather than as S or VP.

(90) a.   I believe there [to be a problem here]/*[to like Sandy].

   b.   I believe it [to be raining]/*[to like Sandy].

   c.   It's unlikely [for there [to be a solution here]/*[to like Sandy]].

   d.   Close tabs seem [to have been kept on Kim]/*[to bother them].

Yet when a *to*-phrase appears in a non-raising context (e.g. those in (91)), the unexpressed subject of the infinitival phrase (always a clause on our analysis) must be referential.

(91) a.   *To run* would be wonderful.

   b.   I want *to be running*.

   c. A: What do you want now?

      B: *To run*.

      B′:   *To bother them*.

Thus when the verb heading the complement of *to* selects for a nonreferential subject, such *to*-phrases are systematically ill-formed:

(92) a.   *To rain* would be wonderful. (cf. *For it to rain* would be wonderful.)

   b.   *I want *to be raining*. (cf. I want it to be raining.)

   c. A: What do you want now?

      B: *To rain*.

      B′:   *To bother them that I'm not there*.

Moreover, the requirement that an unexpressed subject must be referential applies to all clauses in English, even those embedded within *wh*-questions (e.g. to all *to*-phrases other than raising complements), as the following additional examples illustrate:

(93) a.   *a yard [in which [to be a party]]. (cf. a yard [in which [to have a party]])

   b.   *I wonder [where [to be a riot]] (cf. I wonder [where [there is a riot]])

   c.   *Bother you(rself) that Kim left!

   d.   *[Raining] would bother them.

In our analysis, these facts are all accounted for by a constraint governing all clauses:

(94)   Clause Constraint:

            clause:

            $\left[\text{SUBJ} \quad list(noncan\text{-}ss) \right] \rightarrow \quad \cdots$

The Clause Constraint says that the SUBJ value of all clauses must be a list each of whose members is of type (i.e. belongs to some subtype of) *noncan-ss*. Given that a SUBJ list has at most one member, the effect of (94) is to guarantee that a clause's SUBJ value is one of the following:

(95)   a. $\langle \ \rangle$ b. $\langle$ *pro-ss* $\rangle$ c. $\langle$ *gap-ss* $\rangle$

This follows because *pro-ss* and *gap-ss* are the only two subtypes of *noncan-ss* and the empty list is also a subtype of *list(noncan-ss)*.

Both a *gap-ss* element (corresponding to an extracted element, which can never be an expletive pronoun) and an unexpressed pronominal are referential in our analysis. In fact, elements of type *pro-ss* are always reflexive and *accusative*. The following constraint encodes these properties of unexpressed pronominals.

$$(96) \quad \textit{pro-ss} \ \Rightarrow \ \begin{bmatrix} \text{HEAD}|\text{CASE} \ \textit{acc} \\ \\ \text{CONT} \begin{bmatrix} \textit{reflexive} \\ \text{INDEX} \ \textit{ref} \end{bmatrix} \end{bmatrix}$$

Since a *pro-ss* must have a referential index, it is inconsistent with the subject specification of any dummy-selecting predicate. Hence no infinitival clause can have a head daughter of the sort that would normally combine with an expletive subject (e.g. *to be raining*). This is a correct consequence, as we have seen. Moreover, the requirement that the CONTENT value of *pro-ss* be of type *reflexive* guarantees that the binding and control assignment behavior of *pro-ss* interact to explain 'Visser's Generalization' (Bresnan (1982a)) in its full generality, as discussed in P&S–94, chaps. 6–7.[58]

The Clause Constraint plays an important role in our theory. It interacts with other, independently motivated constraints to limit the possible SUBJ values of the particular clausal constructions that we analyze. Basically, the Clause Constraint guarantees that clauses either (1) are 'subject-saturated' (i.e. have an empty SUBJ list), (2) have an unexpressed 'PRO' subject, or else (3) have a subject that is extracted, corresponding to the three options shown in (95). The Clause Constraint will in fact guarantee that the only option for clausal *to*-phrases is to have a singleton SUBJ list containing a *pro-ss*. This follows because (1) the lexical entry for *to* ((82)) bars 'slashed' subjects,[59] while *gap-ss* elements are always slashed (see Chapter 5) and (2) the type *decl-hd-su-cl* discussed earlier allows only finite instances—thus there is no way in our grammar to build up a clause like *Sandy to leave*.

Since there is no way to construct a phrase like *Sandy to leave* in our analysis, there is no way that such a sequence can satisfy the specification [VFORM *inf*, SUBJ ⟨ ⟩]. This is a desired result, enabling us to specify '(*for* NP) *to* VP' as a natural class: [VFORM *inf*]. This class, excluding 'NP *to* VP' sequences, is relevant for the grammar of such constructions as purpose clauses and infinitival relatives:[60]

(97) a. I bought it [to go to California in].

      b. I bought it [for us to go to California in].

      c. *I bought it [us to go to California in].

(98) a. The car [to go to California in] is a Lincoln.

      b. The car [for us to go to California in] is a Lincoln.

      c. *The car [us to go to California in] is a Lincoln.

---

[58] And, because *pro-ss* elements must be accusative, it follows that there are no unexpressed subject clauses headed by finite verbs (which require nominative subjects), e.g. no clauses like (i).

    (i) *Kim wanted/tried/... goes to the store.

This familiar correlation follows from the interaction of (95), the Clause Constraint, and the lexical constraint requiring that finite verbs have nominative subjects.

[59] This is actually a more general constraint, we believe, applying to all nonfinite verbal forms, and is independently motivated by the interaction of raising and extraction, as discussed briefly in Chapter 5. This analysis of raised subjects might benefit from the introduction of a new synsem type—*raised-synsem*, which is specifed as [SLASH { }] and [WH { }], but we will not explore this refinement here.

[60] See Green 1991 and Johnston 1999.

Of course, we can still distinguish between *to*-phrases and *for*-phrases via the SUBJ value of a [VFORM *inf*] phrase or by specifying the HEAD value as *v* vs. *c*. Thus it is straightforward to write a lexical entry for a verb like *try*, which cannot take a *for-to*-clause as complement:

(99) a. I tried [to go to California].

  b. *I tried [for us to go to California].

  c. *I tried [us to go to California].

2.9 Proposition-Embedding Verbs

A phrase like (83) (*to go to the* UK) can serve as the complement of most raising verbs. For example, the lexeme *believe* will include the information in (100), some of which is derived via constraint inheritance.[61]

(100)

$$
\begin{bmatrix}
\text{PHON } \langle \text{ believe } \rangle \\
\text{SS|LOC|CONT} \begin{bmatrix} soa \\ \text{NUCL} \begin{bmatrix} believe\text{-}rel \\ \text{BELIEVER} \quad i \\ \text{COG(NITIVE)-ARG} \quad j \\ \text{PROP-ARG} \begin{bmatrix} proposition \\ \text{SIT } s \\ \text{SOA } \boxed{1} \end{bmatrix} \end{bmatrix} \end{bmatrix} \\
\text{ARG-ST } \left\langle \text{NP}_i , \left[\text{LOC } \boxed{2}\right], \begin{bmatrix} \text{VP} \\ \text{VFORM} \quad inf \\ \text{SUBJ} \quad \langle [\text{LOC } \boxed{2}] \rangle \\ \text{CONT} \quad \boxed{1} \end{bmatrix} \right\rangle
\end{bmatrix}
$$

Because the *to*-phrase here is not a clause, the Clause Constraint is inapplicable. Therefore the unexpressed subject of the VP[*inf*] argument and the object of *believe* are free to be of any type. This allows for nonreferential objects in examples like (101).

(101) a. We believe [it] [to be obvious that Brooke is the one].

  b. Fergie believed [there] [to be no solution to this problem].

  c. Jan believes [it] [to be snowing now].

Similarly, a *soa*-denoting *to*-phrase may serve as complement of the complementizer *for*, as shown in (76) above. But a *pro-ss* is ruled out in both (76) (*for them to go to the* UK) and (101), as the object of *for* or *believe* must be an overt element, i.e. a *sign*,[62] and hence [SYNSEM *canon*].

---

[61]We follow Cooper and Ginzburg (1996), who assume that attitudinal predicates carry an argument, labeled here as COGNITIVE-ARG, filled by a contextually supplied mental situation of the reported agent. For further discussion, see Chapter 8, note 35.

[62]Note, however, that a raised element whose LOCAL value is shared with that of the unexpressed subject of a *to*-phrase can be extracted, as shown in (i):

  (i) Who did you believe __ to be the best candidate?

This follows, given our treatment of raising as sharing of LOCAL values, (NB: not SYNSEM values). When there is extraction of a raised object, the object argument of the raising verb will be of type *gap-ss* (see section 5.1), and hence slashed. But this *synsem* is distinct from the subject of the infinitive, which is unslashed.

These predictions follow from the interaction of the Principle of Canonicality in (49) and the constraints stated directly on the type *hd-comp-ph* ((34) above).

Next consider a proposition-embedding verb like *think*. Its lexical entry includes the information in (102).

$$
(102) \quad
\begin{bmatrix}
\text{PHON} & \langle\, \text{think}\, \rangle \\[2ex]
\text{SS|LOC|CONT} &
\begin{bmatrix}
soa \\
\text{NUCL} &
\begin{bmatrix}
\textit{think-rel} \\
\text{THINKER} & i \\
\text{COG-ARG} & j \\
\text{PROP-ARG} & \boxed{1}\,\textit{proposition}
\end{bmatrix}
\end{bmatrix} \\[6ex]
\text{ARG-ST} &
\left\langle\, \text{NP}_i\,,\,
\begin{bmatrix}
\text{VFORM} & \textit{fin} \\
\text{CONT} & \boxed{1}
\end{bmatrix}
\,\right\rangle
\end{bmatrix}
$$

In the system developed in this chapter, there are only two kinds of phrase that potentially satisfy the selectional requirements of this verb: *that*-clauses and indicative instances of the type *decl-hd-su-cl*.[63] The predictions are the following (an asterisk here indicates information of the complement that is incompatible with the properties selected by *think*):

(103) a. They think [that Leslie is winning].   (CP[*fin*]:*proposition*)
    b. They think [Leslie is winning].   (S[*fin*]:*proposition*)
    c. *They think [Leslie be winning].   (S[*fin*]:**outcome*)
    d. *They think [that Leslie be winning].   (CP[*fin*]:**outcome*)
    e. *They think [Leslie to be winning].   (no such clause)
    f. *They think [to be winning].   (VP[**inf*]:*proposition*)
    g. *They think [for her to be winning].   (CP[**inf*]:**outcome*)

The lexical entry for a proposition-embedding verb like *claim*, however, differs from that in (102) in that it lacks the [VFORM *fin*] restriction on its complement. This produces the following paradigm for *claim*:

(104) a. They claim [that Leslie is winning].   (CP[*fin*]:*proposition*)
    b. They claim [Leslie is winning].   (S[*fin*]:*proposition*)
    c. *They claim [Leslie be winning].   (S[*fin*]:**outcome*)
    d. *They claim [that Leslie be winning].   (CP[*fin*]:**outcome*)
    e. *They claim [Leslie to be winning].   (no such clause)
    f. They claim [to be winning].   (VP[*inf*]:*proposition*)
    g. *They claim [for her to be winning].   (CP[*inf*]:**outcome*)

---

[63] For the moment, we ignore sentences like (i), which involve extraction of an embedded subject:

(i) Who did you think [__ was winning]?

These examples are discussed in section 5.1.

Again, these contrasts seem precisely in accord with intuition.

Finally, consider the lexical entry for a verb like *insist* in its 'demand' sense:

(105)
$$
\begin{bmatrix}
\text{PHON} & \langle \text{ insist } \rangle \\
\text{SS|LOC|CONT} & \begin{bmatrix} soa \\ \text{NUCL} & \begin{bmatrix} insist\text{-}rel \\ \text{INSISTOR} & i \\ \text{COG-ARG} & j \\ \text{OUTCM-ARG} & \boxed{1}\,outcome \end{bmatrix} \end{bmatrix} \\
\text{ARG-ST} & \left\langle \text{NP}_i \,, \begin{bmatrix} \text{VFORM} & fin \\ \text{CONT} & \boxed{1} \end{bmatrix} \right\rangle
\end{bmatrix}
$$

Our system allows exactly two kinds of clause as the complement of verbs like (105), as shown in (106)a,b:

(106) a.   They insist [he stay outside].   (S[*fin*]:*outcome*)

   b.   They insist [that he stay outside].   (CP[*fin*]:*outcome*)

   c.   *They insist [Leslie to stay outside].   (no such clause)

   d.   *They insist [to stay outside].   (VP[**inf*]:*outcome*)

   e.   *They insist [for him to stay outside].   (CP[**inf*]:*outcome*)

   f.   They insist [that they're incompetent].   (CP[*fin*]:**proposition*|**fact*)

   g.   They insist [they're incompetent].   (S[*fin*]:**proposition*|**fact*)

The last two examples are not unacceptable, of course. Rather they illustrate a different sense of the verb *insist*—one we may paraphrase as 'maintain the truth of'. In this sense, the verb takes a proposition-denoting complement.

2.10   Fact-Denoting Declarative Clauses

In the next chapter, we will provide evidence that finite declarative clauses lead a double semantic life as *fact*s, a type of message distinct from *proposition* and *outcome*. To accommodate this evidence, we introduce a new clausal type—a subtype of both *core-cl* and *hd-only-ph*—which 'promotes' a proposition-denoting sentence to one that denotes a fact. The constraints idiosyncratic to this construction are illustrated in (107).

(107)   *factive-cl*:
$$
\begin{bmatrix}
\text{HEAD} & \begin{bmatrix} verbal \\ \text{VFORM} & fin \end{bmatrix} \\
\text{CONT} & \begin{bmatrix} fact \\ \text{PROP} & \boxed{1} \end{bmatrix}
\end{bmatrix} \rightarrow \mathbf{H}\begin{bmatrix} \text{CONT} & \boxed{1} \end{bmatrix}
$$

This construction applies to both CPs and Ss (both main and embedded), allowing us to assign a *fact*-type meaning to all finite declarative clauses.

In providing a second semantic life for declarative clauses as factives, our analysis leads us to the view that such sentences have a semantic overlap with exclamatives, which we treat uniformly as having a *fact*-type meaning. This is an intuitive result, as exclamatives always seem to have paraphrases that have the outward appearance of declaratives:

(108) a. Is Kim clever!

      b. Kim IS CLEVER.

(109) a. How clever Kim is!

      b. Kim is truly clever.

      c. Mmm. Mmm. KIM...IS...CLEVER.

These effects rely on context, and sometimes in addition on the presence of emphatic modifiers or the pragmatic help of intonation.

2.11 Summary

This chapter has built up an analysis of the basic declarative clause constructions in English. The system of clausal features and types presented here makes it possible to specify natural classes for purposes of lexical selection. Following the approach articulated by Grimshaw (1979) and others, this selection is partly semantic and partly syntactic. Semantic types and VFORM distinctions play a significant role in our account of this, as does our theory of declarative clause types.

The various phrasal types we have proposed are summarized in (110):

(110)

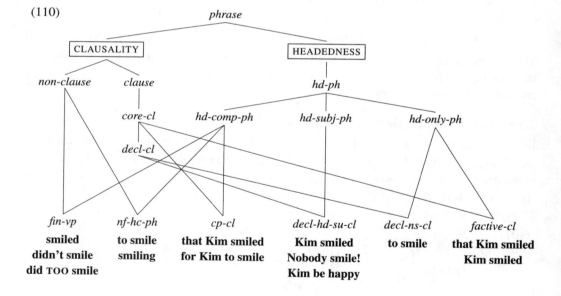

3

A Semantic Ontology

3.1 Introduction: Semantic Theory and Ontology

This chapter has two main aims. The first is to develop an ontology of semantic types for the main clausal constructions in English, with particular focus on interrogative clauses and the predicates that embed them. Our second aim is to construct a semantic universe in which the fundamental properties of the semantic entities we posit can be explicated. Once again, our most important topic will be *questions*. Fulfilling these two aims will enable us to specify a semantic theory for a comprehensive fragment of English. We start by setting these goals and the way we hope to achieve them within a wider setting. Initially, we compare them with the basic tasks of semantic theory, as conceived within a framework such as Montague Semantics (Montague 1974b, Dowty et al. 1981). We conclude with some comments on cognitive aspects of a semantic theory.

The semantic theory developed by Montague consists of two main components: a syntax/semantics interface and a model theory. The model theory explicates which class of set-theoretic structures can function as possible models. The syntax/semantics interface consists of a set of rules that associate with an NL expression ϕ an entity $[\![\phi]\!]$ (the denotation of ϕ) in any of the class of possible models. In practice, the syntax/semantics interface is formulated by means of a translation procedure that associates with each NL expression an intensional logic formula. This simplifies the statement of the rules associating model theoretic entities with NL expressions, because the intensional logic formulas have a transparent model theoretic interpretation.

The models are the basis for explicating what have been taken to be core semantic notions such as synonymy, truth, and entailment. Though synonymy is a complicated notion whose application in practice is tricky, it is one that applies generally and indiscriminately to relate all types of expressions. Truth and entailment, on the other hand, are notions that apply only to declarative sentences; indeed, they apply only to uses of declarative sentences in context.[1,2] In a given context, uttering any of the examples in (1) seems to involve making the same claim about the world:[3]

(1) a. A: Jill is the president.

   b. A: [Pointing at Jill] She is the president.

   c. A: That tall woman over there is the president.

---

[1] In section 3.2 we will see examples of non-sentential expressions to which truth and entailment are applicable.

[2] How relativization to context is handled within our account is discussed in section 3.6.

[3] Of course, these sentences do have different *meanings* in a sense made precise by Montague, Kaplan and others. See section 3.6 for additional discussion of the meaning/content distinction.

The claim common to a given class of declarative utterances is often called a *proposition*. The idea of positing such entities goes back at least to Frege 1892, where they are termed *thoughts*.[4] Consequently, it turns out to be useful to think of truth and entailment not as metalinguistic notions applying to expressions, but rather as semantic notions that characterize the class of propositional entities. Developing a theory of truth and entailment on the class of propositions is one of the basic means of explicating what such entities are. In turn, determining what propositions are is a core ingredient of a theory of the understanding of declarative sentences in any natural language. Montague explicated propositions in terms of possible worlds: a proposition is a set of possible worlds: p is true in world w iff $w \in p$; p entails q iff $p \subset q$. This explication can be extended straightforwardly to provide a theory of properties as well.

Thus, one way to view the model theory developed by Montague for the PTQ fragment is as a theory of natural language ontology. Following Turner (1997), a Montagovian structure can be presented as a relational structure of the form (2):[5]

(2) $[D, Prop, True, \rightarrow, \Pi_T]$
    where:

1. D is a set representing the universe.
2. $Prop$ is the power-set of the set of possible worlds ($\mathcal{P}(W)$ for some set W).[6]
3. $True$ is $\{W\}$.
4. For each type T, Π_T is a function from $P^{[\![T]\!]}$ to $Prop$ which, given as input a function f from $[\![T]\!]$ to $\mathcal{P}(\mathcal{W})$, returns W just in case for all d in $[\![T]\!]$, $f(d) = W$. Otherwise f returns the empty set.
5. $\rightarrow$ is a function from $Prop$ to $Prop^{Prop}$ representing entailment:
    $\rightarrow (A, B) = (W \setminus A) \cup B$.[7]

Such structures explicate the nature of propositions and properties using standard set theoretic tools. The account is based on an ontology where worlds are taken as basic, i.e. they constitute a distinguished subset of the domain of individuals. Since Montague's pioneering efforts in the early 1970s, it has been recognized that there is a need for a wider range of entities in the ontology than those Montague originally allowed for. At the same time, as Bach (1981) and others have observed, the ontological theory needed to explain talk in natural language is not obviously the same ontological theory as that needed by physical science. Following Bach's terminology, we call the former theory *natural language metaphysics*. The first part of this chapter, section 3.2, is devoted to an empirical investigation of the natural language metaphysics needed for a semantic theory of finite clauses in English, with particular emphasis on interrogatives and declaratives.

With this task accomplished, we have a specification of the various entities required by natural language metaphysics. In addition to properties and propositions, these will include questions, facts, outcomes, and situations/events. Explicating the nature of such entities involves introducing abstract properties akin to truth, such as answerhood, facthood, and fulfilledness. Our task will then be to offer a formal analysis of these entities and abstract properties.

By analogy with Montague, our formal analysis will involve positing a structure that contains certain classes of elements as basic and certain set-theoretic operations through which the

---

[4]Somewhat misleadingly, since Frege clearly views such entities as non-psychological.
[5]See Turner 1997, definition 3.1.3.1.
[6]Given a set X, $\mathcal{P}(X)$ denotes the power-set of X, the set of all subsets of X.
[7]'\' here denotes set difference.

'non-basic' entities get constructed. The main divergences from Montague will be that: (1) different entities are taken as basic and (2) the theory will make use of certain distinct set-theoretic operations, which are based on recent advances in non-well founded set theory (Aczel 1988, Barwise and Moss 1996). As we explain below, the ontology that emerges (which is particularly inspired by situation theoretic work) provides solutions to a number of fundamental semantic problems that beset the possible worlds framework, particularly those involving attitude contexts.

Our main innovation will be in the characterization of questions we put forward: we propose to identify questions with *propositional abstracts*. We will show that this approach, which, as we pointed out in Chapter 1, has a long history but which has been hampered by a host of technical and conceptual problems, actually provides an account of questions that is simpler and more empirically successful than other existing analyses.

The final task we undertake in this chapter is to show how the entities of our semantic universe can be represented within the framework of typed feature structures. This will render our account compatible with recent work in HPSG, specifically as sketched in the previous chapter. The role played by the typed feature structure semantic representations is akin to the function of intensional logic expressions in Montague's theory: to facilitate the statement of rules associating syntactic and semantic/contextual information. We specify a mapping that assigns an interpretation to each of the various typed feature structures which serve as values for the CONTENT attribute in HPSG.

Our emphasis in this introductory section has been on a traditional perspective of semantics, one particularly inspired by work in philosophical logic. Although it was once assumed that the 'realist' perspective prominent in logically inspired views of semantics is antagonistic to the cognitive perspective championed by psychologists and AI workers (two recent proponents of this view are Tomasello (1998) and Gärdenfors (2000)), in fact many of the problems that inspire the approach to semantics developed here have their origin in a cognitive approach to semantics. Our ontology and the notions of content that we use avoid certain problems that challenge the construal of Montague semantics as a cognitive theory. As discussed in section 3.4.3, a semantic theory of the kind described here has been used for developing accounts of mental state representation, as part of a theory of attitude reports. Moreover, the theory of questions we develop here is motivated to a large extent by the need to allow for the pragmatic relativization that plays a key role in interrogative attitude reports, as well as by the need to develop notions of answerhood that can sustain a theory of querying in dialogue interaction. Some applications of our semantic framework to the description of linguistic phenomena characteristic of conversational interaction—for instance reprise utterances and fragments—can be found in Chapters 7 and 8, as well as in Ginzburg 2001. The framework can also be easily adapted for computational applications and may well have more general implications for research into the evolution of communicative interaction (Ginzburg 2000).

3.2 An Ontology for Finite Clauses in English

Starting with the work of Hamblin and Karttunen in the mid 1970s, it has been common to recognize a distinction in semantic type between questions and propositions—the latter being the familiar denotata of declarative clauses. We will briefly reiterate the arguments that led to adopting this distinction and then examine the issue more closely. Although the evidence for maintaining the question/proposition distinction is compelling, we will suggest, *contra* Karttunen, that there is equally compelling evidence to suggest that on some uses interrogatives and declaratives have the same semantic type. In previous work, most influentially that of Hintikka and Groenendijk and Stokhof, this semantic type has been taken to be a proposition.

We will argue against this position. Building on insights originally due to Vendler, we recognize a third ontological category, distinct from both questions and propositions, that of facts. We provide a variety of arguments for distinguishing such entities. For example, we will show: (1) that certain speech acts take facts as their descriptive content, (2) that certain predicates select for facts, but for neither propositions nor questions, and (3) that certain clause types, including exclamatives and certain declaratives, denote facts. With interrogatives, the situation is more subtle. We argue that certain predicates coerce the denotation of an interrogative clause they combine with into a fact, though the 'stand alone' denotation of an interrogative clause will be a question, not a fact. We will also briefly consider the semantic status of infinitives, subjunctives, and imperatives, proposing that there exists a single semantic type common to these clause types. We call this type of entity an *outcome*—intuitively, a specification of a situation which is futurate relative to some other given situation. The analysis of subjunctives as outcomes, taken together with the view developed below, that questions are constructed from propositions, will provide a simple account of the striking fact that there are no subjunctival interrogatives.

3.2.1 Distinguishing Questions from Propositions

Our initial aim in this chapter is to develop and apply an ontology that enables us to capture the fundamental properties of interrogative and declarative clauses and the predicates that embed them. As we will see, this is a complicated enterprise because there are grounds for maintaining a distinction between the denotation type of interrogatives and that of declaratives, but there are also grounds for maintaining a uniform denotation. We argue: (1) that all uses of an interrogative denote a question, a semantic object ontologically distinct from a proposition, and (2) that only some uses of any given declarative denote a proposition, which we take to be the kind of object that can be true or false.

Interrogatives and declaratives also have a class of uses in which a fact gets 'semantically contributed'. For declaratives, this actually involves the possibility of a distinct fact-denoting denotation, whereas for interrogatives, facts get contributed in embedded contexts only, via coercion. The distinct mechanisms we propose for interrogative- and proposition-related facts will serve to explain why some predicates subcategorize for both interrogative and declarative clauses, as illustrated in (3):[8]

(3) a. Jamie forgot that/whether the Pope likes stuffed cabbage.
    b. Merle knows who insulted the Mayor/whether the Mayor was insulted/that the Mayor's honor was at stake.
    c. Brendan discovered when the tube shuts down/that the tube shuts down before midnight.

Early work on interrogative semantics in the 1960s actually took data such as (3) as motivation for assuming that interrogatives, like declaratives, denote propositions. An influential proposal by Hintikka proposed the following paraphrase:

---

[8]We use the term 'subcategorization' as a cover term for the syntactic requirements placed on its complements by a predicate and the term 'selection' for the corresponding semantic requirements.

(4) a. Ashley **V**s who came ↔ Any person is such that if (s)he came, then Ashley **V**s that (s)he came.

b. Ashley **V**s whether it is raining ↔ If it is raining, then Ashley **V**s that it is raining, and if it is not raining, then Ashley **V**s that it is not raining. (Hintikka 1976)

That there are grounds for actually positing an ontological distinction between questions and propositions was first argued in detail by Hamblin (1973) and by Karttunen (1977). Karttunen's main argument is based on the existence of a class of predicates which embed interrogative but not declarative complements:

(5) a. Brooke asked/wondered/investigated who left.

b. #Brooke asked/wondered/investigated that Drew left.

Moreover, although one might attempt to provide a semantics for some of these predicates by means of lexical decomposition, Karttunen claims that there is no obvious way to lexically decompose predicates such as those in (6) in a similar way:[9]

(6) a. Who wins the race depends upon who enters it.

b. When Mary will arrive will be influenced by who drives the bus.

We believe, with the vast literature that builds on Karttunen's work, that this argument as a whole is compelling. This type of argument—establishing the ontological distinctness of two clause types by exhibiting a class of predicates that are consistently compatible with one but not the other—is one we will appeal to repeatedly in arguing for our own ontology of semantic types. Nonetheless, what Karttunen's argument does not prove is that *all* embedded interrogative uses involve selection for questions. Such a position, which we will refer to as the Interrogative Uniformity Hypothesis, might seem attractive *prima facie* on grounds of parsimony. Parsimony, however, is to some extent in the eye of the beholder and various researchers, starting with Boër (1978), were disturbed by the fact that any approach like Karttunen's, adhering to the Interrogative Uniformity Hypothesis, needs to posit dozens of doublet relations: one doublet for each member of the class of predicates (*know*, *discover*, *tell*, etc.) that subcategorize for both interrogative and declarative clauses. That is, Karttunen posits a relation know^{question} to analyze interrogative-subcategorizing uses of *know* and a relation know^{proposition} for the corresponding declarative-subcategorizing uses. Karttunen proposed that such uses be related via meaning postulate.

However, questions of parsimony aside, we believe that Karttunen's hypothesis about uniform selection for questions can actually be refuted empirically. Our argument involves considering nominal complements in addition to the clausal complements of interrogative-subcategorizing predicates. This wider perspective reveals a fundamental bifurcation among interrogative-subcategorizing predicates. One class consists of factive and resolutive predicates[10] such as *know*, *discover*, *forget*, *tell*, *guess*, *predict*. Distinguished from these is a second class of verbs which we call Question Embedding (QE) predicates, e.g. *ask*, *wonder*, *investigate*, and *discuss*. Our basic

---

[9]However, see Boër 1978 and Hand 1988 for a semantics for predicates like *depend*. These proposals share important assumptions with Hintikka's interrogative semantics.

[10]The class of predicates that behave 'factively' with interrogatives is somewhat wider than the class of factive, declarative-subcategorizing predicates. We dub those predicates, including *tell*, *guess*, *announce*, *predict* and *report*, which exhibit such behavior with interrogatives but not with declaratives 'resolutive' since they carry a presupposition that the embedded question is resolved, as we discuss in more detail in section 3.2.3.

claim is that a member of the QE class simply takes a question as its argument, whereas the resolutives and factives take as their argument a fact that constitutes an answer to the question denoted by the interrogative. The content of the complement clause does not serve as a 'genuine argument' of the predicate. Rather, the complement's content—a question—is coerced into a fact resolving that question.

In order to ground this intuition in concrete data we appeal to a basic semantic notion originally put forward by Quine (1963), who equates a complement's being a 'genuine argument' of a predicate—in his terms, the complement's occurring purely referentially—with the complement passing the tests of substitutivity and existential generalization.[11] Using this criterion, questions can be shown to be genuine arguments of QE predicates. More precisely, QE predicates treat question-denoting nominals as arguments that are purely referential:[12]

(7) a. **Substitutivity**:

Jean asked/investigated/was discussing an interesting question.
The question was who left yesterday.
Hence: Jean asked/investigated/was discussing who left yesterday.

b. **Existential Generalization**:

Jean asked/investigated/was discussing who left yesterday.
Hence, there is a question/issue that Jean asked/investigated/was discussing yesterday. Which question?
The question was who left yesterday.

Resolutive and factive predicates treat question-denoting nominals quite differently. For a start, many such predicates cannot felicitously take question-denoting nominals as complements:[13]

(8) a. #Jan told me/forgot/guessed an interesting question.
b. #Brooke predicted/stated a strange issue.

More crucially, even those factive/resolutive predicates which can take question-denoting nominals as complements treat them in a markedly distinct way from QE predicates—both substitutivity and existential generalization fail:[14]

---

[11] See, for example, Quine 1963: 139–145 for discussion.

[12] The verb *wonder* does not subcategorize for NP arguments, but does subcategorize for PP arguments. With the requisite modifications, it also passes these tests.

[13] In case the question-denoting NP is definite, the felicity of the predication improves:

(i) Jan guessed the question.
(ii) Brooke stated the issue with some precision.

This, we believe, is due to the fact that in such a case the question nominal can be coerced to be a 'concealed question' (See Baker 1970, Grimshaw 1979, Heim 1979, and Pustejovsky 1995)—a coercion which allows such predicates to take definite NP complements whose N' (the property denoted by it) is virtually arbitrary:

(iii) Jan guessed the color of Jo's eyes.
(iv) Brooke stated Mo's weight with some precision.

Concealed questions are discussed more fully in Chapter 8.

[14] In fact, 'V *about*' passes pure referentiality tests in cases where V is a resolutive predicate. However, as noted already by Boër (1978), in such cases 'V *about*' manifests significantly distinct behavior from 'V'. For instance, *Alexis managed to make a guess about who showed up to the party* does not imply that Alexis' guess was correct, in contrast to *Alexis managed to guess who showed up to the party*. See section 8.3 for further discussion of how *about* fits into the picture in connection with *concealed questions*.

(9) a. **Substitutivity**: Jean discovered/revealed an interesting question.

The question was who left yesterday.

It does not follow that: Jean discovered/revealed who left yesterday.

b. **Existential Generalization**:

Jean discovered/knows who left yesterday.

It does not follow that: there is a question/issue that Jean discovered/knows.

These data pose an intrinsic problem for Karttunen's strategy of treating all interrogative-embedding predicates as involving predications of questions. Presumably the simplest way to explain the behavior of QE predicates is to assume that interrogatives have a use in which they denote the same class of objects (questions) that question-denoting nominals do. What a QE predicate selects for is then simply a question, though the precise range of complements such a predicate can co-occur with is apparently subject to syntactic factors as well.[15] If Karttunen's proposal were correct, then we would expect the class of entities that factive/resolutive predicates select for to include, *inter alia*, the class of questions. The fact that question-denoting complements do not sanction substitutivity and existential generalization argues strongly against the hypothesis that resolutives select for questions and, by extension, against the Interrogative Uniformity Hypothesis.[16]

3.2.2 Do Interrogatives Ever Denote Propositions?

Rejecting the Interrogative Uniformity Hypothesis, as we have argued one should, leads to the recognition that on some uses, the content supplied by an interrogative is not a question. What is it in such cases? It has commonly been proposed (see, for example, Hintikka 1976, 1983, Boër 1978, and Groenendijk and Stokhof 1984, 1997) that interrogatives embedded by factives and resolutives actually denote propositions.[17] We believe that there is an important intuition behind this view, namely that a unified semantic type exists for which factive predicates select. This explains why this class of predicates predominantly subcategorizes both for declaratives and for interrogatives. However, as we will demonstrate, basing this explanation on the assumption that

---

[15]The verb *wonder*, for instance, is incompatible with nominal complements, whereas *investigate* is incompatible with PP complements, while *answer* can only cooccur with non-clausal question-denoting complements:

(i) Bo wondered #(about) the question.

(ii) Bo investigated (#about) the question.

(iii) Bo answered #(the question concerning) who inhaled.

[16]This argument might not, in and of itself, refute the Interrogative Uniformity Hypothesis. Our argument also requires some appeal to explanatory simplicity. Thus, an adherent of the Interrogative Uniformity Hypothesis could in principle assume that for each QE predicate there are actually two manifestations: one predicate that selects for a question, and another selecting for a distinct class of entity, assumed to be the denotation of question nominals. The two predicates would be related by means of a meaning postulate, though of course it remains unclear what class of entities would constitute the denotation of question nominals, if the latter is distinct from the denotation of interrogatives. Factive/resolutive predicates, on this story, would then have to involve at least THREE manifestations, one as a predicate of questions, one as a predicate of (the denotation of) certain nominals, and one as a predicate of whatever one takes declaratives to denote, say propositions. Given the failure of pure referentiality, there would be no systematic connection between the predicate of questions and the predicate of nominals, whereas there would be a meaning postulate relating the predicate of questions and the predicate of propositions. The redundancy and arbitrariness inherent in such a system speaks strongly against adopting it.

[17]Groenendijk and Stokhof differ from Hintikka and Boër in accepting the force of Karttunen's argument that on some uses interrogatives do in fact denote an entity that is distinct from a proposition.

interrogatives possess a propositional denotation leads to a highly unsatisfactory theoretical picture. There are two main reasons for this. One reason is that precisely the predicates that can be argued on independent grounds to select for propositions are incompatible with interrogative complements. This class of predicates, which we call TRUE/FALSE (TF) predicates, includes *believe*, *assert*, *deny*, and *prove*. Secondly, there are data parallel to examples (7)–(9) that demonstrate that factive predicates do not treat proposition-denoting complements purely referentially. These two sets of data, to which we now turn, argue strongly against the assumption that interrogatives ever denote propositions.

An initial consideration to support the assumption that TF predicates select for propositions was originally pointed out by Vendler (1972). These predicates impose an appropriateness condition on their nominal arguments, namely the condition that truth or falsity can be predicated of them. This is, of course, the hallmark of a proposition. The examples in (10) show that, in contrast to factive predicates, TF predicates can only co-occur with nominal complements of which truth can be predicated:

(10)   a.   #Jackie believed/doubted/assumed/proved Bo's weight/my phone number.
       b.   Jackie knows/discovered Bo's weight./my phone number.
       c.   #Billie's weight/my phone number is true/false
       d.   Jo believed/doubted/assumed Billie's story/the claim/the hypothesis/the charges/the forecast.
       e.   Billie's story/the claim/the hypothesis/the charges/the forecast is true/false.

Relatedly, free relatives headed by such verbs can have truth/falsity predicated of them:

(11)   What Jo believed/doubted/assumed/proved was true/false.

Indeed such predicates satisfy the following inference pattern relating their nominal complements to an embedded clause:

(12)   a.   Jean believed a certain hypothesis.
            Hence, Jean believed that that hypothesis is true.
       b.   Merle denied a certain claim.
            Hence, Merle denied that that claim is true.
       c.   Bo proved Merle's conjecture.
            Hence, Bo proved that Merle's conjecture is true.

Let us dub this inference schema for future reference **T-Pred**:

(13)   **T-Pred** Inference Schema:

       NP V the $\bar{\text{N}}$.
       Hence, **NP V** that the $\bar{\text{N}}$ is true

Interestingly, factive predicates do not obey **T-Pred**:

(14)   a.   Jean discovered a certain hypothesis.
            It does not follow that Jean discovered that that hypothesis is true.
       b.   Bo forgot Merle's conjecture.
            It does not follow that Bo forgot that Merle's conjecture is true.
       c.   Merle revealed a certain claim.
            It does not follow that Merle revealed that that claim is true.

A second consideration which supports the assumption that TF predicates select for propositions is that they treat proposition-denoting complements purely referentially:

(15) a. **Substitutivity**:

 The Fed's forecast was that gold reserves will be depleted by the year 2000.

 Brendan believes/denies the Fed's forecast.

 Hence, Brendan believes/denies that gold reserves will be depleted by the year 2000.

 b. **Existential Generalization**:

 Brendan believes/denies that gold reserves will be depleted by the year 2000.

 Hence, there is a claim/hypothesis/prediction that Brendan believes.

If interrogatives have a propositional denotation, it is surprising that TF predicates, which without exception select for propositional arguments, cannot co-occur with interrogative complements:[18]

(16) a. #Bo supposes/assumes the question/issue of which pitcher will play tomorrow.

 b. #Bo supposes/assumes which pitcher will do what tomorrow.

 c. #Carrie claimed/argued who came yesterday.

 d. #Carrie denies/doubts who stole Mo's key.

 e. #Tony believes/suggests whether Bo stole Mo's key.

These facts are stable across a wide range of languages, including English, Hebrew, Japanese, Greek, and Turkish. In fact, we will hypothesize below that this generalization, the inability of TF predicates to license interrogative complements, constitutes a linguistic universal. Assuming this to be the case, we believe that the generalization should be captured in terms of a sortal incompatibility between the embedding predicate and the denotation of the interrogative complement. It does not seem amenable to an explanation in terms of syntactic subcategorization or pragmatics. Thus, any attempt to explain the inability of TF predicates to license interrogative complements simply as a consequence of putative syntactic incompatibility between TF predicates and interrogatives will founder due to the fact that the incompatibility is maintained under pronominalization. Example (17a) shows that the proposition expressed by a declarative can be picked up by a pronoun, which is the complement of a TF predicate.

(17) a. A: Jo left yesterday.

  B: Bo believes that.

 b. A: Who left yesterday?

  B: #Bo believes that.

 c. A: Who left yesterday?

  B: Bo knows that.

---

[18]We should note here that the verb *prove* is subject to speaker variation. There are speakers, usually ones with significant exposure to mathematical discourse, who accept locutions such as (i) and (ii):

 (i) Jo proved that fact.

 (ii) Bo proved that fact to be true.

Such speakers also accept sentences such as (iii) and (iv), where *prove* takes an interrogative complement:

 (iii) Jo proved whether Bo committed the crime.

 (iv) Jo proved who did what.

The account we will propose below correlates the ability of a predicate to take interrogative complements with its compatibility either with questions or with facts. Thus, our account will lead to the expectation that speakers who reject (i) and (ii) should equally reject (iii) and (iv).

In contrast, (17b) demonstrates that the denotation of an interrogative cannot serve as an antecedent for a pronoun embedded by a TF predicate, though it is perfectly acceptable when embedded by a factive.[19]

The pragmatic explanation which most readily suggests itself for the incompatability of interrogatives with TF predicates is that it arises out of the conflict between a principle like the following, with some sort of factivity inherent in interrogatives:[20]

> "Do not fill the cognitive argument of a TF predicate with material already present in the common ground."

The main problem for such an explanation is that, although the complements of TF predicates tend to constitute non-presupposed material, this is no more than an easily overriden tendency. This matter is treated in greater detail in Ginzburg 1993, where the following examples are discussed:

(18) a. For a long time there had been allegations that Dana was seeing a certain journalist. It's turned out that the allegations are well founded. Thus, even though we all know they're true, Brett, staunchly loyal, doesn't accept the allegations.

   b. Bo's claim was that Merle was ill. I discovered that, in fact, Merle was ill. After that, everyone accepted the claim.

   c. Bo is usually so wrong-headed, but for once he actually believes something we all accept without batting an eyelash, namely that the sun will rise tomorrow.

   d. Now that she's been shown the evidence, and let me assure you it conclusively establishes his guilt, Jo won't deny that Bo could have committed the crime.

However, even in a context that establishes the veridicality of a certain item of information, the incompatibility of interrogatives with TF predicates remains, in contrast to the declarative case:

(19) a. Fergie knows who left: Birch, Alexis and Gerry.
      So, it is also true to say that #Fergie believes/assumes who left.

   b. Fergie knows that Jo left.
      So, in particular, it is also true to say that Fergie believes/assumes that Jo left.

   c. #Fergie correctly believes/assumes who left.

We note some additional considerations against the assumption that interrogatives possess a propositional denotation. First, that assumption leaves unexplained the fact that interrogatives cannot be used equatively with proposition-denoting nominals:[21]

---

[19] Of course we cannot absolutely rule out the possibility of a syntactic explanation of the inability of TF predicates to license interrogative complements. That is, one can certainly assume that there is some abstract morphosyntactic property common to TF predicates that renders them incompatible with interrogatives. One such account is perhaps the proposal of Huang's (1982) that attitude predicates be distinguished according to whether they subcategorize for a [WH −] or [WH +] complementizer. An ontologically-based account of the kind we suggest is needed does not necessarily conflict with such a morphosyntactically based one, although it arguably renders it superfluous. Indeed, to some extent, which type of account is to be preferred is a question of methodological predeliction, correlating with whether one has more confidence in the independent justification for the ontology or for the morphosyntactic theory employed. One *prima facie* advantage for ontologically-based accounts of such facts is that they have greater applicability across languages with diverse morphosyntactic systems and lexicons.

[20] Such an explanation is offered by Boër (1978).

[21] For that matter, interrogatives cannot be used equatively with fact nominals, either. In Chapter 8, we will take this as motivation for a coercion analysis, which is triggered by the embedding predicate:

(i) #The fact is who left.

(20) a.   The question is who left.

  b.   The claim is that Bill left.

  c.   #The claim is who left.

And of course, interrogatives cannot be used assertorically, as would be expected if they in fact allowed a propositional reading:

(21)   I'm going to make the following claim: #who left this building dirty/#Did someone leave this building dirty.

We now turn to a related issue (which in fact motivated the interrogatives-as-proposition idea in the first place): the independent and deep-seated assumption that factive predicates select for propositional arguments. The only motivation we are aware of for this assumption is simple *declarative uniformity*; the assumption that since some uses of declaratives denote propositions, all uses of declaratives denote propositions. We already saw above that factives do not directly predicate truth of their arguments, as indicated by the data in (14). However, as we shall now show, there is evidence to suggest that factives do not even treat propositions as genuine arguments as they clearly fail at least one test for the pure referentiality of their proposition-denoting complements, namely substitutivity. This is regardless of whether the context indicates that the proposition at issue is true:[22]

(22)   **Substitutivity**:

  The Fed's forecast was that gold reserves will be depleted by the year 2000.
  (The Fed's forecast is true).
  Brendan discovered/was aware of the Fed's forecast.
  It does not follow that: Brendan discovered/was aware that gold reserves will be depleted by the year 2000.

To conclude this section: we considered the standard alternative to the Karttunen-inspired Interrogative Uniformity Hypothesis, namely the position that when embedded by resolutive predicates interrogatives denote propositions. We suggested that this view is highly problematic for three main reasons. First, those predicates that uncontroversially select for propositions, the class of predicates we have dubbed TF predicates, are incompatible with interrogatives. This cross-linguistically highly stable incompatibility does not seem to lend itself to either a syntactic or a pragmatic explanation, and hence calls for an explanation based on sortal incompatibility. Second, interrogatives lack properties that are characteristic of truth-bearing expressions. They cannot be used equatively with proposition-denoting nominals, although they can be so used with question-denoting nominals. Nor can interrogatives be used assertorically. Third, those predicates that motivated positing a propositional denotation for interrogatives, namely factives, actually appear not to select for propositional arguments.

---

[22]The situation with existential generalization is somewhat trickier. Is the inference pattern in (i) a reasonable one? Intuitions are difficult because of the (minimally) awkward nature of predications such as (ii)

  (i)   Kylie forgot that the party would take place before the Millenium. Hence, there is a true
        claim/hypothesis/statement/report that Kylie forgot.
  (ii) ?Kylie forgot a hypothesis/statement/report.

3.2.3 The Missing Semantic Type: Facts

So far, our discussion of the ontological status of interrogatives and declaratives has yielded both positive and negative conclusions. On the positive side, we have seen reason to endorse the existence of a semantic type distinction between some uses of interrogatives and declaratives. We have provided grounds for assuming that there is a class of predicates that select for questions and a class disjoint from this whose members select for propositions. On the other hand, we have provided arguments for rejecting two commonly assumed positions, the Karttunen-inspired Interrogative Uniformity Hypothesis and the position, stemming from the work of Hintikka and Groenendijk and Stokhof, that interrogatives possess a propositional denotation. Rejecting the latter position while endorsing an insight that underlies it, namely that factives select for the same type of semantic object when they embed either interrogatives or declaratives, immediately raises two related questions:

1. What do interrogatives denote when embedded by factives?, and
2. More generally, what semantic type do such predicates select for?[23]

Our task in this section is to offer an answer to these questions that will lead us to a general discussion of the ontological space that we need to posit.

The approach we take is generally in line with what is by now a significant body of work, pioneered by Vendler (1968, 1972), both in the formal semantics and philosophical literature (e.g. Asher 1993, 1996 and Peterson 1997) and in computational lexical semantics (e.g. Pustejovsky 1995). This work, the 'Vendlerian Turn', has demonstrated the need for an ontology of 'abstract entities' intrinsically richer than that extant in Montague's intensional logic, which as we mentioned in Chapter 1 is an intensionalized version of the austere ontology of Wittgenstein's *Tractatus*.

Work in the Vendlerian Turn articulates a distinction between a class of entities called *events* (sometimes called *eventualities*), a more general term meant to accommodate states as well, and the classes of *facts/possibilities* and *propositions*. These distinctions cut across syntactic categories. For example, there are NPs that can have denotations in all three classes and POSS-*ing* gerunds can also fluctuate between an eventive and a factive denotation.

We now examine some of the key properties of the various classes. First, the eventualities are taken to be 'semi-concrete' objects which are spatio-temporally located and can be modified by concrete adjectives:

(23) a. The wedding lasted a long time/was lavish/took place in Sheikh Jarah.
b. Tony's savaging of the party has lasted for years/is bloody/is not limited to London.

In contrast, facts/possibilities and propositions are not spatio-temporally located and resist modification by concrete adjectives:

(24) a. #The fact that Tony savaged the party has lasted for years/is bloody/is not limited to London.
b. #Tony's savaging the party has lasted for years/is bloody/is not limited to London.
c. #That Tony savaged the party lasted a long time/was lavish/took place in Sheikh Jarah.
d. The hypothesis was that Glyn is dangerous. #That hypothesis has lasted for years/is bloody/is not limited to London.

---

[23]The same issues of course arise for non-factive, resolutive predicates such as *tell*, *guess*, and *predict*, though there the answers that arise are subtly different. We suggest in section 3.6.3 that resolutives select for various kinds of entity, including propositions, facts, and (in some cases) events.

Among the abstract entities, a crucial distinction is drawn between facts/possibilities and propositions. The former have causal powers which the latter lack entirely:

(25) a. The fact that Tony was ruthless made the fight against her difficult.

  b. Tony's being ruthless frightened Glyn.

  c. The possibility that Glyn might get elected made Tony's hair turn white.

  d. #The claim/hypothesis/proposition that Tony was ruthless made the fight against her difficult.

Truth is predicable only of propositional entities, not of facts/possibilities:

(26) a. #The fact that Tony was ruthless is true.

  b. #Tony's being ruthless is true.

  c. #The possibility that Glyn might get elected is true.

  d. The claim/hypothesis/proposition that Tony was ruthless is true/false.

In what follows, a three-way distinction is drawn between events, facts/possibilities, and propositions. In particular, we distinguish between a class of entities that contains all possibilities (factual/realized and otherwise) and the class of propositional entities. Although they will play an important role in our ontology, as *situations*, we will not discuss eventive denotations in detail. In a more comprehensive treatment, one might plausibly treat this class of entities as the denotation type of certain types of phrase, such as POSS-ing gerund and naked infinitive phrases.

Using the proposition/fact distinction, let us return to consider the semantic nature of the complements of factive predicates. We have seen that such predicates embed neither question-denoting complements nor proposition-denoting complements purely referentially. This does not mean that such predicates are 'hyperintensional', but only that we have so far failed to provide them the type of complement that they actually select for. When one supplies the appropriate kind of complement, i.e. one that denotes a fact, we can once again see the effects of pure referentiality, as illustrated in (27):

(27) a. Jean is aware of/reported/revealed an alarming fact.

      That fact is that Brendan has been working hard to destroy the company.

      Hence, Jean is aware/reported/revealed that Brendan has been working hard to destroy the company.

  b. Jean knows two facts about Marin Marais.

      One is that he was a student of Saint Colombe, the other is that he composed music for the viola da gamba.

      Hence, Jean knows that Marin Marais was a student of Saint Colombe and Jean knows that he composed music for the Viola da gamba.

  c. Jean regrets/remembers well a troubling fact about the McCarthian era.

      That fact is that everyone was required to sign the pledge.

      Hence, Jean regrets/remembers well that everyone was required to sign the pledge.

(28) a. Philippe knows/discovered that Marin Marais composed music for the Viola da gamba.
Hence, there is a fact that Philippe knows/discovered.
Which fact?
The fact that (indicating/proving that) Marin Marais composed music for the Viola da gamba.

b. Philippe knows/discovered whether Emanuelle was in town.
Hence, Philippe knows/discovered a fact that indicates/proves whether Emanuelle was in town.

c. Philippe knows/discovered who attended the WTO meeting.
Hence, Philippe knows/discovered a fact, one that resolves the issue of who attended the WTO meeting.

d. Dominique revealed to me when the train is leaving.
Hence, Dominique revealed a fact to me, one that resolves the issue of when the train is leaving.

The data in (28) reflect a common intuition. When factive predicates embed an interrogative, they are predicating something of a fact that constitutes an answer to the question expressed by the interrogative (i.e. an answer that *resolves* that question). Declaratives work similarly. When such predicates embed a declarative, there seems to be a predication of a fact that proves the associated proposition true. We might schematize these inference patterns as follows:

(29) a. Brendan **V**s/has **V**ed (knows/discovered/told me/reported/managed to guess) that p.
So, Brendan **V**s/has **V**ed a fact that proves the proposition p.

b. Brendan **V**s/has **V**ed q.
So, Brendan **V**s/has **V**ed a fact that resolves the question q.

The most direct way to account for these inference patterns is to assume that factives select for fact-denoting arguments. How are we to reconcile this with our previous assumption that interrogatives denote questions and declaratives denote propositions? In principle, two strategies are open to us: one is to assume that a given clause-type can denote more than one semantic type; the other is to assume that no such ambiguity exists and that a factive predicate can coerce clauses so that their denotation becomes fact-denoting.[24] We believe that the two strategies each have a role to play: the coercion strategy for interrogatives, the ambiguity strategy for declaratives. This conclusion goes against the proposals of Groenendijk and Stokhof, who advocate the ambiguity strategy for interrogatives. Within their system the intensions of interrogatives denote questions and the extensions denote propositions.

There are three noticeable differences between declaratives and interrogatives which lead to this conclusion. First, declaratives but not interrogatives can be used equatively with fact-denoting nominals:

(30) a.   The fact is that Tony vanquished the anti-Leninist faction.

b. #The fact is whether Tony vanquished the anti-Leninist faction.

c. #The fact is who vanquished the anti-Leninist faction.

Second, whereas interrogatives can be used as complements of nouns such as *question* and *issue*, they cannot be complements of the noun *fact*, which can of course take a declarative complement:

---

[24]See Pustejovsky 1995 for a relevant notion of 'coercion'.

(31) a.   The question of who hacked into turing.stanford.edu.

     b.   #The question that Bo hacked into turing.stanford.edu.

     c.   The fact that Bo hacked into turing.stanford.edu.

And third, declaratives, but not interrogatives, can participate in anaphora with fact-denoting nominals:

(32) a. A: I'd like to point out a crucial fact to you.

       B: Go on.

       A: The Pope is waiting for you in my office.

     b. A: I'd like to point out a crucial fact to you.

       B: Go on.

       A: #Who is waiting for you in my office.

These data pinpoint that there is a need for a 'stand alone' fact-denotation for declaratives, but not for interrogatives, which in contrast seem to require a fact-denotation only in embedded contexts. We have already seen in Chapter 2 that the denotation type of simple a declarative clause is the semantic supertype *austinian*, which subsumes both *proposition*, and *outcome*.[25,26] There are additional considerations that argue against attempting to explicate the fact-contributing potential of interrogatives in terms of a constructional ambiguity. For example, any such analysis would produce fact-denoting interrogative clauses that would be selectable by any fact-selecting predicate.

The first consideration arguing against a fact-denoting analysis of interrogatives is that there exists a class of predicates, including *intrigue*, *mystify*, and *puzzle*, that are compatible with both questions and facts. These predicates satisfy pure referentiality arguments with interrogatives, though not with declaratives:

(33) a.   The question is who entered the building last night.

         That question intrigues me.

         Hence, it intrigues me who entered the building last night.

     b.   The claim is that Jerry entered the building last night.

         That claim intrigues me.

       #Hence, it intrigues me that Jerry entered the building last night.

     c.   That Jerry entered the building last night intrigues me.

         Hence, there is a fact that intrigues me, namely the fact that Jerry entered the building last night.

Second, the class of emotive predicates selects for facts. But for many speakers, emotive predicates are incompatible with interrogatives (Lahiri 1991, Peterson 1997):[27]

---

[25]Recall, however, that a finite declarative clause will invariably be either proposition-denoting or outcome-denoting, depending on whether the verb is indicative or subjunctive. We posited a phrasal type *factive-cl*, which builds a fact-denoting clause from a proposition-denoting phrase.

[26]The system developed by Asher (1993) also builds in an ambiguity for declaratives. In Asher's system, a declarative potentially denotes any of the various abstract entities he motivates, including propositions and facts.

[27]There is little controversy that emotives resist polar interrogatives. There are, however, speakers who accept examples such as the following:

     (i) Jo really regretted which student was picked for the job.

     (ii) Bo resented/was surprised who ate what at the cheese fair.

(34) a. #Jo resents/regrets when Billie left the party.

    b. #Mo regrets/resents whether Dominique joined the reformist wing.

By limiting the coercion mechanism to a selected class of predicates, we can accommodate such data. The coercion mechanism allowing interrogative clauses to provide fact-denoting arguments is discussed in Chapter 8.

We conclude this section by providing additional motivation for incorporating facts into our ontology for messages. The most commonly studied speech act is assertion, an act which is typically analyzed as having a proposition as its descriptive content. An informal, partial characterization of assertion might run as follows:

(35) **Assertion**

    a. Point: Convince the audience that p is true.

    b. Sincerity condition: The speaker believes that p.

    c. Preparatory condition: It has not been accepted in the context that either (a) $\neg p$ is true or (b) p is true.

By the same token, there exist types of speech act that seem best analyzed as having a fact as their descriptive content. We mention two here: *reminding* and *exclaiming*. Consider first reminding:

(36) **Reminding**

    a. Point: Speaker brings a fact f presumed to be in the conversational common ground to the addressee's attention.

    b. Preparatory condition: f is in the common ground.

    c. Sincerity condition: Speaker believes f is in the common ground.

The evidence for treating the descriptive content of a reminding as a fact is primarily based on the assumption that such acts involve the factive predicate *remind*:

(37) a. Fergie: Why don't the vendors here speak Straits Salish?

       Bo: We're in New York City, for pete's sake.

    b. Bo reminded Fergie (of the fact) that they were in New York City.

Exclaiming differs from reminding in that the speaker expresses astonishment (or at the very least surprise) about a certain fact f_0. At the same time, there is the potential for disagreement between speaker and addressee about the factuality of f_0. Since f_0 is striking, at least for the speaker, it is apt to be non-mundane, relatively improbable, and frequently will concern matters whose objective verification is difficult:

(38) a. That's such an amazing play!

    b. Look at that. Bo really gets the most out of the musicians!

    c. Oh boy, that's such an inefficient way to run a university!

There can be disagreement about what the background facts are and this is why remindings and exclamations can be challenged:

(39) a. A: That's such an amazing play!

       B: [yawns] Rather mundane for my taste.

    b. A: Why do they look at us with hostility?

       B: Remember: we're American nationals.

       A: Oh, but I gave up my citizenship a while back.

This points to the need to ensure that 'facthood' is somehow defeasible. Indeed, this will be captured in our semantic ontology in virtue of the assumption that facts belong to a wider class of entities, the possibilities. The question of which such entities manifest the property of being realized/factual is typically contingent. This sort of assumption is needed independently, in order to explain presupposition projection and anaphora. In (40a) what is predicated of Kimmo is potential regret of a possibility, which at utterance time is unknown to be factual, whereas we take the anaphora in (40b) to refer to a possibility whose factuality is controversial:

(40) a. If Sandip leaves, Kimmo will regret that fact bitterly.
      b. A: I regret the fact that Kim left.
          B: It's not a fact. She's hiding in my cupboard.

Given our assumption that an indicative declarative clause can denote a fact (as an option to denoting a proposition), it is straightforward to explain reminding and exclamative uses of declaratives. However, declaratives are not the only means for expressing exclamative speech acts. There exists a clause-type often called an 'exclamative' clause, analyzed in Chapter 6, whose matrix uses involve exclamations:

(41) a. What an amazing play Frayn has written!
      b. How inefficiently they run this place!

Not surprisingly, in light of our discussion above concerning exclamations and their descriptive content, we assume that exclamatives denote facts. This assumption receives independent support from a variety of phenomena. First, exclamatives can be used equatively with fact-denoting nominals, but not with question or proposition-denoting nominals:

(42) a. The amazing fact I noticed during my visit was how modest all Ruritanians are.
      b. A striking fact I became aware of is what a reputation Bo has carved out for herself among computational ethologists.
      c. #An interesting claim Mo has put forward is what a reputation Bo has carved for herself among computational ethologists.
      d. #An intriguing question I've been investigating is what a reputation Bo has carved for herself among computational ethologists.

Second, the inferential behavior of exclamatives seems to resemble that of interrogatives and declaratives embedded by factives/resolutives:[28]

(43) a. Merle is struck by how incredibly well Bo did in the elections.
      b. Hence, Merle is struck by a fact, a fact that demonstrates that Bo did very well in the elections.

(44) a. Bo told us a fact. This fact shows that Micky did very badly on the exam.
      b. Hence, Bo told us just how badly Micky did on the exam.

Third, exclamatives cannot be used assertorically, to provide new information:

---

[28] As discussed in Chapter 6, *wh*-clauses such as (43a) and (44b) have two analyses, one as an exclamative and one as an interrogative.

(45) a. A: #I'd like to make the following claim: what a big building that is.
   b. A: I've got some news for you about Lee's injury.
      B: uh huh.
      A: Lee is badly injured./Lee is injured to a fairly significant extent./
           #How badly Lee is injured!

Fourth, neither QE predicates nor TF predicates are compatible with such clauses;

(46) a.   #Jo wondered/asked what a runner Dana is.
   b.   #Jo wondered/asked how very well Merle did in the elections.
   c.   #Jo believes/claims what an artist Dana is.
   d.   #Jo believes/claims how very well Merle did in the elections.

Fifth, both resolutive, factive and indeed emotive predicates are compatible with exclamatives:

(47) a.   Jo finally discovered what a runner Dana is.
   b.   Merle knows how incredibly well Merle did in the elections.
   c.   Brendan forgot what an artist Dana is.
   d.   Lou told us how very badly Micky did on the exam.
   e.   Kim actually managed to predict what a mess the Prime Minister would cause.
   f.   Taylor regrets what a horrible mess he created in the Senate.
   g.   Gerry resents just how much better Dana gets paid than she does.

The fact that exclamative utterances can be challenged, as in (48), is closely related to the data discussed above concerning the defeasibility of facts:

(48) Watson: What a queer, scrambling way of expressing his meaning!
      Holmes: On the contrary, he has done remarkably well.
           (*The Valley of Fear*, A. Conan Doyle.)

   This section has suggested the need to introduce facts into the semantic ontology. Following a significant body of work inspired by Vendler, such entities are taken to be distinct both from events and from propositions. We have suggested that facts are among the entities selected by factive predicates and that certain speech act types have facts as their descriptive content. We argued that two distinct types of clause—declaratives and exclamatives—may take a fact as their denotation. Interrogatives, by contrast, do not actually denote facts but can be associated with appropriately resolving facts when they are embedded as complements of factive and resolutive predicates.

3.2.4 Outcomes

We move now to discuss briefly two more clause types relevant to the syntax and semantics of interrogatives: infinitivals, which allow interrogatives, and subjunctives, which do not:

(49) a.   I wonder who to invite to the party.
   b.   I wasn't sure whether to leave the anarchist faction.
   c.   *Billie wonders whether Mo leave the anarchist faction.
   d.   *Billie wonders who be invited to the party.

We posit a class of abstract entities called *outcomes* as the denotata of subjunctives and certain uses of infinitives.[29],[30] Intuitively, an outcome is a specification of a situation which is futurate relative to some other given situation:

(50) a. Bo demanded that Mo be released.

  b. Kjell demanded to leave the party.

  c. The regulations require that Luca resign next week.

  d. The citizens of Worms prayed that Solomon's book be found.

  e. Glen ordered that we be brought to see her.

  f. Glen ordered Billie to be brought to see her.

The argumentation for the existence of outcomes as distinct entities in the ontology is entirely parallel to the one we used above to motivate the existence of questions. There exists a semantically coherent class of predicates (mandatives), including *demand*, *require*, *prefer*, and *instruct*, which are incompatible with indicative declaratives but which allow subjunctive declaratives:

(51) a. #Bo demanded that Mo is released.

  b. #Kjell demanded that Billie left the party.

  c. #The citizens of Worms prayed that Solomon's book was found.

  d. #The regulations require that Luca resigns next week.

  e. #Glen ordered that Billie was brought to see her.

These predicates exhibit purely referential behavior with outcome-denoting nominals:[31]

(52) a. One possible outcome is for Jo to get the position.
        I prefer/want that outcome.
        Hence, I want Jo to get the position.

  b. One conceivable outcome was that Bo be given the position.
        Lynn actually demanded that outcome.
        Hence, Lynn demanded that Bo be given the position.

  c. There are two possible outcomes, that Mo be expelled from the party or that he be put on trial by the central committee.
        I prefer the former outcome.
        Hence, I prefer that Mo be expelled from the party.

---

[29] For an account of subjunctives and infinitives which has partly inspired our own see Portner 1997.

[30] Recall that we argued in Chapter 2 that infinitivals also manifest a reading as a SOA, which can subsequently be used to build the propositional argument of a raising verb.

[31] The verb *want* subcategorizes for infinitives but not for subjunctives. We assume that this is a syntactic idiosyncrasy, describable by restricting *want*'s subcategorization to nonfinite clauses. Verbs close in meaning to *want* (such as *wish*, *desire*, and *prefer*) are compatible with subjunctives, as well as infinitives:

 (i) I desire/wish/prefer that Taylor leave immediately.

Moreover, in many other languages, verbs similar in meaning to *want* do select for finite clauses corresponding to English subjunctives, for example the Modern Hebrew verb *raca*, which selects for (morphologically) future tense finite clauses:

 (ii) raciti   še tistaleq   mipo   od   etmol
      wanted-1-sg that leave-fut-2-sg from-here already yesterday
      I wanted you to leave yesterday.

(53) a. Lynn demanded that Bo be given the position.

Hence, there is an outcome that Lynn demanded, the one in which Bo gets the position.

    b. Jo wants to be promoted.

Hence, there is an outcome Jo wants, one in which she gets promoted.

How do imperatives fit into the picture? We believe that the descriptive content of a directive speech act is also an outcome. This provides a description of an eventuality typically involving the addressee, which is futurate to the utterance situation, and which the speaker would like to see realized.[32] We offer two arguments for this view of imperatives. The first is that imperative uses can often be paraphrased using the mandative predicate *order*, which can be shown to select for an outcome:

(54) a. Chris: Go home Leslie!

Chris ordered Leslie to go home.

    b. Chris ordered that Leslie go home.

    c. Bo: Don't touch the ball with your hands, Dana; you'll be sent off.

    d. Bo implored Dana not to touch the ball with his hands.

    e. Bo suggested to Dana that he not touch the ball with his hands.

Moreover, from a semantic perspective, this view of imperatives provides a straightforward analysis of negative and stative imperatives such as (55) below, which a view of imperatives in terms of actions (common in speech act based treatments; see e.g. Allen and Perrault 1980) are unable to give:

(55) Don't worry; be happy!

We return to explain how facts such as those in (49) can be accounted for once we offer a semantic explication of what questions and outcomes amount to in the following sections.

3.2.5 Interim Summary and Implications

Let us summarize the main conclusions of this section:

1. Interrogatives and declaratives need to be distinguished denotationally: interrogatives unambiguously denote questions, whereas indicative declaratives denote either propositions or facts.

---

[32]Indeed in some languages, e.g. Modern Hebrew, there is no imperative/subjunctive distinction, their function is subsumed by indicative future tense:

  (i) tistaleq   mipo
      Get out-2nd-fut from-here
      Go away!

  (ii) ani tove'a   še tistaleq   mipo
       I   demand-1st-sg that Get-out-2nd-fut from-here
       I demand that you leave.

Note though that this 'future tense' form, as with *roce*('want') in footnote 31 above, can be used for past tense mandative predicates:

  (iii) jihad tava   še nistaleq   mipo
       Jihad demanded-3rd-pst that get-out-1st-pl-fut from-here
       Jihad demanded that we leave.

Modern Hebrew possesses an additional, morphologically distinct set of imperative forms. But, with some exceptions, these are perceived as archaic and are falling out of use.

2. Factive predicates select for facts: this type of entity can be provided directly by fact-denoting expressions such as NPs, indicative declarative clauses and exclamative clauses, or else via coercion of an interrogative clause.

3. Non-finite declaratives, as well as imperatives and certain uses of infinitives, denote outcomes.

3.3 Building an Ontology of Semantic Types: Basic Tools

In section 3.2 we provided linguistic motivation for an ontology that distinguishes questions, propositions, facts, situations/events and outcomes. Our task in this section is to show how to construct a semantic universe in which distinctions between abstract entities such as these can be captured.

3.3.1 Basic Strategy

The strategy we adopt, in common with past work in Situation Theory (ST)[33] and in Property Theory,[34] is to characterize semantic objects such as properties and propositions, and in our case, also questions, facts, and outcomes in a way that treats their identity conditions very much on a par with 'ordinary' individuals. Such entities are taken as basic, but they are *structured objects*. That is, they arrive on the scene with certain constraints that 'define them' in terms of other entities of the ontology. In this way, various foundational problems that beset classical theories of properties, propositions and (in particular given current concerns) questions can be circumvented. For propositions, these problems typically center around doxastic puzzles such as logical omniscience and its variants such as Soames' puzzle (Soames 1985).[35]

A key innovation of ST, the distinction between SOAs and propositions, provides a solution to the 'Paradox of the Liar'.[36] This distinction, combined with an innovative theory of abstraction, also enables us to develop a theory of questions which reconstructs an old intuition: that questions are akin to open propositions. Our view of questions will be compared to the most influential formal semantic characterization, one based on entities that encode Exhaustive Answerhood Conditions (EAC). We will show that our approach affords a solution to a number of fundamental problems besetting EAC approaches, including problematic characterizations of answerhood and the misplaced identification of positive and negative polar questions.

We adopt the approach to modeling situation theoretic universes developed in Seligman and

---

[33]See, for example, Barwise and Etchemendy 1987, Barwise and Cooper 1991, Cooper and Poesio 1994, and Seligman and Moss 1997.

[34]See, e.g. Bealer 1982, Chierchia and Turner 1988, and Chierchia 1994.

[35]See footnote 76 for discussion of this puzzle.

[36]In this book, soas are discussed in two distinct settings, at the level of typed feature structures and at the level of the semantic universe we build up. Of course the former is used to model aspects of the latter, so we try to maintain terminological consistency across the two levels. In order to prevent confusion, however, we introduce the following notational convention:

  (i) SOA names a feature.

  (ii) *soa* names a type, which the feature SOA takes as value.

  (iii) **Soa** names a (3-place) structural relation of SITSTRs.

  (iv) SOA names those (real world) entities structurally built up by means of the structural relation **Soa**.

A final terminological remark. The term SOA originated as an acronym for *state-of-affairs*. However, despite the etymology, SOAs are intended to be neutral with respect to the stative/eventive distinction.

Moss 1997 (S&M–97), which we recommend to our formally inclined readers.[37] We proceed somewhat informally here, employing simplified definitions when appropriate. A semantic universe is identified with a relational structure S of the form $[A, S_1, \ldots, S_m; R_1, \ldots, R_m]$. Here A—sometimes notated also as $|S|$—is the universe of the structure. From the class of relations we single out the $S_1, \ldots, S_m$ which are called the *structural relations*, intended as they are to capture the structure of certain elements in the domain. Specifically, for our purposes, we use structural relations first to 'build' SOAs up from relations and assignments of entities to the argument roles of the relations. Subsequently, SOAs and situations serve as the 'basic building blocks' from which the requisite abstract entities of our ontology are constructed. Each S_i can be thought of as providing a condition that defines a single structured object in terms of a list of n objects $x_1, \ldots, x_n$. For instance, a SOA σ is built up from a relation R and an assignment f (of entities to the argument roles of the relation). The structural relation **Soa**, consequently, ensures that σ is a structured object whose components are R and f.

We proceed incrementally, first explaining what a Situation Structure (SITSTR) is. We then introduce notions of abstraction and application; a structure closed under such operations will be called a λ(lambda)-structure. We then define our semantic universe, building from a λ–SITSTR a Situational Universe with Abstract Entities (SU+AE), which contains facts, propositions, and outcomes. Since the SU+AE is a λ-structure, it will automatically also contain questions, given our identification of these with proposition abstracts.

A word about the consistency of our semantic theory. S&M–97 show how to build a SITSTR. This same technique can be used to expand a SITSTR to an SU+AE. They also prove that any extensional structure can be expanded to a λ-structure.[38] Thus, at all steps the consistency of our theory is as safe as the consistency of set theory.[39] In particular, the step we make in expanding the universe to include questions involves no danger, as far as consistency goes. Some additional discussion of these issues is provided in Appendix B.

3.3.2 Situation Structures

The most basic relational structure which underpins our modeling, following Seligman and Moss, is a SITSTR. Intuitively, a SITSTR is simply a universe which contains among its entities a class of temporally located entities called situations and a class of entities called SOAs. The SOAs, as we have noted, are structured objects, constructed from a relation R and an assignment α, that assign a set of entities from the universe to a set of argument roles that they are appropriate for. Indeed, the assignment itself is taken to be a structured object characterized in terms of the ordered

---

[37] For an earlier approach, which attempts to linguistically motivate an ST universe, see Cooper and Poesio 1994.

[38] The universe is said to be EXTENSIONAL if structured objects are defined uniquely: for any structural relation S_i and list of n objects $x_1, \ldots, x_n$ there is at most one object y such that $S_i(x_1, \ldots, x_n, y)$. As S&M–97 note 'The extensionality condition is a form of Leibniz's Law: objects that are indistinguishable on the basis of their structural relationships are identical'. (S&M–97, p. 260)

[39] The set theory in question is ZFC⁻ + AFA: ZFC⁻ is Zermelo Fraenkel set theory with the axiom of choice but without the axiom of foundation. AFA is the anti-foundation axiom proposed by Aczel (1988). AFA is an alternative to the axiom of foundation. The axiom of foundation stipulates that set theoretic membership cannot involve cycles—for instance, cases like $a \in a$ or $a \in b \in a$ are excluded. AFA, by contrast, allows such cycles to occur and consequently enables circularity to be modeled. This makes it a highly useful tool for modeling circular phenomena, such as those that occur in NL semantics, in computational processes, in legal reasoning and so forth. Aczel has shown that ZFC⁻ + AFA is consistent iff ZFC⁻ is. For a highly readable introduction to non-well-founded set theory and its applications see Barwise and Moss 1996.

pairs that make its graph: for a role i and entity a, **Sel(ectionally)Ad(equate)Val(ue)**(i, a, α) will mean that a satisfies the selectional restrictions of role i and that they are elements of the assignment α's graph; α will of course be required to be functional. One crucial departure from the familiar Montagovian set-up is that relations, in contrast to assignments, are here taken as unstructured atomic individuals, rather than as intensionalized sets of tuples of individuals.[40]

Situations are partial, temporally located, actual entities, whose role is to explicate such objects as states or events.[41] SOAs perform the function of designating *properties* that situations might possess, as illustrated by the two SOAs depicted in (56):[42]

(56) a. ⟨⟨See; see-er:jo, seen:bo⟩⟩

      b. ⟨⟨Hot; location:holborn station, time:3:45 gmt⟩⟩

It is worth emphasizing that these are solely depictions of SOAs. Far from being sentences in a formal language, they are non-linguistic abstractions individuated in terms of real-world objects. To take a rather familiar example, the Roman philosopher Cicero is occasionally referred to by the anglicized form of his middle name, Tully. Example (57a,b) shows two depictions of a single SOA that could be used to predicate of a situation that it includes Cicero sleeping.

(57) a. ⟨⟨Sleep; sleep-er:cicero⟩⟩

      b. ⟨⟨Sleep; sleeper:tully⟩⟩

This is because the constituent of the SOA is the individual Marcus Tullius Cicero, regardless of how we manage to refer to him.[43,44] One final condition on α as the assignment of a SOA is that the assignment itself be appropriate: we place no constraints on what components make up an assignment. Examples of possible assignments are given in (58):

(58) a. runner:tully,time:3:45 gmt

      b. seer:tully,seen:seneca

      c. runner:tully,seen:seneca

      d. seer:tully,eaten:salome

Of these only (58a,b) are appropriate in the sense that they involves a coherent set of roles.

We should mention an additional important function which SOAs fulfill, already alluded to in Chapter 2, footnote 14, namely that they serve as 'semantic common denominators' among distinct semantic abstract entities. A long standing and often repeated assumption of Speech Act

---

[40] An additional mechanism for building up relations, namely abstraction, is discussed below. Unlike abstracts in Montague Semantics, which are construed as sets, our abstracts are structured objects.

[41] Their most important innovative semantic use has been to serve as denotations of naked infinitive clauses (see, for example, Barwise and Perry 1983 and Cooper 1998), and to explicate domain restriction in quantification (Cooper 1996). We return to the matter of domain restriction in Chapter 4.

[42] A somewhat more precise, albeit more pedantic, notation for the SOAs in (56) would be:

(i) ⟨⟨See; { see-er:jo, seen:bo }⟩⟩

(ii) ⟨⟨Hot; { location:holborn station, time:3:45 gmt }⟩⟩

This is more precise because it emphasizes that a SOA consists of two components (the relation and the assignment) and that the latter is itself a structured object.

[43] We emphasize this familiar point here because it plays a considerable role in the way we model propositions and facts. Note that the approach developed here differs from many others that might appear similar in certain respects, notably Discourse Representation Theory (Kamp and Reyle 1993). See section 3.4.3 below.

[44] However, see section 3.6 for a discussion of how naming information associated with uses of proper names gets packaged in HPSG.

Theory (see e.g. Searle 1969, Searle and Vanderveken 1985), which in fact originates with Frege (1918), is the assumption that assertions, polar queries, and commands differ on the level of illocutionary force, but share the same descriptive/propositional content. Applied, for instance to (59), the claim amounts to saying that (uttered in the same context), the declarative, the interrogative, and the imperative have the same content, namely some proposition p. The difference between these potential utterances, on this view, is that (59a) will be used to assert p, whereas (59b) will be used to ask p, and (59c) to command p:

(59) a. Bo will go away.
   b. Will Bo go away?
   c. Go away Bo!

   This view, the Frege-Searle Propositional Content Hypothesis, is untenable, as it stands; we already provided evidence in section 3.2.4 that showed that the denotata of indicative and subjunctive declaratives/imperatives should be distinguished. We now show the weaknesses of identifying the denotation of a polar interrogative with that of the corresponding declarative.[45] An obvious problem with such an identification is this: if the difference between a declarative and a polar interrogative is merely one of illocutionary force, then an utterance of the latter should be paraphrasable using a proposition-denoting *that*-clause. As (60) shows, this is not the case; such a paraphrase requires a *whether*-clause:

(60) a. A: Did Bo leave?
   b. A asked whether/#that Bo left.

That this difference between *that* and *whether* is semantically significant is illustrated by the fact that (61a) differs from (61b) in allowing for the possibility that Jo didn't leave:

(61) a. Bo knows whether Jo left.
   b. Bo knows that Jo left.

Another problem with the Frege-Searle Propositional Content Hypothesis is this: if a polar question denotes a proposition it should be assertible and bear a truth value, neither of which is the case:

(62) a. I wish to make the following claim: #Did Bo leave?
   b. #It is true/false whether Bo left.

   The thesis about denotational identity across declaratives, interrogatives, and imperatives is, then, fallacious. This does not mean, however, that the intuition which underlies it, the existence of a 'common semantic denominator' cannot be salvaged. Indeed, on our account, one will be able to characterize this common denominator in terms of a SOA, which is a component of the respective proposition, polar question, and outcome posited to capture the distinct denotations. As already mentioned in Chapter 2, footnote 14, the existence of such a common denominator is of considerable importance, in that it provides a uniform account of the role of quantification and of adverbial modification in declarative, interrogative, and imperative clauses.

---

[45]Indeed in Chapter 7, we even argue against identifying the denotations of declaratives and of 'intonation' questions such as (i):

   (i) Bo is leaving?

Moving on to relate SOAs and situations: the notation in (63) indicates that a situation s is correctly classified by a SOA σ:

(63) $s \models \sigma$

This is sometimes referred to as the situation *supporting* the SOA or making the SOA *factual*. If a situation fails to be correctly classified by a SOA σ, we notate this as follows:

(64) $s \not\models \sigma$

Negation plays an important role in explicating what questions are. Thus it is important to understand how the effects of negation fit within our framework. We assume that SOAs come in pairs—positive and negated—as regulated by the *NegOf* relation introduced below. In developing our grammatical framework we will depart from most of the existing work in Situation Semantics which marks polarity overtly (via 1/+ and 0/− or else a feature POLARITY taking such elements as its value). Rather, we will take positive SOAs as literally unmarked and build negative SOAs by means of an adverbial-like operator that takes the positive SOA as its argument. We notate the SOA dual to σ as $\overline{\sigma}$. Our assumptions (see below) about symmetry, functionality, and duals' sharing of defining relation and assignment will yield the familiar cancellation of double dualization:

(65) $\overline{\overline{\sigma}} = \sigma$

We will assume that all situations are consistent in the following sense:

(66)   If $s \models \sigma$, then $s \not\models \overline{\sigma}$

Because situations are partial, there is a difference between a situation failing to be correctly classified by σ and being correctly classified by $\overline{\sigma}$. For any situation s and SOA σ, (67a) holds, but (67b) does not generally hold:

(67)   a. Either $s \models \sigma$ or $s \not\models \sigma$
        b. Either $s \models \sigma$ or $s \models \overline{\sigma}$

The intuition is that classifying s with $\overline{\sigma}$ means that that s actually possesses information which rules out σ, rather than simply lacking concrete evidence for σ. To take a simple example, a situation in which some individual *kiko* is running will typically support both the SOA (68a) and also (68b); however, it will support neither (68c) nor (68d):

(68)   a. $\langle\langle \text{Run; runner:kiko} \rangle\rangle$

        b. $\langle\langle \text{Alive; agent:kiko} \rangle\rangle$

        c. $\langle\langle \text{Sleep; sleeper:cicero} \rangle\rangle$

        d. $\overline{\langle\langle \text{Sleep; sleeper:cicero} \rangle\rangle}$

Cooper (1998), motivated in part by data from naked infinitive clauses, has proposed a pair of axioms that attempt to capture this intuition. (69a) states that if a situation s supports the dual of σ, then s also supports positive information that precludes σ being the case:

(69)   a. $\forall s, \sigma[s \models \overline{\sigma} \text{ implies } \exists(Pos)\psi[s \models \psi \text{ and } \psi \Rightarrow^{\neg} \sigma]]$
        b. $\forall s, \sigma[s \models \overline{\sigma} \text{ implies } \exists(Pos)\psi[s \models \psi \text{ and } \psi > \sigma]]$

(69b) tells us that if a situation s supports the dual of σ, then s also supports information that defeasibly entails that σ is the case.[46]

To these two dualization axioms, one might add a third, which is a converse of (69a): if a situation s supports a SOA which is incompatible with σ, then s supports $\overline{\sigma}$:[47]

(70) $\quad \forall s, \sigma \exists \psi [s \models \psi$ and $\psi \Rightarrow^{\neg} \sigma]$, then $s \models \overline{\sigma}$.

Given that SOAs encode different ways situations could be (in other words, they are potential properties of external reality), they play a role similar to possible worlds in possible worlds semantics. In particular, they will be a key component in the explication of what propositions are. Nonetheless, there are two obvious differences between SOAs and possible worlds.[48] First, SOAs are structured objects; second, their 'informational range' is microscopic compared to a possible world, which determines the resolution of each conceivable issue (and then some). The SOAs defined in definition 3 are all *basic* SOAs—their direct components are simply a relation and an assignment of entities to the argument roles of that relation. In many ST accounts, it is assumed that in addition to basic SOAs, there also exist compound SOAs, built structurally; but we do not make this assumption here. Although compound SOAs play no role in any of our analyses, we take no stand on the issue of whether such entities should be avoided on general theoretical grounds, as suggested by Devlin (1991).[49]

Before summarizing our assumptions about SITSTRs,[50] we review a few preliminaries about structural relations:[51]

Definition 1 Structural Sorts

Given a structural relation S, the class S^* consists of those objects a such that $S(\overrightarrow{x}, a)$ holds for some sequence $\overrightarrow{x}$ of elements of A. The elements $\overrightarrow{x}$ will be called the components *of a. The classes S_i^* constitute the* structural sorts *of the relational structure S.*[52]

Definition 2 Extensionality

In general, we will assume that the relational structures we define are extensional: *structured objects are determined uniquely. That is, given a structural relation S_i and a sequence of objects $\overrightarrow{x}$, there exists at most one y such that $S_i(\overrightarrow{x}, y)$.*

---

[46]Suppose, for example, that we say (i):

  (i) Jo saw Bo not stop at the traffic lights.

Here we are typically talking about a situation where Bo approaches a red traffic light, a situation that usually involves stopping. We leave the notion of defeasible entailment unanalyzed here. Various notions could be used, however, for instance the notion of defeasible entailment developed within Barwise and Seligman's Channel Theory (Barwise and Seligman 1996).

[47]This property of dualization would follow directly if one assumed the class of SOAs to be a Heyting algebra, with dualization constituting a pseudo-complement operation. For one such set-up, see Barwise and Etchemendy 1990.

[48]We mentioned above that situations are usually taken to be ACTUAL. However, there is nothing in the theory that rules out postulating non-actual situations. Nonetheless, as Cooper (1993) shows, one can recast Montague's theory of modality in situation theory without making this additional assumption, in which case the 'possibilities' would all be explicated by means of SOAs. For recent discussions of modality in ST, see Barwise 1997 and Vogel and Ginzburg 1999, where the use of non-actual situations is entertained.

[49]For discussion, see Barwise 1989b.

[50]The definition here involves the minimum conditions for a structure to be a SITSTR. Some additional assumptions that would typically be assumed have been discussed above.

[51]See definition 3.2 of Seligman and Moss.

[52]It should be emphasized that structural sorts are merely a metatheoretical device, useful for talk about structural relations. When talking about a class of relational structures, we will sometimes find it convenient to discuss it in terms of its associated structural relations; on other occasions it will be more convenient to formulate discussion in terms of structural sorts.

The assumptions about a SITSTR have been partitioned into four categories. The first two groups concern the nature of SOAs and negation, respectively. The third group imposes certain obvious sortal requirements, while the fourth specifies certain basic assumptions about temporal structure.[53]

Definition 3 A Situation Structure (SITSTR)

A Situation Structure (SITSTR) is a relational structure of the following type:[54]
$$[\ \mathcal{A}, \ \mathbf{SelAdVal^3}, \mathbf{Soa^3}, \mathbf{Pos^1}, \mathbf{Neg^1}; \ Sit^1, \models^2, Rel^1, ArgRole^1, Approp^1, NegOf^2,$$
$$Time^1, Timespan^2, Anterior^2 \ ] \ such \ that:$$

1. *Basics concerning SOAs:*
   (a) *If* $\mathbf{Soa}(R, \alpha, \sigma)$, *then* $Rel(R)$ *and* $Approp(\alpha)$.
   (b) *If* $\mathbf{SelAdVal}(i, a, \alpha)$, *then* $ArgRole(i)$.
   (c) *If* $\mathbf{Soa}(R, \alpha, \sigma)$, *then for any i,a,b such that* $\mathbf{SelAdVal}(i, a, \alpha)$ *and* $\mathbf{SelAdVal}(i, b, \alpha)$
       it follows that $a = b$.
   (d) *If* $s \models \sigma$, *then* $Sit(s)$ *and there exist* R, α *such that* $\mathbf{Soa}(R, \alpha, \sigma)$.[55]
   (e) *Notation: If* $\mathbf{Soa}(R, \alpha, \sigma)$, *then we write:* $\sigma = \langle\langle R; \alpha \rangle\rangle$

2. *Negation and SOAs:*
   (a) *If for some* $R, \alpha \ \mathbf{Soa}(R, \alpha, \sigma)$, *then exactly one of the following:* $\mathbf{Pos}(\sigma)$ *or* $\mathbf{Neg}(\sigma)$
   (b) *The NegOf relation is symmetric and functional (If* $NegOf(\sigma, \tau)$, *then* $NegOf(\tau, \sigma)$;
       If $NegOf(\sigma, \tau)$ *and* $NegOf(\sigma, \tau')$, *then* $\tau = \tau'$)
   (c) *Dual SOAs are constituted from the same SOA and role assignment: If* $\mathbf{Soa}(R, \alpha, \sigma)$,
       then there is a SOA $\overline{\sigma} \neq \sigma$ *such that* $NegOf(\sigma, \overline{\sigma})$ *and* $\mathbf{Soa}(R, \alpha, \overline{\sigma})$

3. $\mathbf{Soa^*}$ *and* $\mathbf{SelAdVal^*}$ *are disjoint.*

4. *Temporal Structure:*
   (a) *If* $Timespan(s, t)$, *then* $Sit(s)$ *and* $Time(t)$. *Timespan relates a situation to the
       times occurring within it.*
   (b) *If* $Anterior(s_1, s_2)$, *then* $Sit(s_1)$ *and* $Sit(s_2)$. *Anterior is a partial ordering on
       the class of situations in terms of temporal constitution such that* $Anterior(s_1, s_2)$
       intuitively means that the temporal instants of s_1 *precede the temporal instants of* s_2.

3.3.3 Simultaneous Abstraction

The final component we need before we can fully define our semantic universe is the notion of *simultaneous abstraction*. Simultaneous abstraction will play a pivotal role in providing a viable notion of *propositional abstract*, one which can be used to overcome the formal and conceptual problems involved in previous 'open proposition' accounts of questions. Simultaneous abstraction, first introduced by Aczel and Lunnon (1991), is a generalization of unary abstraction (familiar from the λ-calculus) with two crucial differences. First, instead of abstracting over a single

---

[53]These latter assumptions are novel to our account and not in S&M–97.

[54]We adopt the notational convention that structural relations are depicted in boldface and have numerical superscripts corresponding to their r-ity. We will typically omit the latter.

[55]An alternative approach we could adopt, discussed in S&M–97, is to view Sit and $\models$ as structural relations. The idea behind this is that situations are then taken to be structurally determined by the SOAs they support. This has the advantage of pinning down in very concrete terms the identity conditions of situations.

variable, one abstracts over a set.[56] Second, an abstract is not construed functionally, but rather by means of structural relations that relate it to its body and the (abstracted) roles. Thus, if the universe contains objects of sort ϕ (e.g. SOAs or facts or propositions), then abstraction constitutes an operation that potentially expands the universe to contain also objects of sort ϕ-*abstract*. Such objects can be applied to an assignment f to yield objects of sort ϕ in which substitution as specified by f has taken place. We proceed to clarify the nature of the closely related notions of substitution and abstraction.

Substitutions and Simulations

Given an extensional structure $[\mathcal{A}, S_1, \ldots, S_m; \ldots]$, a substitution is simply a mapping f between elements of the universe $\mathcal{A}$. A relation g that extends f is called an f-simulation if it relates two elements a and b just in case a and b are identical modulo 'substitutions induced by f'.[57]

What this amounts to is the following:[58]

Definition 4 f-Simulation

Given a mapping f, a binary relation G is an f-simulation just in case: if $G(a,b)$ holds, then

1. if $a \in Dom(f)$, then $b = f(a)$
   Otherwise:

2. $a = b$, for an unstructured object a

3. If a is a structured object, then whenever $S(x_1, \ldots, x_n, a)$ for some structural relation S, then there exist $y_1, \ldots, y_n$ such that $S(y_1, \ldots, y_n, b)$ and for each i: $G(x_i, y_i)$

4. Conversely, whenever $S(y_1, \ldots, y_n, b)$, there exist $x_1, \ldots, x_n$ such that $S(x_1, \ldots, x_n, a)$ and for each i: $G(x_i, y_i)$

5. Given a substitution f, if there exists an f-simulation that relates a to b, we write this as $b = a\{f\}$.

To make this concrete, let us take a simple example with a SITSTR. If f is the mapping in (71), then, by clause 2 of definition 4, a relation G_0 can be an f-simulation only if it relates any ordinary, unstructured individual a other than kim and lou to itself:

(71) $f : [\text{kim} \mapsto \text{sam}, \text{lou} \mapsto \text{billie}]$

Now consider SOAs, the prime example so far of a structured object. For simplicity, we restrict our attention to simple SOAs, where the elements in the range of the role assignment mapping are unstructured. Any such SOA whose role assignment mapping does not contain either kim or lou in its range can only be related to itself. This is because a SOA σ's components are the relation R and the role assignment mapping α. R is unstructured, and (by our previous discussion) can only be related to itself by G_0; the components of α are the roles and the elements in the range of α. These are all, by our assumption, unstructured and distinct from kim and lou. And so again, by our previous discussion, these can only be related to themselves by G_0. A SOA such as (72a), which does contain kim as a constituent of its role assignment mapping, would need to be related by G_0 to (72b), whereas a SOA like (72c) would need to be related to (72d):

---

[56]A related notion does exist in certain versions of the lambda calculus, which allows for the product operation. See, for example, Barendregt 1984.

[57]The notion of an *f-simulation* is closely related to the notion of *bisimulation* discussed in Appendix B.

[58]See S&M–97 definition 3.11.

(72) a. $\langle\langle \text{Sleep; sleeper:kim}\rangle\rangle$

 b. $\langle\langle \text{Sleep; sleeper:sam}\rangle\rangle$

 c. $\langle\langle \text{See; see-er:kim, seen:lou}\rangle\rangle$

 d. $\langle\langle \text{See; see-er:sam, seen:billie}\rangle\rangle$

These examples illustrate that two objects related by means of an f-simulation are indeed identical, modulo 'substitutions induced by f'.

Abstraction and Application: Initial Notions

With this in hand, we can now turn to abstraction.[59] We start with unary abstraction. Recall that in a framework such as Montague Semantics, abstracts have no ontological status as such. λ-terms function as useful *notation* for functions. For instance, (73a) is construed as (73b):[60]

(73) a. $\lambda x. See(x, j)$

 b. the function $h : D_e \rightarrow \{0, 1\}$ such that $h(a) = [\![See(x, j)]\!]^{M, g_x^a}$

Although one could develop a variant of this 'functional' approach for our framework, we will adopt a strategy where abstraction is a semantic operation akin to substitution; the main difference is that the element which gets 'substituted in' functions as a place holder, not a regular role filler. There are a number of reasons for adopting such an approach. For a start, it can be argued to be conceptually simpler, directly expressing the intuition that abstraction over an entity of type ϕ creates an 'open ϕ'. The functional view further requires that the domain of the function be explicitly computed. This conceptual advantage of the substitutional approach has concrete ramifications: a functional construal of an abstract involves an unmotivated loss of semantic grain. This is because intuitively distinct descriptions of the domain of the function can end up being instantiated by the same set. For instance, if we interpret the interrogatives in (74) as abstracts and in turn construe these abstracts functionally, then the two denotations will be identified.[61] Such a conflation will not arise on the approach we develop here:[62]

(74) a. Which primes smaller than five are divisors of 9?

 b. Which numbers smaller than 4 are divisors of 9?

How are we to formalize our notion of abstraction? Given the modeling strategy so far, it is clear that abstracts will be specified using structural relations. At first, one might think that in view of the notation $\lambda b.p$, one could simply posit a three place structural relation **Abst** such that **Abst**(p, b, a) would mean that a arises by abstracting b from p. But such an approach will not quite work. The reason for this is quite simple: structured objects are required to have a unique set of components. For instance, the SOA which we depict as $\langle\langle R, f\rangle\rangle$ is built from the relation R and the assignment f. But by its very nature, an 'abstract' is not uniquely determined by the single entity it has been 'abstracted from'. After all, abstraction, as its name implies, 'generalizes' over

---

[59]Our presentation here, on the formal side, is highly dependent on S&M–97. However, the formulation we provide differs slightly from theirs: the way we set things up makes the introduction of restrictions on abstracts somewhat simpler. Moreover, it will help us ensure—for reasons explained below—that an abstract is necessarily distinct from the entity it is abstracted from. This means that S&M–97's theorem that every extensional structure can be extended to a λ-structure needs to be modified subtly, though not in a way that hampers our application of it, as we show in Appendix B.

[60]One could make the comparison to the current framework even more direct by substituting for $\{0, 1\}$ a sort such as **SOA***.

[61]The denotation will be the function $x : \{2, 3\} \mapsto Divide(x, 9)$.

[62]Actually, the approach we discuss in this chapter does not provide a fully satisfactory account of abstraction with restrictions. A minor adjustment, presented in Chapter 4, will provide the requisite notion.

a whole class of entities. $\lambda x \langle\langle$See; see-er:x, seen:bo$\rangle\rangle$ can no more be structurally determined by $\langle\langle$See; see-er:jo, seen:bo$\rangle\rangle$ than by $\langle\langle$See; see-er:mo, seen:bo$\rangle\rangle$.

A more successful method is to specify abstraction using two structural relations, one of which involves an essential self reference. Think of an abstract as a structured object containing a place-holder.[63] In turn, think of the place-holder as specified in terms of an entity which contains the place-holder as a component. This latter entity, the body of the abstract, is the substitution instance of the various entities which the abstract generalizes over.[64]

In order to characterize a structure with an abstraction operation, one which we will call an *abstraction structure*, we posit two structural relations: $\mathbf{PlaceHolder}^2(b, \pi)$, which relates the body b and the place-holder π, and $\mathbf{Abst}^2(b, a)$, which relates the body b and the abstract a. Objects of sort $\mathbf{PlaceHolder}^*$ are called place-holders and objects of sort $\mathbf{Abst}^*$ are called abstracts.

In order that these specifications serve to define an abstraction operation we need to impose certain conditions on these relations. First, we want to ensure that a place-holder is on one hand a component of the body of the abstract; conversely, it does not have any other structural description:

(75) a. If $\mathbf{Abst}(b, a)$, then $b \neq a$ and there exists π such that $\mathbf{PlaceHolder}(b, \pi)$.

     b. If $\mathbf{PlaceHolder}(b, \pi)$, then the only sort of π is $\mathbf{PlaceHolder}^*$.

Second, we want to ensure that the result of applying the abstract will be well defined. This we achieve by requiring that a place-holder can occur in only one body:

(76)   If $\mathbf{PlaceHolder}(b, \pi)$ and $\mathbf{PlaceHolder}(b', \pi)$, then $b = b'$.

Finally, and most crucially, we want to ensure that the body of the abstract is indeed a substitution instance of the various entities which the abstract generalizes over. This is what will ensure that the result of applying an abstract is the intended one, namely that it involves substituting a non place-holder in place of the abstract's place-holder.[65] We state this as follows:

(77) a. Given an abstraction structure $\mathcal{S}$ and two objects a and c, an abstract τ is THE AB-STRACTION OF b FROM σ if there exist π and c such that

       1. $b = a\{c \to \pi\}$
       2. $\mathbf{PlaceHolder}(b, \pi)$
       3. $\mathbf{Abst}(b, \tau)$
       4. The only sort of π is $\mathbf{PlaceHolder}^*$.

     b. Given an abstract a in an abstraction structure $\mathcal{A}$, a substitution $\pi \to d$ is an appropriate assignment to a if there exists b such that

       1. $\mathbf{PlaceHolder}(b, \pi)$
       2. $\mathbf{Abst}(b, a)$
       3. $b\{\pi \mapsto d\}$ exists.

     c. If $b\{\pi \mapsto d\}$ exists, we call it the application of a to the substitution $\pi \mapsto d$.

---

[63] Also known as a ROLE INDEX in Aczel and Lunnon 1991 and Cooper 1993 and as a POINTER in S&M–97.

[64] Recall that the set theory which formally underpins our account accommodates non-well-founded phenomena.

[65] Indeed the distinction between the body and the abstract will become more pronounced once we introduce abstraction with restrictions in Chapter 4. The restrictions will be components of the abstract which delimit the possible substitutions which the abstract can be applied to. However, they will not in general be components of the body or of substitution instances of the abstract.

Let us consider a simple example. Abstraction over the SOA in (78a) yields a SOA abstract that we notate as (78b). The place-holder involved in this abstraction 'occupies' the role previously filled by jo:

(78)   a. $\langle\langle$See; seer:jo, seen:bo$\rangle\rangle$
       b. $\lambda\{\text{jo} \mapsto \pi\}\langle\langle$See; see-er:jo, seen:bo$\rangle\rangle$

Whereas, applying (78b) to (79a) would yield (79b):

(79)   a. $f : [\pi \mapsto \text{kim}]$
       b. $\langle\langle$See; seer:kim, seen:bo$\rangle\rangle$
       c. $f_0 : [\text{jo} \mapsto \text{kim}]$

Note that this is identical with the result of starting out with a substitution f_0 as in (79c) and—via a f_0-simulation—replacing *jo* in the original SOA (78a) with *kim*.

As we have noted, **PlaceHolder** and **Abst** are structural relations. This implies that b being abstracted out of σ yields a unique place-holder and a unique abstract. This, in turn, implies that in creating a structured object, abstraction 'forgets' the original fillers of the argument role. Thus, the abstract (80a) can be shown to be identical to (80b), a property analogous to α-equivalence in λ-calculus:

(80)   a. $\lambda\{\text{billie} \mapsto r_1\}\langle\langle$See; seer:billie, seen:bo$\rangle\rangle$
       b. $\lambda\{\text{jo} \mapsto r_2\}\langle\langle$See; seer:jo, seen:bo$\rangle\rangle$

Moreover, there is no need to reify as members of the universe 'parameters' or similar variable-like entities to fill the roles over which abstraction takes place (cf. Barwise and Cooper 1991). Rather, place-holders are modeled as structured objects, postulated to be entities which have no other sort.[66] A consequence of the unique definability of place-holders is a notational convention we will often adopt: unless reference to the place-holder is of import in a particular discussion, we will omit the place-holder from the notation for abstracts. (81b) will serve as the notation for (81a):

(81)   a. $\lambda\{\text{billie} \mapsto r_1\}\langle\langle$See; seer:billie, seen:bo$\rangle\rangle$
       b. $\lambda\{\text{billie}\}\langle\langle$See; seer:billie, seen:bo$\rangle\rangle$

Simultaneous Abstraction

We can now turn to simultaneous abstraction. This turns out to be a straightforward generalization. Abstracting a set of entities $c_1, \ldots, c_n$ from an object $\sigma(c_1, \ldots, c_n)$ of which they are components, is equivalent to the existence of a $[c_1 \mapsto r_1, \ldots, c_n \mapsto r_n]$-simulation which relates $\sigma(c_1, \ldots, c_n)$ to the body of the abstract:

Definition 5 Simultaneous Abstraction

In an abstraction structure $\mathcal{S}$, given a and a set C (= $\{c_1, \ldots, c_n\}$), an abstract τ is the abstraction of C from σ if there is an injective function $\pi : C \to |\mathcal{S}|$ (the PlaceHolder function) and b such that:

   1. $b = \sigma\{c_1 \mapsto \pi(c_1), \ldots, c_n \mapsto \pi(c_n)\}$.
   2. For each c_i: **PlaceHolder**$(b, \pi(c_i))$.

---

[66]This elegant view of abstraction, which does not presuppose the existence of parameters 'prior' to the abstraction is due to Seligman and Moss. For a detailed and insightful development of a related view, see Crimmins 1993a.

3. **Abst**(b, τ).

4. *For each c_i: the only sort of $\pi(c_i)$ is* **PlaceHolder***.

The abstraction of C (= $\{c_1, \ldots, c_n\}$) from σ is notated as either $\lambda C.\sigma$ or as $\lambda\{c_1, \ldots, c_n\}\sigma$.

An appropriate assignment f for a simultaneous abstract is a function whose domain includes the roles of the abstract. In addition, $b\{f\}$ must exist, for b—the body of the abstract. The formal definition is identical *mutatis mutandis* to (77b).[67] For instance, abstraction over the SOA in (82a) yields the SOA abstract in (82b). Applying this abstract to the assignment in (82c) is identical to the result of substituting the objects *kim* and *lou* for the objects *bo* and *jo* abstracted out of the SOA (82a), as shown in (82d):

(82) a. $\langle\langle\text{See}; \text{seer:jo}, \text{seen:bo}\rangle\rangle$

  b. $\lambda\{\text{jo} \mapsto r_1, \text{bo} \mapsto r_2\}\langle\langle\text{See}; \text{seer:jo}, \text{seen:bo}\rangle\rangle$

  c. $f : [r_1 \mapsto \text{kim}, r_2 \mapsto \text{lou}]$

  d. $\langle\langle\text{See}; \text{see-er:kim}, \text{seen:lou}\rangle\rangle$

Ontology and λ-Structures

Definition 3 postulated that one of the components of a SOA is a relation, a postulate we repeat here as (83a). To this we add an additional natural assumption, given in (83b), that ensures that SOAs are closed under substitutions:

(83) a. If **Soa**(R, α, σ), then $Rel(R)$.

  b. If **Soa**(R, α, σ) and if $\alpha\{f\}$ exists, then **Soa**$(R, \alpha\{f\}, \sigma)$.

Let us consider the ontological status of SOA abstracts. Given a SOA $\sigma = \langle\langle R; \alpha\rangle\rangle$, abstraction over a set B yields an object $\rho = \lambda B\langle\langle R, \alpha\rangle\rangle$. If there exists f, an appropriate assignment for ρ, it follows from (83b) that $\rho\{f\}$ is a SOA; indeed it is $\langle\langle R; \alpha\{f\}\rangle\rangle$. Consequently, given our assumption in (83a), it follows that ρ is a relation. This emphasizes that the ontological status of abstracts is, at least in part, determined by assumptions concerning other structural relations.

One additional point to note, which will be of relevance in our treatment of polar questions, concerns 0-ary abstraction. Definition 5 does not require that the set of elements abstracted away be nonempty. We will assume that the 0-ary case is to be construed as follows: a 0-ary abstract $Ab^0(\sigma) = \lambda\{\}\sigma$ involves a place-holder function that is a mapping from the empty set into the universe. This picks out a PlaceHolder π_0, an element of the universe which points at no component of σ, the body of $Ab^0(\sigma)$. The structural relations that hold by virtue of the definition (5) are these:

(84) a. **PlaceHolder**(σ, π_0)

  b. **Abst**$(\sigma, Ab^0(\sigma))$

  c. The only sort of π_0 is **PlaceHolder***

Given the basic characteristic of the structural relation **Abst** that requires the body to be distinct from the abstract, it will also be the case for 0-ary abstracts that σ is distinct from $Ab^0(\sigma)$.

In Montague's IL, as in various other type theories, it is assumed that the domain is closed under functional type formation: 'if a is a type and b is a type, then so is $< a, b >$'. The analogous

---

[67] In Chapter 4 a definition of application for simultaneous abstraction with restrictions will be provided.

assumption for abstraction, which we will assume our semantic universe to obey, is *closure under simultaneous abstraction*:[68]

Definition 6 A λ-Structure

> An extensional structure S is a lambda structure (λ-structure) if for every element a of $|S|$, the universe of S, and every set C of elements of $|S|$, the simultaneous abstraction $\lambda C.a$ exists.

3.4   A Situational Universe with Abstract Entities

Before we proceed to construct the semantic universe we use to ground our theory of questions, it may be useful to digress briefly into what might be called the Austinian strategy—the approach we adopt toward the abstract objects in our ontology.

3.4.1   The Austinian Strategy

This approach has two components. First, propositions, facts, and outcomes will be assumed to be situationally relativized—a particular situation will be one of their defining components. Second, a distinction is drawn between 'pure' informational units, as represented by the SOAs, and the entities which carry information, the situations. The first component of the strategy is not particularly idiosyncratic; there has been a fair amount of work over the last 10 years that has motivated the need for relativization to events/situations. This includes work on definite reference and anaphora inspired by situation semantics (for some recent examples see Poesio 1993, Cooper 1996, Milward 1995, Recanati 1996). But also there is a vast amount of work based on a Davidsonian strategy, wherein predications involve relativization to events (although these get existentially closured at some stage of a semantic derivation. (See, for example, Parsons 1994, Kamp and Reyle 1993.) Cooper (1998) observes that there are important parallels between the Davidsonian strategy and the Austinian one, though in certain key cases (Cooper focuses on the treatment of naked infinitives) the two approaches generate subtly distinct predictions. The debate on the issue of reference vs. existential closure to situations/events is still ongoing and difficult to resolve conclusively. Given this, we should point out that we could adopt a more complex modeling strategy, in which relativization to situations would not involve indexicality but would incorporate situational existential closure in some fashion. Such a move, possibly eschewing any situational relativization, might be needed independently to cope with general sentences, such as *Two and two are four* or *Fish swim*.[69]

   As for the second component of the Austinian strategy, the distinction between information and its carriers, such a modeling strategy was pioneered by Barwise and Etchemendy (1987). They provided the first detailed formalization and used it to provide a constructive solution to the Liar's Paradox, a foundational conundrum that has no general solution in more familiar forms of semantics, such as possible worlds semantics. As we discussed above in section 3.3.2, in relation to the Frege-Searle propositional content hypothesis, the distinction is of considerable utility: it provides a means for capturing semantic generalizations about and operations on the entire class of abstract entities.

---

[68]In fact, given the notion of simultaneous abstraction with restrictions introduced in Chapter 4, we will ultimately require closure under this latter notion.

[69]This was recognized already by Barwise and Perry (1985). See Glasbey 1998 and Kim 1998 for proposals that some propositions are Austinian, whereas others (e.g. mathematical and individual-level statements) are Russellian (in Barwise and Etchemendy's (1987) sense; that is, they do not make reference to a particular situation).

3.4.2 Basic Definition

We now specify the semantic universe that grounds our grammatical framework. A Situational Universe with Abstract Entities (SU+AE) is a SITSTR closed under abstraction (a λ-SITSTR) with some additional structural sorts. Before presenting these in detail, we provide a brief overview. **Proposition***, **Possibility***, and **Outcome*** are sorts whose elements represent, respectively, the propositions, possibilities, and outcomes of the universe. For the two sorts **Proposition***, **Outcome***, we also posit a corresponding sort **At-...** (viz. **AtProposition***, **AtOutcome***), whose elements are 'atomic'—'basic' in some terminologies—members of the corresponding sort. Atomic propositions are structurally determined by a situation and a SOA; atomic outcomes by a situation and a SOA abstract (one in which the temporal argument is abstracted away). This latter class of entities will be characterized by means of a structural sort **Irr(ealis)Soa***.[70] The atomic/non-atomic distinction is needed because we will subsequently posit the existence of 'compound' members of these sorts. Possibilities are structurally determined by a proposition, atomic or otherwise.

Following our discussion in section 3.2.3, we will also posit a property *Fact*, applicable to the class of possibilities. Those possibilities that are factual will constitute the facts of the universe. Analogously, there will be properties *True* and *Fulfill*, which capture the notions of truth and fulfilledness for propositions and outcomes.[71] The notation '$\rightarrow_{prop}$' represents a concept of entailment on propositions.[72]

We bring questions into the picture in section 3.5, but, since we will take them to be proposition abstracts, and given that a SU+AE must be closed under abstraction, they will automatically exist in any SU+AE.

The foregoing paragraphs can be summarized by the following definition: A SU+AE is an extensional relational structure of the type given in Definition 7:

Definition 7 Situational Universe with Abstract Entities

A SU+AE is a relational structure of the following type:
[$\mathcal{A}$, **Possibility^2**, **AtProposition^3**, **Proposition^1**, **AtOutcome^3**, **Outcome^1**, **IrrSoa^3**; $Fact^1, True^1, Fulfill^1, \rightarrow^2_{prop}$], *where $\mathcal{A}$ is a λ-SITSTR and in addition:*

1. **Possibility***, **Proposition***, **Outcome***, **Soa***, **SelAdVal*** *are pairwise disjoint.*
2. **AtProposition*** ⊂ **Proposition***; **AtOutcome*** ⊂ **Outcome***;
3. *If* $\rightarrow^2_{prop}$ (p, q), *then* **Proposition**(p) *and* **Proposition**(q); $\rightarrow^2_{prop}$ (p, q) *if* $True(p)$ *implies* $True(q)$
4. *. . . (additional conditions stated below)*

3.4.3 Possibilities, Facts, and Propositions

The first notion we characterize pertains to what we will call an *atomic proposition*. The semantic setup we have provides a fairly direct conceptualization; recall that the SOAs constitute the properties that can hold of situations. Consequently, we assume that a situation s and a SOA σ serve to define a proposition, which we will notate as prop(s, σ), the proposition that s is a

---

[70]The *r-soa/i-soa* type distinction was discussed in Chapter 2.

[71]Neither *Fact*, nor *True* or *Fulfill* for that matter, are structural relations. This reflects the (not incontrovertible) intuition that identity conditions and truth conditions are orthogonal.

[72]As will become clear, we offer only the barest specification possible for such a notion. For discussion as to how to port a logic into the current setup see S&M–97.

situation of the type designated by σ. This assumption amounts to the following requirements on the structural relation **AtProposition**:[73]

(85) a. If **AtProposition**(s, σ, p), then $Sit(s)$ and there exist R, α such that **Soa**(R, α, σ)

  b. If $Sit(s)$ and there exist R, α such that **Soa**(R, α, σ), then there exists p such that **AtProposition**(s, σ, p)

Truth for atomic propositions is straightforwardly definable as follows:

(86) If there exists s, σ such that **AtProposition**(s, σ, p), then $s \models \sigma$ if and only if $True(p)$.

Note that because our semantic universe is extensional, structured objects are defined uniquely. Hence, in particular, we can talk about the sole proposition defined by a situation, SOA pair (s, σ).

What are possibilities? The account we adopt here follows the correspondence theory of truth, namely that a proposition is true in virtue of the existence of a fact (see, for example, Russell 1949 and Mulligan et al. 1984). In our account, this is made concrete by assuming that possibilities are structurally determined by propositions.[74] The possibility defined by a proposition is a *fact* just in case the corresponding proposition is true:

(87) a. If **Possibility**(p, f), then **Proposition**(p)

  b. If **Proposition**(p), then there exists f such that **Possibility**(p, f)

  c. $Fact(f)$ iff there exists p such that **Possibility**(p, f) and $True(p)$

  d. Notation: poss(p) denotes the possibility individuated by the proposition p.

Note that by treating facts as a subclass of the possibilities, we have a straightforward account of the defeasability of facts in dissent and projection phenomena discussed above (see examples (40), repeated here as (88)):

(88) a. A: I regret the fact that Kim left.
    B: It's not a fact.

  b. If Sandip leaves, Kimmo will regret that fact bitterly.

In cases like (88a), we assume that the reference is to a possibility and the discussion pertains to whether it is also a fact. Similarly, in (88b) what is predicated of Kimmo is potential regret of a possibility, which at utterance time is not known to be factual.

Let us consider some of the fundamental characteristics of the current theory of propositions and possibilities. In contrast to possible worlds semantics, propositions are individuated with finer grain than truth conditions. By extensionality there will be exactly one proposition defined in terms of its basic components: a situation and a SOA. The SOAs in (89a,b) hold in all possible worlds, but neither they nor the corresponding propositions (and by extension facts) are identified. Thus, logical omniscience, the most intrinsic problem besetting possible worlds semantics,

---

[73]Actually, we could get by without STIPULATING that (85b) is the case. As we discuss in Appendix B, we can always build models ('anti-founded structures'), where such requirements hold.

[74]Our ontologically scrupulous readers might wonder why we assume possibilities to be structurally determined by propositions and not, say, vice versa. In fact, one could construct an ontology of the latter kind and, as far as we are aware, it would be as viable as the one we define in the text. The main advantage gained by basing things on propositions is a certain simplicity when dealing with questions, whose status as *propositional* abstracts we will argue for.

does not arise for a situation theoretic universe:[75]

(89)   a. $\langle\langle$ SelfIdentical;marais $\rangle\rangle$

     b. $\langle\langle$ SelfIdentical;poulenc $\rangle\rangle$

Indeed, avoiding logical omniscience can be achieved simply by taking propositions to be sets of situations. However, as Soames (1985) observes, such a move does not escape what has come to be known as Soames' puzzle. An Austinian view of propositions evades this difficulty.[76] But not all doxastic puzzles can be solved just by adopting an improved ontology, the prime example being Kripke's Pierre puzzle (Kripke 1979). This is actually a family of puzzles revolving around an agent's failure to identify a single object that has distinct 'presentations': two distinct names, or tokens of names, or even two distinct smells, for a canine agent. The most well known form of the puzzle involves the Frenchman Pierre who works near Trafalgar Square in London. After witnessing the foul state of Nelson's Column, he is moved to affirm (90a):[77]

(90)   a. I believe that Nelson's Column is fouled up.

     b. Je ne crois pas que le Column de Nelson est sale.

     c. $\mathrm{prop}(s_{\mathrm{trafalgar-sq}}, \langle\langle \mathrm{Ugly;nc} \rangle\rangle)$

     d. Pierre believes that Nelson's Column is fouled up.

At the same time, Pierre, who was educated in a monolingual school in France, retains his school-boy belief about a pristine marble arch he knows as the *Column de Nelson*, which he does not connect with Nelson's Column. In conversation with his French ex-school mates, Pierre will affirm (90b). However, the Austinian propositions associated with the embedded clauses of (90a) and (90b) are identical—for example, (90c), and so a potential paradox looms when trying to assess if (90d) is true.

Actually, the paradox just described arises only if (ignoring tense) one takes attitude predicates to be dyadic: relations between an agent and an abstract entity (proposition/fact/question etc). Thus, one way around the paradox (following Crimmins and Perry 1989, Crimmins 1993b, and Cooper and Ginzburg 1996) is to jettison the assumption of dyadicity. Instead, the assumption can be made that an additional, implicit argument exists for such predicates, one that is filled by a particular information state of the reported agent. The attitudinal relation is then taken to involve an agent, an information state IS (belief, knowledge, wondering etc), and an abstract object α (proposition, fact, question) such that IS has α as its content.

On this view, a single agent can rationally possess distinct information states, even though these may possess contradictory contents. This approach also explains why substitutivity of co-

---

[75]Logical omniscience is the identification contentwise of logically equivalent sentences, as is the case in possible worlds semantics.

[76]Soames' puzzle arises by considering the chain of inferences in (i) to (iv):

  (i) The Babylonians believed that 'Hesperus' referred to Hesperus and that 'Phosphorus' referred to Phosphorus.

  (ii) The Babylonians believed that 'Hesperus' referred to Hesperus and that 'Phosphorus' referred to Hesperus.

  (iii) The Babylonians believed that 'Hesperus' referred to something$_i$ and that 'Phosphorus' referred to it$_i$.

  (iv) The Babylonians believed that 'Hesperus' and 'Phosphorus' were co-referential.

(i) is clearly true and (iv) clearly false, given that the Babylonians had distinct names for Venus. The puzzle is to find the fallacious inferential link. See Soames 1985 for discussion of the puzzle. In fact, in order to defuse the puzzle, it is sufficient to take (uses of) sentences to denote SOAs, as in 'Russellian' approaches to propositions.

[77]Strictly speaking, this is a variant on Kripke's own example, in which the belief at issue is whether London is pretty or not. That particular formulation of the puzzle, however, can straightforwardly be defused using Austinian propositions.

referring terms can be legitimate, but need not be. This follows because in attitude reports it is typical that the reporter chooses words so as to transparently reflect the representational structure of a particular information state of the cognizer. Using the name *Nelson's Column* in a belief report like (90d), implicates that this is a name by means of which Pierre would refer to the London monument. Nonetheless, this implicature is cancellable, for instance by adding *though he wouldn't phrase it this way*.

This discussion is relevant to an issue that our modeling of possibilities and propositions brings up. We have assumed explicitly that possibilities and propositions are distinct but bijectively related. In this we deviate from a number of past proposals. Asher (1993, 1996) suggests that beliefs are individuated with finer grain than facts and possibilities. Thus, with respect to the Tully/Cicero conundrum, Asher suggests that (91a) constitutes a distinct propositional entity from (91b), but that the fact represented by (91c) is identical to the one represented in (91d):

(91)   a. The belief that Tully was a famous orator
       b. The belief that Cicero was a famous orator
       c. The fact that Tully was a famous orator
       d. The fact that Cicero was a famous orator

One problematic consequence of this suggestion, given Asher's assumption that attitude predicates are dyadic, is that it predicts differences in granularity between predicates selecting for propositions and predicates selecting for facts. Assuming (91a) to be distinct from (91b) immediately explains a discourse such as (92a):

(92)   a. Tom holds that belief.
          Which belief?
          The belief that Tully was a famous orator.
          Hence, Tom believes Tully was a famous orator, though not (necessarily) that Cicero was a famous orator.
       b. Tom is aware of that fact.
          Which fact?
          The fact that Tully was a famous orator.
          Hence, Tom is aware that Tully was a famous orator.
          Hence, Tom is aware that Cicero was a famous orator.

However, the assumption that (91c) and (91d) are identical leads to the acceptance of (92b). This predicted asymmetry between TF predicates and factives seems incorrect. On the other hand, if we follow the suggestion that attitude predicates are triadic, then we can accept that the propositional objects at issue in (91) are identical (as are the facts) without difficulty.

In ST, it has often been common to call factual SOAs *facts*, not as we have been doing here.[78] Identifying facts with factual SOAs is, however, problematic if one attempts to treat facts, as we do here, as abstract entities that are known, discovered, and so forth. If one assumes, in the spirit of the Austinian program, that atomic propositions are individuated in terms of a situation and a SOA, but facts are SOAs, one predicts an asymmetry between propositional and factive predicates as far as the 'situatedness' of the attitude. Propositional attitudes, on this view, involve

---

[78]The connection between facts in ST and the philosophers' facts (e.g. those of Austin and Vendler) is discussed by Barwise (1989a).

situationally relativized entities, whereas factives involve *situationally absolute* entities. Once again, there seems no evidence to support such an asymmetry for a pair such (93a,b); insofar as Kimmo's belief concerns a particular arrival event, so does her knowledge:

(93) a. Kimmo believes that Sandheep arrived on time.

     b. Kimmo knows that Sandheep arrived on time.

3.4.4 Outcomes

We move now to consider how outcomes should be modeled. In Chapter 2 we discussed the class of *irrealis* SOAs. In fact, *irrealis* SOAs will not be SOAs, but rather SOA abstracts—SOAs out of which the temporal argument has been abstracted away. For notational ease we employ a circumflexed $\hat{t}$ to notate the unary abstraction operator in the case of such SOA abstracts. An irrealis SOA $\hat{t}\sigma$ is characterized as an entity whose PlaceHolder r is one for which a time is selectionally adequate and such that substituting a time for r yields a SOA:

(94) If **Irrsoa**$(c, r, \hat{t}\sigma)$, then:

    1. **Abst**$(c, \hat{t}\sigma)$,

    2. **PlaceHolder**(c, r), and

    3. there exists t_0, R, μ such that: (a) $Time(t_0)$ and (b) **Soa**$(R, \mu, \hat{t}\sigma\{r \to t_0\})$.

Our constraints will, for example, associate the irrealis SOA in (95) with the subjunctive verb *leave* (b denotes the individual supplied by the subject):

(95) $\hat{t}\langle\langle\text{Leave; leaver:b, time:}t\rangle\rangle$

We will treat outcomes as structured objects, constructed from an irrealis SOA $\hat{t}\sigma$ and a situation s. $\hat{t}\sigma$ provides a condition that is uninstantiated within the timespan of the situation:

(96) a. If **AtOutcome**$(s, \hat{t}\sigma, o)$, then there exist c,r such that:

       (a) $Sit(s)$ and (b) **Irrsoa**$(c, r, \hat{t}\sigma)]$ and there is no t_0 such that: (a) $Timespan(s, t_0)$ and (b) $s \models \hat{t}\sigma\{r \to t_0\}$

     b. Notation: If **AtOutcome**$(s, \hat{t}\sigma, o)$, then we use the notation out$(s, \hat{t}\sigma)$ to stand for o.

Thus, intuitively, an outcome allows us to represent a possible path of evolution for a situation. Outcomes are distinct from possibilities and propositions, hence neither factuality nor truth is applicable. There is, nonetheless, a somewhat analogous notion which is readily definable—the conditions according to which an atomic outcome is fulfilled. For an outcome out$(s_0, \hat{t}\sigma)$, this involves the existence of a situation s_1 which is situated temporally after s_0 such that s_1 supports an instantiation of $\hat{t}\sigma$. This is the sense in which outcomes are 'futurate'.

(97) *Fulfilled(o)* iff there exist $s_0, s_1, \hat{t}\sigma, c, r, t_0$ such that:

    a. **AtOutcome**$(s_0, \hat{t}\sigma, o)$ and

    b. **Irrsoa**$(c, r, \hat{t}\sigma)$ and

    c. $Anterior(s_0, s_1)$ and $s_1 \models \hat{t}\sigma\{[r \to t_0]\}$

Our constraints associate the outcome in (98) with the subjunctive clause *that Billie leave* (s_0 denotes a contextually supplied situation):

(98) out$(s_0, \hat{t}\langle\langle\text{Leave; leaver:b, time:}t\rangle\rangle)$

3.4.5 Compounding Operations on propositions

We further assume that propositions and outcomes can be compounded.[79] We consider here only propositions, since the minimal structure we impose on them will be of some importance when we come to discuss questions. It would be a routine exercise to define an analogous construction for outcomes.

The following definition allows for set-theoretic structure on propositions, imposes familiar truth conditions on the meet and join of a set of propositions, ensures that these exist, and imposes certain conditions on propositional negation:[80]

Definition 8 A De Morgan $\bigwedge / \bigvee$-closed Situation Structure with Abstract Entities

An SU+AE $\mathcal{S}$ of type [$\mathcal{A}$, $\mathbf{Set}^1$, ϵ^2, $\mathbf{ConjOf}^2$, $\mathbf{DisjOf}^2$; $NegationOf^2$] is De Morgan $\bigwedge / \bigvee$ closed iff:

1. *(a) $\mathbf{ConjOf}^* \subset \mathbf{Proposition}^*$; (b) $\mathbf{DisjOf}^* \subset \mathbf{Proposition}^*$; (c) $\epsilon^* \subset \mathbf{Set}^*$.*

2. *The elements of $\mathbf{Set}^*$ are regulated by the axioms of the set theory ZFC^-.*

3. *If $\mathbf{Set}(X)$ and for each $p \in X$, $\mathbf{Proposition}(p)$, then there exist $\bigwedge X$ and $\bigvee X$ such that for each $p \in X$ $\mathbf{ConjOf}(p, \bigwedge X)$, $\mathbf{DisjOf}(p, \bigvee X)$.*

4. *If $\mathbf{Set}(X)$ and $\mathbf{Proposition}(p)$ for each $p \in X$, then: $True(\bigwedge X)$ iff for each $p \in X$, $True(p)$.*

5. *If $\mathbf{Set}(X)$ and $\mathbf{Proposition}(p)$ for each $p \in X$, then: $True(\bigvee X)$ iff $True(p)$ for some $p \in X$*

6. *The $NegationOf$ relation is symmetric and functional (If $NegationOf(p,q)$, then $NegationOf(q,p)$; If $NegationOf(p,q)$ and $NegationOf(p,q')$, then $q = q'$)*

7. *Dual atomic propositions are constituted from the same situation and SOA:*
   If $\mathbf{AtProposition}(s, \sigma, p)$ then there is a proposition $\neg p \neq p$ such that $NegationOf(p, \neg p)$ and $\mathbf{AtProposition}(s, \overline{\sigma}, \neg p)$

8. *If $\mathbf{Set}(X)$ and $\mathbf{Set}(Y)$ and for each $p \in X \cup Y$, $\mathbf{Proposition}(p)$, and*
   (a) for each $p \in X$ there is a $q \in Y$ such that $NegationOf(p,q)$, and
   (b) for each $q \in Y$ there is a $p \in X$ such that $NegationOf(p,q)$
   then: $NegationOf(\bigwedge X, \bigvee Y)$

Note that we now have two negation-like notions around: the *NegOf* operations on SOAs and the relation *NegationOf* on propositions. The latter is dependent on the former, since for atomic propositions the relation NegationOf is defined on the basis of *NegOf*. This leads to a negation operation on propositions that is classical in the respect that, for atomic propositions at least, $\neg\neg p$ is identical to p. However, in contrast to most work in ST, the space of propositions that emerges is not quite classical, since it will not in general be the case that:

(99)   p is true iff $\neg p$ is false

Rather, we only have the weaker:

(100)   a. If p is true, then $\neg p$ is false.
         b. If $\neg p$ is true, then p is false.

---

[79]Given that possibilities are constructed from propositions, any expansion of the universe that results in additional propositions will 'trigger' a concomitant expansion of the sort **Possibility***.

[80]This definition is closely modeled on definitions 3.16 and 3.17 in S&M–97.

We believe that this deviation from standard ST practice is required if, as we suggest later, questions are taken to be proposition abstracts. This is required empirically both for an adequate definition of answerhood and for an account of the properties of polar questions.

3.4.6 Summary

In this section, we have provided a sketch of the semantic universe that underlies the grammar we develop in the following chapters. The semantic universe, technically a Situational Universe with Abstract Entities, is a λ-SITSTR with additional structural sorts. These sorts are used to explicate propositions, possibilities, outcomes, and in the next section, questions. Atomic propositions have as their defining components a situation and a SOA. An outcome has as its defining components a situation and a SOA abstract whose temporal argument is abstracted away. Possibilities, a subclass of which constitute the domain of facts, are built out of propositions. We have also sketched rudimentary notions of compounding and negation on the class of propositions.

3.5 Questions

What is a question? There have been dozens of answers to this question, motivated, for the most part, as attempts to explicate one or more of the following sets of phenomena.

Short Answers. One of the most obvious ways in which an interrogative use changes the context is to enable elliptical follow-ups (*short answers*): phrasal utterances used to respond to queries. The nature of the question asked strongly influences the semantic type, and to some extent, the form of the short answer. A polar question gives rise to short answer responses that can be a sentential modifier; a unary *wh*-question gives rise to a short answer whose semantic type matches that of the *wh*-phrase in the interrogative (*who*: animate NPs, *when*: temporal phrases, etc.); a multiple *wh*-question gives rise to a pair of phrases, each of which matches one *wh*-phrase in the interrogative and so forth.

(101) a. A: Did Bo attend the meeting?
           B: Yes./Maybe./Probably.
       b. A: Who attended the meeting?
           B: Mo/No students./A friend of Jo's.
       c. A: When did Bo leave?
           B: Yesterday./At two.
       d. A: Who was interacting with whom at the party?
           B: Bo with Mo./Some of my friends with each of her friends.
       e. A: Why did Carrie cross the road?
           B: Because she thought no cars were passing.

Resolvedness/Exhaustivity. In section 3.2, we discussed the fact that an interrogative complement embedded by a factive predicate supplies that predicate with an argument that is (pretheoretically) an answer resolving the question denoted by the complement. An inference pattern illustrating this is given in (102a).[81] Such an answer is commonly also referred to as *exhaustive*. In what follows, we will reserve the term 'exhaustive' as a technical term (to be defined below), using 'resolving' as the pretheoretical notion. An important task for any theory of questions is to characterize this answerhood relation. One needs to explain why the second utterances in (102b,c) are typically intuited to constitute facts that resolve the questions *whether Terry left*

---

[81]Note that the inference also goes in the other direction: (102a(iii)) entails (102a(i)) and (102a(ii)).

and *who will help the President* respectively, whereas the responses in (102d,e) are examples of facts that would not usually be taken to resolve these questions:

(102) a. (i) I know/discovered a particular fact.
   (ii) This fact resolves the question whether Terry left/of who will help the President.
   Therefore, (iii) I know/discovered whether Terry left/who will help the President.

   b. Bo knows/discovered whether Terry left.
   Terry did (didn't) leave.
   Therefore, Bo knows/discovered that Terry did (didn't) leave.

   c. Sandy: Who will help the President?
   Jackie: His close friends./Bo Derek and Bo Diddley./A number of high powered lawyers.
   Jackie indicated to Sandy who would help the President.

   d. Lee: Did Terry leave?
   Chris: It's not very likely.
   Chris did not actually indicate whether Terry left.

   e. Whitney: Who will help the President?
   Kim: Few people that the two of us know.
   Kim couldn't quite tell Whitney who would help the President.

Aboutness. Many factors go into characterizing the full range of options available to someone responding to a query. Particularly complex is the matter of figuring out what an optimal response might be. Nonetheless, even someone who is not clued in to either the querier's goals or to her belief/knowledge state can distinguish a certain class of propositions that are, quite independently of their truth or specificity relative to current purposes, intimately related to the specific question posed, call it q_0. This class consists of those propositions characterizable as providing information ABOUT or CONCERNING q_0. The aboutness criterion is illustrated in (103) and (104)

(103) a. Jo: When is the train leaving?
   Carrie: At 2:58, 17.333398 seconds, according to our caesium clock./At 2:58./In about an hour./In a short while.
   Carrie provided information (whose accuracy I will not vouch for) about when the train is leaving.

   b. Chris: Did Merle leave?
   Kim: Yes./Probably./It's not likely./No.
   Kim provided information (whose accuracy I will not vouch for) about whether Merle left.

   c. Sandy: Who will help the President?
   Tracy: His close friends./Few people we know./Merle Africa or Merle Haggard.
   Tracy provided information (whose accuracy I will not vouch for) about who will help the President.

(104) a. Jo: When is the train leaving?
   Lee: I don't have a clue./We should be informed of this quite soon./Why do you ask?/Go talk to that guard over there; she'll put you on it.
   Lee responded to the question, but could/did not provide any information about when the train is leaving.

These examples also show that the 'aboutness' answerhood relation is a less restrictive condition than the 'resolving' answerhood relation. Thus, responses that provide information that are neither useful nor even factual can sometimes be described as being 'about' the question, as long as their subject matter is appropriate. Conversely, many felicitous responses, even helpful ones, cannot be described as providing information 'about' the question, even if they can be described as suggesting how to obtain information about the question.

3.5.1 Questions as Exhaustivity Encoders

In this section, we compare two ways of conceptualizing what questions are. The first derives from a common intuition, triggered in part by short answer phenomena, that a question is somehow akin to an open proposition.[82] Making sense of this basic intuition has proved remarkably difficult within standard semantic ontologies. In opposition to this first approach lies an approach (motivated primarily by exhaustivity phenomena) that seeks to explain questions as semantic entities that encode Exhaustive Answerhood Conditions (EAC). This approach was originally pioneered by Åqvist and Hintikka, whose accounts did not include an ontological distinction between questions and propositions. The approach has been most influential through the proposals of Hamblin (1958, 1973), Karttunen (1977) and Groenendijk and Stokhof (1984, 1997).

These latter proposals explicitly develop a distinction between questions and propositions. Questions are specified as properties of propositions; concretely, the property of being the *exhaustive answer* to the question. It is probably true to say that this latter explication is the most widely accepted in contemporary formal semantics. The popularity of the EAC view notwithstanding, we will show that the semantic setup described in the previous sections provides a formally explicit and conceptually viable version of the 'questions as open propositions' view, one that is, we will argue, conceptually simpler, and empirically superior to the EAC alternative. In this section we focus on some problematic aspects of the EAC view. In the following section, we provide our own explication of what questions are.

EAC Basics

In order to make the discussion concrete, we start with a brief survey of the EAC view as formulated by Groenendijk and Stokhof (Gr & St). Two key assumptions are the following:

(105) a. **Semantic absoluteness of embedded answerhood:** Resolving answerhood conditions can be characterized in purely semantic terms, rather than as also involving complex 'pragmatic' factors that depend heavily on context.

  b. **Aboutness is reducible to resolvedness:** the notion of answerhood relevant to query uses is derivative, and can be deduced from or explained in terms of the notion of answerhood associated with clauses embedded by factive/resolutive predicates.

To this one should add a specific empirical claim:[83]

(106) A fact f resolves a question q iff f is an *exhaustive answer* to q:

  a. For a polar interrogative $p?$: f entails p if p is true; otherwise f entails $\neg p$

  b. For a *wh*-interrogative *who* $\mathbf{V}s$: f entails *whether* $a_1\mathbf{V}s$ for all a_1 in the relevant domain.

---

[82] See Jespersen 1965 and Cohen 1929 for early statements of such a view.

[83] Karttunen argues for a somewhat different characterization of *wh*-interrogatives. But his approach is equally committed to there being a simple semantic formula for calculating exhaustiveness.

Given the assumptions in (105) and in (106), Gr & St's theory is simple and elegant: the extension of an interrogative is identified with the exhaustive answer. Hence, the intension of an interrogative is that function which maps a world to the proposition that constitutes the exhaustive answer in that world. Within a possible worlds semantics, the picture that emerges is this: the extension of an interrogative at w is a set of worlds, those that determine the extension of the queried property equivalently. The intension of the interrogative is the partition of the set of possible worlds induced by this equivalence relation.

(107) a. whether Morgan likes Bo.

   Extension at i: $\lambda j.[like(m, b)(j) = like(m, b)(i)]$
   (All worlds j that agree with respect to the truth value of $like((m, b)$ at i.)
   Intension: $\lambda i.\lambda j.[like(m, b)(j) = like(m, b)(i)]$

   b. who likes Bo. Assumed paraphrasable as: for all x whether x likes b.

   Extension at i: $\lambda j.[\lambda x.like(x, b)(j) = \lambda x.like(x, b)(i)]$
   (All worlds j that agree with respect to the extension of $like(x, b)$ at i.)
   Intension: $\lambda i.\lambda j.[\lambda x.like(x, b)(j) = \lambda x.like(x, b)(i)]$

Gr & St assume that the notion of answerhood relevant for querying (*partial answerhood*) is derivative from exhaustive-answerhood: a 'partial answer' is a disjunction of some, but not all possible exhaustive answers defined by the question. In terms of partitions, it is a proposition that eliminates at least one partition from further consideration as an exhaustive answer.

Exhaustivity

The simplicity of the EAC view is also the source of its theoretical vulnerability. This weakness derives from the fact that a question is identified with a semantic object primarily on the basis of one essential class of phenomena associated with interrogatives, namely the semantic properties of interrogatives embedded by factive and resolutive predicates. The attractiveness of the strategy depends on two assumptions: (1) that resolutive embedding is purely referential, and (2) that resolving answerhood can be characterized in purely semantic terms, as mentioned previously.

If factives/resolutives embedded interrogative complements purely referentially, this would provide some evidence identifying the semantic object which is posed in a query—a question— with an object that encodes exhaustive answerhood conditions. However, as we saw in section 3.2.1, this assumption is false. The issue of the semantic nature of resolvedness is complex. There have been a number of works arguing forcefully that the resolving answerhood conditions for many types of interrogatives cannot be reduced to the simple semantic formula assumed by Hintikka, Karttunen, and Groenendijk and Stokhof. This class of interrogatives includes:

- *who is I*: Boër and Lycan (1985) discuss examples like (108a,b):

   (108) a. Who is that man?

      b. Bertie knows who Quine is. (Boër and Lycan 1985: 96, example (11))

   It is clear that the answer specified by (108b) cannot be characterized in terms akin to (106) above, i.e. as an answer that entails for each possible property P, whether or not Quine has P. Without knowledge of the background surrounding a statement like (108b) (Is Bertie a professional philsopher, an undergraduate, or a newspaper vendor?), it is virtually impossible to predict the nature of the answer Bertie knows.

- *why S*: Bromberger (1992) and Ginzburg (1995a) discuss examples like (109):

(109) a. Why is there something rather than nothing? (M. Heidegger)

  b. Why has there never been a President of the United States named Clovis? (Bromberger 1992: 92)

  c. We have been told why he is writing this paper. (Ginzburg 1995a)

- *where S*: Ginzburg (1995a) discusses examples like (110a) and shows that whether (110b) is judged to be exhaustive varies with context:

(110) a. Jo knows where she is.

  b. Jo is in Helsinki. (resolving: Jo about to step off a plane in Helsinki; non-resolving: Jo steps out of a taxi in Helsinki.)

- *how S*: Hintikka (1976) and Asher and Lascarides (1998) discuss examples such as (111):

(111)   Jo knows how to get from London to Oxford.

Here, as Hintikka points out, a proposition that provides a single route can be resolving. As Asher and Lascarides point out, however, this is not simply an ambiguity. In certain contexts (Jo is a travel guide, say), a resolving answer must be exhaustive, providing every single route, as well as indicating which routes to avoid.

In all these cases there are a multiplicity of possible resolving answers. Moreover, audience background and interests seem crucially involved in determining which ones are resolving answers appropriate for a given context.

In fact, Ginzburg and, more circumspectly, Asher and Lascarides suggest that this pragmatic indeterminacy extends to interrogatives in general. Ginzburg discusses examples such as (112) and suggests that any of (112b-d) can constitute resolving answers reportable as (112e):

(112) a. Who attended the lecture?

  b. Bo: A number of important Swan and Ubikh specialists along with their students.

  c. Bo: A mix of the old and new generation from among the local researchers

  d. Bo: Gia, Leila, Zurab, Nino, . . .

  e. Bo revealed who attended the lecture.

Which of these would qualify as a resolving answer in a particular context requires reference to highly particularized details about the context and the conversationalists' background knowledge, interests and the like.

For the sake of the argument, let us momentarily assume that a purely semantic notion of exhaustiveness does provide an adequate characterization of the resolvedness conditions of regular *who*-interrogatives. It still remains the case that there is no straightforward general semantic characterization of the resolvedness conditions of a large class of interrogatives (including *who is P-*, *when-*, *where-*, *how-*, and *why*-interrogatives). For these, one needs an account that is relativized to unquestionably pragmatic or agent-specific parameters such as goals and background beliefs. Thus, the EAC strategy offers at best an insufficiently general account of resolvednessness conditions. Consequently, it cannot provide a general account of what a question is.

To summarize, the EAC approach treats the content of an interrogative as an entity intended to fix the resolvedness conditions of a question. Given what we have seen about these, the EAC approach amounts to positing a *semantic* denotation whose value—for at least a significant number of cases—is only fixed relative to unquestionably *pragmatic*, agent-specific parameters. Such a strategy raises some significant methodological questions, which at present remain unanswered. For instance, how does one talk about questions in a way that is independent of the existence of agents? How do agents share questions? Other things being equal, a semantic ontology which does not require answers to such questions would be preferable.

Polar Interrogatives

So far we have suggested that the basic motivation for the EAC approach is flawed. We now point to two additional problems. The first concerns identity conditions of polar interrogatives; the second involves the aboutness conditions specified by interrogatives.

In approaches where questions are characterized in terms of exhaustive answerhood conditions, it follows that when two interrogatives carry the same exhaustive answerhood conditions, the questions they denote must be regarded as identical. This predicts that positive and negative polar interrogatives such as (113a,b) are deemed to have the same content:

(113) a. whether Morgan likes Bo.
   Extension at i: $\lambda j.[like(m,b)(j) = like(m,b)(i)]$
   (All worlds j that agree with respect to the truth value of $like(m,b)$ at i.)
   Intension: $\lambda i.\lambda j.[like(m,b)(j) = like(m,b)(i)]$

   b. whether Morgan doesn't like Bo.
   Extension at i: $\lambda j.[\neg like(m,b)(j) = \neg like(m,b)(i)]$
   (All worlds j that agree with respect to the truth value of $\neg like(m,b)$ at i.)
   Intension: $\lambda i.\lambda j.[\neg like(m,b)(j) = \neg like(m,b)(i)]$

Let us call this hypothesis Negative-Positive Interrogative Synonymy (NPIS). NPIS initially appears unproblematic, perhaps even a favorable consequence as far as interrogatives embedded by resolutives go, since it predicts that (114a,b) have identical truth conditions:

(114) a. Ronnie knows whether Morgan likes Bo.

   b. Ronnie knows whether Morgan does not like Bo.

But there are phenomena which suggest that any such identification is problematic. Przepiórkowski (1999) points out that, contrary to the claims that are standardly made, negative interrogatives can trigger negated answers:

(115) a. A: I wonder whether Sanca really didn't get married ...
      B: Yes, she didn't. (Przepiórkowski's (4.7))

   b. A: I wonder whether Sanca really got married ...
      B: #Yes, she didn't. (Przepiórkowski's (4.7))

   c. A: I suppose Mo DIDN'T go to the store.
      B: Yes, she didn't. (Przepiórkowski's (4.8))

   d. A: I suppose Mo went to the store.
      B: #Yes, she didn't. (Przepiórkowski's (4.8))

We can strengthen these observations with further data involving intonation questions. These provide further support for the claim that negation need not be neutralized in polar interrogatives. An example like (116a) is well paraphrased by (116c) and (116d), but far less successfully by (116e) and (116f), where the content of latter examples is a positive polar:

(116) a. A: In the end Kim and Sandy didn't leave yesterday?
       b. B: Right, (they're still here.)
       c. A asked whether Kim and Sandy had actually not left.
       d. A checked if Kim and Sandy had not in the end left.
       e. ?A asked if Kim and Sandy left.
       f. ??A checked if Kim and Sandy had in the end left. (? marks inaccurate paraphrase)

It is also worth noting that the common belief underlying NPIS—that the response patterns triggered by the two types of polars are identical—ignores a small but important fact. In a language like modern English, which lacks a word like *si/doch*, responding *tout court* with *yes* frequently results in ambiguity. This is illustrated by the following dialogue, whose initial query is a negative polar question, expressed either as an interrogative sentence or by means of an intonation question:

(117) A: She's not annoyed?/Isn't she annoyed?
       B: Yes.
       A: She is or she isn't annoyed?

The essence of our account of this phenomenon, further articulated in Chapter 8, is simply this: the semantics we provide associates distinct contents for positive and negative polars. However, the answerhood relations we posit will turn out to yield identical exhaustive answers for p? and $\neg p$?. These basic facts will allow us to develop an account that can distinguish the contexts created by uses of p? and $\neg p$?, while at the same time capturing the identity of truth conditions associated with pairs like (114a,b).

Aboutness

An additional problem we mention here concerns aboutness. Ginzburg (1995a) shows in detail that both Karttunen's and Gr & St's accounts underdetermine the notion of aboutness needed to explain coherence intuitions in querying. Consider first polar interrogatives. Propositions such as the one expressed by the responder in (118), although frequently not fully satisfying the goal which leads to asking the question, seem to be entirely coherent responses, i.e. they seem to constitute information about the question.

(118) Pat: Is Dominique leaving tomorrow?
      Stevie: Possibly/It's unlikely

Responses like these represent information that any competent speaker of the language associates with the question in virtue of their knowledge of meaning.[84]

However, Gr & St's system does not recognize such information as answers to the question, partial or otherwise. The reason for this is that a partial answer needs to eliminate at least one partition. However, since a polar question consists of only two partition blocks (propositions entailing p and propositions entailing $\neg p$), the only answers which can eliminate partitions are exhaustive answers. That is, the prediction of Gr & St's system is that no partial answers exist, contrary to (118).

---

[84]Although Stevie's response in (118) is really rather UNUSEFUL, responses such as (i) and (ii) have similar modal force, but could be quite useful—despite the fact that they entail neither 'yes' nor 'no':

  (i) If she finds her rail ticket in time.
  (ii) Only if she manages to write the two remaining sections of her paper.

For a *wh*-interrogative, partial answerhood is a richer notion than exhaustive answerhood. Thus, for an interrogative like *who left*, a Gr & St partial answer will have a form paraphrasable as:[85]

(119) $p =$ No one left or only Leslie left or only Leslie and Chris left or ... or only Leslie and Chris and Tracy left or ...

This means that only one type of answer can be accommodated, namely 'exhaustified' answers:

(120) a. 'Only several firemen left' $\leftrightarrow$ The (set of) leavers consisted of several firemen (and no one else).
   b. 'Only few journalists left' $\leftrightarrow$ The (set of) leavers consisted of few journalists (and no one else). (That is, either no one left or the ones who left were journalists and few.)
   c. 'Only every student left' $\leftrightarrow$ The (set of) leavers consisted of every student (and no one else).

What this notion of partial answer fails to accommodate is non-exhaustified information about the question that need not be construed as in (120a,b). But non-exhaustified partial answers certainly exist, as shown in (121):

(121) Q: Who left?
       A: (All I know is that) several firemen left/few journalists left.

A Computational Argument

Bos and Gabsdil (2000) point out a computational problem for an EAC approach such as Gr & St's that seriously threatens its construal in cognitive terms. A natural way of computationally implementing the partition view of questions is to identify a partition with a set of sets of first order formulas, where each set of formulas represents a propositional condition characteristic of a single block of the partition. For a unary *wh*-question and a domain of size n, there will be 2^n partition blocks. In the general case this means that partitions are intractably big, unless for some reason the domain happens to be very small.

Summary

Let us briefly review our claims concerning the EAC approach to questions. We have argued that the motivation for identifying a question—the semantic object associated with the attitude of wondering and the speech act of asking—with an entity that encodes exhaustive answerhood conditions is flawed. We have shown that, in fact, most classes of interrogatives clearly resist an analysis of their resolving answerhood conditions in the purely semantic terms assumed by EAC approaches.

We have noted further empirical problems facing such approaches:

1. An EAC analysis presupposes a notion of answerhood that mischaracterizes intuitions about coherence of responses to queries.
2. Despite the existence of data to the contrary, an EAC analysis depends on the assumption that positive and negative polar interrogatives are synonymous.
3. At least on one construal, the EAC analysis is problematic from a computational point of view.

We now show that an older and more basic intuition about what questions are avoids such prob-

---

[85] In other words, such an answer is a disjunction of one or more exhaustive answers.

lems, without in any way forgoing an adequate characterization of notions related to answer-hood—including the conditions under which an answer is resolving.

3.5.2 Questions as Propositional Abstracts

The view of questions as akin to open propositions has frequently been put forward. However, given certain technical and conceptual problems it faces, it has not been influential among semanticists. One obvious issue is how to construe the notion of 'open proposition'. There seem to be two main options. The first option, let us call it the Uninstantiated Variable (UV) view, is to construe an open proposition in a fairly literal minded spirit as a structured object that contains variable-like objects which are uninstantiated.[86] One obvious problem for such an approach are embedded uses of interrogatives, such as (122):

(122)   Bo knows who left.

The content associated with the entire sentence needs to be a proposition. However, the prediction of the UV view is that it is a question, since the variables associated with the embedded interrogative remain unbound.

A second issue which has typically remained unexplored within UV proposals is the fate of polar interrogatives. The most obvious proposal would be to say that polar interrogatives constitute the limiting case where the number of uninstantiated variables is 0. But this involves identifying polar questions with the queried proposition, which is untenable, as we mentioned above in our discussion of the Frege-Searle propositional content hypothesis.

A second strategy for implementing the open proposition approach, which has been widely explored, is to abstract over the variables rather than keep them uninstantiated. (See, for example, Keenan and Hull 1973, Hull 1975, Hausser 1983, and Hausser and Zaefferer 1979.) This strategy seemed crucially flawed when viewed from an early 1980s Montagovian perspective as emphasized by Groenendijk and Stokhof (1984, 1989). Within a type theory such as Montague's intensional logic, the type of any two interrogatives differing in r-ity (e.g. unary/binary/ternary *wh*-interrogative-sentences) or in the type of argument (e.g. adverbial vs. argumental *wh*-phrase) is distinct. This contradicts a popular methodological constraint stating that a given syntactic category should map onto a single semantic type. In addition, there is a related empirical problem concerning coordination: how does one interpret a coordinate structure consisting of conjuncts of distinct semantic type? To these problems, which are actually surmountable, one can add a third—one of ontology. Questions seem quite incontrovertibly distinct entities from relations:

(123)   a.   The question is who is happy—This question is unresolved.
                #The property of being happy is unresolved.
                #To be happy is unresolved.

        b.   Can you tell me something about who is happy? $\not\Rightarrow$ Can you tell me something about being happy.

        c.   Some man is happy.
                So we know that happiness and manfulness are not incompatible.
                #So we know that the question of who is happy and who is a man are not incompatible.

---

[86]For a recent proposal that adopts such a strategy, see Kempson et al. 2000. The UV theorist is not forced to take a structured object perspective. One could construe such an object as the set of all its instantiations, like open formulas are treated in first order logic.

    d. A: What was Bill yesterday?

        B: Happy.

        B: #The question of who is happy.

    e.   Bill and Phil are almost identical: the only property Bill has that Phil doesn't is happiness.

        #The only question Bill has that Phil doesn't is who is happy.

A final problem concerns answerhood. If one views a question as an abstract of some kind, then it does not encode in any direct way a notion of exhaustiveness. Neither does the set of substitution-instances of an abstract come close to providing an adequate characterization of the notion of aboutness—the range of propositions coherently connected to a question.

Within the universe that we have built up, however, there are solutions to all four problems: characterizing the semantic distinctness of polar interrogatives and propositions, maintaining the uniform type hypothesis, allowing for the ontological distinctness of questions and relations, and explicating answerhood. Let us start with the ontological problem. Within ST, as mentioned above, SOA abstracts are treated as relations. Paired with an appropriate assignment, a SOA abstract yields a SOA. Crucially, our ontology provides a sharp distinction between propositions and SOAs. Consequently, within our system, propositional abstracts are ontologically distinct from SOA abstracts, and more generally from relations. Consequently, no ontological objection stands in the way of our identifying questions with proposition abstracts.[87] We will see in Chapter 7 that the assumption that questions are abstracts over propositions, as opposed to facts or outcomes, makes some interesting predictions about the construal of in-situ *wh*-phrases in English.

It is worth emphasizing that within the basic approach to semantic modeling adopted here, even if there are strong links tying questions to propositional abstracts, one could forgo identifying the two, and merely view the former as structurally determined by the latter. However, in the absence of strong reasons to the contrary, given the considerable simplification that results, we will proceed to identify questions with the class of proposition abstracts. Although this could not be done uniformly in Montague's intensional logic, we can offer the following simple characterization in terms of simultaneous abstraction:[88]

Definition 9 Questionhood

Given an SU+AE $\mathcal{S}$: **Question**(q) *iff there exist a set* B, $B \subset |\mathcal{S}|$, $p, c \in |\mathcal{S}|$, *and a function* $\pi : B \to |\mathcal{S}|$ *such that:*

1. *For each* $b \in B$: **PlaceHolder**(c, b).
2. **Abst**(c, q).
3. $q\{\pi\} = p$.
4. **Proposition**(p).

In such a case, we say that p *is a* propositional instantiation *of* q *(denoted as:* $PropInst(p, q)$*).*

---

[87]In the ST literature there have been proposals to utilize proposition abstracts to explicate (non-interrogative) quantification. Both Gawron and Peters (1990) and Cooper (1996) have proposed that determiners be analyzed as denoting relations between proposition abstracts and SOA abstracts (that is, as relations). However, as we will see in Chapter 4, the purpose intended for propositional abstracts by Gawron and Peters and by Cooper—essentially to encode domain selection—is achieved equally well by using FACT ABSTRACTS.

[88]Note though that this definition does not mean that we are postulating **Question** as an additional structural relation. Rather, it constitutes a 'derivative' notion: since we explicate questions as propositional abstracts and SU+AEs are required to be λ-structures, any SU+AE will necessarily contains the class of questions. We, nonetheless, use boldface for the relation 'Question', since it is defined in terms of the structural relations **Abst** and **Proposition**.

Ginzburg (1992), in a related proposal, shows ways to define coordination operations simultaneously for questions and propositions. Definition 10 for conjunction is based on the definition for type conjunction in Cooper 1993. Note that the definition makes sense because we assume the existence of a meet operation on propositions and that the SU+AE is a λ-structure. An entirely analogous definition can be given for disjunction:

Definition 10 A Conjunction Operation for Questions

Given a question q_1 (= $\lambda A.\sigma$) and a question q_2 (= $\lambda B.\tau$), where $A \cap B = \emptyset$:[89]

$$\bigwedge(\lambda A.\sigma, \lambda B.\tau) =_{def} \lambda A \cup B. \bigwedge\{\sigma, \tau\}$$

The coordination of interrogatives is a fertile area with various interesting puzzles that we cannot enter into here. Probably the most fundamental of these is the question of how to provide a definition that uniformly applies to propositions and questions. In this respect, the simplicity of the account provided here is interesting to compare with the complicated regime of type shifting required by an EAC account, as demonstrated in detail in Groenendijk and Stokhof 1989.[90]

What of polar questions? We will treat these as propositional abstracts where the set of abstracted elements is the empty set. Given our assumption that the semantic universe is a λ-universe, it follows that such abstracts exist. In general, given our assumptions about the abstraction operation, it follows that an abstract is distinct from its body. This holds also for 0-ary abstracts, as we remarked in section 82. Therefore, in particular, a polar question is distinct from a proposition.

The constraints we posit below will associate:[91]

(124) a. a use of *Did Bo scream* with the propositional abstract
    $\lambda\{\ \}\mathsf{prop}(s, \langle\langle \text{Scream; screamer: } b\rangle\rangle)$

   b. a use of *Who left?* with the propositional abstract
    $\lambda\{b\}\mathsf{prop}(s, \langle\langle \text{Leave; leaver: } b\rangle\rangle)$

   c. a use of *Who annoyed whom?* with the propositional abstract
    $\lambda\{b,a\}\mathsf{prop}(s, \langle\langle \text{Annoy;annoyance: } b, \text{annoyed: } a\rangle\rangle)$

3.5.3 Notions of Answerhood

In the previous section, we addressed three of the problems faced by an 'open proposition' approach to questions. We turn now to the most fundamental issue for any theory of questions, namely answerhood. When thinking about answerhood, we move away from the assumption that there is a unique answerhood relation that a question needs to encode. Rather, we take the strategy, initiated by Ginzburg (1995a), of viewing answerhood as any of a variety of propositional

---

[89]Given that the notion of abstraction we employ respects α-equivalence, it is unproblematic to ensure that this assumption is satisfied.

[90]Recall that the object which constitutes a question in their theory is a partition on the set of possible worlds—type $<< s,t >, t >$ in Montagovian terms. Generalized conjunction applied to a partition yields a new, more refined partition. Hence, conjunction applies smoothly to interrogatives to yield a conjoined question. However, generalized disjunction does not, in general, yield as output a partition. Thus, in order to accommodate disjunction Groenendijk and Stokhof are required to posit that this takes place at a higher type, essentially the type of sets of partitions. The consequence of this is, for instance, that within Groenendijk and Stokhof's system a verb like *know* can be specified to be of type $<< s,t >, < e,t >>$ for embedded atomic interrogatives and embedded conjunctive interrogatives, but needs to be type lifted to type $<<<< s,t >,t >,t >, < e,t >>$ to deal with embedded disjoined interrogatives.

[91]This is actually still an approximation that abstracts away from the issue of the 'restrictor information' introduced by *wh*-phrases, a matter we return to in Chapter 4.

properties that can be defined in terms of the question and the semantic structure provided by the universe. Given this, our simple view of what questions are will provide the basis for a rich theory of answerhood that is not constrained by the assumption that one particular notion of answerhood is primary.

Here we consider three notions of answerhood. First, we show how to reconstruct the notion of *strong exhaustiveness*, which is Groenendijk and Stokhof's characterization of the exhaustive answerhood conditions of a question. The emerging notion benefits, we believe, from the partiality that our semantic universe provides. We then show how to define a more inclusive and contextually relativized notion of resolvedness. Finally, we offer a proposal for what *aboutness* amounts to. This constitutes the weakest, i.e. most inclusive notion of answerhood, required in order to characterize the range of coherent, 'direct' responses to a query.

Strong Exhaustiveness

In order to define the various notions of answerhood, we first introduce two auxiliary notions: *atomic answer* and *simple answer*. A proposition p is an atomic answer to q if it is either an instantiation of q or a conjunct of such an instantiation. A proposition p is a simple answer to q if it is either an atomic answer or a negation of such an answer:

Definition 11 Atomic and Simple Answerhood

    a. $AtomAns(p, q)$ *iff* $\exists r[ConjOf(p, r)$ and $PropInst(r, q)]$

    b. $NegAtomAns(p, q)$ *iff* $\exists r[r = \neg p$ and $AtomAns(r, q)]$

    c. $SimpleAns(p, q)$ *iff* $AtomAns(p, q)$ or $NegAtomAns(r, q)$

    With these notions in hand, we can define the *strongly exhaustive answer* as the meet of the set of true, simple answers:

Definition 12 Strong Exhaustiveness

$StrongExhAns(f, q)$ *iff* $f = \bigwedge\{p \mid True(p)$ and $SimpleAns(p, q)\}$

In order for this definition to make sense, the set of true, simple answers needs to be nonempty. We call a question for which this is the case *decided*:

Definition 13 Decidedness Conditions for a Question

    A question q is decided iff $\{p \mid True(p)$ and $SimpleAns(p, q)\} \neq \emptyset$

    One difference between the semantic setting in which our semantic theory is formulated and possible worlds theory is that in our account, not all questions are decided.[92] When we discuss the embedding of interrogatives by factive/resolutive predicates in Chapter 8, we suggest that such predicates introduce a presupposition that the requisite question is decided. This is why in such cases the exhaustive answer is well-defined and can serve as an argument to the predicate.

    Let us now consider some examples. For a polar question, the strongly exhaustive answer is whichever polar answer is true:

(125) a. $q = \lambda\{\}\mathsf{prop}(s, \langle\langle\text{Tall};m\rangle\rangle)$ (*whether Mo is tall*)

        b. $AtomAns(p_0, q)$ iff $p_0 = \mathsf{prop}(s, \langle\langle\text{Tall};m\rangle\rangle)$

        c. If $True(p_0)$, then $StrongExhAns(f, q)$ iff $f = \bigwedge\{p_0\} = p_0$;

           If $True(\neg p_0)$, then $StrongExhAns(f, q)$ iff $f = \bigwedge\{\neg p_0\} = \neg p_0$

        d. q is decided iff either $True(p_0)$ or $True(\neg p_0)$.

---

[92]This is because it is possible that for some proposition p, neither p nor its negation $\neg p$ is true.

Let us consider now a conjunction of polar questions. The strongly exhaustive answer is simply the conjunction of the strongly exhaustive answers to each question:

(126) a. $q_1 = \lambda\{\ \}\mathsf{prop}(s_0, \langle\langle\text{Tall};\text{b}\rangle\rangle)$ (*whether Bo is tall*)

b. $q_2 = \lambda\{\ \}\mathsf{prop}(s_1, \langle\langle\text{Hungry};\text{k}\rangle\rangle)$ (*whether Kim is hungry*)

c. $q = \bigwedge\{q_1, q_2\} =$ (by definition 10)
$\lambda\{\ \}\bigwedge\{\mathsf{prop}(s_0, \langle\langle\text{Tall};\text{b}\rangle\rangle), \mathsf{prop}(s_1, \langle\langle\text{Hungry};\text{k}\rangle\rangle)\}$

d. $\{p \mid AtomAns(p, q)\} = \{\mathsf{prop}(s_0, \langle\langle\text{Tall};\text{b}\rangle\rangle), \mathsf{prop}(s_1, \langle\langle\text{Hungry};\text{k}\rangle\rangle)\}$

e. $StrongExhAns(f, q)$ iff $f = \bigwedge\{p \mid True(p)$ and $[p = \mathsf{prop}(s_0, \langle\langle\text{Tall};\text{b}\rangle\rangle)$ or $p = \mathsf{prop}(s_0, \overline{\langle\langle\text{Tall};\text{b}\rangle\rangle})$ or $p = \mathsf{prop}(s_1, \langle\langle\text{Hungry};\text{k}\rangle\rangle)$ or $p = \mathsf{prop}(s_1, \overline{\langle\langle\text{Hungry};\text{k}\rangle\rangle})]\}$

For a *wh*-question, the strongly exhaustive answer involves conjoining the true atomic answers—instantiations of the propositional abstract, if any such exist—along with those negations of instantiations of the propositional abstract that are true.

(127) a. $q_1 = \lambda\{\text{b}\}\mathsf{prop}(s_0, \langle\langle\text{Available};\text{b}\rangle\rangle)$ (*who is available*)

b. $AtomAns(p_0, q_1)$ iff $\exists a[p_0 = \mathsf{prop}(s_0, \langle\langle\text{Available};\text{a}\rangle\rangle)]$

c. $StrongExhAns(f, q)$ iff $f = \bigwedge(\{p \mid True(p)$ and $\exists a[p = \mathsf{prop}(s_0, \langle\langle\text{Available};\text{a}\rangle\rangle)$ or $p = \mathsf{prop}(s_0, \overline{\langle\langle\text{Available};\text{a}\rangle\rangle})]\})$

This characterization of strong exhaustiveness makes a subtle but important point concerning negative answers. Due to partiality, viz. the fact that p being false does not make $\neg p$ true, the negative answers that are conjuncts of the exhaustive answer are true propositions of the form $\mathsf{prop}(s, \overline{\langle\langle Available; a\rangle\rangle})$. In section 3.3.2, we outlined the ST assumptions about when $\overline{\langle\langle Available; a\rangle\rangle}$ is supported by a given situation. This holds just in case s carries positive information indicating that a fails to be available and also that he might be expected to be available. Thus, in our account, the strongly exhaustive answer to a *wh*-question such as *who is available* combines positive information about individuals, concerning those individuals that the situation indicates are available, with a limited amount of negative information, concerning those individuals whose unavailability is explicitly indicated in the situation. This is a useful refinement of Groenendijk and Stokhof's notion of strong exhaustiveness, which is a proposition entailing information about every individual in the world, detailing whether or not they manifest the property at issue.[93]

Finally, an example of conjoining a *wh*-question and a polar question. The strongly exhaustive answer is once again simply the conjunction of the strongly exhaustive answers to each question:

---

[93] As far as *wh*-questions are concerned, our account as it stands is incomplete. We have not as yet incorporated any notion of domain selection—or any other restrictions on the roles abstracted away beyond those that come from the relation. This means that our answerhood notions will be too inclusive: in (127), for instance, any proposition whatever of the form $\mathsf{prop}(s_0, \langle\langle Available; x\rangle\rangle)$ counts as an atomic answer. In general, given that s_0 is a situation, and therefore, in principle, a partial entity, only a limited number of such propositions and their negations will come out as true. Hence, for an answerhood notion which is based on true answers—such as exhaustiveness—domain selection is relatively unproblematic. However, with respect to other notions of answerhood, such as *aboutness*, where truth does not come into the picture, domain selection is crucial in limiting the answerhood space. The necessary refinement will be introduced in Chapter 4.

(128) a. $q_1 = \lambda\{b\}\text{prop}(s_0, \langle\langle\text{Tall};b\rangle\rangle)$ (*who is tall*);

   $q_2 = \lambda\{\}\text{prop}(s_1, \langle\langle\text{Hungry};k\rangle\rangle)$ (*whether Kim is hungry*);

   $q = \bigwedge\{q_1, q_2\}$

   b. $\{p \mid AtomAns(p, q)\} =$

   $\{p \mid \exists a[p_1 = \text{prop}(s_0, \langle\langle\text{Tall};a\rangle\rangle)\} \cup \{\text{prop}(s_1, \langle\langle\text{Hungry};k\rangle\rangle)\}$

   c. $StrongExhAns(f, q)$ iff

   $f = \bigwedge\{p \mid True(p) \text{ and } [\exists a[p = \text{prop}(s_0, \langle\langle\text{Tall};a\rangle\rangle) \text{ or } p = \text{prop}(s_0, \overline{\langle\langle\text{Tall};a\rangle\rangle})]$

   $\text{or } p = \text{prop}(s_1, \langle\langle\text{Hungry};k\rangle\rangle) \text{ or } p = \text{prop}(s_1, \overline{\langle\langle\text{Hungry};k\rangle\rangle})]\}$

Resolvedness

What we have seen so far in this section is that we can reconstruct the notion of strong exhaustiveness that underlies Groenendijk and Stokhof's semantics. We can adopt this as the fundamental
notion we use to specify the content of interrogatives embedded by factive/resolutive predicates.
Alternatively, in light of the data discussed in section 3.5.1, we can adopt a more inclusive and
pragmatically relativized notion of exhaustiveness—the notion of *resolvedness* introduced by
Ginzburg (1995a). On this view, the notion of *resolvedness* required for explicating the basic
inferential properties of interrogative factive complements is a relative notion: information resolves a given question relative to a goal and an attitudinal (belief/knowledge) state. That is, a
given question defines a class of propositions each of which is potentially resolving. Whether a
given member of this class, p, is actually a resolving answer in a given context depends on two
additional factors. The first is the goal g_0, which determines a lower bound for p. The second
factor is the information state, IS_0, which determines the resources relative to which p has g_0 as
a consequence.

   Devising a successful empirical characterization of potential resolvedness is tricky. For example, to say that an item of information τ is not potentially-resolving requires one to consider all
possible goal/belief-state combinations and to decide that in none of them would the information
provided by τ be deemed resolving. The difficulty involves only *wh*-questions, however, since it
seems clear that for polar questions, potential resolvedness reduces to strong exhaustiveness.

   We sketch here one characterization of potential resolvedness, that of Ginzburg (1995a), on
the basis of which we will be able to define resolvedness. The intuition is that a potentially resolving answer is one that either indicates that the question is positively resolved or alternatively
one that indicates that the question is negatively resolved. What does a question being positively
resolved amount to? For a polar question $\lambda\{\ \}p$, this amounts to entailing p; for a *wh*-question
$\lambda\{x\}p(x)$, this amounts to entailing that $\lambda\{x\}p(x)$ can be instantiated, and moreover providing some additional sortal information about the instantiator(s) that distinguishes it (them) from
other potential instantiators. This intuition can be traced back to Belnap (1982).[94] Examples of
positively resolving answers are given in (129b–e) and (130b–d). We claim that, given the right
pragmatic circumstances, these examples count as resolving the question, hence licensing utterances such as (129f) and (130e).

---

[94]"One appealing conjecture is that all and only existence-entailing (or presupposing) terms can be short answers to
what-questions [Here 'short answer' means roughly, in current terms, 'term that provides resolving information and can
be used to respond to a query use of the question'—J.G & I.A.S]. . . . Perhaps each term must be formed from a sortal in
the sense of Gupta 1974, together with an existence entailing (or presupposing) quantifier." (Belnap 1982: 196)

(129) a. [Aagje is about to give a talk in Odense.]
          Aagje: Who will show up for the talk?

      b. Bo: Arne Ness.

      c. Bo: Several senior Danish logicians.

      d. Bo: Either Ebbe Sand or Stig Tofting.

      e. Bo: Every student of Nielsen's.

      f. Bo explained to us who would show up for the talk.

(130) a. Leigh: When is the train leaving?

      b. Morgan: Within 20 minutes.

      c. Morgan: In a short while.

      d. Morgan: After the 16:24 shows up.

      e. Morgan indicated to us when the train would leave.

Note that these examples resolve the questions independently of whether the answers provided in (129) constitute exhaustive information.[95] Hence, this notion of potential resolvedness is a more inclusive notion than exhaustiveness—strong or otherwise. Note also that, according to this definition, answers like the one in (131) are not positively resolving, since they provide no sortal information beyond that already encoded in the question:[96]

(131) a. Morgan: Who will show up for the talk?
          Bo: Someone.

      b. Leigh: When is the train leaving?
          Morgan: At some time.

We now turn to negative resolvedness. For a polar question $\lambda\{\ \}p$, this amounts to entailing $\neg p$; for a *wh*-question $\lambda\{x\}p(x)$ this amounts to entailing that $\lambda\{x\}p(x)$ is uninstantiable:

(132) a. Aagje: Who will show up for the talk?
          Bo: No one, alas.

      b. Leigh: Why is the train delayed?
          Morgan: Apparently, for no reason.

The notion of potential resolvedness we have sketched here excludes propositions that are neither positively-resolving nor negatively-resolving, e.g. (133b–e). That is, the notion predicts that propositions would not license attitude reports such as (133f):

(133) a. A: Who will show up for the talk?

      b. B: Maybe Ebbe Sand.

      c. B: It's unlikely anyone will show up.

      d. B: Few people. No one with any knowledge of Category Theory.

      e. B: Either Ebbe Sand or no one.[97]

      f. B explained to us who would show up for the talk.

---

[95] Exhaustiveness is harder to test for a question like (130a), which has a unique answer.

[96] See Ginzburg 1995a for arguments as to why this is not a pragmatic epiphenomenon, and also for arguments against the common assumption that *wh*-interrogatives carry an existential presupposition.

[97] This example is like one proposed to us by Adam Przepiórkowski (personal communication).

For some of these cases, such as (133b,c), the prediction seems intuitively correct. For cases like (133d,e) intuitions are less clear cut. Insofar as there might be an inclination to view (133d) as potentially resolving, this could be explained away by assuming that it licenses an implicature that strengthens its interpretation to (134), which positively resolves the question since it entails that the question is instantiable.

(134)   Stevie: Those who show up will be few and they will lack any knowledge of Category Theory.

However, no such explanation extends to (133e). For those speakers who feel it to be potentially resolving, a more inclusive notion of potential resolvedness would need to be provided.[98] All these propositions will, in any case, be characterized as constituting information about the question, as discussed below.

We turn now to formalizing and briefly illustrating the notion of potential resolvedness that we have been discussing. The following definition provides a unified proposal for polar and *wh*-questions:

Definition 14 Potential Resolvedness
$PotResAns(p, q)$ *iff* **Proposition**(p) and **Question**(q) and

1. *Either: $PositivelyResolves(p, q)$. That is, both a. and b. hold:*
   a. **p witnesses q**: $p \rightarrow_{prop} \bigvee\{r \mid AtomAns(r, q)\}$.
   b. **p sortalizes q**: *If $|\{r \mid AtomAns(r, q)\}| \geq 2$, then there exists at least one r such that $AtomAns(r, q)$ and $r \not\rightarrow_{prop} p$.*
2. *Or: $NegativelyResolves(p, q)$. That is, $p \rightarrow_{prop} \bigwedge\{r \mid NegAtomAns(r, q)\}$.*

Note that potential resolvedness does indeed reduce to strong exhaustiveness for a polar question $\lambda\{\ \}p$:[99]

(135)   a. If $q = \lambda\{\ \}p$, then:
        b. $AtomAns(r, q)$ iff $r = p$; $NegAtomAns(r, q)$ iff $r = \neg p$.
        c. $PotResAns(\psi, q)$ iff **Proposition**(ψ) and **Question**(q) and $True(\psi)$ and:
           either: $\psi \rightarrow_{prop} \bigvee\{r \mid AtomAns(r, q)\}$, i.e. $\psi \rightarrow_{prop} \bigvee\{p\}$; i.e. $\psi \rightarrow_{prop} p$;
           or: $\psi \rightarrow_{prop} \bigwedge\{r \mid NegAtomAns(r, q)\}$, i.e. $\psi \rightarrow_{prop} \bigwedge\{\neg p\}$; i.e. $\psi \rightarrow_{prop} \neg p$.

For a simple unary *wh*-question such as *who is available*, the proposal leads to the following characterization:

(136)   a. $q_1 = \lambda\{b\}\mathsf{prop}(s_0, \langle\langle Available;b\rangle\rangle)$ (*who is available*)
        b. $AtomAns(r, q)$ iff $\exists a[r = \mathsf{prop}(s_0, \langle\langle Available;a\rangle\rangle)]$
        c. $PositivelyResolves(p, q)$, that is both (1) and (2) hold:
           (1) **p witnesses q**: $p \rightarrow_{prop} \bigvee\{r \mid AtomAns(r, q)\}$,
               i.e. $p \rightarrow_{prop} \bigvee\{r \mid \exists a[r = \mathsf{prop}(s_0, \langle\langle Available;a\rangle\rangle)]\}$
           (2) **p sortalizes q**: There exists at least one r such that $AtomAns(r, q)$ and $r \not\rightarrow_{prop} p$.
        d. $NegAtomAns(r, q)$ iff $\exists a[r = \mathsf{prop}(s_0, \overline{\langle\langle Available;a\rangle\rangle})]$
        e. $NegativelyResolves(p, q)$ iff $p \rightarrow_{prop} \bigwedge\{r \mid \exists a[r = \mathsf{prop}(s_0, \overline{\langle\langle Available;a\rangle\rangle})]\}$

---

[98] We wish to thank Eric Potsdam and Adam Przepiórkowski for alerting us to this problem.

[99] But the sortal condition does not come into the picture, because the cardinality of the set of atomic answers is 1.

Let us consider this example in more detail. To begin with, consider the answer that B provides in (137a).

(137)　　A: Who is available?

  a. B: Ebbe Sand

  b. B: Either Ebbe Sand or Stig Tofting.

  c. B: Several senior Danish logicians.

  d. B: No one.

This is a member of the set of atomic answers. Hence, in particular, it is potentially resolving. Similar remarks apply to (137b); assuming there are other individuals in the domain apart from Ebbe Sand and Stig Tofting, the proposition expressed by (137b) entails the join of the set of atomic answers, whose truth requires simply the truth of at least one element of the set.

In order to consider the status of answers like (137c,d), we need to consider how quantificational propositions are represented in ST. Cooper (1996) provides a variety of arguments for a reformulation of Generalized Quantifier (GQ) theory using ST tools. Here we present a simplified version of this proposal, mainly because for the moment we will ignore domain selection.[100] A quantified statement denotes a proposition of the form in (138a):

(138)　a. $\mathsf{prop}(s, \langle\langle \mathrm{QuantRel}; \tau, \varrho \rangle\rangle)$

  b. $\mathsf{prop}(s, \langle\langle \mathrm{Every}; \lambda\{b\}\langle\langle \mathrm{Student};b \rangle\rangle, \lambda\{c\}\langle\langle \mathrm{Run};c \rangle\rangle \rangle\rangle)$
   (*every student runs*)

  c. $\mathsf{prop}(s, \langle\langle \mathrm{Some}; \lambda\{b\}\langle\langle \mathrm{Student};b \rangle\rangle, \lambda\{c\}\langle\langle \mathrm{Run};c \rangle\rangle \rangle\rangle)$
   (*some student runs*)

  d. $\mathsf{prop}(s, \langle\langle \mathrm{Several}; \lambda\{b\}\langle\langle \mathrm{SeniorDanishLogician};b \rangle\rangle,$
   $\lambda\{c\}\langle\langle \mathrm{Available};c \rangle\rangle \rangle\rangle)$
   (*several senior Danish logicians are available*)

Here the quantified SOA begins with *QuantRel*, a relation provided by the quantificational determiner. Its relata, τ and ϱ, are one place SOA abstracts, i.e. properties. Simple examples are provided in (138b,c,d).

Cooper suggests that the truth conditions of a quantificational statement can be given in terms of constraints that relate the GQ account to the classical set-theoretic based account. The basic idea is simply that with each determiner relation q we associate a set theoretic relation $q^\dagger$ whose relata are sets.

(139)　a. $s \models \langle\langle \mathrm{QuantRel}; \tau, \varrho \rangle\rangle$ iff $\mathrm{QuantRel}^\dagger(\{x \mid s \models \tau\{x\}\}, \{x \mid s \models \varrho\{x\}\})$
  b. $s \models \overline{\langle\langle \mathrm{QuantRel}; \tau, \varrho \rangle\rangle}$ iff
   it is not the case that: $\mathrm{QuantRel}^\dagger(\{x \mid s \models \tau\{x\}\}, \{x \mid s \models \varrho\{x\}\})$

Thus, if we take Every[†] to be set inclusion, Some[†] to be non-empty intersection, and Several[†] to be intersection with cardinality greater than 1, we have a straightforward treatment of the truth conditions of the propositions in (138b-d). Concretely, we can take the truth conditions of (138d) to be as given in (140):

(140)　　$|\{b \mid s \models \langle\langle \mathrm{SeniorDanishLogician};b \rangle\rangle\}| \cap \{c \mid s \models \langle\langle \mathrm{Available};c \rangle\rangle\}| \geq 2$

---

[100] Accounting for domain selection is one the most important motivations for the ST-based formulation. We will return to this issue in Chapter 4.

Given (140), it is clear that (137c) entails the join of the set of atomic answers. Moreover, assuming the universe is not composed exclusively of senior Danish logicians, (137c) sortalizes the question. Hence, (137c) is potentially resolving.

Given partiality and our approach to negation, a negative quantifier such as *no* needs to be characterized in terms that require the supporting situation to actually support a set of negative SOAs about the relevant individuals, as in (141a):

(141)   a. $s \models \langle\langle \mathrm{No}; \tau, \rho \rangle\rangle$ iff $\{x \mid s \models \tau\{x\}\} \subset \{x \mid s \models \overline{\rho\{x\}}\}$
        b. $s \models \langle\langle \mathrm{No}; \tau, \rho \rangle\rangle$ iff $(\{x \mid s \models \tau\{x\}\} \cap \{x \mid s \models \rho\{x\}\}) = \emptyset$

Simply assuming (141b) leads to overly weak truth conditions.

Given (141a), it follows that (137d) will be true just in case (142) is true:

(142) $\{\mathrm{b} \mid s \models \langle\langle \mathrm{Person;b} \rangle\rangle\} \subset \{\mathrm{c} \mid s \models \overline{\langle\langle \mathrm{Available;c} \rangle\rangle}\}$

Assuming that s contains persons, i.e. that the set $\{\mathrm{b} \mid s \models \langle\langle \mathrm{Person;b} \rangle\rangle\}$ is non-empty, it will follow that (137d) is potentially resolving.

The notion of resolvedness emerges by relativizing potential resolvedness to agent information states that supply the necessary knowledge and goal parameters. Nonetheless, one can also show that in many cases such additional parameters are fixed in such a way as to mask their presence. For example, if the goal is assumed to be transparently expressed by the denoted question q_0, and the limited nature of informational resources is ignored, then resolvedness reduces to exhaustiveness. Thus, the pervasive intuitions about exhaustiveness need not be ignored; they can be seen as default inferences. The following is the definition of *resolves* that can be adopted, stated relative to a notion of consequence and an agent's information state that supplies a GOAL g.[101]

Definition 15   Resolving a Question

p is a proposition that resolves a question q relative to an information state is, just in case the following conditions hold:

   a.   *Semantic Condition: $True(p)$ and $PotResAns(p, q)$.*
   b.   *Pragmatic Relativization: p enables the current goal (in IS) to be fulfilled relative to the available inferential resources (of IS).*

Aboutness

We turn now to *aboutness*, the notion of answerhood that we take to underlie the coherence of 'direct answers' to queries. We propose the following characterization:

Definition 16   Aboutness

$About(p, q)$ *iff* **Proposition**(p) *and* **Question**(q) *and* $p \rightarrow_{prop} \bigvee \{r \mid SimpleAns(r, q)\}$.

The most obvious difference between aboutness and the other notions we have discussed above is that aboutness says nothing about truth. Given (143a), all simple answers are automatically characterized as being about the question. In order to appreciate this, recall from our earlier discussion that:

---

[101]The notion of 'goal' here is identified with an *outcome* which, intuitively, describes a (typically epistemic) state the agent would like to attain, e.g. *to find Mo's house this afternoon, to know the identity of the President's dinner guests*, etc. See Ginzburg 1995a for discussion and further illustration.

(143)   a. For a polar question: $\{r \mid SimpleAns(r, \lambda\{\ \}p)\} = \{p, \neg p\}$
       b. For a unary *wh*-question: $\{r \mid SimpleAns(r, \lambda\{b\}p(b))\} =$
          $\{p(a_1), \ldots, p(a_n), \neg p(a_1), \ldots, \neg p(a_n)\}$

However, aboutness is a more inclusive condition than being a *SimpleAns*. Thus, in order for a proposition to be about a polar question $\lambda\{\ \}p$, it must entail the proposition $\bigvee\{p, \neg p\}$ (i.e. the proposition $p \vee \neg p$). On a traditional model-theoretic conception, this defining condition is vacuous. However, in the current context, given that p being false does not require that $\neg p$ be true, the condition is restrictive. For instance, it will not generally be the case that (144) is true.

(144) $\mathsf{prop}(s, \langle\langle \text{Leave};j \rangle\rangle) \rightarrow_{prop} \bigvee\{\mathsf{prop}(s, \langle\langle \text{Tall};j \rangle\rangle), \mathsf{prop}(s, \overline{\langle\langle \text{Tall};j \rangle\rangle})\}$

This is because a situation's containing information about J's leaving does not mean that it must contain information about J's being tall or not tall.

Let us now consider what answers this characterization admits. For a polar question $\lambda\{\ \}p$, we obtain the following:

(145) $(About(r, \lambda\{\ \}p))$ iff $(r \rightarrow_{prop} \bigvee\{p, \neg p\})$

It straightforwardly follows that both p and $\neg p$ are about $\lambda\{\ \}p$. What is more interesting is that— unlike all previous accounts we are aware of—we can also accommodate answers that are weaker than the two polar propositions. Thus, we want to show that 'weak' modal information, e.g. *possibly/probably/unlikely p*, is *about* $\lambda\{\ \}p$. We confine ourselves here to showing the existence of a notion of *possibly*, whose definition we restrict for simplicity to basic propositions. As is easy to verify, aboutness is upward monotone closed: if $p \rightarrow_{prop} r$ and r is about q, then p is *About* q. Hence, given that *probably p* $\rightarrow_{prop}$ *possibly p*, once we show that *possibly p* is *about* $\lambda\{\ \}p$, it will follow that *probably p* is *about* $\lambda\{\ \}p$.

In order to do this, we need a semantics for *possibly* which is compatible with the situation semantics framework that we have adopted. For this purpose, we outline a simplified version of the analysis developed in Vogel and Ginzburg 1999, which builds on Kratzer 1981.[102] Asserting of a proposition $\mathsf{prop}(s, \sigma)$ that it is *possible* involves drawing attention to the fact that σ is one of the existing alternatives for describing s and, moreover, that some other situation causally linked to s does not support $\overline{\sigma}$ being the case. For example:

(146) $True(Possibly(\mathsf{prop}(s, \sigma)))$ iff there exist τ, s' such that:
       a. $CausallyLinked(s, s')$.
       b. $s' \not\models \overline{\sigma}$.
       c. $True(\bigvee\{\mathsf{prop}(s, \sigma), \mathsf{prop}(s, \tau)\})$.
       d. τ and σ are incompatible. That is, for all s: $True(\mathsf{prop}(s, \tau)) \rightarrow_{prop} True(\mathsf{prop}(s, \overline{\sigma}))$ and $True(\mathsf{prop}(s, \sigma)) \rightarrow_{prop} True(\mathsf{prop}(s, \overline{\tau}))$.

It follows from this definition that:[103]

---

[102]Vogel and Ginzburg's analysis is formulated using notions from Channel Theory (Barwise and Seligman 1996) that provide an account of the notion of a causal link between situations—an important component of a theory of modality. We abstract away from such notions here, in so far as this is possible.

[103]To prove (147a): if $\mathsf{prop}(s, \sigma)$ is true, then take $\overline{\sigma}$ for τ in (146) and s to be s'. The truth of $Possibly(\mathsf{prop}(s, \sigma))$ is immediate. To prove (147b): if $Possibly(\mathsf{prop}(s, \sigma))$ is true, then according to (146) there exists τ which is incompatible with σ such that $True \bigvee\{\mathsf{prop}(s, \sigma), \mathsf{prop}(s, \tau)\}$. In section 3.3.2, we postulated that if a situation s supports a SOA that is incompatible with σ, then s supports $\overline{\sigma}$. Hence, it follows that $\bigvee\{\mathsf{prop}(s, \sigma), \mathsf{prop}(s, \overline{\sigma})\}$ is true.

(147) a. $\text{prop}(s, \sigma) \rightarrow_{prop} Possibly(\text{prop}(s, \sigma))$, but not vice versa.

   b. $Possibly(\text{prop}(s, \sigma)) \rightarrow_{prop} \bigvee \{\text{prop}(s, \sigma), \text{prop}(s, \overline{\sigma})\}$

Hence, *Possibly p* is *about* $\lambda\{\ \}p$, at least for basic propositions. Thus, we have a notion that begins to capture the meaning of *possibly*, a non-polar modality at any rate, which is an answer about the corresponding polar question.

By similar reasoning, it emerges for *wh*-questions that certain propositions that are not *potentially resolving*, are nonetheless *about*. Example (148) illustrates this:

(148) a. A: Who will come?

      B: Possibly John.

   b. A: Who will show up?

      B: Either Ebbe Sand or no one.

3.5.4 Recap

We have presented a view of questions as propositional abstracts. We have shown how within the ontological setup of ST—in particular the fact that SOAs are distinct from propositions and the closure of the universe under simultaneous abstraction—we can surmount various problems that beset earlier attempts at formalizing the intuition of questions as 'open propositions'. We have shown how to:

1. ontologically distinguish questions from relations,
2. define a uniform semantic type for questions which covers both polar and *wh*-questions,
3. provide a simple theory of coordination.

Most crucially, given that we do not take any single notion of answerhood as *the* basic, semantic notion of answerhood, we can explicate the variety of answerhood relations needed for semantic and pragmatic theory. The notion of question we have developed constitutes a means of *under-specifying* answerhood.

3.6 A TFS Version of the Ontology

In this section, we show how to embed our proposal for a semantic universe into a framework of typed feature structures (TFSs); hence, we render it compatible with recent work in HPSG (for example, Pollard and Yoo 1998 and Sag 1997) and with the overall grammar architecture that we employ throughout this work. This demonstration will involve two tasks: (1) developing a hierarchy of semantic types on the basis of which we can encode semantic objects and (2) providing an interpretation function that maps type feature structures to elements of the semantic universe. To reiterate the analogy with Montague Semantics pointed out in section 3.1: the type feature structures correspond to logical forms of intensional logic; our semantic universe corresponds to a Montagovian structure like (2) above.

Before we turn to these two tasks, a few remarks about context and its role in determining content are in order. Montague (1974a)—and, perhaps more influentially, Kaplan (1989)—distinguish between *meaning* (Kaplan's term is *character*) and *content*. The semantic object associated with an expression context independently is its meaning. Given a context c, a meaning can be used to evaluate the content of an expression ϕ in c. Thus, a common formalization of a meaning is as a *function* from from contexts to contents.[104] To a first approximation, then, what the *content* attribute of a sign encodes is the value the meaning function takes, given the values of the contextual parameters, whose values are represented in the attribute C(ONTEXTUAL)-INDICES and in the attribute B(A)CKGR(OUN)D.

This represents a simplification of the meaning/context/content interrelationship. For example, it assumes that *sentences* have contents, rather than viewing content as a notion conversationalists associate with utterances—spatio-temporally located speech events—they perceive. This latter perspective, which as we mentioned in Chapter 1 was pioneered in Barwise and Perry 1983, is required if conversational phenomena such as corrections or requests for clarification are to be accommodated—phenomena that arise because conversationalists do not classify the content of a commonly perceived utterance identically. Adopting such a perspective, one can say that signs as conceived of in this book specify a speaker-oriented view of the conventional content information pertaining to an utterance. That is, we do not, for the most part, make allowance for communicative problems that might lead to an imperfect perception of an utterance on the phonological, syntactic, or semantic level.[105] We will, nonetheless, offer an account of one phenomenon which turns crucially on the existence of a mismatch between speaker and addressee. These are reprise utterances which we discuss in Chapters 7 and 8.

In addition, the view of content we assume here does not in and of itself offer an explanation of how content can have an impact on context, a topic that much research has focussed on since the pioneering work on pronominal anaphora in Discourse Representation Theory, Dynamic Predicate Logic, and Situation Semantics (e.g. Kamp 1981, Heim 1982, Barwise 1985, and Groenendijk and Stokhof 1991b). Although 'dynamic concerns' are not a central part of the current work, we do provide a brief sketch of a dynamic view of how context evolves in a dialogue setting, based on the framework developed in Ginzburg 2001. We use this to develop a fairly detailed account of non-sentential utterances in Chapter 8. A novel and interesting feature of our account of ellipsis is that the dynamic effects involve both the semantic and syntactic levels. What gets projected into the context from an utterance comprises syntactic as well as semantic information.

3.6.1 Basic Setup

The content of a clause will always be some subtype of the semantic type *message*; an initial sketch of a hierarchy of semantic types is sketched in (149). As we will see shortly, this hierarchy can also be used to specify classes of abstract entities selected by predicates.

(149)

---

[104]Recent work in situation semantics (e.g. Cooper and Poesio 1994 and Ginzburg 1998) formalize meanings as abstracts (in a sense explained above in section 3.3.3), where entities abstracted away from content represent the contextual parameters. We abstract away from the differences between these two formalizations in the current work.

[105]For certain purposes—for instance, describing dialogue interaction—it is more convenient to set things up so that signs specify meanings, not contents (see, for example, Ginzburg 1998, 2001). We could implement such an account without significant complication.

Message is the semantic type that is the most basic to communication—its (maximal) sub-types constitute the descriptive contents of basic illocutionary acts such as assertion, query-ing, commanding, exclaiming and the like;[106] it is also the general semantic type of all finite clauses.

The type *message* has a variety of subtypes: one we postulated already in Chapter 2 is the type *austinian*. *austinian* has as its maximal subtypes *proposition* and *outcome*. These introduce two features, the feature SIT, whose value will be the situation involved in the relevant proposition or outcome, and the feature SOA. All SOAs, following P&S–94, will be treated in terms of feature structures that allow the features QUANT(IFIER)S and NUCL(EUS), both of which are discussed further in Chapters 4 and 5. In addition, *i-soa*s are specified for the feature T(EMPORAL)-PARAM, whose value corresponds to the temporal parameter of the SOA, which gets abstracted away. In concrete terms the value of T-PARAM is a parameter whose restriction is a temporal fact—a fact which restricts the (range of entities anchorable to) the parameter to be temporal.[107] We deviate somewhat from P&S–94 in locating the CTXT feature at the level of the *sign*, not *synsem*. Moreover, the BCKGRD feature will be assumed to be a non-local feature whose value is a set of facts rather than of propositions. Motivation for these changes is provided in Chapters 5 and 8 respectively; Chapter 8 contains additional discussion and refinement of the representation of context.

The other subtype of *message* is the type *prop(ositionally)-constr(ucted)*, so called because its maximal subtypes, *fact* and *question*, involve a proposition in their construction.[108] Concretely, both types introduce a feature PROP, whose value is a proposition. Recall that on our semantic theory questions are identified with proposition abstracts. Given this, the type *question* is also appropriate for a feature PARAMS, whose value will be a (possibly empty) set of parameters—restriction-bearing indices—corresponding to the set of entities that gets abstracted away. Exten-sive motivation for this view of the feature PARAMS, the *wh*-phrase analogue of QUANTS, will

---

[106] We should stress that the hierarchy presented here is still incomplete in its characterization of the semantic types which can serve as descriptive contents of (conventionalized) illocutionary acts. There clearly exist act-types whose descriptive content is neither a proposition, outcome, fact, or question. Apologies, for instance, can be argued to have an event or situation as their descriptive content. Similarly, calls—exemplified by *Jo! (A call from Batumi for you.)*—can be argued to involve a communicative agent as their descriptive content.

[107] Restriction-bearing indices are discussed in more detail in Chapter 4. We omit the restrictions when they are empty.

[108] Note that we have postulated a type *fact* and not a type *possibility*. In our semantic universe it is this latter which constitutes the more general sort, of which facts are a subclass; semantic arguments for this view of facts were given in e.g. (40). However, in developing the grammatical type system we restrict attention to facts since, as far as the grammar developed in the current work goes, the more general type does not seem to be required, e.g. there is no clause type which needs *possibility* rather than *fact*. It is certainly possible that once additional constructions or lexical items receive serious attention, one might need to modify this decision. To take one simple example, one might argue that a predicate such as *hope*, which subcategorizes for declarative clauses, does not select propositions. As (ii) and (iii) show, *hope* resists proposition-denoting nominals and free relatives headed by it cannot have truth/falsity predicated of them:

(i)   Bo hoped that Mo survived the yachting accident.

(ii)   #Bo hoped (for) the claim/hypothesis/forecast.

(ii)   #What Bo hoped (for) was true.

What these data suggest is that when *hope* embeds a(n indicative) declarative clause its semantic argument is not a proposition, nor given the nature of *hope* is it a fact. We leave open the issue of whether one can find additional evidence supporting the need for possibility as a type of denotation. If one did find such evidence, one could accommodate it, for instance, by postulating a supertype *possibility* which would subsume *fact* and a new type *unsubstantiated*.

be provided in Chapter 4.[109] The feature declarations just introduced are summarized in (150). ('IST' again indicates immediate supertype relations.)

(150)   Some Basic Semantic Types:

TYPE	FEATURES/VALUE TYPE	IST
sem-obj		
message		*sem-obj*
austinian	$\begin{bmatrix} \text{SIT} & situation \\ \text{SOA} & soa \end{bmatrix}$	*message*
proposition	$\begin{bmatrix} \text{SOA} & r\text{-}soa \end{bmatrix}$	*austinian*
outcome	$\begin{bmatrix} \text{SOA} & i\text{-}soa \end{bmatrix}$	*austinian*
prop-constr	$\begin{bmatrix} \text{PROP} & proposition \end{bmatrix}$	*message*
fact		*prop-constr*
question	$\begin{bmatrix} \text{PARAMS} & set(param) \end{bmatrix}$	*prop-constr*
soa	$\begin{bmatrix} \text{QUANTS} & list(quant\text{-}rel) \\ \text{NUCL} & rel(ation) \end{bmatrix}$	*sem-obj*
r-soa		*soa*
i-soa	$\begin{bmatrix} \text{T-PARAM} & param \end{bmatrix}$	*soa*
scope-obj	$\begin{bmatrix} \text{INDEX} & index \\ \text{RESTR} & set(fact) \end{bmatrix}$	*sem-obj*
quant-rel		*scope-obj*
param(eter)		*scope-obj*

Recall from Chapter 2 that an instance of a specific type must bear an appropriate specfication for all features specified as appropriate for that type, as well as for those features that are appropriate for each supertype of that type. Thus, in virtue of inheritance and the type hierarchy given in (150), we permit semantic objects like the following, which are the feature structure analogues of propositions, facts, outcomes, and questions discussed earlier.

---

[109]Note that although the feature SIT is not appropriate for *fact* and *question*, tokens of these types *are* situationally relativized, the relativization emerging from the proposition serving as value of PROP.

(151) a. *Brendan left.*

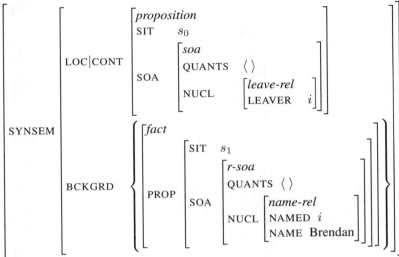

   b. *Brendan left.*

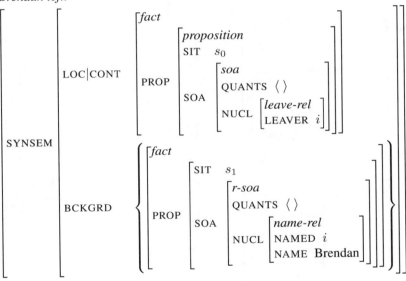

(152) a. *Did Brendan leave?*

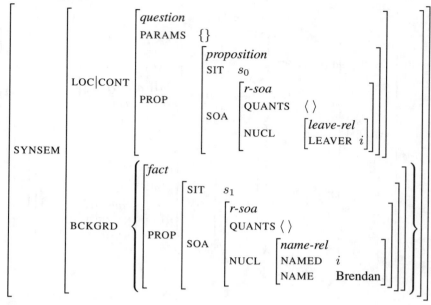

b. *Leave!*

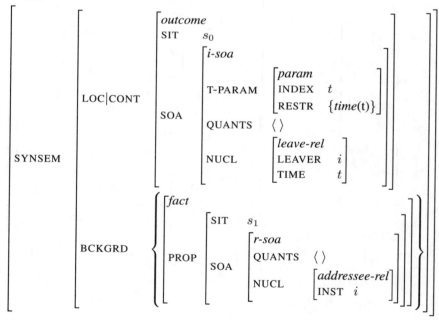

In (152b) we employ an attribute T-PARAM, whose value is the parameter whose index is abstracted over within the outcome. Although one might base a treatment of tense on the assumption that all (temporally located) soas include a specification for this attribute, we will supress any such specification here and in subsequent discussions, as it is not our intention to offer a treatment of tense.

3.6.2 Interpreting Typed Feature Structures

In this section, we show how to define an interpretation function that maps type feature structures to elements of the semantic universe.[110] For the most part, the definition is straightforward and closely reflects our discussions in previous sections. The exceptions are the clauses for quantification, questions, and negation. These are included here primarily for the sake of completeness. The treatment of questions and quantification is explained in Chapter 4, whereas negation is discussed further in Chapter 8.

Definition 17 An Interpretation Function for TFSs

Let $M = \langle \ SU+AE_0, I \ \rangle$ where $SU+AE_0$ is a situational universe plus abstract entities, as outlined in section 3.4, and I is an interpretation function defined below. c is a context, specifying speaker, hearer, loc-utt, etc, as well as an assignment function c_f from indices to the universe of $SU+AE_0$. The BACKGROUND specifies a set of facts that must hold in c.

We define $[\![a]\!]^c$—the interpretation of a (a a feature structure, feature, or type) with respect to a context c:

1. If a is a (subtype of the type) relation, then $[\![a]\!]^c = I(a)$ and $Rel(I(a))$.
2. If a is a role feature, then $[\![a]\!]^c = I(a)$ and $ArgRole(I(a))$.
3. If a is an index, then $[\![a]\!]^c = c_f(a)$, where $c_f(a) \in |SU+AE_0|$.
4.
   If a is of the form:
   $$\begin{bmatrix} \rho \\ F_1 & v_1 \\ \dots & \\ F_n & v_n \end{bmatrix},$$
   where ρ is a subtype of relation,
   then $[\![a]\!]^c = \left\langle\!\!\left\langle \ [\![\rho]\!]^c; [\![F_1]\!]^c : [\![v_1]\!]^c, \dots, [\![F_n]\!]^c : [\![v_n]\!]^c \right\rangle\!\!\right\rangle$ (a SOA).

5.
   If a is of the form:
   $$\begin{bmatrix} soa \\ \text{QUANTS} & \langle\,\rangle \\ \text{NUCL} & b \end{bmatrix}$$
   then $[\![a]\!]^c = [\![b]\!]^c$ and $\mathbf{Pos}([\![a]\!]^c)$.

6.
   If a is of the form:
   $$\begin{bmatrix} soa \\ \text{QUANTS} & \begin{bmatrix} \text{FIRST} & not\text{-}rel \\ \text{REST} & b \end{bmatrix} \\ \text{NUCL} & g \end{bmatrix}$$
   then $[\![a]\!]^c = \overline{h}$ (the dual of the SOA h),
   where $h = \left[\!\!\left[\begin{bmatrix} soa \\ \text{QUANTS} & b \\ \text{NUCL} & g \end{bmatrix} \right]\!\!\right]^c$.

---

[110]Here we follow the program for semantics outlined in Nerbonne 1992 and related work. Semantic interpretation is defined on totally well-typed and sort-resolved feature structures, not on feature structure descriptions.

7. *If a is of the form:*

$$\begin{bmatrix} soa \\ \text{QUANTS} \begin{bmatrix} \text{FIRST} \begin{bmatrix} \delta \\ \text{IND} & i \\ \text{RESTR} & \Sigma \end{bmatrix} \\ \text{REST} & b \end{bmatrix} \\ \text{NUCL} & g \end{bmatrix},$$

where δ is a subtype of quant-rel,

then $[\![a]\!]^c = \left\langle\!\!\left\langle \; [\![\delta]\!]^c; \lambda\{\, c_f(i)\,\} [\![\Sigma]\!]^c, \lambda\{\, c_f(i)\,\} \begin{bmatrix} \begin{bmatrix} soa \\ \text{QUANTS} & b \\ \text{NUCL} & g \end{bmatrix} \end{bmatrix}^c \right\rangle\!\!\right\rangle.$

8. *If a is of the form:*

$$\begin{bmatrix} proposition \\ \text{SIT} & s \\ \text{SOA} & \sigma \end{bmatrix}$$

then $[\![a]\!]^c = \mathsf{prop}([\![s]\!]^c, [\![\sigma]\!]^c).$

9. *If a is of the form:*

$$\begin{bmatrix} fact \\ \text{PROP} & p \end{bmatrix},$$

then $[\![a]\!]^c = \mathsf{poss}([\![p]\!]^c)$ *and* $Fact([\![a]\!]^c).$

10. *If a is a set of elements of type fact*
then $[\![a]\!]^c = \mathsf{poss}(p)$ *and* $Fact([\![a]\!]^c),$
where $p = \bigwedge\{g \mid \exists h[h \in a \text{ and } [\![h]\!]^c = \mathsf{poss}(g)]\}.$

11. *If a is of the form:*

$$\begin{bmatrix} outcome \\ \text{SIT} & s \\ \text{SOA} & b[\text{T-PAR}|\text{INDEX} \quad t] \end{bmatrix},$$

then $[\![a]\!]^c = \mathsf{out}([\![s]\!]^c, \lambda\{\, c_f(t)\,\} [\![b]\!]^c).$

12. *If a is of the form:*

$$\begin{bmatrix} question \\ \text{PARAMS} & \Sigma \\ \text{PROP} & b \end{bmatrix}$$

then: $[\![a]\!]^c = \lambda\{\mathbf{indices}(\Sigma)\}[\mathbf{facts}(\Sigma)][\![b]\!]^c$ *and* $\mathbf{Question}([\![a]\!]^c)$
where **indices** *is the function that maps a set of parameters to the set of indices that it contains and* **facts** *is the function that maps set of parameters to the set of facts that it contains:*
$\mathbf{indices}(\Sigma) =_{def} \{i \mid \exists p\,[p \in \Sigma \text{ and } \text{INDEX}(p) = x \text{ and } i = c_f(x)]\}$
$\mathbf{facts}(\Sigma) =_{def} \bigcup\{F \mid \exists p, g\,[p \in \Sigma \text{ and } \text{RESTR}(p) = g \text{ and } F = [\![g]\!]^c]\}$

3.6.3 Semantic Universals: selection and clause denotations

We turn finally to two fundamental issues for a semantic framework. The first concerns the description of semantic categories for purposes of semantic selection; the second involves capturing what appear to be semantic universals concerning clausal denotations and selectional properties of predicates. Let us take these points in turn.

As far as we are aware, previous work has not attempted to provide a comprehensive system of semantic categories which would partition the class of clausal embedding predicates according to their selectional requirements.[111] The type distinctions introduced in Montague Semantics, for instance between propositions and questions, provide a starting point for such a system. However, as we have argued in detail in section 3.2, one needs a significantly more refined ontology than Montague Semantics provides. We have motivated the existence of four distinct abstract entity semantic types that clauses can take as their denotation type: questions (q), facts (f), outcomes (o), and propositions (p). Our argumentation rested, in part, on exhibiting classes of predicates that select for one of these semantic types. This provides an additional step toward the development of a system of semantic categories for clausal embedding predicates. Indeed, it raises the issue of what additional, more complex categories exist ('complex' in the sense that they involve entities of more than one class—selection for both facts and propositions, or for both questions and outcomes, etc.). The table in (153) below suggests that such complex categories do exist:[112] these include the resolutive predicates, which select for facts and propositions; decidative predicates, which select for questions and outcomes; and predicates such as *intrigue*, which appears to select for questions, facts, and outcomes.[113] And yet, it is also apparent that not all logically possible categories are instantiated: of the 15 logically possible categories,[114] there is convincing evidence for the existence of 8 classes.

We must leave as an important task for future work—supported by cross-linguistic and corpora-based investigation—a formal characterization of the space of instantiated categories. We hypothesize that the basic ingredients for this characterization will be the (types of) entities we have postulated in our ontology. Note that this will have to involve not solely the four abstract entity semantic types discussed above. For instance, in order to distinguish emotives from other factives one apparently needs to consider event/situation-denoting expressions.[115]

---

[111]Though there do exist many useful, though not formally grounded, partial categorizations. See, for example, Vendler 1972, Karttunen 1977, and Grimshaw 1979.

[112]This table was compiled on the basis of casual introspection, not on the basis of a corpus study. Given this, our conclusions must be viewed as tentative.

[113]The data regarding this class, specifically whether it actually selects for outcomes is quite subtle and apparently liable to variation across speakers. In the table, we provide what seems to be a relatively acceptable *for*-clause complement. We find similar examples with subjunctives less acceptable:

    (i) #It astounded me that Bo be promoted while we remain on 4 shillings a week.

This might suggest that this class actually does not select for outcomes but rather for the type *prop-constr*, which at present remains uninstantiated.

[114]The remaining category involves those predicates that select for none of the 4 abstract entities.

[115]Thus, a 'pure' factive such as *discover* and an emotive such as *regret* differ in their ability to license event-denoting nominals:

    (i) Bo regrets/#discovered Mo's departure

A similarly bifurcation affects the class of resolutives:

    (ii) Bo announced/#told me Mo's departure

For additional data from Modern Greek bearing on this issue see Ginzburg and Kolliakou 1998.

(153)

Name of class	Repr. members	Evidence	Type selected
+q (QE predicates)	*ask, wonder investigate*	section 3.2.1	*question*
+p (TF predicates)	*believe, deny prove*	section 3.2.2	*proposition*
+f (factives)	*know, discover forget*	section 3.2.3	*fact*
+o (mandatives)	*demand, require want*	section 3.2.4	*outcome*
+q,+p	??	??	—
+o,+f	??	??	—
+o,+p	*be-conceivable be-reasonable*	It is conceivable: that Bo arrived safely that Bo be promoted soon #whether Bo is promoted #That fact is conceivable	*austinian*
+p,+f (resolutives)	*tell, guess predict*	What Bo told me was false Bo told me: an interesting fact who left #that Mo be promoted #Mo's departure #a question	?
+q,+f	??	??	*prop-constr*
+q,+o (decidatives)	*be-resolved decided*	The question was who to fire The issue is resolved/decided; So: it was resolved who to fire It was resolved that Billie be fired #The fact is resolved; #The claim is resolved #It is resolved that Billie left	?
+q,+f, +o	*intrigue, astound*	examples (33) above; For Bo to get the job would astound me	?
+q,+f,+o	??	??	—
+o,+p,+f	??	??	—
+o,+p,+q	??	??	—
+f,+p,+q	??	??	—

As we have shown in the course of this chapter, there exist various general patterns concerning subcategorization by clause-embedding predicates. We conjecture that, with possible minor riders—e.g. *in a language with a CN corresponding to 'fact', 'question'*—the following are universal:

1. There are no subjunctive interrogatives (in English).[116]
2. TF predicates do not coocur with interrogatives or exclamatives.
3. QE predicates coocur with interrogatives and question nominals.
4. Factives cooccur with declaratives, interrogatives, exclamatives and fact nominals.

The generalization about the lack of subjunctive interrogatives is captured within our system in virtue of the fact that questions are proposition abstracts and, hence, contain an *r-soa* as a constituent. Attempting to build a question out of a subjunctive will fail since the non-finite verb that heads it denotes an *i-soa*. The generalization about TF predicates follows because selection in our system is partly semantic: all TF predicates select for propositions, which neither interrogative nor exclamative clauses denote (see Chapter 6). The generalizations about QE predicates and factives are explained in Chapter 8. These are accounted for via a combination of semantic selection and the denotations we associate with various clause types.

---

[116]In this case some additional care is needed in pinning down the category *subjunctive*. Roughly, we might link this with the clause type subcategorized for by mandative predicates which is distinct from (indicative) declarative, assuming such exists.

4

Wh-Phrase Meaning

In this chapter, we explain how *wh*-phrases are to be treated in our theory, postponing a detailed discussion of our proposed scoping mechanism to Chapters 5 and 6. We argue that *wh*-phrases have three distinct uses: an *independent* use (our focus in this book), a *functional(ly dependent)* use, and a *reprise* use, discussed in detail in Chapter 7. Common to all these uses is the type of *message* that gets expressed, namely a *question*.[1] In Chapter 3, we identified questions with abstracts, discussing how they emerge by simultaneous abstraction from a proposition. This view leads to a simple picture of a *wh*-phrase's semantic contribution. A *wh-phrase* does two things: (1) it enables an abstraction to occur over the parameter that the *wh*-phrase associates with the semantic argument role it fills and (2) it introduces certain restrictions over that argument-role—personhood for *who*, inanimateness for *what*, the common-noun property for *which*-phrases, etc.[2] To develop this view of *wh*-phrase meaning, we make a few assumptions—originally presented in Ginzburg 1992—that depart in important ways from much of the literature. In particular, we argue that:

- *wh*-phrases should be treated non-quantificationally, in terms of a parameter that introduces a restriction, and
- *wh*-phrases scope wider than generalized quantifiers (GQs).

We start by subtly refining the view of GQs we described in Chapter 3, in order to take the phenomenon of domain selection into account. These same considerations also apply to interrogatives. In order to accommodate domain selection, we introduce one minor and independently motivated refinement of the notion of abstraction introduced in Chapter 3: abstraction with restrictions. We then develop our account of the semantic contribution of *wh*-phrases, considering along the way some phenomena related to scopal interaction among *wh*-phrases and between *wh*-phrases and GQs. Finally, a number of apparent counterexamples to our theory are considered and reanalyzed in terms of functional uses of *wh*-phrases.

---

[1] The meaning of *wh*-phrases is constant across reprise and independent uses. The only differences that arise are ones that derive from general, constructional characteristics of reprise utterances.

[2] As discussed in Chapter 5, *wh*-phrases used in exclamative clauses behave differently; we assume they denote generalized quantifiers. These differences arise both lexically—there are only a handful of *wh*-phrase-types that can occur in exclamatives—and constructionally—the exclamative construction allows only one *wh*-phrase per clause.

4.1 Quantification and Domain Selection

In the previous chapter, we sketched a simplified formulation of a proposal based on Cooper 1996 to recast generalized quantifier theory using situation theoretic tools. On that account, a quantified statement denotes a proposition of the form in (1a):[3]

(1) a. $\mathrm{prop}(s, \langle\langle \mathrm{QDet}; \rho, \tau \rangle\rangle)$

    b. $s \models \langle\langle \mathrm{QDet}; \rho, \tau \rangle\rangle$ iff $\mathrm{QDet}^\dagger(\{x \mid s \models \rho\{x\}\}, \{x \mid s \models \tau\{x\}\})$

    c. $s \models \overline{\langle\langle \mathrm{QDet}; \rho, \tau \rangle\rangle}$ iff it is not the case that $\mathrm{QDet}^\dagger(\{x \mid s \models \rho\{x\}\}, \{x \mid s \models \tau\{x\}\})$

Here the quantified SOA has its relation provided by the quantificational determiner. Its relata— τ and ρ—are one-place SOA abstracts, i.e. properties. The truth conditions of a quantificational statement can be given in terms of constraints that relate the GQ account to the classical set-theoretic based account. Thus with each determiner relation QDet, we associate a set theoretic relation $\mathrm{QDet}^\dagger$ whose relata are sets R and T. R and T contain those individuals that instantiate ρ and τ (respectively) in s, the described situation of the proposition.

The most significant simplification in our presentation of Cooper's proposal concerns the issue of domain selection. (1) embodies the assumption that the situational component of a proposition (intuitively, the described situation of an assertion or belief) is necessarily the situation that restricts the quantifier. However, as discussed by Barwise and Perry (1983) and argued in detail in Cooper 1996, this need not be the case:

(2) a. Everything is on the table. (Cooper 1996, (22))

    b. Every linguist voted for the linguist and every philosopher voted for the philosopher. (Cooper 1996, (19))

In (2a), the table at issue is included in the situation described by the sentence. However, the only plausible way to understand the sentence is by assuming that the table is *not* included in the domain of the universal quantifier. Example (2b) is readily understood in a scenario where a cognitive science department is engaged in a job search. Once again, in such a scenario, the sentence is plausible only if the candidates voted for are not included in the range of the quantifiers *every linguist* and *every philosopher*.

In order to accommodate this, Cooper, following Gawron and Peters 1990, proposes to treat the restrictor argument of a *QDet* not as a relation, but as a propositional abstract ζ, say $\lambda\{x\}\mathrm{prop}(s_1, \rho)$. The situational component of such an abstract can be distinct from the situational component of the entire proposition. The relevant restrictor set R arises by selecting those elements that truly instantiate ζ. Making this particular move is not natural for us, given that we identified propositional abstracts with questions, which do not seem to play the role of restrictors. However, it is arguably the case that Cooper's (and Gawron and Peters') choice of *propositions* as the entities to abstract over is not optimal. The elements needed for the restrictor set are not the individuals a for which the substitution $\lambda\{x\}\mathrm{prop}(s_1, \rho)\{x \to a\}$ constitutes a proposition, but all such a for which $\lambda\{x\}\mathrm{prop}(s_1, \rho)\{x \to a\}$ constitutes a *true* proposition. This effect would be attained directly, if the entity over which the abstraction is made were a *fact*. Once we make this minor analytic adjustment, we can adopt the proposal that a *QDet* is a relation between a fact

---

[3]Recall from Chapter 3 that $\sigma\{f\}$ denotes the application of σ to f.

abstract and a property (i.e. a unary SOA abstract):[4]

(3) a. prop(s, $\langle\langle$ *QDet*; *fact-abstract*, *SOA-abstract* $\rangle\rangle$)

    b. $s \models \langle\langle QDet; \rho, \tau \rangle\rangle$ iff $QDet^\dagger(\{x \mid \rho\{x\}\}, \{x \mid s \models \tau\{x\}\})$

    c. $s \models \overline{\langle\langle QDet; \rho, \tau \rangle\rangle}$ iff it is not the case that $QDet^\dagger(\{x \mid \rho\{x\}\}, \{x \mid s \models \tau\{x\}\})$

For example, (4a) might be uttered at a party:[5]

(4) a. Several Danish logicians are attending that.

    b. prop(s_{party}, $\langle\langle$ Several; $\lambda\{b\}$fact(prop(s_{dasl}, $\langle\langle$DanishLogician; b$\rangle\rangle$)),

              $\lambda\{c\}\langle\langle$Attend; attender:c, event:e$\rangle\rangle$ $\rangle\rangle$)

The information that the group referred to by such an utterance consists of Danish logicians need not be included in the party situation s_{party}. Rather, the information about their being Danish logicians might be better treated as part of the database of the Danish Association for Symbolic Logic, s_{dasl}.[6] Consequently, we represent the content of (4a) as (4b).

Similar considerations can apply to interrogatives. In accordance with Chapter 3, we associate questions with unrestricted propositional abstracts, as seen in (5):

(5) a. Who knew Bo?

    b. $\lambda\{a\}$prop(s, $\langle\langle$Know; knower:a, known:b$\rangle\rangle$)

An entity c that can be substituted for this role must satisfy the selectional restrictions associated with being a *knower*—animacy for instance. Otherwise, the substitution $\{a \rightarrow c\}$ will not exist.

But the roles associated with questions can also carry additional restrictions, most obviously those emanating from the *wh*-phrase. For instance, in order to capture the content of (5a), the only potential instantiators must be *human*. Indeed, as with GQs, one needs to restrict attention to humans from some situation or other. In some cases, this situation is the same as the described situation of the queried proposition. But, as the examples in (6) suggest, this need not always be the case:

(6) a. Which foreign students were rejected by the university?

    b. Who attended the meeting?

Consider (6a) uttered in a university admissions office. The situation associated with the query as a whole, on the basis of which answers will be derived, is university-internal (the university database). Applicants who were not admitted to the university do not count as students for university-internal purposes, for example, they might not be admitted to the university library. However, they can still count as students relative to other situations, such as obtaining discounted airline tickets. Example (6b) might involve reference to a big meeting of trapeze artists from all over Europe as it is uttered by one of two Slovenian trapeze artists, where the querier's interest is restricted to fellow Slovenian trapeze artists. Once again, the situation associated with the

---

[4]Cooper suggests that there may be grounds for distinguishing the described situation from the situation associated with the nuclear scope. Consequently, in his constraints, on which (3b,c) are modeled, the situation from which the nuclear scope set is constructed is quantified away. We maintain the simpler view of identifying the described situation and that of the nuclear scope, since it simplifies the characterization of quantified propositions as answers (as in section 3.5.3).

[5]We use the notation fact(p) to denote the possibility $a = $ poss(p), restricted to satisfy *Fact*(a).

[6]For the relation between situations and databases, see Rounds 1991.

query as a whole—the one which includes the meeting and on the basis of which answers will be derived—is distinct from a situation internal to Slovenia.

The most straightforward way to accommodate such restriction is to refine the notion of unrestricted abstraction introduced in Chapter 3. Such a notion has already been proposed by S&M–97, whose definition we adopt with minor modifications:[7]

Definition 18 Restricted Abstraction

1. *A SU+AE $\mathcal{S}$ has* restricted abstraction *if it has an additional structural relation* $\mathbf{Res}^2$ *such that if* $\mathbf{Res}^2(\sigma, a)$, *then a is an abstract and σ is a possibility. In such a case a is a* restricted abstract *and σ is a* restriction *of a. For each object χ, a set $C (= \{c_1, \ldots, c_n\})$ in $\mathcal{S}$ and a set of facts Σ, an abstract τ is* the simultaneous abstraction of C from χ restricted by Σ *if there is an injective function $\pi : C \rightarrow |\mathcal{S}|$ and b such that:*

   (a) $b = \chi\{c_1 \mapsto \pi(c_1), \ldots, c_n \mapsto \pi(c_n)\}$

   (b) *For each $\sigma \in \Sigma$:* $\mathbf{Res}(\sigma\{c_1 \mapsto \pi(c_1), \ldots, c_n \mapsto \pi(c_n)\}, \tau)$

   (c) $\mathbf{Abst}(b, \tau)$

   (d) *For each c_i:* $\mathbf{PlaceHolder}(b, \pi(c_i))$

   (e) *For each c_i: the only sort of $\pi(c_i)$ is* $\mathbf{PlaceHolder}^*$

2. *The abstraction of C from χ restricted by Σ is notated $\lambda C[\Sigma].\chi$*

3. *Given an abstract $a = \lambda C[\Sigma].\chi$ in $\mathcal{S}$, a substitution $f : \Pi \mapsto D$ is an* appropriate assignment *to a if there exists b such that*

   (a) *For each $\pi \in \Pi$:* $\mathbf{PlaceHolder}(b, \pi)$

   (b) $\mathbf{Abst}(b, a)$

   (c) *For each $\sigma \in \Sigma$:* $Fact(\sigma\{f\})$

   (d) $b\{f\}$ *exists.*

   If $b\{f\}$ exists and f is appropriate, then $b\{f\}$ is the application *of a to f.*

4. *We will require of our SU+AE $\mathcal{S}$ that it be* closed under abstraction with restrictions: *for every element a of $|\mathcal{S}|$, every set Σ of possibilities and every set C of elements of $|\mathcal{S}|$, the simultaneous abstraction with restrictions $\lambda C[\Sigma].a$ exists.*

This definition of restricted abstraction would then allow the following analysis:

(7) a. Which foreign student was rejected?

  b. $\lambda\{b\}[\mathsf{fact}(\mathsf{prop}(s_{europe}, \langle\langle\mathsf{ForeignStudent}; b\rangle\rangle))]\mathsf{prop}(s_{univ}, \langle\langle\mathsf{Reject}; \mathsf{rejected}:b\rangle\rangle)$

Here, the university-internal situation is designated s_{univ} and the abstract is restricted by a fact pertaining to a distinct situation designated s_{europe}. As for (8), the situation including the meeting is designated $s_{euro-meet}$:

(8) a. Who attended the meeting?

  b. $\lambda\{b\}[\mathsf{fact}(\mathsf{prop}(s_{slov-tr}, \langle\langle\mathsf{Person}; b\rangle\rangle))]$
    $\mathsf{prop}(s_{euro-meet}, \langle\langle\mathsf{Attend}; \mathsf{attender}:b, \mathsf{event}:a\rangle\rangle)$

---

[7]See S&M–97, definition 4.3, p. 285. Restricted abstraction was originally introduced as a means of characterizing the contextual components of a meaning. In approaches such as Situation Semantics, where meanings are taken to arise by abstracting a set of contextual parameters from a content, the restrictions are used to encode additional conditions on the contextual parameters—those facts that need to hold in a context for felicitous use of an expression whose meaning is given by a given abstract.

The abstract is restricted by a fact pertaining to Slovenian trapeze artists, designated $s_{slov-tr}$.

Finally, we note that with this modified notion of question, there is an immediate solution for one of the problems that we noted for our definitions of answerhood in Chapter 3 (see section 3.5.3). In particular, we can now resolve the problem that too many propositions were taken into consideration as potential answers. With the improvements just sketched, the propositions that constitute instantiations of the question all involve entities taken from either the queried situation or the restrictor situation.

4.2 The Semantic Contribution of *Wh*-Phrases

In the previous section, we described our approach to analyzing restrictions and domain selection for both quantified propositions and *wh*-questions. In both cases, situationally relativized restrictions are introduced by combining abstraction with facts. Specifically, GQs are analyzed by treating the restrictor role of a determiner relation as filled by a fact abstract. *Wh*-questions are analyzed as restricted propositional abstracts. We can now complete the explanation we began in the preceding chapter of how to represent semantic objects by means of Typed Feature Structures (TFSs).

A GQ is represented by means of an AVM of the form specified in (9):

$$(9) \quad \begin{bmatrix} quant\text{-}rel \\ \text{INDEX} & index \\ \text{RESTR} & set(fact) \\ \dots & \dots \end{bmatrix}$$

By means of constraints discussed in Chapter 5, such a semantic object, together with possibly other quantifiers, gets scoped in to yield a SOA, whose TFS representation is, for example, as shown in (10a):

$$(10) \quad a. \quad \begin{bmatrix} \text{QUANTS} & \left\langle \begin{bmatrix} every\text{-}rel \\ \text{INDEX} & \boxed{1} \\ \text{RESTR} & \{\ poet(\boxed{1})\ \} \end{bmatrix}, \begin{bmatrix} some\text{-}rel \\ \text{INDEX} & \boxed{2} \\ \text{RESTR} & \{\ poem(\boxed{2})\ \} \end{bmatrix} \right\rangle \\ \text{NUCL} & \begin{bmatrix} think\text{-}up\text{-}rel \\ \text{THINKER} & \boxed{1} \\ \text{THOUGHT} & \boxed{2} \end{bmatrix} \end{bmatrix}$$

b. $\langle\langle$ Every; $\lambda\{b\}$fact(prop(s_0, $\langle\langle$Poet; b$\rangle\rangle$))),
$\lambda\{b\}\langle\langle$ Some;$\lambda\{a\}$fact(prop(s_1, $\langle\langle$Poem; a$\rangle\rangle$))),
$\lambda\{a\}\langle\langle$Think-up; thinker:b, thought:a$\rangle\rangle$ $\rangle\rangle$ $\rangle\rangle$

Recall from Chapter 3 that an entity of type *soa* is appropriately specified for the features QUANTS (taking a list of quantifiers as value), and NUCL (taking an element of type relation as value). The ordering inherent in QUANTS is intended to be construed as scopal ordering. Note that although our TFS representations of GQs specify nothing about their *nuclear* scope, the definition given in Chapter 3 (definition 17, the relevant clause of which we repeat here as (11)) guarantees that a (TFS) quantificational content like (10a) is interpreted as in (10b):[8]

(11)

If a is of the form:

$$\begin{bmatrix} soa \\ \text{QUANTS} \begin{bmatrix} \text{FIRST} \begin{bmatrix} \delta \\ \text{IND} & i \\ \text{RESTR} & \sigma \end{bmatrix} \\ \text{REST} & b \end{bmatrix} \\ \text{NUCL} \quad g \end{bmatrix},$$

where δ is a subtype of *quant-rel*,

then $[\![a]\!]^c = \left\langle \left\langle \; [\![\delta]\!]^c; \lambda\{\, c_f(i)\,\} [\![\sigma]\!]^c, \lambda\{\, c_f(i)\,\} \begin{bmatrix} soa \\ \text{QUANTS} & b \\ \text{NUCL} & g \end{bmatrix}^c \right\rangle \right\rangle$

In other words, the index associated with each quantifier is bound both within the restrictor and within the nucleus.[9]

But what about questions? As we have seen, questions share some crucial properties with quantified SOAs, but there are also some important differences. We capture the contribution of *wh*-phrases in questions by requiring that questions are appropriately specified for the feature PARAMS, whose value is a set of parameters. Each *wh*-word will introduce one parameter, which performs two of the tasks associated with *wh*-phrases: (1) linking one of the abstracted arguments to an argument position r within the *proposition* and (2) introducing additional restrictions that entities associated with r must satisfy. Note that the value of PARAMS is a set, *not* a list, in contrast to QUANTS. Moreover, the 'scope' of PARAMS is a proposition, not a SOA.

In the TFS content representations, the fact that both GQs and *wh*-phrases are not role fillers but rather involve abstraction is captured by positing a type *scope-obj(ect)*. This type subsumes both *quant-rel*, the type of all quantificational *soa*s, as well as *parameter*. As posited in Chapter 3, *scope-obj* declares the feature RESTR as appropriate. Objects of type *scope-obj* are the only objects that can belong to the sets that serve as values of the feature STORE. As our interpretation of TFS representations make clear, quantification involves a determiner relation associating two abstracts—a fact abstract and a SOA abstract. *Wh*-words are intrinsically different: they lack a quantificational force; they do not take scope over one another; and their scopal interaction with GQs is of a limited and 'non-standard' kind. We will explain these aspects of our analysis shortly, as well as their empirical consequences. But first let us give a couple of illustrations:

---

[8]Here and throughout, we use '*person* ($\boxed{1}$)' as a shorthand for a fact of the following form:

(i)
$$\begin{bmatrix} fact \\ \text{PROP} \begin{bmatrix} \text{SIT} & s \\ \text{SOA} \begin{bmatrix} \text{QUANTS} & \langle\,\rangle \\ \text{NUCL} \begin{bmatrix} person\text{-}rel \\ \text{INSTANCE} & \boxed{1} \end{bmatrix} \end{bmatrix} \end{bmatrix} \end{bmatrix}$$

[9]In order to accommodate phenomena pertaining to presupposition, this rule could be modified to allow restrictions pertaining to quantificational indices to be included in the restrictor.

(12) a. *Who left?* ↦

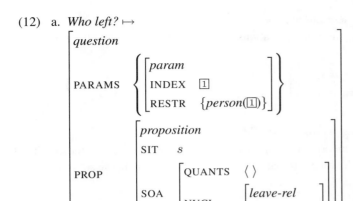

b. *Did someone leave?* ↦

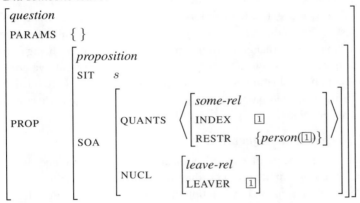

Note that polar questions are treated uniformly in terms of an empty PARAMS value. Conversely, multiple *wh*-questions are straightforwardly accommodated in terms of a non-singleton PARAMS value:

(13)   *Who greeted who?* ↦

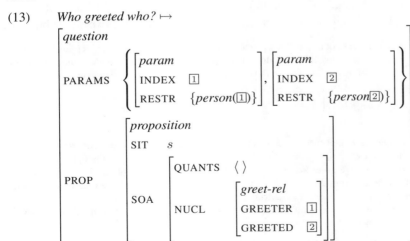

For convenience, we repeat here the most general formulation of the relationship between TFS question representations and their interpretations as SU+AE entities, originally provided in definition 17 in Chapter 3:[10]

(14)

If a is of the form:
$$\begin{bmatrix} question & \\ \text{PARAMS} & \sigma \\ \text{PROP} & b \end{bmatrix},$$

then: $[\![a]\!]^c = \lambda\{\text{indices}(\sigma)\}[\text{facts}(\sigma)][\![b]\!]^c$ and $\textbf{Question}([\![a]\!]^c)$

where **indices** is the function that maps a set of parameters to the set of indices that it contains and **facts** is the function that maps a set of parameters to the set of facts that it contains. (See Chapter 3 for details.)

4.3 The (Non)-Quantificational Nature of *Wh*-Phrases

Do *wh*-phrases behave semantically as quantifiers? Much of the syntactic literature—following in particular Chomsky (1977)—assumes this to be true primarily because of the corresponding assumption that *wh*-phrases are syntactic operators. We return to the latter issue in Chapter 7, where we argue against the belief that English unary *wh*-interrogatives require the fronting of the *wh*-phrase (with the echo readings that arise from pure in-situ interrogatives being either ignored or else regarded as outside the domain of 'core grammar'). For the present, we concentrate on semantic issues. We begin by evaluating how well *wh*-phrases fit the mold provided by quantification theory. We then argue that *wh*-phrases are better analyzed as non-quantificational elements that do not enter into scope relations.

4.3.1 *Wh*-Phrases as Generalized Quantifiers?

One of the important achievements of quantification theory, following Frege, was the ability to provide a straightforward interpretation procedure for sentences containing *arbitrarily many* quantifiers; these are simply interpreted by multiple iterations of the procedure for interpreting unary quantification.[11] Assuming the principles of GQ theory, the basic explanation for this can be described in the following way: the content created by a quantifier is of the same semantic type (*soa*, in our system) as a content created in an ordinary predication. Thus, the *output* of any quantified content can serve as the *input* for another quantifier. This allows us to explain why a given sentence containing more than one quantifier phrase, say exp_1 and exp_2, is liable to be

---

[10]Note that our formulation makes use of the auxiliary functions **indices** and **facts**. We could reformulate this in a way that would dispense with these functions. Such a modification would require us to rearrange the feature geometry of the PARAMS set to consist of a set of indices and a set of facts, in order to correspond to abstraction with restrictions, as shown in (i):

(i)
$$\begin{bmatrix} \text{PARAMS} & \begin{bmatrix} \text{INDICES} & set(index) \\ \text{RESTR} & set(fact) \end{bmatrix} \end{bmatrix}$$

Although this is only an issue for multiple *wh*-questions, such a change is easy to implement. The only consequence would be a slight complication in the existing formulation of the Interrogative Retrieval Constraint (governing retrieval of the stored parameters of interrogative *wh*-expressions) discussed in Chapter 6. Instead of identifying PARAMS with a (possibly empty) set of parameters from the store (as the constraint specifies at present), we need to state seperate constraints requiring set union of the indices and the restrictions that have been retrieved.

[11]We cast some of this discussion in 'procedural' terms for purely expository reasons. The entire discussion applies equally to a purely declarative view of interpretation.

ambiguous. As a rule, one can equally create a content in which $\exp_1$ scopes wider than $\exp_2$,[12] or vice versa. This idea is quite standard, though our particular formulation, following P&S–94's use of the features QUANTS and NUCL, is not.[13]

We claim that *wh*-phrases do not fit into this picture naturally. The basic assumption made by a quantificational view of *wh*-phrase meaning can be summarized in our terms as follows:

(15) a. Wh-Quantification (WHQ): a *Wh*-determiner maps a fact abstract and a property to an object of message type q(uestion).

  b. Wh: (fact-abstracts $\times$ properties) $\rightarrow$ q

  c. $Wh_i[FactAbstract](P(\ldots t_i \ldots))$

It is important to note that there is no obvious quantificational force to assign to *wh*-phrases. While it is certainly *possible* to treat a *wh*-phrase as an existential, as in Karttunen 1977, this is an artificial 'raising' which plays no semantic role and needs to be syncategorematically 'lowered' again. Semantically, as discussed in detail in Chapter 3, *all that is required is the requisite abstraction*. Although we present empirical arguments for the non-quantificational position in the following sections, it is important to emphasize that, *ceteris paribus*, the non-quantificational approach is the more restrictive position to adopt. This is because it requires us to forgo the existence of ordering, and more generally structure, on the PARAMS set of a given interrogative content. Therefore, even if a non-quantificational approach and a quantificational approach have similar empirical coverage, the former is to be preferred.

A second and more general point concerns sentences containing multiple uses of *wh*-phrases and GQs. This point applies to the view that a *wh*-phrase has no quantificational force, but still bears its own scope, as in the commonly assumed categorial grammar denotation $\lambda P \lambda x.P(x)$ (see Hausser 1983). In most semantic theories, the semantic type of an interrogative is distinct from the propositional type in order to account for the fact that interrogatives do not bear a truth value. Consequently, no expression whose scope is propositional can be assigned a scope wider than the scope of the *wh*-phrase simply on the basis of a WHQ rule like (15). In (16), Quant$_j$ is a quantifier that requires its scope to be propositional; without some additional mechanisms, it cannot be quantified into an interrogative content:

(16)   # Quant$_j[Wh_i \ldots (P(\ldots t_i, \ldots t_j))]$

Without making additional assumptions, (17a) can be assigned only one reading, where the *wh*-phrase takes wide scope. Example (17b) cannot be assigned any reading at all:

(17) a. Who proved each theorem?

  b. Who proved what?

On a purely technical level, one could defuse this argument in a number of ways, most simply by assuming that the semantic type of interrogatives *is* after all propositional or else (which amounts to the same thing) that interrogatives and declaratives live within the same type. Either way, two questions concerning the semantics of non-interrogative quantifiers remain unan-

---

[12]That is, one in which the entire content created by $\exp_2$ is a constituent of the scope of the content created by $\exp_1$.

[13]A full account of natural language quantification may need to appeal to a larger arsenal of semantic tools, e.g. polyadic quantification, branching quantification, and so forth. See Keenan and Westerståhl 1997 for a review of the current state of the art. Moreover, one might choose to adopt a non-standard view of what quantificational scope amounts to, as in skolemized or dependency-based accounts, which we discuss briefly below.

swered: (1) what mechanism ensures that when such a quantifier scopes *wider* than an interrogative content—as illustrated in (17a)—the whole content becomes interrogative and (2) what denotation should be assigned to a non-interrogative quantifier so that it can scope *wider* than an interrogative content in a semantically meaningful way?[14]

Of course, this impasse can be avoided by adopting additional special purpose semantic mechanisms. We are aware of two types of approaches. The first, proposed by Higginbotham (1996)[15] and Rexach (1997),[16] postulates a special semantic rule that allows non-interrogative quantifiers to outscope *wh*-phrases in a way that yields an interrogative content. Higginbotham does not explicitly discuss how to interpret multiple *wh*-interrogatives. However, his rule of *wh*-quantification (used to interpret unary *wh*-interrogatives) can be adapted to account for a subclass of multiple *wh*-interrogatives—those that can be input to the rule of *absorption* (see Higginbotham and May 1981), which we discuss in connection with *which*-phrases below. Absorption creates a single polyadic quantifier from a sequence of unary quantifiers.[17] In Rexach's system, an n-ary multiple question has a distinct type from an m-ary multiple question (for $m \neq n$). Each *wh*-phrase can shift its type, depending on the arity of the question it is building up. The problem of quantifying a *wh*-phrase into an interrogative content is solved at the price of positing a massive type ambiguity for *wh*-phrases.

An alternative approach (see Karttunen and Peters 1979 and Groenendijk and Stokhof 1984) is to postulate a rule of '*Wh*-Quantifying-In' (WH-QI) that uniformly enables either a *wh*-phrase or a GQ to quantify into and get as output an interrogative content. Essentially, this approach assumes that when a narrower scoping *wh*-phrase exists, GQs mutate into *wh*-phrases.

Is there any theoretical gain to be made by postulating such behavior? The evidence taken to show that there *is* motivation for this involves multiple *wh* sentences. These are often assumed to be synonymous with a pair-list/functional reading of a corresponding mixed universal quantifier/interrogative sentence where the quantifier (putatively) scopes over the *wh*-phrase. In the following two subsections, we provide data that we believe refute this assumption and which do not fit well into a quantificational view of *wh*-phrase meaning. We reiterate that we do not claim that *wh*-phrases cannot be squeezed into the generalized quantifier mold; we are merely observing that a system in which *wh*-phrases are not quantifiers is simpler.

4.3.2 The Non-Synonymy of Multiple *Wh*-Interrogatives and *Wh*/GQ-Interrogatives

First, we consider 'disjunction resolution' contexts—contexts in which disjunctive information is salient. Multiple *wh*-sentences used in such contexts do not elicit pair-list responses. In the same contexts, a unary *wh*-interrogative containing a quantifier would be inappropriate as a means of

---

[14]Nelken and Francez (1998) propose a system based on a five-valued logic (True, False, Undecided, Resolved, UN-resolved) in which declaratives and interrogatives (or their logical syntax counterparts) are all expressions of type t. In this system, it is unproblematic to quantify into interrogatives. On the other hand, such a system allows the emergence of scope relations among *wh*-phrases in multiple *wh*-interrogatives, which—as we show below—is a problematic consequence. An earlier attempt along these lines, using 4-valued logic, was made by Hoepelmann (1983).

[15]See his rule (75), p. 378.

[16]See his definition 54, PAIR-LIST LIFT, p. 444.

[17]Absorption is not applicable to multiple *wh*-interrogatives where one *wh*-phrase carries a dependency on the other, as in (i):

(i) Which student saw which one of her friends?.

See Higginbotham 1991 for an explicit proposal for multiple *wh*-interrogatives along these lines.

resolving the disjunction; such questions are preferably followed by pair-list responses.

Thus, in the context provided in (18), the natural response to (18a) would be (19a).

(18)   a. [It is known that Robin phoned Dale or Dale phoned Robin.]
Who phoned whom?

   b. [Same context:] Who did each person phone?

(19)   a. Well, it's Robin who phoned Dale.

   b. Robin phoned Dale, while Dale phoned Zhang.

On the other hand, in the same context, the preferred response to (18b) is still (19b). Indirectly, this last utterance could be taken to resolve the disjunction by implicating, for instance, that Dale did *not* phone Robin. But this sentence contains fundamentally different information than that of (19a), which is a felicitous response to (18a). Moreover, disjunction resolution contexts are not the only ones that elicit non-pair-list responses, as seen in the following example from the BBC:

(20)   A: Later on today an Italian court will start proceedings concerning the disappearance of an Italian businessman 7 years ago in London. Brian, who is going to be investigating what? (BBC World Service, Eight O'Clock News. Dec. 1998)

Higginbotham (1996), who motivates the need for a distinctive rule for quantifying non-interrogative quantifiers into interrogative contents, provides a similar argument. He suggests that (21a) and (21b) are not synonymous; although (21a) can be used in a situation in which I know what two of three salient persons said, (21b) cannot:

(21)   a. I have some information about who said what. (Higginbotham's (73))

   b. I have some information about what everybody said. (Higginbotham's (74))

Finally, let us mention another basic difference between multiple *wh*-interrogatives and mixed *wh*-GQ interrogatives. As we discuss in section 4.4.3 below, certain mixed *wh*-GQ interrogatives give rise to short answers which express so called *functional* answers. For example, (22b) is a possible response to (22a), where the bare NP *her karate instructor* is understood to vary with all Japanese women in the domain:

(22)   a. A: Who does each Japanese woman admire most?

   b. B: Her karate instructor

In contrast, multiple *wh*-interrogatives never allow single functional answers:

(23)   a. A: In your experience which person does which Japanese woman typically admire most?

   b. B: #Her karate instructor.

   c. B: The academic woman admires Banana Yoshimoto, whereas the businesswoman admires Hiday Nakata.

This contrast will be explained directly on our account, as *wh*-phrases always contribute a parameter into the PARAMS set—whether they are used independently or functionally. Thus, A's question in (23) involves a 2-element PARAMS set, i.e. is a 2-place proposition abstract. Conversely, only *wh*-phrases contribute elements to PARAMS and so a question like the one posed in (22a)—on whatever reading—involves a singleton PARAMS set (i.e. it is a 1-place proposition abstract).

4.3.3 Presuppositions of *Which*-Interrogatives

Interrogative sentences containing *which*-phrases with a singular common noun phrase manifest a uniqueness presupposition, as originally discussed in Higginbotham and May's seminal 1981 paper.[18,19] We argue that phenomena revolving around uniqueness provide support for the non-quantificational nature of *wh*-phrase meaning. Uniqueness considerations also point to the need to recognize a fundamental ambiguity between independent and functional readings.

The simplest case concerns unary *which*-interrogatives. For example, the speaker in (24a) presupposes that at most one student dropped out:

(24) a. Which student dropped out?

   b. Which student read which book?

The presuppositions associated with (24b) are more complex; a speaker who uses this sentence presupposes the existence of a set of students that can be mapped bijectively onto a set of books they read. Such a presupposition must make reference to a 2-place 'nuclear scope'. This goes against the assumption that one of the *wh*-phrases takes scope over the other.

Many accounts of the meaning of *which*-phrases in the formal semantic literature address only the unary case (e.g. Karttunen and Peters 1979) or fail to take into account these presuppositions (see, for example, Groenendijk and Stokhof 1984, Engdahl 1986).[20] Accounts that have recognized the need to capture these presuppositions begin with the assumption that *wh*-phrases are quantifiers, but they continue by introducing mechanisms that (either syntactically or semantically) create a polyadic quantifier from the multiply occurring *which*-phrases (see Higginbotham and May 1981, May 1989, Srivastav 1991 and Rexach 1997). Polyadic quantification, however, is a way of bypassing scopal dependence by quantifying over n-tuples.

Higginbotham and May suggest that sentences containing multiple *which*-phrases are ambiguous. They argue that such sentences allow both a polyadic reading and one that arises by iteratively scoping in the *which*-phrases (in the latter case, the presupposition exhibited is *absolute uniqueness*). We will dispute this account, suggesting that only the polyadic reading exists.

---

[18]We would like to thank Stanley Peters and Carl Pollard for useful discussions on this topic which have led to a substantial revision of this section.

[19]We discuss *which*-phrases with a PLURAL common noun phrase later on in this section.

[20]Engdahl recognizes that uniqueness is exhibited in unary *wh*-interrogatives but suggests that this need not be built into the meaning of the interrogative. She proposes that uniqueness arises via (conversational) implicature, but she does not attempt to elucidate her proposal. Engdahl's justification for the treatment via implicature is two-fold. First, she claims that uniqueness is not maintained in multiple *wh*-interrogatives. Her evidence for this is (i), which she suggests could not be responded to with (ii):

(i) Which table ordered which wine?

(ii) Table A ordered the Ridge Zinfandel

If one assumes a quantificational treatment of *wh*-phrases, this argument has some merit; the lack of absolute uniqueness for multiple *which*-interrogatives is surprising. However, below we will see evidence that multiple *which*-interrogatives can give rise to (absolute) uniqueness expectations.

Engdahl's second argument is that relativized uniqueness need not apply. She claims that when using (i) a querier does not exclude the possibility that some table ordered more than one kind of wine. Here we disagree, on the basis of differing intuitions about the relevant data. We believe that a speaker who does not wish a relativized uniqueness presupposition to emerge would be required to use sentences such as (iii) or (iv):

(iii) Which table ordered which wines?

(iv) Which tables ordered which wines?

Of course, an adequate account for *which* must explain how absolute uniqueness for the unary case typically gets 'relativized' in many cases of multiple *which*-interrogatives. This is a challenge we take up in this section.

The cases claimed to necessitate the iterative reading—which exhibit absolute uniqueness—can be explained in other ways. In certain cases, absolute uniqueness comes from the interaction of other presuppositional factors; elsewhere, the claimed generalizations about the data are simply inaccurate. The polyadic reading will require no special mechanisms in our account, given our non-quantificational view of *wh*-phrases. The presupposition will arise as a consequence of a constraint we associate with questions containing parameters introduced by singular *which*-phrases.

It is worth noting that if, following Engdahl, we were to deny the existence of these uniqueness presuppositions, then an extremely simple view of *wh*-phrase meaning could be entertained. Although it is often assumed that the possibility of providing pair-list responses in interrogatives correlates with scopal ambiguity, this is not actually the case. Certain pair-list uses *can* be explained as normal (independent) uses of *wh*-phrases. Thus, in (25a), if we assume an independent use of both *wh*-phrases does not involve scoping between the *wh*-phrases, then the question is a 2-place proposition abstract:

(25) a. A: Who admires whom in this department?
         B: Millie admires Brendan, Sigmund admires Carl . . .
      b. A: Who do the police officers in this precinct hate?
         B: Serpico hates Mancetti, Harry hates Goldfarb . . .

In such a case, a pair-list response is nothing more than a response that provides a sequence of atomic answers. Similarly, a pair-list reading for (25b) can be explained as arising from a combination of two factors: the possibility of using *who* to specify an aggregate or sum and a cumulative reading of the VP. This latter explanation could also account for the possibility of a pair-list response such as (26c).

(26) a. Who does every Englishwoman admire most?
      b. Posh Spice, Ruth Lawrence, and Peter Mandelson.
      c. Mrs. Thatcher admires herself; the Queen admires Mrs. Thatcher and Alex Ferguson, Nigella Lawson admires Doris Lessing, . . .

The response here enumerates a set that the set of Englishwomen admire cumulatively. A system of this type, where *wh*-phrases have just one type of use and are never outscoped by GQs, could be argued to have significant empirical coverage. Moreover, the only price that would be paid for achieving this coverage would be the assumption that *wh*-phrases range over sets, an assumption that is independently motivated, as we will see. The only class of phenomena that one would not obviously get a handle on is functional responses, further discussed in section 4.4.3 below.

Although we do not advocate such a sparse system, we believe it is only once one takes uniqueness phenomena seriously that it becomes necessary to recognize an ambiguity in interrogatives, such as in (26a). Examples (27) and (28) provide arguments for the position that singular *which* $\bar{N}$ phrases carry a uniqueness presupposition:[21]

---

[21]More precisely, uniqueness in this context is not 'exactly one', but rather 'at most one' given that the existential implicature is cancellable:

(i) Which applicant, if any, should I select for the position?

We use 'uniqueness' in the 'at most one' sense throughout this section, though conversational implicature will often strengthen the force to 'exactly one'.

(27) a. A: Which student left yesterday?
   B: Bo.
   Valid inference: Bo is the student that left.

   b. A: #Which book have you been reading over the last few years?
   (Strange because people rarely read a single book for a few years; cf. the perfectly normal: *Which books have you been reading over the last few years?*)

(28) a. A: Which undergraduate student are you inviting for Thanksgiving dinner?
   B: Bo.
   A: #Which other undergraduate students are you inviting for your dinner?

   b. A: Who are you inviting for your Thanksgiving dinner?
   B: Bo.
   A: Who else?

Examples like (27) show that an answer to a unary *which*-question licenses the inference that the queried property (restricted by the *which*-phrase's restrictor property) is uniquely instantiated in the current context. The examples in (28) demonstrate a contrast between a unary *which*-interogative and a unary *wh*-interogative with respect to uniqueness.

If we assume that (singular) *which* $\bar{N}$ carries a uniqueness presupposition, then the normal 'wide scope' reading for (29a) should carry the presupposition that there exists at most one student m such that m impressed each lecturer:

(29) a. Which student impressed each lecturer?

   b. Carrie impressed Fergie, Dana impressed Glen . . .

But a pair-list response such as (29b) to (29a) violates this presupposition. Given that such a response does not seem to require significant presuppositional adjustment, it would seem that (29a) has another reading in which the above presupposition is absent. Specifically, it appears as if the presupposition is relativized, so that the uniqueness is no longer absolute but relative to each lecturer. Hence, an interrogative like (29a) must be assumed to be ambiguous.

Let us now consider sentences containing multiple occurrences of *which*-phrases. Higginbotham and May 1981 (henceforth H&M–81) propose a semantic system that treats *wh*-phrases as unary quantifiers. In particular, they build in a uniqueness presupposition for singular *which*-phrases. Within this system, applying the quantification rule iteratively will lead to the prediction that a sentence such as (30a) presupposes that a unique man/woman pair saw each other. However, as they point out, (30a) readily accepts pair-list answers such as (30b):

(30) a. Which man saw which woman? (H&M–81's (1.11))

   b. John saw Mary and Bill saw Sally. (H&M–81's (1.13))

   c. John saw Mary and he also saw Sally, as did Bill.

H&M draw two conclusions from these data. First, a mechanism needs to be proposed to account for this unexpected presupposition, which they term the *bijective reading* of the sentence ('bijective', since a response such as (30c) seems to go against the querier's expectations). Second, H&M conclude that sentences such as (30a) are ambiguous. They suggest that such sentences presuppose absolute uniqueness—a reading they term the *singular reading*. As evidence, they put forward (31A), which presupposes an answer like (31B), but not one like (31B′).

(31) A: In *Gone with the Wind*, which character admired which character?
            (H&M–81's (1.14))[22]

   B: Ashley Wilkes admired Rhett Butler (H&M–81's (1.15))

   B′:   #Ashley Wilkes admired Rhett Butler and Melanie Wilkes admired Scarlet O'Hara.
            (H&M–81's (1.16); H&M's judgement.)

More generally, they suggest that the bijective reading is available only when the domains of quantification associated with the *which*-phrases are disjoint.

Within H&M's system, the *singular* reading is of some importance, since its existence accords with the prediction of iterative quantification. However, we are skeptical that such a distinct *reading* exists. For a start, the judgement that (31B′) is anomalous seems suspect. Moreover, we believe that counterexamples to H&M's generalization about the unavailability of the bijective reading are not difficult to construct. (32a) is an example from H&M's own paper, which they acknowledge exhibits a bijective understanding:

(32) a.   [Asked of a gossip columnist] Which guest is going home with which guest?
            (H&M–81, nt. 3)

   b.   Which female guest is going home with which male guest?

But H&M argue that, given the social norms (e.g. of the 1980s), the sentence is usually understood as (32b), and therefore does not go against their generalization. However, we contend that bijective understanding is possible even in a society such as ours, where heterosexual preference is no longer a default. Example (33) can also be understood bijectively, but there is no clear argument that the associated domains of quantification are distinct:

(33) A: We need to be prepared for all possible contingencies. What if the trampolene gives way and the human pyramid collapses? Do you have any idea what will happen?

   B: You mean that we need to worry about which trapeze artist will end up crushing which trapeze artist?

For theory-internal reasons, H&M predict that interrogatives where one *which*-phrase depends anaphorically on another cannot get bijective understandings as seen in (34a,b). Judgements about this vary, however; example (34c), from Engdahl 1986, seems quite acceptable:

(34) a.   Which boy likes which one of his sisters? (H&M–81's (1.32))

   b.   #John admires his sister Mary and Fred admires his sister Sally. (H&M–81's (1.40); H&M's judgement.)

   c.   Bill likes his elder sister; Mike likes his younger sister,....

Now consider the following example:

(35) A: Sir, there's some bad news. A student has smashed one of the double-glazed windows in the quad.

   B: OK tell me, which student smashed which window?

Though the singular understanding of (35B) is implied by the context, the bijective understanding is still hard to evade. For example, one is tempted to understand B to be implicating that A has been hiding worse news and that probably more than one window was broken.

---

[22]H&M–81's example actually has *admires* where we have *admired*, but this seems to be a typographical error, given the answers they provide, which we reproduce verbatim. It is possible that using the present tense biases one to prefer an answer such as (31B) over (31B′), since the question then resembles a quizmaster question. We discuss this issue further in this section.

Of course, we do not deny that singular understandings are sometimes possible. These cases typically have a 'quizmaster question' feel to them, as in (36a,b):

(36)   a.   Which French emperor inspired which great Austrian composer to write which string quartet?

b.   In the 1920's which American inventor promoted which European right wing political ideology?

The pragmatic background to such a use, e.g. the implausibility of believing that a specific propositional abstract should have more than one true instantiator, helps to foster a singular understanding.

Also relevant are interrogative Bach-Peters sentences like (37a):

(37)   a.   Which director who produced it backed out of which highly publicized movie that was causing him losses?

b.   Coppola was the director, the movie was *Hammett*.

c.   #Coppola (was the director who) backed out of *Hammett*, Ponti (was the director who) backed out of *The Bicycle Thief*,...

Many speakers find such cases to be marginal. However, those who do not (for instance, Ginzburg 1992, which is our source for these examples) report that, when understood with crossing coreference, only a singular understanding is possible. Example (37a) is similar to (36) since both are 'quizmaster questions', which we suggested introduce an expectation for uniqueness. We support this explanation semantically. As we show below, even if one assumes that sentences containing multiple *which*-phrases exhibit only a bijective reading, there are independent presuppositional factors—namely the uniqueness presuppositions introduced by pronouns—which interact to yield a singular understanding of the sentence. We conclude that semantically sentences containing (singular) *which*-phrases are unambiguously bijective.

It is important to note that these data constitute an argument for the non-quantificational nature of *wh*-phrases. More precisely, they support the claim that *wh*-phrases do not scope over one another. This is because the presupposition is unscoped: it concerns an n-ary abstract (or open sentence). H&M's account for this reading involves postulating the operation of *absorption*. Absorption, as defined by H&M, creates a polyadic quantifier expression out of unary quantifier expressions.[23] H&M defined the operation on the (syntactic) level of logical form, though it can also be defined semantically. The following (superficially modified) definition from Rexach 1997 incorporates the semantics proposed by H&M:

(38)   Let E be a domain, $R \subset E^n$, $Z_1, \ldots, Z_n \subset E$.
Then, $\mathrm{Bij}(which_1(Z_1), \ldots, which_n(Z_n))$ is an n-ary quantifier
(i.e. is of type $[\mathcal{P}(E^n) \to q]$, where q is the type of questions, $\mathcal{P}(E^n)$ is the power-set of E^n).
$\mathrm{Bij}(which_1(Z_1), \ldots, which_n(Z_n))(R)$ presupposes that
$\forall \alpha_i \exists! < \alpha_1, \ldots, \alpha_{i-1}, \alpha_{i+1}, \ldots, \alpha_n > \in Z_1, \ldots, Z_{i-1}, Z_{i+1}, \ldots, Z_n$ such that
$< \alpha_1, \ldots, \alpha_n > \in R$ (See Rexach 1997, definition 52, p. 441.)

---

[23]H&M offer an independent, non-interrogative use for absorption in explicating such phenomena as Bach-Peters sentences. We provide an entirely different use for absorption in Chapter 8.

There are two points to be made with respect to (38). The first concerns the generalization of bijectivity to an n-place abstract. We claim that the condition proposed in (38) is not quite correct.[24] This condition requires each entity α_i occurring in the i-th place of an n-tuple of the queried predicate to be uniquely completed as an n-tuple. As seen below in (39), this rules out an answer where an entity (*Anna Karenina*) occurs in two distinct tuples:

(39) A: Which student read which book for which course?

     B: Kim read *Anna Karenina* for Russian Lit 413 and she read *To Mageio* for Greek Lit 169, whereas Sandy read *Anna Karenina* for Women's Studies 305 and he read *White Teeth* for Women's Studies 510. (Example due to Carl Pollard (p.c.))

However, an alternative notion proposed to us by Pollard allows for the answer provided in (39). This notion, which we call *n-jectivity*, is given in (40):

(40)   A propositional abstract μ ($= \lambda\{b_1, \ldots, b_n\}p$) is n-jective iff the following condition holds:

    whenever

        1. two assignments f_1 and f_2 are appropriate for μ,

        2. both $\mu[f_1]$ and $\mu[f_2]$ are true propositions, and moreover

        3. f_1 and f_2 are identical on $n - 1$ roles,

    then f_1 and f_2 also agree on the nth role.

    That is, if for some subset of indices $\{i_1, \ldots, i_{n-1}\}$ $f_1(x_{i_j}) = f_2(x_{i_j})$, for $1 \leq j \leq n - 1$, then also $f_1(x_{i_n}) = f_2(x_{i_n})$

If two assignments to the abstract agree on all but one coordinate, then they must also agree on the remaining one. As defined in (40), the relation of n-jectivity reduces to uniqueness for $n = 1$, to bijectivity for $n = 2$, but for $n = 3$, it diverges from bijectivity.

A second, more methodological point to make about (38) is this: in contrast to systems that treat *wh*-phrases as quantifiers, a system like ours, where *wh*-phrases do not bear scope relative to each other, requires no additional scoping mechanism (such as absorption) to capture n-jectivity. N-jectivity follows from the one rule of *wh*-retrieval we posit, combined with a single presupposition-triggering constraint associated with questions introduced by singular *which*-phrases. The constraint will state that if at least one singular *which*-phrase gets retrieved, then a presupposition is introduced that the question is n-jectively instantiated.[25]

We then assume that what triggers the presupposition is the singular nature of the restrictor common noun phrase in a singular *which*-phrase. For this assumption to be plausible, we must provide evidence that the distinction between singular and plural *which*-phrases is semantically significant. Such evidence is not difficult to find. Singular and plural *which*-phrases contrast minimally with respect to plural entities. Singular *which*-phrases cannot be used with intrinsically collective predicates, whereas plural *which*-phrases can:

(41) a. #Which student surrounded the mayoral candidate as he got out from his taxi?

     b.   Which students surrounded the mayoral candidate as he got out from his taxi?

     c.   #Which politician has the same height?

     d.   Which politicians have the same height?

---

[24]We owe this observation to Carl Pollard.

[25]Note that because our propositions are Austinian, this means that instantiation possibilities for the abstract are relativized to a situation. In this respect, we follow the situation semantics analysis of definites.

Conversely, using a plural *which*-phrase involves the assumption that the question is not uniquely instantiated. Example (42a) can only be understood if either two elections took place in 1960 or if the United Fruit Company has a collective leadership:

(42) a. Which senators were elected president of the United Fruit Company in 1960?

  b. #Which natural numbers precede all others?

  c. Which natural number precedes all others?

Similarly, (42b) is incomprehensible because, in contrast to the unique minimal natural number zero, there is no distinguished group of minimal natural numbers. *Who* and *what* are intermediate cases, both usable with intrinsically collective and uniquely satisfiable predicates:

(43) a. What is the first natural number?

  b. Who was elected president of the United Fruit Company in 1960?

  c. Who surrounded the mayoral candidate as he got out from his taxi?

The data in (41) and (42) indicate that the semantic contribution of singular and plural *which*-phrases is fundamentally distinct. Using the perspective on the singular/plural distinction outlined in Link 1983, we state this distinction as follows:

(44) a. Singular *which*-phrases specify indices restricted to atomic individuals.

  b. Plural *which*-phrases specify indices restricted to non-atomic individuals.

  c. *Who* and *what* specify indices underspecified for the atomic/non-atomic distinction.

Trying to make a distinction at the level of indices[26] is not sufficient. It does not permit us to distinguish singular *which*-phrases from *who/what* on uses where the index of the latter is resolved to be atomic, e.g. by a singular, non-collective verb.[27] In order to distinguish singular *which*-phrases from plural *which*-phrases, and *who* and *what*, we examine the singular/plural distinction of common noun phrases (following Link 1983).[28] Link and others (see Landman 1989 and Lönning 1997) have proposed that (45a) denotes a property applicable only to atomic individuals, whereas (45b) is applicable to atomic and non-atomic individuals. This latter property arises via an operation on atomic properties denoted by suffixing a '^{b}':

(45) a. *student* $\mapsto$ Student

  b. *students* $\mapsto$ Student^b

We use this basic distinction to partition the type *count-rel*, a subtype of *rel*, into two distinct subtypes: *atomic-rel* and *non-atomic-rel*. The former subsumes the contents of singular common noun phrases; the latter applies to the content of all other common noun phrases. We can then

---

[26]See P&S–94, Chapter 2 for a detailed discussion of agreement, including a singular/aggregate distinction among the (referents of) indices.

[27]We do not appeal here to any notions pertaining to 'definiteness' or 'specificity', notions that have been regularly associated with *which*-phrases since Katz and Postal 1964. An influential proposal by Pesetsky (1987) distinguished *which*-phrases from most other *wh*-phrases in terms of a notion he called D-linking. A *wh*-phrase is D-linked if its use requires the existence of a salient set of potential instantiators for the role with which it is associated. Pesetsky suggested that positive or negative specification for D-linking could be used to explain contrasts distinguishing *which*-phrases from *who* and *what*, especially with respect to *superiority*. We discuss D-linking in Chapter 6.

[28]Rexach (1997) follows a similar strategy.

associate the following contents with the different classes of *wh*-phrase:[29]

(46) a. *which CN[sg]*

$$
\begin{bmatrix}
param \\
\text{INDEX} \quad \boxed{1}[3rd,sg] \\
\text{RESTR} \quad \left\{ \begin{bmatrix} fact \\ \text{PROP|SOA|NUCL} \quad \begin{bmatrix} atomic\text{-}rel \\ \text{INST} \quad \boxed{1} \end{bmatrix} \end{bmatrix} \right\}
\end{bmatrix}
$$

b. *who*

$$
\begin{bmatrix}
param \\
\text{INDEX} \quad \boxed{1}[3rd] \\
\text{RESTR} \quad \left\{ \begin{bmatrix} fact \\ \text{PROP|SOA|NUCL} \quad \begin{bmatrix} person^b\text{-}rel \\ \text{INST} \quad \boxed{1} \end{bmatrix} \end{bmatrix} \right\}
\end{bmatrix}
$$

c. *which CN[pl]*

$$
\begin{bmatrix}
param \\
\text{INDEX} \quad \boxed{1}[3rd,pl] \\
\text{RESTR} \quad \left\{ \begin{bmatrix} fact \\ \text{PROP|SOA|NUCL} \quad \begin{bmatrix} non\text{-}atomic\text{-}rel \\ \text{INST} \quad \boxed{1} \end{bmatrix} \end{bmatrix} \right\}
\end{bmatrix}
$$

(To enhance readability, here and throughout we will supress the distinction between atomic and non-atomic relations, except where it is of immediate relevance.)

This framework allows us to define the constraint that triggers the n-jectivity presupposition. However, we should emphasize that our framework does not fully address the various issues raised by the singular/plural divide. In particular, our treatment of the interrelationship among *wh*-retrieval, distributivity and plural NPs is minimal. Nonetheless, we hypothesize that our framework can be extended to provide an adequate account of such issues.

Our formulation is motivated by the need to avoid linking the emergence of the *which*-presupposition to a particular syntactic context, as would be the case were we to associate its triggering with a particular construction type. Since the presupposition arises with any interrogative clause that contains a singular *which*-phrase, it is appropriate to associate the presupposition directly with the questions that serve as the denotata of *which*-interrogatives. More precisely, we state the constraint as an additional subcase in the TFS to SU+AE mapping defined in definition 17 of Chapter 3. A TFS *a* of type *question* that has in its PARAMS set at least one parameter re-

---

[29]This simplified representation abstracts away from issues pertaining to storage and scoping. As we explain in Chapters 5 and 6, the content associated with a *wh*-phrase involves a restriction-less parameter and a parameter which includes the restriction(s). The former is introduced as a role filler in the NUCLEUS of a *soa*, whereas the latter gets retrieved into the PARAMS set of a question.

stricted by an *atomic-relation* involves the presupposition that the question—*a*'s denotation—is n-jectively instantiated:

(47)   Singular *Which* Presupposition Constraint (WH-PRC):

Let M = ⟨ SU+AE, I ⟩ where SU+AE is a situation universe plus abstract entities, *I* the interpretation function defined in section 17, and *c* a context.

$$
\text{If } a = \begin{bmatrix} question \\[4pt] \text{PARAMS} \quad \left\{ \dots \begin{bmatrix} param \\ \text{RESTR} \quad \{ \dots [\text{NUCL} \quad atomic\text{-}rel] \dots \}, \dots \end{bmatrix} \right\} \end{bmatrix}
$$

then there must exist a situation *s* such that *c* contains a certain fact *f*, where
$$f = \text{fact}(\text{prop}(s, \langle\langle \text{N-Jective}; \llbracket a \rrbracket^c \rangle\rangle))$$

From the WH-PRC, it follows that (48a) carries the presupposition that for any company official who gave a gift to a man, she gave that man a unique gift.[30] The content and contextual background associated with (48a) are given in (48b):

(48)   a. Which company official gave which gift to which man?

   b.
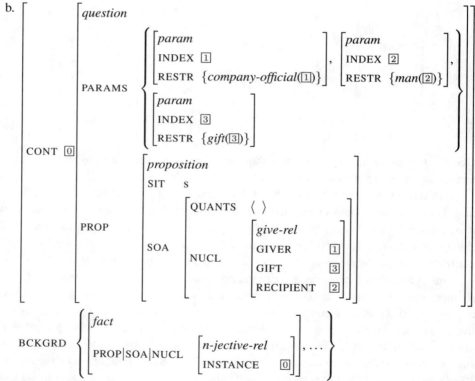

We can also offer a semantic explanation for interrogative Bach-Peters sentences with crossing coreference. Examples like (37), repeated here as (49), exhibit a presupposition of absolute uniqueness, i.e. that there exists at most one pair that instantiates the propositional abstract:

---

[30]See section 4.5 for an additional example that combines n-jectivity with a functional reading.

(49) a.   Which director who produced it backed out of which highly publicized movie that
          was causing him losses?

     b.   Coppola was the director, the movie was *Hammett*.

     c.   #Coppola (was the director who) backed out of *Hammett*, Ponti (was the director who)
          backed out of *The Bicycle Thief*, ...

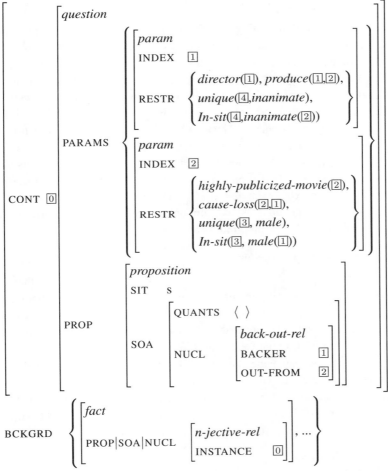

According to our account, the two *which*-phrases do not bear scope relative to each other.
Therefore, it is simple to derive the crossing coreference. A detailed account of this requires a
careful discussion of the uniqueness associated with singular pronouns, which we will not provide. For concreteness, we follow the SitSem account developed by Gawron and Peters (1990).
We assume that, for some contextually supplied situations, pronouns carry uniqueness restrictions. In such instances, there is a situationally unique male/female/inanimate. This assumption
involves adding restrictions to the *which*-phrases: in some situation, tagged with index [3] in (49d),
[1] is the unique male, and in some other situation, tagged with index [4], [2] is the unique inani-
mate. Given n-jectivity, the consequence of this is the emergence of absolute uniqueness as the
presupposition.

Finally, given the above interpretation, we provide an explanation for the distinct presuppositions that arise with sentences containing singular and plural *which*-phrases, seem in (50). Example (50a) involves a bijectivity presupposition. However, (50b,c) can be read as neutral:

(50) a. Which student read which book?
      b. Which student read which books?
      c. Which students read which books?

Given the presence of a singular *which*-phrase in (50b), the n-jectivity presupposition will be triggered. However, since a plural *which*-phrase specifies a group, (50c) involves a bijection between a set of students and a set of sets of books. This means that the n-jectivity presupposition has been filtered away. To support this explanation, we need to refine the semantic contribution we have associated with plural *which*-phrases. In contents where the role associated with a plural *which*-phrase is understood distributively, we must ensure that the filler of that role is specified to be *maximal*, otherwise inconsistency will result. Consider (50b). In such a case, n-jectivity tells us that for each student a there is a unique set of books P such that $\forall z{:}P(z)\langle\langle \text{Read},a,z\rangle\rangle$. But then it follows that $\forall z{:}P'(z)\langle\langle \text{Read},a,z\rangle\rangle$, for any P' such that $P' \subset P$. This contradicts the uniqueness of P required by n-jectivity. This problem is avoided if the specification for P included the condition that P is the maximal set such that $\forall z P(z)\langle\langle \text{Read},a,z\rangle\rangle$; the subsets of P', then, no longer need be taken into account. The assumption that interrogatives encode exhaustivity is of course common. We make this assumption merely for plural *which*-phrases.[31]

4.4   *Wh*-phrase and GQ Interaction

We now turn to the scopal interaction of *wh*-phrases with GQs. We claim that, within a single sentential content (i.e. ignoring the effect of sentence embedding), *wh*-phrases scope wider then GQs.[32] As background, we first mention one additional class of readings for *wh*-phrases—functional readings—to which we argue that *all* cases where *wh*-phrases do not *seem* to exhibit widest scope can be reduced. In our treatment of functional readings, the (functional) index contributed by a *wh*-phrase scopes wider than any GQ in that sentential content. We consider two phenomena that have been claimed to show that *wh*-phrases can scope narrower than GQs: (1) the interaction of *wh*-phrases with adverbs and (2) the phenomenon of pair-list readings. We consider whether pair-list readings motivate a semantic mechanism above and beyond the one that accounts for functional readings. We argue against the need for any such additional mechanism.

4.4.1   Functional Readings

In section 4.3.3, we established that, in order to elicit a pair-list response, an interrogative sentence like (51) must be analyzed as ambiguous:

(51)   Which student does each lecturer find most impressive?

This ambiguity has often been taken as evidence for the existence of a reading in which the GQ *outscopes* the *wh*-phrase. However, as noted in section 4.3.1, such a conclusion is unnatural

---

[31] For analogous requirements of maximality with respect to dynamic semantic treatments of plural pronouns, see van den Berg 1993, Kibble 1997.

[32] As noted above, this issue is independent from the issue of whether *wh*-phrases are quantifiers. It is possible that *wh*-phrases scope wider then GQs and are quantificational in addition. Conversely, one might also entertain the view that *wh*-phrases are not quantificational but *wh*-phrases do not necessarily scope wider then GQs.

from a semantic point of view since it relies on the assumption that GQs behave differently in interrogative contexts.

Elisabet Engdahl (1980, 1986) was the first to propose an alternative source for such uses. Engdahl observed that sentences such as (51) could (in addition to a pair-list response) elicit a response such as (52). Example (52) could be read to mean that every lecturer is impressed by a student in her own class. However, explicating the source of readings of the latter type in terms of the GQ outscoping the *wh*-phrase is undesirable; an agent can respond with (52) only with rudimentary knowledge of the domain over which the quantifier ranges:[33]

(52)   The student who writes the shortest term paper.

Engdahl proposed to analyze the sentence as a *functional* reading; the queried property in such a case is not a property of individuals, but rather a property of functions between individuals.

Example (51) could be interpreted as "What is a function f such that each lecturer x is impressed by f(x)?" Engdahl also pointed out that functional responses are not simply stylistic variants of pair-list responses since sentences like (53) exist. These sentences elicit functional responses, but not pair-list responses:[34]

(53)   a.   Who does no Englishwoman admire?
       b.   Her headmistress.
       c.   #Mrs. Thatcher admires Mr. Heath, the Queen admires Nigel Dempster, . . .
       d.   #Mrs. Thatcher doesn't admire Mr. Heath, the Queen doesn't admire
            Nigel Dempster, . . .

Nor are functional readings a 'notationally variant' means of assigning wide scope to the GQ, as some might think, since they arise by means of a process akin to skolemization. What Skolem showed was that any first order formula in prenex form can be associated with a truth-conditionally equivalent second order formula, in which narrowly scoped (first order) existential quantifiers are replaced by wide scoping existential quantifiers over functions. For a large class of cases (e.g. for characterizing the truth conditions of declarative sentences containing NPs denoting first order quantifiers), it makes little difference whether one takes a first order formula—$\forall x \exists y P(x, y)$—or the corresponding skolemized formula—in this case $\exists f \forall x P(x, f(x))$—as a logical form. However, there are cases where a skolemized formula is not reducible to a first order formula, as emphasized in the Game Theoretic Semantics literature (surveyed in Hintikka and Sandu 1997). Moreover, in semantic settings that distinguish contents in terms of information structure or dynamic effects, a 'skolemized' formula will not be a 'syntactic variant' of a first order formula. There have also been proposals—most prominently those by Hobbs (1983, 1996)—to explicate underspecification of quantifier scoping by means of skolem-like dependencies.

Though the current work makes no such claim, skolemization may play a significant role in the analysis of quantification and other related phenomena in natural language semantics. Be that as it may, as far as interrogatives are concerned, 'skolemization' is by no means innocuous. For example, there is no obvious first order analog of the 'skolemized' $\lambda f \forall x P(x, \mathbf{f}(x))$. We speculate

---

[33]Thus, such an agent is not answering a question paraphrasable as "For every lecturer j, who is it that j finds most impressive?"

[34](53) contains a potential 'negated' pair-list to show that the problem is not related to the polarity of the response.

that a system where all 'scope ambiguities' are handled in terms of skolemization will emerge as a competitive alternative to existing accounts.

4.4.2 *Wh*-Phrases and Adverbs

Adverbs have been a source of conflicting claims about the scopal nature of *wh*-phrases. Let us consider first embedded clauses. Berman (1990, 1991) argues that when embedded by factive predicates, *wh*-phrases are bound by adverbs of quantification. Specifically, he argues for the existence of a fundamental bifurcation among embedded interrogative clauses (the 'quantificational variability effect' (QVE)). Berman claims there is a crucial difference between question predicates and resolutives: in a clause embedded by a question predicate (e.g. (54a)), an adverb of quantification is interpreted as quantifying over cases/events/situations (henceforth the *cases* reading), whereas a clause embedded by a resolutive predicate (e.g. (54b)) displays an additional reading (the QV reading) paraphrased in (54c):

(54)   a. Jill to some extent/usually/for the most part wonders which students cheat on the exam.

   b. Jill to some extent/usually/for the most part knows which students cheat on the exam.

   c. For some/most students x that cheat on the exam, Jill knows that x cheats on the exam.

Ginzburg (1995b) argues that this view of adverbial modification of interrogatives is erroneous. He disputes the claim of the existence of a resolutive/question predicate asymmetry and rejects the truth conditions Berman proposes for the QV reading. With respect to the latter issue, Ginzburg argues against an analysis involving 'quantificational variability'.[35] He points out that (55) licenses (56a,b):

(55)   Celia: All I know is that some rather unruly linguists showed up, though I don't know who.

(56)   a. Celia could tell (only) to some extent/ to a limited extent who showed up last night.

   b. Celia knew (only) to some extent/to a limited extent who showed up last night.

If the quantificational variability paraphrase were correct, (56) should entail (57).

(57)   For some x who showed up last night Celia told me/knew that x showed up last night.

However, given the context of (55), such a paraphrase in (57) is not warranted.

Moreover, Ginzburg suggests that by moving away from a view of QV readings as involving quantificational variability, it becomes apparent that question predicates can manifest a reading which is distinct from the cases reading. Example (58) exemplifies a QV reading for the predicate *investigate*

(58)   a. There have been many issues for us to investigate, far too many for us to do a thorough job. We have to some extent investigated who committed the crime, we have fully investigated who was at the scene of the crime, but only to a limited extent when the suspects were in town.

   b. Hence, what has taken place is: partial investigation of the first issue, complete investigation of the second issue, limited investigation of the third issue.

---

[35]The analysis in terms of quantificational variability was first proposed by Berman and endorsed by Lahiri (1991) and Groenendijk and Stokhof (1993).

Ginzburg proposes an account that links QV readings to adverbial modification of the embedding *predicate*, tying together cases like (59a) with non-interrogative examples like (59b):[36]

(59) a. The scientist has to some extent established which person committed the crime. (The scientist has established a fact that goes some way toward resolving the question of which person committed the crime.)

b. The scientist has to some extent established that unpasteurized milk causes botulism in rats. (The scientist has established a fact that goes some way toward proving the claim that unpasteurised milk causes botulism in rats.)

If such an account is correct, we can maintain the assumption that *wh*-phrases do not get bound by adverbs of quantification. This assumption should be distinguished from the claim that *wh*-phrases are always understood independently (i.e. non-functionally) when occurring in construction with an adverb of quantification (see Berman 1990, Ginzburg 1992). Sentences such as (60a,b,c) are most readily understood when the adverb becoming part of the proposition over which the interrogative parameter gets abstracted:

(60) a. Which regular customer rarely tips big?

b. Who rarely supports the government's tax-cutting proposals?

c. Which spectator fails to laugh at the right moment whenever you watch a performance of a play by Mamet?

Example (60a) can convey 'who has the property of being both a regular customer and rarely tipping big'; (60b) queries for an individual who occasionally supports the government's tax-cutting moves; and (60c) is a question about the ultimate philistine—a spectator equipped with sense of humor so deficient that it leads him/her to mislaugh at performance after performance:

Below, the sentences in (61) weakly manifest a 'specific indefinite' reading. The most prominent reading, however, is construable with the adverb taking widest scope:

(61) a. A regular customer rarely tips big.

b. Everyone rarely supports the government's tax-cutting proposals.

c. Some spectator fails to laugh at the right moment whenever you watch a performance of a play by Mamet.

Example (61a) can be paraphrased as "It is rarely the case that there is a regular customer *i*, such that *i* tips big".

We claim that it is inaccurate to conclude that sentences such as those in (60) are unambiguous. In fact, the questions in (60) can elicit responses such as those in (62), which are instances

---

[36]In Ginzburg 1995b, an account of how the QV reading arises for predicates such as *know, discover, tell* and *establish* is developed, based on two essential components. The first is a notion of a fact f_1 subsuming-to-Q-extent a fact f_0. The second is a meaning postulate posited to be applicable to such predicates, which equates *V'ing-to-Q-extent* of a fact f with V'ing a fact f_1 which subsumes-to-Q-extent f. This allows an account that is applicable simultaneously to interrogative, declarative and NP complements. It also allows a more detailed account of lexical variation concerning QV readings than the accounts cited above. For instance, accommodating the fact that with factive predicates such as *amaze* and *disgust*, the QV reading does not involve V'ing a 'weaker' fact—(i) does not entail (ii):

(i) Jo was to some extent disgusted by who showed up to the party.

(ii) Jo was disgusted by a fact that partially resolves the issue of who showed up to the party.

of the functional readings we discussed in the previous section.[37]

(62) a. A: Which regular customer rarely tips big?
          B: The customer who enters the shop last every day.

      b. A: Who usually cooks the dinner around here?
          B: The person who arrives home first from work.

      c. A: Who rarely supports the government's tax-cutting proposals?
          B: The people who stand to gain least from them.

      d. A: Which spectator fails to laugh at the right moment whenever you watch a performance of a play by Mamet?
          B: The guy sitting just behind you.

Such readings, as emphasized above in the related case of quantificational NPs, are best analyzed in terms of a functional parameter that scopes wider than the quantificational adverb.

In conclusion, we propose that the data from adverbs is consistent with our assumptions about the scopal interaction between *wh*-phrases and GQs. Within a single sentential content, a parameter originating with a *wh*-phrase (either an ordinary or a functional parameter) always scopes wider than the operators associated with a quantificational NP or adverb.

4.4.3 Pair-List Readings: Evidence for Quantifying In?

The data in (53) show that grammar must provide a mechanism for generating functional readings, one that is independent of the mechanism for pair-list readings. In fact, a number of researchers have suggested the converse approach, namely to view pair-list responses as special cases of functional uses, since there are few, if any, cases of interrogative sentences that allow for pair-list responses, but not for functional ones. Chierchia (1991, 1993) presents two arguments for such a view. The first is essentially methodological: as noted by Groenendijk and Stokhof (1984), who do propose an independent mechanism for generating pair-list readings, the class of GQs that allow for pair-list responses in an interrogative is limited to universal quantifiers. The consequence is that the pair-list scoping mechanism must be applicable solely to such quantifiers. Moreover, methods of preventing such a rule from applying to polar interrogatives must be developed, since these seem not to allow for pair-list readings.[38] This is a task whose successful or insightful accomplishment Chierchia is dubious of.

---

[37]Berman proposed to account for the (putatively) unambiguous nature of the interrogative sentences in an essentially syntactic manner. According to his account, the reason that *wh*-phrases must be scoped wider than the adverb is that they move at LF to a position outside its scope. Apart from the empirical problems posed by (62), this analysis is problematic since it does not address in-situ uses of *wh*-phrases. (We discuss this issue in Chapter 7.) Both reprise and non-reprise uses of in-situ *wh*-phrases manifest the same lack of adverbial scope interaction that fronted *wh*-phrases exhibit. But positing dislocation for such cases is also problematic given that the *wh*-phrases can occur in essentially all environments from which dislocation is illicit:

  (i)   You seldom used to go for a drink with WHICH PERSON? (The preferred reading for this query is: "Which person did you say you seldom went out with?" The *wh*-phrase does not get the force of *seldom*.)
  (ii) Billie seldom used to go for a drink with an educated person. (The indefinite can be outscoped by *seldom*.)
  (iii) A quadratic equation usually has HOW MANY solutions? (This query has the force of: "How many solutions did you say a quadratic equation usually has?" The *wh*-phrase does not get the force of *usually*.)
  (iv) A quadratic equation usually has two solutions. (The indefinite can be outscoped by *usually*.)

[38]This is a subtle issue about which a number of researchers have expressed differing opinions. See Belnap 1982, Higginbotham 1996, Hornstein 1995 for further discussion.

Chierchia's second argument is that if pair-list readings are reduced to functional readings, then there is a simple account for the subject/object asymmetry (whose existence May (1985) argued for) concerning the availability of pair-list readings. This involves the claim that sentences such as (63a) elicit pair-list responses, while sentences such as (63c) do not:[39]

(63) a. Who does everyone like?

   b. For which f: everyone$_x$ [x likes f(x)]

   c. Who likes everyone?

   d. For which f: everyone$_x$ [f(x) likes x]

Chierchia's argument assumes that, at a level of LF, functional readings involve representations that include 'layered' traces bound by functional interrogative operators (as seen in (63b) and (63d)). The LF structure posited for (63a) is legitimate, whereas the corresponding LF structure for (63c) creates a *weak crossover* violation.

   Saito (1997) proposed an additional argument against viewing pair-list responses as having been derived from a scope ambiguity. He suggests that while it is difficult for subjects to scope out of embedded clauses, as in (64a), the corresponding interrogative in (64b) easily exhibits a pair-list use:

(64) a. Someone thinks that everyone bought a book.

   b. What does Jean think everyone bought?

---

[39]May claimed that (ii) is a possible direct response to (i), but that (v) is an inappropriate direct response to (iii) (cf. (iv)).

   (i) A: What did everyone bring?

   (ii) B: Merle brought a cake, Jarle brought some beer.

   (iii) A: Who brought everything?

   (iv) B: Fred, he's so generous.

   (v) B: Merle brought the cake, whereas Jarle brought the beer.

   (vi) B: The cake, Merle brought; and as for the beer, Jarle brought it.

We reserve judgement about whether (v) is actually infelicitous as a response to (iii). To our ears, (vi) certainly seems felicitous. In addition, there are further examples—pointed out by Lappin (1991) and Ginzburg (1992)—that might lead one to be skeptical about the subject/object asymmetry:

   (vii) A: Who proved each lemma?

      B: Gauss proved the snake lemma, Cauchy proved the enumeration lemma . . .

   (viii)   John claims to know who was elected mayor of every city in Ontario. (Lappin 1991)

   (ix)   Please inform me for every plane that gets downed who you think shot it.

These examples make it doubtful that the asymmetry needs should be captured in terms of inviolable syntactic principles, as May and Chierchia suggest. The asymmetry may simply reflect a tendency akin to the preference for narrow scope interpretation of object GQs in standard GQ/GQ interaction. Further problematic data for a syntactic account of the asymmetry is provided by examples (x) and (xi).

   (x) A: Which book did everyone buy for Meredith?

      B: #Dale bought Maus, Carrie bought Fritz the Cat . . .

   (xi) A: Which person bought everything for Meredith?

      B: #Dale bought the cakes, Carrie bought the beer . . .

As we have already emphasized (in section 4.3.3 above), the best diagnostic that a pair-list response does not arise from an independent use of a *wh*-phrase is the existence of such uses associated with singular *which*-N̄ phrases (because of the uniqueness presupposition associated with such *wh*-phrases). The putative subject/object asymmetry for pair-list readings is significantly weakened with such NPs. This weakens considerably the motivation for assuming that the grammatical mechanism responsible for NON-independent (e.g. functional) uses of *wh*-phrases is sensitive to some notion of argument structure or obliqueness hierarchy.

In contrast to these arguments against explicating pair-list responses in terms of ambiguity stands recent work by Krifka (1999) and Parsons (1999). They propose (resurrecting an idea hypothesized in passing by Karttunen (1977)) that pair-list responses arise from a mechanism separate from the functional one. This mechanism is quantifying into query speech acts. In briefly evaluating this idea, we focus exclusively on Krifka's proposal; but as far as we can tell, our comments apply equally to Parsons' proposal.

Krifka argues against treating pair-list responses in terms of functional readings, citing the need to explain the generalization that the pair-list reading[40] is restricted to universal quantifiers (and, correspondingly, to definite plurals). As seen below, this generalization is somewhat questionable and, even if it is true, it is amenable to an explanation grounded in quantifier presuppositions and the pragmatics of querying.[41]

Krifka observes that universal quantifiers are the only ones that can be expressed by conjunction alone. He suggests that conjunction is the one Boolean operation that is well-defined on queries, and more generally on speech acts. Given this, he suggests that a question like (65a) can also be interpreted as (65b), where the universal scopes over the speech act:

(65) a. Who did each person see?
      b. Each person x: I ask who did x see?
      c. Who did Bo see and who did Leslie see and who did Jo see and ...

This results in a conjoined speech act, as in (65c), with the conjunction ranging over the members of the domain of the quantifier.

Moreover, Krifka claims that conjoined queries cannot elicit functional responses:

(66) A: Which dish did Bo make, which dish did Leslie make, and which dish did Jo make?
      B: *His/*Their favourite dish (Krifka's 21; his judgements)

We are skeptical about this latter claim and believe that with proper contextualization these responses can become appropriate:

(67) A: So, about the cookery competition, can you give us your predictions: Which dish will Merle make, which dish will Dana make, and which dish will Chris make?
      B: Not surprisingly, given the fraught circumstances, I think it's safe to say for each of them: their favorite dish.
      B′: Without a doubt, they'll play it safe: I'd say for sure—their favourite dish.

In addition, Krifka's 'decompositional' analysis of universal quantifiers is questionable. The fact that universals have similar truth conditions to conjunctions of instantiations ranging over the entire domain does not require the acceptance of such a decomposition. After all, the determiner *all* heads NPs that express universal quantifiers, ones which tend to be interpreted collectively, but which also allow distributive readings, as in (68):

(68)   All children I know have their own favorite story: Pat likes *Peter Pan*, Sandy likes *Emil and the Detectives*, ...

---

[40]We use this term for convenience in the discussion, without committing ourselves to the position that such a separate reading actually exists.

[41]It should be noted that Krifka provides additional arguments against conflating pair-lists with functional readings. However, these all concern specific details of Chierchia's account that are absent from our proposal.

But *all* seems to resist pair-list responses:[42]

(69)   A: Which story do all children you know adore most?

         B: *Peter Pan.*

         B′:   #Pat likes *Peter Pan*, Sandy likes *Emil and the Detectives*, . . .

Similarly, a negative universal can be decomposed by conjunction of negated propositions, yet *no* clearly resists pair-list responses:

(70)   a.   No boy came ↔ Bo didn't come and Mo didn't come and . . .

      b. A: Which book did no boy read?

         B: The one his Latin teacher gave him

         B′:   #Bo didn't read Disgrace and Mo didn't read To Mageio and . . .

A significant problem for Krifka's conjunctive decomposition is that, in contrast to universal quantifiers like *each* or *every*, a unary *which*-sentence with a conjoined NP does not relativize the absolute uniqueness presupposition. Thus, (71a) suggests (despite the pragmatic implausibility) that Searle, Derrida, Himmelfarb, and Greer collaborated in writing a single book:

(71)   a.   Which book did John Searle and Jacques Derrida and Gertrude Himmelfarb and Germaine Greer write last year?

      b.   Which goal did Rivaldo and David Beckham and Roy Keane and Ole Gunnar Solskjaer score last year?

Example (71b) is similar, despite the even greater pragmatic implausibility.

It is crucial to consider examples like (71), where the *wh*-phrase is a singular *which*-phrase. Such cases are the only ones where a pair-list answer clearly involves a genuinely distinct reading. As emphasized in section 4.3.3, when the *wh*-phrase is *who*, *what* or a plural *which*-phrase, one can explain pair-list responses in terms of cumulativity.

Krifka emphasizes that he does not intend to conflate the pair-list contents of interrogatives containing universals with those of conjoined interrogatives. Rather, he claims "that asking the explicitly conjoined question is communicatively equivalent to asking the question with a quantifier."[43] Given this rider, it is unclear how to evaluate the proposal, since of course in one sense an explicitly conjoined sequence of queries is equivalent to the pair-list content of a universal-containing interrogative: they elicit similar responses. What one can point to are aspects of context which, given an utterance of the one, do not apply to a context in which the other has been uttered.

The examples in (72) show that both the querier and the responder can treat a conjoined interrogative as a plural object:

(72)   a. A: So, who is responsible for the fiasco and what will be their fate?

         B: These are interesting issues for sure. I don't have very much new to add.

      b.   The questions to ponder are who is responsible for the fiasco and what will be their fate?

---

[42] Krifka has suggested to us (e-mail message of December 16, 1999) that (i) allows a pair-list reading, but this judgment is not shared by the native speakers we have consulted (or by the authors).

   (i) Which present did all the children get?

[43] Krifka (e-mail message of December 16, 1999).

However, (73) shows that this is not the case for a universal-containing interrogative:

(73) a. A: So, which book did each person here write?

B: #These are interesting issues for sure. I don't have very much new to add.

b. #The questions to ponder are which professor did each student meet this afternoon?

Embedded interrogatives provide a domain for evaluating the need for a special purpose pair-list reading, given that they are shielded from effects that arise solely from illocutionary action. Groenendijk and Stokhof (1984) have argued, with respect to examples such as (74), that two types of knowledge can be described: Bo can know a functional description of admiration tendencies among sane Canadians without knowing a pair-by-pair description, and vice versa. Hence, Groenendijk and Stokhof claim, there is a need for an ambiguity to capture the difference:

(74) Bo knows which politician every sane Canadian admires.

This argument contradicts a fundamental assumption of theories that assume pair-list responses involve different mechanisms from functional readings. This is the assumption that only universal GQs allow for pair-list responses. This assumption is what has led to the positing of mechanisms that will generate the pair-list reading only for universal QNPs. The contradiction arises because the same need for distinguishing functional from pair-by-pair knowledge can be constructed, as seen in (75a) and (75b), where the 'pair-list' construal is not supposed to exist:

(75) a. Bo knows which politician most sane Canadians admire

b. Bo knows which politician exactly thirteen sane Canadians admire.

Clearly, Bo can have a pair-list knowledge of the political admirations of a set of sane Canadians from either of the quantifier sets 'most sane Canadians' or from 'exactly thirteen sane Canadians' without knowing a functional description, and vice versa. If these different psychological states reflect a grammatical ambiguity, then they pose a difficulty for theories that include a separate mechanism for generating pair-list responses—a mechanism which is applicable only to universal quantifiers. Such theories will not be able to produce the required 'pair-list' psychological state reading for cases such as (75a) and (75b). Of course, one might claim that interrogatives embedded by resolutive predicates allow 'pair-list construals' that are missing from both query uses of interrogatives and from interrogatives embedded by question predicates. Such a claim has been made by Szabolcsi (1993) and endorsed by Krifka (1999), who attempts to offer an explanation.

However, there are significant empirical problems for such a claim. For example, a putative contrast offered in support of the claim is the following:

(76) a. *Which dish did most boys make?

b. *Doris wondered/asked which dish most boys made

c. Doris found out which dish most boys made (She found out that Al made hamburgers and that Bill made french fries.) (Krifka's 56, 57; the judgements are Krifka's).

As noted in our discussion of examples (74) and (75), we are skeptical as to whether the grammar really allows discrimination of a functional from a pair-list reading in embedded cases such as (76c). It seems clear that an equally appropriate text can be constructed to demonstrate the putative availability of a pair-list-like reading embedded under a question-embedding verb:

(77)   Doris was in a whirl. The party would start in less than an hour. She hadn't started cooking yet. She couldn't quite remember everyone who was invited, but could remember a large number of them. She started wondering which dish most boys invited to come might decide to make: she was thinking about Drew—what would he make and Francis—what would he make and Les . . .

A crucial problem for the putative resolutive/question predicate-asymmetry arises from the fact that queries can be asked indirectly by means of a polar interrogative or imperative that embeds an interrogative under a resolutive predicate. Such embeddings maintain the independent/functional ambiguity:

(78)   a. A: Do you know which teacher each student here admires most?
           B: Yo Fujimura/His first trigonometry tutor/Robbie admires Yo, Lonnie admires Mo,. . .

        b. A: Tell me please which teacher each student here admires most?
           B: Yo Fujimura/His first trigonometry tutor/Robbie admires Yo, Lonnie admires Mo,. . .

If a 'pair-list' construal did exist, limited to interrogatives embedded by resolutive predicates, one would be able to elicit pair-list responses by means of queries similar to those in (78). However, as (79a,b) show, this is not the case:

(79)   a. A: Do you know which teacher most students here admire most?
           B: Yo Fujimura/Their first trigonometry tutor/#Robbie admires Yo, Lonnie admires Mo,. . .

        b. A: Tell me please which teacher most students here admire most?
           B: Yo Fujimura/Their first trigonometry tutor/#Robbie admires Yo, Lonnie admires Mo,. . .

Hence, the data above provide no evidence for the existence of a resolutive/question predicate asymmetry regarding 'pair-list' construals.

Finally, let us turn to one of the basic issues involved in the pair-list/functional debate: what is behind the generalization that only universal GQs allow for pair-list uses? One strategy for explaining this is to assume that a hard grammatical principle is involved and to propose a mechanism in which only universal GQs can legitimately participate. This strategy has been advocated by Groenendijk and Stokhof and most recently by Krifka. However, there are alternative ways of explaining the relevant data which are not nearly as clear cut as has been supposed.[44]

A fundamental characteristic of pair-list responses is that they involve enumerating a function that maps a witness set for the quantifier GQ to a set of individuals associated with the interrogative, relative to a condition provided by the question. For a pair-list response to be available, the responder must be able to deduce from the context which witness set the querier has in mind. We call this task the *pair-list-domain-selection-problem*. As noted by Groenendijk and Stokhof (1984), the domain selection problem is particularly simple for universal quantifiers (and definite plurals)—such NPs are the only ones that (in generalized quantifier terms) 'live on' a unique set that automatically provides a domain for the pair-list enumeration.[45] In contrast, negative universals like *no girl* or *no boy* involve a difficult pair-list domain selection problem, given that a

---

[44] Similar explanations have been proposed in the aforementioned works by Chierchia and Ginzburg.

[45] In an example like *Who does every Englishwoman admire*, *every Englishwoman* 'lives on' the set of all Englishwomen. A pair-list use involves relating each Englishwoman to a person she admires.

witness for such a set is one that contains anything but girls (for *no girl*) or boys (for *no boy*), etc. Related to pair-list domain selection problems are certain pragmatic considerations: if a querier really *is* interested in getting a pair-list response, she should signal the domain she is interested in, a task she can always achieve by using a definite plural or a universal determiner and a suitably restricted common noun phrase or partitive. This is what we believe underlies the difficulty in eliciting a pair-list response from (80a) and the need to use (80b) for such a purpose:

(80) a. Which person do most people here admire?
     b. I'd be really grateful if most people here were to say which person they support.
     c. Which person do each of the people sitting over there admire?

If (80a) is to elicit a pair-list response, then the querier wants the responder to pick an arbitrary witness set for *most people here* from the multitude of such sets available to serve as domain for the pair-list. This is a highly unlikely thing for a querier to want.

In any case, one *can* point to examples of pair-list readings with non-universal GQs, as in (81) and (82):

(81) A: Most people here have submitted a paper to a journal.
     B: Which journal?
     A: Alexis to *Psychic Review*, Pat to *Post-Modern Letters*, . . .

(82) A: Do you know which person each committee member is going to support?
     B: Nope.
     A: OK, can you tell me at least as far as most committee members go which person is going to get supported?
     B: Well, let me think: Alex is going to support Hilary, Dana is going to support Ronnie, . . .

Example (81) illustrates a pair-list response arising from a so-called sluiced *wh*-phrase whose antecedent is a sentence containing a non-universal GQ. Offering a precise analysis of this depends upon the specific analysis one chooses for sluicing. If one opts for an account involving syntactic reconstruction/deletion (Ross 1969, Levin 1982, Chung et al. 1995), then presumably one concludes that pair-lists are available with non-universals. Alternatively, adopting a non-syntactic approach (e.g. that of Ginzburg 1992; see also Chapter 8), we actually have an additional argument for the position that the pair-list reading does not involve a scope ambiguity.

We conclude that the unavailability of pair-list readings can be explained as a pragmatic epiphenomenon. This is a consequence of the difficulty of the domain-selection problem raised by non-universal NPs.

In summary, it is difficult to determine whether pair-list readings in mixed GQ/*wh*-interrogatives involve a mechanism distinct from the one commonly thought to underlie the possibility of functional responses. We have argued that, to date, no convincing data or theory has been proposed to support a pair-list/functional ambiguity. Thus, the phenomenon of pair-list responses in mixed GQ/wh-sentences does not pose a problem for an account like ours, which assumes that *wh*-phrases are never outscoped by GQs. In our earlier analysis of pair-list uses, we claim that it is the functional dependency index that receives widest sentential scope. In the following section, we sketch an extension of our framework that allows functional readings to be generated. In this way, our account provides a way of maintaining the relevant generalizations about the relative scope of *wh*-phrase/GQs.

4.5 Describing Functional Uses

We assume that all cases where *wh*-phrases do not have the widest sentential scope can be analyzed as *functional* uses, a type of use discussed extensively by Engdahl (1986).[46] We offer a sketch of how functional uses can be captured.[47] The basic difference between an *independent* and a *functional(ly dependent)* use of a *wh*-phrase is that the content of the former involves a simple index, whereas the content of the latter is an index that is functionally dependent on the indices of one or more NPs. For simplicity, we confine our attention to dependence on a single NP.[48] In addition, independent and functional uses differ regarding the parameters that are involved. For an independent use, the parameter (that is stored and retrieved into PARAMS) packages an index and its restriction; for a functional use, the parameter's index f corresponds to the functional dependency and the parameter's restriction is a a characterization of f.

In our analysis, a functional use is specified as follows:[49,50]

(83) *who*: functional use

$$
\begin{bmatrix}
\text{CONTENT} & \begin{bmatrix} parameter \\ \text{INDEX} & \boxed{f}(x) \\ \text{RESTR} & \{\} \end{bmatrix} \\
\text{STORE} & \left\{ \begin{bmatrix} parameter \\ \text{INDEX} & \boxed{f} \\ \text{RESTR} & \{\, \forall z(z \in Dom(\boxed{f}) \rightarrow person^b(\boxed{f}(z))) \,\} \end{bmatrix} \right\}
\end{bmatrix}
$$

In (83), there are three essential components: the index $\boxed{f}$, the restriction on $\boxed{f}$, and the index x. The stored parameter with index $\boxed{f}$ is subject to retrieval in the same way as 'ordinary', independently used *wh*-phrases. Hence, it will become a member of the PARAMS set of the question. x is the index of another NP, prototypically a quantified NP whose scope will contain $\boxed{f}(x)$. Thus, a

---

[46] Other detailed analyses are in Engdahl 1980, Groenendijk and Stokhof 1984, Chierchia 1993, Ginzburg 1992.

[47] An important issue we do *not* address is the nature of the syntactic/semantic interface conditions. Clearly, restrictions exist, as shown in works following May's original claims about subject/object asymmetry in the availability of pair-list readings (see Chierchia 1993, Hornstein 1995, Beghelli 1997). As suggested in footnote 39, a structural account of such restrictions is unlikely. We speculate that future accounts of this will be no less complex than existing characterizations of the restrictions on quantifier scope ambiguities (see Kurtzman and McDonald 1993) and we are obliged to leave this issue to further research.

[48] Engdahl demonstrated that the dependence could be on more than one NP with examples such as (i) below:

(i) A: What does every parent wish for her children?
     B: That they leave home by the time they're 18.

[49] We would like to thank Carl Pollard for useful suggestions relating to this specification.

[50] For expository convenience, we abuse TFS notation and employ the first order logic notation $\forall z(z \in Dom(\boxed{f}) \rightarrow person^b(\boxed{f}(z)))$. This serves to abbreviate (i):

(i)
$$
\begin{bmatrix}
fact \\
\text{PROP} & \begin{bmatrix} \text{SIT} & s \\ \text{SOA} & \begin{bmatrix} \text{QUANTS} & \left\langle \begin{bmatrix} every\text{-}rel \\ \text{IND} & z \\ \text{RESTR} & \{ z \in Dom(\boxed{f}) \} \end{bmatrix} \right\rangle \\ \text{NUCL} & person^b(\boxed{f}(z)) \end{bmatrix} \end{bmatrix}
\end{bmatrix}
$$

functional use of the *wh*-phrase in (84a) will yield the content in (84b):

(84)   a.   Who proved each theorem?

b.
$$
\begin{bmatrix}
\textit{question} \\[4pt]
\text{PARAMS} \quad
\left\{
\begin{bmatrix}
\textit{parameter} \\
\text{INDEX} \quad \boxed{f} \\
\text{RESTR} \quad \{ \forall z (z \in Dom(\boxed{f}) \rightarrow person^{b}(\boxed{f}(z))) \}
\end{bmatrix}
\right\} \\[10pt]
\text{PROP} \quad
\begin{bmatrix}
\textit{proposition} \\
\text{SIT} \quad s \\[4pt]
\text{SOA} \quad
\begin{bmatrix}
\text{QUANTS} \quad
\left\langle
\begin{bmatrix}
\textit{each-rel} \\
\text{INDEX} \quad \boxed{2} \\
\text{RESTR} \quad \{\textit{theorem}(\boxed{2})\}
\end{bmatrix}
\right\rangle \\[12pt]
\text{NUCL} \quad
\begin{bmatrix}
\textit{prove-rel} \\
\text{PROVER} \quad \boxed{f}(\boxed{2}) \\
\text{PROVED} \quad \boxed{2}
\end{bmatrix}
\end{bmatrix}
\end{bmatrix}
\end{bmatrix}
$$

The presupposition associated with a sentence containing a functional use of a *which*-phrase, as in (85), follows directly from the WH-PRC in (47) above—without any additional or modified mechanisms.

(85)   a.   Which student proved each theorem?

b.
$$
\begin{bmatrix}
\text{CONT} \; \boxed{1}
\begin{bmatrix}
\textit{question} \\[4pt]
\text{PARAMS} \quad
\left\{
\begin{bmatrix}
\text{INDEX} \quad \boxed{f} \\
\text{RESTR} \quad \{ \forall z (z \in Dom(\boxed{f}) \rightarrow student(\boxed{f}(z))) \}
\end{bmatrix}
\right\} \\[10pt]
\text{PROP} \quad
\begin{bmatrix}
\textit{proposition} \\
\text{SIT} \quad s \\[4pt]
\text{SOA} \quad
\begin{bmatrix}
\text{QUANTS} \quad
\left\langle
\begin{bmatrix}
\textit{each-rel} \\
\text{INDEX} \quad \boxed{2} \\
\text{RESTR} \quad \{\textit{theorem}(\boxed{2})\}
\end{bmatrix}
\right\rangle \\[12pt]
\text{NUCL} \quad
\begin{bmatrix}
\textit{prove-rel} \\
\text{PROVER} \quad \boxed{f}(\boxed{2}) \\
\text{PROVED} \quad \boxed{2}
\end{bmatrix}
\end{bmatrix}
\end{bmatrix}
\end{bmatrix} \\[16pt]
\text{BCKGRD} \quad
\left\{
\begin{bmatrix}
\textit{fact} \\
\text{PROP|SOA|NUCL} \quad
\begin{bmatrix}
\textit{n-jective-rel} \\
\text{INSTANCE} \quad \boxed{1}
\end{bmatrix}
\end{bmatrix}, \; ...
\right\}
\end{bmatrix}
$$

The basic triggering for the emergence of the presupposition—an atomic-relation—is present in the (nucleus of) the restrictions of the PARAMS set of the question. In such cases, the question is an abstract pertaining to functions. The force of the presupposition for a unary abstract is, as we mentioned above, uniqueness—there exists a single function that instantiates the abstract. This function maps theorems to students such that for any theorem t, $\boxed{f}(t)$ is the student that proved t. Given the uniqueness of $\boxed{f}$, a relativized uniqueness effect arises: it is presupposed that for each theorem there exists exactly one student who proved it.

4.6   Summary and General Architecture

In this section, we have developed a non-quantificational approach to *wh*-phrase meaning and have compared it with the quantificational approach assumed in most of the syntactic and semantic literature. In our proposal, *wh*-words do not take scope over one another, nor do real quantifiers ever take widest scope in an interrogative content. Although the quantificational view is so familiar as to constitute the 'common sense' view, we have argued that it actually involves more complexity and is, in certain respects, empirically inferior to our non-quantificational approach.

- **Independent motivation**: There is no independent semantic motivation for assigning *wh*-phrases a quantificational force.

- ***Wh*-quantifying-in**: We have provided data that challenge the commonly assumed independent motivation for a special rule of *wh*-quantifying-in, namely the putative synonymy of a multiple *wh*-sentence with a pair-list/functional reading of a corresponding mixed universal quantifier/interrogative sentence.[51]

- **Uniqueness**: The presuppositions associated with (singular) *which*-phrases are unscoped. Quantificational approaches require recourse to polyadic mechanisms to capture this. Our account allows us to capture such presuppositions straightforwardly by positing that a question, an n-ary propositional abstract, bears the property of *n-jectivity*, which reduces to uniqueness for $n = 1$. We have shown how to trigger this presupposition based on independently motivated distinctions relating to the singular/plural divide. Our proposal also extends to functional uses of *wh*-phrases where uniqueness is relativized.

- **'Narrow scope' uses of *wh*-phrases**: Even in this domain, the apparent advantage of a quantificational approach turns out to be illusory. A sentence like *Who proved each theorem?* (seen in example (84a)) does *not* involve a *straightforward* scope ambiguity. Whenever a GQ appears to outscope a *wh*-phrase, special purpose mechanisms need to be invoked to ensure (a) that the meaning one gets is a question (*not* a proposition) and (b) that the resulting quantification is semantically meaningful. Our account, by contrast, provides a way of accounting for the relevant generalizations in terms of *functional* uses of *wh*-phrases. Quantificational approaches must appeal to the existence of functional uses for reasons originally discussed by Engdahl (1980, 1986).

Our view of *wh*-phrase meaning is further supported in Chapter 7, where we consider another pervasive use for *wh*-phrases—the *reprise* or *echo* use. Reprises involve questions where one or more of the semantic roles of the prior utterance is abstracted over, typically because the person making the reprise is unable to resolve the requisite referential acts. These uses of *wh*-phrases are most naturally thought of as *not* involving scopal interaction between the reprised *wh*-phrases.

---

[51]This assumption is also held by researchers who eschew *wh*-quantifying-in. See Hornstein 1995.

Our own proposal accounts for them, once we incorporate certain assumptions applicable to all reprise uses.

The results established in this section lead to the following decision concerning quantifier scoping: retrieval of generalized quantifiers in our system is *lexical* and retrieval of the parameters of questions is *phrasal*. This is one way of ensuring that GQs never have the potential of outscoping *wh*-phrases in any clausal content. We propagate both kinds of elements—parameters and generalized quantifiers—'up through' phrases via a single 'store'. The mechanisms are described in section 5.3.

5

Unbounded Dependencies

There are two kinds of unbounded dependencies that are relevant to the grammar of interrogative clauses: those between fillers and gaps ('extraction' dependencies) and those involving *wh*-interrogative words whose presence (at arbitrary depth of embedding) is mandated in a particular kind of *wh*-constructions (so-called 'pied piping' effects). Before proceeding, we must consider how each phenomenon is to be treated.

5.1 Extraction Dependencies

P&S–94 (Chap. 4) provide a uniform, if somewhat cumbersome characterization of NONLOCAL feature inheritance in terms of the features INHERIT and TO-BIND and their NONLOCAL Feature Principle. The present proposal, based on that of Bouma et al. (2001), presents a significant simplification of the relevant feature structures and provides solutions to a number of problems that were unsolved in the P&S–94 account, as noted by Hukari and Levine (1995, 1996a).

5.1.1 Extracted Arguments

The HPSG analysis of extraction, building on earlier work in the GPSG tradition, involves specifications for the feature SLASH that are projected upward in a syntactic structure, as indicated via shading in (1) on the following page. All signs must have a SYNSEM value of type *canonical*, according to the Principle of Canonicality presented in Chapter 2. The second argument of the verb *visits* in (1), however, is an object of type *gap-ss*, which must bear a nonempty value for the feature SLASH. This nonempty SLASH value is amalgamated by the verb, i.e. it is also the verb's SLASH value. Further, the verb's SLASH value is passed up from head daughter to mother throughout extraction structures, as indicated by the shading in (1). (This will be explained below.) Extraction is thus treated entirely in terms of the inheritance of SLASH specifications; 'binding off' of the SLASH specification occurs at an appropriate point HIGHER in the structure, where a compatible filler constituent must occur.[1]

---

[1] In fact, the analysis of extraction we adopt here extends to various cases of 'subbinding', where the binder is not in a superordinate position in the phrasal structure. Examples of this include *an easy person to please* __ , *too tall for anyone to be able to dance with* __ , and French *en*-cliticization (e.g. *La surface* __ *en-brille* 'the surface of-it-shines'). For further discussion, see Bouma et al. 2001 and Miller and Sag 1997.

(1)

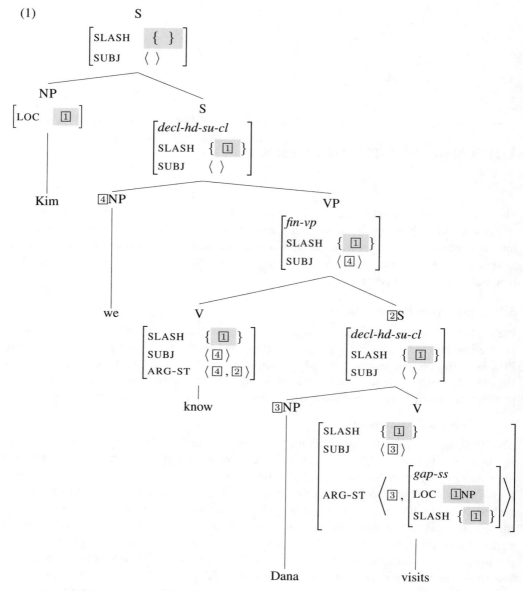

In the analysis of Bouma et al. (2001), words are subject to a constraint (originally suggested in Sag 1997) that defines their SLASH value in terms of the SLASH values of their arguments, i.e. the SLASH values of the members of their ARG-ST list.[2] This SLASH-'amalgamation' constraint can be stated as follows:[3]

---

[2]Bouma et al. (2001) use a further feature DEPENDENTS, whose value is a list consisting of the argument structure plus optionally selected adjuncts. We have eliminated this feature here, in favor of an analysis that distinguishes the ARG-ST of a lexeme from the extended ARG-ST of a word derived from that lexeme.

[3]Here and throughout, we use indexed Σs as tags designating sets. Bouma et al. (2001) assume a slightly more complicated version of (2), where predicates like *tough* may 'subtract' an NP element from the amalgamation of the arguments' SLASH values. For expository simplicity, we ignore this refinement here, though we assume that the lexical binding properties of such predicates simply supersede the default constraint in (2).

(2)   SLASH-Amalgamation Constraint:

$$word \Rightarrow / \begin{bmatrix} \text{SS}|\text{SLASH } \boxed{\Sigma_1} \cup \cdots \cup \boxed{\Sigma_n} \\ \text{ARG-ST } \left\langle [\text{SLASH } \boxed{\Sigma_1}], \ldots, [\text{SLASH } \boxed{\Sigma_n}] \right\rangle \end{bmatrix}$$

According to (2), if all the arguments of a verb have an empty SLASH value, then (by default) so does the verb itself. By contrast, if any one of the complements of a verb is 'slashed' (i.e. has a nonempty SLASH value), then the verb itself is slashed. For example, the SLASH value of the verb *know* in (1) must contain the element $\boxed{1}$ because its sentential complement's SLASH value is $\{\boxed{1}\}$.[4] Lexicalized SLASH-amalgamation thus allows us to simplify the statement of the inheritance of SLASH specifications. In fact, the inheritance of SLASH specifications from the verb to the VP and the S that it projects, shown in (3), already follows from the GHFP, as it affects two constructions discussed in Chapter 2:

(3) a. *fin-vp*:

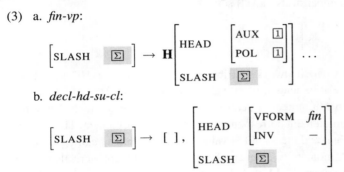

b. *decl-hd-su-cl*:

The GHFP thus guarantees the inheritance of SLASH values sketched in (4).

(4)

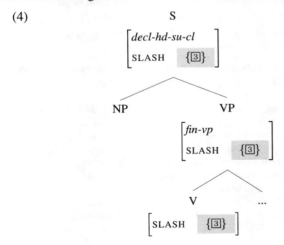

---

[4]The SLASH value of any word whose ARG-ST list is empty is the empty set, as guaranteed by an independent lexical constraint.

In any headed phrase whose SLASH value includes that of a non-head daughter, the inheritance is mediated by the head daughter, whose SLASH value includes that of the non-head daughter whenever the latter is a subject, complement, or specifier.[5]

A verb like *visits* in (1) has two notable properties: (1) it is slashed (as guaranteed by the SLASH-Amalgamation Constraint), giving rise to the inheritance of nonempty SLASH specifications, according to the GHFP and (2) it does not combine locally with its object NP. Our theory must guarantee that this absence of local realization and the inheritance of nonempty SLASH specifications are correlated. The key to understanding how this comes about is the type *gap-ss*—a subtype of *noncan-ss* which was introduced in Chapter 2.

The ARG-ST specifications in lexical entries in general require only that each argument be of type *synsem*. This leaves open the possibility that a given argument can be resolved to the type *canon-ss* or else to some subtype of *noncan-ss*, e.g. *gap-ss*. Such a resolution will cause the verb to be slashed, because an object of type *gap-ss* is subject to a further constraint identifying its LOCAL value with the single member of its SLASH set:

$$(5) \quad \textit{gap-ss} \quad \Rightarrow \quad \begin{bmatrix} \text{LOC} & \boxed{1} \\ \text{SLASH} & \{\boxed{1}\} \end{bmatrix}$$

Because a *gap-ss* argument is slashed, it always contributes an element to the verb's SLASH value, which is an amalgamation of the arguments' SLASH values, according to (2).

But if an element of a verb's argument structure is resolved to *gap-ss*, then that verb can never combine with an overt complement corresponding to the *gap-ss* argument. This is because overt elements are all of type *sign*, and the SYNSEM value of all signs must be of type *canonical* (according to the Principle of Canonicality). Hence, if the *gap-ss* argument were also to appear on the COMPS list, then no structure could be built. This is because the constraint on head-complement phrases given in (34) of Chapter 2 requires that each member of the head daughter's COMPS list be unified with the SYNSEM value of some complement daughter. Thus one of the arguments of a verb can be resolved to a *gap-ss*, but when this happens, this argument must not be included in the verb's COMPS list.

In order to allow *gap-ss* arguments to absent themselves from a verb's COMPS list,[6] we reformulate the Argument Realization Principle (originally (7) in Chapter 2) as follows:[7]

---

[5]If, following P&S–94, the SLASH value of the mother of a head-adjunct phrases must include the SLASH value of the head daughter and that of the modifier daughter, then a constraint to this effect—which must override the GHFP—may be placed on the type *hd-adj-ph*. Alternatively, if gaps in adjunct phrase are possible, but are pronominal (Cinque 1990, Postal 1998) and parasitic on the presence of a distinct gap in the modified phrase, then the GHFP need not be overriden. Rather, a pronominal SLASH element coindexed with the head daughter's SLASH element must be allowed as an option. We make no attempt to resolve these options here. Note further that specific head-adjunct phrases may be extraction 'islands', in which case their adjunct daughter is constrained to be [SLASH { }].

[6]For English, the particular subtype of relevance is *gap-ss*, but argument-drop languages are naturally analyzed by generalizing the constraint we propose to allow *pro-ss* ARG-ST elements to be unrealized on valence lists, as well. Similarly, Miller and Sag (1997) treat French pronominal affixes (so-called 'clitics') in terms of affixal (*aff-ss*) arguments that do not appear on valence lists.

[7]Here '$\ominus$' designates a relation of contained list difference. If λ_2 is an ordering of a set σ_2 and λ_1 is a subordering of λ_2, then $\lambda_2 \ominus \lambda_1$ designates the list that results from removing all members of λ_1 from λ_2; if λ_1 is not a sublist of λ_2, then the contained list difference is not defined. For present purposes, $\ominus$ is interdefinable with the sequence union operator ($\bigcirc$) of Reape (1994) and Kathol (1995):

$$(A \ominus B = C) \quad \Leftrightarrow \quad (C \bigcirc B = A)$$

(6)   Argument Realization Principle (final version):

$$
word \Rightarrow \begin{bmatrix} \text{SS}|\text{LOC}|\text{CAT} & \begin{bmatrix} \text{SUBJ} & \boxed{A} \\ \text{SPR} & \boxed{B} \\ \text{COMPS} & \boxed{C} \;\ominus\; list(\textit{gap-ss}) \end{bmatrix} \\ \text{ARG-ST} & \boxed{A} \;\oplus\; \boxed{B} \;\oplus\; \boxed{C} \end{bmatrix}
$$

The effect of (6) is to constrain the ARG-ST value to be equal to the result of appending the COMPS list to the SUBJ and SPR lists, except for the possible difference that one or more elements of type *gap-ss* may be present in the ARG-ST list, but absent from the COMPS list. (As in Chapter 2, the empty SPR value of verbs will be ignored.) Note that (6) need not stipulate that all elements of type *gap-ss* be removed from the COMPS list—this follows immediately from the interaction of the Principle of Canonicality with the constraint on head-complement phrases, as just noted. The SLASH-Amalgamation Constraint in (2) and the revised ARP thus interact to ensure that when a verb's (nonsubject) argument is resolved to *gap-ss*, the verb's SLASH value must be nonempty and the *gap-ss* argument cannot be realized locally as a complement.

So a lexeme like (7) will give rise to inflected words (related to it by inflectional rules) like the one illustrated in (8):

(7)
$$
\begin{bmatrix} \textit{v-lx} \\ \text{PHON} & \langle \text{ visit } \rangle \\ \text{SS}|\text{LOC} & \begin{bmatrix} \text{CAT} & \begin{bmatrix} \text{HEAD} & \textit{verb} \\ \text{SUBJ} & \langle\text{XP}\rangle \end{bmatrix} \\ \text{CONT} & \begin{bmatrix} \textit{soa} \\ \text{NUCL} & \begin{bmatrix} \textit{visit-rel} \\ \text{VISITOR} & i \\ \text{VISITED} & j \end{bmatrix} \end{bmatrix} \end{bmatrix} \\ \text{ARG-ST} & \langle \text{ NP}_i \text{ , NP}[acc]_j \rangle \end{bmatrix}
$$

(8)
$$
\begin{bmatrix} \textit{word} \\ \text{PHON} & \langle \text{ visits } \rangle \\ \text{SS}|\text{LOC} & \begin{bmatrix} \text{CAT} & \begin{bmatrix} \text{HEAD} & \begin{bmatrix} v \\ \text{VFORM} & \textit{fin} \end{bmatrix} \\ \text{SUBJ} & \langle\text{XP}\rangle \end{bmatrix} \\ \text{CONT} & \begin{bmatrix} \textit{r-soa} \\ \text{NUCL} & \begin{bmatrix} \textit{visit-rel} \\ \text{VISITOR} & i \\ \text{VISITED} & j \end{bmatrix} \end{bmatrix} \end{bmatrix} \\ \text{ARG-ST} & \langle \text{ NP}[nom]_i \text{ , NP}[acc]_j \rangle \end{bmatrix}
$$

Such words must also satisfy the Argument Realization Principle in (6), which can be done in several distinct ways.

One way of satisfying the constraints in (8) and the ARP is illustrated in (9):

(9)

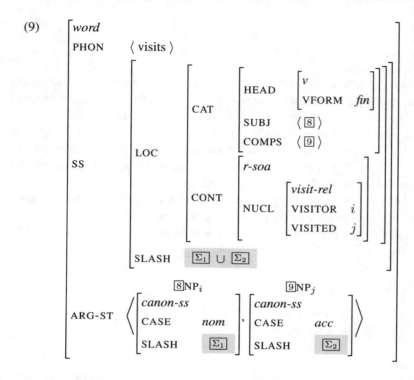

This instantiation of the lexical entry in (8) gives rise to unslashed sentences like (10a) and slashed examples like (10b).

(10)   a. Merle visits Dominique.

       b. Which of the prisoners do you think Pat visits [relatives of __]?

In the former case, the SLASH-Amalgamation Constraint is satisfied, because each argument has the empty set as its SLASH value, and hence the verb does, too ($\{\ \} \cup \{\ \} = \{\ \}$). In the latter case, the direct object argument is slashed (it is a *canon-ss* phrase that properly contains a gap). This gives rise to the SLASH amalgamation and inheritance pictured in (11):

(11)

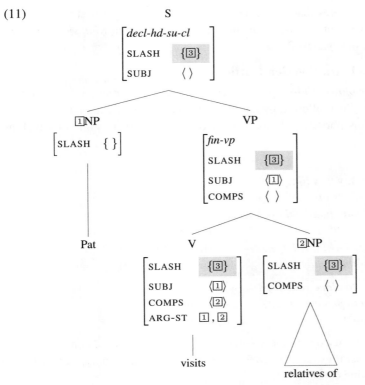

A second way of satisfying the constraints in (8) and our other principles is shown in (12):

(12)

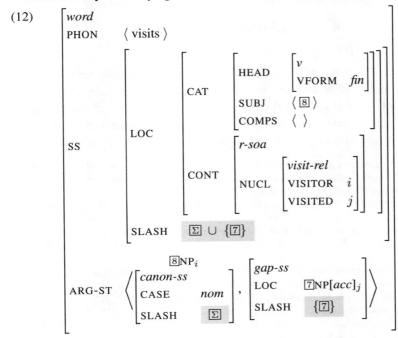

This is the instantiation of features that results when the word *visits* appears at the bottom of an extraction dependency (without any locally realized object NP), e.g. in *Kim, we know Dana visits*, which was illustrated in (1) above.[8]

5.1.2 'Topicalization': an Extraction Construction

The phrasal type *head-filler-phrase* (*hd-fill-ph*) defines the general construction that introduces an 'extracted' element (the filler) followed by a sentential head that is missing an element corresponding to that filler. This phrase type has many subtypes in English, some of which are illustrated in (13) and (14):

(13) a. *These bagels, I like.*   (topicalization)
      b. *These bagels, they say they like.*   (topicalization)
      c. the baker *whose bagels I like*   (*wh*-relative)
      d. the baker *from whom I bought these bagels*   (*wh*-relative)
      e. *Whose bagels do you like?*   (*wh*-interrogative)
      f. *From whom did you buy these bagels?*   (*wh*-interrogative)
      g. *What great bagels they bought!*   (*wh*-exclamative)

(14) a. the baker *in whom to place your trust*   (*wh*-relative)
      b. I wonder *in whom to place my trust*   (*wh*-interrogative)
      c. I wonder *who to trust*   (*wh*-interrogative)

In this section, we will discuss just one of these—the so-called 'topicalization' construction.[9]

We treat all the clauses just illustrated in terms of the type *hd-fill-ph*, a subtype of *hd-ph* that is associated with the following constraint:[10]

(15)   *hd-fill-ph*:

$$
\begin{bmatrix} \text{SLASH} & \boxed{\Sigma_2} \end{bmatrix} \rightarrow \begin{bmatrix} \text{LOC} & \boxed{1} \end{bmatrix}, \text{H} \begin{bmatrix} phrase \\ \text{HEAD} & v \\ \text{SLASH} & \{\boxed{1}\} \uplus \boxed{\Sigma_2} \end{bmatrix}
$$

The constraint in (15) says first that the head daughter (and hence the head-filler phrase itself) must be a verb projection. (15) also states that one member of the head daughter's SLASH set is identified with the LOCAL value of the filler daughter and that whatever other elements might be in the head daughter's SLASH must constitute the SLASH value of the mother of the head-filler phrase. Except in cases of multiple extraction, this SLASH value will be the empty set.[11]

---

[8] Note that there is no VP constituent in (1)'s embedded clause. This is because transitive verbs whose object is extracted behave like strict-intransitive verbs; that is, they may function as the head daughter of a head-subject phrase.

[9] On the discourse properties of this construction, see Prince 1981.

[10] Here '⊎' designates the operation of disjoint set union, which is just like familiar set union, except that the disjoint union of two sets with a nonempty intersection is undefined.

[11] There is an issue as to whether the filler daughter should be able to contribute to the SLASH value of a head-filler phrase. At stake are examples like the following, where the filler contains a new gap associated with a distinct filler higher in the tree:
  (i) ??[Dignitaries this famous]$_i$, I never know [[how many pictures of _ $_i$]$_j$ I should take _ $_j$].
  (ii) ??[Dignitaries this famous]$_i$, I never know [[how many pictures of _ $_i$]$_j$ to take _ $_j$].
  (iii) ??[A Dignitary like this]$_i$, [[how many pictures of _ $_i$]$_j$ do you think we should take _ $_j$]?
  (iv) ??[Gangsters that dangerous]$_i$, [[pictures of _ $_i$]$_j$, only a fool would take _ $_j$].
We will treat these examples as ungrammatical here. For a modification of (15) that allows the non-head daughter's SLASH value to be included in that of the clause, and hence predicts that these examples are grammatical, see Bouma et al. 2001.

The first subtype of *hd-fill-ph* to consider is the topicalization construction, illustrated by the examples in (13a,b). To treat such examples, we posit a type *topicalized-clause* (*top-cl*). *Top-cl* is a subtype of both *hd-fill-ph* and *core-cl* (*n.b*—not of *decl-cl*):

(16)

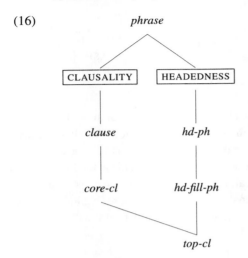

Instances of this type obey the following construction-particular constraint:

(17)   *top-cl*:

$$[\ ] \rightarrow \begin{bmatrix} \text{WH} & \{\ \} \end{bmatrix},\ \text{H} \begin{bmatrix} \text{VFORM} & fin \\ \text{IC} & + \\ \text{SUBJ} & \langle\ \rangle \end{bmatrix}$$

Topicalized clauses can thus only be built from (i.e. have as a head daughter) independent ([IC +]) finite clauses, e.g. the declarative head-subject clauses discussed in Chapter 2. Additionally the 'filler daughter' of the topicalized clause construction is constrained to be [WH { }]. The effect of the latter constraint is to prevent any WH-specified interrogative or exclamative words from appearing as the filler or an element contained within the filler. This is a key difference between topicalized clauses and other kinds of head-filler phrase. Finally, the various identities will hold between the head daughter and mother of this type of phrase—courtesy of the GHFP. These identities include the CONTENT value, as well as the [IC +] and [SUBJ ⟨ ⟩] specifications illustrated in (18):

(18)   **GHFP** & *hd-fill-ph* & *clause* & *top-cl*:

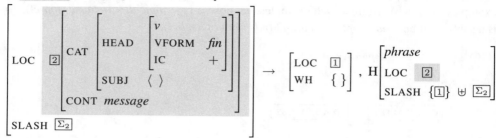

Note that the ⊎ operation is undefined if its arguments have any member in common; hence '{$\boxed{1}$} ⊎ $\boxed{\Sigma_2}$' must be distinct from '$\boxed{\Sigma_2}$'. The constraint in (15) thus entails that the mother and head daughter have distinct SLASH values. Given this, the effect of the GHFP is to 'push down' so as to require identity of the LOCAL value of mother and head daughter. This is the highest level within the synsem where identity is consistent with all inherited nondefeasible constraints.

A typical example of topicalization can now be analyzed as follows (where shading illustrates the percolation and 'binding off' of SLASH elements, rather than the effects of the GHFP):

(19)

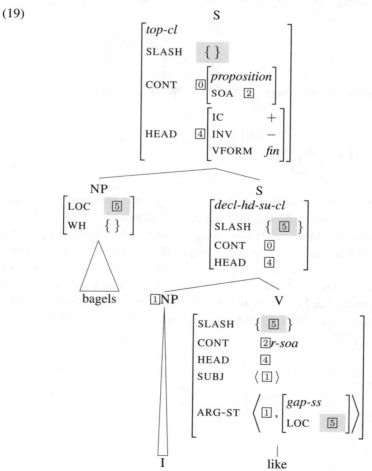

Because the GHFP requires that the SUBJ value of mother and head daughter both be the empty list, there are no topicalized clauses produced via subject extraction. That is, examples like (20) have only one analysis: they are unambiguously instances of the type *decl-hd-su-cl*.

(20) Bagels(,) always upset my stomach.

This is precisely the result argued for on purely theoretical grounds by Lasnik and Saito (1992).

Because the only restriction placed upon the CONTENT value of a topicalized phrase (inherited from the type *clause*) is that it be some subtype of *message*, it is also possible for the head daughter to be a subjunctive clause. As noted in Chapter 2, though subjunctive instances of *decl-hd-su-cl* generally appear in embedded environments, there are certain environments where [IC +] subjunctives may appear. As it turns out, in just these environments, subjunctive topicalized clauses are well-formed:

(21) a. We suggested that *people like that, he be wary of __* .
     b. I prefer that *proposals of this kind, I be kept informed of __*
     c. Proposals of this kind, nobody be taken in by __ !

This is precisely as predicted by our analysis.

There are also instances of (subjectless) imperative topicalizations, as in (22a,b), as well as interrogative [(22c–e)] and exclamative [(22f,g)] topicalizations.

(22) a. People that smart, always pay attention to __ !
     b. The Roman Forum, be sure to visit __ when you're in Rome!
     c. That kind of antisocial behavior, can we really tolerate __ in a civilized society?
        (Radford 1988)
     d. This report, shouldn't you have already read __ ?
     e. That kind of behavior, who could object to __ ?
     f. People that stupid, am I ever fed up with __ !
     g. (?)His valiant efforts, how many people have overlooked __ !

Because topicalized phrases are *clauses*, but not instances of *decl-cl*, they may have any subtype of *message* as their CONTENT value. Thus any independent clause can in principle serve as the head daughter of a topicalized phrase.[12] In addition, the head daughter of a *top-cl* can be a coordination of two clauses, as in examples like (23), as predicted.

(23) Bagels, [[Kim likes __] and [Pat hates __]].

The generality of the topicalized clause construction thus appears to be adequately accommodated by our analysis.

5.1.3 Some Constraints on Extraction

In our earlier discussion of the lexeme *visit* in (7) above, we failed to consider a third possible instantiation, shown in (24), which is the key to our treatment of subject extraction:

---

[12]We return to the analysis of exclamative clauses below and in the next chapter.

(24)

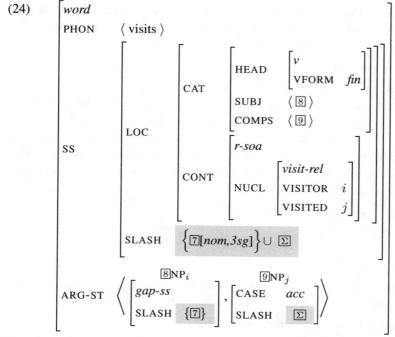

Here the subject argument is a *gap-ss*, yet it appears on the verb's SUBJ list (since the ARP does not subtract any argument from the SUBJ list). This instantiation is initially perplexing: Although it can give rise to an *r-soa*-denoting verb phrase of the kind shown in (25), this *fin-vp* cannot combine with an overt subject, whose *synsem* type would have to be *canon-ss*, which is in conflict with the *gap-ss* on the SUBJ list (of the verb and the VP) in (25).

(25)

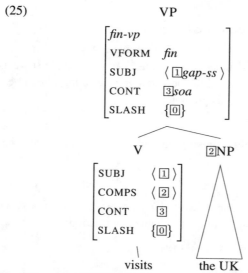

Although a VP like (25) cannot combine with a subject in a declarative head-subject clause (or any other kind of *hd-subj-ph*), in fact nothing blocks such a VP from serving as head daughter of a declarative non-subject clause (introduced in section 2.4.3). To see this, consider (26), which is the result of unifying the constraints on *decl-ns-cl* with relevant constraints inherited from its supertypes:

(26)   **GHFP** & *decl-cl* & *hd-only-ph* & *decl-ns-cl*:

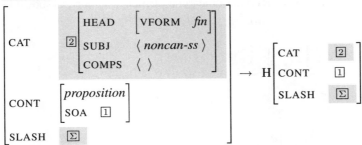

Note that here the GHFP interacts with the constraint on *decl-cl* that embeds the head daughter's CONTENT value into that of the mother. Since the two CONTENT values must be distinct (circular structures are ill-defined), the default unification required by the GHFP identifies only the CATEGORY value of the mother and head daughter, as shown in (26).

In sum, the type *decl-ns-cl* was used in Chapter 2 to license infinitival clauses. This same type also licenses finite clauses like (27), where the SUBJ list of the mother contains not a *pro-ss* element, but rather an element of type *gap-ss* (Shading again illustrates inherited SLASH elements.):

(27)   'S'

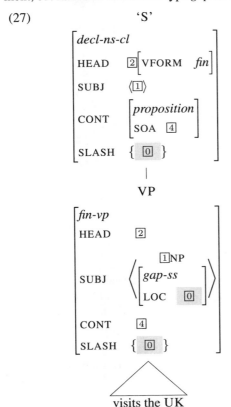

visits the UK

Phrases like this cannot function as independent utterances, because they are slashed and stand-alone expressions must all be [SLASH { }]. However, such a phrase may serve as the complement of a verb like *think*, which selects for finite *proposition*-denoting phrases (see section 2.9). Verbs like *think* thus allow extraction of their complement's subject, as shown in (28):

(28)

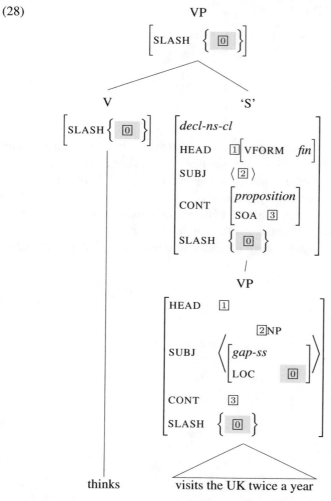

Clauses like (27) thus give rise to sentences like the following:

(29) a. That's the UN delegate that Terry thinks [visits the UK twice a year].

    b. Which UN delegate did you say Terry thinks [visits the UK twice a year]?

Subjunctive clauses whose subject is extracted have a similar analysis:

(30) Which people did you insist [be invited to the party]?

As we will see shortly, subject-extracted declarative clauses also occur in a variety of other contexts.

This analysis of extraction is unusual in that extracted subjects are never cancelled from the SUBJ list and clauses whose subject is extracted are readily distinguishable from others (as [SUBJ ⟨ *gap-ss* ⟩] rather than [SUBJ ⟨ ⟩]). As Bouma et al. (2001) argue, this analysis provides an immediate account of such phenomena as the so-called '*that*-trace effect'. Because a complementizer like *that* selects a [SUBJ ⟨ ⟩] complement (see (67) in Chapter 2), examples like the following are correctly ruled out:[13]

(31) a. *That's the UN delegate that Terry thinks that [visits the UK twice a year].

    b. *Which UN delegate did you say Terry thinks that [visits the UK twice a year]?

That-trace facts are thus reduced to category selection of a familiar sort.

Bouma et al. (2001) also suggest that the present analysis can account for the so-called 'adverb amelioration effect' (see Culicover 1993, among others) illustrated in (32):

(32) This is the kind of person who I doubt that, under normal circumstances, would have anything to do with such a scheme.

When an adverb intervenes between that *that* and a subject position, extraction of that subject is apparently possible.

One analysis of this phenomenon that is consistent with our overall extraction analysis involves simply positing a second entry for the complementizer *that*:

(33)
$$\begin{bmatrix} \text{PHON} & \langle\,\text{that}\,\rangle \\ \text{ARG-ST} & \left\langle \text{ADV} \,, \begin{bmatrix} & \text{'S'} \\ \text{SUBJ} & \langle\,\textit{gap-ss}\,\rangle \end{bmatrix} \right\rangle \end{bmatrix}$$

This lexical entry obligatorily selects an adverb and a clause whose subject is extracted.

More interesting than this ad hoc proposal, however, is one along the lines suggested by Bouma et al. (2001). This involves tuning the constraints on the adverb 'preposing' construction. Assume that this construction (a kind of *hd-fill-ph*) states that its mother is [SUBJ ⟨ ⟩], but that its head daughter is specified as [SUBJ ⟨(*gap-ss*)⟩].[14] In this case, when there is adverb fronting within a clause, it is [SUBJ ⟨ ⟩], and hence selectable by the complementizer *that*, even if its subject is extracted. Examples like (33) would thus have a structure like (34):

---

[13]This account also extends to the analysis of the *que/qui* alternation in French filler-gap constructions, as Bouma et al. (2001) show.

[14]In order for this analysis to work, the SUBJ value of mother and head daughter must be 'deidentified', enabling the GHFP to be overridden. For discussion of a similar issue that arises in our treatment of in-situ interrogatives, see section 7.2.

(34)

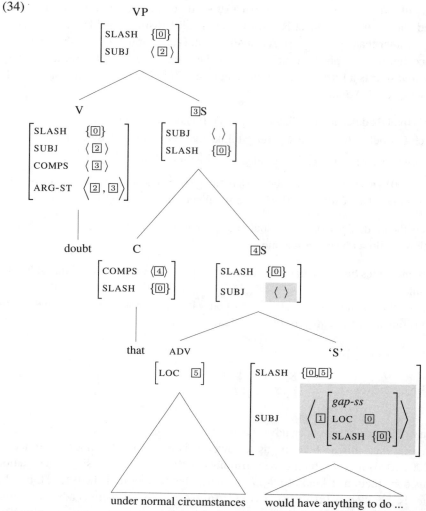

Though there remains some residual worry about the generality of the adverb amelioration effect,[15] it nonetheless seems that the basic phenomenon is amenable to treatment within our analysis.

In sum, our theory of extraction, unlike many of its GPSG and HPSG forbears, treats all cases of missing subjects in terms of a *gap-ss* element on the SUBJ list of a verb and the VP it projects. Because of the SLASH amalgamation that is central to our proposal, whenever a verb's subject is missing in an extraction construction, that verb is slashed. As Hukari and Levine (1995, 1996b) argue at length, this is precisely the generalization about subject extraction that is motivated on cross-linguistic grounds and precisely the generalization missed by earlier treat-

---

[15]For example the decreased acceptability of examples like the following:

(i)??This is the kind of person who I doubt that last year had anything to do with such a scheme.

(ii)??Who do you think that happily visited museums?

(iii)*Which people at the conference did they think that in Paris visited museums?

ments in G/HPSG. Our analysis allows a uniform account of extraction-sensitive phenomena (Kikuyu downstep suppression, Chamorro/Palauan verb morphology, and related cross-linguistic phenomena) in terms of SLASH specifications.

There are other constraints on extraction (i.e. 'island constraints') that have a natural account in the extraction analysis outlined here. As Bouma et al. (2001) show, the Coordinate Structure Constraint and its 'across-the-board' exceptions are a consequence of the requirement that a coordinate structure and all its conjuncts must share a single value for the feature SLASH. In addition, since there are no *wh*-traces in this system, there is no sign that can serve as a conjunct in examples like (35), which either are left undiscussed or else are incorrectly generated in many extraction analyses.

(35) a. *[Which of her books]$_i$ did you find both [[a review of __ $_i$] and __ $_i$]?
 b. *[Which of her books]$_i$ did you find [__ $_i$ and [a review of __ $_i$]]?
 c. *[Which rock legend]$_i$ would it be ridiculous to compare [__ $_i$ and __ $_i$]?
  (cf. [Which rock legend] would it be ridiculous to compare __ $_i$ with himself$_i$?)

More generally, our extraction analysis is unusual in that it provides a natural account of the fact, emphasized by Postal (2001), that island phenomena are heterogeneous. Postal shows in detail, through an examination of an extensive and diverse set of syntactic phenomena, that islands are not a unified class. Rather, specific constructions constitute islands for certain kinds of syntactic dependencies, and not for others, a fact that is difficult to reconcile with many familiar treatments of extraction.

In the present account, by contrast, island phenomena are a consequence of particular type constraints. These constraints may be imposed on a high-level type—so as to affect a large class of constructions—or, in the limiting case, on a particular construction, as is the case, for example, with the Coordinate Structure Constraint. If a particular kind of phrase is an absolute extraction island, then it is subject to a type constraint requring it to be specified as [SLASH { }]. An extraction non-island is left unconstrained with respect to the feature SLASH. A construction that allows, say, only pronominal extraction dependencies—terminated in a pronominal, rather than a gap—is specified as [SLASH *set(pron)*], where *pron* is the type of pronominal *local* objects proposed by Abeillé et al. (to appear) in order to explicate 'Clitic Left Dislocation' and related phenomena in French. Similarly, constructions that allow only NPs to be extracted from them (e.g. so called 'weak islands') are specified as [SLASH *set*(NP)].

There are further island phenomena that could be considered here, but these would take us too far afield. The bare-bones sketch of the grammar of extraction just outlined should provide a sufficient platform for the presentation of our treatment of interrogative constructions. For further discussion of the issues discussed in this section, see Bouma et al. 2001.

5.2 Pied Piping

The second unbounded dependency to be discussed in this chapter is pied piping. A number of *wh*-constructions are head-filler phrases whose initial (filler) daughter is typically simply an appropriate *wh*-word, as in (36).

(36) a. I wonder [[*what*] inspired them].   (*wh*-interrogative)
      b. I wonder [[*why*] they did that __].   (*wh*-interrogative)
      c. [[*How*] they stink]!   (*wh*-exclamative)
      d. the book [[*which*/*what] inspired them]...   (*wh*-relative)

Yet in all such constructions, the required *wh*-word may be properly contained within the filler daughter, as in (37).

(37) a. I wonder [[*whose* cousin] they like __ best].
      b. I wonder [[*how* quickly] they did that __].
      c. the person [[*whose* cousin] ate the pastry]...
      d. the person [[to *whom*] they dedicated the building __]...
      e. [[*How* tall] they are __]!
      f. [[[*What* a] fool] Pat is __]!

Moreover, there is no upper bound on how deeply the *wh*-word may be embedded within the filler daughter, as shown in (38).

(38) a. I wonder [[[*whose* cousin]'s friend's ...dog] ate the pastry].
      b. I wonder [[[[[*how*] much] more] likely] Kim is __ to do that].
      c. the person [[[*whose* cousin]'s friend's ...dog] ate the pastry]...
      d. That's the very report [[the height [of [the [lettering [on [the [covers [of [*which*]]]]]]]]] the CIA prescribes __].
      e. [[[[*How* honest] a] person] she is __]!

It is in this sense that the dependency between the top of the construction and the presence of the appropriate *wh*-word within the filler daughter is unbounded in nature.

   This unbounded dependency, which (following Ross 1967) we refer to as 'pied piping', has been analyzed within HPSG just as extraction dependencies are treated—via the inheritance of feature specifications. For instance, the head-filler constructions we introduce in the next chapter for *wh*-interrogative and *wh*-exclamative clauses define structures like (39):

(39)

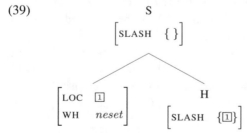

The *neset* in (39) will be resolved as {*param(eter)*} for interrogative clauses and {*unusual-rel*} for exclamative clauses, where *unusual-rel* is a kind of *generalized-quantifier (GQ)*.[16] As we will show directly, {*param*} is an appropriate WH value for interrogative *wh*-words and {*unusual-rel*} is the appropriate WH value for all exclamative *wh*-words. Thus the simple examples in (36a–c) are simply accounted for.

---

[16]The feature WH, as noted earlier, corresponds to the feature QUE utiliized by P&S–94, who did not provide an account of exclamatives.

The examples in (37) and (38) are more challenging. What is required is a way of guaranteeing that the constructional WH requirement trickles down appropriately through a filler daughter like the one shown in (40) to ensure that there is an embedded *wh*-word with the appropriate WH specification:

(40)

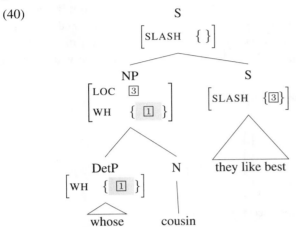

Put differently, our grammar must include constraints guaranteeing that whenever a WH-specified word (one with a non-empty value for WH) is present, its WH specification is passed up through the tree so as to WH-specify phrases that contain that WH-specified word as well. Conversely, it must follow that when no *wh*-word is present within a given phrase, that phrase must be [WH { }], and hence unsuitable as a filler daughter in a *wh*-construction.

5.2.1 *Wh*-Words

Before formulating constraints on the inheritance of WH-specifications, let us first examine more closely the lexical entries of *wh*-words. The interrogative and exclamative *wh*-words are distinguished from other words in that they allow nonempty specifications for the feature WH. As just noted, WH takes as its value a set that contains either a parameter (in the case of a fronted interrogative *wh*-word) or a quantifier (in the case of an exclamative *wh*-word) or else is empty. We formulate the lexical entry for interrogative *who* in (41):

(41)   Interrogative *who*:

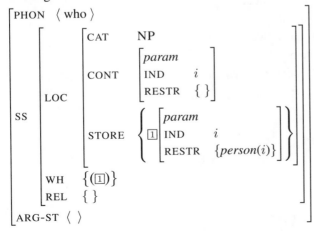

Similar lexical entries are assumed for all interrogative *wh*-words, including *what*, *which*, *whose*, *where*, *when*, *why*, and *how*.

The type *param* (roughly equivalent to the restricted parameters of the Situation Semantics literature and to the type *nom-obj* of P&S–94) is the type of the CONTENT value of all NPs. In (41), the index of the *wh*-word is identified with that of the parameter that is contributed to the STORE. Once a parameter is in the STORE, it is 'passed up' (via principles explained in the next section) to be incorporated into a question somewhere 'higher' in the sentence structure. In this way, an interrogative *wh*-word in a syntactically embedded context can receive wide scope in examples like the following:

(42) a. [You said [you believe [you saw WHO]]]?

b.
$$\begin{bmatrix} question \\[2pt] \text{PARAMS} \quad \left\{ \begin{bmatrix} param \\ \text{INDEX} \quad \boxed{1} \\ \text{RESTR} \quad \{person(\boxed{1})\} \end{bmatrix} \right\} \\[2pt] \text{PROP} \quad \textbf{say(you,[believe(you,[see(you,}\boxed{1}\textbf{)])])} \end{bmatrix}$$

Note further that according to (41) the WH value of a *wh*-interrogative word may also be the empty set, though a variety of constraints will interact to determine a unique value for a *wh*-word's WH value in any given linguistic context. The generalization that follows from our analysis is that only the first interrogative *wh*-word in an interrogative clause will bear a nonempty WH value. All in-situ occurrences of interrogative *wh*-words—those in reprise questions like (43) or those in multiple *wh*-questions (section 6.6)—will be [WH { }]. This distinction is fundamental to the grammar of *wh*-interrogatives presented in subsequent chapters.

Exclamative *wh*-words are similar, except—according to Quirk, Greenbaum, Leech, and Svartvik (1985: 833)—there are only two of them: the degree element *how* and the predeterminer *what*. These words always have a quantifier as their WH value. We will name this quantifier *unusual-rel*. The intuition underlying this involves examples such as (43a,c,e), which can be paraphrased as in (43b,d,f):

(43) a. What a performance I've just heard!
　　b. There's an unusual performance I've just heard.
　　c. What a sunset I've just seen.
　　d. There's an unusual sunset I've just seen.
　　e. How hard this problem is!
　　f. There's an unusual extent such that this problem is hard to that extent.

This motivates the following lexical entry for exclamative *what a*:

(44) Exclamative *what a*:

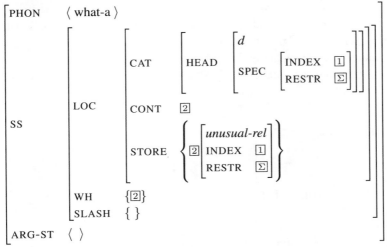

This is a determiner very similar to *every*, *some* or *the*: it combines with an N̄, which it selects via the feature SPEC and identifies that N̄'s RESTR value with that of the stored quantifier. Exclamative *wh*-words also behave in a way that closely resembles their interrogative counterparts: they contribute a quantifier to the STORE and also to the WH-value. The stored exclamative quantifier is 'passed up' in accordance with constraints described in the next section and integrated into the meaning of an exclamative clause via a construction-specific constraint formulated in the next chapter. In contrast to interrogative *wh*-words, exclamative *wh*-words obligatorily have a non-empty WH specification. Since elements with non-empty WH specifications have a highly restricted distribution (as we will soon see), our analysis predicts that there are no in-situ uses of exclamative *wh*-words.

The lexical entry for exclamative *how* is sketched in (45):

(45) Exclamative *how*:

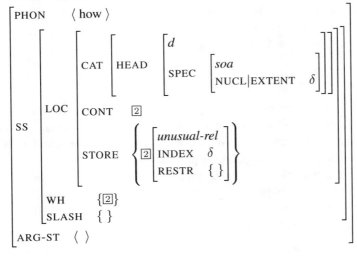

Note that exclamative *how* is a specifier that also selects its head via the feature SPEC. However, since the value of SPEC must be a *soa* whose nucleus allows the feature EXTENT—i.e. it must be a gradable adjective or adverb, exclamative *how* combines as a specifier only with APs and ADVPs headed by semantically gradable items.

Relative pronouns are somewhat different from the previous two kinds of *wh*-word. They have an empty STORE and they are [WH { }]. They also must have a parameter as their REL value, as shown in (46):

(46)   Relative *who*:

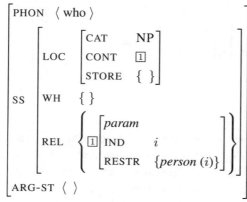

Similar entries are assumed for the other relative *wh*-words *which* and *whose*. A relative *wh*-word's nonempty REL value must be passed up through pied-piping structures in the same way that WH-specifications are, though there are slightly different constraints at work in the two cases.

Because *wh*-relative words have an empty STORE, they also do not contribute to the content of a phrase in the same way that interrogative and exclamative *wh*-words do. Their contribution will come entirely from constraints on the various types of relative clause identifying the index of the WH value with that of the nominal being modified. Moreover, because the distribution of expressions with nonempty REL values, like WH-specified expressions, is highly constrained, relative words do not have in-situ uses in English. As explicated in Chapters 6 and 7, this possibility exists for interrogative *wh*-words only because they also allow a [WH { }] specification (note the optionality of the WH member in (41)), an option that is unavailable for the REL value of relative *wh*-words.[17]

5.2.2   WH Percolation

We may now ask how WH-specifications are 'percolated' in pied piping structures. Put simply, the answer to this question is that the percolation is mediated by lexical heads. That is, a noun selecting a specifier takes on the specifier's WH value because there is a constraint (similar to the SLASH-Amalgamation constraint discussed in the previous section) requiring words to amalgamate the WH values of their arguments (including specifiers). Thus once a noun combines with a [WH {*param*}] determiner, the noun itself is [WH {*param*}]. And once the noun is so specified, the phrases projected by that noun are also [WH {*param*}], courtesy of the GHFP. The GHFP thus interacts with lexical constraints to account for WH-percolation without introducing any

---

[17]For convenience, since we will have no further discussions of *wh*-relatives, we will henceforth omit all mention of the feature REL.

new mechanisms into our grammar. However, as we will see, there is more than one pattern of lexical constraint that we must recognize in order to predict the different properties of pied piping in nominal, verbal, prepositional and other structures.

We posit three constraints governing the distribution of WH specifications in lexical entries. The first of these is the WH-Amalgamation Constraint, which ensures that by default the WH value of any word is the union of the WH values of that word's arguments:

(47)   WH-Amalgamation Constraint:

$$word \Rightarrow / \begin{bmatrix} \text{SS}|\text{WH} & \boxed{\Sigma_1} \cup \ldots \cup \boxed{\Sigma_n} \\ \text{ARG-ST} & \left\langle [\text{WH } \boxed{\Sigma_1}], \ldots, [\text{WH } \boxed{\Sigma_n}] \right\rangle \end{bmatrix}$$

Note that the interrogative and exclamative *wh*-words just presented override the constraint in (47).[18]

The WH-Amalgamation Constraint applies to feature structures of type *word* (n.b.—not *lexeme*), as does the following constraint:

(48)   WH-Subject Prohibition (WHSP):

$$word \quad \Rightarrow \quad \left[\text{SS}|\text{LOC}|\text{CAT}|\text{SUBJ} \quad list([\text{WH } \{ \}]) \right]$$

The WHSP prevents subjects from being WH-specified. This has the effect, for example, that all *wh*-phrases that appear to be WH-specified subjects (e.g. *Who left?*) are really extracted phrases. That is, any such *wh*-phrase is the filler of a head-filler construction, not the subject of a head-subject construction.

The final general constraint on WH specification is the following:

(49)   WH-Constraint (WHC):
        Any non-initial element of a lexeme's ARG-ST list must be [WH { }].

The WHC, which can be formalized in several ways,[19] ensures that only the initial member of a lexeme's ARG-ST can be WH-specified. The three constraints just adumbrated interact with the properties of specific lexical classes to explain the subtly different pied piping behavior found in various kinds of phrases.

NPs

As argued by Pollard and Sag (1992, 1994), nominal specifiers must be part of a noun's argument structure in order to account for binding data like that in (50).[20]

(50)   a.   His$_i$ picture of himself$_i$ was pretty ugly.

        b.   *Their$_i$ pictures of them$_i$ were on sale everywhere.

        c.   *They$_i$ knew my pictures of each other$_i$ were on sale everywhere.

---

[18]In section 5.4 below, we collapse the SLASH-Amalgamation Constraint and the WH-Amalgamation Constraint into a single principle amalgamating the values of non-LOCAL features.

[19]For example, the WHC could be formulated as an RSRL-style implicational constraint. The alternative that we will adopt involves positing a list type *arg-st-list* with two subtypes: *elist* and *n(on)e(mpty)-arg-st-list*. The latter is constrained as follows:

(i)   *ne-arg-st-list* $\Rightarrow$ $\left[\text{REST} \quad list([\text{WH } \{ \}]) \right]$

[20]For a recent critical discussion of binding effects in nominal phrases, see Keller and Asudeh 2000.

Hence, the lexical entry for a common noun lexeme like *cousin* is as shown in (51):[21]

(51)
$$
\begin{bmatrix}
\textit{cn-lx} \\
\text{PHON} \quad \langle\, \text{cousin} \,\rangle \\
\text{SS|LOC|CAT|HEAD} \; n \\
\text{ARG-ST} \quad \langle\, \text{Det} \,\rangle
\end{bmatrix}
$$

This lexeme gives rise to the (nonpredicative) singular word shown in (52) via a lexical rule that we may formulate as in (53):

(52)
$$
\begin{bmatrix}
\textit{word} \\
\text{PHON} \quad \langle\, \text{cousin} \,\rangle \\
\text{SS} \quad
\begin{bmatrix}
\text{LOC|CAT}
\begin{bmatrix}
\text{SPR} \quad \left\langle \begin{bmatrix} \boxed{2}\text{Det} \\ \text{WH} \quad \boxed{\Sigma} \end{bmatrix} \right\rangle \\
\text{SUBJ} \quad \langle\,\rangle \\
\text{COMPS} \quad \langle\,\rangle \\
\text{HEAD}
\begin{bmatrix}
n \\
\text{PRED} \quad - \\
\text{AGR} \quad [\text{NUM} \; sg]
\end{bmatrix}
\end{bmatrix} \\
\text{WH} \quad \boxed{\Sigma}
\end{bmatrix} \\
\text{ARG-ST} \quad \langle\, \boxed{2} \,\rangle
\end{bmatrix}
$$

(53) Singular Attributive Noun Lexical Rule:

$$
\begin{bmatrix}
\textit{lx} \\
\text{SS|LOC|CAT|HEAD} \quad n
\end{bmatrix}
\Longrightarrow_{LR}
\begin{bmatrix}
\textit{word} \\
\text{SS|LOC|CAT}
\begin{bmatrix}
\text{HEAD}
\begin{bmatrix}
\text{AGR|NUM} \; sg \\
\text{PRED} \quad -
\end{bmatrix} \\
\text{SPR} \quad \langle\boxed{1}\rangle \\
\text{SUBJ} \quad \langle\,\rangle
\end{bmatrix} \\
\text{ARG-ST|FIRST} \quad \boxed{1}
\end{bmatrix}
$$

Several points are noteworthy. First, the LR in (53) produces a singular word as its output.[22] Second, the LR also identifies the noun's first argument with the specifier that the noun selects. Because of the WH-Amalgamation Constraint, this specifier and the noun share their WH value, as indicated in (52). Third, because the LR preserves the ARG-ST of the input lexeme in the output word, the noun in (52) has a singleton ARG-ST list. Hence, because the LR also specifies an empty SUBJ value for the derived word, the Argument Realization Principle guarantees that the latter's COMPS value is also empty, as indicated.

The effect of WH-amalgamation is to ensure that a noun like (52) is WH-specified whenever it combines with a WH-specified determiner. The WH-specified noun then passes up its nonempty

---

[21] We use 'Det' to abbreviate the synsem of a sign (either *word* or *phrase*) whose HEAD value is of category *d*.
[22] We adopt an AGR-based analysis of agreement here merely for convenience.

WH value to the nominal phrases it projects, as required by the GHFP. This provides an account of simple pied piping in NPs like (37a) above.

Not all noun lexemes have singleton argument structures, however. The lexical entry for the lexeme *picture* is illustrated in (54):

(54)
$$\begin{bmatrix} cn\text{-}lx \\ \text{PHON} \quad \langle \text{ picture } \rangle \\ \text{SS|LOC|CAT|HEAD} \quad n \\ \text{ARG-ST} \quad \langle \text{ Det } (, \text{PP}[of]) \rangle \end{bmatrix}$$

Such lexemes give rise to nonpredicative singular words in like fashion. Note, however, that the WHC requires that the PP[*of*] must be [WH { }].

The lexemes just described also give rise (again by inflectional rule) to plural words that differ from their singular counterparts only in their number specification. The interaction with WH-amalgamation again accounts for the pied piping effect, this time in NPs like (55).

(55)　a.　I wonder [[*whose* pictures (of Sandy)] Pat likes].

　　　b.　I wonder [[[*whose* friend's] pictures (of Sandy)] Pat likes].

Plural and mass singular nouns may also give rise to determinerless phrases like (56):

(56)　[Pictures (of Sandy)] are cheap.

These are analyzed in terms of a non-branching construction (a *hd-only-ph*) in which a [SPR ⟨ Det ⟩] head daughter projects an NP that is [SPR ⟨ ⟩], as shown in (57):

(57)　*bare-nom-ph*:

$$\begin{bmatrix} \text{SPR} \quad \langle \rangle \end{bmatrix} \rightarrow \text{H} \begin{bmatrix} \text{HEAD} \quad n \\ \text{SPR} \quad \left\langle \begin{bmatrix} \text{Det} \\ \text{WH} \{ \} \end{bmatrix} \right\rangle \end{bmatrix}$$

Note the interaction with the GHFP, which ensures, *inter alia*, that specifications for all valence features other than SPR are percolated from head daughter to mother:

(58)　ECC & GHFP & *hd-only-ph* & *bare-nom-ph*:

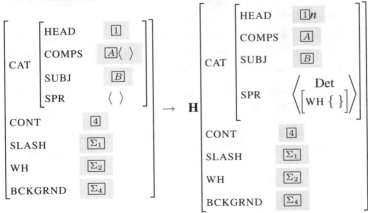

The analysis provided for a 'bare plural' NP is thus as shown in (59):

(59)

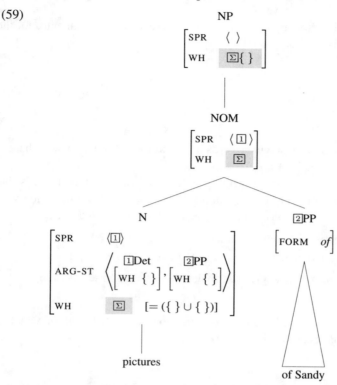

The *bare-nom-ph* construction imposes the further requirement that the head daughter's SPR value is ⟨[WH { }]⟩, as indicated. This further ensures (courtesy of WH-amalgamation and the GHFP) that the head noun and its projections are all [WH { }], and hence unsuitable as fillers in *wh*-interrogative clauses like (60), even though another interrogative *wh*-word may be present:[23]

(60) a. *I wonder [[pictures of *Pat*] they were admiring __ .]

      b. *I wonder [[pictures of *whom*] they were admiring __ .]

In (60b), the PP *of whom* and the NP *whom* must both be [WH { }], as required by the WHC and its interaction with the other principles already illustrated.

    We now make the further proposal that possessive *'s* is a determiner that obligatorily selects an NP specifier argument. From this it follows, again by the Argument Realization Principle and WH-amalgamation, that *'s* must be WH-specified whenever its specifier is, as shown in (61):[24]

---

[23]Note further that examples like (i) are blocked because proper nouns are lexically specified as [WH { }].

   (i) *I wonder [[*Pat*] they were admiring __ .]

[24]This analysis of possessive *'s* is proposed independently by Fillmore et al. (to appear). An alternative account of pied piping in possessive phrases, based on the ideas of Zwicky (1987), is also possible within our approach.

(61)

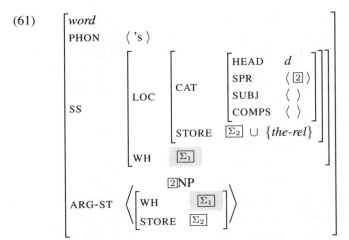

Therefore, again by the GHFP, the determiner *'s* must pass up its WH value to the DetP it projects.

Our treatments of common nouns and the possessive determiner interact to account for unbounded pied piping within NPs, as illustrated in (62):

(62)

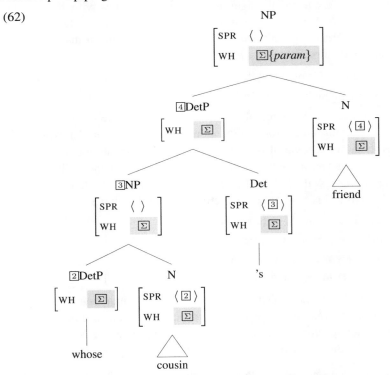

Our system of constraints also ensures that when *whose* is replaced by the [WH { }] determiner *my*, the resulting phrase—*my cousin's friend*—is [WH { }], which makes it unsuitable as a filler in any *wh*-construction.

Similarly, the exclamative determiner *how*—lexically specified as [WH {*unusual-rel*}]—may be selected as a specifier by a gradable determiner like *few*. Again it follows from the interaction of the Argument Realization Principle and WH-amalgamation that the WH value of *few* will in this case also be *unusual-rel*. Hence the DetP *how few* will be [WH {*unusual-rel*}], as will any noun that selects *how few* as its specifier. Therefore, again via the GHFP, NPs like those bracketed in (63a,b) are all [WH {*unusual-rel*}] and may serve as the filler daughter in a *wh*-exclamative clause. Similar further identifications ensure unbounded pied piping in exclamatives as well, providing an account of (63c,d).[25]

(63) a.   [[How few books] they've read]!

  b.   [[How many people] have remembered your birthday]!

  c.   [[How many people's birthdays] she remembers __]!

  d. (?)[[How many students' parents' suggestions] you take __ into account]!

There is a further point about pied piping in the NP that must be noted. An adequate analysis must ensure that all other (i.e. non-initial) arguments of nouns be specified as [WH { }]. It is not that multiple *wh*-expressions are impossible within an NP, as examples like (64) show.[26]

(64)   I wonder [[*whose* pictures of *whom*] they were admiring __].

The point is rather that the second *wh*-expression in (64) is not WH-specified—it is in situ. This claim can be verified by the test discussed at length in the next chapter, involving the possibility of modification by *the hell, the devil, in the world*, etc. Expressions such as these can only modify words that are [WH {*param*}]. Hence the following contrasts confirm that the second *wh*-expression in (64), but not the first, is [WH { }].

(65) a.   I wonder [[*who the hell*'s pictures] they were admiring __].

  b.   *I wonder [[whose pictures of *who the hell*] they were admiring __].

The WHC in (49) above ensures that noninitial members of a noun lexeme's ARG-ST list must be [WH { }]. This renders them unsuitable for modification by *the hell* and similar expressions. The WHC also plays a role in our account of key contrasts in the interpretation of multiple *wh*-interrogatives. Both of these matters are taken up in detail in the next chapter. Finally, since exclamative *wh*-words are never specified as [WH { }], the WHC also predicts that there are no in-situ exclamatives within NPs. This is a correct prediction, as the following examples show:

(66) a.   *[[Pictures of how few churches] they've seen __]!

  b.   *[[How few pictures of how few churches] they've seen __]!

  c.   *[[Letters to what a great senator] they've written __]!

  d.   *[[What a great letter to what a great senator] they've written __]!

We also treat predicative NPs lexically. That is, we assume that common noun lexemes also give rise to predicative nominal words. But the lexical rule that creates predicative nouns prefixes a subject argument to the noun lexeme's ARG-ST list. This allows predicative NPs to function like other subject-selecting predicating expressions (e.g. VPs). Unifying in the effects of the

---

[25]For some speakers, it appear that acceptability decays with depth of embedding more rapidly in the case of exclamatives than with interrogatives or relatives. We have no explanation for this fact at present.

[26]Note that examples like (i) are already properly accounted for, as the noun *picture* must be [WH { }], agreeing with its specifier *Pat's*.

  (i) *I wonder [[Pat's pictures of whom] Sandy likes __].

Since *picture* is [WH { }], so is the NP it projects, rendering that NP unsuitable as a filler daughter in a *wh*-interrogative clause, e.g. the one bracketed in (i).

Argument Realization Principle, WH-amalgamation, and the WHSP [(48)] we have the following description for the predicative noun *cousin*:

(67)

$$
\begin{bmatrix}
word \\
\text{PHON} \quad \langle \text{ cousin } \rangle \\
\text{SS} \begin{bmatrix}
\text{LOC|CAT} \begin{bmatrix}
\text{HEAD} \begin{bmatrix} noun \\ \text{PRED} + \\ \text{AGR} \quad [\text{NUM} \quad sg] \end{bmatrix} \\
\text{SPR} \quad \langle \boxed{2} \rangle \\
\text{SUBJ} \quad \langle \boxed{5} \rangle \\
\text{COMPS} \quad \langle \, \rangle
\end{bmatrix} \\
\text{WH} \quad \boxed{\Sigma}
\end{bmatrix} \\
\text{ARG-ST} \quad \left\langle \begin{matrix} \boxed{5}\text{NP} \\ [\text{WH} \quad \{ \}] \end{matrix} , \begin{matrix} \boxed{2}\text{Det} \\ [\text{WH} \quad \boxed{\Sigma} \,] \end{matrix} \right\rangle
\end{bmatrix}
$$

Note that in (67), the noun's WH value is identified with that of the specifier (the second member of the ARG-ST list). This follows because WHSP ensures that the first argument's WH value is { } (and because { } ∪ $\boxed{\Sigma}$ = $\boxed{\Sigma}$). Note further that this analysis provides an account of examples like the following, if we assume that complements of the identity copula are also predicative NPs.

(68)   I wondered [*whose cousin*] *she was pretending to be* __ .

Below we show how this analysis extends to pied piping in uncontroversially predicative NPs like the one italicized in (69).

(69)   I wonder [*how good a candidate*] *he would be* __ .

PPs

Different lexical classes exhibit different constraints vis à vis the feature WH. 'Case-marking' prepositions, for example, take on the WH value of their first argument (their object NP), as illustrated in (70).

(70)   a. I wonder [[to *whom*] they sent presents __ .]

b. I wonder [[to *whose* friends] they sent presents __ .]

c.

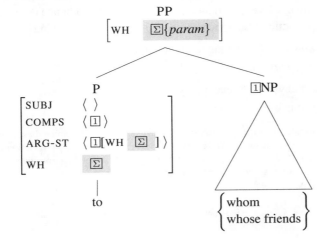

'Head-object' WH-agreement in the case of case-marking prepositions is a consequence of WH-amalgamation. This lexical agreement interacts with the GHFP to ensure that examples like (70a,b) are correctly treated. In addition, the proposed treatments of nouns and prepositions interact to account for a distinct pattern of unbounded pied piping in interrogatives, as illustrated in (71)–(72).[27]

(71) a. I wonder [[to [*whose* friends]] they sent presents __].

      b. I wonder [[to [[*whose* friends'] children]] they sent presents __].

      c. I wonder [[to [[[*whose* friends'] children's] pets]] they sent presents __].

Exclamatives in PPs work similarly, though acceptability again decays more rapidly with depth of embedding:

(72) a. [[To [[*how* many] children]] they've sent presents __]!

      b. [[To [[[*how* many] children's] schools]] they've sent donations __]!

Predicative prepositions—those with two NPs on their ARG-ST list, have lexical entries like the following:

$$
(73) \quad
\begin{bmatrix}
\text{PHON} & \langle\, in\,\rangle \\[2pt]
\text{SS} &
\begin{bmatrix}
\text{LOC}|\text{CAT} &
\begin{bmatrix}
\text{HEAD} & \begin{bmatrix} p \\ \text{PRED} & + \end{bmatrix} \\
\text{SUBJ} & \langle\, \boxed{1}\,\rangle \\
\text{COMPS} & \langle\, \boxed{2}\,\rangle
\end{bmatrix} \\
\text{WH} & \{\,\}
\end{bmatrix} \\[2pt]
\text{ARG-ST} & \left\langle \boxed{1}\text{NP}\begin{bmatrix}\text{WH} & \{\,\}\end{bmatrix}, \boxed{2}\text{NP}\begin{bmatrix}\text{WH} & \{\,\}\end{bmatrix}\right\rangle
\end{bmatrix}
$$

The effect of the WHC is indicated in (73) (the object NP must be [WH { }], as it is a non-initial argument of the prepositional lexeme). In addition, predicative prepositions, like all other predicatives, select for a subject that is identified with the first member of the ARG-ST list. Thus under our analysis it follows—from the interaction of the WHSP and WH-amalgamation—that predicative prepositions are always [WH { }] (since { } ∪ { } = { }) and hence do not appear in pied piping structures. This prediction also appears to be correct, as the following data suggest.[28]

(74) a. ?*I wonder [[in [[*how* many] synagogues]] they have been __].

      b. *I wonder [[about [*what*]] this book is __].

(75) a. I wonder [[[*how* many] synagogues] they have been in __].

      b. I wonder [[*what*] this book is about __].

---

[27]Some case marking prepositions allow non-*wh* specifiers such as *right* or *straight*. Assuming these to be specified as [WH { }], the WH-Amalgamation Constraint and the WHC would interact to ensure that any preposition cooccurring with such a specifier would also be specified as [WH { }]. This leads to the prediction that these specifiers cannot appear in pied piping structures. As examples like (i) show, this prediction appears to be correct.

   (i) *I wonder [right [to [*whom*]] they threw the ball __].

[28]It should be noted that there is some variation in judgment across speakers with respect to certain of these examples.

In examples (75a–b), the preposition's second argument is of type *gap-ss*, a type which is constrained to be [WH { }]. Hence in these examples, the WHC is not violated.

APs

Let us now turn to adjectives, which also project phrases that contain pied piping of unbounded depth, as shown in (76).

(76) a. I wonder [[how happy] Sandy is __].
      b. [[How happy] is Sandy __]?
      c. I wonder [[[how much] smarter (than Pat)] Sandy really is __].
      d. [[[How much] smarter (than Pat)] do you think Sandy really is __]?
      e. (?)I wonder [[[[how many] times] smarter than Pat] Sandy really is __].
      f. (?)[[[[How many] times] smarter than Pat] do you think Sandy really is __]?

(77) a. [[How happy] Sandy is __]!
      b. [[[How much] smarter (than Pat)] Sandy is __]!
      c. (?)[[[[How many] times] smarter than Pat] Sandy seems to be __]!

Like pied piping within the NP, pied piping in an AP is possible only if the *wh*-word is the adjective's specifier or a specifier within the adjective's specifier. Thus examples like the following are systematically ill-formed.

(78) a. *I wonder [[(so) proud of whom] Sandy really is __].
      b. *[[Proud of whom] do you think Sandy really is __]?

As noted in section 2.2, there are argument structure parallelisms between adjectives and verbs. To capture these similarities, we proposed there, following standard practice in HPSG, that adjective lexemes should be assigned ARG-ST values parallel to those of verbal lexemes. On this view, the ARG-ST of a strict intransitive adjective, e.g. *big*, is analogous to that of a simple intransitive verb, i.e. $\langle NP \rangle$, while that of a subject control adjective like *eager* is $\langle NP_i, [SUBJ \langle NP_i \rangle] \rangle$, analogous to that of the verb *try*. This account of adjectival lexemes accounts for subcategorizational generalizations cross-cutting the two lexical classes, but it leaves no room for specifiers, which all gradable adjectives (but no verbs) can select for.

Our approach to this discrepancy is to formulate the lexical rules deriving adjectival words so that they insert a specifier into the second position of the argument structure. On this view, an adjective lexeme like *happy* in (79) is mapped into the predicative word described in (80) (again with the effects of the Argument Realization Principle, WHSP and WH-amalgamation unified in):

(79)
$$
\begin{bmatrix}
a\text{-}lx \\
\text{PHON} \quad \langle \text{ happy } \rangle \\
\text{SS|LOC|CAT|HEAD } a \\
\text{ARG-ST} \quad \langle \text{ NP } \rangle
\end{bmatrix}
$$

(80)

$$
\begin{bmatrix}
word \\
\text{PHON} \quad \langle \text{ happy } \rangle \\
\text{SS} \begin{bmatrix}
\text{LOC|CAT} \begin{bmatrix}
\text{HEAD} \begin{bmatrix} a \\ \text{PRED} \quad + \\ \text{DEG} \quad \boxed{4} \end{bmatrix} \\
\text{SUBJ} \quad \langle \boxed{1} \rangle \\
\text{SPR} \quad \langle \boxed{2} \rangle
\end{bmatrix} \\
\text{WH} \quad \boxed{\Sigma}
\end{bmatrix} \\
\text{ARG-ST} \quad \left\langle \begin{bmatrix} \boxed{1}\text{NP} \\ \text{WH} \ \{\ \} \end{bmatrix}, \begin{bmatrix} \boxed{2}\text{Det} \\ \text{WH} \quad \boxed{\Sigma} \\ \text{DEG} \quad \boxed{4} \end{bmatrix} \right\rangle
\end{bmatrix}
$$

Note that the predicative adjective in (80) shares its WH value with its second argument. This follows from the WHSP and WH-amalgamation ($\{\ \} \cup \boxed{\Sigma} = \boxed{\Sigma}$). In addition, we have introduced a feature DEG for which degree determiners like *so*, *too*, and *how* are positively specified. Because of the agreement for DEG indicated in (80), an adjective will be [DEG +] whenever it combines with such a determiner.

Although (gradable) adjectives and nouns do not always cooccur with an overt specifier, on our analysis their ARG-ST list always includes an appropriate degree phrase specifier. A non-branching construction, similar to that used for bare plural constructions, will sanction [SPR $\langle\ \rangle$] APs whose head daughter is [SPR $\langle$Det$\rangle$]:

(81)   *bare-adj-ph*:

$$
\begin{bmatrix} \text{SPR} \quad \langle\ \rangle \end{bmatrix} \rightarrow \text{H} \begin{bmatrix}
\text{HEAD} \begin{bmatrix} a \\ \dots \end{bmatrix} \\
\text{SPR} \quad \left\langle \begin{bmatrix} \text{Det} \\ \text{DEG} \quad - \\ \text{CONT} \quad some\text{-}rel \\ \text{WH} \quad \{\ \} \end{bmatrix} \right\rangle
\end{bmatrix}
$$

This construction provides the requisite existential interpretation for the unexpressed quantifier (lexically amalgamated by the adjectival head daughter). The sentence *Kim is tall* is assigned a content roughly paraphrasable as 'there is a degree δ, sufficient in the relevant context, such that Kim is tall to degree δ'.

This analysis provides an account of bare adjective phrases like the one sketched in (82).

(82)

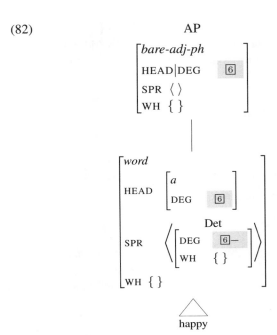

happy

The inheritance of DEG specifications shaded in (82) follows from the interaction of the DEG value identity specified in (80) and the GHFP.

Given that gradable adjectives always have a nonempty SPR value, obligatorily selecting a (degree) determiner as specifier, WH-amalgamation and the GHFP interact to provide an account of pied piping in APs like (83) as well.

(83)

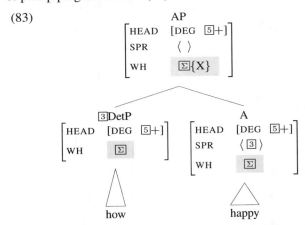

how   happy

This structure can be the filler daughter of a *wh*-interrogative or *wh*-exclamative clause. In the interrogative clause of (84a), the WH element X is a parameter; in the exclamative cases [(84b)], it is the quantifier unusual.

(84) a. I wonder [[*how* happy] they really are __].

  b. [[*How* happy] they seem __]!

The structure for *too happy* is the same as (83), except that the WH value is { }, a consequence of the differing lexical WH-specfication of the non-*wh*-degree word *too*. In addition, gradable adverbials like those in (85) allow all the same WH possibilities as gradable adjectives and may be given an analogous treatment.

(85) a. [[*How* quickly] can they get the job done __]?
     b. [[*How* quickly] they get the job done __]!
     c. [They got the job done [*too* quickly].]

Predeterminers

An AP like (83) can also serve as the specifier of the determiner *a* in examples like (86).[29]

(86) a. I wonder [[[*how* big] a risk] they really are/took __].
     b. They are/took [[*too* big] a risk].
     c. They are/took [[*such*] a risk].

To account for the complex phrases in examples like (86), we allow the determiner *a* to optionally select a gradable AP as its specifier. When this option is exercised, we derive (unifying in the Argument Realization Principle and the WH-Amalgamation Constraint once again) the constraints shown in (87):

(87)

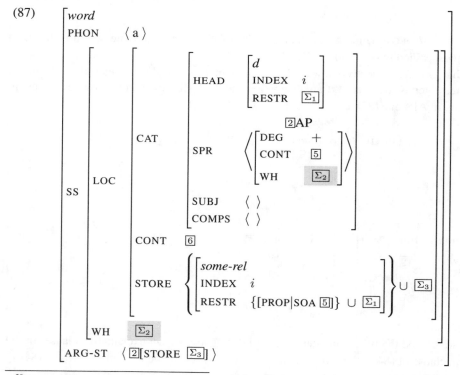

---

[29]Steps must be taken to prevent such APs from appearing between the determiner and the noun:

  (i) *I wonder [[a [*how* big] risk] they really are/took __].
  (ii) *They are/took [a [*too* big] risk].
  (iii) *They are/took [a [*such*] risk].

A constraint on the prenominal adjective construction requiring the modifier daughter to be [DEG −] may well suffice for this purpose.

The STORE value of determiners and their inheritance in larger grammatical structures are discussed in the next section. Here, the important point to see is that the lexical entry in (87) allows *a* to combine with a [DEG +] AP as 'predeterminer', giving rise to determiner phrases like the following, where the AP *how big* functions as the specifier of *a*:

(88)

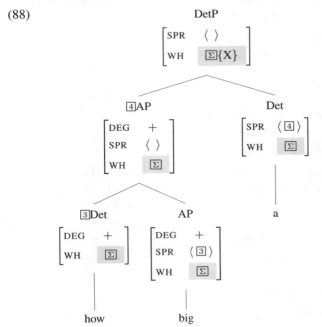

And this DetP can be selected as a specifier by a noun like *risk*, whose WH value is shared with the DetP in (88) (again by WH-amalgamation) and then passed up via the GHFP, producing an analysis of *how big a risk* as an NP whose WH value is either a parameter (in interrogative clauses) or the quantifier *unusual* (in exclamatives). A similar analysis is provided for *too big a risk*, except the shared WH value is { }. Note that exactly the same pattern of feature inheritance is true of *such a risk*, under the assumption that *such* leads a life as an appropriate specifier, lexically specified as [WH { }].

By treating predeterminers as AP specifiers selected by the determiner *a*, we make the further correct prediction that other determiners disallow such predeterminers. That is, we predict the impossibility of examples like (89).

(89) a. *I wonder [[[[*how* big] some] eater] he is __].

     b. *We like [[[*too* big] all] eaters].

     c. *[[[[*How* big] the] eater] he is __]!

This same distributional pattern appears to be true of *what*-exclamatives:

(90) a. [[[*What a*] fool] he is __]!

     b. [[*What* fools] they are __]!

On our analysis, this is because exclamative *what a* and its plural analog *what* uniformly function as the specifier of a nominal phrase. There is thus a fundamental asymmetry in the analysis of exclamative *how*—the specifier of a specifier in *how big a...* and *what a*, which is simply lexicalized as a complex determiner.

VPs

Finally, let us turn to the matter of WH percolation in verb phrases. As the following data show, interrogative and exclamative pied piping is impossible in VPs:

(91)   a. *I wonder [[*who(m)* leaving] upset Sandy].

     b. *I wonder [[(Kim) talking to *who(m)*]] upset Sandy].

     c. *I wonder [[to love *who(m)*]] would please Sandy].

(92)   a. *It's amazing [[[*what* a nice guy] leaving] Sandy was upset by _].

     b. *[[*What* a nice guy] leaving] Sandy was upset by _ !

     c. *[Talking to [*what* a nice guy]] Sandy was upset by _ !
        (cf. What a nice guy Sandy was upset by talking to _ !)

It already follows from our analysis that none of the indicated *wh*-words can be WH-specified, as each of them is either a subject, and hence required to be [WH { }] by the WHSP, or else a non-initial argument of a verbal lexeme, and hence [WH { }], according to the WHC. Hence it follows from WH-amalgamation that subject-selecting verbs are themselves all [WH { }]. And since verbs and the phrases they project are all [WH { }], it follows from WH-amalgamation that a complementizer like *that*, which selects an S as its only argument, must also be [WH { }], thus blocking pied piping in examples like (93).

(93)   a. *I wonder [[that who left] upset Sandy].

     b. *I wonder [[that Kim loves who(m)] upset Sandy].

The only apparent exception to the pattern shown in (92) is verbal gerunds with possessive determiners, illustrated in (94).

(94)   a. I wonder [[whose leaving the room] upset Sandy].

     b. *I wonder [[my talking to who(m)] upset Sandy].

     c. *I wonder [[who(m) leaving the room] upset Sandy].

     d. *I wonder [[me talking to who(m)] upset Sandy].

As the contrast in (94) shows, when these gerunds take specifiers (typically possessors), they follow the same pattern as NPs, allowing pied piping of the specifier argument only. But when gerunds take NP[*acc*] subjects, they behave like other nonfinite verbal forms: they and all their arguments are [WH { }].

Our account of the contrasts in (94) builds on the analysis of verbal gerunds developed by Malouf (1998, 2000), who assigns verbal gerunds to a distinct part of speech, referred to earlier as *g*. Words assigned to this part of speech share properties with (and form a natural class with) both nouns and verbs. For example verbal gerunds, like nouns, identify their first ARG-ST member with the specifier that the gerund selects, as shown in (95):

(95)
$$
\begin{bmatrix}
\textit{word} \\
\text{PHON} \quad \langle\,\text{walking}\,\rangle \\[4pt]
\text{SS} \quad
\begin{bmatrix}
\text{LOC}|\text{CAT}
\begin{bmatrix}
\text{HEAD}
\begin{bmatrix}
g \\
\text{PRED} \quad - \\
\text{AGR} \quad [\text{NUM} \ \textit{sg}]
\end{bmatrix} \\[10pt]
\text{SPR} \quad \left\langle\,
\begin{array}{l}
\boxed{2}\text{Det} \\
[\text{WH} \quad \boxed{\Sigma}\ ]
\end{array}
\,\right\rangle \\[8pt]
\text{SUBJ} \quad \langle\ \rangle \\
\text{COMPS} \quad \langle\ \rangle
\end{bmatrix} \\[20pt]
\text{WH} \quad \boxed{\Sigma}
\end{bmatrix} \\[10pt]
\text{ARG-ST} \quad \langle\,\boxed{2}\,\rangle
\end{bmatrix}
$$

Crucially, such words also obey the WH-Amalgamation Constraint (as indicated in (95)) and hence may take on the [WH {*param*}] specification of an appropriate determiner like *whose*. This is sufficient to predict that gerunds exhibit pied piping behavior analogous to nouns, i.e. to predict the grammaticality of examples like (94a).

But gerunds may also, like verbs, select a first argument via SUBJ, rather than SPR. In this case, gerunds obey the same constraints as other verbal forms. That is, because of the WHSP, the SUBJ value—corresponding to the subject *who(m)* in (94c) and *me* in (94d)—must be [WH { }]. Similarly, the object *who(m)* in (94d) must be [WH { }], according to the WHC. And finally (again by WH-amalgamation), the gerund, like all other verbal words, must itself be [WH { }]. For these reasons, there is no way for a subject-selecting verbal gerund to appear in a pied piping construction.

The analysis we have developed in this section provides a unified picture of phrases containing interrogative and exclamative *wh*-words. The filler daughter of a *wh*-construction must be WH-specified and the WH value of the filler phrase is identified with exactly one *wh*-word within it—the leftmost *wh*-word. Our theory of WH-specification ensures that all non-initial interrogative *wh*-words within a clause are [WH { }]. This fact enables us to predict certain restrictions on the interpretation of multiple *wh*-constructions and related constraints on the distribution of *the hell* modifiers, as detailed in the next chapter. It also provides the basis for distinguishing those *wh*-expressions that induce reprise interpretations, as explained in Chapter 7.

5.3 Quantifier Scope

The theory of quantifier scope presented in Chapter 8 of P&S–94 is based on the technique of quantifier storage pioneered by Cooper (1975, 1983). 'Cooper storage' is a method allowing a variable to go proxy for a quantifier's contribution to the semantic content of a sentence, while the quantifier which binds that variable is placed in a 'store'.[30] Stored quantifiers are gathered up and passed up to successively higher levels of structure until an appropriate scope assignment locus is reached—for example a clause (as in the version of Cooper storage developed by P&S–94). There, quantifier(s) may be retrieved from storage and integrated into the meaning, receiving a wide scope interpretation. Quantifier scoping is thus treated as a semantic unbounded

---

[30]The highly procedural character of this discussion is entirely metaphorical, though hopefully intuitive. The effects of 'storage', 'inheritance' and 'retrieval' are all consequences of declarative constraints.

dependency, though many orthogonal factors obscure its fundamentally unbounded nature. Our version of storage is slightly different from the standard one. It incorporates the innovations we introduced in Chapters 3 and 4, including our generalization of storage to admit parameters as possible members of the set values of the feature STORE.

We may assume that a determiner like *every* introduces a generalized quantifier in its STORE value, as shown in (96):

(96)
$$
\begin{bmatrix}
d\text{-}lx \\
\text{PHON} \quad \langle\, every\, \rangle \\
\text{SS|LOC}
\begin{bmatrix}
\text{CAT}
\begin{bmatrix}
\text{HEAD}
\begin{bmatrix}
d \\
\text{SPEC}
\begin{bmatrix}
\text{INDEX} & \boxed{1} \\
\text{RESTR} & \boxed{\Sigma}
\end{bmatrix}
\end{bmatrix}
\end{bmatrix} \\
\text{CONT} \quad \boxed{2} \\
\text{STORE} \quad
\left\{
\boxed{2}
\begin{bmatrix}
every\text{-}rel \\
\text{INDEX} & \boxed{1} \\
\text{RESTR} & \boxed{\Sigma}
\end{bmatrix}
\right\}
\end{bmatrix} \\
\text{ARG-ST} \quad \langle\ \rangle
\end{bmatrix}
$$

This will serve as the specifier of a nominal element with which it combines (via a nominal *hd-spr* construction) to form an NP like (97):

(97)
$$
\begin{bmatrix}
hd\text{-}spr\text{-}ph \\
\text{SS|LOC}
\begin{bmatrix}
\text{CAT}
\begin{bmatrix}
\text{HEAD} & n \\
\text{SPR} & \langle\ \rangle \\
\text{COMPS} & \langle\ \rangle
\end{bmatrix} \\
\text{CONT}
\begin{bmatrix}
param \\
\text{INDEX} & \boxed{1} \\
\text{RESTR} & \{\ \}
\end{bmatrix} \\
\text{STORE}
\left\{
\begin{bmatrix}
every\text{-}rel \\
\text{INDEX} & \boxed{1} \\
\text{RESTR} & \{person(\boxed{1})\}
\end{bmatrix}
\right\}
\end{bmatrix}
\end{bmatrix}
$$

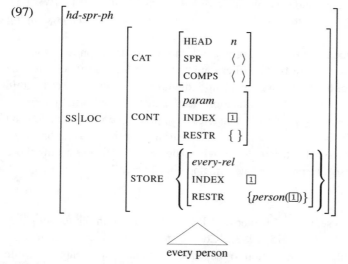

every person

Note that this NP has the indicated CONTENT and STORE values because the INDEX and RESTR of the stored quantifier in (96) are identified with those of the determiner's SPEC value, which in turn is identified with (the synsem of) the head daughter *person*.

This treatment incorporates many features of the analysis developed by Pollard and Yoo (1998), who modify the treatment of storage developed in P&S–94 in order to overcome a number of difficulties originally pointed out by Bob Carpenter in unpublished work. First, as shown in (97), they make STORE a feature of *local* objects, rather than a feature of the highest level of grammatical structure—the *sign*, as P&S proposed. This revision has the consequence that stored quantifiers are identified within raising and extraction constructions. That is, the STORE value of the subject of *seems* in a nest of raising structures like (98) is also the STORE value of the (unexpressed) subjects of *to*, *be*, and the verb *approaching*.

(98)   A unicorn [seems [to [be [approaching]]]].

Thus if the NP *a unicorn* in (98) has an existential quantifier in its STORE, so does the SUBJ value of the lowest verb in (98)—the verb that assigns a semantic role to the index bound by that quantifier.

Pollard and Yoo also propose to change the way storage works, so that unscoped quantifiers are passed up to the mother in a headed structure not from all the daughters (as in Cooper's account or in that of P&S), but only from the semantic head daughter (the adjunct-daughter, if there is one; the syntactic head daughter, otherwise). To achieve this, they constrain the STORE value of a verb, requiring that it be the set union of the STORE values of the verb's ARG-ST members. We may adapt this proposal in terms of the Store Amalgamation Constraint formulated in (99):[31]

(99)   Store Amalgamation Constraint (preliminary version):

$$
word \quad \Rightarrow \quad / \begin{bmatrix} \text{SS|LOC|STORE} & \boxed{\Sigma_1} \cup \cdots \cup \boxed{\Sigma_n} \\ \text{ARG-ST} & \langle\, [\text{STORE } \boxed{\Sigma_1}],...,[\text{STORE } \boxed{\Sigma_n}]\, \rangle \end{bmatrix}
$$

On this approach, the STORE of the verb in (100) is nonempty and is passed up the tree (according to a store inheritance principle) from head daughter to mother as shown in (100):

(100)

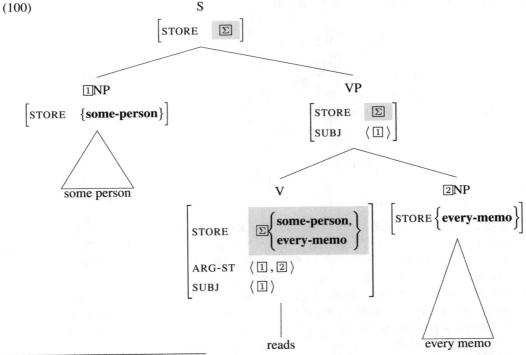

---

[31] This proposal is somewhat more general than the one Pollard and Yoo actually propose, in that it applies to all words (by default).

Note that exactly the same amalgamation will allow common nouns to incorporate into their own STORE value the stored quantifiers of the determiner specifier that they select for:

(101)

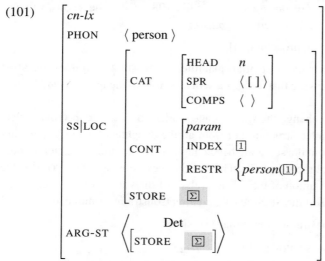

Let us continue to ignore adjuncts for present purposes, considering only the case where the syntactic head and 'semantic head' are the same, as in a structure like (100). S-level retrieval of stored quantifiers is always in accordance with the constraint sketched in (102):

(102)   Pollard/Yoo Quantifier Retrieval:

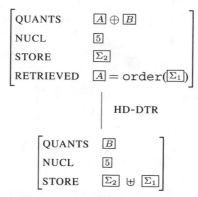

(102) says that the mother's QUANTS value is a list differing from the head daughter's QUANTS list ($\boxed{B}$) only in that a list of quantifiers ($\boxed{A}$) has been prepended to the latter. This preserves the daughter's quantifiers in the meaning of the mother. Moreover, the list of additional quantifiers (the RETRIEVED value) must be an ordering of the set of quantifiers ($\boxed{\Sigma_1}$) that constitutes the difference between the head daughter's STORE value and the mother's STORE value ($\boxed{\Sigma_2}$). This ensures that the extra quantifiers in the mother's meaning all come from the daughter's STORE. In addition, it guarantees that any element removed from the daughter's STORE is integrated into the mother's meaning.

If we now reconsider the tree in (100) in light of the constraints on retrieval sketched in (102), we can see the possibility of S-level quantifier retrieval of the sort shown in (103):

(103)

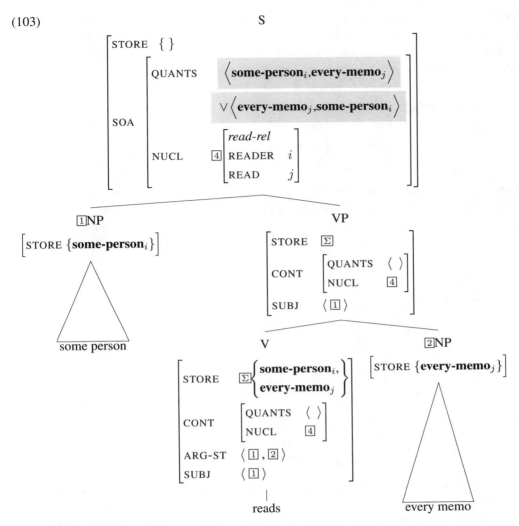

This correctly allows for both possible scopings of (103). It also assigns to (98) a reading where the subject has narrow scope with respect to *seems*. This follows because STORE is part of the LOCAL value and the SUBJ value of *seems* (which includes the LOCAL value) is the SUBJ value of *to, be* and *approaching*.

There is a difficulty with this approach, however: it allows retrieval in too many places. That is, unless one adds further constraints, this system (like the one in P&S–94) produces multiple analyses of every available reading. For example, allowing both S and VP retrieval in structures like (103) produces each possible scoping in three different ways (each retrieval order at one node, or one quantifier retrieved at each node).

This problem is noted and addressed by Manning et al. (1999), who propose to eliminate the redundancy by making retrieval and scope assignment entirely lexical in nature. They state lexical constraints to the effect that a word's QUANTS value is an ordering of some set of generalized quantifiers subtracted from the union of the STORE values of the verb's arguments. (The feature

RETRIEVED is eliminated entirely.) A lexical head passes up in its STORE value whatever quantifiers from its arguments are not already scoped in that word's QUANTS value. These unscoped quantifiers are thus passed up into the STORE value of the phrase projected by the lexical head. At this point, they can be retrieved in the next higher syntactic domain.

This proposal assumes the following modified Store Amalgamation Constraint.[32]

(104) Store Amalgamation Constraint (final version):

$$word \Rightarrow / \begin{bmatrix} \text{SS|LOC} & \begin{bmatrix} \text{CONT} & [\text{QUANTS order}(\boxed{\Sigma_0})] \\ \text{STORE} & (\boxed{\Sigma_1} \cup \ldots \cup \boxed{\Sigma_n}) \doteq \boxed{\Sigma_0} \end{bmatrix} \\ \text{ARG-ST} & \langle [\text{STORE } \boxed{\Sigma_1}], \ldots, [\text{STORE } \boxed{\Sigma_n}] \rangle \end{bmatrix}$$

Note that words whose ARG-ST list is empty override this constraint. Some such words (e.g. determiners, as described above) have a nonempty store; others (e.g. proper nouns) have an empty store. Words whose CONTENT value is not of type *soa* also override this constraint.

In consequence of the revision in (104), the lexical entry for *reads* is constrained as shown in (105).

(105)
$$\begin{bmatrix} word \\ \text{PHON} & \langle \text{ reads } \rangle \\ \text{SS|LOC} & \begin{bmatrix} \text{STORE} & (\boxed{\Sigma_1} \cup \boxed{\Sigma_2}) \doteq \boxed{\Sigma_0} \\ \text{CONT} & \begin{bmatrix} r\text{-}soa \\ \text{QUANTS order}(\boxed{\Sigma_0}) \\ \text{NUCL} & \begin{bmatrix} read\text{-}rel \\ \text{READER} & i \\ \text{READ} & j \end{bmatrix} \end{bmatrix} \end{bmatrix} \\ \text{ARG-ST} & \left\langle \begin{matrix} \text{NP}_i \\ [\text{STORE } \boxed{\Sigma_1}] \end{matrix}, \begin{matrix} \text{NP}_j \\ [\text{STORE } \boxed{\Sigma_2}] \end{matrix} \right\rangle \end{bmatrix}$$

Other aspects of the Pollard/Yoo theory remain unchanged, though we may in addition require of semantically vacuous (non role-assigning) elements—like *to*, *be*, and *do*—that their content be identified with the content of their non-subject complement. These elements continue to satisfy STORE-amalgamation, but they are prevented from subtracting out any quantifiers from their complement's STORE. Thus, a lexical head other than *to*, *be* and *do*, gets a chance to scope the quantifiers of its role-assigned arguments, and the quantifiers from those arguments that are not scoped remain in the verb's STORE to be passed up to higher levels of structure.[33] Finally, notice

---

[32]We use the symbol '$\doteq$' to designate a relation of contained set difference that is identical to the familiar notion of set difference ($\Sigma_1 - \Sigma_2$ = the set of all elements in Σ_1 that are not in Σ_2), except that $\Sigma_1 \doteq \Sigma_2$ is defined only if Σ_2 is a subset of Σ_1.

[33]A caveat should be added here about raising verbs. Some steps must be taken to ensure that elements in the STORE of raised arguments, e.g. the subject argument of *seem*, do not enter into the semantics of a sentence twice. One could, following Przepiórkowski (1998), formulate a constraint requiring that quantifiers be amalgamated from all but the 'raised' argument of the verb (the one not assigned a semantic role by the raising predicate). In this way, quantifiers in the STORE of a raised argument would be amalgamated by the lowest predicate in a raising construction and could be scoped there or higher. The raising verb, because it does not amalgamate the stored quantifiers of the raised argument could never 'reintroduce' such quantifiers into the semantic analysis.

However, the stipulations involved in any such proposal seem unnecessary, once we introduce independently motivated

that the inheritance of STORE specifications from head daughter to mother is already accounted for by the GHFP. This is the last piece of our treatment that needs to be put into place.

In our analysis, there are exactly as many scope assignment points in a sentence as there are role-assigning verbs (or other lexical heads with a *soa* as their semantic type). And since there is no structure-based retrieval of quantifiers, sentences like those we have just been considering have no spurious semantic derivations. The constraints that are part of the lexical entry of the word *reads* can simply be satisfied in two distinct ways, allowing the two scopal readings (corresponding to two distinct orderings of the quantifiers on the verb's QUANTS list). Note further that the modification of the Pollard/Yoo theory proposed by Manning et al. (1999) still guarantees the correct two readings for *A unicorn seems to be approaching*, either *seems* or *approaching* is allowed to assign scope to **some-unicorn**. The latter option is illustrated in (106):

(106)

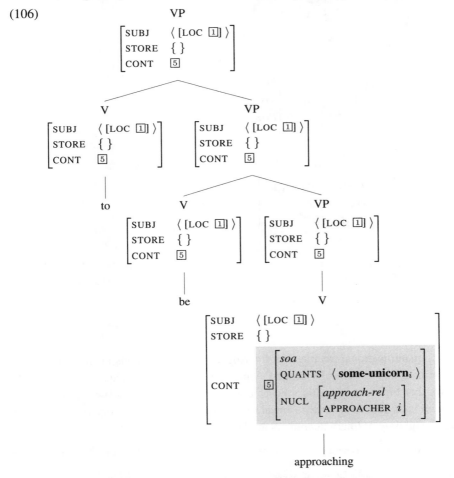

---

modifications of our semantic analysis to take into account the resource-sensitive nature of quantification. One such proposal, which immediately explains the observed behavior of raised quantifiers, is the analysis in terms of 'minimal recursion semantics' introduced by Copestake et al. (2000). Under their proposal, quantifier scope is underspecified and a given quantifier can enter into the resolution of scope only once. Unfortunately, incorporating such a far-reaching (though otherwise harmonious) modification of our semantic analysis is beyond the scope of the present study. We must therefore leave this issue unresolved here.

The alternate scoping is illustrated in (107):[34]

(107)

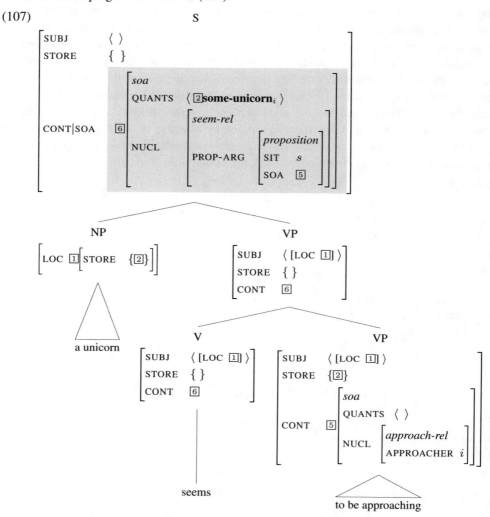

Given the nonquantificational treatment of interrogative *wh*-expressions justified in Chapter 4 and the requirement that all lexically scoped elements be generalized quantifiers (not parameters), it follows that ordinary quantifiers never outscope a *wh*-expression within a question. Hence, there is no need for 'structural' retrieval of ordinary quantifiers. In our analysis of *wh*-interrogatives, all and only ordinary quantifiers are lexically scoped.[35]

---

[34]Recall that raising verbs like *seems* must not amalgamate their 'raised' argument's (in this case the subject's) stored quantifiers.

[35]For a distinct (but related) account of lexical scoping in which *wh*-expressions are treated as quantifiers, not as parameters, see Przepiórkowski 1998.

5.4 Context

Certain kinds of utterances have particular usage restrictions because they contain certain words or phrases (e.g. honorific pronouns or verb forms). In order to allow the appropriateness conditions associated with individual words and constructions to be passed up within linguistic structures, P&S–94 (p. 333) propose the following principle:

(108) Principle of Contextual Consistency:
The CONTEXT|BACKGROUND value of a given phrase is the union of the CONTEXT|BACKGROUND values of the daughters.

The idea here is that a given word, e.g. French *vous* ('you (sg.,polite)') or German *du* ('you (sg.,familiar)'), introduces appropriateness conditions that are inherited by the phrases that contain them and ultimately by entire utterances like those in (109).

(109) a. Vous amusez vous, n'est-ce pas? "You are having fun, aren't you?" [appropriately uttered only to someone to whom politeness is owed]

      b. Bist du müde? "Are you tired?" [appropriately uttered only to someone with whom a certain intimacy is established]

As Wilcock (1999) observes, however, a certain uniformity is gained if the BACKGROUND value of a given head is defined to be the amalgamation of the BACKGROUND values of its arguments, just as we have proposed for the values of the features SLASH, WH and STORE. Integrating Wilcock's proposal into our analysis turns out to be straightforward. In fact, if we depart from P&S–94's analysis slightly and make BACKGROUND, like SLASH and WH, a non-LOCAL feature of *synsem* objects, then we may generalize the amalgamation of SLASH, WH and BACKGROUND as follows:[36]

(110) Non-LOCAL Amalgamation Constraint:
For every non-LOCAL feature **F**:

$$word \Rightarrow / \begin{bmatrix} \text{SS}|\mathbf{F} \; \boxed{\Sigma_1} \cup \ldots \cup \boxed{\Sigma_n} \\ \text{ARG-ST} \; \left\langle [\mathbf{F} \; \boxed{\Sigma_1}], \ldots, [\mathbf{F} \; \boxed{\Sigma_n}] \right\rangle \end{bmatrix}$$

Once we have a principle like (110), we have no need for P&S–94's Principle of Contextual Consistency or for Wilcock's proposed alternative constraint. The inheritance of BACKGROUND specifications (a set of facts), will be successively inherited from head daughter to mother within headed structures by the GHFP. Moreover, since the GHFP is a default constraint, we leave open the possibility that some construction might override the default, adding appropriateness conditions of its own to the set of pooled background conditions. In Chapter 7, we will treat certain uses of in-situ interrogatives in terms of a construction that does precisely this.

5.5 Summary

In this chapter we have outlined the basic treatment of three kinds of unbounded dependency: filler-gap (or extraction) dependencies, pied piping, and quantifier scoping. These dependencies are encoded via the features SLASH, WH, and REL, each of which is subject to particular constraints. However, the bulk of the analytic burden throughout this chapter has been carried by a

---

[36]This proposal excludes STORE amalgamation from the proposed generalization. Note also that BACKGROUND has been removed from CONTEXT, which we take to be a *sign*-level feature (See Chapter 2).

single theoretical principle—the GHFP, which unifies the account of the inheritance of feature specifications. We believe that the analyses we have presented have the virtue of reconciling analytic generality and explanation with the need to scale up to matters of detail that are usually left undiscussed in the literature.

6

Basic Interrogatives and Exclamatives

6.1 Introduction

This chapter contains a detailed presentation of our analysis of the basic kinds of interrogative clause in English: polar and *wh*-interrogatives. It also includes a sketch of our treatment of closely related constructions—notably exclamatives—and the interrogative complementizers *whether* and *if*. In the final section, we present an account of multiple *wh*-questions and superiority effects, which differs from various well-known treatments in a number of important respects.

Recall from the discussion at the end of Chapter 3 that the CONTENT type of all interrogatives is *question*. Polar questions are treated in terms of feature structures like (1), where the components are an empty PARAMS set and a (parametric) proposition:

(1)
$$
\begin{bmatrix}
question \\
\text{PARAMS} & \{\ \} \\
\text{PROP} &
\begin{bmatrix}
proposition \\
\text{SIT} & s \\
\text{SOA} & soa
\end{bmatrix}
\end{bmatrix}
$$

Wh-questions are similar, but their PARAMS set is nonempty:

(2)
$$
\begin{bmatrix}
question \\
\text{PARAMS} & \{\pi_1, ...\} \\
\text{PROP} &
\begin{bmatrix}
proposition \\
\text{SIT} & s \\
\text{SOA} & soa
\end{bmatrix}
\end{bmatrix}
$$

The hierarchy of phrasal types that we propose for interrogative clauses is sketched in (3):

(3)

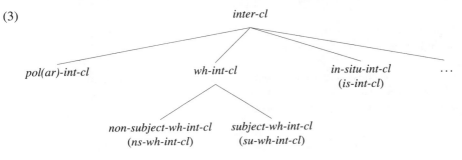

213

The in-situ clauses, of which there are two varieties—reprises and non-reprises, are discussed in the next chapter. Chapter 8 introduces another type of interrogative construction in order to analyze the phenomenon of 'sluicing' (Ross 1969).

As justified in Chapter 3, we treat exclamative constructions in terms of semantic objects like (4):

(4)
$$\begin{bmatrix} fact \\ \\ \text{PROP} \begin{bmatrix} proposition \\ \text{SIT} \quad s \\ \text{SOA} \quad soa \end{bmatrix} \end{bmatrix}$$

The two types of exclamative clauses discussed in this chapter—both subtypes of *excl-cl*—differ only in that the proposition within the content of *wh*-exclamatives includes the quantifier *unusual-rel* introduced by the nonempty WH specification of the exclamative *wh*-phrase, as described in section 5.2 above.

6.2   *Wh*-Complementizers

Before considering interrogative-particular construction types, let us first turn to the *wh*-comple-mentizers *whether* and *if*. The lexical entry for the former is as shown in (5):[1]

(5)
$$\begin{bmatrix} \text{PHON} \quad \langle \text{ whether } \rangle \\ \\ \text{SS} \begin{bmatrix} \text{LOC} \begin{bmatrix} \text{CAT} \begin{bmatrix} \text{HEAD} \begin{bmatrix} c \\ \text{IC} \quad - \\ \text{VFORM} \quad \boxed{2} \end{bmatrix} \end{bmatrix} \\ \text{CONT} \begin{bmatrix} question \\ \text{PARAMS} \quad \{ \} \\ \text{PROP} \quad \boxed{1} \end{bmatrix} \end{bmatrix} \\ \text{WH} \quad \{ \} \end{bmatrix} \\ \\ \text{ARG-ST} \quad \left\langle \begin{bmatrix} \text{HEAD} \begin{bmatrix} \text{INV} \quad - \\ \text{VFORM} \quad \boxed{2} \end{bmatrix} \\ \text{SUBJ} \quad \langle (pro\text{-}ss) \rangle \\ \text{CONT} \quad \boxed{1} \end{bmatrix} \right\rangle \end{bmatrix}$$

The word *whether* can head a phrase of type *cp-cl* (see Chapter 2), giving rise to structures like the one shown in (6):

---

[1]We provide no treatment here of other uses of *whether*, e.g. in concessive conditionals like (i).

(i) Whether or not they are on time, I refuse to participate.

For a treatment of this construction, see Gawron to appear.

(6)

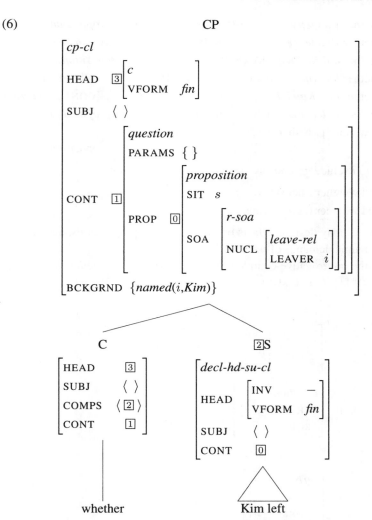

CP

The content of such a clause is identified with that of the word *whether*. That is, the clause's content is a polar question whose PROP value is determined by the content of *whether*'s clausal complement.

Now consider the possible choices for the complement of *whether*. This complement must satisfy the description of the ARG-ST element in (5), and hence must denote a proposition. In addition, it must be *verbal* (projected by a verb or a complementizer); this follows from the fact that only elements of this type allow specifications for INV. Furthermore, the complement of *whether* must be indicative (its SOA value must be an *r-soa*), it must be specified as [INV −], and its SUBJ value must either be the empty list or ⟨ *pro-ss* ⟩. The following data are therefore predicted: (Conflicting and nonconflicting properties of the *whether*'s complement are indicated in parentheses.)

(7) a. I wonder [whether *Kim left*].   (S, [SUBJ ⟨ ⟩], [CONT *proposition*], [INV −])

   b. *I wonder [whether *Kim leave*].   (S, [SUBJ ⟨ ⟩], *[CONT *outcome*], [INV −])

   c. *I wonder [whether *did Kim leave*]. (S, [SUBJ ⟨ ⟩], [CONT *proposition*],[2] *[INV +])

   d. *I wonder [whether *for Kim to leave*].   (*CP, [SUBJ ⟨ ⟩], *[CONT *outcome*])

   e. *I wonder [whether *that Kim left*].   (*CP, [SUBJ ⟨ ⟩], [CONT *proposition*])

   f. I wonder [whether *to leave*].   ('S', [SUBJ ⟨*pro-ss*⟩], [CONT *proposition*], [INV −])

   g. *Who did you wonder [whether *died*].

          ('S', *[SUBJ ⟨*gap-ss*⟩], [CONT *proposition*], [INV −])

There is an issue of how to exclude gerunds as the complement of *whether*:

(8) a. *Kim wondered whether (them) leaving.

   b. *Kim wondered whether their leaving.

We will assume that gerunds may designate facts or events, but not propositions, and are hence incompatible with the semantic demands of *whether*.[3]

   The lexical entry for the interrogative complementizer *if* is similar to *whether*, but the complement of *if* must be [VFORM *fin*] and [SUBJ ⟨ ⟩]:

(9)
$$
\begin{bmatrix}
\text{PHON} & \langle \text{if} \rangle \\[2pt]
\text{SS} &
\begin{bmatrix}
\text{LOC} &
\begin{bmatrix}
\text{CAT} & \begin{bmatrix} \text{HEAD} & \begin{bmatrix} c \\ \text{IC} & - \\ \text{VFORM} & \boxed{2}\,fin \end{bmatrix} \end{bmatrix} \\[6pt]
\text{CONT} & \begin{bmatrix} question \\ \text{PARAMS} & \{\ \} \\ \text{PROP} & \boxed{1} \end{bmatrix}
\end{bmatrix} \\[6pt]
\text{WH} & \{\ \}
\end{bmatrix} \\[6pt]
\text{ARG-ST} & \left\langle \begin{bmatrix} \text{HEAD} & \begin{bmatrix} verb \\ \text{INV} & - \\ \text{VFORM} & \boxed{2} \end{bmatrix} \\ \text{SUBJ} & \langle\ \rangle \\ \text{CONT} & \boxed{1} \end{bmatrix} \right\rangle
\end{bmatrix}
$$

These small lexical differences serve to predict the following data:

(10) a. I wonder [if *Kim left*].   (S, [SUBJ ⟨ ⟩], [CONT *proposition*], [INV −])

   b. *I wonder [if *Kim leave*].   (S, [SUBJ ⟨ ⟩], *[CONT *outcome*], [INV −])

   c. *I wonder [if *did Kim leave*].   (S, [SUBJ ⟨ ⟩], [CONT *proposition*], *[INV +])

   d. *I wonder [if *for Kim to leave*].   (*CP, [SUBJ ⟨ ⟩], *[CONT *outcome*])

   e. *I wonder [if *that Kim left*].   (*CP, [SUBJ ⟨ ⟩], [CONT *proposition*])

   f. *I wonder [if *to leave*].   ('S', *[SUBJ ⟨*pro-ss*⟩], [CONT *proposition*], [INV −])

   g. *Who did you wonder [if *died*]. ('S', *[SUBJ ⟨*gap-ss*⟩], [CONT *proposition*], [INV −])

---

[2]The analysis of inverted clauses as propositions is discussed in the next section.

[3]It is also possible to modify (5) to require that the selected argument be [VFORM *clausal*].

The correct syntactic behavior of such phrases is thus guaranteed by lexical specifications and constructions that we have already motivated.[4]

As a final illustration of a *wh*-complementizer, we offer a speculative treatment of *how come*, the element that appears in examples like (11):

(11) a. How come they didn't believe you?

b. I wonder [how come they didn't believe you].

The analysis of the type *root* sketched in Chapter 2 (see also the revision presented in the next chapter) specifies that an independent utterance can in principle be a CP, as well as an S. However, *that*-clauses, *whether*-clauses, etc. cannot function as independent utterances. This is because their lexical entry includes the specification [IC −], which is percolated to the clausal level by the GHFP.

This makes available a lexical treatment of *how come* based on the lexical entry in (12):[5]

(12)
$$
\begin{bmatrix}
\text{PHON} & \langle \text{ how-come } \rangle \\[2ex]
\text{SS} & \begin{bmatrix}
\text{LOC} & \begin{bmatrix}
\text{CAT} & \begin{bmatrix} \text{HEAD} & \begin{bmatrix} c \\ \text{VFORM} & \boxed{2}\textit{fin} \end{bmatrix} \end{bmatrix} \\[2ex]
\text{CONT} & \begin{bmatrix} \textit{question} \\ \text{PARAMS} & \left\{ \begin{bmatrix} \text{INDEX} & \boxed{0} \end{bmatrix} \right\} \\ \text{PROP} & \mathbf{cause}(\boxed{0},\boxed{1}) \end{bmatrix}
\end{bmatrix} \\[2ex]
\text{WH} & \{ \}
\end{bmatrix} \\[2ex]
\text{ARG-ST} & \left\langle \begin{bmatrix} \text{HEAD} & \begin{bmatrix} v \\ \text{INV} & - \\ \text{VFORM} & \boxed{2} \end{bmatrix} \\ \text{SUBJ} & \langle \, \rangle \\ \text{CONT} & \boxed{1} \end{bmatrix} \right\rangle
\end{bmatrix}
$$

Crucially, (12) is unspecified for the feature IC, and hence is compatible with either a positive or negative specification for that feature. It follows that *how-come*-clauses may be either independent utterances (as in (11a)) or selected interrogative complements (as in (11b)).

Contrasts like those in (13), noted by Culicover (1999), also follow from this treatment:

(13) a. Why the hell did you do that?

b. *How come the hell you did that?

c. *How the hell come you did that?

As explained below, our analysis of modifiers like *the heck* requires that they adjoin to a WH-specified lexical item. Since complementizers are not WH-specified, i.e. their WH value is

---

[4] Apparently, there is some variation in judgment regarding (10f). This variation is purely lexical under our account.

[5] Here **cause**($\boxed{0}$,$\boxed{1}$) is a shorthand for the proposition that $\boxed{0}$ caused $\boxed{1}$.

always { }, it follows that examples like (13b) (or (13c)) are systematically ruled out and differentiated from true ('fronted') *wh*-words like *why*.

6.3 Polar Interrogatives

Our analysis of polar questions is based on a type of clause that we call *polar-interrogative-clause* (*pol-int-cl*). Every inverted 'yes-no' interrogative is an instance of this type, which is a subtype of, and hence inherits constraints from, the types *inter-cl* and *sai-ph* (and their supertypes):

(14)

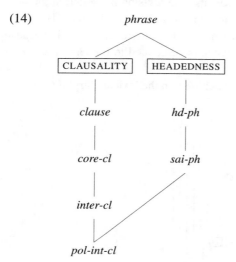

Recall from Chapter 2 that all instances of the type *sai-ph* are constrained as follows:

(15)   *sai-ph*:

$$
\left[\text{SUBJ} \ \langle \ \rangle \right] \rightarrow \mathbf{H} \begin{bmatrix} word \\ \text{INV} & + \\ \text{AUX} & + \\ \text{SUBJ} & \langle \boxed{0} \rangle \\ \text{COMPS} & \boxed{A} \textit{nelist} \end{bmatrix}, \boxed{0}, \boxed{A}
$$

Thus the only construction-specific constraint that needs to be stated is the following:

(16)   *pol-int-cl*:

$$
\left[\text{CONT} \begin{bmatrix} \text{PARAMS} \ \{ \} \\ \text{PROP} \begin{bmatrix} proposition \\ \text{SOA} & \boxed{1} \end{bmatrix} \end{bmatrix} \right] \rightarrow \mathbf{H} \begin{bmatrix} \text{IC} & + \\ \text{CONT} & \boxed{1} \end{bmatrix}, \dots
$$

That is, the only constraints that are specific to the *pol-int-cl* construction are (1) that it is an independent clause and (2) that its CONTENT is a polar question built from a proposition constructed from its head daughter's SOA value.

Polar interrogative clauses thus inherit the constraints illustrated in (17):

(17) ECC & GHFP & *sai-ph* & *core-cl* & *inter-cl* & IRC & *pol-int-cl*:

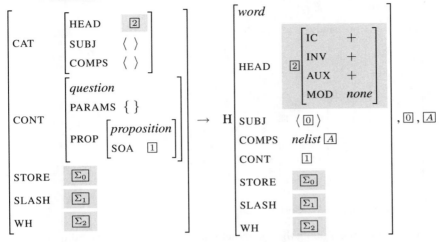

Note that some valence specifications of the mother and head daughter (e.g. their SUBJ and COMPS values) are required to be distinct, as are their CONTENT values. Thus, the GHFP has the effect of identifying only the HEAD, SLASH, BACKGRND, and WH values of the head and mother in this construction.

A typical 'inverted' polar interrogative clause, satisfying all the inherited constraints, is sketched in (18):

(18)

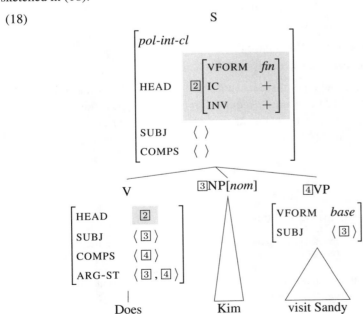

Observe in particular that the HEAD specification is passed up from the lexical head to its mother by the GHFP. Because it is specified as [IC +], a clause like (18) must be an independent clause—

it cannot appear in embedded interrogative environments:

(19) a. *They wondered [had she left].

  b. *No one knew [is that possible].

And the semantics that our analysis assigns to (18) is shown in (20):

(20)

$$
\begin{bmatrix}
question \\
\text{PARAMS} \quad \{\ \} \\
\text{PROP} \quad
\begin{bmatrix}
proposition \\
\text{SOA}
\begin{bmatrix}
\text{QUANTS} \ \langle\ \rangle \\
\text{NUCL}
\begin{bmatrix}
visit\text{-}rel \\
\text{ACTOR} \quad i \\
\text{UNDGR} \quad j
\end{bmatrix}
\end{bmatrix}
\end{bmatrix} \\
\text{BCKGRND} \quad \{named(i, Kim), named(j, Sandy)\}
\end{bmatrix}
$$

There is little more to say about this construction, except, as argued by Fillmore (1999), that it is related to a number of sister constructions (all subtypes of *sai-ph*) that include, *inter alia*, exclamatives like (21), 'blesses, wishes and curses' like (22), and auxiliary conditionals like (23):

(21) a. Boy, *was I stupid*!

  b. Wow, *can she sing*!

(22) a. May they live forever!

  b. May I live long enough to see the end of this job!

  c. May your teeth fall out on your wedding night!

(23) a. *Were they here now*, we wouldn't have this problem.

  b. *Should there be a need*, we can always call for help.

Each of these involves a distinct subtype of *sai-ph* (not all of which are [IC +], as (23) shows). The inverted exclamatives like (21), for example, require a construction type that is also a subtype of *excl-cl*, from which it inherits the constraint that its CONTENT is of type *fact* (see Chap. 2). This leaves only the constraints shown in (24) as particular to the inverted-exclamative construction:[6]

(24) *inv-excl-cl*:

$$
\begin{bmatrix} \text{CONT}|\text{PROP}|\text{SOA} \ \boxed{1} \end{bmatrix} \rightarrow \mathbf{H} \begin{bmatrix} \text{IC} & + \\ \text{CONT} & \boxed{1} \end{bmatrix}, \ldots
$$

The semantics we associate with instances of this type is illustrated in (25):

---

[6]Huddleston (1993a) argues that inverted exclamatives are really interrogatives that give rise to exclamative meaning via pragmatic inference. We could adopt Huddleston's analysis—it would in fact simplify our grammar by eliminating a construction. However, one problem with assuming polar exclamatives arise via pragmatic inference from interrogative content is that it leads to the expectation that this type of inference should be applicable cross-linguistically, whenever polar interrogative content is expressed. However, as the Hebrew example in (i) illustrates, this expectation is not met. (i) can only be understood as a polar question:

(i) ha'im omer yaxol laruc
  the-if omer can run
  Can Omer run

(25) a. Does Kim stink!

b.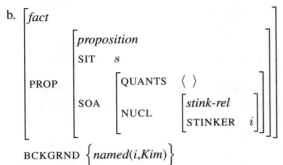

To the family of subject-auxiliary inversion constructions studied by Fillmore, we add another: a slashed, proposition-denoting clause that will be part of our treatment of negative adverb preposing constructions like (26a) and main clause *wh*-questions like (26b).

(26) a. Under no circumstances *did she think they would do that*.

b. Whose book *are you reading*?

This type, which we call *inverted-declarative-clause* (*inv-decl-cl*), is a subtype of both *sai-ph* and *decl-cl*:

(27)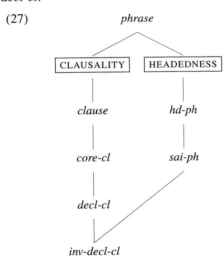

Since *inv-decl-cl* inherits from the *decl-cl* a constraint requiring that its CONTENT be of type *austinian*, it must be further constrained as follows:

(28)   *inv-decl-cl*:

$$\left[\text{SLASH } neset\right] \rightarrow \mathbf{H}\left[\text{IC } +\right], \dots$$

This type of clause, illustrated in (29), has a highly restricted distribution—it occurs only in slashed independent clauses, i.e. root clauses that contain an extraction dependency:[7]

(29)

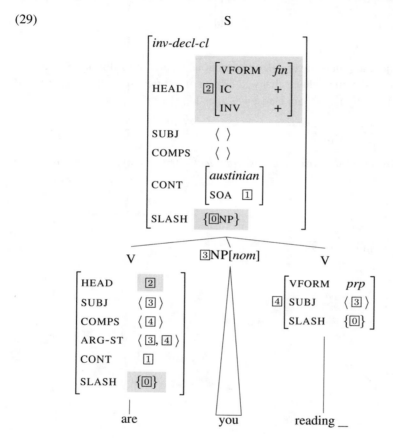

---

[7]Note that since inverted verbs are all indicative in English, their CONTENT value is always an *r-soa*. Hence the content of an *inv-decl-cl* is always a *proposition* (never an *outcome*).

6.4   *Wh*-Exclamative Phrases

In Chapter 5, we presented the basics of our analysis of filler-gap dependencies in terms of the construction type *hd-fill-ph*. There we considered only 'topicalized' clauses like those in (30).

(30) a. Bagels, I like __ .

     b. People that smart, always pay attention to __ !

     c. That kind of antisocial behavior, can we really tolerate __ in a civilized society?

     d. That kind of behavior, who could object to __ ?

     e. People that stupid, am I ever fed up with __ !

In this section, we will consider the analysis of *wh*-exclamatives like (31a,b).

(31) a. [How tall] they are __ !

     b. [What a great smile] you have __ !

    Examples like these, we treat in terms of the *wh-exclamative-clause* (*wh-excl-cl*) construction, a distinct subtype of *hd-fill-ph*. *Wh-excl-cl* is also a subtype of *excl-cl*, from which it inherits the constraint that its CONTENT value must be of type *fact*:

(32)

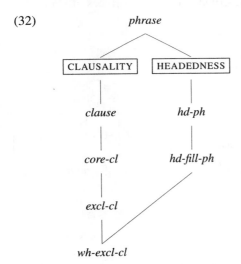

Otherwise, it is quite similar to the topicalization construction discussed in the previous chapter. For example, an instance of *wh-excl-cl* (and its head daughter, by the GHFP) must be uninverted.

One distinctive feature of *wh-excl-cl* is that the WH value of its filler daughter must be a quantifier that gets added to the head daughter's QUANTS list, as shown in (33):

(33) *wh-excl-cl*:

$$
\begin{bmatrix}
\text{HEAD}|\text{INV} & - \\
\text{PROP}|\text{SOA} & \begin{bmatrix} \text{QUANTS} & \langle \boxed{0} \rangle \oplus \boxed{A} \\ \text{NUCL} & \boxed{2} \end{bmatrix} \\
\text{STORE} & \boxed{\Sigma_1} \\
\text{SLASH} & \{\ \}
\end{bmatrix}
\rightarrow
\begin{bmatrix} \text{WH} \{\boxed{0}\} \end{bmatrix},\ \mathbf{H}
\begin{bmatrix}
\text{SOA} & \begin{bmatrix} \text{QUANTS} & \boxed{A} \\ \text{NUCL} & \boxed{2} \end{bmatrix} \\
\text{STORE} & \{\boxed{0}\textit{quant-rel}\} \uplus \boxed{\Sigma_1} \\
\text{SUBJ} & \langle\ \rangle
\end{bmatrix}
$$

We have also assumed that *wh-exclamatives* are extraction islands, and hence are [SLASH { }], as indicated in (33).

If we now unify (33) with relevant constraints inherited from the supertypes of *wh-excl-cl*, we arrive at (34):

(34) GHFP & *hd-fill-ph* & *excl-cl* & *wh-excl-cl*:

$$
\begin{bmatrix}
\text{CAT} & \boxed{5} \begin{bmatrix} \text{HEAD}|\text{INV} & - \\ \text{SUBJ} & \langle\ \rangle \end{bmatrix} \\
\text{CONT} & \begin{bmatrix} \textit{fact} \\ \text{PROP} & \begin{bmatrix} \text{SOA} & \begin{bmatrix} \text{QUANTS} & \langle \boxed{0} \rangle \oplus \boxed{A} \\ \text{NUCL} & \boxed{2} \end{bmatrix} \end{bmatrix} \end{bmatrix} \\
\text{STORE} & \boxed{\Sigma_1} \\
\text{SLASH} & \{\ \} \\
\text{WH} & \boxed{\Sigma}
\end{bmatrix}
\rightarrow
\begin{bmatrix} \text{LOC} & \boxed{4} \\ \text{WH} & \{\boxed{0}\} \end{bmatrix},\ \mathbf{H}
\begin{bmatrix}
\text{CAT} & \boxed{5} \\
\text{CONT} & \begin{bmatrix} \text{SOA} & \begin{bmatrix} \text{QUANTS} & \boxed{A} \\ \text{NUCL} & \boxed{2} \end{bmatrix} \end{bmatrix} \\
\text{STORE} & \{\boxed{0}\textit{quant-rel}\} \uplus \boxed{\Sigma_1} \\
\text{SLASH} & \{\boxed{4}\} \\
\text{WH} & \boxed{\Sigma}
\end{bmatrix}
$$

The identification of the mother and head daughter's CAT and WH values (as shaded in (34)) is a consequence of the GHFP. Finally, note that the head daughter's SLASH value is resolved as a singleton set: it must contain the filler daughter's LOC value and whatever other elements it contains must be included in the mother's SLASH value, which must be empty.

As noted in Chapter 5, requiring that the non-head daughter be specified as [WH {*quant-rel*}] will ensure that there is an exclamative *wh*-word present somewhere within that constituent. (33) further guarantees that the quantifier in the WH value of that *wh*-word is integrated into the clause's content, as illustrated via shading in (35):

(35)

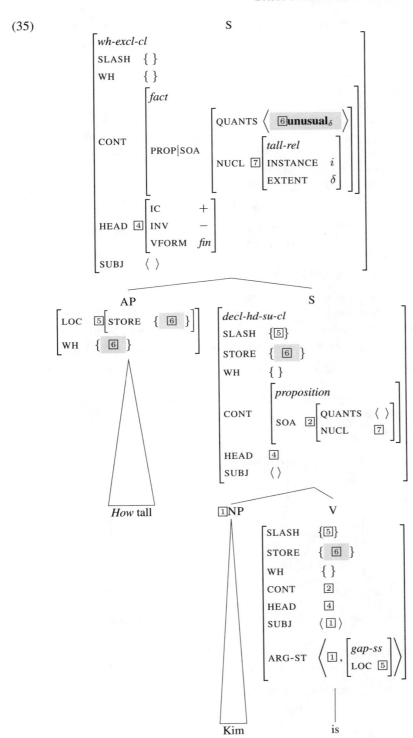

The semantic effect of this construction is to associate an example like (36a) with a CONTENT value like (36b):

(36) a.   How tall Kim is __ !

      b.

$$\begin{bmatrix} fact \\ \text{PROP} \begin{bmatrix} proposition \\ \text{SIT} \quad s \\ \text{SOA} \begin{bmatrix} \text{QUANTS} \left\langle \begin{bmatrix} unusual\text{-}rel \\ \text{IND} \quad \delta \\ \text{RESTR} \quad \{\,\} \end{bmatrix} \right\rangle \\ \text{NUCL} \begin{bmatrix} tall\text{-}rel \\ \text{INSTANCE} \quad i \\ \text{EXTENT} \quad \delta \end{bmatrix} \end{bmatrix} \end{bmatrix} \\ \text{BCKGRND} \quad \{named(i,Kim)\,\} \end{bmatrix}$$

The generalized quantifier *unusual-rel* holds of a fact-abstract and a SOA-abstract, according to the analysis of Chapter 3. *Unusual-rel* is existential in nature. Thus, in the case of (36) the truth conditions that result require that there be an unusual degree such that Kim is tall to that degree.

What a exclamatives work similarly. The semantic analysis we assign to (37a) is (37b):

(37) a.   What a sunset Kim painted __ !

      b.

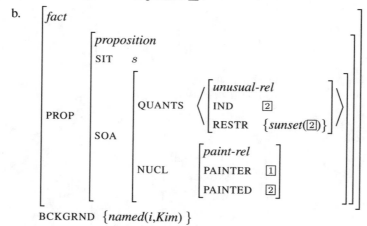

Unusual-rel holds of the relevant pair of abstracts just in case there is an unusual sunset that Kim painted.

The constraints in (34) require that the head daughter be specified as [SUBJ ⟨ ⟩]. This correctly ensures that there are no *wh*-subject exclamatives, as the contrasts in (38)–(39) indicate.

(38) a.   [How many birds] there are __ on the fence!

      b. ?*[How many birds] __ are on the fence!

(39) a.   [What a nice guy] he is __ !

      b. ?*[What a nice guy] __ walked into the room!

Examples like the following may appear to be counterexamples to the claim that subject exclamatives do not exist:

(40)   a.   It's amazing [[how many birds] __ are on the fence].

        b.   It's amazing [[how many people's cars] __ will fail this test.]

However, as argued persuasively by Huddleston (1993b), predicates like *amazing* allow either interrogative or exclamative clauses as their complement. The semantics in the case of an interrogative complement, according to Huddleston, is roughly 'the answer to the question ... is amazing'.[8]

Assuming then that the complements in (40) are only interrogative clauses (as analyzed in the next section) and that there are no subject exclamatives, we predict contrasts like the following:

(41)   a.   It's amazing [[what a nice guy] he is __].

        b.   *It's amazing [[what a nice guy] __ walked into the room].

The predeterminer *what* occurring in *what a nice guy* can only be exclamative, as we know from the ungrammaticality of (42a,b):

(42)   a.   *[What a nice guy] is he __ ?

        b.   *I wonder [[what a nice guy] he is __].

Therefore the ungrammaticality of examples like (41b) is properly explained by assuming the constraint against subject exclamatives that we have included in (33) (the condition that the head daughter's SUBJ value be $\langle \ \rangle$).

6.5 *Wh*-Interrogatives

6.5.1 General Constraints

As noted in section 6.1, *inter-cl* is the most general type of interrogative clause in our phrase hierarchy. Hence the constraints that we place on the type *inter-cl*, one of which is shown in (43), reflect the properties common to all interrogative clauses in English:

(43)   Interrogative Retrieval Constraint (IRC)

inter-cl:

$$\begin{bmatrix} \text{STORE} & \boxed{\Sigma_1} \\ \text{CONT} & \begin{bmatrix} \text{PARAMS} & \boxed{\Sigma_2} \end{bmatrix} \end{bmatrix} \rightarrow \ \dots \ \mathbf{H}\begin{bmatrix} \text{STORE} & \boxed{\Sigma_1} \uplus \boxed{\Sigma_2} \end{bmatrix} \dots$$

The content of an interrogative clause is necessarily a question, as guaranteed by the constraint placed on the type *inter-cl* in Chapter 2. The IRC is the further requirement that the STORE value of an *inter-cl* be the head daughter's STORE value, minus some set of parameters that is the clause's PARAMS set. Put differently, the clause's STORE value and the clause's PARAMS set add up to be the head daughter's STORE. The IRC applies to the 'extracted' *wh*-constructions that we turn to immediately, to the in-situ *wh*-interrogatives discussed in the Chapter 7, and to the construction we introduce in Chapter 8 to handle sluicing. Note that we intentionally allow the set of retrieved parameters to be the empty set. Thus clausepolar interrogative clauses, whose PARAMS set must be empty, also satisfy this constraint by 'passing up' to the clause's STORE all parameters that are in the head daughter's STORE.

---

[8]See Chapter 8 for our analysis of interrogatives embedded by factive and resolutive predicates.

All extracted *wh*-interrogatives—those that consist of a *wh*-specified non-head daughter followed by a sentential head daughter that contains a gap—are treated as instances of a particular subtype of interrogative clause that we will refer to simply as *wh-interrogative-clause* (*wh-int-cl*). We now expand the hierarchy introduced in section 6.1 so as to include relevant supertypes:

(44)

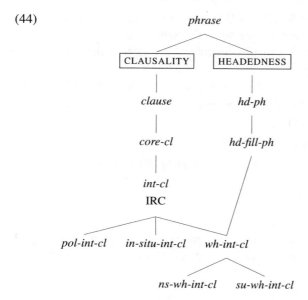

All instances of *ns-wh-int-cl* and *su-wh-int-cl* are thus constrained by the IRC. And since *wh-int-cl* is also a subtype of *hd-fill-ph*, instances of this type must also obey the general constraints on head-filler phrases already illustrated.

In addition, instances of the type *wh-int-cl* must satisfy a constraint we call the 'Filler Inclusion Constraint':

(45) Filler Inclusion Constraint (FIC):

wh-int-cl:

$$\left[\text{CONT} \quad \left[\text{PARAMS} \; \{\boxed{1}\} \uplus \textit{set} \right] \right] \; \rightarrow \; \left[\text{WH} \quad \{\boxed{1}\} \right], \; \mathbf{H}$$

The FIC guarantees that the non-head daughter of a *wh*-interrogative clause (always the filler daughter of a head-filler phrase) must be WH-specified, and hence that the filler constituent either is or properly contains an interrogative *wh*-word (as explained in the previous chapter). The FIC further ensures that (1) the filler daughter's WH value must contain a parameter and (2) that parameter must be included in the PARAMS value (a set of parameters) of the clause's content. It also crucially leaves open the possibility that other parameters in the head daughter's STORE are included in the clause's PARAMS set.[9] Without further stipulation, this will allow for multiple *wh*-questions (section 6.6 below) as well as for reprise questions like (46) (discussed in the next chapter), where the embedded *wh*-interrogative word WHO outscopes the WH-specified filler in the embedded interrogative clause.

---

[9]It may not be obvious at first how the filler daughter's WH member (corresponding to the leftmost *wh*-word within that phrase) can be included in the clause's STORE, given that (by (43)) all members of the clause's PARAMS must be included in the head daughter's STORE. This is explained in more detail in the next section.

(46)   You asked [[which book] Sandy gave to WHO]?

In addition to the FIC, *wh*-interrogative clauses in our analysis are subject to the following constraint, which identifies the head daughter's CONTENT value with the clause's PROP value:

(47)   Propositional Head Constraint (PHC):

wh-int-cl:

$$\left[\text{CONT} \quad \left[\text{PROP} \quad \boxed{2}\right]\right] \rightarrow \ldots \mathbf{H}\left[\text{CONT} \quad \boxed{2}\right]$$

Since the value of the feature PROP must be a proposition, the PHC simultaneously resolves the head daughter's content to be of type *proposition* and guarantees that that proposition is the one the clause's content (a question, as guaranteed by *inter-cl*) is based on.

In the previous chapter, we proposed a number of lexical constraints on the distribution of WH specifications. The WHC in particular requires that all noninitial arguments of a lexeme be specified as [WH { }]. This might at first appear to rule out all in-situ occurrences of *wh*-words, e.g. the one in (46), but it does not.

To see this, recall that interrogative *wh*-words may be WH-specified or not. That is, according to lexical constraints, they may be specified either as [WH {*param*}] or else as [WH { }]. This is crucial to our analysis of *wh*-interrogative clauses, where the leftmost *wh*-word will always be WH-specified, but all in-situ occurences of interrogative *wh*-words will be specified as [WH { }]. This distinction plays an important role in our account of the fact (Brame 1978) that certain items, e.g. *the hell/heck*, can modify a 'fronted' *wh*-expression, but not one that remains in situ:[10]

(48)   a.   [Who the heck/hell/devil] do you think they visited?

  b.   *Who visited [who the heck/hell/devil]?

  c.   *Sandy visited [WHO the heck/hell/devil]?

In our analysis, such modifiers are lexically restricted as shown in (49):

(49) $\left[\text{SS|LOC|CAT|HEAD|MOD} \quad \left[\text{WH} \quad \{param\}\right]\right]$

These contrasts involving *the hell* and the like provide independent motivation for our distinguishing between 'fronted' and in-situ *wh*-expressions via their WH specifications.

These modifiers must be further constrained so as to modify interrogative *wh*-words (not *wh*-phrases), as the following contrasts show:

(50)   a.   [Who the hell] did they visit __ ?

  b.   *[Which book the hell] did they read __ ?

  c.   [[Which the hell] book] did they read __ ?

(51)   a.   *[How many books the hell] did they read __ ?

  b.   *[How many the hell books] did they read __ ?

  c.   [How the hell] many books did they read __ ?

(52)   a.   [[who the hell]'s books] did they read __ ?

---

[10]The set of such modifiers is larger than generally appreciated. It includes numerous expressions that have the feel of curses (real or surrogate): *the devil, the fuck, in the world, in God's name, in tarnation, the blazes, in blue blazes, the deuce*.

    b. %[[whose the hell] books] did they read __ ?[11]
    c. *[whose books the hell] did they read __ ?

There are of course further constraints on the distribution of these modifiers. For example, a semantic distinction something like the distinction between 'open' and 'closed' questions proposed by Huddleston (1993b)[12] is needed to explain why fronted (WH-specified) *wh*-words like those in (53b) and (54b) cannot be modified by *the hell* and the like.

(53)   a.   I wonder [[*who* the hell] they were talking to].
         b. #I found out [[*who* the hell] they were talking to].

(54)   a.   I don't know [[*what* in the world] they were talking about].
         b. #I know [[*what* in the world] they were talking about].

Whatever semantic or pragmatic factors are at work here, we assume they will interact smoothly with the grammatical constraints we formulate in terms of varying WH-specifications.[13]

    The diverse possibilities for WH-specification illustrated here seem difficult to reconcile with the suggestion made by Bresnan (2000) that elements modified by *the hell* and the like all bear an appropriate 'discourse function', a kind of grammatical relation native to LFG's functional structure. Perhaps there is a deeper explanation for which elements can be WH-specified in English. In fact, we think any such explanation is likely to rely on semantics or pragmatics, rather than functional structure relations. In any case, at present, the nature of such a deeper explanation remains obscure.

6.5.2 Nonsubject *Wh*-Interrogatives

The first subtype of *wh-int-cl* that we must consider is *ns-wh-int-cl*, which we use to analyze nonsubject *wh*-interrogatives like (55a,b).

(55)   a.   [Who [will Sandy visit __]]?
         b.   They wonder [who [Sandy will visit __]].

Instances of *ns-wh-int-cl* come in two varieties: independent clauses and embedded clauses. The primary difference between the two is that the head daughter of the former kind must be inverted, while the head daughter of the latter kind cannot be:[14]

---

[11]The observed variation here can be analyzed in lexical terms. Those varieties that include *whose the hell* have lexicalized *whose*; in other varieties, *whose* comes about through the syntactic combination of *who* and the possessive marker *'s*.

[12]See also Bolinger 1978.

[13]Some speakers find a contrast between pairs like the following:
    (i)   ??I wondered whether the hell they were real.
    (ii)   *I wondered if the hell they were real.

However, speakers tend to agree that *whether* does not allow the full range of modifiers that true (interrogative) *wh*-words allow:
    (iii)   *I wondered whether in the world/blue blazes/tarnation they were real.
    (iv)   *I wondered whether the devil/deuce they were real.

Thus whatever increased acceptability might inhere in examples like (i), it cannot provide serious motivation for treating *whether* as being WH-specified. More likely, *whether the hell*—for those speakers that find it fully acceptable—is a lexicalized remnant of an earlier grammar where *whether* was a true *wh*-word.

[14]This is a bit of an oversimplification, as inverted interrogative clauses may sometimes be embedded, as in dialectal variants like (i)–(ii), which seem to exist in some varieties of English in a kind of 'semi-indirect style' (a blend of direct and indirect speech):
    (i)   I wonder [what did they want].
    (ii)   I wonder [did they leave].

(56) a. [Who [will Sandy visit __]]?

b. *[Who [Sandy will visit __]]?

c. They wonder [who [Sandy will visit __]].

d. *They wonder [who [will Sandy visit __]].

To account for these contrasts, we posit the following constraint:

(57)   Inversion Constraint (INVC):

ns-wh-int-cl:

$$[\ ] \quad \rightarrow \quad \ldots \quad \mathbf{H}\begin{bmatrix} \text{IC} & \boxed{1} \\ \text{INV} & \boxed{1} \end{bmatrix}$$

The INVC guarantees that main-clause ([IC +]) questions are inverted and that embedded ([IC −]) questions are uninverted. This rules out (56b), where the clause and its bracketed head daughter are [INV −] but [IC +]. Conversely, if the interrogative clause is embedded, i.e. [IC −], then it must also be [INV −]. The complement of *wonder* in (56d), as well as its bracketed head daughter, is [INV +], in violation of the INVC.

One further property of nonsubject *wh*-interrogatives is shown in (58):

(58)   Optional *Pro* Condition (OPC):

ns-wh-int-cl:

$$[\ ] \quad \rightarrow \quad \ldots \quad \mathbf{H}\big[\text{SUBJ} \ \langle\, (pro\text{-}ss)\, \rangle\big]$$

(58) guarantees that the head daughter's SUBJ list is either empty (making it a saturated clause) or else a singleton list containing an element of type *pro-ss*. The latter instantiation will be relevant for infinitival *wh*-questions, which we turn to in a moment.

In (59) we illustrate the unification of key constraints inherited by instances of the type *ns-wh-int-cl*. These include the IRC, the FIC, the constraints in (47) above, the OPC, and the SLASH-binding constraint on head-filler phrases:

(59) ECC & GHFP & *core-cl* & *inter-cl* & IRC & *hd-fill-ph* & FIC & PHC & *ns-wh-int-cl*:

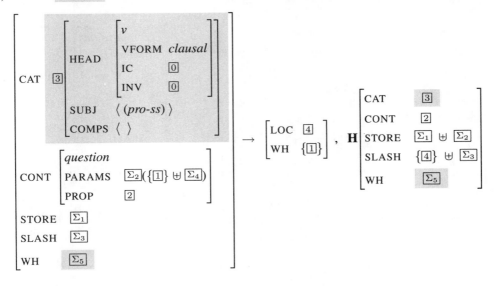

Note that since the various constraints specify that mother and head daughter diverge on values for STORE, CONTENT, and SLASH, the effect of the GHFP is to 'push down' so as to require identity of CAT and WH. The constraints in (59) also allow the SUBJ value of mother and head daughter to be [SUBJ ⟨ *pro-ss* ⟩]. However, when the head daughter is finite, as in the following example, that option always produces a case clash (finite verbs select nominative subjects; *pro-ss* must be accusative). Matrix instances of this construction thus always have the general shape illustrated in (60):

(60)

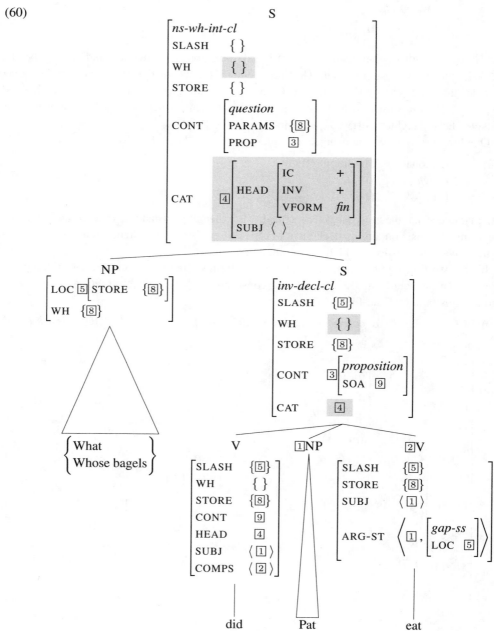

This example illustrates the highly interactive nature of our analysis. For example, the interaction of type constraints guarantees all of the following divergences between head daughter and mother:

(61) a. The SLASH value of the *ns-wh-int-cl* differs from that of its head daughter because *ns-wh-int-cl* inherits the SLASH-binding constraint from the type *hd-fill-ph*.

   b. The CONTENT value of the *ns-wh-int-cl* differs from that of its head daughter because the *ns-wh-int-cl*'s content is a *question* (via constraint on the supertype *inter-cl*) and that question's PROP value is identified with the head daughter's CONTENT value (by the PHC in (47)).

   c. The STORE value of the *ns-wh-int-cl* differs from that of its head daughter because *ns-wh-int-cl* inherits the IRC constraint in (43), again from its supertype *inter-cl*

In all other cases, the feature specifications of the head daughter are identified with those of the mother via the GHFP, as indicated. Note further that the head daughter of the *ns-wh-int-cl* must express a proposition, and hence must be constructed as an *inv-decl-cl*, not as a *pol-int-cl*.

There is a crucial constraint interaction illustrated in (60). Because the feature STORE is a feature of *local* objects (as explained in section 5.3), the STORE value of the *gap-ss* in (60) contains the element 8 that is in the STORE of the clause's filler daughter. This is a consequence of the extraction theory outlined in the previous chapter: the inheritance of SLASH values throughout the extraction path results in an identification of the two indicated LOCAL values (tagged 5). Furthermore, the *gap-ss* has the parameter 8 in its STORE, which is amalgamated into the STORE of the inverted auxiliary verb and then passed up to the S[INV +] (by the GHFP). Because of this interaction, the parameter of the *wh*-word within the clause's filler daughter is also in the STORE of the clause's head daughter, whence it is retrieved in accordance with the FIC (45), which affects all clauses of type *wh-int-cl*. The effect of the FIC therefore is to guarantee that the WH value of the phrase's filler daughter is within the PARAMS value of the interrogative clause. In this case, the filler's parameter is the only member of the PARAMS set, i.e. Σ_4 in (59) is the empty set in (60).

The content of the phrase in (60) is shown in (62):

(62)

$$
\begin{bmatrix}
question \\
\text{PARAMS} \quad \left\{ \begin{bmatrix} \text{IND} & j \\ \text{RESTR} & \{thing(j)\} \end{bmatrix} \right\} \\
\text{PROP} \quad \begin{bmatrix} \text{SIT} & s \\ \text{SOA} & \begin{bmatrix} \text{QUANTS} & \langle\,\rangle \\ \text{NUCL} & \begin{bmatrix} eat\text{-}rel \\ \text{EATER} & i \\ \text{EATEN} & j \end{bmatrix} \end{bmatrix} \end{bmatrix} \\
\text{BCKGRND} \quad \{named(i,Pat)\}
\end{bmatrix}
$$

Consider now the embedded analogue of this same interrogative. The phrase in (63) is also an instance of the type *ns-wh-int-cl*, but it is uninverted, as explained above:

(63)

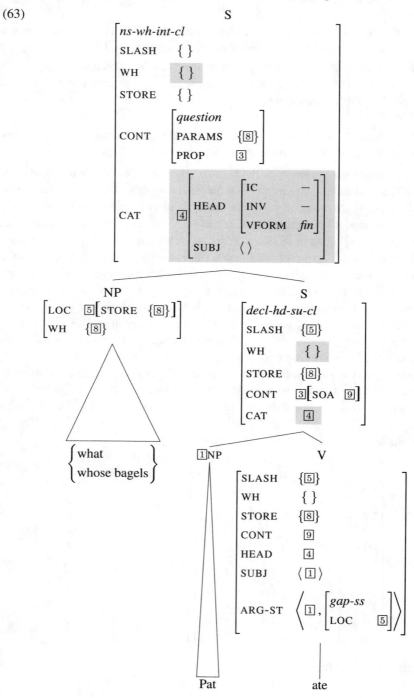

All other relevant properties of this phrase are the same as those just described for its inverted counterpart, except that the clause's head daughter is an instance of the type *decl-hd-su-cl* (which satisfies the [INV −] constraint), rather than an *inv-decl-cl* (which cannot satisfy that constraint).

Note that the INVC has an effect analogous to that of head movement in *wh*-interrogative clauses. In a main ([IC +]) clause, the verb must precede the subject because the [INV +] constraint constrains what kind of construction can appear 'at the next level down'. Conversely, in an embedded *wh*-interrogative clause the verb can never precede the subject because the [INV −] constraint ensures that the the next constituent down is incompatible with the type *sai-ph*. Movement is thus an illusion caused by the interaction of constraints.

Finally, it should also be noted that the INVC applies more generally in other Germanic languages, deriving well-known movement effects in declarative clauses, as well as interrogatives. Moreover, the analysis of movement phenomena in this way is in no sense more stipulative than the transformational alternatives. In movement-based theories, it must be stipulated that main clauses are rooted in CP[*fin*] (or TP), while embedded and nonfinite clauses lack the appropriate movement triggers. These stipulations are similar to the constraint on the type *root* formulated in Chapter 2, some analog of which must be part of any empirically adequate grammar, as far as we can see.

There is one further way that the constraints on the type *ns-wh-int-cl* can be satisfied. Because there are proposition-denoting *to*-clauses—the subjectless declarative clauses discussed in Chapters 2 and 5, these may also serve as the head daughter of an *ns-wh-int-cl*. Since we have no head-subject clauses that consist of a subject followed by VP[*to*], the only infinitival clauses that can function as head daughters of non-subject *wh*-interrogative clauses are those constructed as instances of the type *decl-ns-cl*, as illustrated in (64):[15]

---

[15]Gerund phrases are ruled out as possible head daughters here: (1) they do not denote propositions and (2) they are incompatible with the [VFORM *clausal*] constraint inherited from the supertype *core-cl*.

(64)

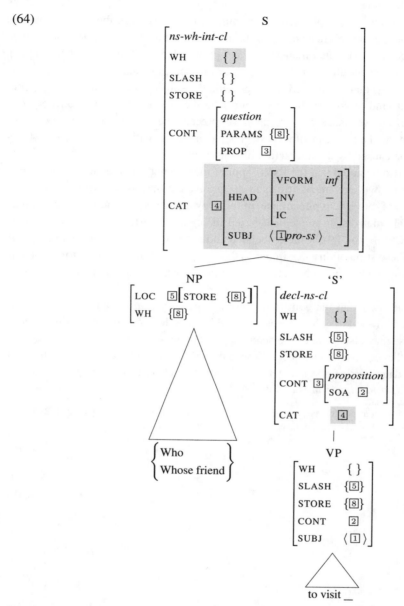

Notice that the FIC is obeyed here, as are all other constraints inherited from the supertypes of *ns-wh-int-cl*. Here again, the GHFP identifies all specifications of head daughter and mother, except for those discrepancies that are induced by specific constraints of the grammar.

6.5.3 Subject *Wh*-Interrogatives

We now turn to the second subtype of *wh-int-cl*, the type *su-wh-int-cl*, which we use to analyze interrogatives where the obligatory *wh*-word functions as a subject:

(65) a. *Who* visits Merle?

 b. *Whose friends* left?

(66) a. I wonder [*who* visited Merle].

 b. I wonder [*whose friends* left].

First, we can be sure that the *wh*-phrases in these examples are WH-specified, as they allow *the hell* and the like as modifiers:

(67) a. I wonder [*who the heck/hell/devil* would eat that].

 b. *Who the heck/hell/devil* would eat that?

By treating subject *wh*-questions as a kind of *wh-int-cl* we predict this, because the bracketed constituents must be WH-specified, according to the FIC in (45).

 Note that we cannot treat subject *wh*-questions as a kind of *hd-subj-ph*, because the WHSP (discussed in section 5.2) requires that all SUBJ values be [WH { }]: the WH-specified subject could not combine directly with a VP specified as [SUBJ ⟨ [WH { }] ⟩]. Rather, we treat this kind of interrogative as a head-filler construction where the subject is extracted:

(68) *su-wh-int-cl*:

$$\begin{bmatrix} \text{SUBJ} & \langle \, \rangle \end{bmatrix} \rightarrow \begin{bmatrix} \text{LOC} \; \boxed{4} \end{bmatrix}, \; \mathbf{H}\begin{bmatrix} \text{SUBJ} & \left\langle \begin{bmatrix} \textit{gap-ss} \\ \text{LOC} \; \boxed{4} \end{bmatrix} \right\rangle \end{bmatrix}$$

 We illustrate in (69) the unification of key constraints on supertypes that are inherited by this construction. These again include the IRC, the FIC, the PHC, and the SLASH-binding condition on head-filler phrases:

(69) ECC &   GHFP   & *hd-fill-ph* & *core-cl* & *inter-cl* & IRC & FIC & PHC & *su-wh-int-cl*:

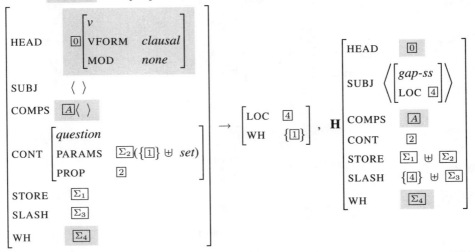

Because the head daughter of this construction must have a CONTENT value of type *proposition* and must in addition have a non-empty SUBJ list, one of the few possible expansions of this head daughter will be via the *decl-ns-cl* construction discussed in Chapter 2. This is illustrated in (70):

(70)

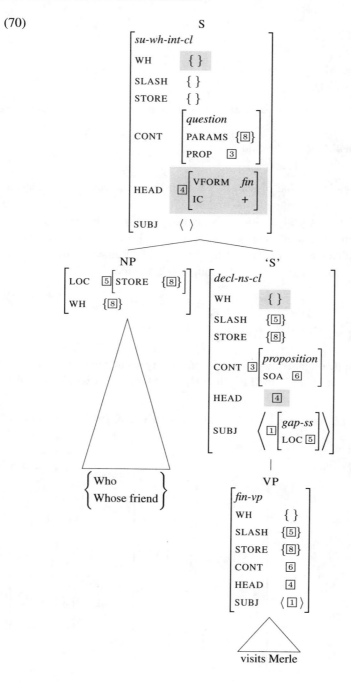

Thus in all subject *wh*-questions, the subject NP is in fact extracted and the verb heading such a question is slashed. This treatment is thus consistent with the generalizations of Hukari and Levine (1996a,b), who observe that extraction-sensitive phenomena, in all languages where they exist, manifest themselves in subject *wh*-interrogative constructions like these, as well as in constructions containing object or adverbial gaps.

Moreover, since no constraint requires an instance of *su-wh-int-cl* to be an independent clause, it follows that such clauses may also be [IC −]. This provides an account of embedded subject *wh*-interrogatives like those in (71).

(71) a. I wonder [*who* visits Merle].

  b. I wonder [*whose friends* left].

The semantics we provide for an interrogative clause like (70) or (71a) is shown in (72):

(72)
$$
\begin{bmatrix}
\textit{question} \\[4pt]
\text{PARAMS} \quad \left\{ \begin{bmatrix} \text{IND} & i \\ \text{RESTR} & \{ person\,(i) \} \end{bmatrix} \right\} \\[20pt]
\text{PROP} \quad \begin{bmatrix}
\text{SIT} & s \\[4pt]
\text{SOA} & \begin{bmatrix}
\text{QUANTS} & \langle\,\rangle \\[4pt]
\text{NUCL} & \begin{bmatrix} \textit{visit-rel} \\ \text{VISITER} & i \\ \text{VISITED} & j \end{bmatrix}
\end{bmatrix}
\end{bmatrix} \\[30pt]
\text{BCKGRND} \quad \{ named(j,Merle) \}
\end{bmatrix}
$$

Finally, note that the lower VP in (70) is an instance of the *fin-vp* construction discussed in Chapter 2. Since phrases of this type are [AUX −] unless they are polarized (see Chapter 2), it follows that unfocussed *do* (lexically specified as [AUX +]) can never head such a phrase unless it is polarized. As a consequence of this, there can be no subject *wh*-questions like those in (73a,b).

(73) a. *Who dĭd leave?

  b. *I wonder [who dĭd leave].

  c. Who dĭdn't leave?

  d. Who dĭd not leave?

  e. Who DID leave?

  f. I wonder [who dĭdn't leave].

  g. I wonder [who dĭd not leave].

  h. I wonder [who DID leave].

Again, key data that have been analyzed in the literature in terms of complex interactions of movement transformations (e.g. head movement and Affix 'Hopping') or else in terms of 'optimization' are here analyzed simply via the simultaneous satisfaction of grammatical constraints.

6.6 Multiple *Wh*-Questions

As we noted above, multiple *wh*-questions can be treated straightforwardly in our analysis. In this section, we outline the basics of our account and address certain issues in the grammar of multiple *wh*-questions that have been much discussed under such rubrics as 'superiority effects' and 'D-Linking'.

6.6.1 The Basic Analysis of Multiple *Wh*-Questions

In our analysis, there is only one *wh*-word per interrogative clause that is WH-specified. This follows from the interaction of the GHFP with the various lexical constraints discussed in the previous chapter (specifically WH-Amalgamation, the WHSP, and the WHC), which ensure that the arguments of verbs (except the specifiers of verbal gerunds) are all [WH { }]. It is only within the initial phrase (the filler daughter) of a *wh*-interrogative clause that WH-specified phrases may appear. This means first that there can only be one exclamative *wh*-word per exclamative clause, as these words must be WH-specified. However, since interrogative *wh*-words are optionally WH-specified, they may appear in unfronted positions. Such in-situ *wh*-words, though not WH-specified, will nonetheless have a parameter in their STORE. This parameter is amalgamated into the STORE of the lexical head that combines with the in-situ *wh*-word and is consequently (by the GHFP) part of the STORE of the phrases that that lexical head projects.

In the case of the famous ambiguities discussed by Baker (1970), e.g. (74), the parameter of an embedded *wh*-interrogative word may be retrieved from storage at the level of the embedded clause or the highest clause.

(74) Who wondered who saw what?

Such parameters can thus become part of the meaning of either interrogative clause. Consider first the possibility that the parameter of *what* is inherited via STORE and retrieved in the lower interrogative clause, as indicated via shading in (75):

(75)

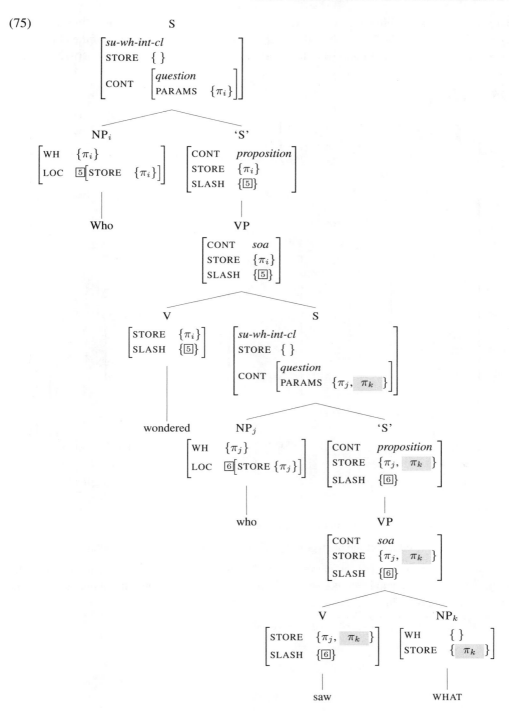

Here the analysis of both subject *wh*-interrogative clauses is just as described in the previous section.[16] Notice that the FIC is obeyed in both clauses. When the parameter of the object in the lower clause is retrieved in the lower clause, as indicated in (75), the resulting CONTENT value is (76):

(76)

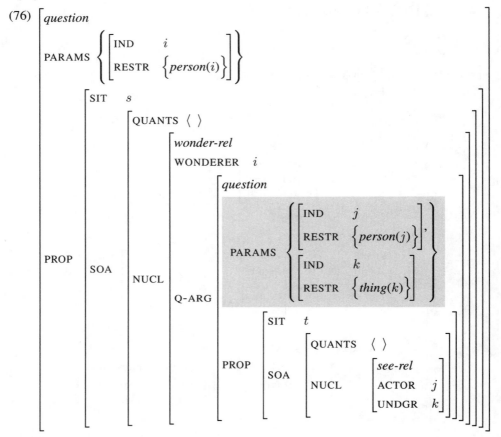

This is the reading of (74) that can be paraphrased as:

(77) Who wondered about the answer to the following question: Who saw what?

But nothing requires that the parameter π_k be retrieved in the lowest clause. If it is not, it continues being passed up in STORE (by the GHFP) and is retrieved into the content of the higher interrogative clause. This alternative analysis is illustrated in (78):

---

[16]The focussed nature of the in-situ *wh*-word *what* is discussed in the next section.

(78)

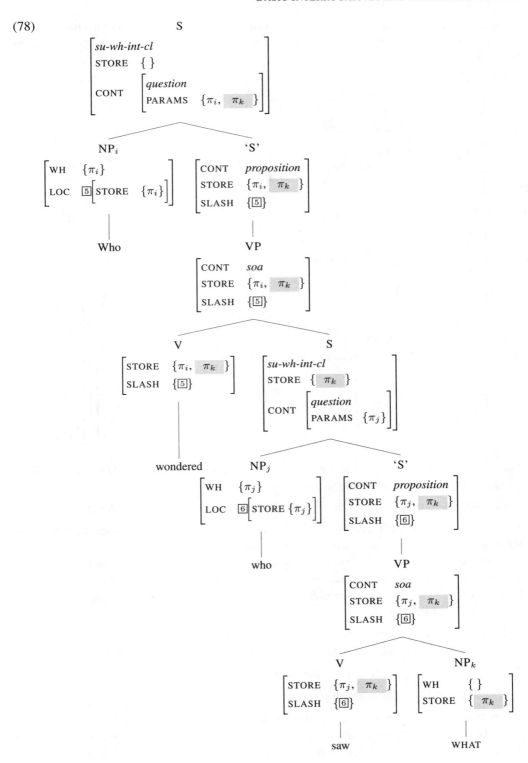

Nothing has changed here, other than the indicated inheritance and retrieval of the parameter π_k. When this parameter is retrieved in the higher clause, as shown in (78), the CONTENT value that results is (79).

(79)

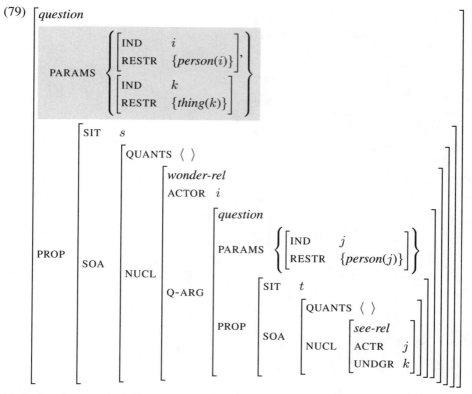

This is the alternate 'pair list' reading of (74) that is appropriately answered (see Chapter 4) by citing pairs of wonderers and things, as in (80):

(80)   Bo wondered who saw the Picasso; Dana wondered who saw the Monet; ....

The ambiguity just described follows without stipulation from our analysis, since the IRC allows optional retrieval of stored parameters in either *wh*-interrogative clause.

The FIC plays a crucial role in our analysis as well—it ensures that the index of the WH-specified *wh*-word (i.e. the leftmost interrogative *wh*-word) is retrieved at the lowest possible level in the tree. This is a correct prediction of our analysis, as the Baker example in (74) has no pair-list reading like (81).

(81)   a. For which persons x and y, did x wonder what was seen by y.

       b. Bo wondered what was seen by Kim; Dana wondered what was seen by Lee; ....

The way to ask such a question in English is of course with (82).

(82)   Who asked what was seen by WHO?

And in (82), the lower *who* is in situ, and hence not WH-specified on our analysis. It is therefore free to be retrieved from STORE at the highest interrogative clause in (82), as required to produce the reading described in (81). By contrast, the word *what* in (82)—because it is the filler of the lower interrogative clause—must be WH-specified in our analysis, and hence must be retrieved within the lower interrogative clause. This correctly predicts that (82) lacks the reading in (79), i.e. the reading indicated in (83).

(83)   For which person x and which thing y, did x ask who saw y.

These data, much discussed in the syntactic literature since Baker 1970, follow to the letter from our proposal.

In addition, it should be noted that our analysis provides a correct account of the ambiguity of examples like (84) (due to Engdahl 1986), where the in-situ *wh*-word is properly contained within the clause's filler daughter.

(84)   Who remembers [whose recordings of which Beethoven symphony] Leslie prefers?

Because the entire STORE of the bracketed NP in (84) is amalgamated into the store of the lowest verb *prefers*, the parameter associated with the NP *which Beethoven symphony* 'starts out' in storage there and may be retrieved at any higher node. This parameter can thus be part of the PARAMS set of either question; the account is essentially identical to the one just illustrated.

Another descriptive advantage of our approach, already mentioned above, is that it accounts for the fact that *the hell* and the like can modify a 'fronted' *wh*-expression, but not one that remains in situ. The consequences of this are pervasive in multiple *wh*-questions and include an explanation of contrasts like the following.

(85) a.   [Who the heck/hell/devil] does the cooking around here?
      b.   [Who the heck/hell/devil] does WHAT around here?
      c. * Who does [what the heck/hell/devil] around here?
      d. *[Who the heck/hell/devil] does [what the heck/hell/devil] around here?

Our analysis explains these contrasts because it distinguishes 'fronted' *wh*-expressions from in-situ *wh*-expressions via their WH specifications.[17]

Finally, note that our treatment of multiple *wh*-questions makes a surprising prediction about gerunds. On Malouf's (1998) analysis, as modified slightly in the preceding chapter, gerunds select accusative subjects as in (86a)—via the SUBJ feature, but they select possessive NPs, as in (86b), via the SPR feature.

(86) a.   Sandy/them winning the election...
      b.   Sandy's/their winning the election...

Given the WHSP, which disallows WH-specified subjects, and the WHC, which ensures that all non-initial members of an ARG-ST list are specified as [WH { }], examples like (87) are predicted to be ungrammatical.

---

[17]It is tempting to provide a similar account of the obligatory fronting of *why*:

(i)   Why did Sandy leave?
(ii)   *Who left why? (cf. Who left WHEN?)

This contrast would be accounted for if *why* were specified as in (iii).

(iii) $\left[\text{SS}|\text{WH} \ \{param\}\right]$

This treatment is not yet satisfactory, however, as the specification in (iii) leaves unexplained why other in-situ occurrences of *why*, discussed more fully in Chapter 7, are possible:

(iv)   A: Bo left because she was exasperated.
        B: Right; and Sandy left WHY?

We leave this matter to future research.

(87) *I wonder [[*who(m)* winning the election] Chris wrote about].

This follows because there is no way for the gerund phrase to be WH-specified: a subject-selecting gerund and all its arguments must be [WH { }].

By contrast, a gerund cooccurring with a *wh*-word as specifier is WH-specified just in case its specifier is. This follows from WH-amalgamation and the absence of any constraint requiring the gerund's specifier to be [WH { }]. We thus correctly predict that pied piping from the possessor should be possible:

(88) I wonder [[whose winning the election] Chris wrote about __].

There is a further prediction made by our analysis, taken together with Malouf's theory of gerunds. In a sentence like the following, the clausal head *wrote* and its PP argument must be [WH { }] (this follows from the WHC, the WHSP, and their interaction with WH-amalgamation).

(89) Pat wonders who wrote about [WHOSE winning the election].

But because the PP is [WH { }], so is the preposition *about* (this follows from the GHFP). And because such prepositions identify their WH value with that of their object argument (see section 5.2), it follows that the gerund phrase *winning the election* is [WH { }], and hence its head (again by the GHFP) and its specifier *whose* (by WH-amalgamation) are [WH { }]. In other words, in this kind of example, the *wh*-word *whose* is in situ.

Moreover, as Malouf (1998, 2000) notes, multiple *wh*-interrogatives like (90) are also possible.

(90) Pat wonders who wrote about [WHO(M) winning the election].

This too is predicted, because we allow optional WH-specification for interrogative *wh*-words. Hence no constraints of our theory are violated in structures like (91).

(91)

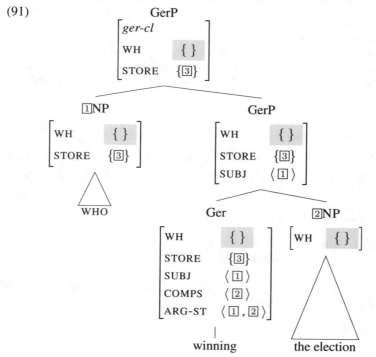

6.6.2 Superiority Effects

Contrasts like the following have been known for some time (Kuno and Robinson 1972, Chomsky 1973):

(92) a. Who __ saw what?

     b. *What did who see __ ?

Chomsky (1973) proposes to account for such contrasts in terms of a 'superiority' condition which prevents a transformation from applying to a given phrase if it could also have applied to a superior phrase, i.e. one closer to the root sentence. Because of the way superiority is defined,[18] the superiority condition blocks (92b), but allows both the examples in (93) (Chomsky's (71)–(72)).

(93) a. John remembers where Bill bought which book __ .

     b. John remembers to whom Bill gave which book __ .

Chomsky (1980) assumes that the contrast between (92a) and (92b) represents a subject/object asymmetry and offers an alternative account on the basis of the Empty Category Principle (ECP). However, as Hornstein (1995: 124) argues (following Hendrick and Rochemont 1982), similar contrasts like (94), where neither *wh*-expression is in subject position, are not easily amenable to analysis in terms of the ECP.

(94) a. Who did you persuade __ to buy what?

     b. *What did you persuade who to buy __ ?

The literature on the superiority phenomenon is considerable and we cannot do justice to it here. However, in our view, this phenomenon has not yet been adequately analyzed, despite frequent assertions to the contrary.

There are a number of reasons why we say this, not the least of which is the difficulty in coming up with a clear characterization of what the data actually are. There are many potential counterexamples to the basic superiority effect—the generalization that a *wh*-dependency between a binder and a gap may not cross a *wh*-expression that is syntactically superior to the gap. For example, it is generally agreed that *which*-phrases are immune to the effect:

(95) a. I wonder which book *which man* read __ .

     b. To which organization did *which people* give money __

An influential strategy that data like (95) have spawned, following Pesetsky (1987), is to distinguish between inherently D(iscourse)-linked and non-D-linked *wh*-phrases: some interrogative phrases are quantificational and require fronting at LF for their interpretation; others are interpreted like indefinites and do not require fronting at LF. According to Pesetsky's proposal, these latter expressions require 'D-linking'; their use requires a set of possible instantiators for the argument role with which the D-linked expression is associated to be salient. The prototypical D-linked interrogative expressions are *which*-phrases. Pesetsky's conclusion is that an ECP-based account for the asymmetries above can be maintained, albeit restricted to the quantificational interrogative phrases.

---

[18]"A is superior to the category B in the phrase marker if every major (N, V, or A) category dominating A dominates B as well but not conversely." (Chomsky 1973: 246)

We are skeptical about the grammatical viability of the D-linking distinction: although it is clear that *which*-phrases differ *presuppositionally* from *what* and *who* (in that the former carry a uniqueness presupposition that the latter do not carry),[19] there is no independent evidence for interpretational asymmetries (and hence distinct interpretational mechanisms) between the putatively distinct classes of *wh*-phrases. Both *which*-phrases and *who/what* (and indeed all other *wh*-phrases we are aware of) can be used independently, functionally, and to reprise. Moreover, the condition that Pesetsky suggests characterizes felicitous uses of *which*-phrases is incorrect.[20] Thus it is implausible to suggest that in using a sentence such as (96), a speaker has in mind a range of felicitous answers more precise than the range of answers that someone who used any of the examples in (97) might have in mind:

(96)   I don't know anything about cars. Do you have any suggestions about which car, if any, I should buy when I get a raise?

(97) a. I don't know anything about cars. Do you have any suggestions about what car, if any, I should buy when I get a raise?

      b. I don't know anything about cars. Do you have any suggestions about what, if anything, I should buy when I get a raise?

      c. I don't know anything about cars. Do you have any suggestions about how many (cars), if any, I should buy when I get a raise?

Though these varying choices differ little, if at all, with respect to the specificity of the answer set presupposed by the speaker, they apparently have quite different behavior with respect to the possibility of multiple *wh*-questions:

(98) a. Who did which president greet __ ?

      b. */#Who did what president greet __ ?

      c. */#Who did how many presidents greet __ ?

In short, the appeal to D-linking fails to explain such constraints on multiple *wh*-questions in terms of any distinguishing semantic property.

Similarly problematic are claims such as that made by Hornstein (1995), that fronted *wh*-phrases in multiple *wh*-interrogatives must be D-linked, as illustrated by (99):

(99) a. Which recently published reports should be made required reading for which government departments?

      b. Don't just make big claims for the current administration. Tell us specifically: What has the government done in recent years for which underprivileged group?

---

[19] For discussion, see section 4.3.3.

[20] In fact, it is not the case that D-linking, in the sense of linking an NP use with a contextually provided domain, in any way *characterizes* sentences containing *which*-phrases or superiority-violating multiple *wh*-sentences. Any use of a sentence (an episodic sentence, at least) requires for full comprehension the fixing of a domain or situation which the utterance concerns. Without this, the utterance is not felicitous. This applies as much to uses of declaratives as to uses of interrogatives. Thus, out of the blue, an utterance of (i), (ii), or (iii) contains no semantic clues to the domain over which the possible fillers of either the quantifier or interrogated roles vary:

  (i) Who likes whom?
  (ii) Someone was asleep.
  (iii) Who was asleep?

Hence, without further contextual specification of the domain, the corresponding query or assertion will be infelicitous. As these data make evident, this phenomenon is quite orthogonal to the semantics of (multiple) *wh*-interrogatives.

A newly elected public official, ignorant of the available government reports, can utter (99a), whereas (99b) can be uttered by an activist who believes the government has not done anything to help underprivileged groups.

Likewise, it is hard to see why examples like (100) involve mechanisms of interpretation different from those that are relevant to the semantic analysis of the questions in (101).

(100) a. How many students took how many courses?

      b. How many courses did how many students take?

(101) a. Who took what courses?

      b. ?What courses did who take?

Because of problems of this sort, we reject the claim that there are two distinct mechanisms for interpreting *wh*-expressions: quantification and D-linking. The theory we present treats all *wh*-phrases in terms of a single interpretive technique: the abstraction of indices of interrogative parameters.

Moreover, as Bolinger (1978) and others have pointed out, there are other kinds of systematic exceptions to the superiority effect. First, there are echo questions like (102B).

(102) A: What did Agamemnon break?

      B: What did WHO break __ ?

Second, there are 'reference' questions like (103B).

(103) A: What did he break?

      B: What did WHO break __ ?

We discuss and analyze both of these interrogative types in the next chapter.

Third, there are superiority-violating multiple *wh*-questions such as those in (104).

(104) a. Who wondered what WHO was doing?

          (= Who are the x, y pairs such that x wondered what y was doing?)

      b. Who asked how often WHO went to a baseball game?

          (= Who are the x, y pairs such that x asked how often y went to a baseball game?)

In addition, there are single clause interrogatives that violate superiority. As Bolinger (1978: 108) notes, when more than two (interrogative) *wh*-words are present, any of them can appear in fronted position:

(105) a. Who took WHAT WHERE?

      b. What did WHO take __ WHERE?

      c. Where did WHO take WHAT __ ?

It is hard to see how examples like (105b,c) can be squared with any purely syntactic account of superiority, including those of Pesetsky (1987), Lasnik and Saito (1992), Hornstein (1995), or Chomsky (1995b). These theories offer an account of at best a small subset of the phenomena, with no precise alternative offered for the remaining cases.

Notice that in all of the examples we have been considering, accentual prominence typical of focus is evident on the non-fronted *wh*-expressions. That is, the most natural phonetic renditions of all these examples involve the presence—to varying degrees—of a focus-related pitch accent. Perhaps focus holds the key to understanding the exceptions to superiority.

In this connection, it is interesting to consider further counterexamples to superiority offered by Bolinger (1978: 108):

(106)   a.   I know that among all the disasters in that kitchen, Jane scorched the beans and Lydia put salt in the ice tea; but WHAT did WHO BREAK? I know somebody broke some something, so stop evading my question.

        b.   I know what just about everybody was ASKED to do, but what did WHO (actually) DO?

Pesetsky (1987: 109), who agrees fully with Bolinger's claim about the acceptability of these examples, adds a further counterexample of his own:

(107)   I know that we need to install transistor A, transistor B, and transistor C, and I know that these three holes are for transistors, but I'll be damned if I can figure out from the instructions WHERE WHAT goes.

He observes that these require a proper context and that the felicity is particularly evident "if all the *wh*-words are given extremely heavy stress" (Pesetsky 1987: 108).

Now Pesetsky (as well as Hornstein (1995)) sees the absence of superiority effects as an indication of D-linking, a mechanism that has never been made precise and whose motivation we believe is dubious, as previously discussed. However, the intuition behind D-linking may well be related to the focus facts that have been observed.

We suggest that the following generalization is true:

(108)   In a multiple *wh*-interrogative, all *wh*-phrases except the first must be accented.

If we build an analysis that embodies this generalization, then the only thing wrong with examples like (92b) (repeated here as (109a)) is that the second *wh*-word is unaccented.

(109)   a.   *What did whŏ see __ ?
        b.   *What did whŏ break __ ?
        c.   *What did whŏ do __ ?
        d.   *Where did whăt go __ ?

This would account nicely for the contrasts agreed upon by Bolinger and Pesetsky (compare (106) and (107) above).

It is straightforward to modify our analysis to express this generalization. In the previous chapter, we assumed a single lexical entry—with a disjunctively specified WH value—for each interrogative *wh*-word. Suppose instead that we distinguished the WH-specified *who* from its [WH { }] counterpart phonologically. That is, we could posit the following two lexical entries for interrogative *who*.[21]

---

[21]Obviously, the clumsy disjunction '*who*/WHO' should be replaced by an appropriately formulated accentual underspecifation.

(110)   a. WH-Specified Interrogative *who*:

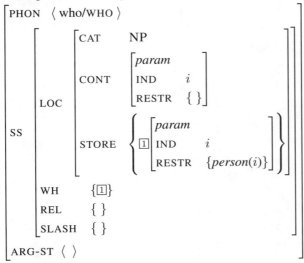

   b. WH-{ } Interrogative *who*:

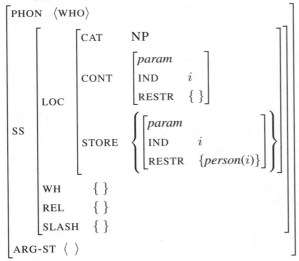

Since our syntactic analysis guarantees that only (110b) can appear in situ, we then immediately predict that in-situ *wh*-words must be accented, while 'fronted' *wh*-words are only optionally so. This, by the way, is precisely the generalization offered by Ladd (1996: 170–172) in his brief discussion of English *wh*-interrogative intonation.

    With this revision in place, we have an analysis of all of the preceding contrasts. The analysis of Bolinger's example (105b), for example, is shown in (111).

(111)

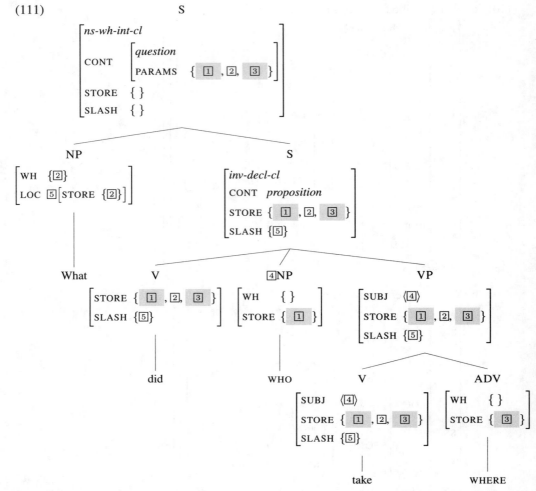

Since both WHO and WHERE are [WH { }], they must be accented, as lexical entries like those in (110) guarantee.

In order to account for the relative ease with which *which*-phrases violate superiority, we need only state that the [WH { }] lexical entry for *which* allows, but does not require, a pitch accent. This will allow us to explain examples like (112).

(112)   a. I wonder which book *which man* read __ .

      b. To which organization did *which people* give money __

This account thus requires no new interpretative mechanism for *which*-interrogatives: *which* differs from other *wh*-expressions only in terms of accentual properties and presupposition. Superiority-violating multiple *wh*-questions like (113) are also now allowed, with focussing of the parameter of the in-situ *wh*-word *who*:

(113)

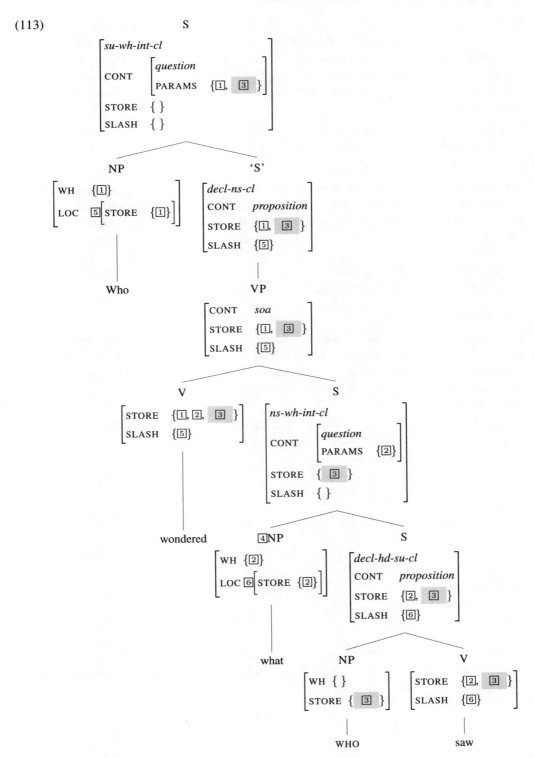

It does not matter at which level of structure the in-situ *wh*-expression's parameter is retrieved. An in-situ *wh*-word (other than *which*) must be accented. A similar interaction will result from the analysis of echo and reference interrogatives developed in the next chapter.

There is one final piece of the prosodic account we have sketched here that needs to be fleshed out. We have been led to the conclusion that in all the examples in (114) (at least) the noninitial *wh*-words are focussed.

(114) a. What did *who* take *where*?
     b. Who gave *what* to *whom*?
     c. Who said *what* about *when*?

Yet the degree of intonational prominence on the penultimate *wh*-expression may be considerably less than that of the final *wh*-word. It seems plausible to attribute this to a prosodic effect that subordinates a given pitch accent to one that follows. That is, our claim about the data here crucially involves FOCUS, which is typically—but not always—associated with a clearly discernable pitch accent. Whether there are other effects (e.g. duration or tempo) that corroborate our claims about the obligatory presence of focus in the examples we have considered is regrettably a matter we must leave to future research.

6.7   Conclusion

In this chapter, we have presented the basics of a grammar of polar and *wh*-interrogative clauses, as well as an account of exclamative clauses—both with and without *wh*-expressions. The overall organization of the clausal types we have posited is sketched in (115). Our analysis includes an account of the ambiguities of multiple *wh*-interrogatives as well as a novel approach to the treatment of superiority effects.

(115)

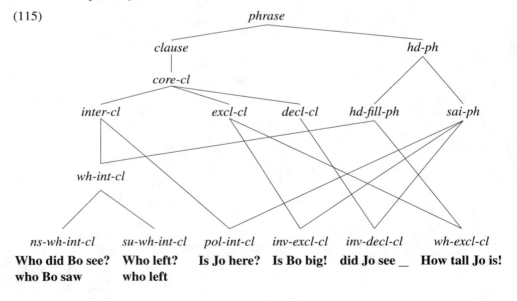

7

In-Situ *Wh*-Phrases

In this chapter we consider the status of sentences like (1).

(1)   Tracy likes WHO?

It has commonly been thought that such sentences can only be used as reprise questions (often equated with 'echo' questions—see below) and/or that the syntax and semantics of such forms are outside the purview of grammar proper. In the Principles and Parameters framework (for particular proposals, see Haegeman 1991, Hornstein 1995) this is a consequence of the θ-criterion, which says that no phrase that is functionally an operator can remain in an A-position at LF. In consequence of the θ-criterion, it is intended that Quantifier Raising apply obligatorily to quantificational expressions (which interrogatives are assumed to be). And, from the perspective of phrase structure grammar, Engdahl suggests:

> Because of their semantic type, *wh*-phrases cannot contribute directly to the meaning of a VP or NP ... We take it to be that the reason we cannot interpret a VP like *kissed who* is that the meaning of *who* is not of the right type to combine with a transitive verb like *kiss*. Rather *who* is a quantifier which necessarily takes scope over a sentence. (Engdahl 1986: 72)

This general strategy appears problematic in that it relies on two questionable assumptions: (1) the assumption that reprise uses involve some intrinsically different interrogative meaning (or different interrogative expressions for that matter) and (2) the assumption that non-fronted (unary) *wh*-interrogative sentences can only be used to make reprises. We will argue that both assumptions are false. We will then show further that our framework is particularly well-suited to account for such facts. There are two reasons for this: (1) scope and dislocation are decoupled and (2) our construction-based approach allows us to impose fine-grained constraints that capture the observed generalizations about the relation between *wh*-word position and semantic interpretation.

Let us begin by clarifying our terminology. We adopt Bolinger's term 'reprise' for the class of queries whose meaning is partially determined directly from the immediately prior utterance. This class includes both echo questions like (2B) and 'ref(erence) questions' (Pope 1976) like (3B).

(2) A: Bustamante y Bacigalupo plays the violin badly.
     B: WHO plays the violin badly?

(3) A: They're mad at Bustamente y Bacigalupo.
     B: WHO's mad at Bustamente y Bacigalupo?

That is, we reserve the term 'echo' for the particular use resulting from mishearing a previous speech act; this use is marked by a characteristic intonation pattern (focus-associated rise with spreading high tone). Ref questions, by contrast, ask for clarification of the reference of some element in the immediately prior utterance and have a distinct intonation pattern (focus-associated fall with spreading low tone).[1] Note that both kinds of reprise question involve accented *wh*-words. As noted in section 6.6.2 of the previous chapter, on our account there is a unidirectional correlation between accent and WH-specification: [WH { }] elements are all accented. We return to this issue below, when we discuss the propensity of reprise uses to license superiority violations. Finally, a point of terminology: we will use the term 'direct' question to designate 'non-reprise' questions, even presupposition-laden examples like (4), which are highly dependent on the (often immediately) previous context.

(4) Which student was riding which motorcycle?

7.1 Reprise Uses of Interrogatives

7.1.1 Background

Our first task is to offer a brief syntactic and semantic analysis of reprise uses. Reprise uses of *wh*-sentences have been given short shrift in much recent literature, either dismissed summarily as 'metalinguistic' and not genuine questions (see Cooper 1983, Engdahl 1986), or else assumed to involve an intrinsically different logical form (Janda 1985). Comorowski (1989) provides a number of important insights on the syntactic nature of reprise phrases which we review below, but in adopting the 'metalinguistic' label, we feel she was led to unnecessary complications. Thus Comorowski assumes (following Karttunen 1977) that an ordinary interrogative denotes a property of propositions. However, for reprise interrogatives like (2B) or (3B) she assumes that they denote a property of properties of propositions. Our basic claim, following Ginzburg (1992), is that reprise (and hence 'echo') uses are metalinguistic only in that the CONTENT that they give rise to contains as a constituent the illocutionary force of the (previous) utterance that it reprises. Beyond that, we claim, there is nothing fundamentally different going on—syntactically or semantically—from other uses of interrogatives. More precisely, reprise uses of *wh*-phrases will introduce a parameter into the STORE value just as in-situ *wh*-phrases do in ordinary multiple *wh*-interrogatives. Moreover, reprise uses will be treated in terms of a construction type that is quite similar to the one we posit for non-reprise uses of *wh*-phrases.

It is also apposite to mention the approach of Reis 1992. In that paper, Reis provides a detailed and insightful discussion of reprise phenomena in German. Reis argues in detail against any marginalization of such phenomena to the extra-grammatical periphery and develops a GB

---

[1]Of course, as Carl Pollard reminds us, all the restrictions we discuss in terms of the previous (or immediately prior) utterance or speech act should ultimately be generalized in terms of a notion of 'text in question', in which the utterer may be unknown or nonexistent. This refinement, which we will not undertake here, is required in order to accommodate data like the following:

(i) [A and B are examining partly illegible text]
   TEXT: Harry Truman didn't put much stock in (illegible).
   B to A: He didn't put much stock in WHAT? (echo intonation)
(ii) [A and B are listening to a 78 rpm record of Cole Porter tunes]
   RECORD: Even educated fleas do it.
   B to A: Even educated fleas do WHAT? (reference resolution intonation)

account. We cannot enter into a detailed comparison here for two reasons: first, Reis's account is developed for German, in contrast to our account for English.[2] Second, Reis does not provide a semantics for her logical forms, which makes it difficult to evaluate her proposal in a number of key respects. We can, nonetheless, point to two fundamental claims she makes (with respect to German) that distinguish her proposal from ours. The first claim concerns the issue of continuity with other interrogative constructions. Reis explicitly denies that reprise interrogatives denote the same type of semantic object as other 'regular' interrogatives. She makes this claim in discussing a proposal by Jacobs (1991), apparently similar in spirit to our own account, within a structured meanings approach.[3] Our claim *for* continuity will rely on one of the most fundamental semantic criteria for content identity, namely the existence of paraphrase relations between reprise and non-reprise interrogatives. The second claim Reis makes that distinguishes her approach from ours concerns the uniformity of 'in-situ phenomena'. Reis's strategy is to provide a uniform analysis for all interrogatives that are not 'canonical' *wh*-interrogatives (in terms of dislocation and intonation). While we must reserve judgement about the German data, we will argue, as already mentioned above, that English 'in-situ phenomena' do *not* constitute a homogeneous class. In particular, there are English *wh*-interrogatives that involve no dislocation, but which do express non-reprise questions.

7.1.2 Syntactic Constraints

One of the main reasons that researchers have assumed reprise uses to be metalinguistic, or 'extragrammatical' is the belief that the strong syntactic constraints that govern independently (and dependently) used interrogative expressions are absent in the case of reprise uses, where 'anything goes'. But it is useful to keep in mind the existence of a distinction between the availability of reprise uses of forms provided by grammar and reprises using 'extragrammatical' forms. It is commonly assumed that not all strings of morphemes that speakers of the language use should be considered 'grammatical'. For example, various false starts, repairs, ellipses, etc. are assumed, for various metatheoretical reasons, to be outside the domain of 'grammatical competence'. How to draw this line is a thorny matter, and such issues apply with special force to domains of 'discourse grammar' such as ellipsis.

Not surprisingly, these issues also crop up with forms that can be used to reprise, which are typically associated with relatively informal settings. Thus, the following kind of example, due to Janda (1985), has been taken as evidence by many for the 'metalinguistic' nature of reprise uses:

(5) A: I've been reading a bit recently about (auditory disturbance in the room) jacency.

    B: Sorry, you've been reading about WHAT-jacency?

Reprise uses can thus apparently enter at a subsyntactic level. Janda takes this as support for the view that sentences used to reprise are assigned contents that vary over linguistic strings, essentially assigning an LF to (5) like (6).

(6)   For which string x, have you been reading about x-jacency

We believe this is an altogether hasty conclusion: most obviously it cannot accommodate the fact that even echos can be responded to quite felicitously by restating the same content using a different form:

---

[2] See Engdahl 2000 for detailed discussion and comparison of the two approaches.

[3] Jacobs' logical forms for reprises also contain an illocutionary operator as a constituent.

(7) A: I like Vyachoslav Voinovich.

    B: (Sorry,) you like WHO?

    A: The Russian you met at the reception.

It can also not accommodate non-echo reprises, such as reference questions or expressions of astonishment, mentioned below. In any case, we are somewhat skeptical about the status of (5) as a well-formed string of English. Rather, we would view it as some kind of extension of the language: a play on words, in a sense discussed at some length by Zwicky and Pullum (1987) with respect to derogatory *schm* (*bagels, schmagels*), borrowed from Yiddish into English. Be that as it may, it seems that anyone who accepts (5) as a *bona fide* sentence of English, also accepts sentences like (8):

(8)   I've been reading about subjacency, abjacency etc. In short, a wide range of [pauses] jacencies. Now you tell me: What kind of jacency have *you* been reading about?

But this expresses a non-reprise query. The fact that (8) explicitly concerns a class of concepts sharing some morphological property is merely a consequence of its punful nature.

We will see below that as far as semantics is concerned, reprise uses exploit the same basic mechanisms as other interrogative contents. A similar point applies to their syntax: many of the syntactic constraints on dislocation of interrogative phrases also apply to reprise uses. Forms violating these constraints cannot be used independently, nor can they be used to reprise. The converse point—that many (if not all) interrogative forms that can be used to reprise can also perform independent, non-reprise functions—will be established in section 7.3 below.

Comorowski (1989) has shown that in Romanian, reprise uses obey constraints on dislocation such as the Coordinate Structure Constraint, the CNPC, and the Unit-Movement Constraint. Moreover, she points out that similar facts hold for English—a 'fronted' *wh*-question that is used to reprise still must obey constraints on extraction:[4]

(9) a. *WHAT$_i$ does the rumor that they might have bought __$_i$ intrigue you? (CNPC/Subject Condition)

     b. *WHO$_i$ do you like Dominique and __$_i$? (Coordinate Structure Constraint)

     c. *WHAT$_i$ did they find a __$_i$? (Unit Movement Constraint)

Putting all this together, Comorowski concludes, persuasively we think, that there is no reason to assume that *wh*-phrases that are used to reprise are intrinsically different *qua* syntactic expressions from *wh*-phrases used otherwise. Nor do they involve a fundamentally distinct scoping mechanism. We will point out further syntactic constraints on reprise uses below.

7.2 The Semantics of Reprise Uses

We view reprising as a subspecies of the clarification acts available to a dialogue participant during the *grounding process* of an utterance (cf. Clark and Schaefer 1989, Traum 1994, Clark 1996). Our analysis of such cases is based on the analysis of utterance interaction developed in Ginzburg 1998, Ginzburg 2001, and Cooper and Ginzburg in preparation, some further discussion of which is provided in Chapter 8. Simplifying somewhat, the basic idea can be described as

---

[4]Similarly, it seems that forms violating the '*wh*-island condition' are only marginally possible reprises:

(i) A: Who broke the Nasazaki?

    B: ??WHAT did you ask who broke?

follows: comprehension of an utterance u involves instantiating the contextual indices $c_1, \ldots, c_n$ of the meaning of u in a way which is compatible with the current context c. If a conversationalist believes she is able to correctly instantiate the meaning, she grounds the utterance, prototypically by providing a response of a type appropriate to the original utterance (an acceptance to an assertion, information about the question asked for a query etc.). Otherwise, utilizing the partial information she possesses about the context, she coerces the content into a clarification question using one of a number of available coercion mechanisms, which we illustrate below.

Ginzburg (1996a) points out that given any utterance u_0 made by speaker A, speaker B has the option of attempting to clarify some aspect of u_0 by repeating (or paraphrasing) any constituent of u_0:[5]

(10) A: Merle attacked Brendan yesterday.
      B: Merle attacked Brendan yesterday?/attacked Brendan?
      B': Merle?/Attacked?/Brendan?/Yesterday?

Let us call such utterances *literal* reprises. When used to clarify the content, the reprising utterance gets a content distinct from what it expresses in a nonreprise use—essentially, the repriser attempts to confirm whether the speaker of the reprised utterance intended to convey a particular content.[6]

While a common cause for clarification acts is the fact that the previous utterance was misheard, there are many other causes ranging from the inability to resolve reference to astonishment, a point which carries over directly to reprise queries. Probably the most obvious reason for the belief that echo uses are metalinguistic is the belief, erroneous as we shall see in section 7.3, that in a *wh*-fronting language like English, a unary *wh*-sentence in which the *wh*-phrase is in situ *cannot* be used to make an 'information query'. We will demonstrate, however, that reprise uses of an interrogative sentence involve semantic objects—questions—of the same semantic type as utilized in independent and functional interrogative uses.

An important set of data for our claim is that reprise sentences can be paraphrased by independent uses of entirely 'normal' fronted interrogative sentences:[7]

(11) a. You like WHO?
      b. Who did you say (just now) that you like?

(12) a. [Go home, Bo!] Go WHERE?
      b. Where did you order me (just now) to go?

(13) a. Who likes WHICH MOVIE?
      b. (?)Which movie did you (just now) ask me who likes?

---

[5]Things are somewhat more subtle because of the effects of indexicality:
(i) A: I_j was annoyed.
     B: #I_j?/ You$_j$?
Such possibilities depend, it seems, on the reprised constituent not changing its content across utterances.

[6]Such utterances have an additional type of use in which the repriser indicates that (s)he has not managed to resolve the content of the particular constituent. In (10B'), for example, the speaker may be trying to resolve who 'Merle' refers to, what the speaker means by 'attack', etc. See Chapter 8 for more discussion of such utterances.

[7]The reprise in (13b) involves a violation of the *wh*-island constraint. As Elisabet Engdahl (p.c.) informs us, analogous sentences in Swedish are fully acceptable. For instance:
(i) Vad var det du undrade vem som gillade?
     What was it you wondered who that liked
     What$_i$ was it you wondered who liked i

Similarly, reprise uses can be reported by embedding an interrogative under *ask*, just like other queries:

(14) a. Tracy: You like WHO?

  b. Tracy was amazed at what I told her, so she asked me who it was that I had said I liked.

(15) a. [Go home Terry!] Go WHERE?

  b. Terry couldn't believe his ears, and asked, utterly incredulously, where I had ordered him to go to.

Thus, the only difference between a literal reprise and a reprise use of an interrogative is that in the latter case one or more of the constituents of the previous content is not reprised,[8] but rather 'replaced' as a consequence of associating that argument role with an interrogative phrase:[9]

(16) a. Prior Utterance: Chris is annoyed with Jan.

  b. Interrogative Reprise: Chris is annoyed with WHO(M)?

  c. Paraphrase of Reprise: Who did you—the previous speaker—assert/say that Chris is annoyed with?

  d. Content of Reprise:

$$
\begin{bmatrix}
question \\
\text{PARAMS} \quad \left\{ \begin{bmatrix} \text{INDEX} & k \\ \text{RESTR} & \{person(k)\} \end{bmatrix} \right\} \\
\text{PROP} \begin{bmatrix} \text{SIT} & s_1 \\ \text{SOA} \begin{bmatrix} \text{QUANTS} \langle \rangle \\ \text{NUCL} \begin{bmatrix} assert\text{-}rel \\ \text{UTTERER} & prev\text{-}spkr \\ \text{MSG-ARG} \begin{bmatrix} proposition \\ \text{SIT} & s_2 \\ \text{SOA} \begin{bmatrix} \text{QUANTS} \langle \rangle \\ \text{NUCL} \begin{bmatrix} annoy\text{-}rel \\ \text{ANNOYED} & j \\ \text{ANNOYANCE} & k \end{bmatrix} \end{bmatrix} \end{bmatrix} \end{bmatrix} \end{bmatrix} \\
\text{BCKGRND} \quad \{named(j,Chris)\}
\end{bmatrix}
$$

---

[8] Or replaced with a coreferential expression.

[9] Here we use *prev-spkr* as a shorthand to identify the speaker of the immediately previous utterance in the conversational context.

Contrary to claims by Authier (1993), reprises *can* also occur multiply, as exemplified in (17). This is accommodated in analogous fashion to independent (non-functional) uses, where neither of two interrogative parameters outscopes the other (see the discussion of *which*-phrases in section 4.3.3 of Chapter 4):

(17) a. Pat gave WHAT to WHOM?

  b.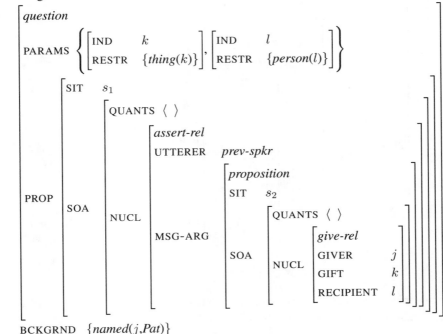

More generally, our theory of reprise questions involves assigning them a content whose type is *question* and whose PROP value is based on the conversational move (or illocutionary) type of the immediately prior utterance in the dialogue, i.e. whether a *proposition* was asserted, a *question* was asked, an *outcome* was ordered and so forth.

To see this, consider what happens when the immediately prior utterance is nondeclarative. This has consequences for the form and content of a subsequent reprise. For example, after an interrogative utterance like (18a), an appropriate reprise would take the form of an interrogative clause like (18b), not a declarative clause like (18c).

(18) a. Who likes barack pálinka?

  b. Who likes WHAT?

  c. #You like WHAT?

Here we have what has been called (by Karttunen 1977) a 'second order' question. On our account, nothing additional has to be said for such contents beyond the usual issues concerning the embedding of interrogative content: since the previous speaker's utterance expressed a question, the MSG-ARG of the subsequent reprise question must be of type *question*. The reprise can be paraphrased by the *wh*-island violating sentence:

(19) ?What (kind of liquor) did you (just now) ask who liked?

The semantic content of (18b) then is the following:

(20)
$$
\begin{bmatrix}
question \\
\text{PARAMS} \quad \left\{ \begin{bmatrix} \text{IND} & k \\ \text{RESTR} & \{thing(k)\} \end{bmatrix} \right\} \\
\text{PROP} \quad \begin{bmatrix}
\text{SIT} & s_1 \\
\text{SOA} & \begin{bmatrix}
\text{QUANTS} \ \langle \ \rangle \\
\text{NUCL} \begin{bmatrix}
ask\text{-}rel \\
\text{UTTERER} & prev\text{-}spkr \\
\text{MSG-ARG} & \begin{bmatrix}
question \\
\text{PARAMS} \left\{ \begin{bmatrix} \text{IND} & j \\ \text{RESTR} & \{person(j)\} \end{bmatrix} \right\} \\
\text{PROP} \begin{bmatrix}
\text{SIT} & s_2 \\
\text{SOA} \begin{bmatrix}
\text{QUANTS} \ \langle \ \rangle \\
\text{NUCL} \begin{bmatrix} like\text{-}rel \\ \text{LIKER} & j \\ \text{LIKED} & k \end{bmatrix}
\end{bmatrix}
\end{bmatrix}
\end{bmatrix}
\end{bmatrix}
\end{bmatrix}
\end{bmatrix}
\end{bmatrix}
$$

Note that this is decidedly different from the content assigned to *Who likes what?* as an instance of the type *su-wh-int-cl* (see section 6.6 of Chap. 6):

(21)
$$
\begin{bmatrix}
question \\
\text{PARAMS} \quad \left\{ \begin{bmatrix} \text{IND} & j \\ \text{RESTR} & \{person(j)\} \end{bmatrix}, \begin{bmatrix} \text{IND} & k \\ \text{RESTR} & \{thing(k)\} \end{bmatrix} \right\} \\
\text{PROP} \quad \begin{bmatrix}
\text{SIT} & s_2 \\
\text{SOA} \begin{bmatrix}
\text{QUANTS} \ \langle \ \rangle \\
\text{NUCL} \begin{bmatrix} like\text{-}rel \\ \text{LIKER} & j \\ \text{LIKED} & k \end{bmatrix}
\end{bmatrix}
\end{bmatrix}
\end{bmatrix}
$$

Similarly, a reprise of an imperative must in general be in the form of an imperative:[10]

(22) a. Try the gulab jamun!
      b. Try the WHAT?
      c. #Will I try the WHAT?
      d. #I will try the WHAT?

Here the semantic content of the reprise utterance is as follows:

(23)
$$
\begin{bmatrix}
\textit{question} \\[2pt]
\text{PARAMS} \quad \left\{ \begin{bmatrix} \text{IND} & k \\ \text{RESTR} & \{\textit{thing}(k)\} \end{bmatrix} \right\} \\[12pt]
\text{PROP} \quad
\begin{bmatrix}
\text{SIT} & s_1 \\[6pt]
\text{SOA} &
\begin{bmatrix}
\text{QUANTS} & \langle \; \rangle \\[6pt]
\text{NUCL} &
\begin{bmatrix}
\textit{order-rel} \\
\text{UTTERER} & \textit{prev-spkr} \\[6pt]
\text{MSG-ARG} &
\begin{bmatrix}
\textit{outcome} \\
\text{SIT} & s_2 \\[6pt]
\text{SOA} & \begin{bmatrix} \text{NUCL} & \begin{bmatrix} \textit{try-rel} \\ \text{TRIER} & j \\ \text{TRIED} & k \end{bmatrix} \end{bmatrix}
\end{bmatrix}
\end{bmatrix}
\end{bmatrix}
\end{bmatrix}
\end{bmatrix}
$$

The fact that the *illocutionary force* or *conversational move type* (CMT) of an utterance is involved in the CONTENT of a reprise utterance might at first glance seem surprising. However, once one explicitly considers the nature of utterance content in conversation, we claim that this is an entirely natural consequence. In order to see this, we need to clarify certain aspects of the notion of utterance content we are assuming. Our discussion here, for obvious reasons of space, is brief; a detailed discussion of the relevant issues can be found in Ginzburg 1998, 2001. Although categorizing utterances in terms of a notion of illocutionary force or conversational move type is common in corpus-based work (for some recently proposed CMT taxonomies, see Carletta et al. 1996, Core and Allen 1997), there exist few attempts to integrate such notions into formal semantic work. In part, this is due to the fact that most previous work has concentrated on monologue or text, where this issue is less pressing than in conversational settings.

A more principled reason for this lacuna is perhaps the phenomenon of *multifunctionality*: it is often the case that a given utterance serves more than one purpose—an assertion can function also as an offer, a query as a suggestion etc. Multifunctionality is certainly one of the most fundamental characteristics of natural language as a communicative interaction system. Recognition

---

[10]But not always, as examples like (i) show.

(i) A: Try the gulab jamun!
     B: I should try WHAT?

This possibility presumably exists because of the close connection between outcomes and propositions whose main relation is that of the deontic modal *should*.

of its existence, particularly in light of Grice's work, has often led to the feeling that issues pertaining to CMT belong entirely to the realm of pragmatics. We think this is the wrong conclusion to draw, for reasons having partly to do with the phenomenon of 'pragmatic intrusion'—the use of pragmatic reasoning to resolve the value of a constituent of content—also affects constituents of content (e.g. tense and anaphora) that belong squarely within the realm of semantics.[11]

Consider first Stina's utterance of (24a) outside a West End theater currently showing a best selling musical:

(24) a. Stina: I have a ticket for tonight's performance.

   b. Stina's claim: she has a ticket for tonight's performance.

   c. Stina's offer: to sell a ticket for tonight's performance

In uttering (24a), Stina seems to be doing two things: making a claim and putting forward an offer. Is the utterance an assertion or an offer? Clearly, in some sense it is both. But if it's both—so goes the worry— then what is *the* illocutionary relation to be used in describing the conventional import of Stina's utterance? Interestingly, as suggested to us by Rich Thomason, it is reprise utterances that provide a probe allowing one to filter the indirect force of an utterance.[12] A reprise utterance of (24a) can be understood as a clarification of the assertion, as in (25b). It cannot be understood as a clarification of the offer, as in (25c,d):[13]

(25) a. Stina: I have a ticket for tonight's performance.
        Belula: You have a ticket for tonight's performance?

   b. Are you claiming that you have a ticket for tonight's performance?

   c. Are you offering me a ticket?

   d. Are you asking if I want to buy it?

This test suggests (not unintuitively) that the assertion and the offer actually have a quite distinct status as contents of the utterance. It upholds the primacy of the assertion as the direct, literal content of the utterance. The test yields similar results with a related example of complex import—(26), originally pointed out by Sperber and Wilson (1986):

(26) 1 Shi: Do you want me to make some coffee?

   2 Alanis: Coffee would keep me awake.

   3 Shi: Coffee would keep you awake?

   4 Alanis: Yes

(27) a. I want/don't want coffee.

   b. Are you claiming that coffee would keep you awake?

   c. Are you saying that you want/don't want coffee?

   d. I'm claiming that coffee would keep me awake.

Alanis' utterance (26[2]) can be understood to convey (27a); whether it is resolved positively or not depends on various additional factors (e.g. Is Alanis in the middle of a night shift or about to leave an extended dinner party?). However, Shi's reprise—(26[3])—merely requests

---

[11]Compare Sperber and Wilson's (1986) concept of 'explicature'. See also Levinson 2000.

[12]Thomason made this suggestion to us at an oral presentation of Ginzburg and Sag 1999.

[13]We assume the verbs *claim*, *say*, and *assert* are close paraphrases of each other, with the former somewhat more natural in ordinary discourse.

clarification of the claim Alanis made; it can be understood solely as (27b), not as (27c). This can be further demonstrated by noting that *yes* in (26[4]) conveys (27d) in this context.[14]

These data provide at least some justification for our assumption that utterances have a well-defined direct CMT or illocutionary force. It is important to emphasize that this is entirely consonant with an essentially Gricean view of communicative interaction, which explicates utterance multifunctionality by assuming conversationalists reason about the plans their interlocuters intend to perform as a consequence of their having performed a given conversational move. Moreover, it is also consistent with a version of this view that does not assume that recognition of the direct conversational move is *prior* to plan recognition, but rather allows for these to take place in parallel. (For such a view see Ginzburg 1998, 2001.)

The simplest way to implement our assumption concerning the direct CMT/force of an utterance is to assume a 1–1 relationship between what we have been calling the CONTENT of a sign, i.e. entities of type *message* (*proposition, question, outcome, fact, . . .*) and CMTs: propositions are associated with the CMT of asserting, questions with asking, outcomes with ordering, and facts with exclaiming. Arguably, such a relationship between message types and CMTs constitutes something like a default. But each of the afore-mentioned subtypes of *message* clearly does have other uses: questions can be used 'rhetorically', outcomes can be suggested and so on. Thus, an adequate view of utterance content needs to allow the CMT associated with a given message-type to be underspecified. For our current purposes, we will maintain the more simplistic view, mentioned in the beginning of this paragraph. Concretely, we posit a type *illoc(utionary)-rel* as the immediate supertype of the four relations mentioned above:[15]

(28)

Each of these types introduces its own constraint on the type of its MSG-ARG value:

(29) a. *assert-rel* ⇒ [MSG-ARG *proposition*]

   b. *ask-rel* ⇒ [MSG-ARG *question*]

   c. *order-rel* ⇒ [MSG-ARG *outcome*]

   d. *exclaim-rel* ⇒ [MSG-ARG *fact*]

---

[14] Our discussion of these data is of necessity all too brief. As we discuss further in Chapter 8, literal reprises have a number of distinct types of readings. One such reading, discussed in footnote 22, involves a request for reformulation of the import of the reprised (sub)-utterance. Thus, for a referential NP utterance, as in (i), this will be understood as a request for reference resolution:

   (i) Andie: Did Jo leave?
   Bo: Jo?
   Andie: Your cousin.

Given this, reprises such as (26[3]) will also yield readings paraphrasable as (ii), where the inferred component of content is *not* necessarily filtered away:

   (ii) Shi: What do you mean by saying *Coffee would keep you awake*?

However, *yes* would be an inappropriate response to this reading of the literal reprise. We wish to thank Annabel Cormack and Dick Hudson for discussion of (26).

[15] Of course this view is also simplistic in that it fails to recognize CMTs such as greeting—a necessary component for explicating the meaning of a word like *hi*, thanking—a necessary component for explicating the meaning of a word like *thanks*, calling—a necessary component for explicating the meanings of utterance-types like *Kim!* and so on. Nothing in the proposed set-up hinders adopting the requisite richer ontology of CMTs.

The final ingredient we need is a constraint that determines the appropriate CONTENT value for utterances, i.e. for root clauses. We propose that the content of every root clause be a proposition whose SOA value is of type *illoc-rel*. This proposition represents the belief an agent forms about the (full, direct illocutionary) content of an utterance. More specifically, this is the content a speaker will assign to her utterance, as will an addressee in case communication is successful. Given (29), this will mean that a root clause will be resolved so as to have as its content a proposition whose SOA value is of one of the subtypes of *illoc-rel*.

This move superficially resembles a group of proposals made in the early 1970s, which came to be known as the *Performative Hypothesis* (PH).[16] Although there are a variety of versions of the PH, they essentially boil down to positing that all (English) matrix sentences have the form *I illoc-verb S*, where *I* is the first person singular pronoun and *illoc-verb* is a verb from the class of performative verbs (e.g. *assert*, *ask*, *order*, *bet*, . . .). For all matrix sentences which do not have this form overtly, the PH involves the assumption that the 'illocutionary prefix' *I illoc-verb* is not realized at the surface but is represented at some other syntactic level. In its formulations in the 1970s, at least, the PH ran into a variety of problems, the most serious of which revolved around the difficulty of maintaining a coherent definition of truth for declaratives. The difficulty arises from the parallelism that the PH enforces between sentences that lack an overt illocutionary prefix (e.g. (30a) and explicit performatives (e.g. (30b):

(30) a. Snow is black.

      b. I claim that snow is black.

Such a parallelism is untenable because it either conflates the truth conditions of quite contingent sentences such as (30a) with those of (30b), which, essentially, become true once they are uttered. Alternatively, the parallelism involves somehow filtering away the semantic effect of the illocutionary prefix. We will not enter here into discussion of the potential for reviving the PH in light of the insights of more recent approaches to grammar. We simply point out that our own proposal is not susceptible to problems such as this, since we will not be making any claims that the requisite information about CMT is *syntactically* represented. Thus, as we now demonstrate, the way in which CMT information enters into the content of a sign does not affect the assignment of (non-illocutionary) content.

In order to ensure that root clauses have contents in which CMT information is represented, we revise the treatment of *root* given in Chapter 2. There we presented *root* as a distinguished type of *sign* that was compatible with only certain construction types. Now we replace the type *root* with a binary feature ROOT and propose a constructional treatment of root utterances in terms of a *hd-only-ph* that embeds message-denoting sentences as arguments of an *illoc-rel*. The constraints idiosyncratic to this construction are illustrated in (31):

---

[16]For a detailed review of this literature see Levinson 1983: 247–263.

(31)   *root-cl*:

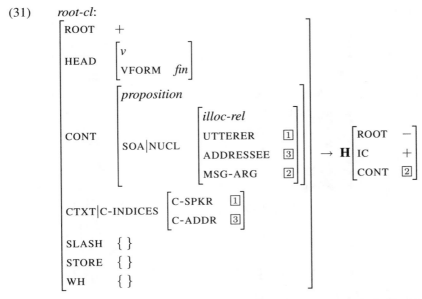

Note that the arguments of the *illoc-rel* are identified with the appropriate individuals in the context of utterance. In addition, we now distinguish root clauses from other independent clauses in terms of positive versus negative specifications for the feature ROOT.[17]

Let us illustrate the effects of the constraint in (31). (32a) has an analysis as a *decl-hd-su-cl* in which it expresses the proposition in (32b):

(32)   a. Jo saw Bo.

b.

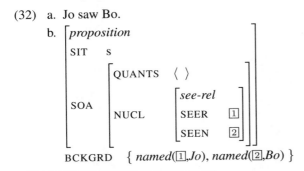

---

[17] On this view, signs are [ROOT −] by default. Since this is the case, we will suppress [ROOT −] specifications on all phrases other than instances of the type *root-cl*.

c.
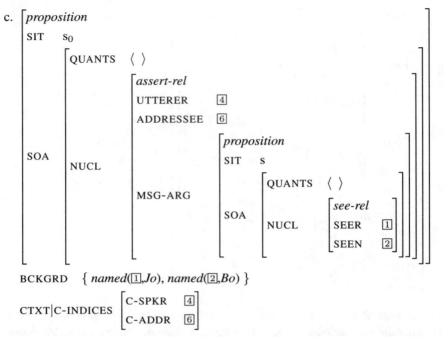

Therefore, given (29) and (31), the content such a clause gets as a root utterance (ignoring tense) is as in (32c).

Similarly, (33a) has an analysis as a *pol-int-cl* in which it expresses the question in (33b).

(33)   a. A: Did Jo leave?

b.
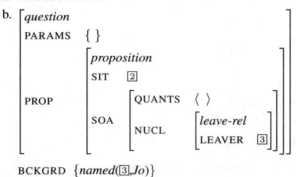

c.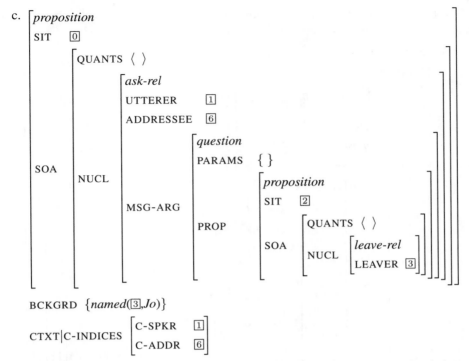

$$
\begin{bmatrix}
\textit{proposition} \\
\text{SIT} \quad \boxed{0} \\
\text{SOA} \begin{bmatrix}
\text{QUANTS} \ \langle \ \rangle \\
\text{NUCL} \begin{bmatrix}
\begin{bmatrix}
\textit{ask-rel} \\
\text{UTTERER} \quad \boxed{1} \\
\text{ADDRESSEE} \quad \boxed{6}
\end{bmatrix} \\
\text{MSG-ARG} \begin{bmatrix}
\textit{question} \\
\text{PARAMS} \ \{ \ \} \\
\text{PROP} \begin{bmatrix}
\textit{proposition} \\
\text{SIT} \quad \boxed{2} \\
\text{SOA} \begin{bmatrix}
\text{QUANTS} \ \langle \ \rangle \\
\text{NUCL} \begin{bmatrix}
\textit{leave-rel} \\
\text{LEAVER} \quad \boxed{3}
\end{bmatrix}
\end{bmatrix}
\end{bmatrix}
\end{bmatrix}
\end{bmatrix}
\end{bmatrix} \\
\text{BCKGRD} \ \{\textit{named}(\boxed{3}, \textit{Jo})\} \\
\text{CTXT|C-INDICES} \begin{bmatrix}
\text{C-SPKR} \quad \boxed{1} \\
\text{C-ADDR} \quad \boxed{6}
\end{bmatrix}
\end{bmatrix}
$$

Therefore, given (29) and (31), the content such a clause gets as a root utterance (again ignoring tense) is (33c). Let us see how such utterances can lead to the emergence of a reprise utterance.

Faced with an utterance of a declarative example like (32), an addressee will respond with a reprise utterance precisely when some aspect of the content of that utterance is unclear. This discrepancy between what was said and what was understood is of course the basic motivation for reprising. Thus our theory of reprising must somehow distinguish the content the speaker would assign to the declarative utterance from the (partial) understanding of it that forms the propositional basis of the reprise question. We do not offer a complete theory here of the nature of such discrepancies,[18] but the constraints that we formulate in terms of the shorthand *perc(eived)-cont(ent)* will interact with other aspects of our theory so as to derive many correct predictions about the nature of reprise utterances.

---

[18] See Chapter 8 for further discussion of related issues; see Ginzburg 2001 and Cooper and Ginzburg in preparation for an explicit account.

Consider first (34a). When this is used to reprise (32a), it has a semantic content—(34b)—containing a proposition that is essentially identical to the root content in (32c).

(34) a. Jo saw WHO?

b.

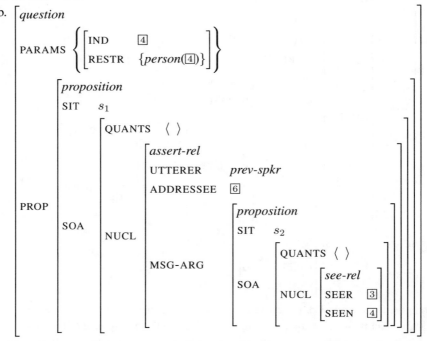

$$\text{BCKGRD} \quad \{named(\boxed{3},Jo)\}$$

Here the proposition within the question must be built up from the components of the reprising utterance, yet it must be compatible with the prior utterance. This is why in general examples like (35) cannot be used to reprise (32a).

(35) a. We saw WHO?

b. Jo likes WHO?

Certain discrepancies are possible, however. For example, in examples like (36), the reprised utterance contains quantification that must be excluded from the proposition within the reprise question:

(36) A: Jo saw absolutely every shaman priest from East Anglia.

B: Jo saw WHO?

That is, we may assume that here B has only understood part of the content of A's utterance and is requesting clarification of the rest via reprising. The content of B's utterance is again (34b), where the proposition inside the question contains no quantification of the kind present in the content of (36a).

And a different partial understanding can give lead to a different reprise, as illustrated in (37):

(37) A: Jo saw absolutely every shaman priest from East Anglia.

B: Jo saw absolutely every shaman priest from WHERE?

Here the proposition within the reprise content must contain the quantification from the content of the prior content. Our analysis will deal with dependencies of the kinds just illustrated in terms of the dyadic predicate *perc-cont*, whose first argument is an utterance and whose second argument is a message reflecting a partial understanding of that utterance.

The general characterization of the content of a *wh*-interrogative sentence S used by a to reprise an utterance S_0 can be described simply as follows:

(38) a. The content of S is a *wh*-question with certain parameters in its PARAMS set.

b. The PROP value of the question is identical to the content value of S_0, as perceived by a.

These desiderata are ensured on our analysis by positing a new construction type—*in-situ-interrogative-clause* (*is-int-cl*)—with a subtype *reprise-interrogative-clause* (*repr-int-cl*). The type *is-int-cl*—a subtype of both *hd-only-ph* and *inter-cl*—is constrained as follows:

(39) *is-int-cl*:

$$\left[\text{CAT} \begin{bmatrix} \text{IC} & + \\ \text{SUBJ} & \langle \, \rangle \\ \text{VFORM} & \textit{fin} \end{bmatrix} \right] \rightarrow \mathbf{H}[\ ]$$

The specification [IC +] in (39) ensures that an in-situ interrogative, including those used to ask reprise questions, cannot function as an embedded interrogative clause. This accounts for the impossibility of examples like the following:

(40) a. *We wondered [Dana saw what]. (cf. We wondered [who Dana saw].)

b. *[Sandy visited who] wasn't clear. (cf. [Who Sandy visited] wasn't clear.)

There is no deep explanation offered here for why in-situ questions cannot be embedded. The construction is simply classified with other 'main clause phenomena'—those constructions that are specified as [IC +]. Our account thus correctly leads us to expect to find languages where in-situ *wh*-interrogatives are embeddable.

In fact, we might even expect to find a language where the 'fronted'/in-situ pattern is reversed. Mandarin is a candidate for just such a language. In Mandarin, interrogative words in direct questions are in situ, as in (41).

(41) Women yao kan duoshao   shu
      we   must read how-many book
      How many books do we have to read?

However, the interrogative word can appear in fronted position in reprise questions:[19]

(42) Duoshao shu women yao kan?
      how-many book we   must read
      We have to read HOW MANY books? (*echo/incredulity*)
      (Yeah, but) HOW many books do we have to read? (*reference-resolving*)

There is thus probably good reason not to design a syntactic theory that seeks to derive from 'deep' principles that fact that English fronting is the norm in direct questions, but not in reprises.

---

[19]Thanks to Carl Pollard for providing these examples.

One might consider adding a [STORE { }] specification to the constraint in (39), which would guarantee that all the stored parameters within an in-situ clause are retrieved.[20] But in fact we will not impose any such condition specific to this type, leaving the [STORE { }] condition to follow from independent constraints that must apply to root utterances in general (see (31) above). By not imposing any such constraint that is particular to this type, we leave open the possibility that non-reprise in-situ *wh*-interrogatives can be reprised, i.e. that a question whose STORE is not empty may be embedded in a reprise construction. We return to this matter in section 7.3 below.

Reprise *wh*-interrogatives are instances of a type *repr-int-cl*. This subtype of *is-wh-cl* is associated with the reprising semantics:

(43)   *repr-int-cl*:

$$\begin{bmatrix} \text{CONT} & \begin{bmatrix} \text{PROP} & \boxed{1}\begin{bmatrix} \text{SOA}|\text{NUCL}|\text{MSG-ARG} & \boxed{2} \end{bmatrix} \end{bmatrix} \\ \text{BCKGRND} & \{ \textit{prev-utt}(\boxed{0}), \textit{perc-cont}(\boxed{0},\boxed{1}) \} \uplus \boxed{\Sigma} \end{bmatrix} \rightarrow \text{H} \begin{bmatrix} \text{CONT} & \boxed{2} \\ \text{BCKGRND} & \boxed{\Sigma} \\ \text{SLASH} & \{ \} \end{bmatrix}$$

The interpretation of reprise questions is thus built from the interpretations that our grammar assigns to various types of clause, with the highest level of the semantics (the outermost question) embedding the content of the clause as the appropriate MESSAGE-ARGUMENT. No further constraints need be placed on this type directly. Rather, because of its place in the hierarchy of construction types, constraint inheritance will ensure that instances of this maximal type must satisfy all the following constraints:

(44)   ECC & GHFP & *hd-only-ph* & *core-cl* & *inter-cl* & IRC & *is-int-cl* & *repr-int-cl*:

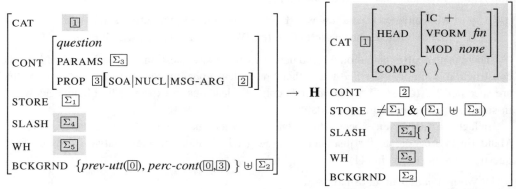

In fact, because this kind of interrogative is always embedded as a daughter of a *root-cl*, whose STORE must be empty, it follows from the GHFP that the $\boxed{\Sigma_1}$ in (44) will always be the empty set. Note further that we can deduce that instances of this type of phrase are also [SUBJ ⟨ ⟩]. Since *repr-int-cl* is also a subtype of *clause*, its SUBJ value (of both daughter and mother, linked by the GHFP) must be either empty or else a list containing an element of type *noncan-ss*, according to the Clause Constraint presented earlier (Chapter 2, example (94)). The only two subtypes of *noncan-ss* are *gap-ss* and *pro-ss*, as explained in Chapter 2. But since a root clause must also be [SLASH { }], according to the constraint in (31) above, this means that the SUBJ element cannot be a *gap-ss*, whose nonempty SLASH specification would be amalgamated by the verb and inherited by both the daughter and mother in (44) (see the discussion in Chapter 5). This leaves *pro-ss*

---

[20]Note that nothing more would then need to be said about the retrieval of parameters, as the IRC (but not the FIC) applies to the supertype *inter-cl*.

as the only possible SUBJ member in (44). However, *pro-ss* is specified as [CASE *acc*], and hence it cannot be the unexpressed subject of a finite clause whose verbal head selects a nominative subject. Therefore it follows that the SUBJ value of all reprise interrogative clauses is the empty list.[21]

So a typical example of a reprise-*wh* question whose basic structure (the head daughter, on our analysis) is a declarative clause is the following:

(45)

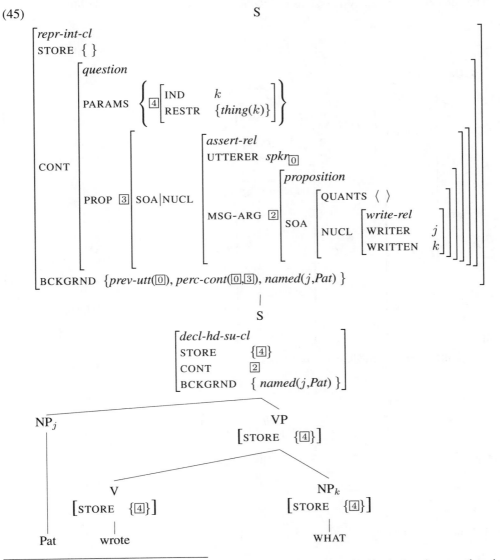

---

[21] This appears to be a wrong prediction, as there are impeccable examples of subjectless reprises, e.g. those in (i) and (ii):

   (i) Went where?

   (ii) Did what?

However, we believe these examples are best analyzed as fragments, that is, elliptical phrases. We will sketch the basics of such an analysis in the next chapter.

The constraint in (43) guarantees that the proposition within the reprise question reflects the speaker's perception of the content of the previous utterance. In addition, note that the previous utterance identified the utterer of the *assert-rel* with the speaker of the previous utterance (this is ensured by the constraint in (31) on the type *root-cl*). Hence, the utterer of the *assert-rel* in the content of the reprise must also be that individual, indicated as $spkr_{[0]}$ in (45).

The content that our analysis assigns to *Who wrote* WHAT? is that shown in (46).

(46)

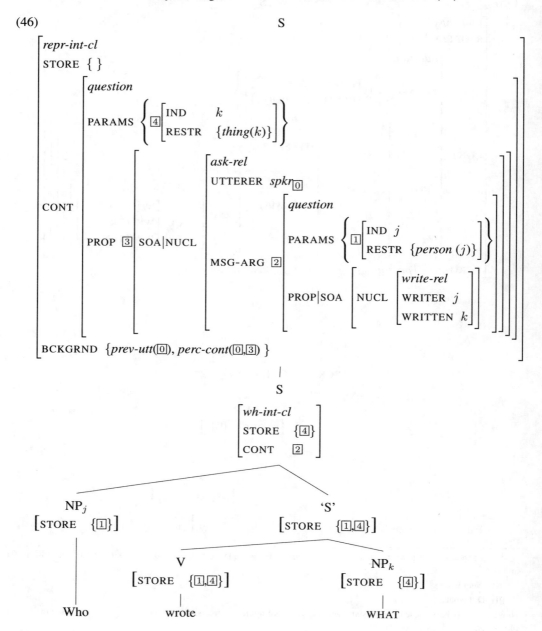

Similar content is produced for other types of reprise. However, note in particular that the reprising phrase in this kind of reprise cannot normally be the first *wh*-expression. This follows because the grammar of *wh*-extraction interrogatives (in particular, the FIC) requires that the WH value be included in the PARAMS value of the interrogative clause (the head daughter of the reprise clause). Thus the only parameter that can remain in STORE in a reprise question like (46) is one that appears elsewhere, i.e. later in the clause. This provides a straightforward account of the oddity of reprises like the following:

(47)   WHO wrote what?

Such examples are not completely excluded, however, as pointed out to us by Adam Przepiórkowski. When the previous utterance is an in-situ non-reprise question, as in (48B), it may be reprised by a question like (47):

(48) A: All these people are writers, you know.

      B: Yeah? And Szczypiorski wrote what?

      A: WHO wrote what?

The possibility of this kind of reprise (and the fact that it is restricted to precisely this kind of context) follows directly from the interaction of our reprise analysis and the treatment of non-reprise in-situ questions presented in the next section.

Our account also allows similar structures for reprise questions that do not exhibit superiority effects. A typical contrast is the following:

(49) a.   *What did whŏ see?

      b.   What did WHO see?

      c.   ?Who is the person that you (just) asked me what they saw?

Example (49a) is ruled out for the reasons discussed the previous chapter—the in-situ *wh*-phrase is [WH { }], which requires that it be accented. Indeed, the reprise in (49b), where the accent on *who* provides the minimal contrast with (49a), is clearly well-formed, though it violates superiority. It is interpreted roughly as the semigrammatical (49c).

This important fact, unaccounted for in all previous theories we are familiar with, follows from the theory we have outlined. Consider the structure in (50).

(50)

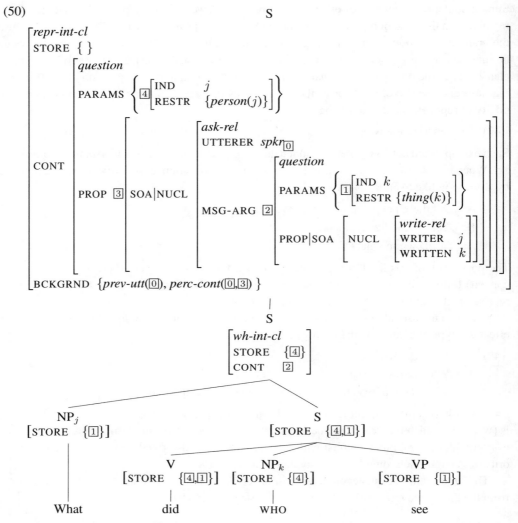

The lexical constraints discussed in Chapter 5 also play a key role in our analysis of reprises. Recall that in a phrase like *whose recipe for what*, for example, only the first *wh*-expression can be WH-specified. Our analysis thus predicts that if a filler phrase (in a *wh*-question) includes two *wh*-expressions, only the second one can be used to reprise, because reprising *wh*-expressions can never be WH-specified (all WH-specified *wh*-phrases function as fillers (or constituents of fillers) in canonical *wh*-clauses (i.e. instances of the type *wh-int-cl*), and hence their parameter is always included in the PARAMS set of a non-reprise question). This is a correct prediction, as examples like the following show:

(51)   a.   #WHOSE recipe for what were they impressed by?
       b.   #You wonder WHOSE recipe for what they were impressed by?
       c.   You wonder whose recipe for WHAT they were impressed by?
       d.   Whose recipe for WHAT were they impressed by?

In examples like (51c,d) the filler's STORE contains a parameter other than the filler's WH value. This parameter is amalgamated into the STORE value of the verb *impressed*, passed up the tree in accordance with the GHFP, and retrieved at the level of the *repr-int-cl*. Hence, examples like these are analyzed in exactly the same way as (46).

Two points about the analysis we have just presented should be emphasized: on the one hand, the descriptive content of a reprise use of an interrogative sentence is a question just like any other interrogative content. On the other hand, the 'wide scope' property associated with reprise uses of interrogative phrases is a direct consequence of the nature of an interrogative reprise, namely that contextual indices of a clausal content get abstracted away. There is absolutely nothing mysterious, then, about why a reprise use of a *wh*-phrase can scope over other, independently used *wh*-phrases.

It should also be noted that our analysis of reprise *wh*-questions immediately allows for what we have called 'literal reprises' (or at least the sentential variety of literal reprises).[22] Because the type *repr-int-cl* is a subtype of *inter-cl*, but not *wh-int-cl*, no constraints (in particular, not the FIC) require the set of retrieved parameters to be nonempty. That is, we allow for reprises like the following, where the reprising content is as indicated:

(52) a. A: Kim is angry.
  B: Kim is angry?!
 b. B asks if A (the previous speaker) asserted/said that Kim is angry.

Our analysis of such an example is as sketched in (53):

(53)

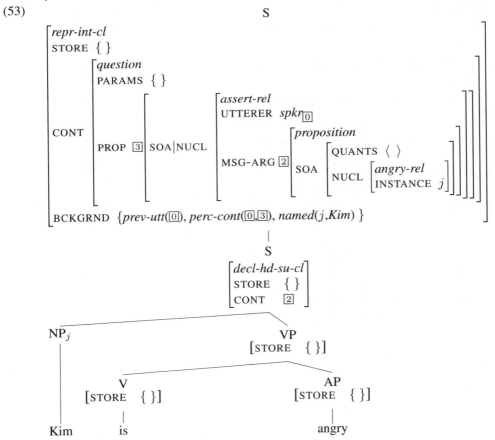

_____
[22] An additional class of (elliptical) literal reprises is analyzed in Chapter 8.

Similarly, we have an account of literal reprises like the following:

(54) a. A: Who left?
          B: Who left?
      b.   Did you (just) ask who left?

(55) a. A: Who saw what?
          B: Who saw what?
      b.   Did you (just) ask who saw what?

And since we treat imperatives as a kind of finite clause (see Chapter 2), our account also extends to cases like the following:

(56) a. A: Leave them alone!
          B: Leave them alone?
      b.   Did you order me to leave them alone?

Such reprises fit into our theory of interrogatives perfectly, as do inverted reprises like (57B).[23]

(57) a. A: Did they talk to Bustamente y Bacigalupo?
          B: Did they talk to WHO?
      b. (?)Who did you (just) ask whether they talked to?

We should also point out that the interrogatives in examples like (58b,c) are not treated as instances of *repr-int-cl* in our analysis, i.e. they are not analyzed grammatically as reprise questions.

(58) a. A: I talked to Bustamente y Bacigalupo.
      b. B: WHO did you talk to?
      c. B: WHO did you say you talked to?

Rather, these are treated as ordinary *wh*-interrogatives—as instances of type *wh-int-cl*. Their echoic character, on our analysis, is intonationally derived. Although this might seem like a

---

[23]Of course a comprehensive theory of reprise utterances presupposes a grammar with exhaustive coverage, an aim which needless to say we do not attain in the current work. Such a grammar would provide analyses of a variety of sentential and non-sentential utterances which allow elliptical exclamations (as in (i) below), greetings (see (ii) below), wishes (e.g. (iii) below), and perhaps even chants (as in (iv) below). With such a grammar in place we hypothesize that our basic approach to reprises would extend to cover the corresponding reprise utterances, all due to Carl Pollard:

  (i) A: What a bove!
       B: What a WHAT? (echo)
  (ii) A: Greetings, fellow hypernychthemerals!
       B: Greetings, fellow WHATs? (echo)
 (iii) A: Oh, that this too solid flesh would melt, thaw, and resolve itself into a dew!
       B: Oh that this too too solid flesh would WHAT? (echo)
 (iv) A: Oo, ee, oo ah ah, ting tang, walla walla bing bang!
       B: Oo, ee, oo ah ah WHAT? (echo)

surprising conclusion, it seems inevitable that some such notion plays a role in a theory of reprise utterances. Consider in particular (58c): the content such an interrogative gets when analyzed as a phrase of type *wh-int-cl* is already a *reprise question*, i.e. one in which the PROP|SOA of the question is an illocutionary relation. If one could somehow modify our constraints to allow an analysis of (58c) as a *repr-int-cl*, this would lead to a content paraphrasable as (59), which is incorrect.

(59)   Who did you say you said you talked to?

The conclusion is that not all utterances that employ a reprise intonation need to be analyzed as instances of the type *repr-int-cl*. This conclusion will be butressed in Chapter 8, where we discuss elliptical reprise utterances, which we show to be analyzable using a phrasal type we motivate for 'short answers'. The situation with (58b) is more complicated, since, in contrast to (58c), its analysis as a *wh-int-cl* does not yield a content which is a reprise question. Indeed, this non-reprise content *does* have a use as a non-reprise utterance, when a question gets reposed for reasons that have nothing to do with clarifying a previous utterance:[24]

(60) B: Who did you talk to?
      A: I talked to Bustamente y Bacigalupo.
      B: No you didn't, you don't know him.
      A: Oh OK, just kidding.
      B: So, WHO did you talk to?

A precise story on how a reprise understanding can also arise for (58b) must await the development of a more explicit theory of intonational meaning.

Finally, we note the existence of examples like the following, again due to Carl Pollard.

(61) A: Hu/Who wrote the most influential Shuihu-zhuan criticism of the early Republican period./?
      B: WHO DOUBLE-YOO AITCH OH (echo) wrote it?

(62) A: Hu/Who wrote the most influential Shuihu-zhuan criticism of the early Republican period./?
      B: HU AITCH YOO (echo) wrote it?

These interesting examples make an important point about context. They would seem to refute what Ginzburg (2001) calls *weak Montagovianism*, a doctrine that most linguistic theories of context subscribe to—namely that only the CONTENT of utterances—*not* their syntactic or phonological properties—contributes information that persists in the context. Our account as it stands cannot accommodate the data in (62), but Cooper and Ginzburg (in preparation) do offer a treatment—based on an HPSG-style representation of signs—that integrates in a single representation information about syntax, phonology, and semantics.

---

[24]The reposed utterance could, but need not involve an additional accent on the auxiliary.

7.3 Non-Reprising In-Situ *Wh*-Interrogatives

Given our discussion in the previous section, where we showed that reprise uses are *bona fide* grammatical entities from a semantic and syntactic point of view, it should be clear that even if in-situ *wh*-sentences such as (1) could only be used to reprise, this would mean that such sentences need to be generated by the grammar. However, we argue—following in the main the arguments first offered by Bolinger (1978)—that the assumption that sentences like (1) have only reprise uses is false.

It is clear that out of the blue an in-situ *wh*-interrogative clause is typically infelicitous. That is, an in-situ *wh*-clause minimally carries a presupposition of a particular kind. Although the nature of this presupposition is difficult to characterize precisely,[25] we believe that the appropriate account of such presuppositions will provide an appropriate pragmatic explanation for the relative rarity of such uses.[26]

Consider (63)–(66):[27]

(63)   a.   A: Well, anyway, I'm leaving.
            B: OK, so you'll be leaving WHEN exactly?
       b.   A: I'm annoyed.
            B: Aha. You're annoyed with WHOM?

(64)   A: My friends, they saw everything.
       B: Yeah, they saw WHAT? [CBS Saturday Night Movie—Jan. 25, 1992]

(65)   A: I'm going to send the sourdough bread to the Southern Bakery, and the croissants to Barringers.
       B: I see, and the bagels you're going to send WHERE?

(66)   Michael Krasny [addressing a guest—WHO HAS NOT SAID ANYTHING YET—about the interim chief of the US Attorney's office]:
       This is a position that is HOW IMPORTANT in your judgment, Rory?
       [Forum KQED—July 29, 1998]

(67)   Lester: I've been working here for 14 years. You've been here for HOW LONG? A month? [from the movie *American Beauty*]

---

[25]The simplest proposal one might consider is that such questions require that another question already be under discussion when they are posed—in terms of the *QUD* component of context discussed in Chapter 8, that QUD be non-empty in a context where such in-situ interrogatives are used.

[26]Various people (see e.g. Vallduví 1992) have proposed that any given utterance-type consists of two components, one of which must be realized, namely the *focus* and the other which is optionally realized, the *ground*. By basic pragmatic principles, in a context where there are two potential utterances u_1 and u_2, whose sole difference is that in u_1 the ground is actually expressed, *ceteris paribus* u_2 will be preferred. This explains, for instance, why 'short-answers' are preferred over their non-elliptical variants.

By the same token, in those contexts which allow non-reprising in-situ *wh*-interrogatives, there usually exists the option of using a form that is *all-focus*, namely a sluice:

(i)   A: I met someone in the office today.
      B: Yeah, WHO?
      B′: Yeah, you met WHO in the office today?

(ii) A: Dana told me that Chris claimed they found something in the office.
      B: Hmm, WHAT?
      B′: Hmm, Dana told you that Chris claimed they found WHAT in the office?

[27]Such examples could be multiplied at will. We thank Emily Bender for (66).

It is evident in all these cases that B has heard and fully understood A's utterance (if there was one at all). On the basis of the information that it provides, B proceeds to query for specific information, in other words, makes an independent use of the *wh*-phrase. These examples *cannot* be analysed as reprise uses. The paraphrase in (68), argued for in section 7.2 as applicable to reprise uses, is clearly not what the above questions mean:

(68) a. When did you say you were leaving?
      b. What did you say your friends saw?
      c. Where did you say you were going to send the Bagels?

(63) might suggest that the factor licensing non-reprising in-situ *wh*-clauses is an overt linguistic expression carrying an existential presupposition of the queried abstract. Examples such as the following cannot be so analyzed, but rather suggest that the factor is more closely related to the salience of the question at hand, i.e. the fact that this question has already been introduced or at least accommodated into the context:

(69) a. [Post-maritally blissful speaker]: We're going to buy a house.
         [Skeptical in-law]: Uh huh. And you're going to pay for it with WHAT?
      b. With what are you going to pay for it?

In (69), due to Bolinger (1978), the first statement establishes the buying of a house as a fact of the discourse situation. This makes the issue of payment for the house fairly accessible for accommodation, and hence licenses the in-situ *wh*-sentence, which appears to carry a different force than the corresponding fronted sentence. Similar remarks apply to the following examples:

(70) a. Mr. Staples says that in a presumably more responsible past film makers changed names or added disclaimers to their productions. And the results were WHAT? [*NY Times*—January 10, 1992]
      b. [Stacy pokes head in office occupied by Jan, who is commonly known to be leaving the area shortly:] Say, Jan, you're leaving WHEN exactly?
      c. [Jan pokes head in office occupied by René. The two have previously committed to a joint activity of unspecified nature the following day:]
         Jan: We're going out tomorrow, right?
         René: I guess so. And we're going to do WHAT exactly?

What we have shown thus far is that non-reprise uses of in-situ *wh*-interrogative clauses are felicitous, subject to certain, not entirely understood, presuppositional factors. From this we conclude that, even ignoring reprise uses, any grammatical principles which *enforce* dislocation of interrogative *wh*-phrases in English are false. And hence our grammar of in-situ *wh*-clauses should involve no such principles.

Our account of non-reprise in-situ *wh*-clauses needs to achieve the two effects sketched in (71) and (72):

(71) It must prevent the clause from functioning as an interrogative clause, unless a WH-specified *wh*-phrase is also present. This is motivated by contrasts such as the following:
      a. Bill assumes (that) Jill met WHO?
      b. *Bill wonders Jill likes WHO.
      c. Bill wonders who exactly knows that Jill met WHO.

(72) It must ensure that an in-situ *wh*-phrase takes as its scope some site where another WH-specified *wh*-phrase appears (in accordance with the analysis of multiple *wh*-questions presented in the last chapter). Alternatively, in the absence of any such phrase, it must be assigned widest scope within a matrix declarative clause:

    a. The bagels, you gave to WHO? (can be used to make a non-reprise query.)

    b. You gave the bagels to WHO? (can be used to make a non-reprise query.)

    c. Who talked to WHO? (can be used to make a non-reprise query.)

    d. Give WHO the book? (can be used *only* to make a reprise query.)

    e. Do I like WHO? (can be used *only* to make a reprise query.)

    f. What a winner WHO is? (can be used *only* to make a reprise query.)

The facts in (72) are particularly interesting from an ontological point of view—they show that questions can only be built from within a proposition-denoting environment. One can not do so from within an outcome-denoting environment (72d)—*a priori* one might expect it to have a reading as a direct question paraphrasable as *who should I give the book to?* if one could simply retrieve a parameter from storage within an 'open outcome' and abstract. Similarly, one cannot build questions from a question-denoting environment (72e), nor from a fact-denoting environment (72f). This provides some interesting support for our view of questions as *propositional* abstracts.

Both this effect and the requirement in (71) are achieved by positing the following clausal type—*direct-in-situ-interrogative-clause* (*dir-is-int-cl*)—as a subtype of *is-int-cl*. This type of interrogative is subject to the following constraint:

(73)   *dir-is-int-cl*:

$$\left[\text{CONT}|\text{PROP}\quad \boxed{1}\right] \;\to\; \mathbf{H}\left[\text{CONT}\quad \boxed{1}\right]$$

Instances of this type are further affected by constraints on the type *is-wh-int-cl*, which requires that the clause be a finite main clause. The superordinate type *inter-cl* allows stored parameters to be retrieved; (73) adds the further constraint that the PROP value of mother and the CONTENT value of the daughter are identified. From this it follows without stipulation that the head daughter must express a proposition. The relevant inherited constraints on this construction are illustrated in (74):[28]

(74)   a. ECC & GHFP & *hd-only-ph* & *core-cl* & *inter-cl* & IRC & *is-int-cl* & *dir-is-int-cl*:

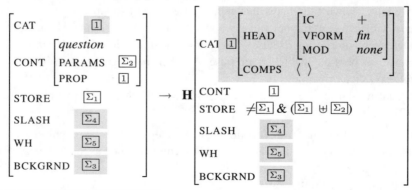

---

[28]Note again that it need not be stipulated in any constructional constraint that the head daughter in (74) must be specified as [SUBJ ⟨ ⟩]. This fact is derived as a theorem by reasoning identical to that outlined in our discussion of (44).

And these constraints give rise to analyses like the following:

(75)

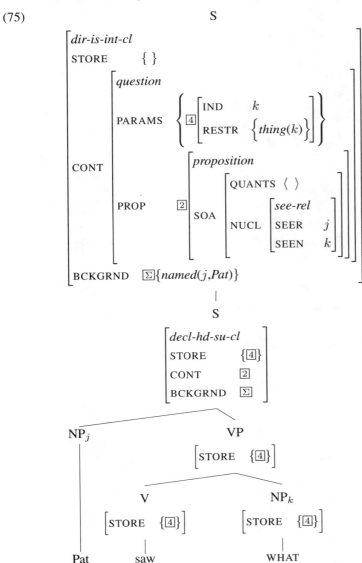

Our analysis thus forces the parameter of a *wh*-phrase to remain in storage as long as the phrase containing it has content of type *proposition*. This will ensure that in (71a) a propositional argument can be formed and embedded under *assume*; a similar effect in (71b) results in ungrammaticality since *wonder* cannot take a proposition as its argument. So—reprises aside—such a *wh*-phrase can then be scoped in two ways: (1) It may be part of an ordinary *wh*-interrogative clause construction, which necessarily involves the existence of a distinct WH-specified *wh*-phrase (and hence a multiple *wh*-interrogative sentence). (2) Alternatively, it may occur within a clause of type *dir-is-int-cl*, as illustrated in (76):

(76)

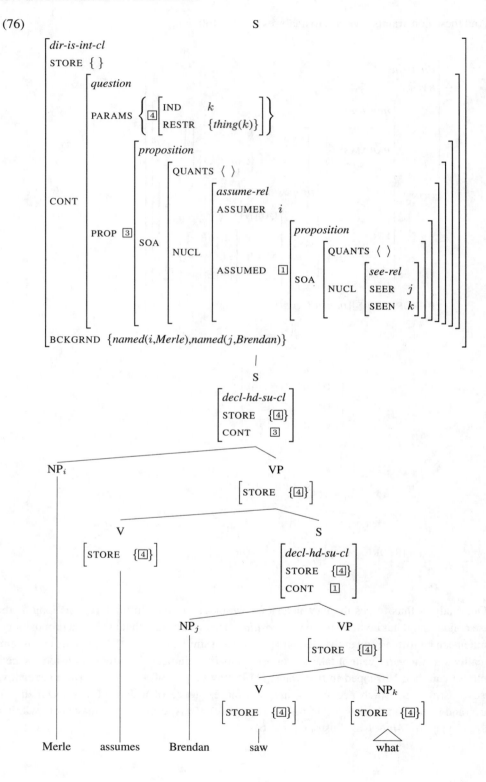

As (76) makes plain, the complement of the verb *assume* is a proposition semantically, and hence can be constructed as an instance of the *decl-hd-su-cl* type. Although this complement clause is propositional, it may contain an in-situ *wh*-expression whose parameter it passes up in STORE, as shown in (76). The reason why a QE predicate like *wonder* cannot embed such a clause is clear: a *decl-hd-su-cl* must express a proposition; QE predicates like *wonder* must select a complement that expresses a question. Given that all instances of *dir-is-int-cl* are [IC +] (this constraint is inherited from the type *is-int-cl*) and the complement of verbs like *wonder* must be [IC −], it follows that examples like (71b) are correctly excluded.

Our analysis of direct in-situ *wh*-interrogatives also extends to so-called 'quizmaster questions' like (77).

(77) [Now trying for the million dollars]
The fingerprints of which Nixon operatives were found in the office of Daniel Ellsberg's psychiatrist?

As far as we can see, although television game shows seem to have developed a characteristic intonation pattern (typically involving a terraced downstep), there is otherwise no reason to assign such questions to a distinct linguistic category. Their content is precisely as guaranteed by our *dir-is-int-cl* construction type.

Let us now return to Przepiórkowski's example in (48), repeated here as (78).

(78) A: All these people are writers, you know.
B: Yeah? And Szczypiorski wrote WHAT?
A: WHO wrote WHAT?

Our analysis of this example embeds a *dir-is-int-cl* within a *repr-int-cl*, as shown in (79):

(79)

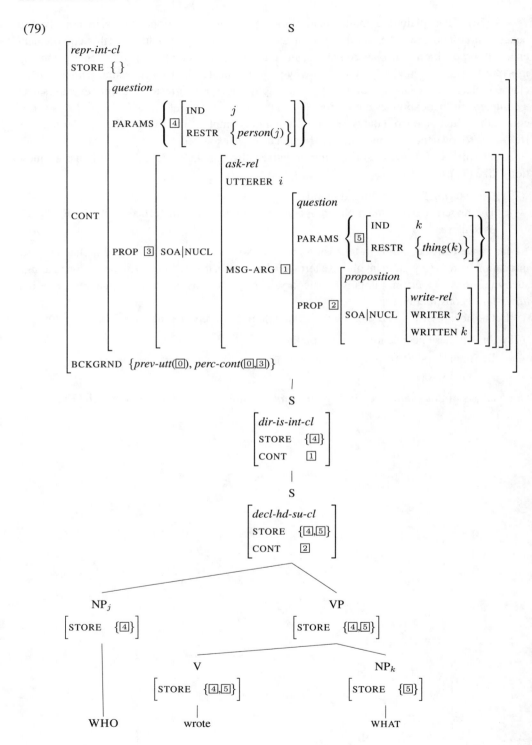

The content associated with this example, i.e. (80), is only appropriate in contexts like the one in (78).

(80)   For which person x, did you ask what x wrote?

Finally, we note that, once again, there is a surprising extension of our analysis to *wh*-less cases. Since nothing requires there to be a retrieved parameter, a clause expressing a *proposition*—for example, a finite declarative clause—can be associated with an interrogative meaning. Indeed, English, along with many other languages, permits finite declarative clauses to be used to query when a suitable intonation is used:

(81)   a. Jean is happy these days?

      b. Everything is going along fine?

Although this construction-type is highly productive both in terms of its frequency in every-day use and cross-linguistically, we are not aware of recent attempts to treat them systematically. This is probably, in part, because as far as their surface syntactic form is concerned, nothing distinguishes an intonation question from a declarative. Therefore, in most treatments of the syntax/semantics interface, there is no elegant way to incorporate a non-propositional meaning for such forms.

Alternatively, it has been proposed that such queries do not involve a distinct semantic content, but rather involve as their descriptive content a proposition embedded under an illocutionary force that is weaker than an assertion (see e.g. Searle and Vanderveken 1985 for an analysis in this spirit). However, such a proposal runs counter to the fact that utterances of this type seem to require disquotation with *whether* if taken to be a query:[29]

(82)   a. Whitney: You're okay?

      b. Whitney asked whether/#that I was okay.

As all in-situ constructions are [IC +], our proposal correctly rules out examples like the following:

(83)   *Whitney asked/wondered [Merle was okay].

Here the embedded clause can only be constructed as an instance of the type *decl-hd-su-cl* and hence must have propositional semantics. But since *ask*, *wonder* and other QE predicates select a

---

[29]This should not be taken to be saying that we rule out the existence of uses of declaratives in which a proposition is embedded under weaker than assertoric force. Such a use presumably occurs in *confirmations*, which indeed can be disquoted either as propositions or as questions:

   (i)   Whitney: You're okay, right?

   (ii) Whitney checked whether/that I was okay.

Similarly, our claim that some uses of 'rising intonation' declaratives express questions does not mean that polar interrogatives and 'rising intonation' declaratives are interchangeable, a point emphasized in the following contrast discussed by Liberman (1975):

   (iii) Hello, my name is Mark Liberman?

   (iv) Hello, is my name Mark Liberman?

However this example simply brings out the fact that rise-intoned declaratives need not be used solely to query (see Bolinger 1989 for extensive arguments to this effect). Note that (iii) above would be disquoted as in (v):

   (v)   Mark stepped into the room and [#inquired whether]/[announced unconfidently that] he was Mark Liberman.

complement whose semantics must be of type *question*, it follows correctly that all such examples are excluded.

The treatment of 'intonation questions' such as (84) is sketched in (85):

(84) Kim is angry?

(85)

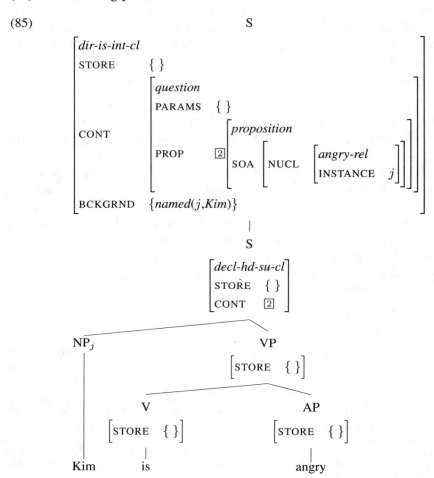

Finally, note that there are also interrogative fragments of various kinds that appear similar to (85). Some of these, thanks once more to Carl Pollard, are shown in (86)–(88).

(86) [To colleague, comparing appointment books while scheduling meeting]
      Wednesday afternoon?

(87) [Unconfident music theory student in aural exam, presented with interval] Flat 13th?

(88) [Guessing answer to riddle]
      Because the turkey was on vacation?

Such examples, discussed more fully in the next chapter, are all analyzed as instances of *dir-is-int-cl*. The difference between these and (85) is that the head daughter is analyzed not as a *decl-hd-su-cl*, but rather as a kind of elliptical declarative clause needed independently for the analysis of sentence fragments.

7.4 Summary of In-Situ Clause Types

In this chapter, we have developed a treatment of two types of in-situ *wh*-clauses. The types that play a role in this analysis are those shown in (89):

(89)

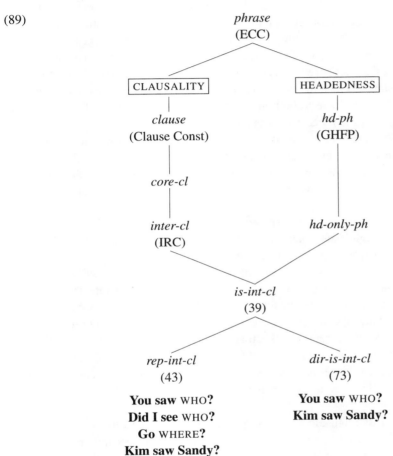

7.5 Cross-Linguistic Variation

The theory of interrogative types developed in this chapter has potential explanatory value for understanding the cross-linguistic variation regarding interrogative constructions. We can see, in particular, that extracted and in-situ clauses share common properties, e.g. they both involve retrieval of parameters from the STORE of their head daughter. The differences among various species of *wh*-interrogative clauses arise from the monotonic interaction of constraints associated with other relevant types, many of which are used to treat non-interrogative constructions as well.

In light of this picture, it is tempting to speculate that these types and some of the constraints associated with them are part of universal grammar. On the strongest interpretation of this idea, the learning of a 'wh-fronting' language consists primarily in recognizing the existence of the wh-extraction type. An 'in situ wh-language' is learned primarily by recognizing the existence of the type is-int-cl. And learning a language like English is more complicated only in that it involves recognizing the existence of both types in a single language.

The logic of the grammar—the partitioning of phrases into CLAUSALITY and HEADEDNESS dimensions—can place further constraints on the learning process, if we assume that this organization is also part of UG.[30] Recognizing the existence of HEADEDNESS types has necessary consequences for the learning of new clause types, since each of these must have a life in the HEADEDNESS dimension as well. If we make strong assumptions about what is innate linguistic knowledge (that many nonmaximal types may be innate, for example), then, the system of types presented here can contribute to both an understanding of the nature of cross-linguistic variation and an account of the process of language learning. If instead we try to explain universal commonalities in more general cognitive and/or functional terms, then the distinctions of CLAUSALITY lend themselves to explanation in terms of communicative needs. The distinctions of HEADEDNESS, by contrast, may be better explained in terms of perceptual factors or more general properties that manifest themselves in cognitive domains other than language as well (see Green 2000).

Our approach also leaves certain other matters to functional, rather than formal explanation. For example, though we might expect that it would be dysfunctional for a language to have many constructional means of expressing a single semantic content, there is no reason why diverse constructional strategies for expressing a single meaning (e.g. a particular wh-question) should not coexist in a given language. That is, given two universally available strategies for expressing the same (or essentially the same) semantic content, nothing in our approach rules out the possibility that a single language might utilize both. Indeed, our analysis of non-reprise in-situ wh-interrogatives leads to the correct prediction that English has two distinct ways of expressing essentially the same interrogative content, e.g. *When did Lee go to Harvard?* and *Lee went to Harvard when?*. Our approach does not countenance any simple distinction between languages that have 'overt movement' versus 'movement in LF'; nor do the observed facts warrant any such distinction.

This picture of the cross-linguistic variation, specifically with respect to the issue of 'movement' versus 'non-movement', fits perfectly with results achieved independently by Johnson and Lappin (1999), building on work of Simpson (1995). In Iraqi Arabic (henceforth IA), both of the following are well-formed wh-questions:

(90) a. Mona shaafat meno
         Mona saw   whom
         Who did Mona see?
      b. Meno shaafat Mona
         Who saw   Mona
         Who did Mona see? *or* Who saw Mona?

---

[30]Though our constraint-based approach to grammar in no way requires that we accept any strong version of linguistic nativism.

As Johnson and Lappin show, current movement-based accounts of *wh*-constructions fail to predict a fundamental aspect of IA interrogatives: that *wh*-'movement' is optional.

Johnson and Lappin's account of IA, by contrast, shares many features with our account of English (though they make certain assumptions that are different from ours in minor ways). In particular, they assume that there are two distinct types of *wh*-clause in IA. the first is a kind of head-subject phrase where the head daughter (the VP) must bear a nonempty WH-specification.[31] Thus a question like (90a) has the following structure.

(91)

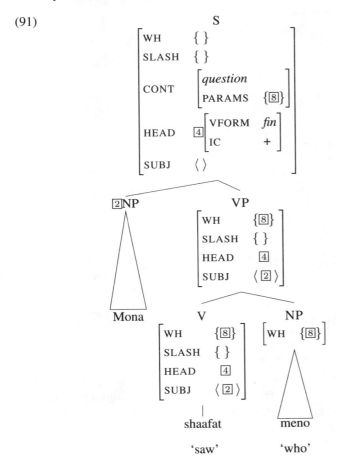

'saw'   'who'

---

[31] Johnson and Lappin follow P&S–94 in using the features QUE and REL instead of WH.

Johnson and Lappin's analysis of (90b), by contrast, involves a head-filler construction whose filler daughter (like its English counterpart) must be WH-specified. The structure of (90b) (on the reading where it paraphrases (90a)) is thus as shown in (92).

(92)

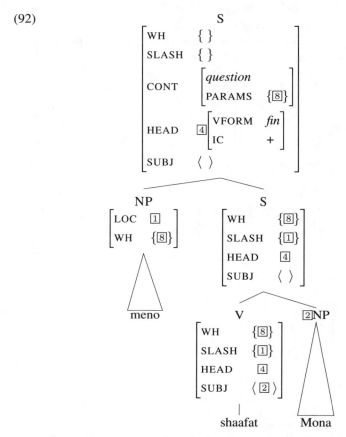

Clearly, their intention is that IA lack any constraint requiring clauses to be [WH { }]. Note further that if one makes this assumption, then it may be possible to treat both examples just illustrated in terms of a single construction, our *dir-is-int-cl*, which would introduce a level of nonbranching structure over both kinds of examples, as shown in (93):

(93)

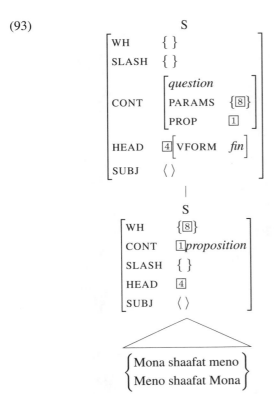

$$
\text{S}
\begin{bmatrix}
\text{WH} & \{\,\} \\
\text{SLASH} & \{\,\} \\
\text{CONT} & \begin{bmatrix} question \\ \text{PARAMS} \quad \{\boxed{8}\} \\ \text{PROP} \qquad \boxed{1} \end{bmatrix} \\
\text{HEAD} & \boxed{4}[\text{VFORM} \quad fin] \\
\text{SUBJ} & \langle\,\rangle
\end{bmatrix}
$$

$$
\text{S}
\begin{bmatrix}
\text{WH} & \{\boxed{8}\} \\
\text{CONT} & \boxed{1}proposition \\
\text{SLASH} & \{\,\} \\
\text{HEAD} & \boxed{4} \\
\text{SUBJ} & \langle\,\rangle
\end{bmatrix}
$$

$$
\left\{ \begin{array}{l} \text{Mona shaafat meno} \\ \text{Meno shaafat Mona} \end{array} \right\}
$$

Whichever of these approaches turns out to be correct, it is clear that the inventory of constructions posited for IA must make available two distinct ways of realizing a particular *wh*-question. Our construction-based approach allows this in principle. The fact that constructions tend overwhelmingly to be interpretationally distinct from one another in any given language (cf. the presuppositional differences between in-situ and 'fronted' *wh*-constructions in English) is to be explained in cognitive and functional terms. This perspective would lead us to look for more subtle semantic/pragmatic differences between the two kinds of IA *wh*-interrogatives, rather than for any formal mechanism that directly relates the two kinds of construction.

8

Extensions

In this final chapter we consider briefly and somewhat speculatively some additional phenomena that have played a role in the discussions of earlier chapters. These constitute an important testing ground for a theory of interrogatives.

We start by considering how to integrate two pervasive elliptical constructions associated with interrogative contexts: *short answers*, a detailed and insightful discussion of which can be found in Morgan 1973, and *sluicing*, first described in detail in Ross 1969. Both of these phenomena raise a variety of interesting questions about the nature of ellipsis resolution that we have pursued, and continue to pursue, elsewhere. Putting most of these issues aside, certain fundamental problems nonetheless fall squarely within the scope of the present inquiry. For example, a theory of interrogatives should clarify the potential that questions have for eliciting responses in the form of short answers. Similarly, sluicing is a highly productive *wh*-construction which, we suggest, does not involve extraction. Our framework is able to provide a relatively straightforward and unified account of these two elliptical constructions.[1]

We then address the interaction of polar interrogatives and negation, picking up on phenomena first discussed in Chapter 3. We saw there that EAC approaches to questions must adopt an assumption we called Negative-Positive-Interrogative-Synonymy (NPIS)—the assumption that a negative polar interrogative has the same content as the corresponding positive polar interrogative. We show that in our framework the contents of negative and positive interrogatives can be distinguished in such a way that the requisite semantic commonalities are still captured.

Finally, we consider two issues involving semantic selection and subcategorization: first, the selection and subcategorization properties of both question-embedding and factive/resolutive predicates and, second, the long-standing puzzle of concealed questions.

8.1 Short Questions and Answers

8.1.1 Ellipsis Resolution

Among the most-frequently used clause types in conversation are two which have come to be called *sluicing*—a term coined by Ross (1969), who presented the first detailed generative discussion of the phenomenon—and *short answers*. Both sluicing and short answers concern XP 'fragments' that receive a 'sentential' interpretation. In the case of sluicing the XP fragment is,

---

[1] See Ginzburg et al. 2000 for a description of SHARDS, a computational implementation based on the grammar described in this chapter.

or contains, a *wh*-phrase, as in (1). 'Short answer' is a more inclusive cover term for XP fragments that typically occur in the context of a response to a query, as in (2):

(1) a. Merle knows that many people failed the test, though she doesn't actually know who.

    b. A: I'm very tired.
       B: Why?/Since when?

    c. A: I can find someone to do the job.
       B: Who?

    d. A: Did Jill phone?
       B: WHO?

(2) a. A: Who attended the meeting?
       B: Millie/No students/A friend of Jill's.

    b. A: Who was interacting with whom at the party?
       B: Bill with Mary/Some of my friends with each of her friends.

    c. A: Did Bill attend the meeting?
       B: Yes/Maybe.

    d. A: Why did Plarr cross the road?
       B: Because she thought no cars were passing.

    e. A: What is the default font-size?
       B: 12 point (, I'm assuming).

    f. A: What does Nixon want for breakfast?
       B: Kissinger says eggs. (Morgan 1973)

The focus of most of the relevant literature has been on the nature of each ellipsis resolution. More specifically, the literature has explored the 'level(s) of representation' that must be postulated in order to explain certain parallelism phenomena between an ellipsis and its source. In fact, sluicing has been used as an argument to justify the existence of Deep Structure for Generative Semantics (Ross 1969), Functional Structure for LFG (Levin 1982), and LF for GB (Chung et al. 1995). Morgan (1973) actually argued that short answers require grammatical rules to make explicit reference to the context of utterance—a highly controversial stance in 1973, perhaps still rejected by certain proponents of strong autonomy, but one which is of course adopted in HPSG.

Sluicing and short answers have thus provided important evidence in the ongoing debate on whether the resolution of ellipsis is syntactic or semantic in nature—that is, whether the 'missing material' needed to assign an interpretation includes syntactic material or else is purely semantic. Purely syntactic and purely semantic approaches both face problems, some of which we point to shortly, but it is important to realize that both types of approach were designed primarily with intra-sentential ellipsis resolution in mind—or, at best, designed for short texts made up of successive or conjoined sentences. This is reflected by the data that have been addressed in the literature. There has been little, if any, detailed linguistic work on short answers since Morgan 1973, and accounts of sluicing have all concentrated on embedded uses such as (1a,b). Virtually no work has been done on matrix sluices like (1c,d).

The reason for this is clear—both short answers and sluices like (1c,d) are intricately tied to a conversational context. Conversation is a medium that requires a different approach to context than does text or monologue. The biggest differences emerge from the fact that conversation involves multiple agents, with distinct information states, who are prone to disagreements and misunderstandings. This forms the background for sluices such as (1c)—B's sluice is felicitous even if she does not accept A's assertion—and (1d)—B's sluice communicates that she has failed to fully understand A's utterance.

Our main contribution here is an account of non-sentential utterances like sluicing and short answers that is based on an independently motivated theory of dialogue context. Our account is designed to avoid certain pitfalls that affect both syntactically-based and semantically-based accounts intended for monologue and text.

For a start, ellipsis resolution in our account is not based on syntactic reconstruction. This is because the infelicity of the putative reconstructed form is not a good predictor of the felicity of either short answers or sluices. Without this, much of the motivation for reconstruction evaporates. Consider (3):

(3) a. A: Did anyone see Mary?
     b. B: Yes.
     c. A: Who?
     d.   *Anyone saw Mary.

Example (3b) could not be the syntactic antecedent of the (3c) sluice, since this would assume that *yes* somehow represents (3d), which is ill-formed.[2] Thus (3a) must be assumed to be or to provide the antecedent. It is at the very least not obvious how a principled reconstruction procedure could be developed to amalgamate (3c) and (3a) to produce a legitimate reconstructed form.

Similarly, the dialogues in (4) show that violations of binding constraints that would otherwise rule out the reconstruction correlate do not entail infelicity of the short answer:[3]

(4) a. A: Who will punish Bill$_i$ if he fails?
         B: He himself/himself/#he/#him.
            (#He himself$_i$/*himself$_i$ will punish Bill$_i$ if he fails.)
     b. A: What caused the computer to break down?
         B: A power surge?
         A: Perhaps, but the most intriguing answer is: [the computer itself]$_i$/itself$_i$/#it.
            (#The computer itself$_i$/*Itself$_i$ caused the computer$_i$ to break down.)
     c. A: Who appeared to be the cause of John and Mary's problems?
         B: Each other. (*Each other appeared to be the cause of John and Mary's problems.)

---

[2] For additional arguments against such a view of *yes*, see Ginzburg 2001.

[3] Fiengo and May's (1994) device of vehicle change will not help here, as the reciprocal and reflexive NPs are lexically realized and thus not subject to variation under reconstruction.

An additional problem for a reconstruction-based approach concerns the existence of felicitous uses of such elliptical forms, as first pointed out by Webber (1978), in cases where either no plausible linguistic antecedent exists, as in (5a-c), or where a linguistic antecedent does exist but from which the requisite resolution cannot be read off, as in (5d):

(5) a. A: I need some sugar for the cake.
    B: I think I bought some yesterday.
    A: [Searching through cupboards] Well, I'm skeptical. If you're so sure, come show me where.

   b. [Milling around on first day of conference, participants ignorant of location of talks go up to harried organiser:] Hey, could you tell us which room so we can go in and wait for things to start?

   c. [In an elevator] What floor?

   d. Films in Germany are sometimes dubbed, sometimes in the original. The program always makes clear which.

Similarly problematic are the *reprise* sluices in (6) where, assuming the analysis of reprise utterances provided in Chapter 7, the resolution involves embedding by an illocutionary operator.

(6) a. A: Did Mary phone you?
    B: When? (= What time t are you asking whether Mary phoned me at t? *cf.* When did you ask whether Mary phoned me?—*"When" cannot modify the embedded clause.*)

   b. A: Who should easily be able to get a job?
    B: Where? (= What place l is A asking about who should easily get a job in l? *cf.* Where does A ask who should easily get a job?—*"Where" cannot modify the embedded clause.*)

   c. A: Go home Billie!
    B: Why? (= Why are you ordering me to go?)

   d. A: Did Billie leave?
    B: WHO? (= Who$_i$ are you asking if she$_i$ left?)

Incidentally, this type of reading is in general unavailable for the non-elliptical correlates of the *wh*-phrase fragment.

Although our account of sluicing does not involve syntactically-based reconstruction, it allows for the existence of connectivity phenomena in which the target displays a certain syntactic parallelism with the source. Accommodating such effects has proven to be an insurmountable obstacle for treatments of ellipsis that are based exclusively on resolution at a level of semantic representation or denotation.[4] Describing ellipsis by using the multi-dimensional sign-based architecture of HPSG means that there is no obstacle, in principle, to developing an account that is sensitive to syntactic parallelism but is not based on a technique like reconstruction.

---

[4] For VPE see Gawron and Peters 1990, Dalrymple et al. 1991, and Shieber et al. 1996.

For sluicing and short answers, the extant parallelism effects involve around category concord between target and source, limited of course to those cases where a linguistic antecedent exists. In languages with rich case systems it is straightforward to demonstrate this: example (7), from Ross 1969, shows that in German both direct sluicing, as in (7a,b), and reprise sluicing, as in (7c), are sensitive to the case requirements of the antecedent NP:

(7) a. Er will jemandem schmeicheln, aber sie wissen nicht wem/#wen.
   He wants someone-dat flatter, but they know not who-dat/#who-acc.
   He wants to flatter someone, but they don't know whom.

b. Er will jemanden loben, aber sie wissen nicht wen/#wem.
   He wants someone-acc praise, but they know not who-acc/#who-dat.
   He wants to praise someone, but they don't know whom.

c. A: Er will dem Hans schmeicheln. B: WEM/#WEN?
   He wants the-dat Hans flatter. who-dat/#who-acc.
   A: He wants to flatter Hans. B: WHOM?

Example (8) illustrates similar case concord in Hebrew short answers:

(8) a. A: lemi hixmeta? B: lemoti/#moti.
   To-who flattered-2nd-sg? to-moti/#moti.
   A: Whom did you flatter? B: Moti.

b. A: et mi šibaxt? B: et moti/#lemoti.
   def-acc who praised-2nd-sg? def-acc moti/#to-moti.
   A: Whom did you praise? B: Moti.

For English NPs the situation is less clear-cut—NPs on the whole do not manifest morphological case. The sole bearers of case are pronouns. Accusative pronouns appear routinely in elliptical utterances:

(9) a. [choosing players for a pick-up soccer game, players gather around team captains, shouting advice and gesturing toward prospective players]:
   #I/Me/#He/Him/#She/Her.

b. A: Who did Bo insult yesterday?
   B: Mo/#I/Me/#He/Him/#She/Her.

c. A: Which cabinet minister did Toni replace?
   B: Mo/#I/Me/#He/Him/#She/Her.

Nominative pronouns, by contrast, are barred from standing alone not only in these examples but also in dialogues like the following, where the pronoun fragment has a nominative antecedent:

(10) a. A: Didn't KIM write that letter?
   B: [pause] Nope. Me/#I/Her/#She/Him/#He.

b. A: Who stole the beer?
   B: Bo/#I/Me/#He/Him/#She/Her.

Cross-linguistically, in languages with strong pronouns, examples like (10) unambiguously call for a pronoun manifesting a particular case, as the following examples from Hebrew show:

(11) a. A: mi šata et hayayin? B: ani/#oti/hu/#oto.

who drank def-acc the-wine? 1st-sg-nom/#1st-sg-acc/3rd-sg-nom/#3rd-sg-acc.

A: Who drank the wine? B: I/#Me/He/#Him.

b. A: mi hu šibeax? B: #ani/oti/#hu/oto.

who he praised? #1st-sg-nom/1st-sg-acc/#3rd-sg-nom/3rd-sg-acc.

A: Whom did he praise? B: #I/Me/#He/Him.

English is in fact cross-linguistically anomalous in allowing divergent case values in dialogues like (10), a fact that we leave unexplained here. Despite this unresolved discrepancy, we must conclude that in general NP short answers should be viewed as exhibiting connectivity effects.[5] We thus build into our account of ellipsis an identity condition between the category of the fragment and that of its antecedent.

8.1.2 General Approach

Our approach to contextual structuring is based on a detailed account of context in dialogue developed in the framework of KOS (Ginzburg 1996b, 2001, Traum et al. 1999). On this view each dialogue participant's view of the common ground is structured by a number of attributes including the following two: FACTS—a set of facts, corresponding to BCKGRD—and QUD ('questions under discussion')—a set consisting of the currently discussable questions, partially ordered by $\prec$ ('takes conversational precedence'). Both querying and assertion involve a question becoming maximal in the querier's or asserter's QUD: the posed question q for a query where q is posed or, similarly, the polar question $\lambda\{ \}p$ for an assertion where p is asserted. Roughly, the responder can subsequently choose either to start a discussion (by providing information σ that is About $q/\lambda\{ \}p$ or by posing a question q_1 on which $q/\lambda\{ \}p$ Depends) or, in the case of assertion, to update her FACTS structure with $fact(p)$.[6] A dialogue participant can downdate $q/\lambda\{ \}p$ from QUD when, as far as her (not necessarily public) goals dictate, sufficient information has been accumulated in FACTS.

For our current purposes, we simply assume that the CTXT attribute contains two additional fields. The first is an attribute MAX-QUD, whose value is of type *question* and represents the question currently under discussion. The second is an attribute SAL(IENT)-UTT(ERANCE), which takes as its value sets of type *local*. SAL-UTT represents the (sub)utterance which receives widest scope within MAX-QUD:[7]

---

[5]Although we do not attempt to develop an account of such fragments here, it is worth noting that connectivity effects extend beyond NPs. For example, the verb *make* subcategorizes for a VP[*bse*] complement, whereas the verb *force* subcategorizes for a VP[*inf*] complement (Pollard and Sag 1987). And despite the fact that the semantic entities specified in the following questions are apparently of identical semantic type, the question *What did you make Bo do?* requires a short answer of category VP[*bse*], whereas *What did you force Bo to do?* requires a short answer of category VP[*inf*]:

(i) A: What did you make Bo do?

B: (#To) leave the flat

(ii) A: What did you force Bo do?

B: (#)To leave the flat

[6]Here Depends is a relation between questions, intuitively corresponding to the notion of 'is a subquestion of'. It can be formalized in terms of the aboutness and resolvedness relations: q_1 depends on q_2 iff any proposition p such that p Resolves q_2, also satisfies p About q_1. See Ginzburg 1996b, 2001 for a discussion.

[7]We discuss how 'deictic' fragments such as (5) should be accommodated below.

- If MAX-QUD is a unary question, i.e. has a singleton PARAMS set, SAL-UTT is the utterance of the phrase associated with the PARAMS set of the question expressed.[8] The prototypical case of this is when MAX-QUD is the content of an interrogative clause, in which case SAL-UTT will simply be identified with the *wh*-phrase utterance associated with the PARAMS set of MAX-QUD.[9] However, we shall also see other cases where MAX-QUD is a question with a singleton PARAMS set but is not the content of a previously uttered interrogative clause. The prime examples of this are questions that enter into the context as a consequence of reprise utterances, as we explain below. In such cases, SAL-UTT will be the utterance of the constituent to be clarified.[10]

- If MAX-QUD is a question with an empty PARAMS set, the context gets a value for SAL-UTT only if the QUANTS list of the open proposition of MAX-QUD is non-empty. In such a case, the value of SAL-UTT is the utterance corresponding to the widest scoping quantifier.

In information-structure terms, SAL-UTT can be thought of as a means of underspecifying the subsequent focal (sub)utterance or as a potential *parallel element* in the sense of Dalrymple et al. 1991 and Shieber et al. 1996.[11] Since SAL-UTT has as its value an object of type *local*, it enables us to encode a limited amount of categorial parallelism. In all cases, however, syntactic parallelism will enter into the picture solely to provide *matching conditions* between a fragment and a prior utterance. In other words, prior syntactic structure will not be used in the *constructing* of the content of a fragmentary utterance; it functions merely to establish its appropriateness. Thus, our approach will be compatible with psycholinguistic work demonstrating the rapid decay of purely structural information (see e.g. Fletcher 1994). Indeed, by tying MAX-QUD and SAL-UTT in the way we do, our approach enables us to make strong predictions about the extent of categorial parallelism.

The innovations to the representation of context discussed in this section can be summarized as follows:

---

[8]We do not discuss here examples with multiple fragments such as (i) and (ii):

(i) A: Who came when?
    B: Bill at 5, Mustafa at 12.
(ii) A: Some student is reported to have quarelled with a famous professor.
    B: Which student with/and which professor?

Hence, in the examples we consider here the value of SAL-UTT will either be singleton or the empty set. For a discussion of examples such as (i) see Ginzburg 1999.

[9]Of course pied piping requires us to sharpen this statement somewhat. The following examples suggest that in such cases the value of SAL-UTT is the most extensive subutterance co-indexed with the PARAMS set:

(i) A: To whom did you give the book?
    B: #(To) Jo
(ii) A: On what does the well-being of the EU depend?
    B: #(On) a stable currency.

[10]Related to this are cases where MAX-QUD is a polar question arising from a form with one or more accented constituents:

(i) A: Does Bo know BRENDAN?
    B: No, (she knows) Frank.

Such cases are naturally treated as involving accommodation of a question with a non-empty PARAMS set). The SAL-UTT in such cases is provided by the accented constituent. For some discussion of such cases within a similar analytical perspective see Engdahl et al. 2000.

[11]Which constituent of a given utterance will be the SAL-UTT need not be viewed as determined *prior* to that utterance's taking place. Typically, as we will see below, the determination of SAL-UTT is a consequence of how a conversationalist decides to structure her context, depending on which question she decides to make maximal in QUD at a given point.

(12)   Contextual Features:

TYPE	FEATURES/VALUE TYPE	IST
conx-obj	$\begin{bmatrix} \text{C-INDICES} & \textit{c-inds} \\ \text{SAL-UTT} & \textit{set(local)} \\ \text{MAX-QUD} & \textit{question} \end{bmatrix}$	*feat-struc*
c-inds	$\begin{bmatrix} \text{C-SPKR} & \textit{index} \\ \text{C-ADDR} & \textit{index} \\ \text{U-LOC} & \textit{index} \end{bmatrix}$	*feat-struc*

8.1.3   Lexical utterances

The simplest kind of case we consider are closely related to utterance fragments. These are words that have stand-alone uses conveying a 'complete' meaning, i.e. a *message*. Prototypical members of this class, which we call *propositional-lexemes*, are words like *yes, no, sure, right, probably not*, and *really*. Such words, although they behave like adverbials semantically, stand alone, without a modified clause and cannot be embedded. Their content is propositional, constructed from a polar question in the context.[12] Thus, a very simple possible analysis of the word *yes* is as follows:

(13)

$$\begin{bmatrix} \text{PHON} & \langle \text{ yes } \rangle \\ \\ \text{SS|LOC} & \begin{bmatrix} \text{CAT} & \begin{bmatrix} \text{HEAD} & \begin{bmatrix} \textit{adv} \\ \text{IC} & + \end{bmatrix} \end{bmatrix} \\ \text{CONT} & \boxed{1} \end{bmatrix} \\ \text{ARG-ST} & \langle \ \rangle \\ \text{CTXT|MAX-QUD} & \begin{bmatrix} \text{PARAMS} & \{ \ \} \\ \text{PROP} & \boxed{1} \end{bmatrix} \end{bmatrix}$$

(14)   a. A: Did Jo leave?
          B: Yes.

   b. A's utterance content:

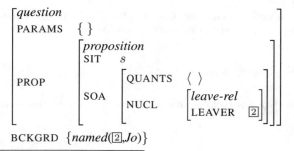

$$\begin{bmatrix} \textit{question} \\ \text{PARAMS} \quad \{ \ \} \\ \\ \text{PROP} \quad \begin{bmatrix} \textit{proposition} \\ \text{SIT} \quad s \\ \\ \text{SOA} \quad \begin{bmatrix} \text{QUANTS} & \langle \ \rangle \\ \text{NUCL} & \begin{bmatrix} \textit{leave-rel} \\ \text{LEAVER} & \boxed{2} \end{bmatrix} \end{bmatrix} \end{bmatrix} \\ \text{BCKGRD} \quad \{\textit{named}(\boxed{2},\textit{Jo})\} \end{bmatrix}$$

---

[12]Such words can also be used to express intonation questions:

   (i) A: Bill left.
        B: Really?

Such uses can be accommodated using the type *dir-is-int-cl* introduced in Chapter 7. As discussed there, *dir-is-int-cl* allows a phrase denoting an intonation question from a phrase denoting the corresponding propositional content.

c. B's utterance:

$$
\begin{bmatrix}
\text{PHON} & \langle \text{ yes } \rangle \\
\text{SS}|\text{LOC} & \begin{bmatrix} \text{CAT}|\text{HEAD} & adv \\ \text{CONT} & \boxed{1} \end{bmatrix} \\
\text{ARG-ST} & \langle \ \rangle \\
\text{CTXT}|\text{MAX-QUD} & \begin{bmatrix} \text{PARAMS} & \{\ \} \\ \text{PROP} & \boxed{1} \end{bmatrix}
\end{bmatrix}
$$

We discuss further subtleties concerning the words *yes* and *no* (as well as their counterparts French *oui/si*, German *ja/doch*, and Georgian *cho/ki*) in section 8.2, where we consider positive and negative polar interrogatives more generally.

A related category is preverbal propositional sentential adverbs like *probably*, *usually*, and *at times*. Such an adverb can modify a proposition-denoting clause, yet it can also function as a stand-alone utterance:

(15) a. Brendan probably left.

   b. A: Did Brendan leave?
     B: Probably.

   c. Merle usually shows up late for work.

   d. A: Does Merle show up late for work?
     B: Usually.

   e. At times Arlene loses control.

   f. A: Does Arlene lose control?
     B: At times.

Many adverbial elements thus lead a double life as modifiers and as *propositional-lexeme*s.

8.1.4 Declarative Fragment Clauses

We now turn to phrases like (16), which, though apparently non-sentential in their outward form, nonetheless convey a *message*:

(16) a. [A: Who left?] B: Dominique./Dominique?

   b. [A: A friend of mine left.] B: Who?/I wonder who.

   c. [A: Did Jo leave.] B: WHO?/JO?

Given the restricted scope of our investigation, we limit our analysis to fragments whose content is of type *param*—primarily NPs and (case-marking) PPs.[13]

---

[13]Thus, we will not be attempting to accommodate cases like the following, which would require us to enter into the semantics of adjuncts:

   (i) A: With whom did Jill go to the store?
     B: With Bill.
   (ii) A: Jill went to the store with a friend of ours.
     B: With who?
   (iv) A: Jill will be arriving tomorrow from Skopje.
     B: From WHERE?

We begin by introducing the phrasal type *headed-fragment-phrase* (*hd-frag-ph*)—a subtype of *hd-only-ph*—governed by the constraint in (17). The various fragments we analyze are either subtypes of *hd-frag-ph* or will contain such a phrase as a head daughter.

(17)   *hd-frag-ph*:

$$\begin{bmatrix} \text{HEAD} & \begin{bmatrix} v \\ \text{VFORM } \mathit{fin} \end{bmatrix} \\ \text{SUBJ} & \langle\,\rangle \\ \text{SPR} & \langle\,\rangle \\ \text{CTXT}|\text{SAL-UTT} & \left\{ \begin{bmatrix} \text{CAT} & \boxed{1} \\ \text{CONT}|\text{INDEX} & \boxed{2} \end{bmatrix} \right\} \end{bmatrix} \rightarrow \mathbf{H}\begin{bmatrix} \text{CAT} & \boxed{1}\begin{bmatrix} \text{HEAD} & \mathit{nominal} \end{bmatrix} \\ \text{CONT}|\text{INDEX} & \boxed{2} \end{bmatrix}$$

This constraint has two significant effects. First, it ensures that the head daughter's category—restricted to be *noun(n)* or *preposition(p)*, the two subtypes of *nominal*—is identical to that specified by the contextually provided SAL-UTT. The mother is specified to be of the same category as finite verbs, which allows such phrases to serve as a stand-alone clause, i.e. to be embedded as the head daughter of a *root-cl* (see the discussion in Chapter 7). Such phrases may also function as the complement of a verb that select for finite sentential clauses, but not for NPs. Second, the constraint coindexes the head daughter with the SAL-UTT. This has the effect of 'unifying in' the content of the former into a contextually provided content.

The first subtype of *hd-frag-ph* we consider is used to analyze short answers and reprise sluices. We introduce (18) as the constraint characterizing *declarative-fragment-clause* (*decl-frag-cl*)—also a subtype of *decl-cl*:

(18)   *decl-frag-cl*:

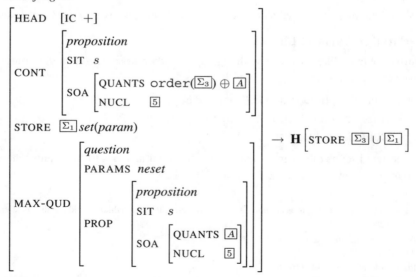

The content of this phrasal type is a proposition. Whereas in most headed clauses the content is entirely or primarily derived from the head daughter, here it is constructed for the most part from the contextually salient question. This provides the concerned situation and the nucleus, whereas if a fragment is or contains a quantifier, that quantifier must outscope any quantifiers already present in the contextually salient question. Finally, the constraint in (18) also ensures that if the head daughter contributes a parameter to the store, due to the presence of a *wh*-phrase, that parameter remains stored, i.e. is included in the mother's STORE value.

The constraint in (18) also requires that phrases of type *decl-frag-cl* be specified as [IC +], This blocks ellipsis in environments other than independent clauses, as in (19):[14]

(19) a. [What do they like?] *I doubt bagels.

     b. [What do they like?] *I wonder if bagels.

Unfortunately, our analysis does not quite make the right predictions here. In Chapter 2, we saw that various 'main clause phenomena' ('topicalization', 'negative adverb preposing', and the like) can appear after the complementizer *that*, subject to pragmatic conditions that are only partially understood. For this reason, our grammar leaves these environments unspecified for the feature IC. This incorrectly allows for the possibility of ellipsis in such environments:

(20) a. [What do they like?] *I think that bagels.

     b. [What do they like?] *I doubt that bagels.

     c. [How does one eat that?] *I gather that with a spoon.

We have no solution to this problem at present.

As with the in-situ phrases discussed in Chapter 7, we must ensure that the GHFP does not identify the mother's STORE value and that of the head daughter. Default unification can succeed in identifying those two STORE values if and only if the set $\boxed{\Sigma_3}$ is empty. This would make the STORE of both mother and head daughter be a set of parameters and would not allow quantifiers to be retrieved in any *decl-frag-cl*, undermining the analysis that follows. Thus, we must introduce a further constraint on phrases of this type in order to block the identification of the mother's and head daughter's STORE values:[15]

(21)   *decl-frag-cl*:

$$\begin{bmatrix} \text{STORE} & \boxed{\Sigma_0} \end{bmatrix} \rightarrow \mathbf{H} \begin{bmatrix} \text{STORE} & \neq\boxed{\Sigma_0} \end{bmatrix}$$

This has the desired effect of preventing the GHFP from identifying the two STORE values.

Given the above constraints, we may illustrate the interaction of all relevant constraints associated with supertypes of *decl-frag-cl*. Phrases of this type are constrained as in (22), where highlighting again shows the effect of the GHFP:

---

[14]Superficially similar examples like (i) and (ii) may all be analyzed as parentheticals:

  (i) [What do they like?] I think bagels.

  (ii) [How will you eat that?] I think with a spoon.

This approach is suggested by the existence—in all such cases, we believe—of paraphrases like (iii) and (iv):

  (iii) [What do they like?] Bagels, I think.

  (iv) [How will you eat that?] With a spoon, I think.

[15]Again, it is important to understand that inequality used here is intensional in nature. In particular, the constraint in (21) allows for the possibility that the two STORE sets have exactly the same members.

(22) ECC & GHFP & *hd-only-ph* & *hd-frag-ph* & *core-cl* & *decl-cl* & *decl-frag-cl*:

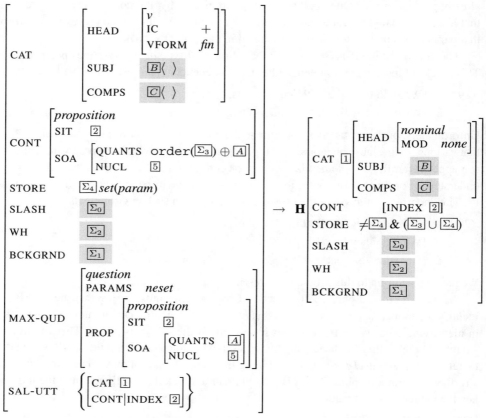

Let us consider the examples in (23). Here A's (sub)utterance of *who* provides the SAL-UTT in (24). And A's full utterance makes the question in (25) the MAX-QUD:

(23)   A: Who left?

        B: Jo

(24)

$$
\begin{bmatrix}
\text{CAT} & \text{NP} \\
\text{CONT} & \begin{bmatrix} param \\ \text{INDEX} & \boxed{1} \\ \text{REST} & \{\ \} \end{bmatrix}
\end{bmatrix}
$$

(25)

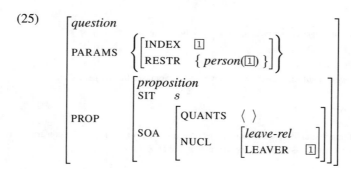

B's utterance thus gets the following analysis:

(26)

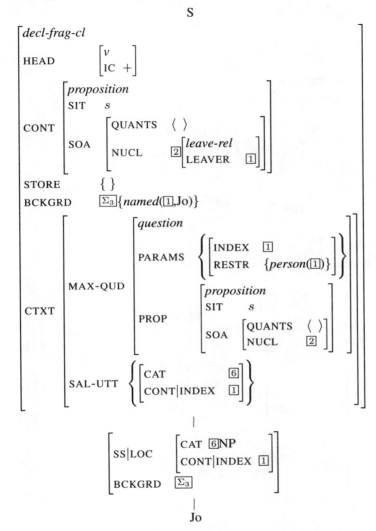

There are some important consequences of the fact that a *decl-frag-cl* is a *hd-frag-ph*. First, the category of the head daughter is NP, as required by the constraint in (17), whereas the category of the clause is *v*. Second, the head daughter gets coindexed with the SAL-UTT, which 'unifies in' the index of the head daughter into MAX-QUD's nucleus and that of the content of the *decl-frag-cl*. The final consequence is that the naming restriction associated with the proper name *Jo* gets incorporated as part of the contextual background of the entire clause.

Let us consider a slightly different example, one where the fragment is a quantificational NP. The only difference between this case and (26) is that the content here arises by retrieving from storage a quantifier introduced by the fragment, as specified by (18):

(27)   A: Who left?

        B: Every student

(28)

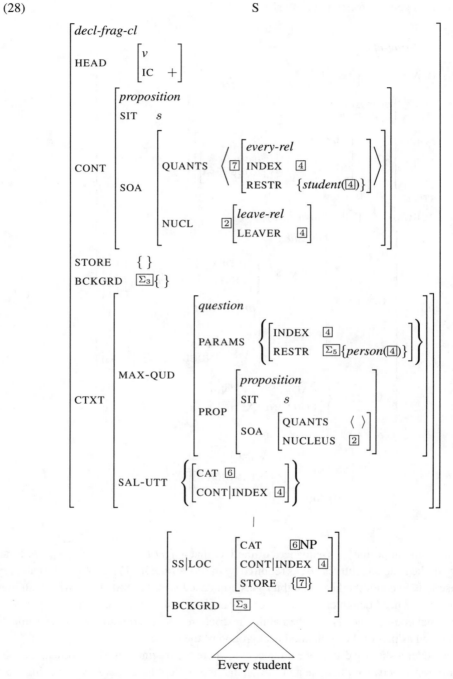

Our analysis further predicts, correctly, that (29a) is unambiguous: it receives only the content in (30), which is equivalent to (29b). This example thus lacks the branching reading which some speakers allow for (29c):

(29) a. A: Who admires no one?

      B: No one.

b. $\forall x[person(x) \rightarrow \exists y[person(y) \text{ and } admire(x,y)]]$

c.   No one admires no one. (Branching reading: there is not a single person who admires anyone.)

(30)

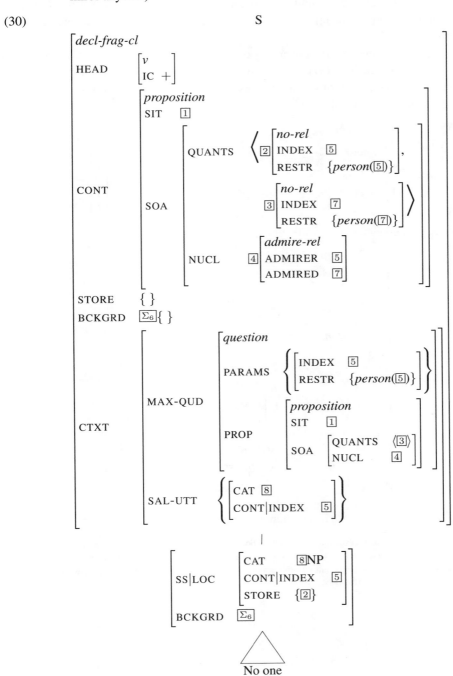

No one

Let us now turn to more complex cases like (31), where the response *a committee* can be understood to vary with each judge:

(31)   A: Who selected each judge?
         B: A committee.

Cases like this may be analyzed by building on our account of the functional uses of *wh*-phrases, if it is complemented with a semantic theory that uses quantificational NPs to denote quantifiers over skolem functions.[16]

Assuming that we allow a 'narrow scope' use of an indefinite to be analyzed as sketched in (32), then a bare-phrase such as (31B) can be interpreted using *decl-frag-cl*, in a manner that entirely parallels our description of functional uses of *wh*-phrases in Chapter 4.

(32)   *a committee*: functional use

$$
\begin{bmatrix}
\text{CONT}|\text{INDEX} & \boxed{f}(x) \\[2ex]
\text{STORE} & \left\{ \begin{bmatrix} some\text{-}rel \\ \text{IND} & \boxed{f} \\ \text{RESTR} & \left\{ \forall z(z \in Dom(\boxed{f}) \rightarrow committee^b(\boxed{f}(z))) \right\} \end{bmatrix} \right\}
\end{bmatrix}
$$

A's utterance in (31) now makes the following question MAX-QUD:

(33)
$$
\begin{bmatrix}
question \\[1ex]
\text{PARAMS} & \left\{ \begin{bmatrix} \text{INDEX} & \boxed{f} \\ \text{RESTR} & \left\{ \forall z(z \in Dom(\boxed{f}) \rightarrow person^b(\boxed{f}(z))) \right\} \end{bmatrix} \right\} \\[3ex]
\text{PROP} & \begin{bmatrix}
proposition \\
\text{SIT} & s \\[1ex]
\text{SOA} & \begin{bmatrix}
\text{QUANTS} & \left\langle \begin{bmatrix} each\text{-}rel \\ \text{INDEX} & \boxed{7} \\ \text{RESTR} & \{judge(\boxed{7})\} \end{bmatrix} \right\rangle \\[3ex]
\text{NUCL} & \begin{bmatrix} appoint\text{-}rel \\ \text{APPOINTER} & \boxed{f}(\boxed{7}) \\ \text{APPOINTED} & \boxed{7} \end{bmatrix}
\end{bmatrix}
\end{bmatrix}
\end{bmatrix}
$$

Whereas the SAL-UTT in this case is the utterance of the *wh*-phrase:

---

[16]An alternative analysis of such cases may be possible. For example, one could alter the specification for QUANTS in the constraint on *decl-frag-cl* given in (21) above. By employing a 'shuffle' operation (e.g. Reape's (1994) sequence union), it would be possible to allow the quantifier originating from the fragment to take narrow scope with respect to the quantifiers originating from MAX-QUD.

(34)
$$
\begin{bmatrix}
\text{CAT} & \text{NP} \\
\text{CONT}|\text{INDEX} & \boxed{f}(\boxed{7}) \\
\text{STORE} & \left\{ \begin{bmatrix} param \\ \text{IND} & \boxed{f} \\ \text{RESTR} & \{\forall z(z \in Dom(\boxed{f}) \rightarrow person^{\flat}(\boxed{f}(z))\} \end{bmatrix} \right\}
\end{bmatrix}
$$

B's utterance gets the following analysis:

(35)   S

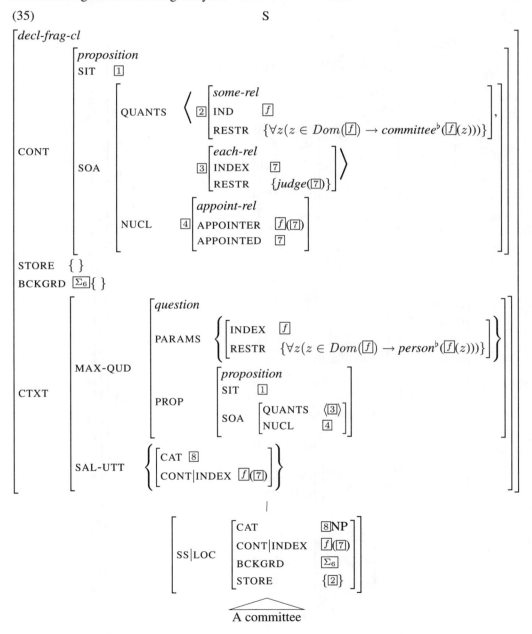

A committee

Our account extends also to examples such as (36), alluded to in Chapter 7:

(36) a. A: Who left?
          B: Jo?
      b. [Unconfident student in an aural exam, presented with an interval:]
          Flat 13th?   (example from Carl Pollard (personal communication))

We analyze B's responses as expressing polar questions. More specifically, these are utterances of type *dir-is-int-cl* with head daughters of type *decl-frag-cl*:

(37)

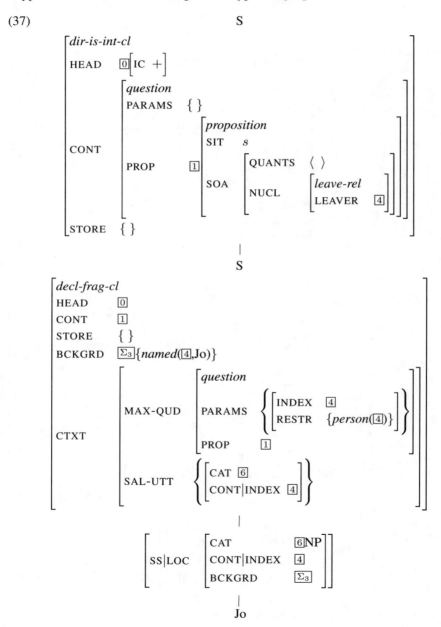

8.1.5 Sluicing: General Strategy

There are two main types of sluices, distinguished perhaps most clearly by whether or not they are used to express reprise questions. Apart from being intonationally distinct, the two kinds of sluice also differ in terms of the contextual background they require and in terms of their ability to appear in syntactically embedded environments.[17] (38a) shows that a non-quantified proposition constitutes a possible antecedent only for a reprise sluice, despite the felicity of a non-elliptical form that seems close in meaning to what the direct sluice might be expected to mean.

(38) a. A: Jo phoned.
          B: WHO?/#Who?/Oh, who is Jo?
      b. A: I ate the raqaqat I found in the fridge.
          B: The WHAT?/#What?
      c. A: I met several of your graduate students at the party.
          B: Who?/WHO?
      d. A: Did anyone phone for me?
          B: Yes.
          A: Aha. Who?/#WHO?

Example (38b) is similar. And (38c) illustrates a context where both a reprise and a direct sluice are appropriate—whereas reprise sluices involve a signaling by the querier of an inability to adequately comprehend the preceding utterance, direct sluices merely involve a request for additional information above and beyond what A originally thought was required. (38d) illustrates a context where, assuming that A has no problems hearing what B says, only the direct sluice is appropriate:

The contrasts in embeddability are illustrated in (39):

(39) a.   Apparently several students called but I wasn't told who.
      b. A: Many doctors want to join up.
          B: I wonder who.
      c. A: Merle saw Mo.
          B: #Does Brendan know WHO? (= Does Brendan know who you claim saw Mo.)
      d. A: Merle saw Mo.
          B: #Brendan also wonders WHO. (= Brendan also wonders who you claim saw Mo.)

---

[17]There exists a third class of clausal bare *wh*-phrases, which we call *exclamative sluices*:

(i)   A: Billie broke the world record for the fifth time last night.
      B: What an athlete!
(ii) A: Merle humiliated Billie again.
      B: What a wimp!

Such phrases share with reprise sluices the inability to appear in non-embedded environments:

(iii) A: Billie broke the world record for the fifth time last night.
      B: #It's amazing what an athlete! (= It's amazing what an athlete Billie is!)
(iv) A: Merle humiliated Billie again.
      B: #It's amazing what a wimp! (= It's amazing what a wimp Merle is!)

Nonetheless, we believe that these differ systematically from both reprise and direct sluices. In contrast to both of these, exclamative sluices do not exhibit connectivity effects—the case of the *wh*-phrase fragment does not vary with respect to the antecedent NP, even in case-rich languages. Moreover, the content is constructed in a distinct way. Oversimplifying somewhat, exclamative sluices merely select a salient entity from the content of some clausal antecedent and predicate of that individual some appropriate property. We disregard this class of sluices in the current work.

These contrasts show that direct sluices do appear in embedded environments, whereas reprise sluices do not, despite possessing contents that would seem appropriate for embedding.

To resolve these differences, our analysis distinguishes constructionally between direct and reprise sluices. One commonality worth noting at the outset relates to the issue of whether or not sluicing involves an unbounded dependency construction (UDC). Most existing accounts of sluicing assume this to be the case, given the assumption that *wh*-phrase interpretation involves dislocation at some syntactic level. In the case of sluicing, the dislocation would arise prior to deletion or after reconstruction.

One piece of evidence against an analysis involving dislocation derives from the fact that sluices quite generally resist modification by fragments like *the hell* and *the heck*:[18]

(40)   a. A: A friend of mine came in.
           B: Who (#the hell/#the heck)?

       b. A: A friend of mine must have stepped in while I was out.
           B: I wonder who (#the hell/#the heck).

       c. A: Jo phoned.
           B: WHO (#the hell/#the heck)?

Note that we argue in Chapter 6 that these elements could modify only *wh*-words in 'extracted' *wh*-phrases, i.e. phrases that introduce a *wh*-interrogative clause. We distinguished these *wh*-phrases via a [WH {*param*}] specification. The fact that fragments like *the hell* and *the heck* cannot appear in sluices is evidence against analyzing sluicing in terms of a reconstruction/deletion operation (as proposed, for example, in Chung et al. 1995 and Reinhart 1997).[19,20] Our account predicts the impossibility of modification in examples like (40), because, as we show below, all such *wh*-phrases are specified as [WH: { }].

---

[18]There are apparent counterexamples to this claim, such as:

   (i) [A arrives at home to find his house covered with toilet paper:] A: What the hell/in tarnation/in the world?

However, these may reasonably be treated as incomplete utterances (perhaps equivalent to *What the hell is going on?*).

[19]The fact that sluicing constructions are productive in so called *wh in situ* languages, such as Mandarin or Japanese (e.g. Takahashi 1994) is itself a significant puzzle for the dislocation strategy.

[20]There is one class of sluices which does pass this test—certain non-pied-piped PP sluices:

   (i)   A: I want to have my omphalos pierced.
         B: What the hell for?
  (ii)   A: I gave my copy of *Maus* to someone, but I can't remember who the hell to.
 (iii)   A: I gave away free copies of *Divergent Series* to some people.
         B: Who on earth to?

However, using a long-distance mechanism to analyze such cases is problematic. A way would be needed to block its application to non-*wh* bare PPs and, perhaps more crucially, to a host of *wh*-PP sluices:

  (iv)   A: I want to have my omphalos pierced.
         B: For Bill's sake?/*Bill's sake for?
   (v)   A: I gave my copy of *Maus* to someone.
         B: To me actually/*me to actually.
  (vi)   A: I put the book under something, but I can't remember under what/*what under. (cf. Which table were they found hiding under?)
 (vii)   A: The instructions say one needs to thread it through some hole.
         B: Through which hole?/*Which hole through? (cf. Which tunnels does the train pass through?)

We leave to future research the problem of how to analyze sluices such as (i)-(iii).

8.1.6 Reprise Sluices

We are about to explain how to analyze reprise sluices, for which our grammar is already sufficient. But, before going into detail, we must amplify the description of the contextual background that underlies a reprise utterance. Ginzburg (1997, 2001) points out the Turn Taking Puzzle (TTP), a phenomenon that indicates an intrinsic asymmetry in contextual access between speaker and addressee. The data at issue concern the resolution of *wh* fragments like those in (41) and (42).

(41) a. A: You're upset. Why? (unambiguously: *Why is B upset?*)

     b. A: You're upset.

        B: Why? (strong preference: *Why does A claim B is upset?*; *Why is B upset?* weakly available)

     c. A: You're upset. Why do I say that?

In examples like (41) two kinds of resolution are in principle available: one where the argument of the operator is the fact associated with the initial assertion (the fact that B is upset); the other where the argument is the fact characterizing the initial utterance (the fact that A asserted that B is upset). (41a), where the original speaker also utters the query, contrasts minimally with (41b), where two distinct speakers are involved.

The examples in (42) are variants of (41) where the initial utterance is a query: in (42a), *why* must pick up on a fact that positively resolves the initial question A poses; but when *why* is uttered by a new speaker, as in (42b), it resolves to a fact characterizing A's initial utterance.

(42) a. A: Where are you buying a house? Why? (= Why is it that <u>you are buying it *there*</u>?)

     b. A: Where are you buying a house?

        B: Why? (= Why do <u>you ask where I am buying a house</u>?)

     c. A: Where are you buying a house? (and) Why am I now asking you this question?

Note that data like (41) and (42) cannot be explained merely as a consequence of the differing coherence of an utterance depending on who utters it: the resolution unavailable to A in (41a) and (42a) is indeed coherent and entirely plausible when it arises from a non-elliptical utterance whose resolution is not so heavily dependent on context, as in (41c) and (42c).

Ginzburg (1997, 2001) develops an account of the TTP based on a fundamental asymmetry in contextual evolution between speaker and addressee. A speaker is obliged to be aware of the content that her utterance communicates. Hence, a speaker immediately integrates the content of her utterance into her representation of the common ground. So, for instance, if she poses a question q then, relative to her view of the common ground, q becomes maximal in QUD.

For the addressee, the situation is different—there is no conversational obligation for him to comprehend the utterance. The obligation is, rather, to consider the issue of whether or not he understands the speaker's utterance. In the view developed by Ginzburg (1997, 2001), understanding an utterance u involves the possession of information that resolves two issues. The first concerns how to instantiate the contextual indices $c_1, \ldots, c_n$ of the meaning of u in a way that is compatible with the current context c. The second, which we put aside in our discussion here, is the issue of what goals the speaker is attempting to achieve by making u. If a conversationalist believes he is able to correctly instantiate the meaning, he 'grounds' the utterance. Otherwise, utilizing the partial information he possesses about the context, he coerces the meaning of u into a clarification question using one of a number of available coercion mechanisms, one of which is illustrated shortly. An addressee's context is, consequently, predisposed to have reprise questions as maximal in QUD in the immediate aftermath of an utterance.

We now illustrate how such coercion takes place.[21] Consider (43a), an utterance of which, if successfully communicated, may have its content specified as (43b):

(43)   a. A: Did Jo leave?

      b.

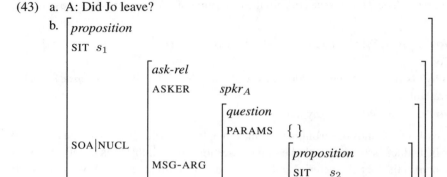

Note that, in line with the specification provided for clauses of type *root-cl* in Chapter 7, the message expressed by this utterance is a proposition whose SOA's NUCLEUS is the illocutionary relation *ask-rel*.

Faced with such an utterance, an addressee who cannot instantiate one or more of the contextual indices, say ③ for concreteness, has only a partial understanding of (43a). In such a situation, as far as the addressee is concerned, the question of resolving the reference of an uncertain index moves to center stage. That is, the following question becomes the maximal question under discussion (MAX-QUD):

---

[21] A detailed account of these coercion mechanisms can be found in Cooper and Ginzburg (in preparation).

(44)

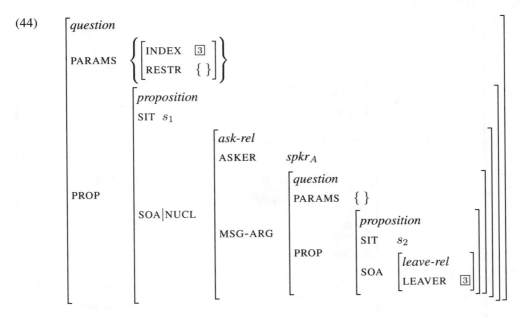

This is, incidentally, the content we proposed for a reprise use of the interrogative (45):

(45)   Did WHO leave?

We are now prepared to analyze reprise sluices. One possible contextual background for B's utterance in (46a), paraphrased as in (46b), is one in which B has introduced as the maximal question in QUD—the current discourse topic—the question in (44):[22]

(46) a. A: Did Jo leave?
          B: WHO?
      b.   Who$_i$ are you asking if i left.

The SAL-UTT derives from A's utterance of the NP *Jo*. We can then analyze the reprise sluice (46) as shown in (47):

---

[22]This sluice can also be understood as expressing the question *who is Jo*, i.e. as signaling a problem with the NP subutterance *Jo*, without being sure that all other constituent subutterances have been comprehended, which would be required if one is to introduce the question in (44). Analyzing this class of readings depends on recognizing an additional coercion mechanism called *parameter value identification* in Cooper and Ginzburg (in preparation). Essentially, this involves constructing a clarification based solely on the content of the given subutterance.

(47)

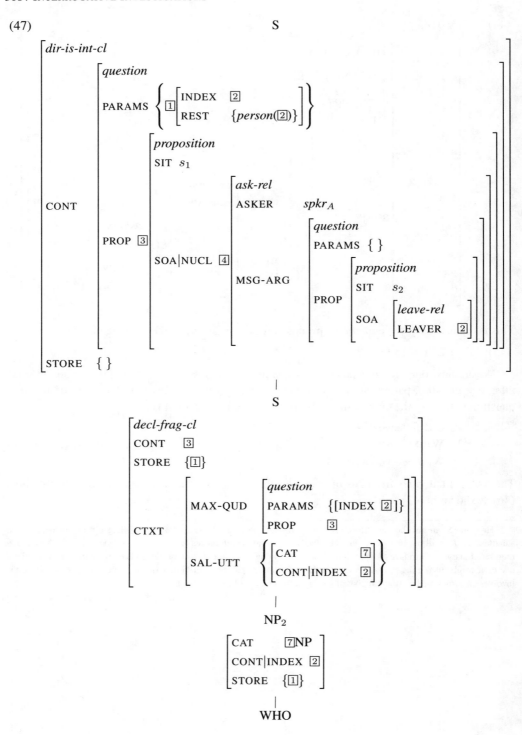

The head daughter of this construction is a *decl-frag-cl* in which the *wh*-phrase's parameter remains in storage. The reprise sluice is then analyzed as a *dir-is-int-cl*, the phrasal type introduced in Chapter 7 to analyze non-elliptical direct in-situ clauses:[23] Note that as a phrase of type *dir-is-int-cl*, the reprise sluice gets specified as [IC +] and we therefore predict correctly facts such as (39c,d) above.

Our analysis extends directly to provide a reading for elliptical literal reprises like (48a), whose non-elliptical counterparts were discussed in Chapter 7.[24]

(48) a. A: Did Jo leave?
          B: Jo?
      b.   Are you asking if JO left?

The analysis we provide for such cases is virtually the same as our treatment of reprise sluices. B introduces as MAX-QUD the question in (44a) and the SAL-UTT derives from A's utterance of the NP *Jo*. The literal reprise is thus analyzed as illustrated in (49):

---

[23]It might seem at first blush somewhat strange that the 'reprise sluice' gets analyzed by means of the non-reprise type *dir-is-int-cl* rather than the reprise type *repr-int-cl*. However, in a *repr-int-cl* those aspects of content which make the utterance a reprise are explicitly introduced by the construction type. In the reprise sluice, however, the reprise aspects of content arise entirely from the context.

[24]This reprise also has a reading which one can paraphrase as *Who is Jo?* The analysis of this reading is analogous to the mechanism discussed in footnote 22.

(49)

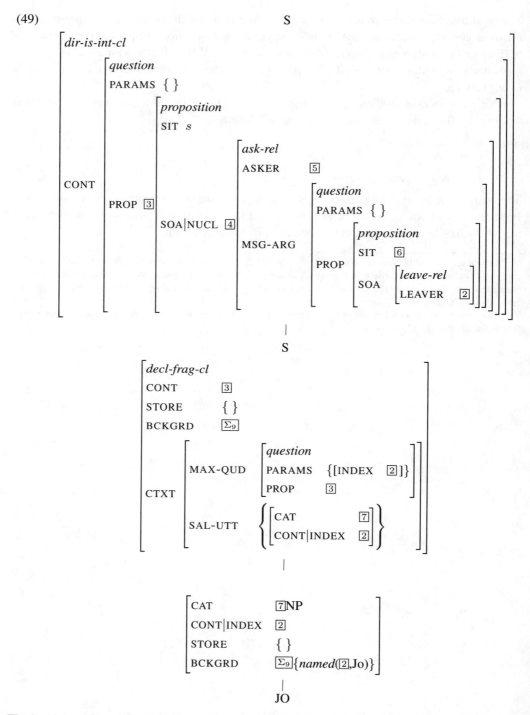

The head daughter of this construction is a *decl-frag-cl*. The polar question arises as a *dir-is-int-cl*.

Finally, let us turn to a potentially surprising prediction of our account—an explanation of why reprise sluices are obligatorily [WH { }], which we take to explain facts such as (40), repeated here as (50):

(50)   A: Jo phoned.
        B: WHO (#the hell/the heck)?

Our analysis treats every reprise sluice as a clause of type *dir-is-int-cl* whose head daughter is a clause of type *decl-frag-cl*. The *decl-frag-cl* in turn has a unique head daughter, which is a *wh*-phrase. The *dir-is-int-cl* is the daughter of a phrase of type *root-cl* in this case, and hence must be specified as [WH { }] by the constraints on *root-cl* presented in Chapter 7. This specification will 'percolate down' to the successive head daughters by the GHFP. Hence the *wh*-phrase is also [WH { }] and cannot be modified by *the hell/heck* and the like.

8.1.7 Direct Sluices

We now turn to direct sluices. We have already hypothesized the existence of four maximal *wh*-interrogative clause types: *ns-wh-int-cl*, *su-wh-int-cl*, *repr-int-cl*, and *dir-is-int-cl*. The last two of these (the subtypes of *in-situ-interrogative-clause*) are restricted to be [IC +], which at the very least means they cannot be used to analyze embedded direct sluices. Attempting to analyze direct sluices using *wh-int-cl* would require us assuming that such sluices are extracted, contrary to the conclusion just reached in considering examples like (40a,b). As a result, we posit an additional type of interrogative clause: *sluiced-interrogative-clause* (*slu-int-cl*). Like *decl-frag-cl*, *slu-int-cl* is a subtype of *hd-frag-ph* and has its content partially determined by the discourse context.

What then is the context for a direct sluice? Virtually all work on sluicing has concentrated on embedded uses, while in monologue this issue has received only cursory attention. The antecedent for a sluice has frequently been assumed to be an existentially quantified declarative logical form or proposition. Some accounts [25] strongly presuppose that *only* existentially quantified logical forms and propositions can serve as antecedents.[26] Glossing over some details of the syntax–semantics interface involved in such accounts, they all assume, in effect, that sluicing involves manipulating an existentially quantified presupposition.

Yet there is reason to doubt whether this correctly describes the contextual background for sluicing. Indeed, quantificational NPs other than existentials can serve as antecedents for sluices:

(51)   a. A: Many dissidents have been released.
           B: Do you know who?
        b. A: Most programs seem to be working, but I can't tell you precisely which ones.
        c. A: Few students have signed up for our courses.
           B: Did Mo actually tell you who?

Two recent accounts, Romero 1998 and Merchant 1999, have sought to frame the antecedency condition for sluicing in terms similar to those proposed by Rooth (1993) for VP ellipsis. The putative analogy between VP ellipsis and sluicing is that in a reconstruction/deletion account, sluicing constitutes S or IP-ellipsis.

---

[25] See e.g. Chung et al. 1995, Reinhart 1997

[26] Chung et al. (1995) assume that existentials are non-quantificational, but denote DRT-style (textually-existentially-closed) variables. Similarly, Reinhart assumes that existentials are non-quantificational and treats them via choice functions rather than quantifier raising. Reinhart suggests this as an explanation for why sluicing is not restricted by constraints on movement.

Both accounts employ an entailment-based notion of *givenness*, developed by Schwarzschild (1999) to help analyze intonational focus marking. To illustrate this approach, consider Merchant's formulation of the antecedency condition:

(52) a. An IP α can be deleted only if α is (or is in) a constituent that is e-GIVEN. (Merchant 1999: 37, (61)).

  b. An expression E is e-GIVEN iff E has a salient antecedent A such that
  (1) A entails F-closure(E) and
  (2) E entails F-closure(A).[27] (Merchant 1999: 36, (42)).

In this view, (53a) can serve as an antecedent for (53b) because: (53a) entails the F-closure of the IP in (53b), given in (53c); and the (existentially closured) IP entails (53a), which in this case is identical with its F-closure.

(53) a. Someone left.

  b. Who$_t$ [$_{IP}$ t left]

  c. $\exists t$ [t left]

Such an account can equally accommodate examples like those in (51), where the antecedent's content is a quantified non-existential proposition.

By the same token, however, a non-quantified antecedent, where the requisite element is focused, is predicted to be an equally appropriate antecedent. (54a) can serve as an antecedent for (54b) because: (54a) entails the F-closure of the IP in (54b), given in (54c); and the (existentially closured) IP is identical with the F-closure of (54a):

(54) a. JO left

  b. Who$_t$ [$_{IP}$ t left]

  c. $\exists t$ [t left]

This incorrectly predicts that a direct sluice should be felicitous in the dialogue (55a) (as an embedded or matrix sluice), with the LF in (54b). Note that a reprise use of the sluice *is* of course possible in such a context.

(55) a. A: JO left.
      B: I wonder who/WHO?

  b. Who$_t$ [you are saying t left]

  c. $\exists t$ [you are saying t left]

Reprise sluices are universally ignored in the above literature, but if our analysis of such readings is utilized—an approximate LF is given in (55b)—the reprise reading is predicted to be inappropriate. That is, neither (54a) or (55a.A) entails (55c), the F-closure of the relevant IP, nor does the reverse entailment hold. Thus, a semantic characterization of the antecedent in terms that merely ensure that it entails a quantified proposition seems problematic.[28]

Our proposal, however, starts out from the observation that sluices do not require the antecedent proposition to actually be presupposed. In (56a), A raises the issue of whether anyone actually showed up for class and continues to be skeptical of this through the utterance of his

---

[27]For an LF E, F-closure(E) is obtained by replacing focussed elements with variables and existentially quantifying over them and any other existing traces.

[28]Of course, one can filter antecedents by adding constraints at a level such as LF, as proposed by Romero (1998) and others. Given our earlier arguments against reconstruction/deletion approaches, however, our concern here is with a semantic characterization of the class of antecedents.

sluice. Similar remarks hold for B's sluice in (56b). In (56d), moreover, the antecedent for the sluice is a polar question:

(56) a. A: Did anyone show up for class today?
          B: Yup.
          A: Really?
          B: Yeah.
          A: Who?
      b. A: Various people support the proposal.
          B: I doubt it.
          A: No, really.
          B: Who?
      c. A: Did anyone call for me during these past hours?
          B: Who, for instance?
      d. A: Is there anyone who could possibly unscrew the hatch?
          B: Gee, I wish I knew who.

What clearly *cannot* be the case for a felicitous direct sluice (in contrast to verb-phrase ellipsis) is that it be *contextually established* that the corresponding property is uninstantiated:[29]

(57) A: No student supported the proposal.
      B: Hmm, #I wonder who. (= I wonder who did.)

We conclude that a more adequate description of the context for sluicing is that it involves the QUD-maximality of a polar question $\lambda\{\ \}p$, where p is a quantified proposition whose widest-scoping quantifier is a positive quantifier.[30] As mentioned above, in the account of dialogue interaction developed in Ginzburg (forthcoming), asserting that p has the initial effect of making $\lambda\{\ \}p$ QUD-maximal. This can lead subsequently either to p's acceptance or to the introduction of a question on which $\lambda\{\ \}p$ **Depends**. Thus, both asserting a non-negative quantified proposition p, as in (51), or posing a polar question $\lambda\{\ \}p$, as in (56), will lead to the QUD-maximality of $\lambda\{\ \}p$. After this point in a dialogue, $\lambda\{\ \}p$ can serve as background for a sluiced utterance.[31]

---

[29]Things seem to improve somewhat if the negative universal is under discussion, as in (i), though one might argue that the sluice becomes felicitous because of the (existential?) whose truth is implicated by B:

(i) A: No students supports the proposal.
     B: I think that's a gloomy assessment of the situation.
     A: Really? Tell me who then?

[30]The distinction between positive and negative quantifiers plays an important role in our treatment of positive and negative polar questions in section 8.2.

[31]Although it does seem that just about any non-negative quantificational NP can serve as an antecedent for direct sluicing, it should be noted that singular definites are exceptions to this—they allow only reprise sluices. This is expected behavior for 'referential' uses of definites, but perhaps less so for 'attributive' uses such as (i):

(i) A: The murderer was obviously a vicious guy.
     B: #Who?/WHO?/#You don't know who?
(ii)   #Which murderer was obviously a vicious guy?

The best explanation we can offer for the impossibility of a direct sluice in (i)B involves a proposed condition concerning which questions can be added to the QUD in a given contextual configuration. This condition would state that one can introduce into the QUD only questions for which a resolving answer is currently not present in the common ground. If A's utterance is understood referentially, then a reprise sluice is felicitous. Otherwise, if A is being attributive, the content our account will associate with the direct sluice will be essentially synonymous with the non-elliptical (ii), which is indeed infelicitous in this context. This seems to be the case because (ii) asks one to select from a set of murderers, where the previous utterance has already indicated that a unique one is known to exist.

We propose (58) as a constraint on the type *slu-int-cl*. As with all interrogative clauses, retrieval is effected as a consequence of the IRC (introduced in Chapter 6), combined with the requirement that the STORE be empty.[32]

(58) *slu-int-cl*:

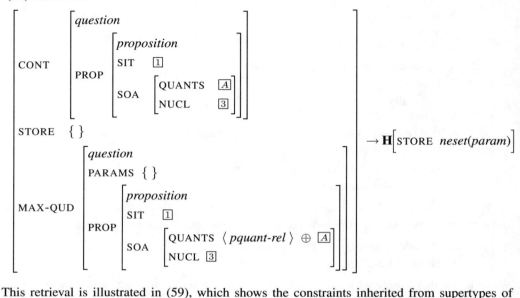

This retrieval is illustrated in (59), which shows the constraints inherited from supertypes of *slu-int-cl*:[33]

---

[32]This latter assumption might be too strong, as the following example suggests:

  (i) A: Several people's birthdays have gone by without acknowledgment recently. Who knows whose?

      B: Well, Jo knows that Bo's birthday went by unnoticed, Mo knows that Merle's was . . . .

[33]It is of course artificial to limit the phenomenon of sluicing to nominal phrases. This must be expanded to include, at least, adverbials of various kinds. There are also some unresolved issues. For example, supposing that (i) is a bona fide instance of sluicing, must (ii) also be so analyzed?

  (i) I wonder why.

  (ii) I wonder how come.

The analysis of *how come* as a complementizer (Chapter 6) allows an alternative analysis of (ii), where the sentential argument of *how come* is simply made optional. We cannot resolve these matters here.

(59) ECC & GHFP & *hd-only-ph* & *hd-frag-ph* & *core-cl* & *inter-cl* & IRC & *slu-int-cl*:

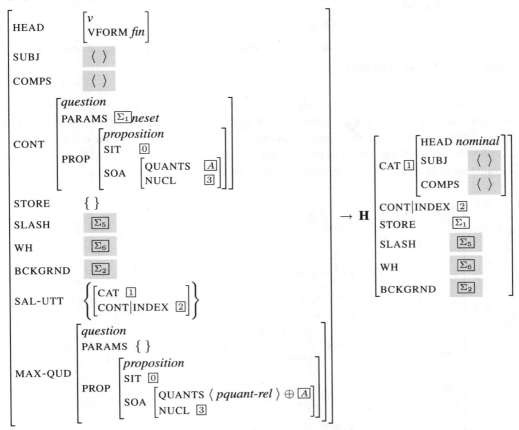

Indeed, the analysis we propose for direct sluices closely resembles the analyses we have provided for short answers. The main difference lies in the somewhat different semantic parallelism linking the QUANTS of the MAX-QUD and the QUANTS of the clause's content. In a short answer, the QUANTS value of the clause arises by retrieving from the head daughter's store the set, possibly empty, of quantifiers and quantifying it in wider than MAX-QUD's QUANTS value. In a direct sluice, by contrast, the widest scoping quantifier of MAX-QUD's QUANTS, call it q_1, is excluded from the QUANTS-list of the clause's content. Thus, the widest scoping quantifier of the open proposition of the question will be whatever quantifier, if any, was previously scoped just narrower than q_1. The commonality uniting these cases is that in each case SAL-UTT derives from the (sub)utterance whose content gets the widest scope in MAX-QUD. For a *slu-int-cl*, the (sub)utterance whose content provided q_1 also provides the SAL-UTT value; for a *decl-frag-cl*, the analogous (sub)utterance is the one whose content provides the interrogative parameter. Notice that our account, in contrast to Reinhart's and Chung, Ladusaw and McCloskey's accounts, does not require any idiosyncratic interpretational mechanism for the antecedents of a sluice.

Note also that because *slu-int-cl* is a subtype of *hd-frag-ph*, all sluiced clauses will be [HEAD *v*]. And because the head daughter must be [HEAD *nominal*] (i.e. an NP or a PP), the GHFP will always be overruled in a *slu-int-cl*. This is important in section 8.3 below, where we consider the selection properties of a verb like *wonder*, which does not select for question-denoting NPs, but is compatible with a sluiced clause:

(60) a. A: A student phoned.
          B: I wonder who.
      b.   B wondered *(about) the question.

As a first illustration of how our analysis works, let us consider a dialogue like (61):

(61)   A: A student phoned.
         B: Who?

Our account of such a case is essentially this: A's assertion changes the context in such a way as to make the issue of *whether a student phoned* maximal in QUD, while SAL-UTT derives from the subutterance *a student*. The content that emerges is the question of who it was that phoned. As with *decl-frag-cl*, we leave it to the dialogue coherence conditions regulated by MAX-QUD to ensure that B intends his question to be asking about students.

(62)

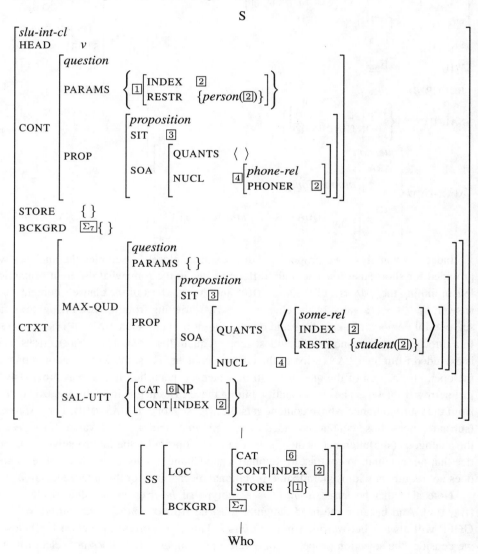

Our account also extends to examples like the following, where the SAL-UTT is a universal NP. Here the reading that emerges is paraphrasable as "Which students will quit?":

(63)   A: (These changes to the program are monstrous.) Every student will quit.
         B: (Really?) Who?

(64)   S

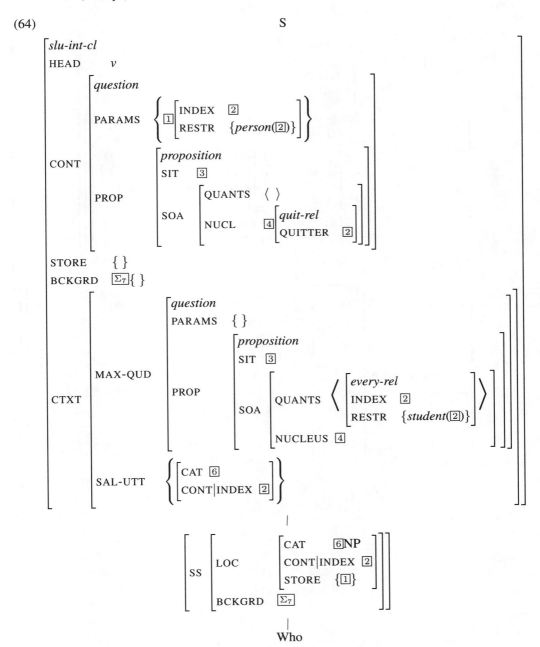

Who

A similar analysis accounts for (65):[34]

(65) A: We've got some good students here. Someone's even read every book by Pinter.
      B: Who?

(66)   S

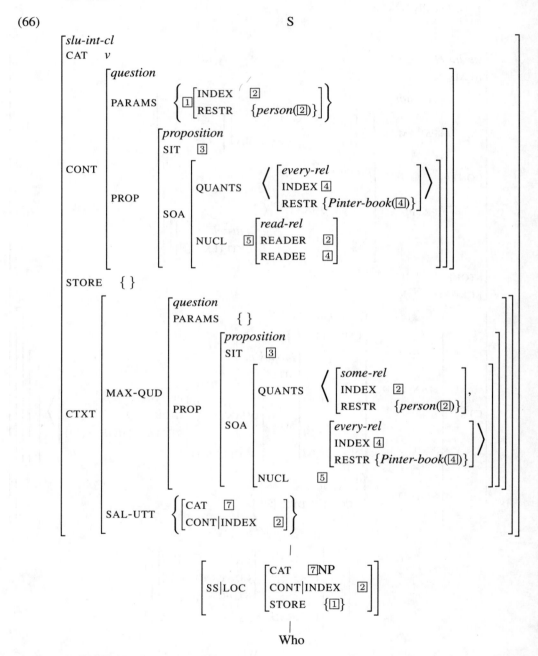

[34]A more detailed analysis concerning the dynamics of the context would also account for the fact that the quantification introduced by the word *someone* in A's second sentence is restricted to range over the salient set of good students.

The type *slu-int-cl* is underspecified for the feature IC. All of the previous examples of *slu-int-cl* would head a *root-cl*, and hence must be specified as [IC +]. Alternatively, a *slu-int-cl* can get the specification [IC −], rendering it a suitable complement to a question-selecting predicate such as *ask* or *wonder* or a factive/resolutive predicate such as *know*, *discover*, and *tell*. For instance, (67) will be treated as shown in (68):[35]

(67)   A: A student phoned. Kim wonders who.

(68)

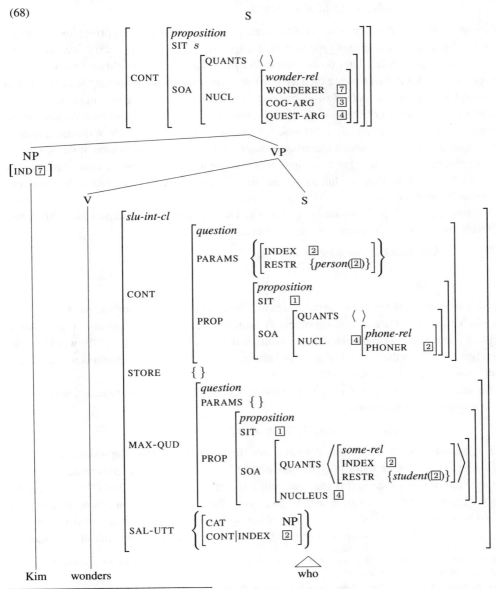

Kim   wonders   who

---

[35] As noted in Chapter 2, we follow Cooper and Ginzburg (1996) in assuming that attitudinal predicates carry an argument (labeled here as COGNITIVE-ARG). This argument is filled by a contextually supplied mental situation of the reported agent. Thus our treatment, which allows reference in attitude contexts to cognitive particulars, as opposed to solely semantic objects such as propositions or questions, provides a compositional implementation of a growing trend in recent work within the philosophical literature on attitude reports.

Let us point to a rather unexpected prediction of our account, already discussed for reprise sluices—direct sluices must be [WH { }]. This explains dialogues such as (40), repeated here in part as (69):

(69) a. A: A friend of mine came in.
   B: Who (#the hell/#the heck)?
   b. A: A friend of mine must have stepped in while I was out.
   B: I wonder who (#the hell/#the heck).

For unembedded direct sluices such as (69a) the same explanation as for reprise sluices applies: since the clause heads a phrase of type *root-cl*, it is specified as [WH { }] (as explained in Chapter 7). This specification 'percolates down' to the *decl-frag-cl* and to the *wh*-phrase that heads it, all courtesy of the GHFP. An example such as (69b) involves a somewhat more detailed explanation. The complete sentence, a *decl-hd-su-cl*, once again heads a *root-cl*, and hence must be [WH { }]. This specification, again courtesy of the GHFP, must be true of the VP and its head daughter— the verb *wonder*. The specification that *wonder* gets for WH must satisfy the WH-Amalgamation Constraint (see Chapter 5), which identifies *wonder*'s WH value as the set union of the WH values of its arguments. This means that no argument of *wonder* in (69b) may bear a non-empty specification for WH. In particular, the sluice must be [WH { }] and consequently so must the *wh*-phrase that heads its head daughter.

We now discuss three tricky cases of sluicing. The first concerns examples like (70), where ostensibly there is no overt expression to provide the SAL-UTT:

(70)   A: And what did you do then?
   B: I ate.
   A: What?

How this is analyzed depends on the treatment of 'object deletion' verbs such as *eat*. One possible analysis is in terms of a new non-canonical synsem type, akin to *gap-ss* or *pro-ss* discussed in Chapters 2 and 5. If this approach can be maintained, then examples such as (70) would receive an analysis similar to the examples discussed above: the element whose synsem is non-canonical would provide the value of SAL-UTT.[36]

An analysis of this sort is harder to maintain for cases like (5) above, repeated here as (71), where no overt utterance exists:

(71)   [A and B are in an elevator] A: What floor?

Here, A assumes that there is some floor B wants the elevator to go to. The general strategy we could adopt is to assume that the QUD gets updated as a result of an accommodation process of some kind. For instance in this case one might suggest that A updates her QUD with a polar question paraphrasable as "Does B want to go to some floor?" The nature of this accommodation process is related to practical reasoning and planning but also probably involves reasoning of a linguistic nature. The latter supposition derives from the fact that it seems difficult to explain, on

---

[36]This would also account for the fact that in case-rich languages, like German, the case information of a 'deleted object' is maintained by the sluice:

(i) A: Als   ich in Mailand war, habe ich auch getrunken. B: Welchen kaffee?
   A: When I   in Milan   was, have I   also drunk.   B: What   coffee-masc-acc?
   A: When I was in Milan, I also drank. B: What coffee?

the basis of semantic and pragmatic reasoning alone, why certain sluice-like utterances are not possible without an overt antecedent. For instance, (72a) seems rather unnatural whereas (72b) is quite infelicitous:

(72) a. [A and B are in an elevator] A: To what floor?
      b. [A and B are in an elevator] A: #Of what floor?

This might suggest, then, that the QUD accommodation process essentially involves the accommodation of an *utterance* or a class of possible utterances. This would imply that SAL-UTT could get a well defined value, which would provide additional parallelism restrictions. This strategy is probably more fruitful than an alternative approach which would analyze sluices that lack overt antecedents as idioms of some kind. This alternative approach is suggested by Chung et al. (1995), following earlier claims by Hankamer and Sag (1976) that sluicing requires an overt antecedent. However, such an approach is difficult to square with the contextual and linguistic variety demonstrated by the examples of antecedent-less sluices provided earlier in this book. We will not try to resolve this debate here and must leave unanswered the question of whether or not utterances such as (71) can be analyzed as instances of *slu-int-cl*.

Finally, we note one other potential extension of our account of sluices. As first noted by Ginzburg (1992), sluices can also exhibit functional readings:

(73) a. A: Every cellist has a favorite piece.
         B: Which piece?
         A: The one she played in her first recital.
      b. A: Most people here have submitted a paper to a journal.
         B: Which journal?
         A: Alexis to *Psychic Review*, Pat to *Post-Modern Letters*, ...

Such cases are of some interest for a number of reasons. As we noted in Chapter 4, if one accepts our arguments that sluicing is not based on reconstruction, then it provides an instance of a pair-list answer that demonstrably does not arise from a scope ambiguity. If, on the other hand, one does not accept our arguments and manages to construct a reconstruction-like approach meeting our objections, then (73b) provides an example of a pair-list answer based on an antecedent that is *not* a universal quantifier. This would contradict the widely assumed generalization discussed in Chapter 4.

If we associate a standard scoped content with "Every cellist has a favorite piece," then our account cannot provide for the requisite functional reading of the sluice. But if—as we speculated above in connection with short answers, as in (32) and (35), one were to interpret 'narrow scope' quantifiers by means of skolemization, one could use *slu-int-cl* together with our analysis of functional uses of *wh*-phrases to directly account for the functional reading. We sketch one possible analysis along these lines:

(74)

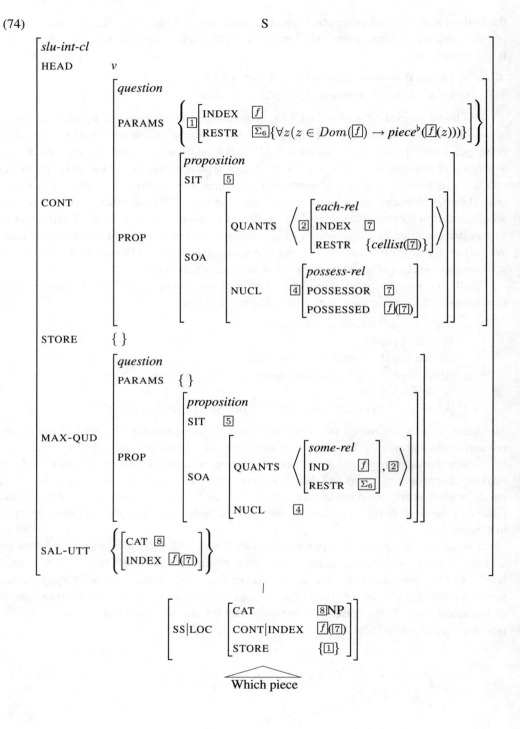

8.1.8 Summary

This section outlined a syntactic, semantic and dialogue-context treatment of several kinds of sentence fragments. This covered both declarative fragments and the phenomenon of sluicing as well as various reprise and functional uses. The overall organization of the clausal types that were posited is sketched in (75).

(75)

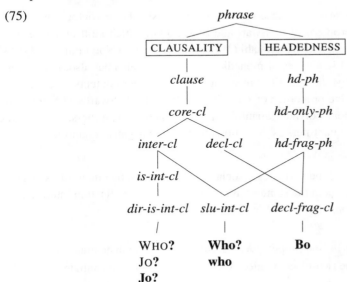

8.2 Negative Questions

8.2.1 Introduction

Chapter 3 contrasted two classes of polar interrogatives—'positive' and 'negative'. We provided evidence, recapitulated below, that for a given proposition p the contents of the interrogatives *whether p* and *whether not p* need to be distinguished. This must be the case, despite the fact that these two classes of interrogatives cannot be distinguished by the answerhood relations they specify. Capturing the difference between positive and negative interrogatives thus poses an intrinsic difficulty for approaches in which questions are reductively explicated in terms of answerhood. This section demonstrates how our approach captures this difference, by recasting the situation-theoretic approach to negation within a polyadic account of negation and negative concord, as developed by de Swart and Sag (2000).

Chapter 3 also discussed the situation-theoretic view of negation. The theory postulates that all SOAs come in pairs: a SOA that carries a positive *polarity*, call it σ, and a distinct SOA: the *dual* of σ, often notated as $\overline{\sigma}$. These are identical in terms of their relation and entity–to–argument-role mapping, but differ in their polarity. The most basic axioms about the dualization operation—introduced as *NegOf* relation in Chapter 3—are those in (76):

(76) a. $\overline{\overline{\sigma}} = \sigma$

  b. If $s \models \sigma$, then $s \not\models \overline{\sigma}$

Axiom (76a) states the assumption that iterating dualization, like classical negation, reverts to the original polarity. (76b) states the assumption that no situation supports both a SOA and its dual. Propositional negation is parasitic on SOA dualization. As in Chapter 3, an atomic (i.e. non-compound) proposition is related to its negative counterpart by the symmetric relation NegationOf: NegationOf(prop(s, σ)) = prop($s, \overline{\sigma}$). A final point to recall in this regard is the constraint associated with the determiner relation *no* (see Chapter 3, example (141a)):

(77) $\quad s \models \langle No; \tau, \rho \rangle$ iff $\{x|s \models \tau\{x\}\} \subseteq \{x|s \models \overline{\rho\{x\}}\}$

No acts as a 'negation operator' for those entities which satisfy the restrictor clause. This ties in interestingly with the proposal of de Swart and Sag (2000), which built on earlier proposals of May (1989) and Keenan and Westerståhl (1997) that Quantified Noun Phrases (QNPs) can interact not merely to build sequences of monadic quantifier contents but also, in restricted circumstances, to construct *polyadic* quantifier meanings, i.e. quantifier contents where the restrictor and nuclear scope involve properties of r-ity distinct from 1. De Swart and Sag restrict the QNPs which can bring about polyadic quantification to negative quantifiers, defining the *resumption* of a set of negative quantifiers as the following polyadic negative quantifier:

(78) $\quad \text{res}(NO_{\sigma_1}^{R_1}, NO_{\sigma_2}^{R_2}, \ldots, NO_{\sigma_n}^{R_n}) =_{def} NO_{\sigma_1 \cup \ldots \cup \sigma_n}^{R_1 \cup \ldots \cup R_n}$

Here, R_i are the restrictors and σ_i the variables associated with the negative quantifiers. Thus, a sentence such as (79a) can yield both the standard iterated monadic quantification interpretation in (79b) and the polyadic interpretation in (79c):

(79) a. No one likes no one.

b. $NO_x[NO_y[likes(x, y)]]$ (the property $\lambda x \neg \exists y.likes(x, y)$ is uninstantiated.)

c. $NO_{x,y} likes(x, y)$ (the two-place relation $\lambda x, y.likes(x, y)$ is uninstantiated)

In case there is a restriction on the QNPs, the polyadic interpretation's restrictor is the cartesian product of the properties contributed by each QNP as illustrated for (80a) in (80b).[37] In so-called negative-concord languages (e.g. Romance) a sentence containing arbitraily many quantifiers, such as (80c), can yield the interpretation in (80d):

(80) a. No student likes no athlete.

b. $NO_{\{x,y\}}^{\{student(x), athelete(y)\}} likes(x, y)$ (the two place relation $\lambda x, y.likes(x, y)$, where x is a student and y is an athlete, is uninstantiated)

c. Personne ne dit jamais rien à personne.

d. $NO_{\{x,y,z,e\}}^{\{human(x), thing(y), human(z), time(e)\}} say(x, y, z, e)$ (the four-place relation $\lambda x, y, z, t.say(x, y, z, e)$, where x is a human, y is a thing, z is a human, and t is a time, is uninstantiated)

The proposal made by de Swart and Sag is to treat sentential negation as a 0-ary negative quantifier—the negation contributes an unrestricted operator which binds no variables. We assume here that this operator is the dualization operator on SOAs just illustrated. The assumption that sentential negation is treated as a 0-ary negative quantifier has the immediate consequence that if it participates in the construction of a negative polyadic quantifier, its contribution is vacuous:

(81) a. No student doesn't like no athlete. (AAVE)

b. $NO_{\{x,y\}}^{\{student(x), athelete(y)\}} likes(x, y)$ (the two-place relation $\lambda x, y.likes(x, y)$, where x is a student and y is an athlete, is uninstantiated)

---

[37]This interpretation is probably unsuitable for standard British or American English, but is possible in a number of varieties such as African American Vernacular English (AAVE).

De Swart and Sag offer an implementation of their proposal in HPSG. This involves the following key components:

- Sentential negation is interpreted by retrieval onto the QUANTS list.
- Retrieval from storage onto QUANTS allows resumption of negative quantifiers. More specifically, they define the following `retrieve` operation:
  - (82) Given a set of GQs Σ and a partition of Σ into two sets Σ_1 and Σ_2, where Σ_2 is a set of negative quantifiers, then
    $$\texttt{retrieve}(\Sigma) =_{def} \texttt{order}(\Sigma_1 \cup \texttt{res}(\Sigma_2)).$$

In addition to this, we introduce a partitioning of the type *soa* into positive and negative subtypes on the basis of a partition of quantifiers into negative and positive. The negative *soa*s are those whose widest scoping quantifier is a negative quantifier, whereas the positive *soa*s are those which either have an empty QUANTS list or whose widest scoping quantifier is positive:[38]

(83)

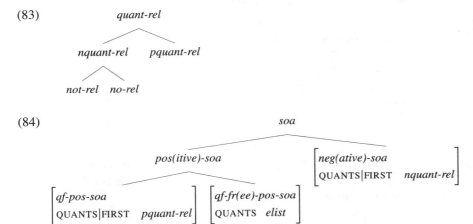

(84)

Two further components addressed here concern the syntactic treatment of sentential negation and the TFS/SU+AE interface. We assume, following Warner (1993), Kim and Sag (1995), Sag and Wasow (1999), Warner (2000), Sag (2000), and Kim and Sag (In press), that the English word *not* is not a modifier of the finite verb but rather is selected as a complement. How this is implemented is not of particular concern here.[39] We assume that the negative operator is retrieved

---

[38]Note that this partition is posited at the level of TFSs. This constitutes one of the few places in our approach where there is a potential mismatch between a semantic account at the denotational level (i.e. relative to the SU+AE, which constitutes our semantic universe) and at the TFS level. As far as its TFS representation goes, a *soa* whose QUANTS value is ⟨*not-rel, not-rel*⟩ is classified as a *neg-soa*. However, the SOA it denotes in the SU+AE is classified as belonging to the sort **Pos** since, as noted above, double dualization reverts to the original polarity. The lexical entries we posit are formulated on the TFS level, so we predict such a content to display the properties of a *neg-soa*. In fact, genuine double negatives, at least in English, are difficult to construct because verbal negation does not iterate. One can construct cases where two negations of distinct kinds are combined:

(i) Isn't it the case that Bo didn't leave?

(ii) Didn't Bo not leave?

These cases intuitively seem to behave as negative polar questions, as the partition at the level of TFSs predicts. We note that our account of answerhood, which predicts that positive and negative polar questions have the same answerhood properties, nonetheless does rely on the iteration property of dualization.

[39]Most analyses developed in HPSG have assumed that a *not*-selecting verb is created by a lexical rule. Warner (2000) accomplishes a similar effect by means of lexical type specification.

onto QUANTS by means of precisely the same mechanisms used for lexical retrieval in Chapter 5. That is, a verb retrieves quantifiers from the STORE values of its arguments. For example:

(85)

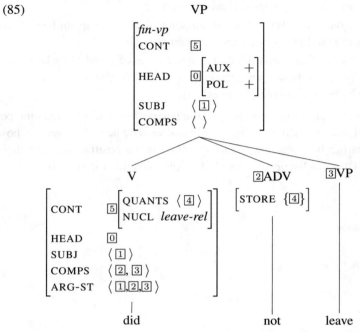

did not leave

In terms of TFS interpretation, the definitions already provided for polarity in Chapter 3, definition 17, are now quite self-explanatory—*soa*s are by default positive but they 'become' negative in virtue of a negative operator represented in QUANTS:

(86) a.

If a is of the form: $\begin{bmatrix} soa \\ \text{QUANTS} & \langle \ \rangle \\ \text{NUCL} & b \end{bmatrix}$,

then $[\![a]\!]^c = [\![b]\!]^c$ and $\mathbf{Pos}([\![a]\!]^c)$

b.

If a is of the form: $\begin{bmatrix} soa \\ \text{QUANTS} & \begin{bmatrix} \text{FIRST} & not\text{-}rel \\ \text{REST} & b \end{bmatrix} \\ \text{NUCL} & g \end{bmatrix}$,

then $[\![a]\!]^c = \overline{h}$ [the dual of the SOA h]

where $h = \left[\!\!\left[\begin{bmatrix} soa \\ \text{QUANTS} & b \\ \text{NUCL} & g \end{bmatrix} \right]\!\!\right]^c$

With this basic treatment of negation, we can now account for the basic properties that distinguish positive from negative polar questions.

8.2.2 A Semantic Analysis of Positive and Negative Polar Questions

We have already analyzed polar questions as 0-ary proposition abstracts. We postulate simply that a *negative question* is a question whose proposition's SOA is a *neg-soa*. For example, (87a) has (87b) as its content, whereas the negative interrogative (87c) has (87d):

(87) a. Did Kim visit Sandy?

     b. $\lambda\{\ \}\mathsf{prop}(s, \langle\langle \mathit{Visit}, \mathit{visitor}{:}k, \mathit{visited}{:}s\rangle\rangle)$

     c. Didn't Kim visit Sandy?

     d. $\lambda\{\ \}\mathsf{prop}(s, \overline{\langle\langle \mathit{Visit}, \mathit{visitor}{:}k, \mathit{visited}{:}s\rangle\rangle})$

These contents have the following TFS representations:

(88) a.

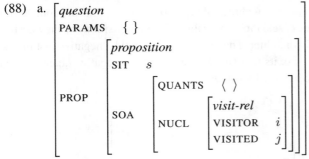

      BCKGRD $\{named(i,Kim), named(j,Sandy)\}$

    b.

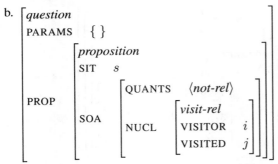

      BCKGRD $\{named(i,Kim), named(j,Sandy)\}$

This yields the desired differentiation between positive and negative, manifested in the distinct appropriate contexts of use and most obviously in elliptical answers with particles like the French *si* and the German *doch*. Moreover, given standard situation theoretic assumptions about the nature of dualization and propositional negation, along with our assumptions about the answerhood relations associated with questions, positive and negative polar questions indeed yield identical answerhood relations. This also helps explain why negation is neutralized in interrogatives embedded by resolutive predicates. In addition, we now can naturally accommodate the fact that non-negated polar interrogatives containing the quantifier *no* behave like negative polar questions. Thus—as with sententially negated interrogatives—responding with *yes* to (89a) leads to confusion, but responding with *no* involves a strong preference for a single-negation reading even though a double-negation reading seems available. In addition, a rising-tone rendition of (89a) involves the negationless expectation (89e):

(89) a. A: Did no one try to help you?

 b. B: Yes.

 c. B: No. (Preferred interpretation *affirms* that no one tried to help B.)

 d. B: No, some guy gave me mouth-to-mouth resuscitation.

 e. Someone tried to help B.

Observe that almost nothing needs to be added to accommodate negative polars.[40] More precisely, since we assume that the morphosyntactic expression of negation is linked to the presence of a negative quantifier in QUANTS, the type constraints previously introduced for polar interrogatives and 'intonation questions' allow us to construct the desired feature structures for negative polars. More concretely, we present three ways of constructing a polar question: as the content of a phrase of type *pol-int-cl*, as the content of a phrase of type *dir-is-int-cl*, or as the content of a CP headed by *whether* or *if*. In all three cases, the SOA (value of the proposition) of the question is identical to the SOA value of the head daughter. The polar question will be negative just in case the head daughter's SOA is a *neg-soa*—i.e. its first QUANTS element is a negative quantifier. We illustrate this for a complement phrase headed by *whether*:

(90)

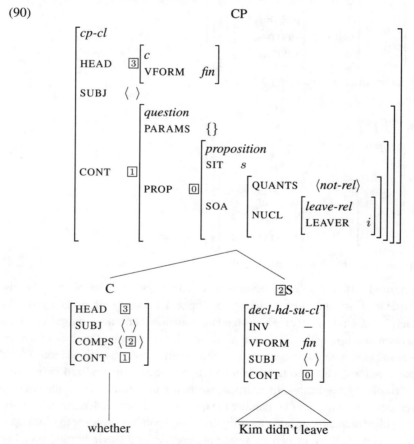

---

[40]The one change that must be made in order to accommodate polyadic quantification is to replace the feature INDEX with the set-valued feature INDICES.

8.2.3 Distinctness in Content and Contextual Appropriateness

One of the main arguments for the synonymy of negative and positive interrogatives, introduced as NPIS in Chapter 3, has been the fact that positive and negative interrogatives *can* elicit similar responses. This is demonstrated by (91a-d), from Hoepelmann 1983, while (91e,f) further show that the *isn't* in (91b) is not answered differently than the *is* in (91a):

(91) a. Is two an even number?
      b. Isn't two an even number?
      c. Yes, two is an even number.
      d. No, two is not an even number.
      e. #No, two is an even number.
      f. #Yes, two is not an even number.

However, Hoepelmann argues at length that NPIS is mistaken, suggesting that the contexts appropriate for a question like (91a) are quite different from those appropriate for (91b). Whereas the former is likely to be asked by a person recently introduced to the odd/even distinction, the latter is not appropriate for such a context. Rather, (91b) is appropriate in a context where, say, the opaque remarks of a mathematician sow doubt on the previously well-established belief that *two is even*.

As a prelude to an explanation for this difference in contextual appropriateness, recall two axioms about dualization, proposed by Cooper (1998), which were discussed in section 3.3.2 of Chapter 3 and are repeated here as (92).

(92) a. $\forall s, \sigma[s \models \overline{\sigma} \text{ implies } \exists (Pos)\psi[s \models \psi \text{ and } \psi > \sigma]]$
      b. $\forall s, \sigma[s \models \overline{\sigma} \text{ implies } \exists (Pos)\psi[s \models \psi \text{ and } \psi \Rightarrow \neg\sigma]]$

(92a) tells us that if a situation s supports the dual of σ, then s also supports information which *defeasibly* entails that σ is the case. We exploit this axiom to identify one of the contexts Hoepelmann identifies as characteristic for using negative questions such (91b). Thus, in considering the question $\lambda\{\}\mathsf{prop}(s, \overline{\sigma})$, one possible source of interest is whether or not s supports information which *defeasibly* entails that σ is the case. In other words, wondering about $\lambda\{\}\mathsf{prop}(s, \overline{\sigma})$ involves wondering about whether s has the characteristics that typically involve σ being the case, but which—nonetheless, in this case—fail to bring about σ.

Similarly, if we consider (92b), what it tells us is that if a situation s supports the dual of σ, then s also supports information that precludes σ. This also has explanatory potential for negative polars: wondering about $\lambda\{\ \}\mathsf{prop}(s, \overline{\sigma})$ can involve, as observed in Przepiórkowski 1999, wondering whether or not s supports information that precludes σ.

Elliptical Responses to Polar Questions

In section 8.1.1, we discussed a class of words we called *propositional-lexemes*—words like *yes*, *no*, *sure*, *right*, *probably not* and *really*, which have uses that convey complete messages. The content a propositional-lexeme gets is propositional, constructed from a polar question derived from the context. The treatment offered above for positive and negative polar questions may now be extended to cover cases attested in languages such as French, German, Old English, and Georgian, where more than one particle is available for responses to polar questions.[41]

---

[41] For discussion of the relevant French and German data see Bäuerle 1979 and Hoepelmann 1983. For a detailed cross-linguistic survey which includes Georgian, see Asatiani 1998.

In such languages, the two positive response particles carry distinct QUD-presuppositions. This amounts to saying the following: French *si*, German *doch*, Georgian *ki* involve the presupposition that the maximal element of the QUD is a negative polar question. The content these particles convey is 'shorn' of this negation. French *oui*, German *ja*, Georgian *xo* involve the presupposition that the maximal element of the QUD is a positive polar question. The queried proposition is affirmed:[42]

(93)
$$
\begin{bmatrix}
\text{PHON} & \langle \text{ si/doch/ki } \rangle \\[2ex]
\text{SS|LOC} & \begin{bmatrix}
\text{CAT} & [\text{HEAD} \quad adv] \\[1ex]
\text{CONT} & \begin{bmatrix}
proposition \\
\text{SIT} \quad s_1 \\
\text{SOA} \quad \begin{bmatrix} \text{QUANTS} & \boxed{A} \\ \text{NUCL} & \boxed{3} \end{bmatrix}
\end{bmatrix}
\end{bmatrix} \\[4ex]
\text{ARG-ST} & \langle \ \rangle \\[2ex]
\text{CTXT|MAX-QUD} & \begin{bmatrix}
question \\
\text{PARAMS} \ \{ \} \\
\text{PROP} \ \begin{bmatrix}
proposition \\
\text{SIT} \quad s_1 \\
\text{SOA} \quad \begin{bmatrix} \text{QUANTS} & \langle nquant\text{-}rel \rangle \oplus \boxed{A} \\ \text{NUCL} & \boxed{3} \end{bmatrix}
\end{bmatrix}
\end{bmatrix}
\end{bmatrix}
$$

(94)
$$
\begin{bmatrix}
\text{PHON} & \langle \text{ oui/ja/xo } \rangle \\[2ex]
\text{SS|LOC} & \begin{bmatrix}
\text{CAT} & [\text{HEAD} \quad adv] \\
\text{CONT} & \boxed{1}
\end{bmatrix} \\[2ex]
\text{ARG-ST} & \langle \ \rangle \\[2ex]
\text{CTXT|MAX-QUD} & \begin{bmatrix}
question \\
\text{PARAMS} & \{ \} \\
\text{PROP} & \boxed{1}[\text{SOA} \quad pos\text{-}soa]
\end{bmatrix}
\end{bmatrix}
$$

In all of the aforementioned languages, as well as in English, there is a single negative response particle. When MAX-QUD involves a positive question, the content is straightforward: a *not-rel* is added to the QUANTS of the SOA of MAX-QUD. Complexity arises with negative questions precisely because in such cases there is potential for ambiguity. As already noted, there is a strong tendency to interpret a negative answer to a negative question as conveying a proposition that has a single negation. Thus, one of the negations is 'absorbed', which is straightforward to conceptualize in the de Swart–Sag account described above. The word *no* can be described as follows: the QUANTS list of MAX-QUD is partitioned into an initial member, which is either a singleton or empty set of negative quantifiers, and the rest. The content of the proposition expressed by *no* involves resumption of *not* with the initial member of MAX-QUD's QUANTS list.

---

[42]Throughout this section we leave propositional lexemes unspecified for the feature IC. Since we have not investigated the embeddability of all the propositional lexemes mentioned here, we leave open the possibility that some must be further constrained as [IC +].

The resulting negative quantifier scopes over all remaining quantifiers from the QUANTS list in the nucleus of the proposition of MAX-QUD:

(95)
$$
\begin{bmatrix}
\text{PHON} & \langle\,\text{no/non/nein/ara}\,\rangle \\
\text{SS|LOC} & \begin{bmatrix}
\text{CAT} & [\text{HEAD}\quad adv] \\
\text{CONT} & \begin{bmatrix}
proposition \\
\text{SIT}\quad s_1 \\
\text{SOA} & \begin{bmatrix}
\text{QUANTS} & \text{order(res(\{\textit{not-rel}\} \cup \boxed{\Sigma})) \oplus \boxed{A}} \\
\text{NUCL} & \boxed{1}
\end{bmatrix}
\end{bmatrix}
\end{bmatrix} \\
\text{ARG-ST} & \langle\,\rangle \\
\text{MAX-QUD} & \begin{bmatrix}
question \\
\text{PARAMS}\ \{\,\} \\
\text{PROP} & \begin{bmatrix}
\text{SIT}\quad s_1 \\
\text{SOA} & \begin{bmatrix}
\text{QUANTS} & \text{order(\boxed{\Sigma}\{(\textit{nquant-rel})\}) \oplus \boxed{A}} \\
\text{NUCL} & \boxed{1}
\end{bmatrix}
\end{bmatrix}
\end{bmatrix}
\end{bmatrix}
$$

When MAX-QUD is a positive polar question no ambiguity is possible. But when it is a negative polar question an ambiguity is triggered by the fact that the constraint in (95) can be satisfied in two distinct ways. If the negative quantifier is included in $\boxed{\Sigma}$ then it is absorbed by the *not-rel* on the QUANTS list of the CONTENT value, which results in a single negation reading. If, on the other hand, the negative quantifier is not included in $\boxed{\Sigma}$ then it is the first member of $\boxed{A}$ and becomes part of the QUANTS list of the CONTENT in addition to the *not-rel*, in which case the double negation reading occurs:

(96) a. A: Did Bo leave?
          B: No.

      b. Content/context of B's response:

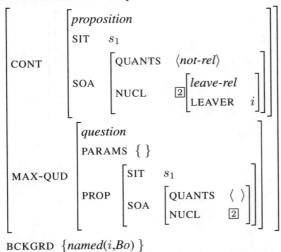

BCKGRD $\{named(i,Bo)\}$

(97) a. A: Didn't Bo leave (in the end)?
      B: No.

   b. Content/context of B's response (double negation reading):[43]

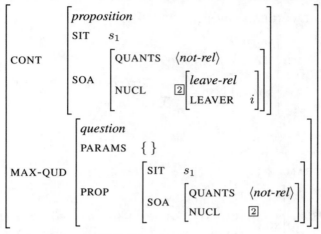

(98) a. A: Didn't Bo leave (in the end)?
      B: No (, he left alright).

   b. Content/context of B's response (double negation reading):

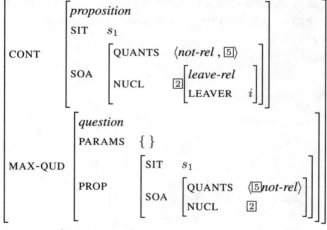

---

[43]Note that the resumption of two 0-ary negative quantifiers is simply a single 0-ary negative quantifier.

As pointed out above, this ambiguity works identically in cases where the polar question is unnegated but contains a negative NP. Our account of these is exactly the same:

(99) a. A: Did no student leave (in the end)?
   B: No.

b. Content/context of B's response (single negation reading):

$$
\begin{bmatrix}
\text{CONT} & \begin{bmatrix} proposition \\ \text{SIT} \quad s_1 \\ \text{SOA} \begin{bmatrix} \text{QUANTS} \left\langle \begin{bmatrix} no\text{-}rel \\ \text{INDICES} \ \{\boxed{4}\} \\ \text{RESTR} \ \{student(\boxed{4})\} \end{bmatrix} \right\rangle \\ \text{NUCL} \quad \boxed{2}\begin{bmatrix} leave\text{-}rel \\ \text{LEAVER} \quad \boxed{4} \end{bmatrix} \end{bmatrix} \end{bmatrix} \\
\text{MAX-QUD} & \begin{bmatrix} question \\ \text{PARAMS} \ \{ \ \} \\ \text{PROP} \begin{bmatrix} \text{SIT} \quad s_1 \\ \text{SOA} \begin{bmatrix} \text{QUANTS} \left\langle \begin{bmatrix} no\text{-}rel \\ \text{INDICES} \ \{\boxed{4}\} \\ \text{RESTR} \ \{student(\boxed{4})\} \end{bmatrix} \right\rangle \\ \text{NUCL} \quad \boxed{2} \end{bmatrix} \end{bmatrix} \end{bmatrix}
\end{bmatrix}
$$

(100) a. A: Did no student leave (in the end)?
   B: No (, some did leave).

b. Content/context of B's response (single negation reading):

$$
\begin{bmatrix}
\text{CONT} & \begin{bmatrix} proposition \\ \text{SIT} \quad s_1 \\ \text{SOA} \begin{bmatrix} \text{QUANTS} \ \langle no\text{-}rel , \boxed{5} \rangle \\ \text{NUCL} \quad \boxed{2}\begin{bmatrix} leave\text{-}rel \\ \text{LEAVER} \quad \boxed{4} \end{bmatrix} \end{bmatrix} \end{bmatrix} \\
\text{MAX-QUD} & \begin{bmatrix} question \\ \text{PARAMS} \ \{ \ \} \\ \text{PROP} \begin{bmatrix} \text{SIT} \quad s_1 \\ \text{SOA} \begin{bmatrix} \text{QUANTS} \left\langle \boxed{5}\begin{bmatrix} no\text{-}rel \\ \text{INDICES} \ \{\boxed{4}\} \\ \text{RESTR} \ \{student(\boxed{4})\} \end{bmatrix} \right\rangle \\ \text{NUCL} \quad \boxed{2} \end{bmatrix} \end{bmatrix} \end{bmatrix}
\end{bmatrix}
$$

Let us return to modern English *yes*. This is, as suggested in section 8.1.1, modeled with the following lexical entry:

(101)

$$
\begin{bmatrix}
\text{PHON} & \langle\,\text{yes}\,\rangle \\[4pt]
\text{SS}|\text{LOC} & \begin{bmatrix} \text{CAT} & [\text{HEAD} \quad adv] \\ \text{CONT} & \boxed{1} \end{bmatrix} \\[12pt]
\text{ARG-ST} & \langle\ \rangle \\[6pt]
\text{CTXT}|\text{MAX-QUD} & \begin{bmatrix} question \\ \text{PARAMS} & \{\,\} \\ \text{PROP} & \boxed{1} \end{bmatrix}
\end{bmatrix}
$$

This means that *yes* can also be used to affirm the negative polar option (as in (115) and (116) from Chapter 3, repeated here):

(102) a. A: I wonder whether Sanca really didn't get married . . .

     B: Yes, she didn't. (Przepiórkowski 1999, (4.7))

   b. A: In the end Kim and Sandy didn't leave yesterday?

     B: Right (, they're still here).

The potential confusion caused by *yes* might be explained in one of two ways. Possibly, *yes* is understood by some speakers as the English version of *oui/ja*, so that it carries a QUD-presupposition that MAX-QUD is a question with a positive polarity. For such speakers, *yes* is simply *inappropriate* as a response to a negative polar. Alternatively, it is possible that some speakers analyze *yes* as the mirror image of *no*, so that *yes* is required to affirm a positive proposition. In either case, the confusion can be traced to the existence of two mildly divergent meanings for a single lexical item.

Different Understandings and Intonation

Are negative interrogatives themselves ambiguous? This is a hypothesis that Przepiórkowski (1999) adopts in order to explain the different possible understandings of negative interrogatives. We prefer instead to link the disparate understandings to presuppositional meaning associated with the distinct intonational tunes used. We assume, following Gussenhoven (1984), Pierre-humbert and Hirschberg (1990), and others, that a tune with a primary fall is used when the di-alogue move does not represent deviation from the existing conversational background, whereas rise involves cases where the move expresses uncertainty. Thus, both negative and positive po-lars intoned with a rise involve a sudden realization that the speaker might need to change their previously held assumption:

(103) a. A: Jo's leaving?! (A is surprised by the possibility that A might be leaving.)

   b. A: Isn't Jo leaving?! (A is surprised by the possibility that A might not be leaving.)

   c. A: Is Jo leaving? (A is surprised by the possibility that A might be leaving.)

   d. A: Is Jo leaving? (A has mild expectation that Jo is leaving.)

   e. A: Isn't Jo leaving (in the end)? (A has mild expectation that Jo is not leaving.)

   f. A: Jo isn't leaving, then? (A has mild expectation that Jo is not leaving.)

To hypothesize that the distinct understandings between (103b) and (103e,f) derive from a semantically manifested ambiguity, we would presumably need to hypothesize the same for the contrast between (103a,c) and (103d). It is not obvious what the source of such an ambiguity would be.[44]

Identical Answerhood Conditions

We have shown how a distinction between positive and negative polar interrogatives can be captured in our approach and why there is a need for such a distinction on the semantic level. We now explain why polar and negative polar questions nevertheless turn out to be like identical twins: distinct but similar in some of their most apparent 'external attributes', which for questions means *answerhood conditions*. In Chapter 3 we laid out the following conditions on the potential resolvedness of polar questions:

(104)   a.   If $q = \lambda\{\ \}p$, then:
   b. $AtomAns(r, q)$ iff $r = p$;
        $NegAtomAns(r, q)$ iff $r = \neg p$
   c. $PotResAns(f, q)$ iff $True(f)$ and:
   d.   Either: $f \rightarrow_{prop} \bigvee\{r \mid AtomAns(r, q)\} = \bigvee\{p\} = p$
   e.   Or: $f \rightarrow_{prop} \bigwedge\{r \mid NegAtomAns(r, q) = \bigwedge\{\neg p\} = \neg p$

Given the assumptions in Chapter 3 about propositional negation, it holds for atomic propositions that double negations cancel out:

(105)   If $NegationOf(p, q)$ and $NegationOf(q, r)$, then $p = r$

Taking (104) and (105) together, it follows that the potential resolvedness conditions of a polar question $\lambda\{\ \}p$ and its negative counterpart $\lambda\{\ \}\neg p$ are identical. A similar demonstration applies to aboutness conditions, as the reader can verify.

The fact that positive and negative polar questions specify identical answerhood conditions explains why, *ceteris paribus*, negation gets neutralized for a polar interrogative clause embedded by a resolutive predicate, like *know* and *discover*. As suggested by (114) in Chapter 3, repeated here as (106), any fact that resolves the positive polar also resolves the negative polar and vice versa.

(106)   a.   Ronnie knows whether Morgan likes Bo.
   b.   Ronnie knows whether Morgan does not like Bo.

Since the content of an interrogative clause that is embedded by a resolutive predicate is coerced to be a fact that resolves the question denoted by the clause, as will be demonstrated in

---

[44]Przepiórkowski's (1999) proposal for the source of the ambiguity in the negative case relies on a 'scope ambiguity' of sorts. He assumes that a case like (103e,f) involves a question whose SOA carries a negative polarity. In order to explain cases like (103b), Przepiórkowski appeals to a notion of polarity that would apply to questions themselves. He symbolizes such contents with formulas such as:

(i) $\langle\langle\ ?, s, \langle\langle\ see, J, M; +\rangle\rangle;\ \rangle\rangle$

Chapter 3 posited distinct dualization operations for SOAs and for propositions. The former is required to explain occurrences of negation in clauses of any subtype of *message*, whereas the latter is justified by the fact that propositions bear a truth value. However, as far as we can tell, the available evidence argues against the existence of a special purpose dualization operation for questions:

(ii)   #The question is false.
(iii) #It is not the case who left/whether Jo left.

the following section, the meanings of positive and negative polar interrogatives embedded by resolutives end up as equivalent.

8.2.4 Conclusion

In this section we have sketched an analysis of negative polar interrogative clauses, focusing on semantic and contextual properties. Our analysis illustrates a small but striking advantage of our general approach to the semantics of interrogatives over EAC approaches such as Karttunen's or Groenendijk and Stokhof's, where questions are analyzed in terms of answerhood conditions. As we have shown, there are a number of phenomena that suggest positive polars should not be conflated with negative polars. We have been able to realize this difference in terms of an independently motivated theory of negation, that of de Swart and Sag, which links the morphosyntactic expression of negation to the presence of a negative quantifier in QUANTS. At the same time, our account ensures that the two types of polars *do* specify identical answerhood conditions. The problem for approaches where questions are analyzed in terms of answerhood conditions is that when two interrogatives carry the same answerhood conditions, as positive and negative polars seem to, the questions denoted must be assumed to be identical. This undesirable consequence for positive and negative polars is straightforwardly avoided under our approach.

8.3 Selection and Coercion

This chapter concludes with a brief account of the basic complementation patterns associated with predicates that subcategorize for interrogative clauses. This is a tricky area because semantics and surface form are, pretheoretically, not perfectly matched. On one hand, as observed in Chapter 3, interrogative clauses do not always 'denote' questions. As we have shown, resolutive predicates (e.g. *discover*, *know*, *tell*) coerce the interrogative to supply a fact. Conversely, interrogative clauses do not exhaust the range of complements that are subcategorized for by question predicates (e.g. *ask*, *wonder*, *investigate*) or resolutives. In particular, both types of predicates can combine with complements that by most syntactic criteria are NPs or PPs:

(107) a. Jo asked a question.
  b. Bo and her doctor discussed Billie's projected birth weight.
  c. Mo found out Merle's address by accident.
  d. Co revealed a number of interesting facts to me.
  e. Yo wondered about that question for a while.

A comprehensive characterization of the range of complements that combine with question and resolutive predicates deserves a monograph of its own and is certainly beyond the scope of the present chapter. Instead, we provide here a tentative discussion of some of the basic issues involved, pointing to certain cases where the relationship between predicate and argument involves coercion of some kind. This includes an explanation of how interrogative clauses embedded by resolutive predicates (*discover*, *know*, *tell*) receive their content. It also contends with the long-standing puzzle of 'concealed question' interpretations of NPs like (107b,c).

8.3.1 Question Predicates

The following is a lexical entry for the verb *ask* that allows *ask* to combine with the full range of interrogative clauses discussed in earlier chapters:

(108)

$$\begin{bmatrix} \text{PHON} & \langle \text{ ask } \rangle \\ \\ \text{SS|LOC|CONT|SOA|NUCL} & \begin{bmatrix} \textit{ask-rel} \\ \text{UTTERER} & \boxed{2} \\ \text{COG-ARG} & \boxed{3} \\ \text{MSG-ARG} & \boxed{1}\textit{question} \end{bmatrix} \\ \\ \text{ARG-ST} & \left\langle \text{NP}_{\boxed{2}}, \begin{bmatrix} \text{IC} & - \\ \text{CONT} & \boxed{1} \end{bmatrix} \right\rangle \end{bmatrix}$$

However, an entry like this potentially misses certain nominal complements allowed by verbs like *ask* and its counterparts across a wide variety of languages):

(109)   Mo asked a/the/that question.

Whether or not (108) actually disallows complements such as those in (109) depends on what semantics is assigned to NPs such as *a question*. Although an NP like *that/the/a question* could conceivably have as its content an object of type *question*, by far the simpler option is to treat these like typical NPs. In HPSG terms, this means that such a content is a parameter that must be anchored to a question or an (in)definite with an analogous restriction. For ease of exposition, we will call a parameter restricted in this way a Question Parameter (QP).

Let us now explore a way of unifying the selection for the two types of complement, NPs whose content is a QP and clauses whose content is of type *question*. This can be done by postulating the existence of a non-branching phrase type *nominalized-interrogative-phrase (nom-int-ph)*—a sub-type of *head-only-phrase*. The mother of a *nom-int-ph* is a sign whose content is of type *question parameter*. Its head daughter, by contrast, has content of type *question*. This construction is constrained as shown in (110):[45]

(110)   *nom-int-ph*:

$$\begin{bmatrix} \text{CONT} & \begin{bmatrix} \textit{param} \\ \text{IND} & \boxed{1} \\ \text{RESTR} & \{\boxed{2} = \boxed{1}\} \end{bmatrix} \end{bmatrix} \rightarrow \mathbf{H}\begin{bmatrix} \text{CONT} & \boxed{2}\textit{question} \end{bmatrix}$$

Since this is both a head-only phrase and a non-clause, it inherits the constraints shown in (111):

(111)   ECC &   GHFP   & *hd-only-ph* & *nom-int-ph*:

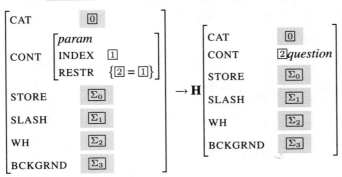

---

[45]For convenience, we do not incorporate here the change from INDEX to INDICES discussed in the previous section.

And this allows structures like the following:

(112)

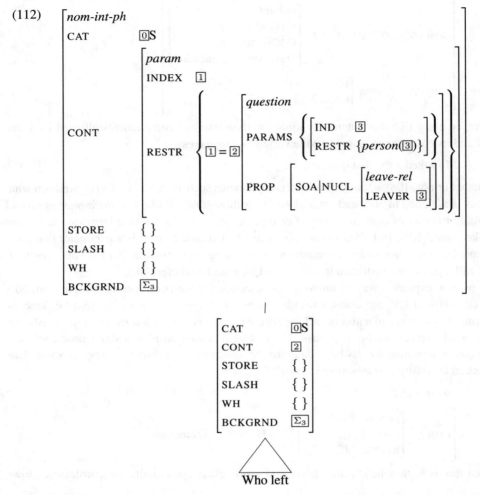

Who left

Once we have nominalized Ss like this, we may revise our lexical entry for *ask* so that it combines only with nominalized complements—i.e. those whose CONTENT is of type *param*, which includes both NPs like *the question* and phrases of type *nom-int-ph*:

(113)
$$
\begin{bmatrix}
\text{PHON} & \langle \text{ ask } \rangle \\
\text{SS|LOC|CONT|NUCL} & \begin{bmatrix} \textit{ask'-rel} \\ \text{ASKER} & \boxed{2} \\ \text{COG-ARG} & \boxed{3} \\ \text{ASKED} & \boxed{1} \end{bmatrix} \\
\text{ARG-ST} & \left\langle \begin{bmatrix} \text{NP} \\ \text{IND} \boxed{2} \end{bmatrix}, \begin{bmatrix} \text{IND} & \boxed{1} \end{bmatrix} \right\rangle
\end{bmatrix}
$$

Note that the content here is not *ask-rel*, the subtype of *illoc-rel* that has figured prominently in our analysis of interrogatives, but rather a distinct relation *ask'-rel*, both of whose arguments are of type *index*. We assume that it is a selectional fact about the ASKED argument that it must be anchored to a question.

Postulating the phrasal type *nom-int-ph* also allows a straightforward account of prepositions like *about*. *About* is compatible with interrogatives, NPs denoting a wide variety of entities (informational and otherwise) and POSS gerunds, but its object cannot be a declarative or an imperative:

(114) a.   We have received information about who attended the mass reincarnation.

       b.   There is some vital information about that question still missing.

       c.   Neeve didn't tell me about Jamie's leaving, nor about any other facts relating to the affair.

       d.   I'm waiting to obtain some information about them.

       e.   #We have no information about (that) Billie left.

       f.   #We received an order about (to) attack the Ruthenian forces.

In lieu of a detailed account of *about*, we note that it is probably best analyzed as an independent predicator that introduces a 'secondary predication' with question predicates. Examples like (115) show that predicates that combine with a PP[*about*] license substitutivity of a question argument, regardless of whether they are themselves question predicates (*wonder*) or resolutive (*know/forget*):

(115)   The question is where can one buy a Havana.

           Bo has been wondering/knows/forgot about that question.

           Hence, Bo has been wondering/knows/forgot about where can one buy a Havana.

Assuming the *nom-int-ph* construction sketched above, all of these facts follow directly if we simply assume that *about* selects as its object a phrase whose content is of type *param*.[46]

Here is another class of complements for question predicates—so-called 'concealed question' (CQ) uses of NPs like (116a–d):[47]

(116) a.   Jo investigated the source of Berlusconi's wealth. (= Jo investigated what the source of Berlusconi's wealth is.)

       b.   Mo asked Mikka's surname. (= Mo asked what Mikka's surname is.)

       c.   The price of beer depends on/influences the price of hops. (= What the price of beer is depends on/influences what the price of hops is.)

       d.   Jo wondered about the source of Berlusconi's wealth. (= Jo wondered about Mikka's surname.)

CQ interpretations do not require the immediate presence of a coercing element. That is, they may appear as the complement of *be* in identity constructions, even as 'stand alone' utterances and queries:

---

[46]We leave undiscussed the fact that exclamatives may also serve as complements of *about*:

    (i) We did receive a report about what a vital role Brendan played in this affair.

[47]For past discussions of this phenomenon, see, for example, Baker 1970, Grimshaw 1979, Heim 1979, Pesetsky 1987, and Pustejovsky 1995.

(117) a. A(1): How are the preparations for the dinner party going?

   B(2): OK, but I'm a bit worried about the ceiling—isn't it too low for some of the guests?

   A(3): I know Merle's height and I know Bo's height. The question we still need to consider is Brendan's height.

   b. A(1): How many of the entries have you read?

   B(2): Most of them.

   A(3): So, I guess the one unresolved question is the winner.

(118) a. A: What question is bothering you at the moment?

   B: Brendan's height.

   b. A: Your name?

The simplest possible treatment of CQs is to assume the existence of a 'coercion mechanism' that alters just the content of a CQ NP, converting it from a definite quantifier to a *question*. We thus postulate a phrasal type *concealed-question-np* (*cq-np*), a subtype of *head-only-ph*, that achieves this effect:[48],[49]

(119) *cq-np*:

$$
\begin{bmatrix}
\text{CONT} & \begin{bmatrix}
\textit{question} \\
\text{PARAMS} \ \{[\text{INDEX} \ \boxed{4}]\} \\
\text{PROP} \begin{bmatrix}
\textit{proposition} \\
\text{SOA} \begin{bmatrix}
\text{QUANTS} \ \langle \boxed{2} \rangle \\
\text{NUCL} \begin{bmatrix}
\textit{identity-rel} \\
\text{ARG1} \ \boxed{3} \\
\text{ARG2} \ \boxed{4}
\end{bmatrix}
\end{bmatrix}
\end{bmatrix}
\end{bmatrix} \\
\text{STORE} \ \boxed{\Sigma_1}
\end{bmatrix}
\rightarrow \mathbf{H}
\begin{bmatrix}
\text{HEAD} \quad n \\
\text{CONT}|\text{INDEX} \ \boxed{3} \\
\text{STORE} \ \boxed{\Sigma_1} \uplus \left\{ \boxed{2} \begin{bmatrix} \textit{the-rel} \\ \text{INDEX} \ \boxed{3} \end{bmatrix} \right\}
\end{bmatrix}
$$

---

[48] One might consider a coercion whose 'output' is content of type *question parameter* in order that *ask* and similar predicates can select for CQ. This is unnecessary, however, since the same effect can be achieved if we postulate that the coercion leads to a *cq-np* with content of type *question*. The *cq-np* can then be embedded as the head daughter of a QP-denoting phrase constructed as a *nom-int-ph*. The direct 'CQ-to-CP' will in any case prove to be problematic once we consider the complements of resolutive predicates.

[49] We do not offer a characterization of the class of definite NPs which yield a CQ interpretation. There appears to be some kind of restriction to definites whose descriptive condition involves an essential or intrinsic relational attribute, hence the contrasts between (i) and (ii) (the # refers to a missing CQ reading):

   (i)   Bo discussed Jo's height/Mo's surname/the registration number of Mo's car/her role in the community/the architect of England's bitterest defeat/the winner of yesterday's playoff game.

   (ii) #Bo discussed Jo's cousin/her dog/the cook of yesterday's meal/her bicycle.

Continuing, (119) inherits constraints as shown in (120):

(120) ECC & GHFP & *hd-only-ph* & *cq-np*:

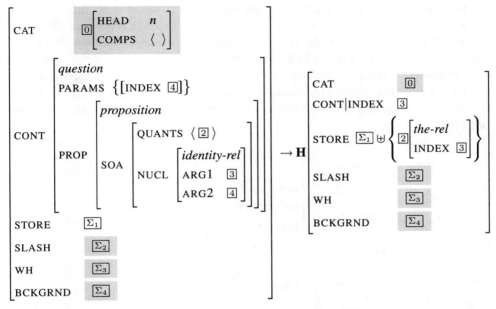

And (119) will yield the interpretation for (121a) sketched in (121b):[50]

(121) a. Mo's height.

   b.

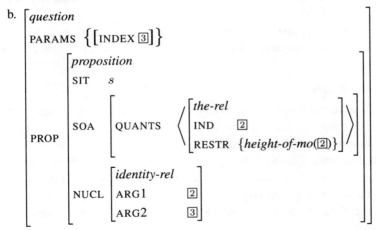

To conclude the discussion of question predicates, consider an additional question predicate whose selectional requirements are subtly different from *ask*. The verb *wonder* is incompatible with question NPs, allowing only clausal complements whose content is of type *question*:[51]

---

[50]Note that we have not specified any restriction for the interrogative parameter. We assume it to be null, i.e. its restrictions are solely those emanating from the definite.

[51]We again leave aside the interaction with prepositions like *about*:

   (i) Kim wondered about that question/Sandy's weight.

(122) a. *Jo wondered that question.

　　　 b. Jo wondered who to visit/whether he knew.

We believe that the most plausible conclusion to draw from this is not that *wonder* behaves semantically in a significantly different way from *ask*.[52] This is a conclusion that in any case is somewhat unattractive given the close synonymy of *ask oneself* and *wonder*. Indeed, in some languages the closest correlate of English *wonder* is simply *ask oneself*. Rather, it reinforces our earlier assumption that the selection properties of the predicates cannot be stated entirely without making reference to categorial features of the complements. In this case, *wonder* requires that its complement (which must have a QUESTION PARAMETER content) must be *verbal* (i.e. an S, 'S' or CP):

(123)

$$
\begin{bmatrix}
lexeme \\
\text{PHON} \quad \langle \text{ wonder } \rangle \\
\text{SS|LOC|CONT|NUCL} \begin{bmatrix} wonder\text{-}rel \\ \text{WONDERER} \quad \boxed{2} \\ \text{COG-ARG} \quad \boxed{3} \\ \text{WONDERED} \quad \boxed{1} \end{bmatrix} \\
\text{ARG-ST} \quad \left\langle \begin{bmatrix} \text{NP} \\ \text{IND} \ \boxed{2} \end{bmatrix}, \begin{bmatrix} \text{HEAD} \begin{bmatrix} verbal \\ \text{IC} \ - \end{bmatrix} \\ \text{CONT|IND} \ \boxed{1} \end{bmatrix} \right\rangle
\end{bmatrix}
$$

Given that the HEAD value of CQ uses is always of type *n*, it follows that *wonder* will not select for such phrases.

Despite the briefness of the above presentation, we hope that the interaction of *cq-np* and *nom-int-ph* will become fully transparent as we add the final component of the story—resolutive predicates.

8.3.2 Resolutive Predicates

Chapter 2 proposed that resolutive predicates do not take questions as their arguments but rather that when they combine with an interrogative complement *I* they 'coerce' it. More precisely, the argument that is semantically embedded as the argument of the resolutive predicate is a fact—a fact that in that context resolves the question denoted by *I*. We pointed out that such a coercion process would be well-defined if and only if the question is *decided*, i.e. the set of simple answers to the question is non-empty.[53] This coercion analysis thus has one important explanatory advantage: the resolvedness presuppositions exhibited by such clauses are explained in a principled manner.

Consider first in general terms what denotation we require the coercion to yield. What actually seems necessary is an *indefinite description* for a resolving fact. The need for a description,

---

[52]The contrast between *ask* and *wonder* holds for the apparent analogues of *ask* and *wonder* in languages such as German, Hebrew, French, and Greek. Hence, one cannot dismiss attempts to find a purely semantic basis for it, as in Pustejovsky 1995. However, the import of Pustejovsky's specific proposal, namely that *ask* selects for a question whereas *wonder* selects for an *attitude* to a question, remains unclear to us.

[53]See definition 13 in Chapter 3.

as opposed to reference, is a direct consequence of the conclusion we pointed to in subsection 3.5.3 of Chapter 3, namely that in general for a given question and agent mental situation there exist a multiplicity of mutually non-entailing facts that resolve the question. Thus, (124a) need not involve more than a claim by the speaker that there exists a fact that resolves the question *who attended the talk* relative to a mental situation of Kazoo's and which Kazoo knows/discovered, whereas (124b) involves the corresponding claim that no such fact exists:[54]

(124) a. Kazoo knows/discovered who attended the talk.

b. Kazoo doesn't know/didn't discover who attended the talk.

This should not be particularly surprising. One of the expressive gains provided by *nominal* quantification is the ability to make statements about arbitrary non-familiar objects, as in (125a). Analogously, one can argue that resolutive complements provide us with the ability to make statements about possibly arbitrary or non-familiar facts that resolve a given question, as in (125b):

(125) a. Some grain of sand will enter my shoe when I go to the beach tomorrow.

b. Max discovered how to prove the theorem a week ago. Of course since I know no mathematics I couldn't tell you anything about it.

The effect required is the following:

(126)

$$
\begin{bmatrix}
\text{SS}|\text{LOC} \begin{bmatrix}
\text{ARG-ST} \left\langle \text{NP}_4, \begin{bmatrix} \text{IC} & - \\ \text{CONT} & \boxed{1}\textit{question} \end{bmatrix} \right\rangle \\[2ex]
\text{CONT} \begin{bmatrix}
\textit{soa} \\
\text{QUANTS} \left\langle \begin{bmatrix} \textit{some-rel} \\ \text{INDEX} & \boxed{2} \\ \text{RESTR} & \{\textit{resolves}(\boxed{2},\boxed{1},\boxed{3})\} \end{bmatrix} \right\rangle \\[2ex]
\text{NUCL} \begin{bmatrix} \textit{resolutive-rel} \\ \text{RESOLVER} & \boxed{4} \\ \text{COGNITIVE-ARG} & \boxed{3} \\ \text{FACT-ARG} & \boxed{2} \end{bmatrix}
\end{bmatrix}
\end{bmatrix} \\
\text{BCKGRD} \ \textit{decided}(\boxed{1})
\end{bmatrix}
$$

In (126) the coercion is stated as a constraint on lexical entries of resolutive predicates. As argued in Chapter 3 and recapitulated below, this is preferable to positing a fact-denoting interrogative phrasal type. We recapitulate the arguments for this position briefly. One line of argument demonstrated that interrogatives only exhibit 'fact-denoting' behavior in embedded contexts. This is captured by limiting the effect of the coercion to embedded contexts where the embedding predicate is resolutive. 'Stand-alone' fact-denoting interrogatives are thus correctly ruled out:

---

[54]The only change needed for an approach that assumes the existence of a unique resolving answer—the *exhaustive* answer as standardly understood—would be that the description become *definite*.

(127) a. #The fact is who left yesterday.

b. #In a moment, I'm going to reveal to you an interesting fact: whether Millie left Mike.

Chapter 3 also noted that predicates such as *intrigue*, *mystify*, and *puzzle* are purely referential in both questions and facts. This provides an important argument for limiting interrogative-to-fact coercion to a selected class of predicates, rather than taking it to be a general characteristic of either interrogative phrasal types or of fact-selecting predicates. Another key consideration, as (128) shows, is that interrogative-to-fact coercion must be applicable to CQ NPs as well. As the content of CQ is of type *question*, the applicability of (126) to such NPs is indeed assured.

(128) a. Jo discovered the source of Berlusconi's wealth.

b. Mo forgot Mikka's surname.

However, this coercion must not be applicable to just any question-denoting expression. This is because if (126) applied to *any* question-denoting complement, we would predict that the assumptions in (129a) should entail (129b) and (129c), contrary to fact:

(129) a. Jill discovered a certain question. The question was who left.

b. Jill discovered a fact that resolves the question of who left.

c. Jill discovered who left.

We do have a principled way of assuring that interrogative-to-fact coercion applies to interrogatives and CQs but not to question-denoting NPs in contexts such as those in (129). This is to assume, as above, that the coercion takes as 'input' elements whose CONTENT value is of type *question*. Interrogative clauses are essentially objects whose content is of type *question*, as are CQs, whereas the CONTENT value of NPs like *that/a question* can only be a *parameter*. This analysis predicts that an NP such as *the question* can come to denote a fact, but only as a CQ. Hence, (130a) can only mean (130b), not (130c):

(130) a. Bill discovered the question. (The question was who left.)

b. Bill discovered what the question was.

c. Bill discovered who left.

Since the lexical entry for a verb like *discover* includes all the information in (126), it will give rise to contents like that shown in (131):

(131)

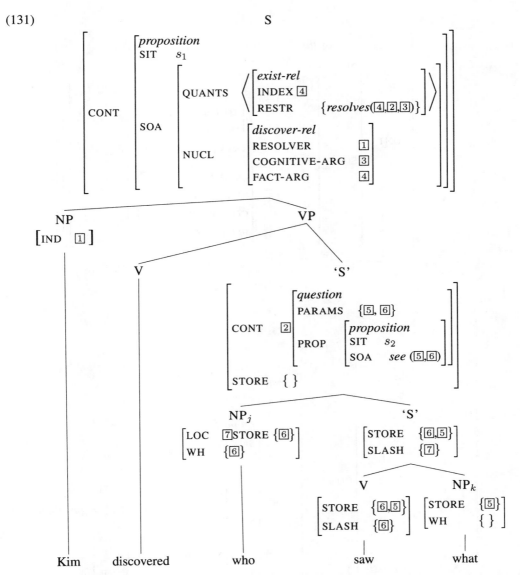

A concealed question embedded by *discover* arises as follows:[55] the NP gets interpreted as a question via *cq-np*. This then gets coerced to denote an existential quantifier over facts that resolve the question via the *nom-int-ph* construction of (110):

[55] A puzzle not addressed here concerns the fact that not all predicates are compatible with CQ interpretations equally readily for a given NP. In particular, resolutive predicates are far more compatible with CQ interpretations than question predicates. Nonetheless, it is clearly not the case that question predicates *lack* the ability to yield CQ interpretations:

   (i) Bo asked Mo/investigated #the winner of yesterday's playoff game/#the architect of England's bitterest defeat/Merle's role in the community/the price of a return ticket/the source of contributions to the Delphic society.

   (ii) Bo told Mo/discovered the winner of yesterday's playoff game/the architect of England's bitterest defeat/Merle's role in the community/the price of a return ticket/the source of contributions to the Delphic society.

(132)

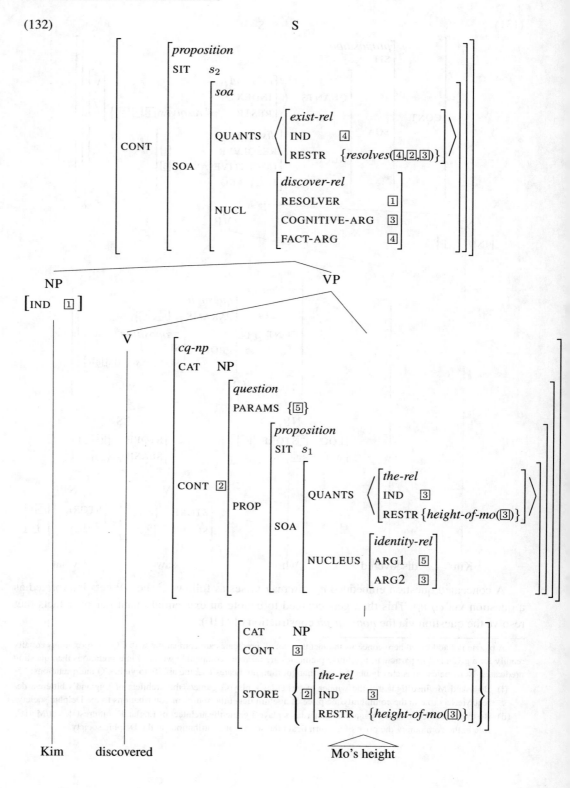

The analysis embodied in (126) yields two further correct predictions. First, it ensures that the coercion also applies to contents that arise anaphorically, an effect required to account for examples like (133):

(133) a. A: Who left yesterday?
           B: Bo knows.
       b. A: Who left yesterday?
           B: Bo knows that.

This result depends on the assumption that the content type of the anaphoric element here is *question*. This seems a natural assumption for null anaphora such as (133a), though perhaps less clearly so for the pronominal element *that* in (133b). Nonetheless, this assumption does receive some support from the behavior of such complements as *wonder*. Verbs of this class, as already seen, resist nominal complements, yet are entirely acceptable with null anaphora and only marginally less so with *that*:

(134) a. A: Who left yesterday?
           B: I've been wondering myself. No data as yet.
       b. A: Who left yesterday?
           B: That's something I've been wondering myself just now.

By contrast, (126) also ensures that complements of *about* do not undergo 'question-to-fact coercion'. This follows because the arguments of *about* have a CONTENT value of type *param* and hence cannot undergo the coercion of (126):

(135)   Bill knows/forgot about who to invite to the party.

           It does not follow that: there exists a fact that resolves the question of who to invite to the party such that Bill knows/forgot that fact.

Note that the ability to capture the array of facts presented in this section depends crucially on the distinction between two manifestations of questions: contents that are a subtype of *message*, i.e. of type *question* and those that are what we have termed *question parameters*. This difference, akin to proposals emanating from property theory that distinguish a property and its nominal correlate, as in Chierchia 1985 and Chierchia and Turner 1988, is a natural consequence of the architecture of semantic types in HPSG. Of some importance to the account developed in this book is a view of complement selection that is primarily semantic, but can take into account local categorial information.

Appendix A: Types

A.1   Some Basic Types

The essentials associated with this type hierarchy are given in sections 2.2 through 2.6. Semantic types are discussed in Appendix B.

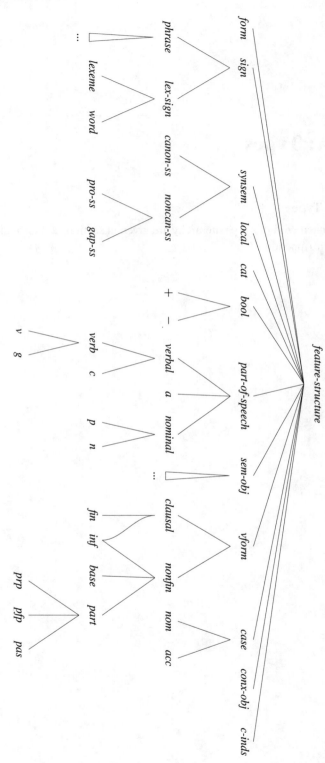

A.1.2 Type Declarations

TYPE	FEATURES/TYPE OF VALUE	IST
form	...	*feat(ure)-struc(ture)*
sign	$\begin{bmatrix} \text{PHONOLOGY} & list(form) \\ \text{SYNSEM} & canon\text{-}ss^1 \\ \text{CONTEXT} & conx\text{-}obj \\ \text{ROOT} & boolean \end{bmatrix}$	*feat-struc*
phrase	[DTRS $\quad$ *list(sign)*]	*sign*
h(eade)d-ph	[HD-DTR $\quad$ *sign*]	*phrase*
lex-sign	[ARG-ST $\quad$ *list(synsem)*]	*sign*
lexeme		*lex-sign*
word		*lex-sign*
synsem	$\begin{bmatrix} \text{LOCAL} & local \\ \text{SLASH} & set(local) \\ \text{WH} & set(scope\text{-}obj) \\ \text{BCKGRND} & set(fact) \end{bmatrix}$	*feat-struc*
canon-ss	...	*synsem*
noncan-ss	...	*synsem*
pro-ss	...	*noncan-ss*
gap-ss	...	*noncan-ss*
loc(al)	$\begin{bmatrix} \text{CATEGORY} & category \\ \text{CONTENT} & sem\text{-}object \\ \text{STORE} & set(scope\text{-}obj) \end{bmatrix}$	*feat-struc*
cat(egory)	$\begin{bmatrix} \text{HEAD} & part\text{-}of\text{-}speech \\ \text{SUBJ(ECT)} & list(synsem) \\ \text{COMP(LEMENT)S} & list(synsem) \\ \text{SP(ECIFIE)R} & list(synsem) \end{bmatrix}$	*feat-struc*
con(te)x(t)-obj(ect)	$\begin{bmatrix} \text{C-INDICES} & c\text{-}inds \\ \text{SAL(IENT)-UTT(ERANCE)} & set(local) \\ \text{MAX(IMAL)-QUD} & question \\ \text{(QUESTION-UNDER-DISCUSSION)} \end{bmatrix}$	*feat-struc*
c(ontextual)-ind(ice)s	$\begin{bmatrix} \text{C-SP(EA)K(E)R} & index \\ \text{C-ADDR(ESSEE)} & index \\ \text{U-LOC(ATION)} & index \end{bmatrix}$	*feat-struc*
bool(ean)		*feat-struc*
+		*bool*
−		*bool*

[1]In Chapter 2, this condition is formulated as a separate constraint called THE PRINCIPLE OF CANONICALITY.

TYPE	FEATURES/TOV	IST
part-of-speech	[PRED *bool*]	*feat-struc*
verbal	$\begin{bmatrix} \text{VFORM} & \textit{vform} \\ \text{I(NDEPENDENT-)C(LAUSE)} & \textit{bool} \end{bmatrix}$	*part-of-speech*
verb	$\begin{bmatrix} \text{AUX(ILIARY)} & \textit{bool} \\ \text{POL(ARIZED)} & \textit{bool} \end{bmatrix}$	*verbal*
c(omplementizer)		*verbal*
v		*verb*
g(erund)		*verb*
d(eterminer)	[SPEC *sem-obj*]	*part-of-speech*
a(djective)		*part-of-speech*
adv(erb)		*part-of-speech*
nominal		*part-of-speech*
p(reposition)		*nominal*
n(oun)	[CASE *case*]	*nominal*
sem-obj(ect)		*feat-struc*
vform		*feat-struc*
clausal		*vform*
fin(ite)		*clausal*
nonfin(ite)		*vform*
inf(initval)		*clausal & nonfin*
base		*nonfin*
part(iciple)		*nonfin*
pr(esent)p(articiple)		*part*
p(er)f(ect)p(articiple)		*part*
pas(sive)		*part*
case		*feat-struc*
nom(inative)		*case*
acc(usative)		*case*

A.1.3 Type Constraints

(1) $\textit{sign} \quad \Rightarrow \quad [\,\text{ROOT} \quad /-\,]$

(2) $\textit{gap-ss} \quad \Rightarrow \quad \begin{bmatrix} \text{LOC} & \boxed{1} \\ \text{SLASH} & \{\boxed{1}\} \end{bmatrix}$

(3) $\textit{pro-ss} \quad \Rightarrow \quad \begin{bmatrix} \text{LOC} & \begin{bmatrix} \text{CAT|HEAD} & \begin{bmatrix} \textit{noun} \\ \text{CASE} & \textit{acc} \end{bmatrix} \\ \text{CONT} & \begin{bmatrix} \textit{reflexive} \\ \text{INDEX} & \textit{ref} \end{bmatrix} \end{bmatrix} \end{bmatrix}$

A.2 Phrase Types

A.2.1 Type Hierarchy

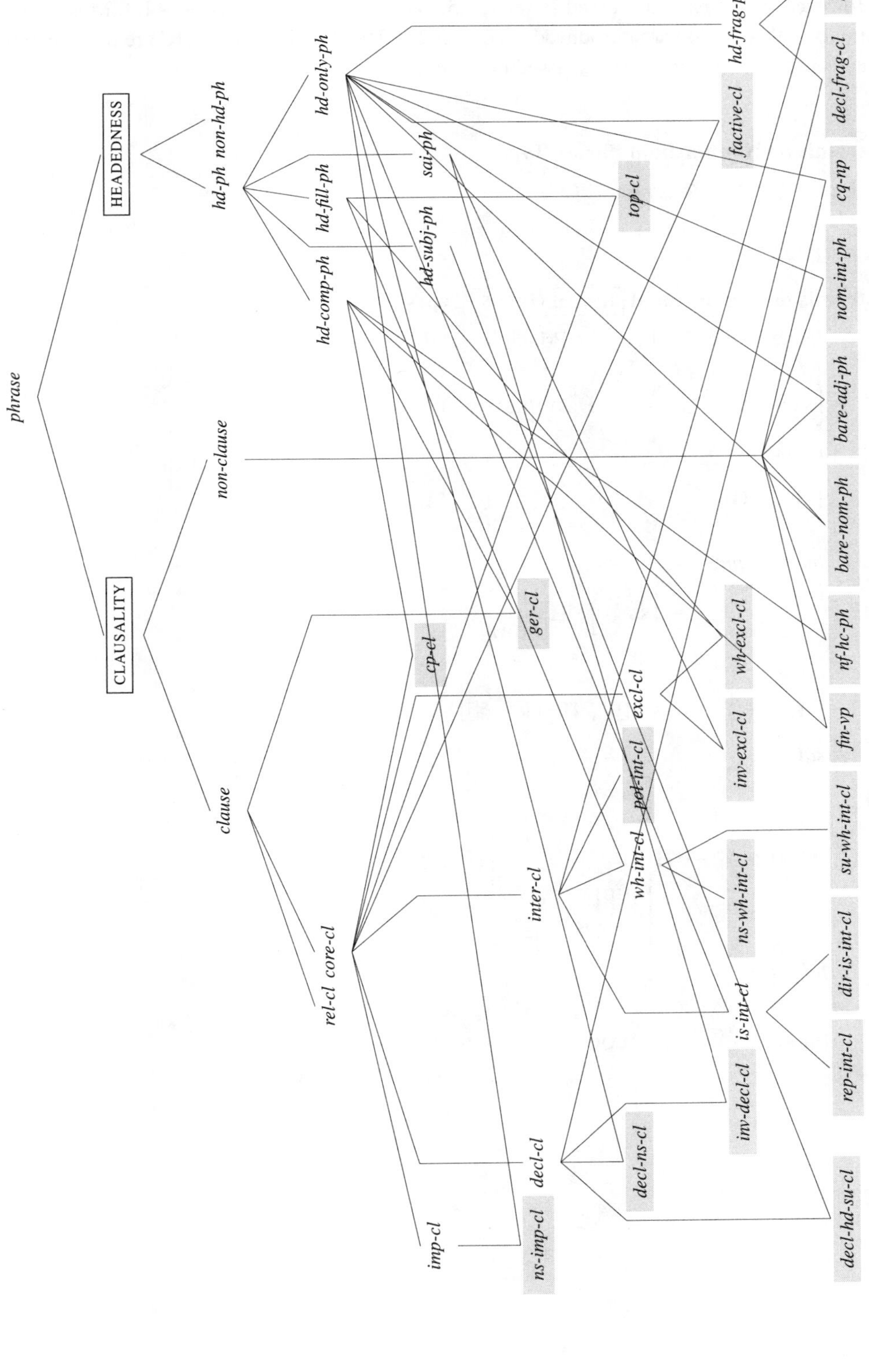

A.2.2 Nonmaximal Phrase Types

Most of the constraints on headed phrases presented in this section are discussed in section 2.5. However, *hd-fill-ph* is discussed in section 5.1 and *hd-frag-ph* in section 8.1.4. Most of the constraints in this section are introduced in section 2.6. The IRC, FIC, and PHC are from section 6.5; the constraint on *is-int-cl* is discussed in section 7.2.

Constraints on Nonmaximal Phrase Types:

(4) Empty COMPS Constraint (ECC):

phrase:

$$\left[\text{COMPS} \ \langle \ \rangle\right] \rightarrow \ \ldots$$

Constraints on Nonmaximal $\boxed{\text{HEADEDNESS}}$ **Types:**

(5) Generalized Head Feature Principle (GHFP)

hd-ph:

$$\left[\text{SYNSEM} \ /\boxed{1}\right] \rightarrow \ \ldots \ \mathbf{H}\left[\text{SYNSEM} \ /\boxed{1}\right] \ \ldots$$

(6) *hd-comp-ph*:

$$[\ ] \ \rightarrow \mathbf{H}\begin{bmatrix}\textit{word} \\ \text{COMPS} \ \textit{nelist}(\boxed{A} \ \oplus \ \textit{list})\end{bmatrix}, \ \boxed{A}$$

(7) *hd-subj-ph*:

$$\left[\text{SUBJ} \ \langle \ \rangle\right] \rightarrow \left[\text{SS} \ \boxed{1}\right], \ \mathbf{H}\begin{bmatrix}\text{SPR} & \langle \ \rangle \\ \text{SUBJ} & \langle \boxed{1} \rangle\end{bmatrix}$$

(8) *hd-spr-ph*:

$$\left[\text{SPR} \ \langle \ \rangle\right] \rightarrow \left[\text{SS} \ \boxed{1}\right], \ \mathbf{H}\left[\text{SPR} \ \langle \boxed{1} \rangle\right]$$

(9) *sai-ph*:

$$\left[\text{SUBJ} \ \langle \ \rangle\right] \rightarrow \mathbf{H}\begin{bmatrix}\textit{word} \\ \text{INV} & + \\ \text{AUX} & + \\ \text{SUBJ} & \langle \boxed{0} \rangle \\ \text{COMPS} & \boxed{A}\end{bmatrix}, \boxed{0}, \boxed{A}$$

(10) *hd-fill-ph*:

$$\left[\text{SLASH} \ \boxed{\Sigma_2}\right] \rightarrow \left[\text{LOC} \ \boxed{1}\right], \ \mathbf{H}\begin{bmatrix}\textit{phrase} \\ \text{HEAD} & v \\ \text{SLASH} & \{\boxed{1}\} \ \uplus \ \boxed{\Sigma_2}\end{bmatrix}$$

(11) *hd-frag-ph*:

$$
\begin{bmatrix}
\text{HEAD} & \begin{bmatrix} v \\ \text{VFORM } \textit{fin} \end{bmatrix} \\
\text{SUBJ} & \langle\ \rangle \\
\text{SPR} & \langle\ \rangle \\
\text{CTXT}|\text{SAL-UTT} & \left\{ \begin{bmatrix} \text{CAT} & \boxed{1} \\ \text{CONT}|\text{INDEX} & \boxed{2} \end{bmatrix} \right\}
\end{bmatrix}
\rightarrow \mathbf{H} \begin{bmatrix} \text{CAT} & \boxed{1}\begin{bmatrix}\text{HEAD} & \textit{nominal}\end{bmatrix} \\ \text{CONT}|\text{INDEX} & \boxed{2} \end{bmatrix}
$$

Constraints on Nonmaximal $\boxed{\text{CLAUSALITY}}$ **Types:**

(12) *clause*:

$$\begin{bmatrix} \text{CONT} & \textit{message} \end{bmatrix} \rightarrow \ \ldots$$

(13) *clause*:

$$\begin{bmatrix} \text{SUBJ} & \textit{list(noncan-ss)} \end{bmatrix} \rightarrow \ \ldots$$

(14) *core-cl*:

$$\begin{bmatrix} \text{HEAD} & \begin{bmatrix} \textit{verbal} \\ \text{VFORM} & \textit{clausal} \\ \text{MOD} & \textit{none} \end{bmatrix} \end{bmatrix} \rightarrow \ \ldots$$

(15) *decl-cl*:

$$\begin{bmatrix} \text{CONT} & \begin{bmatrix} \textit{austinian} \\ \text{SOA} & /\boxed{1} \end{bmatrix} \end{bmatrix} \rightarrow \ \ldots \mathbf{H}\begin{bmatrix} \text{CONT} & /\boxed{1} \end{bmatrix} \ldots$$

(16) *inter-cl*:

$$\begin{bmatrix} \text{CONT} & \textit{question} \end{bmatrix} \rightarrow \ \ldots$$

(17) Interrogative Retrieval Constraint (IRC)

inter-cl:

$$\begin{bmatrix} \text{STORE} & \boxed{\Sigma_1} \\ \text{CONT} & \begin{bmatrix} \text{PARAMS} & \boxed{\Sigma_2} \end{bmatrix} \end{bmatrix} \rightarrow \ \ldots \mathbf{H}\begin{bmatrix} \text{STORE} & \boxed{\Sigma_1} \uplus \boxed{\Sigma_2} \end{bmatrix} \ldots$$

(18) Filler Inclusion Constraint (FIC):

wh-int-cl:

$$\begin{bmatrix} \text{CONT} & \begin{bmatrix} \text{PARAMS} & \{\boxed{1}\} \uplus \textit{set} \end{bmatrix} \end{bmatrix} \rightarrow \begin{bmatrix} \text{WH} & \{\boxed{1}\} \end{bmatrix}, \mathbf{H}$$

(19) Propositional Head Constraint (PHC):

wh-int-cl:

$$\begin{bmatrix} \text{CONT} & \begin{bmatrix} \text{PROP} & \boxed{2} \end{bmatrix} \end{bmatrix} \rightarrow \ \ldots \mathbf{H}\begin{bmatrix} \text{CONT} & \boxed{2} \end{bmatrix}$$

(20) *is-int-cl*:

$$
\begin{bmatrix} \text{CAT} & \begin{bmatrix} \text{HEAD} & \begin{bmatrix} \text{IC} & + \\ \text{VFORM} & \mathit{fin} \end{bmatrix} \end{bmatrix} \\ \text{STORE} & \boxed{\Sigma} \end{bmatrix} \rightarrow \begin{matrix} \mathbf{H} \\ \begin{bmatrix} \text{STORE} & \neq\boxed{\Sigma} \end{bmatrix} \end{matrix}
$$

(21) *excl-cl*:

$$
\begin{bmatrix} \text{CONT} & \mathit{fact} \end{bmatrix} \rightarrow \ \ldots
$$

(22) *imp-cl*:

$$
\begin{bmatrix} \text{CONT} & \mathit{outcome} \end{bmatrix} \rightarrow \ \ldots
$$

(23) *rel-cl*:

$$
\begin{bmatrix} \text{HEAD} & \begin{bmatrix} \text{IC} & - \\ \text{INV} & - \\ \text{MOD} & \begin{bmatrix} \mathit{noun} \end{bmatrix} \end{bmatrix} \\ \text{CONT} & \mathit{fact} \end{bmatrix} \rightarrow \ \ldots
$$

A.2.3 Maximal Declarative-Clause Types

Subtypes of *decl-cl* are first introduced in Chapter 2: *decl-hd-su-cl* is discussed in section 2.6 and *decl-ns-cl* in section 2.8 (see also section 5.1). The types *inv-decl-cl* and *decl-frag-cl* are discussed in sections 6.3 and 8.1.4, respectively. Negative specifications for the feature ROOT, which were suppressed throughout the text, are included in the remainder of this appendix.

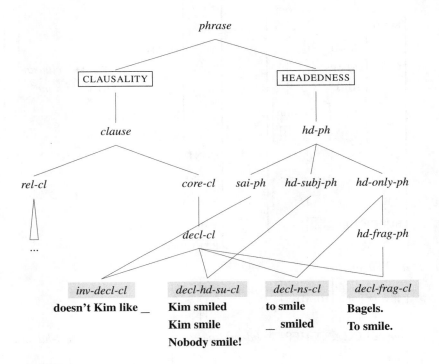

Type Constraints:

(24) a. *inv-decl-cl*:

$$\begin{bmatrix} \text{SLASH} & neset \end{bmatrix} \rightarrow \mathbf{H}\begin{bmatrix} \text{IC} & + \end{bmatrix}, \ldots$$

b. *sign* & ECC & GHFP & *sai-ph* & *core-cl* & *decl-cl* & *inv-decl-cl*:

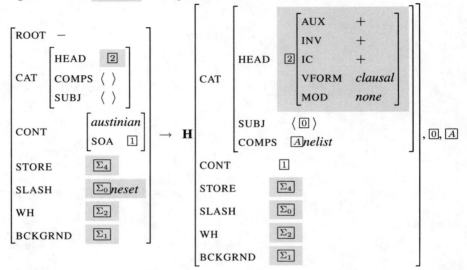

(25) a. *decl-hd-su-cl*:

$$[\ ] \rightarrow [\ ], \begin{bmatrix} \text{HEAD} & \begin{bmatrix} \text{VFORM} & fin \\ \text{INV} & - \end{bmatrix} \end{bmatrix}$$

b. *sign* & ECC & GHFP & *hd-subj-ph* & *core-cl* & *decl-cl* & *decl-hd-su-cl*:

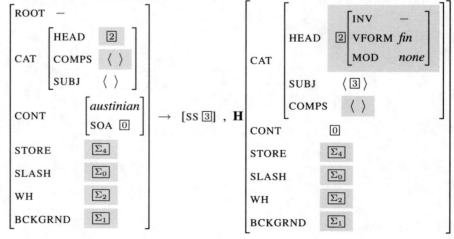

(26) a. *decl-ns-cl*:

$$\begin{bmatrix} \text{HEAD} & \begin{bmatrix} v \\ \text{INV} & - \end{bmatrix} \\ \text{SUBJ} & \langle\, \text{XP}\, \rangle \end{bmatrix} \rightarrow \quad \dots$$

b. *sign* & ECC & ⬛GHFP⬛ & *hd-only-ph* & *clause* & *core-cl* & *decl-cl* & *decl-ns-cl*:

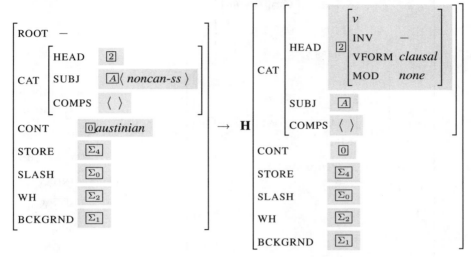

(27) a. *decl-frag-cl*:

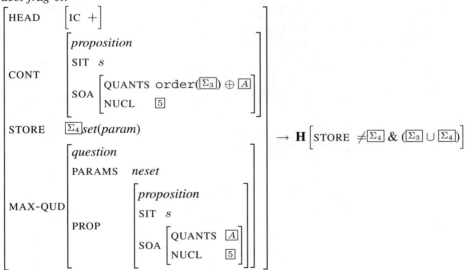

b. *sign* & ECC & GHFP & *hd-only-ph* & *hd-frag-ph* & *core-cl* & *decl-cl* & *decl-frag-cl*:

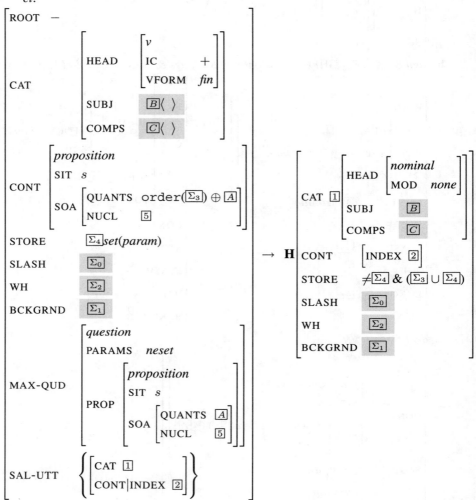

A.2.4 Maximal Interrogative Clauses

Subtypes of *inter-cl* are introduced in Chapter 6: *pol-int-cl* in section 6.3 and *wh-int-cl* (and its subtypes) in section 6.5. For a discussion of *is-int-cl* and its subtypes, see Chapter 7: section 7.2 for *repr-int-cl* and section 7.3 for *dir-is-int-cl*. The type *slu-int-cl* is discussed in section 8.1.7.

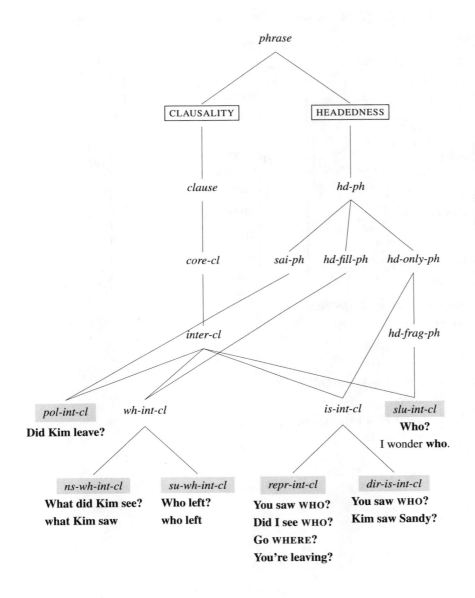

Type Constraints:

(28) a. *pol-int-cl*:

$$
\begin{bmatrix}
\text{CONT} & \begin{bmatrix}
\text{PARAMS} \ \{\ \} \\
\text{PROP} & \begin{bmatrix} proposition \\ \text{SOA} \quad \boxed{1} \end{bmatrix}
\end{bmatrix}
\end{bmatrix}
\rightarrow \ \mathbf{H}
\begin{bmatrix}
\text{IC} & + \\
\text{CONT} & \boxed{1}
\end{bmatrix}, \dots
$$

b. *sign* & ECC & GHFP & *sai-ph* & *core-cl* & *inter-cl* & IRC & *pol-int-cl*:

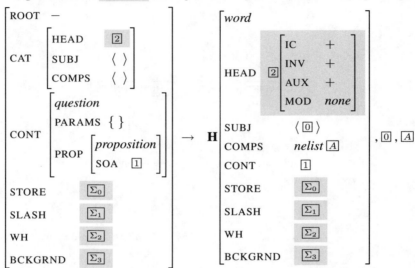

(29) a. Inversion Constraint (INVC):
   ns-wh-int-cl:

$$
[\ ] \ \rightarrow \ \dots \ \mathbf{H}
\begin{bmatrix}
\text{IC} & \boxed{1} \\
\text{INV} & \boxed{1}
\end{bmatrix}
$$

b. Optional *Pro* Condition (OPC):
   ns-wh-int-cl:

$$
[\ ] \ \rightarrow \ \dots \ \mathbf{H}\begin{bmatrix} \text{SUBJ} & \langle\ (pro\text{-}ss)\ \rangle \end{bmatrix}
$$

c. *sign* & ECC & GHFP & *core-cl* & *inter-cl* & IRC & *hd-fill-ph* & FIC & PHC & *ns-wh-int-cl*:

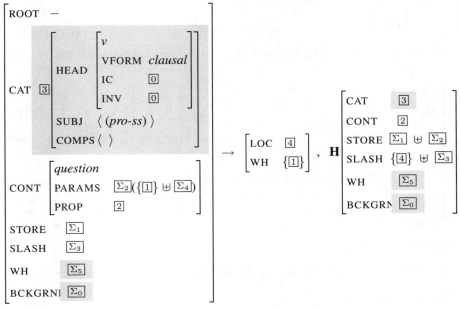

(30) a. *su-wh-int-cl*:

$$\left[\text{SUBJ }\langle\,\rangle\right] \to \left[\text{LOC }\boxed{4}\right],\ \mathbf{H}\left[\text{SUBJ }\left\langle\begin{bmatrix}gap\text{-}ss\\ \text{LOC }\boxed{4}\end{bmatrix}\right\rangle\right]$$

b. *sign* & ECC & GHFP & *hd-fill-ph* & *core-cl* & *inter-cl* & IRC & FIC & PHC & *su-wh-int-cl*:

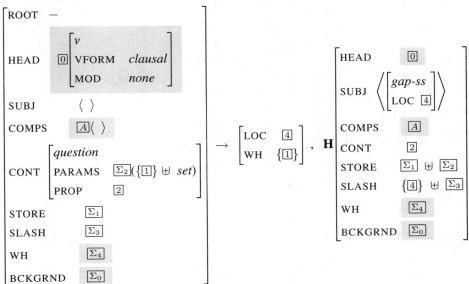

(31) a. *repr-int-cl*:

$$\begin{bmatrix} \text{CONT|PROP} & \boxed{1}\left[\text{SOA|NUCL|MSG-ARG} \quad \boxed{2}\right] \\ \text{BCKGRND} & \left\{\textit{prev-utt}(\boxed{0}), \textit{perc-cont}(\boxed{0},\boxed{1})\right\} \uplus \boxed{\Sigma} \end{bmatrix} \rightarrow \mathbf{H}\begin{bmatrix} \text{CONT} & \boxed{2} \\ \text{BCKGRND} & \boxed{\Sigma} \\ \text{SLASH} & \{\,\} \end{bmatrix}$$

b. *sign* & ECC & GHFP & *hd-only-ph* & *core-cl* & *inter-cl* & IRC & *is-int-cl* & *repr-int-cl*:

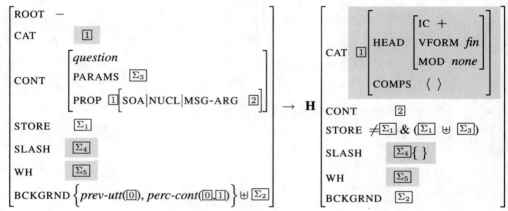

(32) a. *dir-is-int-cl*:

$$\begin{bmatrix} \text{CONT|PROP} & \boxed{1} \end{bmatrix} \rightarrow \mathbf{H}\begin{bmatrix} \text{CONT} & \boxed{1} \end{bmatrix}$$

b. *sign* & ECC & GHFP & *hd-only-ph* & *core-cl* & *inter-cl* & IRC & *is-int-cl* & *dir-is-int-cl*:

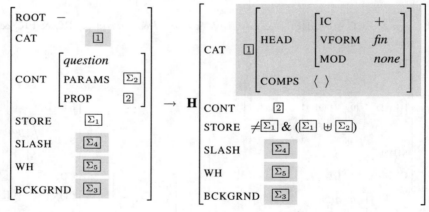

(33) a. *slu-int-cl*:

$$
\begin{bmatrix}
\text{CONT} & \begin{bmatrix} question \\ \text{PROP} & \begin{bmatrix} proposition \\ \text{SIT}\ \boxed{1} \\ \text{SOA}\ \begin{bmatrix} \text{QUANTS} & \boxed{A} \\ \text{NUCL} & \boxed{3} \end{bmatrix} \end{bmatrix} \end{bmatrix} \\[4pt]
\text{STORE}\quad \{\ \} \\[4pt]
\text{MAX-QUD} & \begin{bmatrix} question \\ \text{PARAMS}\ \{\ \} \\ \text{PROP} & \begin{bmatrix} proposition \\ \text{SIT}\ \boxed{1} \\ \text{SOA}\ \begin{bmatrix} \text{QUANTS}\ \langle\ pquant\text{-}rel\ \rangle\ \oplus\ \boxed{A} \\ \text{NUCL}\ \boxed{3} \end{bmatrix} \end{bmatrix} \end{bmatrix}
\end{bmatrix}
\rightarrow \mathbf{H}\begin{bmatrix}\text{STORE}\ \ neset(param)\end{bmatrix}
$$

b. *sign* & ECC & GHFP & *hd-only-ph* & *hd-frag-ph* & *core-cl* & *inter-cl* & IRC & *slu-int-cl*:

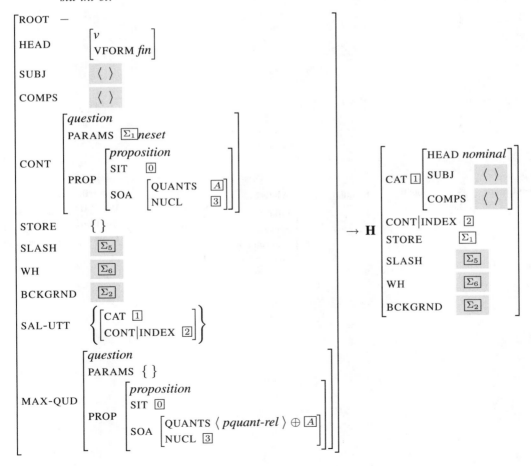

A.2.5 Other Maximal Clausal Types

The subtypes of *excl-cl* are discussed in Chapter 6: *inv-excl-cl* in section 6.3; *wh-excl-cl* in section 6.4. The type *top-cl* is introduced and discussed in section 5.1.2. *Ns-imp-cl*, *cp-cl*, and *factive-cl* originate in Chapter 2; see sections 2.6, 2.8 and 2.10. The type *root-cl* is discussed in section 7.2.

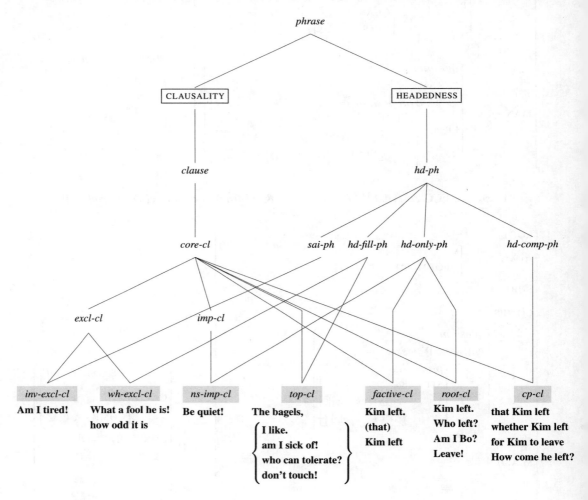

Type Constraints:

(34) a. *inv-excl-cl*:

$$\left[\text{CONT}|\text{PROP}|\text{SOA}\ \boxed{1}\right] \rightarrow \mathbf{H}\begin{bmatrix} \text{IC} & + \\ \text{CONT} & \boxed{1} \end{bmatrix}, \dots$$

b. *sign* & ECC & GHFP & *sai-ph* & *core-cl* & *excl-cl* & *inv-excl-cl*:

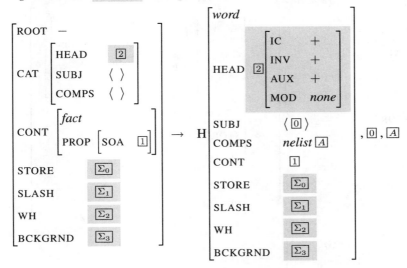

(35) a. *wh-excl-cl*:

$$\begin{bmatrix} \text{HEAD}|\text{INV}\ - \\ \text{PROP}|\text{SOA} \begin{bmatrix} \text{QUANTS} & \langle \boxed{0} \rangle \oplus \boxed{A} \\ \text{NUCL} & \boxed{2} \end{bmatrix} \\ \text{STORE}\ \boxed{\Sigma_1} \\ \text{SLASH}\ \{\ \} \end{bmatrix} \rightarrow \left[\text{WH}\ \{\boxed{0}\}\right], \mathbf{H}\begin{bmatrix} \text{SOA} & \begin{bmatrix} \text{QUANTS} & \boxed{A} \\ \text{NUCL} & \boxed{2} \end{bmatrix} \\ \text{STORE} & \{\boxed{0}quant\text{-}rel\} \uplus \boxed{\Sigma_1} \\ \text{SUBJ} & \langle \ \rangle \end{bmatrix}$$

b. GHFP & *hd-fill-ph* & *excl-cl* & *wh-excl-cl*:

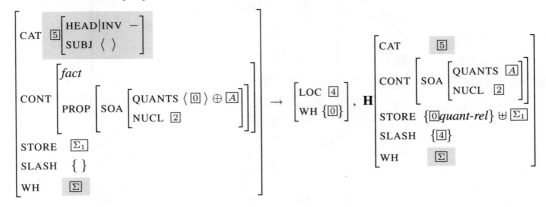

(36) a. *ns-imp-cl*:

$$\left[\text{CONT}|\text{SOA}\ \boxed{1}\right] \rightarrow \begin{bmatrix} \text{VFORM} & \textit{fin} \\ \text{SUBJ} & \langle\ \text{NP}[2nd]\ \rangle \\ \text{CONT} & \boxed{1} \end{bmatrix}$$

b. *sign* & ECC & GHFP & *core-cl* & *imp-cl* & *ns-imp-cl*:

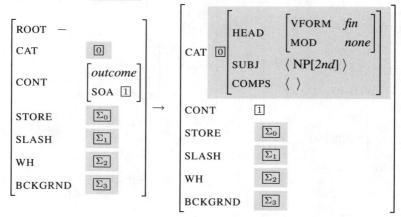

(37) a. *cp-cl*:

$$[\ ] \rightarrow \mathbf{H}\begin{bmatrix} \text{HEAD} & c \\ \text{COMPS} & \boxed{A} \end{bmatrix}, \boxed{A}$$

b. GHFP & *sign* & ECC & *hd-comp-ph* & *clause* & *core-cl* & *cp-cl*:

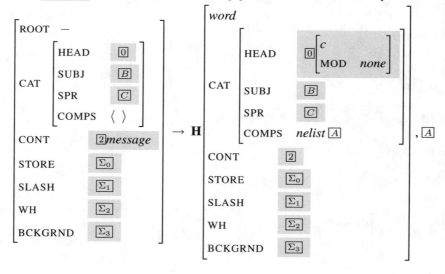

(38) a. *factive-cl*:

$$\begin{bmatrix} \text{HEAD} & \begin{bmatrix} verbal \\ \text{VFORM} & fin \end{bmatrix} \\ \text{CONT} & \begin{bmatrix} fact \\ \text{PROP} & \boxed{1} \end{bmatrix} \end{bmatrix} \rightarrow \mathbf{H}\begin{bmatrix} \text{CONT} & \boxed{1} \end{bmatrix}$$

b. *sign* & ECC & GHFP & *hd-only-ph* & *core-cl* & *factive-cl*:

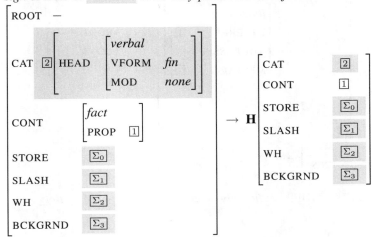

(39) a. *top-cl*:

$$[\ ] \rightarrow \begin{bmatrix} \text{WH} & \{\ \} \end{bmatrix}, \mathbf{H}\begin{bmatrix} \text{VFORM} & fin \\ \text{IC} & + \end{bmatrix}$$

b. *sign* & ECC & GHFP & *hd-fill-ph* & *clause* & *core-cl* & *top-cl*:

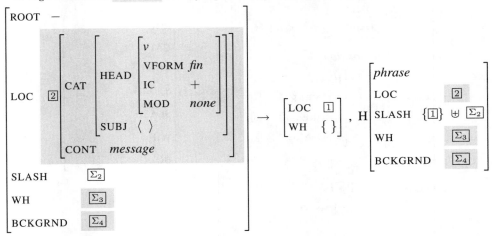

(40)   a.   *root-cl*:

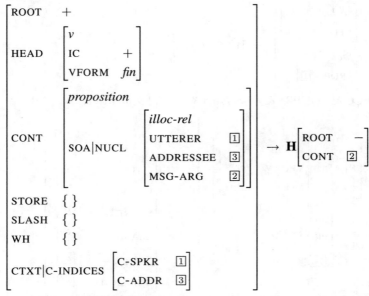

b.   *sign* & ECC &   GHFP   & *hd-only-ph* & *clause* & *core-cl* & *root-cl*:

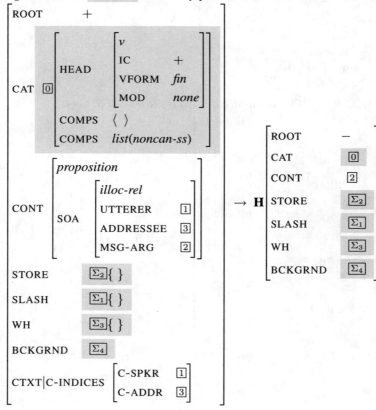

A.2.6 Maximal Nonclausal Types

The types *fin-vp* and *nf-hc-ph* are introduced in section 2.5. *Bare-nom-ph* and *bare-adj-ph* originate in section 5.2. For *nom-int-ph* and *cq-np*, see section 8.3.

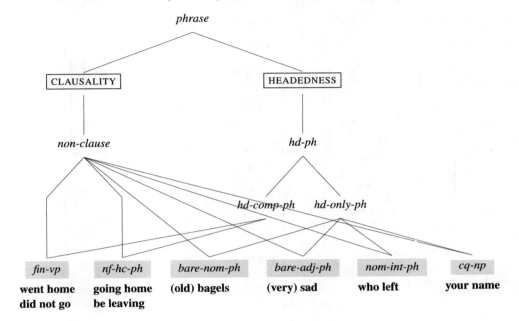

Type Constraints:

(41) a. *fin-vp*:

$$[\ ] \rightarrow \mathbf{H} \begin{bmatrix} \text{HEAD} & \begin{bmatrix} \text{AUX} & \boxed{1} \\ \text{POL} & \boxed{1} \end{bmatrix} \\ \text{COMPS} & \boxed{A} \end{bmatrix}, \boxed{A}$$

b. *sign* & ECC & ⬛ GHFP ⬛ & *hd-comp-ph* & *fin-vp*:

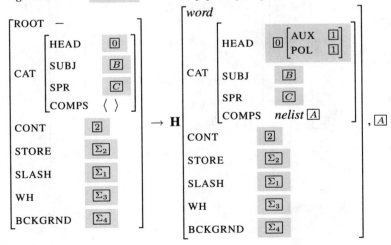

(42) a. *nf-hc-ph*:

$$[\ ] \rightarrow \mathbf{H} \begin{bmatrix} \text{HEAD} & \begin{bmatrix} \text{VFORM} & \textit{nonfin} \end{bmatrix} \\ \textit{comps} & \boxed{A} \end{bmatrix}, \boxed{A}$$

  b. *sign* & ECC & GHFP & *hd-comp-ph* & *nf-hc-ph*:

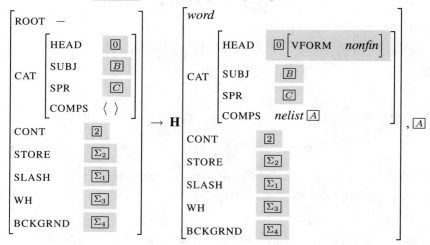

(43) a. *bare-nom-ph*:

$$\begin{bmatrix} \text{SPR} & \langle\ \rangle \end{bmatrix} \rightarrow \text{H} \begin{bmatrix} \text{HEAD} & \begin{bmatrix} \textit{noun} \end{bmatrix} \\ \text{SPR} & \left\langle \begin{matrix} \text{DetP} \\ \begin{bmatrix} \text{WH} \{\ \} \end{bmatrix} \end{matrix} \right\rangle \end{bmatrix}$$

  b. *sign* & ECC & GHFP & *hd-only-ph* & *bare-nom-ph*:

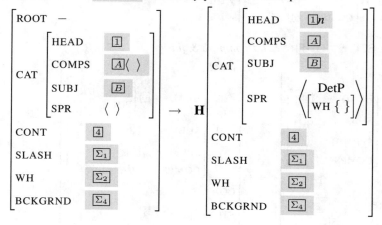

(44) a. *bare-adj-ph*:

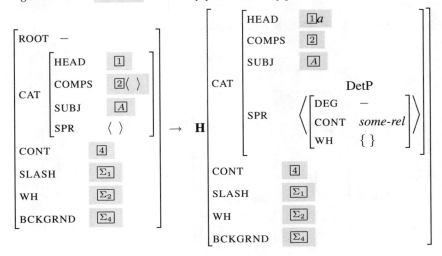

$$\left[\text{SPR} \quad \langle \; \rangle \right] \rightarrow \textbf{H} \begin{bmatrix} \text{HEAD} & \begin{bmatrix} a \\ \dots \end{bmatrix} \\ \text{SPR} & \left\langle \begin{matrix} \text{DetP} \\ \begin{bmatrix} \text{DEG} & - \\ \text{CONT} & some\text{-}rel \\ \text{WH} & \{\;\} \end{bmatrix} \end{matrix} \right\rangle \end{bmatrix}$$

b. *sign* & ECC & GHFP & *hd-only-ph* & *bare-adj-ph*:

$$\begin{bmatrix} \text{ROOT} & - \\ \text{CAT} & \begin{bmatrix} \text{HEAD} & \boxed{1} \\ \text{COMPS} & \boxed{2}\langle\;\rangle \\ \text{SUBJ} & \boxed{A} \\ \text{SPR} & \langle\;\rangle \end{bmatrix} \\ \text{CONT} & \boxed{4} \\ \text{SLASH} & \boxed{\Sigma_1} \\ \text{WH} & \boxed{\Sigma_2} \\ \text{BCKGRND} & \boxed{\Sigma_4} \end{bmatrix} \rightarrow \textbf{H} \begin{bmatrix} \text{CAT} & \begin{bmatrix} \text{HEAD} & \boxed{1}a \\ \text{COMPS} & \boxed{2} \\ \text{SUBJ} & \boxed{A} \\ \text{SPR} & \left\langle \begin{matrix} \text{DetP} \\ \begin{bmatrix} \text{DEG} & - \\ \text{CONT} & some\text{-}rel \\ \text{WH} & \{\;\} \end{bmatrix} \end{matrix} \right\rangle \end{bmatrix} \\ \text{CONT} & \boxed{4} \\ \text{SLASH} & \boxed{\Sigma_1} \\ \text{WH} & \boxed{\Sigma_2} \\ \text{BCKGRND} & \boxed{\Sigma_4} \end{bmatrix}$$

(45) a. *nom-int-ph*:

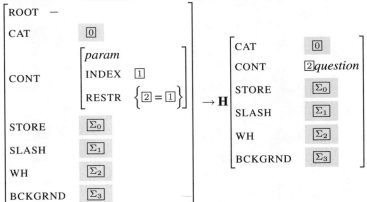

$$\begin{bmatrix} \text{CONT} & \begin{bmatrix} param \\ \text{IND} & \boxed{1} \\ \text{RESTR} & \{\boxed{2} = \boxed{1}\} \end{bmatrix} \end{bmatrix} \rightarrow \textbf{H} \begin{bmatrix} \text{CONT} & \boxed{2}question \end{bmatrix}$$

b. *sign* & ECC & GHFP & *hd-only-ph* & *nom-int-ph*:

$$\begin{bmatrix} \text{ROOT} & - \\ \text{CAT} & \boxed{0} \\ \text{CONT} & \begin{bmatrix} param \\ \text{INDEX} & \boxed{1} \\ \text{RESTR} & \{\boxed{2} = \boxed{1}\} \end{bmatrix} \\ \text{STORE} & \boxed{\Sigma_0} \\ \text{SLASH} & \boxed{\Sigma_1} \\ \text{WH} & \boxed{\Sigma_2} \\ \text{BCKGRND} & \boxed{\Sigma_3} \end{bmatrix} \rightarrow \textbf{H} \begin{bmatrix} \text{CAT} & \boxed{0} \\ \text{CONT} & \boxed{2}question \\ \text{STORE} & \boxed{\Sigma_0} \\ \text{SLASH} & \boxed{\Sigma_1} \\ \text{WH} & \boxed{\Sigma_2} \\ \text{BCKGRND} & \boxed{\Sigma_3} \end{bmatrix}$$

(46) a. *cq-np*:

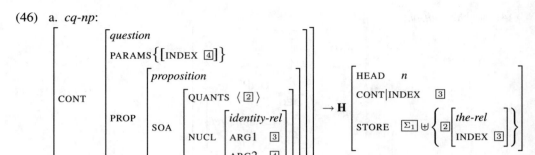

b. *sign* & ECC & GHFP & *hd-only-ph* & *cq-np*:

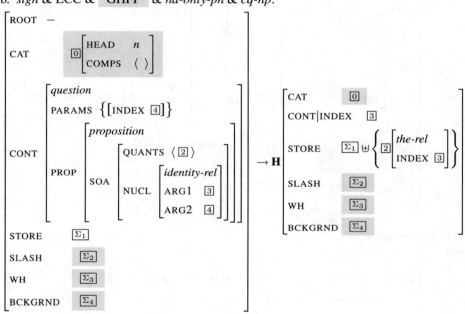

Appendix B: Semantics

B.1 Some Basic Semantic Types

The motivation for the type system described below is given in Chapter 3. In particular, the basic notions related to the message and SOA hierarchies are introduced there (see sections 3.3.2 and 3.4). For SOAs, see also section 2.4.2). The subtypes of *scope-obj* are discussed in section 4.2 and the SOA hierarchy is further refined in section 8.2.

B.1.1 Semantic Type Hierarchy

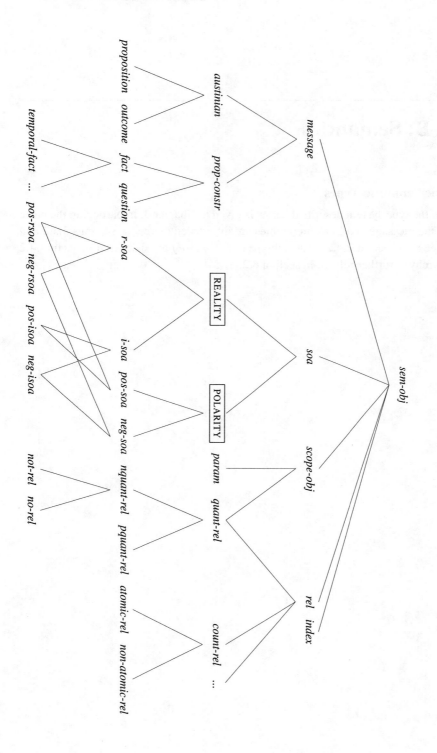

B.1.2 Type Declarations

TYPE	FEATURES/VALUE TYPE	IST
sem-obj		*feature-structure*
message		*sem-obj*
austinian	$\begin{bmatrix} \text{SIT} & situation \\ \text{SOA} & soa \end{bmatrix}$	*message*
proposition	$\begin{bmatrix} \text{SOA} & r\text{-}soa \end{bmatrix}$	*austinian*
outcome	$\begin{bmatrix} \text{SOA} & i\text{-}soa \end{bmatrix}$	*austinian*
prop-constr	$\begin{bmatrix} \text{PROP} & proposition \end{bmatrix}$	*message*
fact		*prop-constr*
question	$\begin{bmatrix} \text{PARAMS} & set(param) \end{bmatrix}$	*prop-constr*
soa	$\begin{bmatrix} \text{QUANTS} & list(quant\text{-}rel) \\ \text{NUCL} & rel \end{bmatrix}$	*sem-obj*
r-soa		*soa*
i-soa	$\begin{bmatrix} \text{T-PARAM} & param \end{bmatrix}$	*soa*
pos-soa		*soa*
qf-pos-soa		*pos-soa*
qf-fr-pos-soa		*pos-soa*
neg-soa		*soa*
scope-obj	$\begin{bmatrix} \text{INDEX} & index \\ \text{RESTR} & set(fact) \end{bmatrix}$	*sem-obj*
rel		*sem-obj*
quant-rel		*scope-obj & rel*
nquant-rel		*quant-rel*
pquant-rel		*quant-rel*
param		*scope-obj*
index		*sem-obj*

B.1.3 Type Constraints

(1)   *qf-pos-soa* $\Rightarrow$ $\begin{bmatrix} \text{QUANTS}|\text{FIRST} & pquant\text{-}rel \end{bmatrix}$

(2)   *qf-fr-pos-soa* $\Rightarrow$ $\begin{bmatrix} \text{QUANTS} & elist \end{bmatrix}$

(3)   *neg-soa* $\Rightarrow$ $\begin{bmatrix} \text{QUANTS}|\text{FIRST} & nquant\text{-}rel \end{bmatrix}$

B.2 Interpreting Typed Feature Structures

Let $M = \langle\, SU+AE_0, I\,\rangle$ where $SU+AE_0$ is a situational universe plus abstract entities, as outlined in section 3.4 and I is an interpretation function defined below. c is a context, specifying speaker, hearer, loc-utt, etc, as well as an assignment function c_f from indices to the universe of $SU+AE_0$. The BACKGROUND specifies a set of facts that must hold in c.

We define $[\![a]\!]^c$—the interpretation of a (a a feature structure, feature, or type) with respect to a context c:

1. If a is a (subtype of the type) relation, then $[\![a]\!]^c = I(a)$ and $Rel(I(a))$.

2. If a is a role feature, then $[\![a]\!]^c = I(a)$ and $ArgRole(I(a))$.

3. If a is an index, then $[\![a]\!]^c = c_f(a)$, where $c_f(a) \in |SU+AE_0|$.

4.

If a is of the form:
$$\begin{bmatrix} \rho & \\ F_1 & v_1 \\ \ldots & \\ F_n & v_n \end{bmatrix},$$

where ρ is a subtype of *relation*,

then $[\![a]\!]^c = \left\langle\!\left\langle\, [\![\rho]\!]^c;\ [\![F_1]\!]^c\!:\![\![v_1]\!]^c, \ldots, [\![F_n]\!]^c\!:\![\![v_n]\!]^c \,\right\rangle\!\right\rangle$ (a SOA).

5.

If a is of the form:
$$\begin{bmatrix} soa & \\ \text{QUANTS} & \langle\,\rangle \\ \text{NUCL} & b \end{bmatrix}$$

then $[\![a]\!]^c = [\![b]\!]^c$ and $\mathbf{Pos}([\![a]\!]^c)$.

6.

If a is of the form:
$$\begin{bmatrix} soa & \\ \text{QUANTS} & \begin{bmatrix} \text{FIRST} & not\text{-}rel \\ \text{REST} & b \end{bmatrix} \\ \text{NUCL} & g \end{bmatrix}$$

then $[\![a]\!]^c = \overline{h}$ (the dual of the SOA h),

where $h = \left[\!\!\left[\begin{bmatrix} soa & \\ \text{QUANTS} & b \\ \text{NUCL} & g \end{bmatrix} \right]\!\!\right]^c$.

7.

If a is of the form:
$$\begin{bmatrix} soa & \\ \text{QUANTS} & \begin{bmatrix} \text{FIRST} & \begin{bmatrix} \delta & \\ \text{IND} & i \\ \text{RESTR} & \Sigma \end{bmatrix} \\ \text{REST} & b \end{bmatrix} \\ \text{NUCL} & g \end{bmatrix},$$

where δ is a subtype of *quant-rel*,

then $[\![a]\!]^c = \left\langle\!\left\langle\, [\![\delta]\!]^c;\ \lambda\!\left\{c_f(i)\right\}[\![\Sigma]\!]^c, \lambda\!\left\{c_f(i)\right\}\!\left[\!\!\left[\begin{bmatrix} soa & \\ \text{QUANTS} & b \\ \text{NUCL} & g \end{bmatrix} \right]\!\!\right]^c \,\right\rangle\!\right\rangle.$

8.
If a is of the form: $\begin{bmatrix} proposition \\ \text{SIT} \quad s \\ \text{SOA} \quad \sigma \end{bmatrix}$

then $[\![a]\!]^c = \mathsf{prop}([\![s]\!]^c, [\![\sigma]\!]^c)$.

9.
If a is of the form: $\begin{bmatrix} fact \\ \text{PROP} \quad p \end{bmatrix}$,

then $[\![a]\!]^c = \mathsf{poss}([\![p]\!]^c)$ and $Fact([\![a]\!]^c)$.

10. If a is a set of elements of type $fact$
then $[\![a]\!]^c = \mathsf{poss}(p)$ and $Fact([\![a]\!]^c)$,
where $p = \bigwedge\{g \mid \exists h[h \in a$ and $[\![h]\!]^c = \mathsf{poss}(g)]\}$.

11.
If a is of the form: $\begin{bmatrix} outcome \\ \text{SIT} \quad s \\ \text{SOA} \quad b\big[\text{T-PARAM}|\text{INDEX} \quad t\big] \end{bmatrix}$,

then $[\![a]\!]^c = \mathsf{out}([\![s]\!]^c, \lambda\{c_f(t)\}[\![b]\!]^c)$.

12.
If a is of the form: $\begin{bmatrix} question \\ \text{PARAMS} \quad \Sigma \\ \text{PROP} \quad b \end{bmatrix}$

then: $[\![a]\!]^c = \lambda\{\mathbf{indices}(\Sigma)\}[\mathbf{facts}(\Sigma)][\![b]\!]^c$ and $\mathbf{Question}([\![a]\!]^c)$
where **indices** is the function that maps a set of parameters to the set of indices that it contains and **facts** is the function that maps set of parameters to the set of facts that it contains:

$\mathbf{indices}(\Sigma) =_{def} \{i \mid \exists p\,[p \in \Sigma$ and $\text{INDEX}(p) = x$ and $i = c_f(x)]\}$
$\mathbf{facts}(\Sigma) =_{def} \bigcup\{F \mid \exists p, g\,[p \in \Sigma$ and $\text{RESTR}(p) = g$ and $F = [\![g]\!]^c]\}$

N-jectivity: A propositional abstract $\mu\ (= \lambda\{b_1, \ldots, b_n\}p)$ is n-jective iff the following condition holds: whenever

1. two assignments f_1 and f_2 are appropriate for μ,
2. both $\mu[f_1]$ and $\mu[f_2]$ are true propositions, and moreover
3. f_1 and f_2 are identical on $n - 1$ roles,

then f_1 and f_2 also agree on the nth role.
That is, if for some subset of indices $\{i_1, \ldots, i_{n-1}\}$ $f_1(x_{i_j}) = f_2(x_{i_j})$, for $1 \leq j \leq n - 1$, then also $f_1(x_{i_n}) = f_2(x_{i_n})$.

Singular *Which* Presupposition Constraint (WH-PRC):

Let M = ⟨ SU+AE, I ⟩ where SU+AE is a situation universe plus abstract entities, I the interpretation function defined in section 17 of Chapter 3, and c is a context.

$$\text{If } a \text{ is of the form:} \begin{bmatrix} question \\[2pt] \text{PARAMS} \quad \left\{ \dots \begin{bmatrix} param \\[2pt] \text{RESTR} \quad \left\{ \dots \begin{bmatrix} \text{NUCL} & atomic\text{-}rel \end{bmatrix} \dots \right\}, \dots \end{bmatrix} \right\} \end{bmatrix}$$

then there must exist a situation s such that c contains a certain fact f, where $f = \mathsf{fact}(\mathsf{prop}(s, \langle\langle \text{N-Jective}; [\![a]\!]^c \rangle\rangle))$.

B.3 Semantic Structures

In this section, we collect the basic definitions that help to characterize an SU+AE and amplify our discussion of a number of formal issues relating to Chapter 3. This section is best read in conjunction with S&M–97.

B.3.1 SU+AE: The Definitions

The semantic universe we have posited is an extensional Situational Universe with Abstract Entities (SU+AE). This is a relational structure of the form $\mathcal{S} = [\ \mathcal{A},\ S, R\ ]$. Here S is the set of *structural* relations specified in (4a). R includes minimally the relations given in (4b). The various conditions these relations need to satisfy, described in Chapters 3 and 4, are repeated here:[1]

(4) a. $\{\mathbf{SelAdVal}^3, \mathbf{Soa}^3, \mathbf{Pos}^1, \mathbf{Neg}^1, \mathbf{PlaceHolder}^2, \mathbf{Abst}^2, \mathbf{Res}^2, \mathbf{Possibility}^2,$
     $\mathbf{AtProposition}^3, \mathbf{Proposition}^1, \mathbf{AtOutcome}^3, \mathbf{Outcome}^1, \mathbf{IrrSoa}^3, \mathbf{Set}^1, \epsilon^2,$
     $\mathbf{ConjOf}^2, \mathbf{DisjOf}^2\}$

  b. $\{Sit^1, \models^2, Rel^1, ArgRole^1, Approp^1, NegOf^2, Time^1,$
     $Timespan^2, Anterior^2, Fact^1, True^1, Fulfill^1, \rightarrow^2_{prop}, NegationOf^2\}$

  1. Basics concerning SOAs:

     (a) If $\mathbf{Soa}(R, \alpha, \sigma)$, then $Rel(R)$ and $Approp(\alpha)$.

     (b) If $\mathbf{SelAdVal}(i, a, \alpha)$, then $ArgRole(i)$.

     (c) If $\mathbf{Soa}(R, \alpha, \sigma)$, then for any i,a,b such that $\mathbf{SelAdVal}(i, a, \alpha)$ and $\mathbf{SelAdVal}(i, b, \alpha)$ it follows that $a = b$.

     (d) If $s \models \sigma$, then $Sit(s)$ and there exist R,α such that $\mathbf{Soa}(R, \alpha, \sigma)$.

  2. Negation and SOAs:

     (a) If for some $R, \alpha\ \mathbf{Soa}(R, \alpha, \sigma)$, then exactly one of the following: $\mathbf{Pos}(\sigma)$ or $\mathbf{Neg}(\sigma)$

     (b) The $NegOf$ relation is symmetric and functional (If $NegOf(\sigma, \tau)$, then $NegOf(\tau, \sigma)$; If $NegOf(\sigma, \tau)$ and $NegOf(\sigma, \tau')$, then $\tau = \tau'$).

     (c) Dual SOAs are constituted from the same SOA and role assignment: If $\mathbf{Soa}(R, \alpha, \sigma)$, then there is a SOA $\overline{\sigma} \neq \sigma$ such that $NegOf(\sigma, \overline{\sigma})$ and $\mathbf{Soa}(R, \alpha, \overline{\sigma})$.

---

[1] Recall that we do not include **Question** as a structural relation given that it constitutes a 'derivative' notion: since we explicate questions as propositional abstracts and SU+AEs are required to be λ-structures, any SU+AE will necessarily contains the class of questions.

3. Temporal Structure:

   (a) If $Timespan(s, t)$, then $Sit(s)$ and $Time(t)$. $Timespan$ relates a situation to the times occurring within it.

   (b) If $Anterior(s_1, s_2)$, then $Sit(s_1)$ and $Sit(s_2)$. $Anterior$ is a partial ordering on the class of situations in terms of temporal constitution such that $Anterior(s_1, s_2)$ intuitively means that the temporal instants of s_1 precede the temporal instants of s_2.

4. Abstraction:

   (a) If **PlaceHolder**(b, π) and **PlaceHolder**(b', π), then $b = b'$.

   (b) If **Abst**(b, a), then $b \neq a$ and there exists π such that **PlaceHolder**(b, π).

   (c) If **Res**(σ, a), then **Possibility**(σ)

   (d) τ is *the simultaneous abstraction of C from χ restricted by* Σ if there is an injective function $\pi : C \to |\mathcal{S}|$ and b such that:

       i. $b = \chi\{c_1 \mapsto \pi(c_1), \ldots, c_n \mapsto \pi(c_n)\}$

       ii. For each $\sigma \in \Sigma$: **Res**$(\sigma\{c_1 \mapsto \pi(c_1), \ldots, c_n \mapsto \pi(c_n)\}, \tau)$

       iii. **Abst**(b, τ)

       iv. For each c_i: **PlaceHolder**$(b, \pi(c_i))$

       v. For each c_i: the only sort of $\pi(c_i)$ is **PlaceHolder**$*$

   (e) Given an abstract $a = \lambda C[\Sigma].\chi$ in $\mathcal{S}$, a substitution $f : \Pi \mapsto D$ is an *appropriate assignment* to a if there exists b such that

       i. For each $\pi \in \Pi$: **PlaceHolder**(b, π)

       ii. **Abst**(b, a)

       iii. For each $\sigma \in \Sigma$: $Fact(\sigma\{f\})$

       iv. $b\{f\}$ exists.

   If $b\{f\}$ exists and f is appropriate, then $b\{f\}$ is the application of a to f.

   (f) $\mathcal{S}$ is closed under abstraction with restrictions: for every element a of $|\mathcal{S}|$, every set Σ of possibilities and every set C of elements of $|\mathcal{S}|$, the simultaneous abstraction with restrictions $\lambda C[\Sigma].a$ exists.

5. Abstract Entities:

   (a) **Possibility**$*$, **Proposition**$*$, **Outcome**$*$, **Soa**$*$, **SelAdVal**$*$ are pairwise disjoint.

   (b) **AtProposition**$* \subset$ **Proposition**$*$; **AtOutcome**$* \subset$ **Outcome**$*$.

   (c) If $\to^2_{prop} (p, q)$, then **Proposition**(p) and **Proposition**(q); $\to^2_{prop} (p, q)$ if $True(p)$ implies $True(q)$.

   (d) If **AtProposition**(s, σ, p), then $Sit(s)$ and there exist R, α such that **Soa**(R, α, σ).

   (e) If there exists s, σ such that **AtProposition**(s, σ, p), then $s \models \sigma$ if and only if $True(p)$.

   (f) If **Possibility**(p, f), then **Proposition**(p)

   (g) If **Proposition**(p), then there exists f such that **Possibility**(p, f).

   (h) $Fact(f)$ iff there exists p such that **Possibility**(p, f) and $True(p)$.

(i) If **Irrsoa**$(b, r, \hat{t}\sigma)$, then:

    i. **Abst**$(b, \hat{t}\sigma)$,

    ii. **PlaceHolder**(b, r), and

    iii. there exists t_0, R, μ such that:

        (a) $Time(t_0)$ and

        (b) **Soa**$(R, \mu, \hat{t}\sigma\{r \rightarrow t_0\})$.

(j) If **AtOutcome**$(s, \hat{t}\sigma, o)$, then there exist b,r such that:

    (a) $Sit(s)$,

    (b) **Irrsoa**$(b, r, \hat{t}\sigma)]$, and

    (c) there is no t_0 such that:

        (a) $Timespan(s, t_0)$ and

        (b) $s \models \hat{t}\sigma\{r \rightarrow t_0\}$.

(k) *Fulfilled(o)* iff there exist $s_0, s_1, \hat{t}\sigma, b, r, t_0$ such that:

    i. **AtOutcome**$(s_0, \hat{t}\sigma, o)$ and

    ii. **Irrsoa**$(b, r, \hat{t}\sigma)$ and

    iii. *Anterior*(s_0, s_1) and $s_1 \models \hat{t}\sigma\{[r \rightarrow t_0]\})$

6. Compounding on Abstract Entities:

    (a) **ConjOf**$^* \subset$ **Proposition***; **DisjOf**$^* \subset$ **Proposition***; $\epsilon^* \subset$ **Set***.

    (b) The elements of **Set*** are regulated by the axioms of the set theory ZFC$^-$.

    (c) If **Set**(X) and for each $p \in X$, **Proposition**(p), then there exist $\bigwedge X$ and $\bigvee X$ such that for each $p \in X$ **ConjOf**$(\mathbf{p}, \bigwedge \mathbf{X})$, **DisjOf**$(\mathbf{p}, \bigvee \mathbf{X})$.

    (d) If **Set**(X) and **Proposition**(p) for each $p \in X$, then:
$True(\bigwedge X)$ iff for each $p \in X$, $True(p)$.

    (e) If **Set**(X) and **Proposition**(p) for each $p \in X$, then:
$True(\bigvee X)$ iff $True(p)$ for some $p \in X$.

    (f) The *NegationOf* relation is symmetric and functional (If *NegationOf*(p, q), then *NegationOf*(q, p); If *NegationOf*(p, q) and *NegationOf*(p, q'), then $q = q'$).

    (g) Dual atomic propositions are constituted from the same situation and SOA:
If **AtProposition**(s, σ, p) then there is a proposition $\neg p \neq p$ such that
NegationOf$(p, \neg p)$ and **AtProposition**$(s, \overline{\sigma}, \neg p)$.

    (h) If **Set**(X) and **Set**(Y) and for each $p \in X \cup Y$, **Proposition**(p), and

        i. for each $p \in X$ there is a $q \in Y$ such that *NegationOf*(p, q), and

        ii. for each $q \in Y$ there is a $p \in X$ such that *NegationOf*(p, q),

    then: *NegationOf*$(\bigwedge X, \bigvee Y)$

B.3.2 Notions related to Questions

1. **Questionhood**: Given an SU+AE $\mathcal{S}$: **Question**(q) iff there exist a set C, $C \subset |\mathcal{S}|$, $p, b \in |\mathcal{S}|$, and a function $\pi : C \to |\mathcal{S}|$ such that:

   (a) For each $c \in C$: **PlaceHolder**(b, c).

   (b) **Abst**(b, q).

   (c) $q\{\pi\} = p$.

   (d) **Proposition**(p).

   In such a case, we say that p is a *propositional instantiation* of q (denoted as: $PropInst(p, q)$).

2. **A Conjunction Operation for questions**: Given a question q_1 $(= \lambda A.\sigma)$ and a question q_2 $(= \lambda B.\tau)$, where $A \cap B = \emptyset$: $\bigwedge(\lambda A.\sigma, \lambda B.\tau) =_{def} \lambda A \cup B. \bigwedge\{\sigma, \tau\}$

3. **Atomic and Simple Answerhood**:

   a. $AtomAns(p, q)$ iff $\exists r[ConjOf(p, r) \text{ and } PropInst(r, q)]$

   b. $NegAtomAns(p, q)$ iff $\exists r[r = \neg p \text{ and } AtomAns(r, q)]$

   c. $SimpleAns(p, q)$ iff $AtomAns(p, q)$ or $NegAtomAns(r, q)$

4. **Strong Exhaustiveness**: $StrongExhAns(f, q)$ iff
   $f = \bigwedge\{p \mid True(p) \text{ and } SimpleAns(p, q)\}$

5. **Decidedness conditions for a question**: A question q is *decided* iff
   $\{p \mid True(p) \text{ and } SimpleAns(p, q)\} \neq \emptyset$

6. **Potential Resolvedness**: $PotResAns(p, q)$ iff **Proposition**(p) and **Question**(q) and

   (a) Either: $PositivelyResolves(p, q)$. That is, both i. and ii. hold:

   i. **p witnesses q**:
   $p \to_{prop} \bigvee\{r \mid AtomAns(r, q)\}$.

   ii. **p sortalizes q**:
   If $|\{r \mid AtomAns(r, q)\}| \geq 2$, then there exists at least one r such that $AtomAns(r, q)$ and $r \not\to_{prop} p$.

   (b) Or: $NegativelyResolves(p, q)$. That is, $p \to_{prop} \bigwedge\{r \mid NegAtomAns(r, q)\}$.

7. **Resolving a Question**: p is a proposition that *resolves* a question q relative to an information state IS just in case the following conditions hold:

   a. Semantic Condition: $True(p)$ and $PotResAns(p, q)$.

   b. Pragmatic Relativization: p enables the current goal (in IS) to be fulfilled relative to the available inferential resources (of IS).

8. **Aboutness** : $About(p, q)$ iff **Proposition**(p) and **Question**(q) and
   $p \to_{prop} \bigvee\{r \mid SimpleAns(r, q)\}$.

B.3.3 SU+AE: Formal Foundations

As mentioned in Chapter 3, in an SU+AE structure, the structural relations are singled out because, intuitively, they 'capture the structure of elements of the domain' (S&M–97, p. 259). The formal underpinning of this intuition is via the notion of a **bisimulation** (S&M–97's definition 3.1):

Definition 19 Bisimulation:

> For a structure S, a binary relation E is a bisimulation *just in case: if E(a,b) holds, then:*
>
> (a) *If a is atomic, then $b = a$.*
> (b) *Whenever $S(x_1, \ldots, x_n, a)$ for S a structural relation, then there exist $y_1, \ldots, y_n$ such that $S(y_1, \ldots, y_n, b)$ and for each i: $E(x_i, y_i)$.*
> (c) *E(b,a).*
>
> *a is bisimilar to b in S iff there is a bisimulation E of S such that $E(a, b)$. S is extensional if it has no distinct entities which are bisimilar.*

Therefore, as S&M–97 point out, '[i]n an extensional structure, the non-atomic objects are individuated according to their structural properties alone'. (S&M–97, p. 260). To rephrase this slightly, if one can prove about two entities of an extensional structure that they satisfy the same structural properties, then they are actually identical.

In building models of our semantic theory, it is useful to introduce two notions: (1) a *unary structural description*, intuitively a specification for an object in terms of the structural relationships it satisfies, and (2) the generalization of this notion to a set of entities, which will be referred to as a *structural description*.[2] The formal definition of the first of these is the following:

Definition 20 Unary Structural Descriptions:

> Given an extensional structure A and an entity x, a unary structural description T is a pair $\langle x, T_x \rangle$ consisting of a set T_x of tuples of the form $\langle S, b_1, \ldots, b_k \rangle$ such that S is a structural relation of A of r-ity $k + 1$ and $b_1, \ldots b_k$ are either x or elements of $|A|$. For each $a \in |A|$, the set $a.T$ consists of tuples of the form $\langle S, b_1[x/a], \ldots, b_k[x/a] \rangle$ for each $\langle S, b_1, \ldots, b_k \rangle \in T_x$. Here $b_i[x/a] = a$ if $b_i = x$, and is b_i otherwise. a satisfies T if for all S and $b_1, \ldots, b_k$:
> $$S(b_1, \ldots, b_k, a) \text{ holds in } A \text{ iff } \langle S, b_1, \ldots, b_k \rangle \in a.T$$

To illustrate this definition, the assignment $f = $ runner:tully,time:3:45 gmt can be described by means of the unary structural description in (5a). The SOA $\sigma = \langle\langle$Run; runner:tully,time:3:45 gmt$\rangle\rangle$ can be described by means of the unary structural description in (5b):

(5) a. $\langle$x, { $\langle$ **SelAdVal**, runner, tully $\rangle$, $\langle$ **SelAdVal**, time, 3:45 gmt $\rangle$ } $\rangle$
     b. $\langle$x, { $\langle$ **Soa**, Run, f $\rangle$ } $\rangle$

In a given structure A we can manufacture a description for any object $a \in |A|$ by collecting all the tuples $\langle S, b_1, \ldots, b_k \rangle$ where $S(b_1, \ldots, b_k, a)$ holds in A. S&M–97 call this the *canonical description* for a.[3] The converse does not hold, however: not every description has a satisfier in a given structure. For certain purposes illustrated below, the following generalization of a unary structural description is useful:

---

[2]These definitions are given in S&M–97, p. 261–262.

[3]To accommodate atoms, one can introduce the identity relation as a structural relation.

Definition 21 Structural Descriptions:

Given an extensional structure $\mathcal{A}$, a structural description T in $\mathcal{A}$ is an indexed family $\{T_x\}_{x \in X}$ of sets T_x of tuples of the form $\langle S, b_1, \ldots b_k \rangle$ such that S is a structural relation of $\mathcal{A}$ of r-ity $k + 1$ and $b_1, \ldots b_k \in |\mathcal{A}| \cup X$. Given a mapping s from X to $\mathcal{A}$, let $s.T$ be the family of sets $s.T_x$ of tuples of the form $\langle S, b_1[s], \ldots b_k[s] \rangle$ for each $\langle S, b_1, \ldots b_k \rangle$ in T_x, where $b_i[s] = s(b_i)$ if b_i is in X and is b_i otherwise. The mapping s satisfies T if for each x in X, $s(x)$ satisfies the unary description $\langle s(x), s.T_x \rangle$

Definition 22 Well-/Anti-foundedness:

A structure $\mathcal{A}$ is well-founded *if it has no infinite descending cycles. That is, if it has no infinite sequence $a_1, a_2, \ldots, a_n, \ldots$ such that for each i, a_i is a component of a_{i+1}. $\mathcal{A}$ is* anti-founded *if every structural description in $\mathcal{A}$ is satisfied.*

S&M–97 prove the following theorem on the basis of which one can construct structures that illustrate our semantic universe:[4]

Theorem 1 *For every extensional structure $\mathcal{A}$, there is a well-founded extensional structure $\mathcal{A}_{wf}$ and an anti-founded extensional structure $\mathcal{A}_{af}$ such that $\mathcal{A}_{wf}$ is isomorphically embedded in $\mathcal{A}$ and $\mathcal{A}$ is isomorphically embedded in $\mathcal{A}_{af}$.*

This theorem is a tool we can use to construct semantic universes of the form we need. Start with a simple relational structure that includes a set of situations, a set of relations, a set of argument roles, and a set of times. The specifications for the requisite structured objects (assignments, SOAs, propositions, outcomes, facts, abstracts, etc.) can be converted to structural descriptions as illustrated in (5) above. Theorem 1 tells us that there exists a structure $\mathcal{S}$ which isomorphically extends the simple relational structure and in which the descriptions have satisfiers.

The final point to consider is why our semantic universe can be assumed to be a λ-structure, a structure that is closed under simultaneous abstraction. This is ensured by a theorem proved by S&M–97 which states:

Theorem 2 *Every extensional structure can be extended to a λ-structure.*

We sketch a slightly modified version of the proof here, modified to accommodate abstraction with restrictions, which is based on a version of (restriction-less) abstraction we have introduced, which is subtly different from S&M–97's. By assumption, $\mathcal{S}$, the structure we constructed above, is anti-founded. In such a structure all the requisite place-holders exist. However, nothing ensures that each place-holder occurs in only one body. In order to ensure that this is the case, we restrict attention to a substructure—call it $\mathcal{S}_l$—which contains only place-holders that occur in a unique body. In order to show that $\mathcal{S}_l$ is a λ-structure, what remains to be shown is that in $\mathcal{S}_l$, for any given set C, set Σ of possibilities, and entity a, $\lambda C[\Sigma].a$ exists. We now provide a structural description, the satisfier of which provides the entity $\lambda B.a$. The description is a union of the following:

1. Singleton requirements $\{\langle \mathbf{PlaceHolder}, a \rangle\}$, for each $c \in C$.
2. The requirement $\{\langle \mathbf{Abst}, a \rangle, \langle \in, a \rangle, \langle \in, \kappa \rangle, \langle \mathbf{Set} \rangle, \{\langle \mathbf{Res}, \sigma \rangle | \sigma \in \Sigma \}\}$, where κ is an atom that is not a hereditary component of a.
3. Canonical descriptions of the (hereditary) components of a that are not in C.

---

[4]This is theorem 3.1, S&M–97, p. 263.

Let S be a satisfier for this description, which must exist, given that S is anti-founded. We need to show that its range is restricted to S_I.

The range of s does not contain any non-uniquely occurring place-holders. This is because for $b \in C$, s finds elements for which the sole structural requirement is $\langle \mathbf{PlaceHolder}, a \rangle$ (i.e. $\mathbf{PlaceHolder}(a\{s\}, s(c))$ is the unique structural relationship that $s(c)$ participates in). Hence, they are indeed uniquely occurring. In the remaining cases, s maps back to the hereditary components of a, which are all in S_I. Given that s is the identity on the components of a that are not in C (since they each are the unique satisfiers of their canonical description) it holds that $a\{s\} = a\{c_1 \mapsto s(c_1), \ldots, c_n \mapsto s(c_n)\}$. Also, for each element $s(c)$, $c \in C$, the only structural relationship it satisfies is $\mathbf{PlaceHolder}(a\{s\}, s(c))$.

Hence, the satisfier of the requirement $\{\langle \mathbf{Abst}, a \rangle, \langle \in, a \rangle, \langle \in, \kappa \rangle, \langle \mathbf{Set} \rangle, \{\langle \mathbf{Res}, \sigma \rangle | \sigma \in \Sigma\}\}$, call it α, is the desired abstract. The only thing that needs to be shown is that α is distinct from $a\{s\}$, the body of the abstract. This follows because by construction $\alpha = \{a\{s\}, \kappa\}$. In a well-founded setting, the required lack of identity would be trivial; here it requires a bit more justification: if $a\{s\}$ is a set, then if it satisfied $a\{s\} = \{a\{s\}, \kappa\}$, then $a = \{a, \kappa\}$. But this would mean that κ is also a hereditary component of a, which directly contradicts our choice of κ. Hence, $a\{s\} \neq \{a\{s\}, \kappa\} = \alpha$, as desired.

Appendix C: Lexicon

C.1   Introduction

This appendix summarizes the lexical analyses sketched at various places in the book. It is no more than a sketch, making little attempt at compact description in terms of type hierarchies and constraint inheritance. This lexicon could be organized in a number of ways that are consistent with the syntactic and semantic theory of constructions summarized in the previous two appendices.

C.2   General Lexical Constraints

(1)   Argument Realization Principle:

$$word \Rightarrow \begin{bmatrix} \text{SS|LOC|CAT} & \begin{bmatrix} \text{SUBJ} & \boxed{A} \\ \text{SPR} & \boxed{B} \\ \text{COMPS} & \boxed{C} \ominus list(gap\text{-}ss) \end{bmatrix} \\ \text{ARG-ST} & \boxed{A} \oplus \boxed{B} \oplus \boxed{C} \end{bmatrix}$$

(See section 5.1.1)

(2)   Store Amalgamation Constraint:

$$word \Rightarrow / \begin{bmatrix} \text{SS|LOC} & \begin{bmatrix} \text{CONT} & [\text{QUANTS} \ \ order\,(\boxed{\Sigma_0})] \\ \text{STORE} & (\boxed{\Sigma_1} \cup \ldots \cup \boxed{\Sigma_n}) \doteq \boxed{\Sigma_0} \end{bmatrix} \\ \text{ARG-ST} & \langle\, [\text{STORE}\ \boxed{\Sigma_1}],...,[\text{STORE}\ \boxed{\Sigma_n}] \,\rangle \end{bmatrix}$$

(See section 5.3)

(3)   SLASH Amalgamation Constraint:

$$word \Rightarrow / \begin{bmatrix} \text{SS|SLASH} & \boxed{\Sigma_1} \cup \ldots \cup \boxed{\Sigma_n} \\ \text{ARG-ST} & \langle [\text{SLASH}\ \boxed{\Sigma_1}], \ldots, [\text{SLASH}\ \boxed{\Sigma_n}] \rangle \end{bmatrix}$$

(See section 5.1.1)

(4)   WH-Amalgamation Constraint:

$$word \Rightarrow / \begin{bmatrix} \text{SS|WH} & \boxed{\Sigma_1} \cup \ldots \cup \boxed{\Sigma_n} \\ \text{ARG-ST} & \langle [\text{WH}\ \boxed{\Sigma_1}], \ldots, [\text{WH}\ \boxed{\Sigma_n}] \rangle \end{bmatrix}$$

(See section 5.2)

(5)   Non-LOCAL Amalgamation Constraint (collapses (3) and (4)):
        For every non-LOCAL feature **F**:

$$word \Rightarrow / \begin{bmatrix} \text{SS}|\mathbf{F} \ \boxed{\Sigma_1} \ \cup \ldots \cup \ \boxed{\Sigma_n} \\ \text{ARG-ST} \ \left\langle [\mathbf{F} \ \boxed{\Sigma_1}], \ldots, [\mathbf{F} \ \boxed{\Sigma_n}] \right\rangle \end{bmatrix}$$

(See section 5.4)

(6)   WH-Subject Prohibition (WHSP):

$$word \ \Rightarrow \ \begin{bmatrix} \text{SS}|\text{LOC}|\text{CAT}|\text{SUBJ} \quad list(\begin{bmatrix} \text{WH} \ \{ \ \} \end{bmatrix}) \end{bmatrix}$$

(See section 5.2)

(7)   WH-Constraint (WHC):
        Any non-initial element of a lexeme's ARG-ST list must be [WH { }].
        (See section 5.2)

C.3   Sample Lexical Entries

C.3.1   Determiners

The lexical entries given here derive from sections 5.2 and 5.3.

(8)
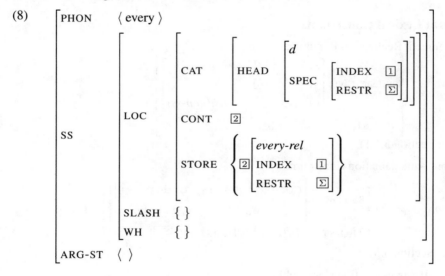

(9)

$$
\begin{bmatrix}
\text{PHON} & \langle\, a\,\rangle \\
\text{SS} & \begin{bmatrix}
\text{LOC} & \begin{bmatrix}
\text{CAT} & \begin{bmatrix}
\text{HEAD} & \begin{bmatrix} d \\ \text{SPEC} & \begin{bmatrix} \text{INDEX} & \boxed{1} \\ \text{RESTR} & \boxed{\Sigma_1} \end{bmatrix} \end{bmatrix} \\
\text{SUBJ} & \langle\ \rangle \\
\text{COMPS} & \langle\ \rangle
\end{bmatrix} \\
\text{CONT} & \boxed{3} \\
\text{STORE} & \boxed{\Sigma_2} \cup \left\{ \boxed{3}\begin{bmatrix} \textit{some-rel} \\ \text{INDEX} & \boxed{1} \\ \text{RESTR} & \left\{\begin{bmatrix}\text{PROP}|\text{SOA} & \boxed{4}\end{bmatrix}\right\} \cup \boxed{\Sigma_1} \end{bmatrix} \right\}
\end{bmatrix} \\
\text{SLASH} & \{\ \}
\end{bmatrix} \\
\text{ARG-ST} & \left\langle \begin{bmatrix} \text{AP} \\ \text{DEG} & + \\ \text{CONT} & \boxed{4} \\ \text{STORE} & \boxed{\Sigma_2} \end{bmatrix} \right\rangle
\end{bmatrix}
$$

(10)

$$
\begin{bmatrix}
\text{PHON} & \langle\, \text{'s}\,\rangle \\
\text{SS} & \begin{bmatrix}
\text{LOC} & \begin{bmatrix}
\text{CAT} & \begin{bmatrix}
\text{HEAD} & \begin{bmatrix} d \\ \text{SPEC} & \begin{bmatrix} \text{INDEX} & \boxed{3} \\ \text{RESTR} & \boxed{\Sigma_1} \end{bmatrix} \end{bmatrix} \\
\text{SPR} & \langle \boxed{2} \rangle \\
\text{SUBJ} & \langle\ \rangle \\
\text{COMPS} & \langle\ \rangle
\end{bmatrix} \\
\text{CONT} & \boxed{1} \\
\text{STORE} & \boxed{\Sigma_2} \cup \left\{ \begin{bmatrix} \textit{the-rel} \\ \text{INDEX} & \boxed{3} \\ \text{RESTR} & \boxed{\Sigma_1} \cup \left\{\begin{bmatrix} \textit{poss-rel} \\ \text{POSS-ER} & \boxed{4} \\ \text{POSS-ED} & \boxed{3} \end{bmatrix}\right\} \end{bmatrix} \right\}
\end{bmatrix} \\
\text{SLASH} & \{\ \}
\end{bmatrix} \\
\text{ARG-ST} & \left\langle \begin{bmatrix} \boxed{2}\text{NP} \\ \text{CONT} & \boxed{1}[\text{IND} & \boxed{4}] \\ \text{STORE} & \boxed{\Sigma_2} \end{bmatrix} \right\rangle
\end{bmatrix}
$$

(11)   Exclamative *what a*:

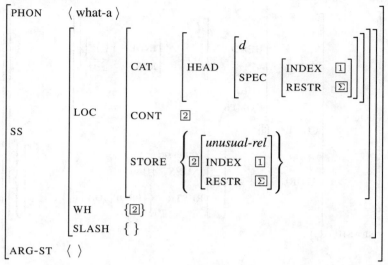

$$
\begin{bmatrix}
\text{PHON} & \langle\, \text{what-a} \,\rangle \\
\text{SS} & \begin{bmatrix}
\text{LOC} & \begin{bmatrix}
\text{CAT} & \begin{bmatrix} \text{HEAD} & \begin{bmatrix} d \\ \text{SPEC} & \begin{bmatrix} \text{INDEX} & \boxed{1} \\ \text{RESTR} & \boxed{\Sigma} \end{bmatrix} \end{bmatrix} \end{bmatrix} \\
\text{CONT} & \boxed{2} \\
\text{STORE} & \left\{ \boxed{2}\begin{bmatrix} unusual\text{-}rel \\ \text{INDEX} & \boxed{1} \\ \text{RESTR} & \boxed{\Sigma} \end{bmatrix} \right\}
\end{bmatrix} \\
\text{WH} & \{\boxed{2}\} \\
\text{SLASH} & \{\ \}
\end{bmatrix} \\
\text{ARG-ST} & \langle\ \rangle
\end{bmatrix}
$$

(12)

$$
\begin{bmatrix}
\text{PHON} & \langle\, \text{which} \,\rangle \\
\text{SS} & \begin{bmatrix}
\text{LOC} & \begin{bmatrix}
\text{CAT} & \begin{bmatrix} \text{HEAD} & \begin{bmatrix} d \\ \text{SPEC} & \begin{bmatrix} \text{INDEX} & \boxed{1} \\ \text{RESTR} & \boxed{\Sigma} \end{bmatrix} \end{bmatrix} \end{bmatrix} \\
\text{CONT} & \boxed{2} \\
\text{STORE} & \left\{ \boxed{2}\begin{bmatrix} param \\ \text{INDEX} & \boxed{1} \\ \text{RESTR} & \boxed{\Sigma} \end{bmatrix} \right\}
\end{bmatrix} \\
\text{WH} & \{(\boxed{2})\} \\
\text{SLASH} & \{\ \}
\end{bmatrix} \\
\text{ARG-ST} & \langle\ \rangle
\end{bmatrix}
$$

(13)   Exclamative *how*:

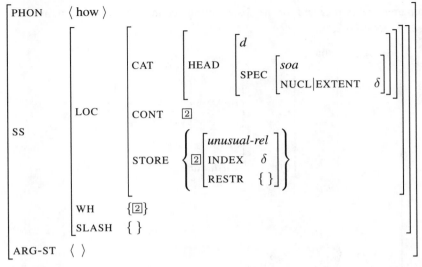

$$
\begin{bmatrix}
\text{PHON} & \langle\, how\,\rangle \\[2pt]
\text{SS} & \begin{bmatrix}
\text{LOC} & \begin{bmatrix}
\text{CAT} & \begin{bmatrix} \text{HEAD} & \begin{bmatrix} d \\ \text{SPEC} & \begin{bmatrix} soa \\ \text{NUCL}|\text{EXTENT} & \delta \end{bmatrix} \end{bmatrix} \end{bmatrix} \\[10pt]
\text{CONT} & \boxed{2} \\[6pt]
\text{STORE} & \left\{ \boxed{2}\begin{bmatrix} unusual\text{-}rel \\ \text{INDEX} & \delta \\ \text{RESTR} & \{\,\} \end{bmatrix} \right\}
\end{bmatrix} \\[20pt]
\text{WH} & \{\boxed{2}\} \\
\text{SLASH} & \{\,\}
\end{bmatrix} \\[10pt]
\text{ARG-ST} & \langle\ \rangle
\end{bmatrix}
$$

C.3.2   Prepositions

This lexical entry and related matters are discussed in section 5.2.

(14)
$$
\begin{bmatrix}
\text{PHON} & \langle\, in\,\rangle \\[4pt]
\text{SS} & \begin{bmatrix} \text{LOC}|\text{CAT} & \begin{bmatrix} \text{HEAD} & \begin{bmatrix} p \\ \text{PRED} & + \end{bmatrix} \end{bmatrix} \end{bmatrix} \\[8pt]
\text{ARG-ST} & \langle\, \text{NP}\,,\text{NP}\,\rangle
\end{bmatrix}
$$

C.3.3 Complementizers

The complementizers *that* and *for* are discussed in section 2.8; *whether*, *if*, and *how-come* are discussed in section 6.2.

(15)

$$
\begin{bmatrix}
\text{PHON} & \langle\, that\,\rangle \\[2pt]
\text{SS} & \begin{bmatrix}
\text{LOC} & \begin{bmatrix}
\text{CAT} & \begin{bmatrix}
\text{HEAD} & \begin{bmatrix} c \\ \text{IC} & - \\ \text{VFORM} & fin \end{bmatrix} \\[6pt]
\text{SUBJ} & \langle\,\rangle
\end{bmatrix} \\[10pt]
\text{CONT} & \boxed{1}\, austinian
\end{bmatrix} \\[8pt]
\text{WH} & \{\,\}
\end{bmatrix} \\[18pt]
\text{ARG-ST} & \left\langle\; \overset{\textstyle S}{\begin{bmatrix}
\text{INV} & - \\
\text{VFORM} & fin \\
\text{SUBJ} & \langle\,\rangle \\
\text{CONT} & \boxed{1}
\end{bmatrix}} \;\right\rangle
\end{bmatrix}
$$

(16)

$$
\begin{bmatrix}
\text{PHON} & \langle\, for\,\rangle \\[2pt]
\text{SS} & \begin{bmatrix}
\text{LOC} & \begin{bmatrix}
\text{CAT} & \begin{bmatrix}
\text{HEAD} & \begin{bmatrix} c \\ \text{IC} & - \\ \text{VFORM} & inf \end{bmatrix} \\[6pt]
\text{SUBJ} & \langle\,\rangle
\end{bmatrix} \\[10pt]
\text{CONT} & \begin{bmatrix} outcome \\ \text{SOA} & \boxed{1} \end{bmatrix}
\end{bmatrix} \\[8pt]
\text{WH} & \{\,\}
\end{bmatrix} \\[18pt]
\text{ARG-ST} & \left\langle\; \begin{bmatrix} canon\text{-}ss \\ \text{LOC} & \boxed{2} \end{bmatrix},\; \overset{\textstyle VP}{\begin{bmatrix}
\text{VFORM} & inf \\
\text{SUBJ} & \langle\,[\text{LOC}\ \boxed{2}]\,\rangle \\
\text{CONT} & \boxed{1}
\end{bmatrix}} \;\right\rangle
\end{bmatrix}
$$

(17)

$$
\begin{bmatrix}
\text{PHON} & \langle\, \text{whether} \,\rangle \\[2pt]
\text{SS} & \begin{bmatrix}
\text{LOC} & \begin{bmatrix}
\text{CAT} & \begin{bmatrix} \text{HEAD} & \begin{bmatrix} c \\ \text{IC} & - \\ \text{VFORM} & \boxed{2} \end{bmatrix} \end{bmatrix} \\[10pt]
\text{CONT} & \begin{bmatrix} question \\ \text{PARAMS} & \{\,\} \\ \text{PROP} & \boxed{1} \end{bmatrix}
\end{bmatrix} \\[20pt]
\text{WH} & \{\,\}
\end{bmatrix} \\[30pt]
\text{ARG-ST} & \left\langle \begin{bmatrix}
\text{HEAD} & \begin{bmatrix} \text{INV} & - \\ \text{VFORM} & \boxed{2} \end{bmatrix} \\
\text{SUBJ} & \langle\, (pro\text{-}ss) \,\rangle \\
\text{CONT} & \boxed{1}
\end{bmatrix} \right\rangle
\end{bmatrix}
$$

(18)

$$
\begin{bmatrix}
\text{PHON} & \langle\, \text{if} \,\rangle \\[2pt]
\text{SS} & \begin{bmatrix}
\text{LOC} & \begin{bmatrix}
\text{CAT} & \begin{bmatrix} \text{HEAD} & \begin{bmatrix} c \\ \text{IC} & - \\ \text{VFORM} & \boxed{2}\mathit{fin} \end{bmatrix} \end{bmatrix} \\[10pt]
\text{CONT} & \begin{bmatrix} question \\ \text{PARAMS} & \{\,\} \\ \text{PROP} & \boxed{1} \end{bmatrix}
\end{bmatrix} \\[20pt]
\text{WH} & \{\,\}
\end{bmatrix} \\[30pt]
\text{ARG-ST} & \left\langle \begin{bmatrix}
\text{HEAD} & \begin{bmatrix} verb \\ \text{INV} & - \\ \text{VFORM} & \boxed{2} \end{bmatrix} \\
\text{SUBJ} & \langle\, \rangle \\
\text{CONT} & \boxed{1}
\end{bmatrix} \right\rangle
\end{bmatrix}
$$

(19)

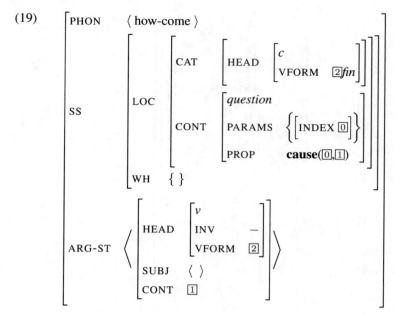

$$
\begin{bmatrix}
\text{PHON} & \langle\,\text{how-come}\,\rangle \\
\text{SS} & \begin{bmatrix}
\text{LOC} & \begin{bmatrix}
\text{CAT} & \begin{bmatrix} \text{HEAD} & \begin{bmatrix} c \\ \text{VFORM} & \boxed{2}\mathit{fin} \end{bmatrix} \end{bmatrix} \\
\text{CONT} & \begin{bmatrix} \mathit{question} \\ \text{PARAMS} & \{[\text{INDEX}\ \boxed{0}]\} \\ \text{PROP} & \mathbf{cause}(\boxed{0},\boxed{1}) \end{bmatrix}
\end{bmatrix} \\
\text{WH} & \{\,\}
\end{bmatrix} \\
\text{ARG-ST} & \left\langle \begin{bmatrix}
\text{HEAD} & \begin{bmatrix} v \\ \text{INV} & - \\ \text{VFORM} & \boxed{2} \end{bmatrix} \\
\text{SUBJ} & \langle\,\rangle \\
\text{CONT} & \boxed{1}
\end{bmatrix} \right\rangle
\end{bmatrix}
$$

C.3.4 Verbs

The verbs discussed here are primarily from sections 2.8 and 2.9. The question selecting verbs and *discover* are from section 8.3.

(20)

$$
\begin{bmatrix}
\text{PHON} & \langle\,\text{visit}\,\rangle \\
\text{SS|LOC} & \begin{bmatrix}
\text{CONT} & \begin{bmatrix}
\mathit{soa} \\
\text{NUCL} & \begin{bmatrix} \mathit{visit\text{-}rel} \\ \text{VISITOR} & i \\ \text{VISITED} & j \end{bmatrix}
\end{bmatrix}
\end{bmatrix} \\
\text{ARG-ST} & \langle\, \text{NP}_i\,,\ \text{NP}[\mathit{acc}]_j\,\rangle
\end{bmatrix}
$$

(21)

$$
\begin{bmatrix}
\text{PHON} & \langle\,\text{to}\,\rangle \\
\text{SS|LOC} & \begin{bmatrix}
\text{CAT} & \begin{bmatrix} \text{HEAD} & \begin{bmatrix} v \\ \text{AUX} & + \\ \text{VFORM} & \mathit{inf} \end{bmatrix} \end{bmatrix} \\
\text{CONT} & \boxed{1}
\end{bmatrix} \\
\text{ARG-ST} & \left\langle \begin{bmatrix} \text{LOC} & \boxed{2} \\ \text{SLASH} & \{\,\} \end{bmatrix},\ \overset{\text{VP}}{\begin{bmatrix} \text{VFORM} & \mathit{base} \\ \text{SUBJ} & \langle\,[\text{LOC}\ \boxed{2}]\,\rangle \\ \text{CONT} & \boxed{1} \end{bmatrix}} \right\rangle
\end{bmatrix}
$$

(22)
$$
\begin{bmatrix}
\text{PHON} \quad \langle\, \text{believe} \,\rangle \\[2pt]
\text{SS|LOC|CONT} \quad
\begin{bmatrix}
\textit{soa} \\[2pt]
\text{NUCL} \quad
\begin{bmatrix}
\textit{believe-rel} \\
\text{BELIEVER} \quad i \\
\text{COG-ARG} \quad j \\
\text{PROP-ARG} \quad
\begin{bmatrix}
\textit{proposition} \\
\text{SIT} \quad s \\
\text{SOA} \quad \boxed{1}
\end{bmatrix}
\end{bmatrix}
\end{bmatrix} \\[4pt]
\text{ARG-ST} \quad \left\langle\, \text{NP}_i\,, \begin{bmatrix}\text{LOC} \; \boxed{2}\end{bmatrix},
\begin{matrix} \text{VP} \\ \begin{bmatrix}
\text{VFORM} \quad \textit{inf} \\
\text{SUBJ} \quad \langle\, [\text{LOC}\;\boxed{2}]\,\rangle \\
\text{CONT} \quad \boxed{1}
\end{bmatrix} \end{matrix} \right\rangle
\end{bmatrix}
$$

(23)
$$
\begin{bmatrix}
\text{PHON} \qquad \langle\, \text{think} \,\rangle \\[2pt]
\text{SS|LOC|CONT} \quad
\begin{bmatrix}
\textit{soa} \\[2pt]
\text{NUCL} \quad
\begin{bmatrix}
\textit{think-rel} \\
\text{THINKER} \quad i \\
\text{COG-ARG} \quad j \\
\text{PROP-ARG} \quad \boxed{1}\textit{proposition}
\end{bmatrix}
\end{bmatrix} \\[4pt]
\text{ARG-ST} \quad \left\langle\, \text{NP}_i\,, \begin{bmatrix}\text{VFORM} \quad \textit{fin} \\ \text{CONT} \quad \boxed{1}\end{bmatrix} \right\rangle
\end{bmatrix}
$$

(24)
$$
\begin{bmatrix}
\text{PHON} \qquad \langle\, \text{insist} \,\rangle \\[2pt]
\text{SS|LOC|CONT} \quad
\begin{bmatrix}
\textit{soa} \\[2pt]
\text{NUCL} \quad
\begin{bmatrix}
\textit{insist-rel} \\
\text{INSISTOR} \quad i \\
\text{COG-ARG} \quad j \\
\text{OUTCM-ARG} \quad \boxed{1}\textit{outcome}
\end{bmatrix}
\end{bmatrix} \\[4pt]
\text{ARG-ST} \quad \left\langle\, \text{NP}_i\,, \begin{bmatrix}\text{VFORM} \quad \textit{fin} \\ \text{CONT} \quad \boxed{1}\end{bmatrix} \right\rangle
\end{bmatrix}
$$

(25)
$$
\begin{bmatrix}
\text{PHON} & \langle\,\text{ask}\,\rangle \\[2mm]
\text{SS|LOC|CONT|NUCL} &
\begin{bmatrix}
\textit{ask'-rel} \\
\text{ASKER} & \boxed{2} \\
\text{COG-ARG} & \boxed{3} \\
\text{ASKED} & \boxed{1}
\end{bmatrix} \\[6mm]
\text{ARG-ST} &
\left\langle
\begin{bmatrix}
\text{NP} \\
\text{IND } \boxed{2}
\end{bmatrix},
\begin{bmatrix}
\text{IND} & \boxed{1}
\end{bmatrix}
\right\rangle
\end{bmatrix}
$$

(26)
$$
\begin{bmatrix}
\text{PHON} & \langle\,\text{wonder}\,\rangle \\[2mm]
\text{SS|LOC|CONT|NUCL} &
\begin{bmatrix}
\textit{wonder-rel} \\
\text{WONDERER} & \boxed{2} \\
\text{COG-ARG} & \boxed{3} \\
\text{WONDERED} & \boxed{1}
\end{bmatrix} \\[6mm]
\text{ARG-ST} &
\left\langle
\begin{bmatrix}
\text{NP} \\
\text{IND } \boxed{2}
\end{bmatrix},
\begin{bmatrix}
\text{HEAD } \textit{verbal} \\
\text{CONT|IND } \boxed{1}
\end{bmatrix}
\right\rangle
\end{bmatrix}
$$

(27)
$$
\begin{bmatrix}
\text{PHON} & \langle\,\text{discover}\,\rangle \\[2mm]
\text{SS} &
\begin{bmatrix}
\text{LOC|CONT} &
\begin{bmatrix}
\textit{soa} \\[2mm]
\text{QUANTS} &
\left\langle
\begin{bmatrix}
\textit{some-rel} \\
\text{INDEX} & \boxed{2} \\
\text{RESTR} & \{\textit{resolves}(\boxed{2},\boxed{1},\boxed{3})\}
\end{bmatrix}
\right\rangle \\[6mm]
\text{NUCL} &
\begin{bmatrix}
\textit{discover-rel} \\
\text{RESOLVER} & \boxed{4} \\
\text{COGNITIVE-ARG} & \boxed{3} \\
\text{FACT-ARG} & \boxed{2}
\end{bmatrix}
\end{bmatrix} \\[6mm]
\text{BCKGRD} & \{\textit{decided}(\boxed{1})\}
\end{bmatrix} \\[6mm]
\text{ARG-ST} &
\left\langle
\text{NP}_{\boxed{4}},
\begin{bmatrix}
\text{CONT} & \boxed{1}\textit{question}
\end{bmatrix}
\right\rangle
\end{bmatrix}
$$

C.3.5 Adjectives

These lexical entries and related matters are discussed in section 5.2.

(28)
$$\begin{bmatrix} a\text{-}lx \\ \text{PHON} & \langle\, happy\, \rangle \\ \text{SS|LOC|CAT|HEAD} & a \\ \text{ARG-ST} & \langle\, \text{NP}\, \rangle \end{bmatrix}$$

(29)
$$\begin{bmatrix} word \\ \text{PHON} & \langle\, happy\, \rangle \\ \text{SS} & \begin{bmatrix} \text{LOC| CAT} & \begin{bmatrix} \text{HEAD} & \begin{bmatrix} a \\ \text{PRED} & + \\ \text{DEG} & \boxed{4} \end{bmatrix} \\ \text{SUBJ} & \langle\, \boxed{1}\, \rangle \\ \text{SPR} & \langle\, \boxed{2}\, \rangle \end{bmatrix} \\ \text{WH} & \boxed{\Sigma} \end{bmatrix} \\ \text{ARG-ST} & \left\langle\, \begin{bmatrix} \boxed{1}\text{NP} \\ \text{WH } \{\,\} \end{bmatrix}, \begin{bmatrix} \boxed{2}\text{DetP} \\ \text{WH} & \boxed{\Sigma} \\ \text{DEG} & \boxed{4} \end{bmatrix}\, \right\rangle \end{bmatrix}$$

C.3.6 Nouns

The *wh*-nouns in this section are discussed in sections 5.2 and 6.6.2. For functional uses of *who*, see section 4.5. The other nouns and related matters are discussed in section 5.2.

(30)
$$\begin{bmatrix} \text{PHON} & \langle\, Kim\, \rangle \\ \text{SS} & \begin{bmatrix} \text{LOC} & \begin{bmatrix} \text{CAT} & \text{NP} \\ \text{CONTENT} & \begin{bmatrix} param \\ \text{INDEX} & \boxed{1} \\ \text{RESTR} & \{\} \end{bmatrix} \\ \text{STORE} & \{\,\} \end{bmatrix} \\ \text{SLASH} & \{\,\} \\ \text{WH} & \{\,\} \\ \text{BCKGRND} & \{\, named(\boxed{1}, Kim)\, \} \end{bmatrix} \\ \text{ARG-ST} & \langle\, \rangle \end{bmatrix}$$

(31)   Unfocussed Interrogative *who*:

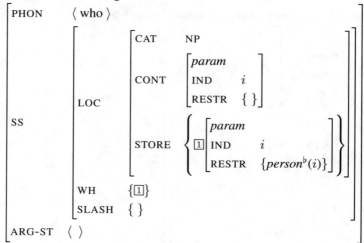

(32)   Focussed Interrogative *who*:

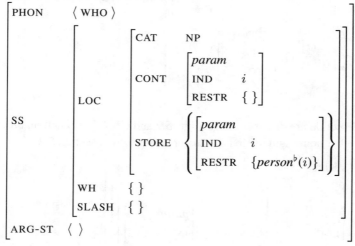

(33)   Interrogative *who* (functional use):[1]

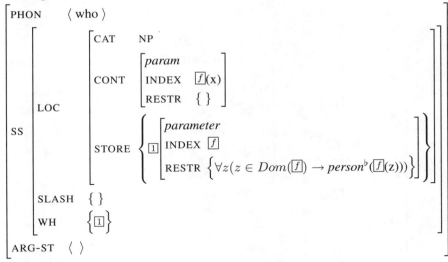

$$
\begin{bmatrix}
\text{PHON} & \langle\,who\,\rangle \\[2pt]
\text{SS} & \begin{bmatrix}
\text{LOC} & \begin{bmatrix}
\text{CAT} & \text{NP} \\[2pt]
\text{CONT} & \begin{bmatrix} param \\ \text{INDEX} & \boxed{f}(x) \\ \text{RESTR} & \{\,\} \end{bmatrix} \\[6pt]
\text{STORE} & \left\{ \boxed{1}\begin{bmatrix} parameter \\ \text{INDEX} & \boxed{f} \\ \text{RESTR} & \{\forall z (z \in Dom(\boxed{f}) \rightarrow person^b(\boxed{f}(z)))\} \end{bmatrix} \right\}
\end{bmatrix} \\[6pt]
\text{SLASH} & \{\,\} \\
\text{WH} & \{\boxed{1}\}
\end{bmatrix} \\[4pt]
\text{ARG-ST} & \langle\,\rangle
\end{bmatrix}
$$

(34)
$$
\begin{bmatrix}
cn\text{-}lx \\
\text{PHON} & \langle\,cousin\,\rangle \\
\text{SS|LOC|CAT|HEAD} & n \\
\text{ARG-ST} & \langle\,\text{DetP}\,\rangle
\end{bmatrix}
$$

(35)   Singular Attributive Noun Lexical Rule:

$$
\begin{bmatrix} lx \\ \text{SS|LOC|CAT|HEAD} & n \end{bmatrix} \Longrightarrow_{LR}
\begin{bmatrix}
word \\
\text{SS|LOC|CAT} & \begin{bmatrix}
\text{HEAD} & \begin{bmatrix} \text{AGR|NUM} & sg \\ \text{PRED} & - \end{bmatrix} \\
\text{SPR} & \langle \boxed{1} \rangle \\
\text{SUBJ} & \langle\,\rangle
\end{bmatrix} \\
\text{ARG-ST|FIRST} & \boxed{1}
\end{bmatrix}
$$

(36)   Singular Predicative Noun Lexical Rule:

$$
\begin{bmatrix} lx \\ \text{SS|LOC|CAT|HEAD} & n \\ \text{ARG-ST} & \langle \boxed{1} \rangle \oplus \boxed{A} \end{bmatrix} \Longrightarrow_{LR}
\begin{bmatrix}
word \\
\text{SS|LOC|CAT} & \begin{bmatrix}
\text{HEAD} & \begin{bmatrix} \text{AGR|NUM} & sg \\ \text{PRED} & + \end{bmatrix} \\
\text{SPR} & \langle \boxed{1} \rangle \\
\text{SUBJ} & \langle \boxed{2} \rangle
\end{bmatrix} \\
\text{ARG-ST} & \langle \boxed{2}, \boxed{1} \rangle \oplus \boxed{A}
\end{bmatrix}
$$

---

[1] It may be possible to collapse this with the previous lexical entries by allowing the identity function to instantiate $\boxed{f}$.

(37)

$$
\begin{bmatrix}
word \\
\text{PHON} \quad \langle \text{ cousin } \rangle \\
\text{SS} \begin{bmatrix}
\text{LOC|CAT} \begin{bmatrix}
\text{SPR} \quad \left\langle \begin{bmatrix} \boxed{2}\text{DetP} \\ \text{WH} \quad \boxed{\Sigma} \end{bmatrix} \right\rangle \\
\text{SUBJ} \quad \langle \, \rangle \\
\text{COMPS} \quad \langle \, \rangle \\
\text{HEAD} \begin{bmatrix} n \\ \text{PRED} \quad - \\ \text{AGR} \quad [\text{NUM} \quad sg] \end{bmatrix}
\end{bmatrix} \\
\text{WH} \quad \boxed{\Sigma}
\end{bmatrix} \\
\text{ARG-ST} \quad \langle \boxed{2} \rangle
\end{bmatrix}
$$

(38)

$$
\begin{bmatrix}
word \\
\text{PHON} \quad \langle \text{ cousin } \rangle \\
\text{SS} \begin{bmatrix}
\text{LOC|CAT} \begin{bmatrix}
\text{HEAD} \begin{bmatrix} noun \\ \text{PRED} \quad + \\ \text{AGR} \quad [\text{NUM} \quad sg] \end{bmatrix} \\
\text{SPR} \quad \langle \boxed{2} \rangle \\
\text{SUBJ} \quad \langle \boxed{5} \rangle \\
\text{COMPS} \quad \langle \, \rangle
\end{bmatrix} \\
\text{WH} \quad \boxed{\Sigma}
\end{bmatrix} \\
\text{ARG-ST} \quad \left\langle \begin{bmatrix} \boxed{5}\text{NP} \\ \text{WH} \quad \{ \} \end{bmatrix}, \boxed{2}[\text{WH} \quad \boxed{\Sigma}] \right\rangle
\end{bmatrix}
$$

C.3.7 Gerunds

This lexical entry and related matters are discussed in section 5.2.

(39)

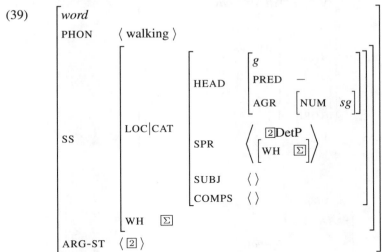

C.3.8 Propositional Lexemes

These words are all discussed in section 8.2.

(40)

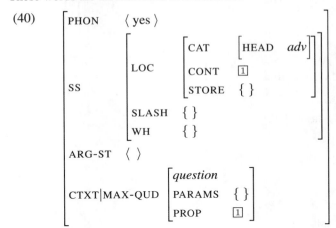

(41)

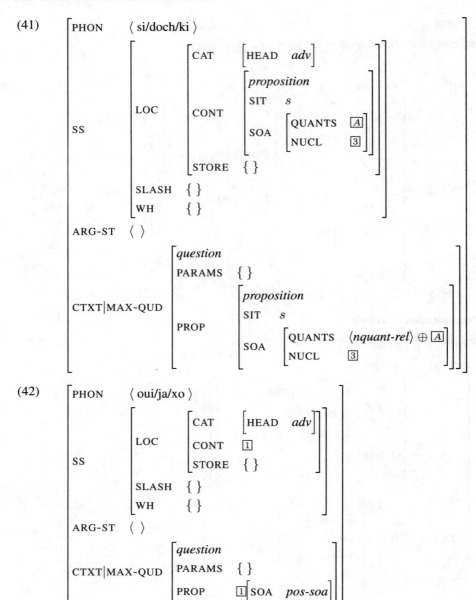

(43)

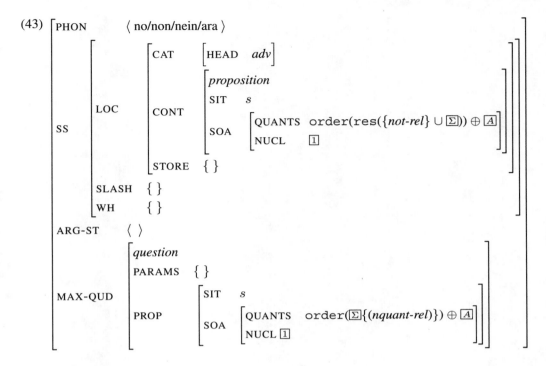

List of Abbreviations

$\oplus$	list addition (append)
$\ominus$	contained list difference
$\uplus$	disjoint set union
$\dot{-}$	contained set difference
a	*adjective*
a-lx	*adjective-lexeme*
ADV	adverb
AFA	Anti-Foundation Axiom
ARG-ST	ARGUMENT-STRUCTURE
ARP	Argument Realization Principle
AtomAns	*AtomicAnswer*
AUX	AUXILIARY
AVM	attribute-value matrix
BCKGRD	BACKGROUND
c	*complementizer*
C-INDICES	CONTEXTUAL-INDICES
canon-ss	*canonical-synsem*
CAT	CATEGORY
CBG	Constraint-Based Grammar
CMT	Conversational Move Type
COMPS	COMPLEMENTS
CONT	CONTENT
core-cl	*core-clause*
cp-cl	*CP-clause*
CQ	concealed question

cq-np	*concealed-question-noun-phrase*
CTXT	CONTEXT
D-linked	Discourse-linked
decl-cl	*declarative-clause*
decl-frag-cl	*declarative-fragment-clause*
decl-hd-su-cl	*declarative-head-subject-clause*
det	*determiner*
dir-is-int-cl	*direct-in-situ-interrogative-clause*
DTRS	DAUGHTERS
dtrv-lx	*ditransitive-verb-lexeme*
EAC	Exhaustive Answerhood Conditions
ECC	Empty COMPS Constraint
ECP	Empty Category Principle
elist	*empty list*
excl-cl	*exclamative-clause*
feat-struc	*feature-structure*
FIC	Filler Inclusion Constraint
fin	*finite*
fin-vp	*finite-verb-phrase*
Functional	functionally dependent
gap-ss	*gap-synsem*
GB	Government and Binding Theory
GHFP	Generalized Head Feature Principle
GPSG	Generalized Phrase Structure Grammar
GQ	generalized quantifier
Gr & St	Groenendijk and Stokhof
H&M	Higginbotham and May
H&M–81	Higginbotham and May 1981
hd-adj-ph	*head-adjunct-phrase*
hd-comp-ph	*head-complement-phrase*
HD-DTR	HEAD-DAUGHTER
hd-fill-ph	*head-filler-phrase*
hd-frag-ph	*headed-fragment-phrase*
hd-only-ph	*head-only-phrase*

hd-spr-ph	*head-specifier-phrase*
hd-subj-ph	*head-subject-phrase*
HPSG	Head-Driven Phrase Structure Grammar
i-soa	*irrealis-soa*
IA	Iraqi Arabic
IC	INDEPENDENT-CLAUSE
illoc-rel	*illocutionary-relation*
imp-cl	*imperative-clause*
inf	*infinitive*
inter-cl	*interrogative-clause*
intr-lx	*intransitive-lexeme*
INV	INVERTED
inv-decl-cl	*inverted-declarative-clause*
inv-excl-cl	*inverted-exclamative-clause*
INVC	Inversion Constraint
IRC	Interrogative Retrieval Constraint
is-int-cl	*in-situ-interrogative-clause*
IST	immediate supertype
LF	Logical Form
MAX-QUD	MAXIMAL-QUESTION-UNDER-DISCUSSION
MOD	MODIFIED
n	*noun*
ne-arg-st-list	*non-empty-argument-structure-list*
NegAtomAns	*NegativeAtomicAnswer*
neg-soa	*negative-soa*
nelist	*non-empty list*
nom-int-ph	*nominalized-interrogative-phrase*
non-hd-ph	*non-headed-phrase*
NPIS	Negative-Positive-Interrogative-Synonymy
nquant-rel	*negative-quantifier-relation*
ns-imp-cl	*no-subject-imperative-clause*
NUCL	NUCLEUS
OPC	Optional *Pro* Condition
orv-lx	*object-raising-verb-lexeme*

p	*preposition*
p-lx	*preposition-lexeme*
P&S	Pollard and Sag
P&S–94	Pollard and Sag 1994
param	*parameter*
PARAMS	PARAMETERS
part	*participle*
pas	*passive-participle*
perc-cont	*perceived-content*
pfp	*perfect-participle*
PH	Performative Hypothesis
PHC	Propositional Head Constraint
POL	POLARITY
pol-int-cl	*polar-interrogative-clause*
PotResAns	*PotentiallyResolvingAnswer*
pquant-rel	*positive-quantifier-relation*
prev-utt	*previous-utterance*
pro-ss	*pronominal-synsem*
PROP	PROPOSITION
prop-constr	*propositionally-constructed*
PropInst	*PropositionalInstantiation*
prp	*present-participle*
QE	Question-embedding
qf-fr-pos-soa	*quantifier-free-positive-soa*
qf-pos-soa	*positively-quantified-soa*
qp	question parameter
QUANTS	QUANTIFIERS
QUD	questions under discussion
QVE	Quantificational Variability Effect
r-soa	*realis-soa*
rel-cl	*relative-clause*
repr-int-cl	*reprise-interrogative-clause*
RESTR	RESTRICTIONS
RSRL	Relational Speciate Reentrant Logic

s-con-lx	*subject-control-lexeme*
S&M–97	Seligman and Moss 1997
s-rsg-lx	*subject-raising-lexeme*
sai-ph	*subject-auxiliary-inversion-phrase*
SAL-UTT	SALIENT-UTTERANCE
sca-lx	*subject-control-adjective-lexeme*
scope-obj	*scope-object*
scv-lx	*subject-control-verb-lexeme*
sia-lx	*strict-intransitive-adjective-lexeme*
SimpleAns	*SimpleAnswer*
sip-lx	*strict-intransitive-preposition-lexeme*
SIT	SITUATION
SitSem	Situation Semantics
SITSTR	Situation Structure
siv-lx	*strict-intransitive-verb-lexeme*
slu-int-cl	*sluiced-interrogative-clause*
SPR	SPECIFIER
sra-lx	*subject-raising-adjective-lexeme*
SRL	Speciate Reentrant Logic
srv-lx	*subject-raising-verb-lexeme*
ST	Situation Theory
stp-lx	*strict-transitive-preposition-lexeme*
str-int-lx	*strict-intransitive-lexeme*
str-trn-lx	*strict-transitive-lexeme*
StrongExhAns	*StronglyExhaustiveAnswer*
stv-lx	*strict-transitive-verb-lexeme*
SU+AE	Situational Universe with Abstract Entities
su-wh-int-cl	*subject-wh-interrogative-clause*
SUBJ	SUBJECT
T-PARAM	TEMPORAL-PARAMETER
TF	True-False
TFS	Typed Feature Structure(s)
top-cl	*topicalized-clause*
trn-lx	*transitive-lexeme*

TTP	Turn-Taking Puzzle
UDC	unbounded dependency construction
UG	Universal Grammar
UV	uninstantiated variable
v	*verb*
v-lx	*verb-lexeme*
VPE	Verb Phrase Ellipsis
wh-excl-cl	*wh-exclamative-clause*
wh-int-cl	*wh-interrogative-clause*
wh-ns-int-cl	*wh-nonsubject-interrogative-clause*
WH-PRC	Singular *Which* Presupposition Constraint
WH-QI	*Wh*-Quantifying-In
WHC	*Wh*-Constraint
WHQ	*Wh*-Quantification
WHSP	*Wh*-Subject Prohibition
ZFC⁻	Zermelo-Fraenkel set theory without the axiom of foundation

References

Abeillé, Anne, Danièle Godard, and Ivan A. Sag. 1998. Two kinds of composition in French complex predicates. In E. Hinrichs, T. Nakazawa, and A. Kathol, eds., *Complex Predicates in Nonderivational Syntax*, pages 1–41. New York: Academic Press.

Ackerman, Farrell and Gert Webelhuth. 1998. *A Theory of Predicates*. Stanford: CSLI Publications.

Aczel, Peter. 1988. *Non-Well-Founded Sets*. Stanford: CSLI Publications.

Aczel, Peter and Rachel Lunnon. 1991. Universes and parameters. In J. Barwise, J. M. Gawron, G. Plotkin, and S. Tutiya, eds., *Situation Theory and Its Applications, II*, CSLI Lecture Notes Number 26, pages 3–24. Stanford: CSLI Publications.

Ades, Antony and Mark Steedman. 1982. On the order of words. *Linguistics and Philosophy* 6:517–558.

Akmajian, Adrian. 1984. Sentence types and the form-function fit. *Natural Language and Linguistic Theory* 2:1–24.

Allen, James and Ray Perrault. 1980. Analyzing intention in utterances. *Artificial Intelligence* 15:143–178.

Asatiani, Rusudan. 1998. The semantics and typology of yes/no particles: A cross-linguistic study. Tech. rep., Institute of Oriental Studies, Georgian Academy of Sciences.

Asher, Nicholas. 1993. *Reference to Abstract Objects in English: a Philosophical Semantics for Natural Language Metaphysics*. Studies in Linguistics and Philosophy. Dordrecht: Kluwer.

Asher, Nicholas. 1996. Events, facts, propositions, and evolutive anaphora. In *Fracas Deliverable D15*. Centre for Cognitive Science, Edinburgh: The Fracas Consortium.

Asher, Nicholas and Alex Lascarides. 1998. Questions in dialogue. *Linguistics and Philosophy* 21:237–309.

Authier, Jean Marc. 1993. Nonquantificational *wh* and weakest crossover. *Linguistic Inquiry* 24:161–168.

Bach, Emmon. 1981. On time, tense, and aspect: An essay in English metaphysics. In P. Cole, ed., *Radical Pragmatics*, pages 63–81. New York: Academic Press.

Baker, C. L. 1970. *Indirect Questions in English*. Ph.D. thesis, University of Illinois at Urbana–Champaign.

Barendregt, Henk P. 1984. *The Lambda Calculus: Its Syntax and Semantics*. Amsterdam: North-Holland.

Barwise, Jon. 1985. Noun phrases, generalized quantifiers, and anaphora. In P. Gärdenfors, ed., *Generalized Quantifiers*, pages 1–29. Dordrecht: Reidel.

Barwise, Jon. 1989a. Notes on branch points in situation theory. In J. Barwise, ed., *The Situation in Logic*, pages 255–276. Stanford: CSLI Publications.

Barwise, Jon. 1989b. *The Situation in Logic*. CSLI Lecture Notes Number 17. Stanford: CSLI Publications.

Barwise, Jon. 1997. Information and impossibilities. *Notre Dame Journal of Formal Logic* 38(4).

Barwise, Jon and Robin Cooper. 1991. Simple situation theory and its graphical representation. In J. Seligman, ed., *Partial and Dynamic Semantics III*, DYANA Deliverable R2.1.C. University of Edinburgh: Centre for Cognitive Science.

Barwise, Jon and John Etchemendy. 1987. *The Liar*. New York: Oxford University Press.

Barwise, Jon and John Etchemendy. 1990. Information, infons, and inference. In R. Cooper, K. Mukai, and J. Perry, eds., *Situation Theory and Its Applications, I*, CSLI Lecture Notes Number 22, pages 33–78. Stanford: CSLI Publications.

Barwise, Jon and Lawrence S. Moss. 1996. *Vicious Circles: On the Mathematics of Non-Wellfounded Phenomena*. Stanford: CSLI Publications.

Barwise, Jon and John Perry. 1983. *Situations and Attitudes*. Bradford Books. Cambridge, MA: MIT Press. Reprinted in 1999 in the David Hume Series. Stanford: CSLI Publications.

Barwise, Jon and John Perry. 1985. Shifting situations and shaken attitudes. *Linguistics and Philosophy* 8:399–452.

Barwise, Jon and Jerry Seligman. 1996. *Information Flow*. Cambridge Tracts in Computer Science. Cambridge: Cambridge University Press.

Bäuerle, Rainer. 1979. Questions and answers. In R. Bäuerle, U. Egli, and A. von Stechow, eds., *Semantics from Different Points of View*, pages 61–74. Berlin: Springer Verlag.

Bealer, George. 1982. *Quality and Concept*. Oxford: Oxford University Press.

Beghelli, Filippo. 1997. The syntax of distributivity and pair-list readings. In A. Szabolcsi, ed., *Ways of Scope Taking*, pages 349–408. Reidel: Kluwer.

Belnap, Nuel. 1982. Questions and answers in Montague Grammar. In S. Peters and E. Saarinen, eds., *Processes, Beliefs and Questions*, pages 165–198. Dordrecht: Reidel.

Bender, Emily. 2000. *Syntactic Variation and Linguistic Competence: The Case of AAVE Copula Absence*. Ph.D. thesis, Stanford University.

Bender, Emily and Daniel Flickinger. 1999. Peripheral constructions and core phenomena: Agreement in tag questions. In G. Webelhuth, J.-P. Koenig, and A. Kathol, eds., *Lexical and Constructional Aspects of Linguistic Explanation*, pages 199–214. Stanford: CSLI Publications.

Berman, Stephen. 1990. Towards the semantics of open sentences: *Wh*-phrases and indefinites. In M. Stokhof, ed., *Proceedings of the 7th Amsterdam Colloquium*. Amsterdam: ILLC.

Berman, Stephen. 1991. *The Syntax and Logical Form of Wh-Clauses*. Ph.D. thesis, University of Massachusetts, Amherst.

Boër, Stephen. 1978. Toward a theory of indirect question clauses. *Linguistics and Philosophy* 2:307–346.

Boër, Steven and William Lycan. 1985. *Knowing Who*. Bradford Books. Cambridge, MA: MIT Press.

Bolinger, Dwight. 1978. On asking more than one thing at a time. In H. Hiz, ed., *Questions*, pages 107–150. Dordrecht: Reidel.

Bolinger, Dwight. 1989. *Intonation and its Uses*. Stanford: Stanford University Press.

Borsley, Robert D. 1993. Heads in Head-Driven Phrase Structure Grammar. In G. Corbett, N. Fraser, and S. McGlashan, eds., *Heads in Grammatical Theory*, pages 186–203. Cambridge: Cambridge University Press.

Bos, Johan and Malte Gabsdil. 2000. First-order inference and the interpretation of questions and answers. In M. Poesio and D. Traum, eds., *Proceedings of Götalog 2000, the 4th Workshop on the Semantics and Pragmatics of Dialogue*, Gothenburg Papers in Computational Linguistics 00-5, pages 43–50. University of Gothenburg.

Bouma, Gosse, Robert Malouf, and Ivan A. Sag. 2001. Satsifying constraints on extraction and adjunction. *Natural Language and Linguistic Theory* 19:1–65.

Bouma, Gosse, Frank van Eynde, and Dan Flickinger. 2000. Constraint-based lexica. In F. V. Eynde and D. Gibbon, eds., *Lexicon Development for Speech and Language Processing*, pages 43–75. Dordrecht: Kluwer.

Brame, Michael K. 1978. *Base Generated Syntax*. Seattle: Noit Amrofer.

Bresnan, Joan. 1976. On the form and functioning of transformations. *Linguistic Inquiry* 7:3–40.

Bresnan, Joan. 1982a. Control and complementation. *Linguistic Inquiry* 13:343–434.

Bresnan, Joan. 1982b. The passive in lexical theory. In J. Bresnan, ed., *The Mental Representation of Grammatical Relations*, pages 3–86. Cambridge, MA: MIT Press.

Bresnan, Joan. 2000. Optimal syntax. In J. Dekkers, F. van der Leeuw, and J. van de Weijer, eds., *Optimality Theory: Phonology, Syntax and Acquisition*. Oxford: Oxford University Press.

Briscoe, Edward, Ann Copestake, and Valeria de Paiva. 1994. *Inheritance, Defaults, and the Lexicon*. Cambridge: Cambridge University Press.

Bromberger, Sylvain. 1992. *Why* questions. In *Essays On What We Know We Don't Know*, pages 75–100. Stanford: CSLI Publications. Originally published in R.G. Colodny, ed., 1966. *Mind and Cosmos: Essays in Contemporary Science and Philosophy*, Vol. 3. University of Pittsburgh: Center for Philosophy of Science.

Callison-Burch, Chris. 2000. *A Computer Model for a Grammar of English Questions*. B.S. Honors thesis, Stanford University.

Carletta, Jean, Amy Isard, Stephen Isard, Jacqueline Kowtko, Gwyneth Doherty-Sneddon, and Anne Anderson. 1996. Map task coder's manual. *HCRC Research Paper* RP-82.

Carnap, Rudolf. 1937. *The Logical Syntax of Language*. London: Routledge and Kegan Paul.

Chierchia, Gennaro. 1985. Formal semantics and the grammar of predication. *Linguistic Inquiry* 16:417–443.

Chierchia, Gennaro. 1991. Functional *wh* and weak crossover. In *Proceedings of the 10th West Coast Conference on Formal Linguistics*, pages 75–90. Stanford: Stanford Linguistics Association.

Chierchia, Gennaro. 1993. Questions with quantifiers. *Natural Language Semantics* 1:181–234.

Chierchia, Gennaro. 1994. Intensionality and context change. *Journal of Logic, Language, and Information* 3:141–168.

Chierchia, Gennaro. 1995. *Dynamics of Meaning*. Chicago: University of Chicago Press.

Chierchia, Gennaro and Ray Turner. 1988. Semantics and property theory. *Linguistics and Philosophy* 11:261–302.

Chomsky, Noam. 1966. *Topics in the Theory of Generative Grammar*. The Hague: Mouton.

Chomsky, Noam. 1973. Conditions on transformations. In S. Anderson and P. Kiparsky, eds., *A Festschrift for Morris Halle*, pages 232–286. New York: Holt, Rinehart, and Winston.

Chomsky, Noam. 1975. *The Logical Structure of Linguistic Theory*. New York: Plenum Publishers. Written in 1955 and widely circulated in mimeographed form.

Chomsky, Noam. 1977. On *Wh*-movement. In A. Akmajian, P. Culicover, and T. Wasow, eds., *Formal Syntax*, pages 71–132. New York: Academic Press.

Chomsky, Noam. 1980. On binding. *Linguistic Inquiry* 11:1–46.

Chomsky, Noam. 1986. *Knowledge of Language*. New York: Praeger.

Chomsky, Noam. 1995a. Bare phrase structure. In G. Webelhuth, ed., *Government and Binding Theory and the Minimalist Program*, pages 383–439. Oxford: Blackwell.

Chomsky, Noam. 1995b. *The Minimalist Program*. Cambridge, MA: MIT Press.

Chomsky, Noam and Howard Lasnik. 1993. Principles and parameters theory. In J. Jacobs, A. von Stechow, and W. Sternefeld, eds., *Syntax: An International Handbook of Contemporary Research*, pages 506–569. Berlin: Walter de Gruyter.

Chung, Sandy, William Ladusaw, and James McCloskey. 1995. Sluicing and logical form. *Natural Language Semantics* 3:239–282.

Cinque, Guglielmo. 1990. *Types of Ā-Dependencies*. Cambridge: MIT Press.

Clark, Herbert. 1977. Bridging. In P. Johnson-Laird and P. Wason, eds., *Thinking*, pages 411–420. Cambridge: Cambridge University Press.

Clark, Herbert. 1996. *Using Language*. Cambridge: Cambridge University Press.

Clark, Herb and Edward Schaefer. 1989. Contributing to discourse. In *Arenas of Language Use*, pages 259–94. Stanford: CSLI Publications. Reprinted from *Cognitive Science*, 13:259–294.

Cohen, Felix S. 1929. What is a question? *The Monist* 39:350–364.

Comorowski, Ileana. 1989. *Discourse and the Syntax of Multiple Constituent Questions*. Ph.D. thesis, Cornell University.

Cooper, Robin. 1975. *Montague's Semantic Theory and Transformational Syntax*. Ph.D. thesis, University of Massachusetts, Amherst.

Cooper, Robin. 1983. *Quantification and Syntactic Theory*. Synthese Language Library. Dordrecht: Reidel.

Cooper, Robin. 1993. Towards a general semantic framework. In R. Cooper, ed., *Integrating Semantic Theories*, vol. R2.1.A. IILC/Department of Philosophy, University of Amsterdam.

Cooper, Robin. 1996. The role of situations in generalized quantifiers. In S. Lappin, ed., *Handbook of Contemporary Semantic Theory*, pages 65–86. Oxford: Blackwell.

Cooper, Robin. 1998. Austinian propositions, Davidsonian events and perception complements. In J. Ginzburg, Z. Khasidashvili, J. J. Lévy, C. Vogel, and E. Vallduví, eds., *The Tbilisi Symposium on Language, Logic and Computation: selected papers*, pages 19–34. Stanford: CSLI Publications.

Cooper, Robin and Jonathan Ginzburg. 1996. A compositional situation semantics for attitude reports. In J. Seligman and D. Westerståhl, eds., *Logic, Language, and Computation*, pages 151–165. Stanford: CSLI Publications.

Cooper, Robin and Jonathan Ginzburg. in preparation. Utterances and attitudes. Manuscript: Gothenburg University and King's College, London.

Cooper, Robin and Massimo Poesio. 1994. Situation theory. In *Fracas Deliverable D8*. Centre for Cognitive Science, Edinburgh: The Fracas Consortium.

Copestake, Ann. 1992. *The Representation of Lexical Semantic Information*. Ph.D. thesis, University of Sussex. Published as Cognitive Science Research Paper, Number 280.

Copestake, Ann and Edward Briscoe. 1992. Lexical rules in a unification based framework. In J. Pustejovsky and S. Bergler, eds., *Lexical Semantics and Knowledge Representation*, Lecture Notes in Artificial Intelligence Number 627, pages 101–119. Berlin: Springer-Verlag.

Copestake, Ann, Dan Flickinger, Carl Pollard, and Ivan Sag. 2000. Minimal recursion semantics: an introduction. Manuscript: Stanford University.

Core, Mark and James Allen. 1997. Coding dialogs with the DAMSL scheme. *Working notes of the AAAI Fall Symposium on Communicative Action in Humans and Machines* MIT, Cambridge, MA, November.

Cresswell, Max. 1973. *Logics and Languages*. London: Methuen.

Crimmins, Mark. 1993a. States of affairs without parameters. In P. Aczel, D. Israel, Y. Katagiri, and S. Peters, eds., *Situation Theory and Its Applications, III*, CSLI Lecture Notes Number 37, pages 55–86. Stanford: CSLI Publications.

Crimmins, Mark. 1993b. *Talk about Beliefs*. Bradford Books. Cambridge, MA: MIT Press.

Crimmins, Mark and John Perry. 1989. The prince and the phone booth: Reporting puzzling beliefs. *Journal of Philosophy* 86:685–711.

Culicover, Peter. 1993. Evidence against ECP accounts of the that-*t* effect. *Linguistic Inquiry* 24:557–561.

Culicover, Peter. 1999. *Syntactic Nuts: Hard Cases, Syntactic Theory and Language Acquisition*. Oxford: Oxford University Press.

Dalrymple, Mary, Fernando Pereira, and Stuart Shieber. 1991. Ellipsis and higher order unification. *Linguistics and Philosophy* 14:399–452.

Davis, Anthony. 1996. *Lexical Semantics and Linking in the Hierarchical Lexicon*. Ph.D. thesis, Stanford University.

Davis, Anthony. 2001. *Linking by Types in the Hierarchical Lexicon*. Stanford: CSLI Publications.

Davis, Anthony and Jean-Pierre Koenig. 1999. Linking as constraints on word classes in a hierarchical lexicon. *Language* 76:56–91.

Devlin, Keith. 1991. *Logic and Information*. Cambridge: Cambridge University Press.

Dowty, David, Robert Wall, and Stanley Peters. 1981. *Introduction to Montague Semantics*. Dordrecht: Reidel.

Emonds, Joseph E. 1976. *A Transformational Approach to English Syntax: Root, Structure-Preserving, and Local Transformations*. New York: Academic Press.

Engdahl, Elisabet. 1980. *The Syntax and Semantics of Questions in Swedish*. Ph.D. thesis, University of Massachusetts, Amherst.

Engdahl, Elisabet. 1986. *Constituent Questions*. Synthese Language Library. Dordrecht: Reidel.

Engdahl, Elisabet. 2000. The role of syntactic features in the analysis of dialogue. Manuscript: Gothenburg University.

Engdahl, Elisabet, Staffan Larsson, and Stina Ericsson. 2000. Focus-ground articulation and parallelism in a dynamic model of dialogue. Tech. rep., University of Gothenburg, Gothenburg. Available from http://www.ling.gu.se/research/projects/trindi.

Fiengo, Robert and Robert May. 1994. *Indices and Identity*. Linguistic Inquiry Monograph Number 24. Cambridge, MA: MIT Press.

Fillmore, Charles. 1999. Inversion and constructional inheritance. In G. Webelhuth, J.-P. Koenig, and A. Kathol, eds., *Lexical and Constructional Aspects of Linguistic Explanation*, pages 113–128. Stanford: CSLI Publications.

Fillmore, Charles, Andreas Kathol, Paul Kay, and Laura Michaelis. to appear. *Construction Grammar*. Stanford: CSLI Publications.

Fillmore, Charles and Paul Kay. 1999. Grammatical constructions and liguistic generalizations: the *what's x doing y?* construction. *Language* 75:1–33.

Fletcher, Charles. 1994. Levels of representation in memory for discourse. In M. A. Gernsbacher, ed., *Handbook of Psycholinguistics*, pages 589–607. New York: Academic Press.

Flickinger, Daniel. 1987. *The Hierarchical Lexicon*. Ph.D. thesis, Stanford University.

Flickinger, Daniel, Stephan Oepen, J.-I. Tsujii, and Hans Uszkoreit, eds. 2001. *Efficiency in Unification-based Processing*. Stanford: CSLI Publications.

Flickinger, Dan, Carl Pollard, and Thomas Wasow. 1985. Structure sharing in lexical representation. In *Proceedings of the 23rd Annual Meeting of the Association for Computational Linguistics*, pages 180–187. Association for Computational Linguistics.

Fodor, Jerry A, Thomas Bever, and Merrill Garrett. 1974. *The Psychology of Language: an introduction to psycholinguistics and generative grammar*. New York: McGraw-Hill.

Frege, Gottlob. 1892. On sense and reference. In P. Geach and M. Black, eds., *Translations from the Philosophical Writings of Gottlob Frege, 3rd Edition*, pages 56–78. Oxford: Blackwell. 1952.

Frege, Gottlob. 1918. Thoughts. In P. Geach and M. Black, eds., *Translations from the Philosophical Writings of Gottlob Frege, 3rd Edition*. Oxford: Blackwell. 1952.

Gärdenfors, Peter. 2000. *Conceptual Spaces*. Cambridge, MA: MIT Press.

Gawron, Mark and Stanley Peters. 1990. *Anaphora and Quantification in Situation Semantics*. CSLI Lecture Notes. Stanford: CSLI Publications.

Gazdar, Gerald. 1981. Unbounded dependencies and coordinate structure. *Linguistic Inquiry* 12:155–184.

Gazdar, Gerald, Ewan Klein, Geoffrey Pullum, and Ivan A. Sag. 1985. *Generalized Phrase Structure Grammar*. Oxford and Cambridge, MA: Blackwell and Harvard University Press.

Gazdar, Gerald, Geoffrey K. Pullum, and Ivan A. Sag. 1982. Auxiliaries and related phenomena in a restricted theory of grammar. *Language* 58:591–638.

Ginzburg, Jonathan. 1992. *Questions, Queries, and Facts: a Semantic and Pragmatics for Interrogatives*. Ph.D. thesis, Stanford University.

Ginzburg, Jonathan. 1993. Propositional and non-propositional attitudes. In P. Aczel, D. Israel, Y. Katagiri, and S. Peters, eds., *Situation Theory and Its Applications, III*, CSLI Lecture Notes Number 37, pages 265–302. Stanford: CSLI Publications.

Ginzburg, Jonathan. 1995a. Resolving questions, I. *Linguistics and Philosophy* 18:459–527.

Ginzburg, Jonathan. 1995b. Resolving questions, II. *Linguistics and Philosophy* 18:567–609.

Ginzburg, Jonathan. 1996a. Dynamics and the semantics of dialogue. In J. Seligman and D. Westerståhl, eds., *Logic, Language, and Computation*, pages 221–237. Stanford: CSLI Publications.

Ginzburg, Jonathan. 1996b. Interrogatives: questions, facts, and dialogue. In S. Lappin, ed., *Handbook of Contemporary Semantic Theory*, pages 385–422. Oxford: Blackwell.

Ginzburg, Jonathan. 1997. On some semantic consequences of turn taking. In P. Dekker, M. Stokhof, and Y. Venema, eds., *Proceedings of the 11th Amsterdam Colloquium on Formal Semantics and Logic*, pages 145–150. Amsterdam: ILLC.

Ginzburg, Jonathan. 1998. Clarifying utterances. In J. Hulstijn and A. Nijholt, eds., *Proceedings of Twen-Dial 98, 13th Twente workshop on Language Technology*, pages 11–30. Twente: Twente University.

Ginzburg, Jonathan. 1999. Semantically-based ellipsis resolution with syntactic presuppositions. In H. Bunt and R. Muskens, eds., *Computing Meaning: Current Issues in Computational Semantics*, pages 255–279. Dordrecht: Kluwer.

Ginzburg, Jonathan. 2000. The evolution of communicative interaction systems: A formal semantics perspective. In J. L. Dassalles and L. Ghadakpour, eds., *Proceedings of the 3rd International Conference on the Evolution of Language*, pages 113–117. Ecole Nationale Supérieure des Télécommunications.

Ginzburg, Jonathan. 2001. *A Semantics for Interaction in Dialogue*. Stanford: CSLI Publications. Draft chapters available from ftp://ftp.cogsci.ed.ac.uk:pub/ginzburg.

Ginzburg, Jonathan, Howard Gregory, and Shalom Lappin. 2000. Shards: Fragment resolution in dialogue. Manuscript: King's College, London.

Ginzburg, Jonathan and Dimitra Kolliakou. 1998. Events and facts: a semantics for *pu* and *oti* clauses in modern Greek. In G. Drachman, A. Malikouti-Drachman, J. Fykias, and C. Klidi, eds., *Proceedings of the 2nd International Conference on Greek Linguistics*, pages 459–470. Graz: N. Neugebauer Verlag.

Ginzburg, Jonathan and Ivan A. Sag. 1999. Constructional ambiguity in conversation. In P. Dekker, ed., *Proceedings of the 12th Amsterdam Colloquium*. ILLC, Amsterdam.

Glasbey, Sheila. 1998. A situation theoretic interpretation of bare plurals. In J. Ginzburg, Z. Khasidashvili, J. J. Levy, C. Vogel, and E. Vallduvì, eds., *The Tbilisi Symposium on Language, Logic and Computation: selected papers*, Foundations of Logic, Language, and Information, pages 35–54. Stanford: CSLI Publications.

Goldberg, Adele. 1995. *A Construction Grammar Approach to Argument Structure*. Chicago: University of Chicago Press.

Green, Georgia. 1976. Main clause phenomena in subordinate clauses. *Language* 52:382–397.

Green, Georgia. 1991. Purpose clauses and their relatives. Manuscript: University of Illinois at Urbana–Champaign.

Green, Georgia. 1996. Distinguishing main and subordinate clause; the root of the problem. Unpublished paper presented at the 3rd International Conference on HPSG, Marseille. Downloadable from http://mccawley.cogsci.uiuc.edu/ green/.

Green, Georgia. 2000. Modelling grammar growth: Universal grammar without innate principles or parameters. Manuscript: University of Illinois at Urbana-Champaign. Revised and expanded version of a paper presented at GALA 97, U. of Edinburgh. Downloadable from http://mccawley.cogsci.uiuc.edu/ green/.

Green, Georgia and Jerry Morgan. 1996. Auxiliary inversion and the notion of 'default specification'. *Journal of Linguistics* 32:43–56.

Grimshaw, Jane. 1979. Complement selection and the lexicon. *Linguistic Inquiry* 10:279–326.

Groenendijk, Jeroen and Martin Stokhof. 1984. *Studies on the Semantics of Questions and the Pragmatics of Answers*. Ph.D. thesis, University of Amsterdam.

Groenendijk, Jeroen and Martin Stokhof. 1989. Type shifting and the semantics of interrogatives. In G. Chierchia, R. Turner, and B. Partee, eds., *Properties, Types, and Meaning*, vol. 2 of *Studies in Linguistics and Philosophy*, pages 21–68. Dordrecht: Kluwer.

Groenendijk, Jeroen and Martin Stokhof. 1991a. Dynamic Montague Grammar. In M. Stokhof, J. Groenendijk, and D. Beaver, eds., *Quantification and Anaphora I, DYANA Report R2.2.A*. Centre for Cognitive Science, University of Edinburgh.

Groenendijk, Jeroen and Martin Stokhof. 1991b. Dynamic predicate logic. *Linguistics and Philosophy* 14(1):39–100.

Groenendijk, Jeroen and Martin Stokhof. 1993. Interrogatives and adverbs of quantification. In K. Bimbó and A. Máté, eds., *Proceedings of the 4th Symposium on Logic and Language*, pages 1–29. Budapest: Áron.

Groenendijk, Jeroen and Martin Stokhof. 1997. Questions. In J. van Benthem and A. ter Meulen, eds., *Handbook of Logic and Language*, pages 1055–1124. Cambridge, MA and Amsterdam: MIT Press and North Holland.

Gupta, Anil. 1974. *The Logic of Common Nouns*. New Haven: Yale University Press.

Gussenhoven, Carlos. 1984. *On the Grammar and Semantics of Sentence Accent*. Dordrecht: Foris.

Haegeman, Liliane. 1991. *Introduction to Government and Binding Theory*. Oxford: Blackwell.

Hamblin, C. L. 1958. Questions. *Australian Journal of Philosophy* 36:159–168.

Hamblin, C. L. 1973. Questions in Montague English. *Foundations of Language* 10:41–53. Reprinted in B. Partee, ed., *Montague Grammar*. New York: Academic Press.

Hand, Michael. 1988. The dependency constraint: a global constraint on strategies in game-theoretical semantics. *Linguistics and Philosophy* 11:395–413.

Hankamer, Jorge. 1978. On the non-transformational derivations of some null NP anaphors. *Linguistic Inquiry* 9:55–74.

Hankamer, Jorge and Ivan Sag. 1976. Deep and surface anaphora. *Linguistic Inquiry* 7:391–426.

Hausser, Roland. 1983. The syntax and semantics of English mood. In F. Kiefer, ed., *Questions and Answers*, pages 97–158. Dordrecht: Reidel.

Hausser, Roland and Dietmar Zaefferer. 1979. Questions and answers in a context-dependent Montague Grammar. In F. Guenthner and M. Schmidt, eds., *Formal Semantics and Pragmatics for Natural Languages*, pages 339–358. Dordrecht: Reidel.

Heim, Irene. 1979. Concealed questions. In R. Bäuerle, U. Egli, and A. von Stechow, eds., *Semantics from Different Points of View*, pages 51–60. New York: Springer Verlag.

Heim, Irene. 1982. *The Semantics of Definite and Indefinite Noun Phrases*. Ph.D. thesis, University of Massachusetts, Amherst.

Heinz, Wolfgang and Johannes Matiasek. 1994. Argument structure and case assignment in German. In J. Nerbonne, K. Netter, and C. Pollard, eds., *German in Head-Driven Phrase Structure Grammar*, CSLI Lecture Notes Number 46, pages 199–236. Stanford: CSLI Publications.

Hendrick, Randall and Michael Rochemont. 1982. Complementation, multiple *wh* and echo questions. Unpublished ms., University of North Carolina and UC Irvine .

Higginbotham, James. 1991. Interrogatives. In L. Cheng, ed., *MIT Working Papers*, vol. 15. Cambridge, MA: MIT.

Higginbotham, James. 1996. The Semantics of Questions. In S. Lappin, ed., *Handbook of Contemporary Semantic Theory*, pages 361–384. Oxford: Blackwell.

Higginbotham, James and Robert May. 1981. Questions, quantifiers, and crossing. *The Linguistic Review* 1:41–80.

Hintikka, Jaakko. 1976. *The Semantics of Questions and the Questions of Semantics*, vol. 28.4 of *Acta Philosophica Fennica*. Amsterdam: North Holland.

Hintikka, Jaakko. 1983. New foundations for a theory of questions and answers. In F. Kiefer, ed., *Questions and Answers*, pages 159–190. Dordrecht: Reidel.

Hintikka, Jaakko and Gabriel Sandu. 1997. Game-Theoretical Semantics. In J. van Benthem and A. ter Meulen, eds., *Handbook of Logic and Language*, pages 361–410. Cambridge, MA and Amsterdam: MIT Press and North Holland.

Hobbs, Jerry. 1983. An improper treatment of quantification in ordinary English. In *Proceedings of the 23rd Annual Meeting of the Association for Computational Linguistics*, pages 57–63.

Hobbs, Jerry. 1996. Monotone decreasing quantifiers in a scope-free logical form. In S. Peters and K. van Deemter, eds., *Semantic Ambiguity and Underspecification*, pages 55–76. Stanford: CSLI Publications.

Hoepelmann, Jacob. 1983. On questions. In F. Kiefer, ed., *Questions and Answers*. Dordrecht: Reidel.

Hooper, Joan and Sandra Thompson. 1973. On the applicability of root transformations. *Linguistic Inquiry* 4:465–498.

Hornstein, Norbert. 1995. *Logical Form*. Oxford: Blackwell.

Huang, James. 1982. Move *wh* in a language without *wh* movement. *The Linguistic Review* 1:369–416.

Huddleston, Rodney. 1993a. On exclamatory inversion sentences in English. *Lingua* 90:259–269.

Huddleston, Rodney. 1993b. Remarks on the construction *You won't believe who Ed has married*. *Lingua* 91:175–184.

Hudson, Richard. 1990. *English Word Grammar*. Cambridge, MA: Blackwell.

Hudson, Richard. 2000. *I amn't. *Language* 76:297–323.

Hukari, Thomas E. and Robert D. Levine. 1995. Adjunct extraction. *Journal of Linguistics* 31:195–226.

Hukari, Thomas E. and Robert D. Levine. 1996a. Phrase structure grammar: the next generation. *Journal of Linguistics* 32:465–496.

Hukari, Thomas E. and Robert D. Levine. 1996b. Subject extraction. Paper presented at the Third International Conference on Head-driven Phrase Structure Grammar, Marseille.

Hull, Rodney. 1975. A semantics for superficial and embedded questions in natural language. In E. Keenan, ed., *Formal Semantics of Natural Language*, pages 33–45. Cambridge: Cambridge University Press.

Jackendoff, Ray. 1997. *The Architecture of the Language Faculty*. Cambridge, MA: MIT Press.

Jacobs, Joachim. 1991. Implikaturen und 'alte information' in *w*-fragen. In M. Reis and I. Rosengren, eds., *Fragesätze und Fragen*. Tübingen: Niemeyer.

Janda, Richard. 1985. Echo questions are about what? In *Papers from the 21st Regional Meeting of the Chicago Linguistic Society*. Chicago: CLS.

Jespersen, Otto. 1924. *A Modern English Grammar on Historical Principles, volumes 1–7*. London: Allen and Unwin. Series published 1909–1949.

Jespersen, Otto. 1965. *The Philosophy of Grammar*. New York: Norton.

Johnson, David and Shalom Lappin. 1999. *Local Constraints versus Economy*. Stanford: CSLI Publications.

Johnson, David and Paul Postal. 1980. *Arc Pair Grammar*. Princeton: Princeton University Press.

Johnston, Michael. 1999. A syntax and semantics for purposive adjuncts in HPSG. In R. D. Levine and G. Green, eds., *Studies in Contemporary Phrase Structure Grammar*, pages 80–118. Cambridge: Cambridge University Press.

Kamp, Hans. 1981. A theory of truth and semantic representation. In J. Groenendijk, ed., *Formal Methods in Semantics*, pages 277–322. Amsterdam Centre for Mathematics.

Kamp, Hans. 1990. Prologmena to a structural theory of belief and other attitudes. In C. Anderson and J. Owens, eds., *Propositional Attitudes: The Role of Content in Logic, Language and Mind*, CSLI Lecture Notes, pages 27–90. Stanford: CSLI Publications.

Kamp, Hans. 1996. Events and related matters. In *Fracas Deliverable D15*. Centre for Cognitive Science, Edinburgh: The Fracas Consortium.

Kamp, Hans and Uwe Reyle. 1993. *From Discourse to Logic: Introduction to Model-theoretic Semantics of Natural Language, Formal Logic and Discourse Representation Theory*. No. 42 in Studies in Linguistics and Philosophy. Dordrecht: Kluwer.

Kaplan, David. 1989. Demonstratives: An essay on the semantics, logic, metaphysics, and epistemology of demonstratives and other indexicals. In J. Almog, J. Perry, and H. Wettstein, eds., *Themes from Kaplan*, pages 481–614. Oxford: Oxford University Press.

Kaplan, Ronald and Joan Bresnan. 1982. Lexical-functional grammar: A formal system for grammatical representation. In J. Bresnan, ed., *The Mental Representation of Grammatical Relations*, pages 173–281. MIT Press. Reprinted in Mary Dalrymple, Ronald Kaplan, John Maxwell, and Annie Zaenen, eds., *Formal Issues in Lexical-Functional Grammar*. Stanford: CSLI Publications. Pages 29–130.

Kaplan, Ronald M. and Annie Zaenen. 1989. Long-distance dependencies, constituent structure and functional uncertainty. In M. R. Baltin and A. S. Kroch, eds., *Alternative Conceptions of Phrase Structure*, pages 17–42. University of Chicago Press. Reprinted in Mary Dalrymple, Ronald Kaplan, John Maxwell, and Annie Zaenen, eds., *Formal Issues in Lexical-Functional Grammar*. Stanford: CSLI Publications. Pages 137–165.

Karttunen, Lauri. 1977. Syntax and semantics of questions. *Linguistics and Philosophy* 1:3–44.

Karttunen, Lauri and Stanley Peters. 1979. Interrogative quantifiers. In C. Rohrer, ed., *Times, Tense, and Quantifiers*, pages 181–205. Tübingen: Niemeyer.

Kathol, Andreas. 1995. *Linearization-Based German Syntax*. Ph.D. thesis, The Ohio State University.

Kathol, Andreas. 2000. *Linear Syntax*. Oxford: Oxford University Press.

Katz, Jerrold and Paul Postal. 1964. *An Integrated Theory of Linguistic Descriptions*. Cambridge: MIT Press.

Keenan, Edward and Rodney Hull. 1973. The logical presuppositions of questions and answers. In J. Petöfi and D. Franck, eds., *Präsuppositionen in der Linguistik und der Philosophie*, pages 441–466. Frankfurt: Athenaeum.

Keenan, Edward and Dag Westerståhl. 1997. Generalized quantifiers in linguistics and logic. In J. van Benthem and A. ter Meulen, eds., *Handbook of Logic and Language*, pages 837–893. Cambridge, MA and Amsterdam: MIT Press and North Holland.

Keller, Frank and Ash Asudeh. 2000. Constraints on linguistic coreference: an experimental investigation of exempt anaphors. Manuscript: University of Edinburgh and Stanford University.

Kempson, Ruth, Wilfried Meyer-Viol, and Dov Gabbay. 2000. *Dynamic Syntax: The Flow of Language Understanding*. Oxford: Blackwell.

Kibble, Rodger. 1997. Complement anaphora, monotonicity and dynamic binding. In S. Ploch and D. Swinburne, eds., *Working Papers in Linguistics and Phonetics*. London: School of Oriental and African Studies.

Kim, Jong-Bok. 1995. English negation from a non-derivational perspective. In *Proceedings of the 21st Annual Meeting of the Berkeley Linguistics Society*, pages 186–196. Berkeley: BLS.

Kim, Jong-Bok and Ivan A. Sag. 1995. The parametric variation of English and French negation. In J. Camacho, L. Choueiri, and M. Watanabe, eds., *Proceedings of the 14th West Coast Conference on Formal Linguistics*, pages 303–317.

Kim, Jong-Bok and Ivan A. Sag. In press. Negation without head-movement. *Natural Language and Linguistic Theory*.

Kim, Yookyung. 1998. Information articulation and truth conditions of existential sentences. *Language and Information* 1.

King, Paul John. 1989. *A Logical Formalism for Head Driven Phrase Structure Grammar*. Ph.D. thesis, University of Manchester.

Koenig, Jean-Pierre. 1999. *Lexical Relations*. Stanford: CSLI Publications.

Koenig, Jean-Pierre and Daniel Jurafsky. 1994. Type underspecification and the on-line type construction in the lexicon. In *Proceedings of the 13th West Coast Conference on Formal Linguistics*, pages 270–285. Stanford: Stanford Linguistics Association.

Kratzer, Angelika. 1981. The notional category of modality. In J. Elkmayer and H. Rieser, eds., *Words, Worlds and Contexts*, pages 33–74. Berlin: De Gruyter.

Krifka, Manfred. 1999. Quantifying into question acts. Handout of talk given at SALT 9, UC Santa Cruz.

Kripke, Saul. 1979. A puzzle about belief. In A. Margalit, ed., *Meaning and Use*, Synthese language Library, pages 239–283. Dordrecht: Reidel.

Kuno, Susumu and Jane J. Robinson. 1972. Multiple *wh* questions. *Linguistic Inquiry* 3:463–487.

Kurtzman, Howard and Mary Ellen McDonald. 1993. Resolution of quantifier scope ambiguities. *Cognition* 48:248–279.

Ladd, D. Robert. 1996. *Intonational Phonology*. Cambridge: Cambridge University Press.

Lahiri, Utpal. 1991. *Embedded Interrogatives and Predicates That Embed Them*. Ph.D. thesis, MIT.

Lambrecht, Knud. 1990. What, me worry? Mad Magazine sentences revisited. In *Proceedings of the 16th Regional Meeting of the Berkeley Linguistics Society*. Berkeley: BLS.

Landman, Fred. 1989. Groups, I. *Linguistics and Philosophy* 12:559–605.

Langacker, Ronald. 1991. *Foundations of Cognitive Grammar, Vol. 2: Descriptive Application*. Stanford: Stanford University Press.

Lappin, Shalom. 1991. Concepts of logical form in linguistics and philosophy. In A. Kasher, ed., *The Chomskyan Turn*, pages 300–333. Oxford: Blackwell.

Lascarides, Alex and Ann Copestake. 1999. Default representation in constraint-based frameworks. *Computational Linguistics* 25:55–105.

Lasnik, Howard and Mamoru Saito. 1992. *Move Alpha: Conditions on its application and output*. Cambridge, MA: MIT Press.

Levin, Lori. 1982. Sluicing: a lexical interpretation procedure. In J. Bresnan, ed., *The Mental Representation of Grammatical Relations*, pages 590–654. Cambridge, MA: MIT Press.

Levinson, Stephen. 1983. *Pragmatics*. Cambridge: Cambridge University Press.

Levinson, Stephen C. 2000. *Presumptive Meanings: the Theory of Generalized Conversational Implicature*. Cambridge, MA: MIT Press.

Liberman, Mark. 1975. *The Intonational System of English*. Ph.D. thesis, MIT. Published in 1979. New York: Garland.

Link, Godehard. 1983. The logical analysis of plurals and mass terms: a lattice theoretical approach. In R. Bäuerle, C. Schwarze, and A. von Stechow, eds., *Meaning, Use, and the Interpretation of Language*, pages 302–323. Berlin: de Gruyter.

Lönning, Jan Tore. 1997. Plurals and Collectivity. In J. van Benthem and A. ter Meulen, eds., *Handbook of Logic and Language*, pages 1009–1053. Cambridge, MA and Amsterdam: MIT Press and North Holland.

MacDonald, Maryellen C., Neal J. Pearlmutter, and Mark S. Seidenberg. 1994. The lexical nature of syntactic ambiguity resolution. *Psychological Review* 101:676–703.

Malouf, Robert. 1998. *Mixed Categories in the Hierarchical Lexicon*. Ph.D. thesis, Stanford University.

Malouf, Robert. 2000. *Mixed Categories in the Hierarchical Lexicon*. Stanford: CSLI Publications.

Manning, Christopher, Ivan A. Sag, and Masayo Iida. 1999. The lexical integrity of Japanese causatives. In R. D. Levine and G. Green, eds., *Readings in HPSG*, pages 39–79. Cambridge: Cambridge University Press.

May, Robert. 1985. *Logical Form*. Cambridge, MA: MIT Press.

May, Robert. 1989. Interpreting logical form. *Linguistics and Philosophy* 12:387–435.

McCawley, James. 1988. Review of *Knowledge of Language*. *Language* 64(2):355–365.

Merchant, Jason. 1999. *The Syntax of Silence: Sluicing, Islands, and Identity in Ellipsis*. Ph.D. thesis, University of California, Santa Cruz.

Meurers, Detmar Walter. 2000. *Lexical Generalizations in the Syntax of German Non-Finite Constructions*. Ph.D. thesis, Universität Tübingen. Published as Arbeitspapiere des SFB 340, Number 145. Universität Tübingen.

Meurers, Walt Detmar and Guido Minnen. 1997. A computational treatment of HPSG lexical rules as covariation in lexical entries. *Computational Linguistics* 23:543–568.

Miller, Philip and Ivan A. Sag. 1997. French clitic movement without clitics or movement. *Natural Language and Linguistic Theory* 15:573–639.

Milward, David. 1995. Integrating situations into a theory of discourse anaphora. In P. Dekker and M. Stokhof, eds., *Proceedings of the 10th Amsterdam Colloquium*, pages 538–519. ILLC, Amsterdam.

Moens, Marc and Mark Steedman. 1988. Temporal reference and temporal ontology. *Computational Linguistics* 14:15–28.

Monachesi, Paola. 1999. Linearization properties of Romanian clitics. In *Proceedings of WECOL 98*. Western Conference on Linguistics.

Montague, Richard. 1974a. Pragmatics. In R. Thomason, ed., *Formal Philosophy*, pages 95–119. New Haven: Yale University Press.

Montague, Richard. 1974b. The proper treatment of quantification in ordinary English. In R. Thomason, ed., *Formal Philosophy*, pages 247–270. New Haven: Yale University Press.

Morgan, Jerry. 1973. Sentence fragments and the notion 'sentence'. In B. Kachru, ed., *Issues in Linguistics: Papers in Honor of Henry and Rene Kahane*. Urbana, IL: University of Illinois Press.

Mulligan, Kevin, Peter Simons, and Barry Smith. 1984. Truth makers. *Philosophy and Phenomological Research* 44:287–321.

Nelken, Rani and Nissim Francez. 1998. Bilattices and the semantics of natural language questions. Tech. rep., Technion, Israel Institute of Technology.

Nerbonne, John. 1992. Constraint-based semantics. In P. Dekker and M. Stokhof, eds., *Proceedings of the 8th Amsterdam Colloquium*, pages 425–444. ILLC, Amsterdam.

Parsons, Terence. 1994. *Events in the Semantics of English: A Study in Subatomic Semantics*. Cambridge, MA: MIT Press.

Parsons, Terence. 1999. Quantification and speech acts. Talk given at SALT 9, UC Santa Cruz.

Pesetsky, David. 1987. *Wh*-in-situ: Movement and unselective binding. In E. Reuland and A. T. Meulen, eds., *The Representation of (In)definiteness*, pages 98–129. Cambridge, MA: MIT Press.

Peterson, Philip. 1997. *Fact, Proposition, Event*. Studies in Linguistics and Philosophy. Dordrecht: Kluwer.

Pierrehumbert, Janet and Julia Hirschberg. 1990. The meaning of intonational contours in the interpretation of discourse. In P. R. Cohen, J. Morgan, and M. E. Pollack, eds., *Intentions in Communication*, pages 271–323. Cambridge, MA: MIT Press.

Poesio, Massimo. 1993. A situation–theoretic formalization of definite description interpretation in plan elaboration dialogues. In P. Aczel, D. Israel, Y. Katagiri, and S. Peters, eds., *Situation Theory and Its Applications, III*, CSLI Lecture Notes Number 37, pages 339–374. Stanford: CSLI Publications.

Pollard, Carl. 1989. The syntax-semantics interface in a unification-based phrase structure grammar. In S. Busemann, C. Hauenschild, and C. Umbach, eds., *Views of the Syntax/Semantics Interface*, pages 167–185. Berlin: Technical University of Berlin.

Pollard, Carl. 1994. Toward a unified account of passive in German. In J. Nerbonne, K. Netter, and C. Pollard, eds., *German in Head-Driven Phrase Structure Grammar*, CSLI Lecture Notes Number 46, pages 273–296. Stanford: CSLI Publications.

Pollard, Carl and Ivan Sag. 1987. *Information-Based Syntax and Semantics*. Stanford: CSLI Publications.

Pollard, Carl and Ivan Sag. 1992. Anaphors in English and the scope of binding theory. *Linguistic Inquiry* 23:261–303.

Pollard, Carl and Ivan Sag. 1994. *Head Driven Phrase Structure Grammar*. Chicago and Stanford: University of Chicago Press and CSLI Publications.

Pollard, Carl and Eun Jung Yoo. 1998. A unified theory of scope for quantifiers and *wh*-phrases. *Journal of Linguistics* 34:415–445.

Pope, Emily. 1976. *Questions and Answers in English*. The Hague: Mouton.

Portner, Paul. 1997. The semantics of mood, complementation, and conversational force. *Natural Language Semantics* 5:167–212.

Postal, Paul M. 1998. *Three Investigations of Extraction*. Cambridge, MA: MIT Press.

Postal, Paul M. 2001. Islands. In M. Baltin and C. Collins, eds., *The Handbook of Syntactic Theory*. Oxford: Blackwell.

Potsdam, Eric. 1996. *Syntactic Issues in the English Imperative*. Ph.D. thesis, University of California, Santa Cruz.

Prince, Ellen F. 1981. Topicalization, focus-movement, and Yiddish movement: a pragmatic differentiation. In D. Alford, ed., *Proceedings of the 7th Regional Meeting of the Berkeley Linguistics Society*, pages 249–264. Berkeley: BLS.

Przepiórkowski, Adam. 1998. 'A unified theory of scope' revisited: quantifier retrieval without spurious ambiguities. In *Proceedings of the Joint Conference on Formal Grammar, Head-Driven Phrase Structure Grammar and Categorial Grammar*. Saarbrücken: University of the Saarland.

Przepiórkowski, Adam. 1999. *Case Assigment and the Complement/Adjunct Dichotomy: A Non-Configurational Constraint-Based Approach*. Ph.D. thesis, Universität Tübingen.

Przepiórkowski, Adam. 1999. Negative polarity questions and Italian negative concord. In V. Kordoni, ed., *Tübingen Studies in Head-Driven Phrase Structure Grammar*, Arbeitspapiere des Sonderforschungsbereichs 340 Bericht Nr. 132, Seminar für Sprachwissenschaft, Universität Tübingen, pages 353–400.

Pullum, Geoffrey K. 1982. Syncategorematicity and English infinitival *to*. *Glossa* 16:181–215.

Pullum, Geoffrey K. 2000. Hankamer was! In *Jorge Hankamer WebFest*. http://ling.ucsc.edu/Jorge/.

Pustejovsky, James. 1995. *The Generative Lexicon*. Cambridge, MA: MIT Press.

Quine, Willard V. O. 1963. *From a Logical Point of View*. New York: Harper and Row. Originally published in 1953 by Harvard University Press. Revised second edition published by Harvard in 1980.

Quirk, Randolph, Sidney Greenbaum, Geffrey Leech, and Jan Svartvik. 1985. *A Comprehensive Grammar of the English Language*. London: Longman.

Radford, Andrew. 1988. *Transformational Grammar: A First Course*. Cambridge: Cambridge University Press.

Reape, Michael. 1994. Domain union and word order variation in German. In J. Nerbonne, K. Netter, and C. Pollard, eds., *German in Head-driven Phrase Structure Grammar*, pages 151–197. Stanford: CSLI Publications.

Recanati, François. 1996. Domains of discourse. *Linguistics and Philosophy* 19:445–475.

Reichenbach, Hans. 1947. *Elements of Symbolic Logic*. New York: Macmillan.

Reinhart, Tanya. 1997. Quantifier scope: How labor is divided between QR and choice functions. *Linguistics and Philosophy* 20:335–397.

Reis, Marga. 1992. Zur grammatik und pragmatik von echo-*w*-fragen. In I. Rosengren, ed., *Satz und Illokution*, pages 213–261. Tübingen: Niemeyer.

Rexach, Javier Guttierez. 1997. Questions and generalized quantifiers. In A. Szabolcsi, ed., *Ways of Scope Taking*, pages 409–452. Reidel: Kluwer.

Richter, Frank. 1999. RSRL for HPSG. In V. Kordoni, ed., *Tübingen Studies in Head-Driven Phrase Structure Grammar*, no. 132 in Arbeitsberichte des SFB 340, pages 74–115. Tübingen: Universität Tübingen.

Richter, Frank. 2000. *A Mathematical Formalism for Linguistic Theories with an Application in Head-Driven Phrase Structure Grammar*. Ph.D. thesis, Universität Tübingen.

Romero, Maribel. 1998. *Focus and Reconstruction Effects in Wh-Phrases"*. Ph.D. thesis, University of Massachusetts, Amherst.

Rooth, Mats. 1993. A theory of focus interpretation. *Natural Language Semantics* 1:75–116.

Ross, John. 1969. Guess who. In *Proceedings of the 5th Annual Meeting of the Chicago Linguistic Society*, pages 252–286. Chicago: CLS.

Ross, John R. 1967. *Constraints on Variables in Syntax*. Ph.D. thesis, MIT. Published in 1986 as *Infinite Syntax!*. Norwood, N. J.: Ablex.

Rounds, William. 1991. Situation theoretic aspects of databases. In J. Barwise, J. M. Gawron, G. Plotkin, and S. Tutiya, eds., *Situation Theory and Its Applications, II*, CSLI Lecture Notes Number 26, pages 229–255. Stanford: CSLI Publications.

Russell, Bertrand. 1905. On denoting. *Mind* 14:479–493. Reprinted in Russell's *Essays in Analysis* (London: Allen and Unwin. 1973. Pages 103-119) and in A. Martinich, ed., *The Philosophy of Language*. New York: Oxford University Press, 1985.

Russell, Bertrand. 1949. *The Philosophy of Logical Atomism*. Minneapolis: Department of Philosophy, University of Minnesota. Reprinted in 1972 as *Russell's Logical Atomism*. Oxford: Fontana/Collins.

Sag, Ivan A. 1976. *Deletion and Logical Form*. Ph.D. thesis, MIT. Published in 1980. New York: Garland.

Sag, Ivan A. 1997. English relative clause constructions. *Journal of Linguistics* 33:431–484.

Sag, Ivan A. 2000. Rules and exceptions in the English auxiliary system. Manuscript: Stanford University.

Sag, Ivan A. 2001. Phrases and constructions. Manuscript: Stanford University.

Sag, Ivan A. and Thomas Wasow, eds. 1999. *Syntactic Theory: A Formal Introduction*. Stanford: CSLI Publications.

Saito, M. 1997. Syntactic chains and quantifier scope. Forum Lecture given at the LSA Linguistic Institute, Cornell University.

Schwarzschild, Roger. 1999. GIVENness, Avoid F and other constraints on the placement of accent. *Natural Language Semantics* 7:141–177.

Searle, John. 1969. *Speech Acts*. Cambridge: Cambridge University Press.

Searle, John and Daniel Vanderveken. 1985. *Foundations of Illocutionary Logic*. Cambridge: Cambridge University Press.

Seligman, Jerry and Larry Moss. 1997. Situation Theory. In J. van Benthem and A. ter Meulen, eds., *Handbook of Logic and Language*, pages 239–309. Cambridge, MA and Amsterdam: MIT Press and North Holland.

Shieber, Stuart, Fernando Pereira, and Mary Dalrymple. 1996. Interactions of scope and ellipsis. *Linguistics and Philosophy* 19:527–552. Reprinted in Shalom Lappin and Elabbas Benmamoun, eds., *Fragments: Studies in Ellipsis and Gapping*. Pages 8–31. New York and Oxford: Oxford University Press.

Simpson, Andrew. 1995. *Wh-Movement, Licensing, and the Locality of Feature Checking*. Ph.D. thesis, School of Oriental and African Studies (SOAS).

Smith, Neil. 1999. *Chomsky: Ideas and Ideals*. Cambridge: Cambridge University Press.

Soames, Scott. 1985. Lost innocence. *Linguistics and Philosophy* 8:59–71.

Soames, Scott and David M. Perlmutter. 1979. *Syntactic Argumentation and the Structure of English*. Berkeley: University of California Press.

Sperber, Dan and Deidre Wilson. 1986. *Relevance: Communication and Cognition*. Oxford: Blackwell. Second edition appeared in 1995. Cambridge, MA: Blackwell.

Srivastav, Veneeta. 1991. Multiple relatives and polyadic quantification. In *Proceedings of the 9th West Coast Conference on Formal Linguistics*, pages 509–522. Stanford: Stanford Linguistics Association.

Steedman, Mark. 1996. *Surface Structure and Interpretation*. Linguistic Inquiry Monograph Number 30. Cambridge, MA: MIT Press.

de Swart, Henriette and Ivan A. Sag. 2000. Negation and Negative Concord in Romance. Tech. Rep. 022, Onderwijsinstituut CKI, Utrecht University.

Szabolcsi, Anna. 1993. Quantifiers in pair-list readings and the non-uniformity of quantification. In P. Dekker and M. Stokhof, eds., *Proceedings of the 9th Amsterdam Colloquium*. ILLC, Amsterdam.

Takahashi, Daiko. 1994. Sluicing in Japanese. *Journal of East Asian Linguistics* 3:265–300.

Tanenhaus, Michael K. and John C. Trueswell. 1995. Sentence comprehension. In J. Miller and P. Eimas, eds., *Handbook of Perception and Cognition (2nd Edition)*, pages 217–262. San Diego: Academic Press.

Thomason, Richmond, ed. 1974a. *Formal Philosophy: The Collected Works of Richard Montague*. New Haven: Yale University Press.

Thomason, Richmond. 1974b. Introduction. In R. Thomason, ed., *Formal Philosophy*. New Haven: Yale University Press.

Tomasello, Michael. 1998. Introduction. In *The New Psychology of Language: Cognitive and Functional Approaches to Language Structure*. Mahwah, NJ: Lawrence Erlbaum.

Traum, David. 1994. *A Computational Theory of Grounding in Natural Language Conversations*. Ph.D. thesis, University of Rochester.

Traum, David, Johan Bos, Robin Cooper, Staffan Larsson, Ian Lewin, Colin Matheson, and Massimo Poesio. 1999. A model of dialogue moves and information state revision. In *Task Oriented Instructional Dialogue (TRINDI): Deliverable 2.1*. Gothenburg: University of Gothenburg. Available from http://www.ling.gu.se/research/projects/trindi.

Turner, Ray. 1997. Types. In J. van Benthem and A. ter Meulen, eds., *Handbook of Logic and Language*, pages 535–586. Cambridge, MA and Amsterdam: MIT Press and North Holland.

Uszkoreit, Hans. 1987. *Word Order and Constituent Structure in German*. CSLI Lecture Notes Number 8. Stanford: CSLI Publications.

Vallduvì, Enric. 1992. *The Informational Component*. New York: Garland.

van den Berg, Martin. 1993. *Plural Dynamic Generalized Quantifiers*. Ph.D. thesis, University of Amsterdam, Amsterdam.

Vendler, Zeno. 1968. *Linguistics in Philosophy*. Ithaca: Cornell University Press.

Vendler, Zeno. 1972. *Res Cogitans*. Ithaca: Cornell University Press.

Vogel, Carl and Jonathan Ginzburg. 1999. A situated theory of modality. In *Proceedings of the Batumi Conference on Logic, Language, and Computation*. Batumi, Adjarian Autonomous Republic, Georgia.

Warner, Anthony. 1993. *English Auxiliaries: Structure and History*. Cambridge and New York: Cambridge University Press.

Warner, Anthony. 2000. English auxiliaries without lexical rules. In R. Borsley, ed., *The Nature and Function of Syntactic Categories*, vol. 32 of *Syntax and Semantics*, pages 167–220. San Diego: Academic Press.

Webber, Bonnie Lynn. 1978. *A Formal Approach to Discourse Anaphora*. Ph.D. thesis, Harvard University. Published in 1979. New York: Garland.

Wechsler, Stephen. 1995. *The Semantic Basis of Argument Structure*. Stanford: CSLI Publications.

Wilcock, Graham. 1999. Lexicalization of context. In G. Webelhuth, J.-P. Koenig, and A. Kathol, eds., *Lexical and Constructional Aspects of Linguistic Explanation*, pages 373–387. Stanford: CSLI Publications.

Zhang, Shi. 1990. The structure of Mad Magazine sentences and unmarked accusative case. In G. Goodall, ed., *Proceedings of the Western Conference on Linguistics*, vol. 3. Fresno: California State University.

Zwicky, Arnold. 1987. Supressing the z's. *Journal of Linguistics* 23:133–148.

Zwicky, Arnold. 1994. Exceptional degree markers: A puzzle in internal and external syntax. In *Ohio State University Working Papers in Linguistics, Vol. 47*, pages 111–123.

Zwicky, Arnold and Geoffrey Pullum. 1987. Plain morphology and expressive morphology. In *Proceedings of the 13th Meeting of the Berkeley Linguistics Society*, pages 330–340. Berkeley: BLS.

Index